Baedeker's

BELGIUM

Hints for using the guide

Following the tradition established by Karl Baedeker in 1846, sights of particular interest and hotels and restaurants of particular quality, are distinguished by one ★ or two ★★.

To make it easier to locate the various places listed in the "A to Z" section of the Guide, their co-ordinates are shown in red at the head of each entry: e.g., Antwerp D 9/10.

Coloured lines down the right-hand side of the page are an aid to finding the main heading in the Guide: blue stands for the Introduction (Nature, Culture, History, etc.), red for the "A to Z" section, and yellow indicates Practical Information.

Only a selection of hotels, restaurants and shops can be given; no reflection is implied therefore on establishments not included.

In a time of rapid change it is difficult to ensure that all the information given is entirely accurate and up-to-date, and the possibility of error can never be entirely eliminated.

Although the publishers can accept no responsibility for inaccuracies and omissions, they are constantly endeavouring to improve the quality of their Guides and are therefore always grateful for criticisms, corrections and suggestions for improvement.

Preface

This guide to Belgium is one of the new generation of Baedeker guides.

These guides, illustrated throughout in colour, are designed to meet the needs of the modern traveller. They are quick and easy to consult, with the principal places of interest described in alphabetical order, and the information is presented in a format that is both attractive and easy to follow.

The subject of this guide is the west European Kingdom of Belgium – from the Ardennes to the North Sea.

The guide is in three parts. The first part gives a general account of the country, its political and geographical divisions, its landscape, climate, flora and fauna, population, educational systems, government and administration, economy, history, famous people, art and culture, and in particular the rich folkloristic life of Belgium. A brief selection of quotations and a

Friendly villages in the Ardennes (left) and a picturesque corner of Brugges (above)

number of suggested itineraries provide a transition to the second part, in which the country's places and features of tourist interest – towns, provinces, scenery – are described. The third part contains a variety of practical information. Baedeker Specials deal with the language differences, Flanders' tapestries, the Battle of Waterloo and Belgian beer. Both the sights and the practical information are listed in alphabetical order.

The new Baedeker guides are noted for their concentration on essentials and their convenience of use. They contain numerous specially drawn plans and colour illustrations; and at the end of the book is a large map making it easy to locate the various places described in the "A to Z" section of the guide with the help of the co-ordinates given at the head of each entry.

Contents

Baedeker Specials

Between the North Sea

... live the Flemings and the Walloons, the two factions who together have constituted the Kingdom of Belgium for rather more than 160 years – and, in defiance of all the prophecies of the doom which will happen if this separatism is allowed to continue, the majority of Belgians seem unprepared to relinquish the status quo. Quite wrongly, this little kingdom is perhaps one of Europe's less popular tourist destinations. When asked what they know about Belgium most people nowadays can only think of Eddy Merckx, Ardennes ham, Brussels lace, the motorways illuminated at night and French fries. Many people know it only as a country through which they pass en route to the Netherlands or to Germany. In fact Belgium's history has made it a country rich in unique places of interest, for it is here that the two major European cultural groups, the Germanic and the Romanic, once met and overlapped. As a result, the country's many cultural attractions and charming countryside make it well worth a visit at any time of the year. In the seaside resorts along the Belgian North Sea coast summer holidaymakers will find long beaches and picturesque dunes to which they can travel in one of the trams which rattle along from one end of the coast to the other. Art lovers can admire magnificent works by all the masters, including Rembrandt, Rubens, van Dyck, as well as more modern painters such as Magritte and Delvaux, in Belgium's

Antwerp

The guild-houses on Grote Markt bear witness to the wealth of the port and home town of Rembrandt

Kortrijk

is just one of the many towns in which the Middle Ages still live on in the Begijnhof

and the Ardennes ...

many museums and collections. The romantically-minded will be thrilled by the historical old town centres, many with rivers and canals and other waterways, and impressive secular and religious buildings like those in Bruges or Ghent. Devotees of the cartoon and the comic strip can spend a whole day in the Comic Museum in Brussels. Those interested in technical achievements will be fascinated by the harbour installations in Antwerp and the bridges, sluices, canals and marine lifting gear such as that at La Louvière or Ronquières, and the coal-mines in the Walloon region. Walkers and nature-lovers will be attracted by the

woodland regions of the Ardennes, where they will find the largest drip-stone cave in Europe, and Spa, a spa town (hence its name) of high quality. Above all, however, visitors will soon realise that the Belgians know how to live. Belgium is famous for its gastronomic delights – per head of population, no other European country can boast as many restaurants awarded stars or medals by international gourmets as Belgium can. And where else does one have to make the agonising choice between more than 400 different beers brewed from age-old recipes, with none tasting exactly like any other and bearing such adventurous names as Verboden Vrucht (Forbidden Fruit), Straffe Hendrik (Tight Henry), Kwak, Judas or even Delirium Tremens and Mort Subite (Sudden Death)?

Flea markets
like this one in Ghent make the collector's heart beat faster

The Maas
Belgium's major river, its banks dotted with proud castles and prosperous towns

Nature, Culture History

Facts and Figures

General

The Kingdom of Belgium lies in the north-west of Central Europe, between 49° 30' and 51° 30' north and 2° 33' and 6° 24' east. In the north and east it has borders with the Netherlands, and further east with Germany and Luxembourg, as well as with France to the south and the North Sea to the west, but only for a length of some 67 km (42 mi.). The total extent of its borders with Germany, Luxembourg and France amounts to 1445 km (898 mi.). Belgium has a small exclave, Baarle-Hertog, on Dutch terrain, within which curiously will be found the two even smaller Dutch exclaves of Baarle-Nassau.

Belgium covers an area of only 30,519 sq. km (11,783 sq. mi.), making it one of the smallest of the European states. Its maximum length is 290 km (180 mi.), from Ostend to Arlon. From the capital Brussels all parts of the country can be reached by car in two hours at the most and by train in two and a half, so Belgium can genuinely be called a "country of short roads".

Topography

From its narrow coastal border Belgium extends well inland to the south-east and then by way of the River Meuse as far as the western foothills of the German low mountain range. In the north the North Sea coast, marshland and coastal moorlands (or "geest") together form a natural continuation of the Netherlands known as Lower Belgium. Central Belgium is a hilly region covered with loess, a fine fertile soil, making them rich agricultural land. The Meuse and Sambre valley is the beginning of Upper Belgium, the Ardennes, divided into the Lower and Upper Ardennes. This ancient mountain massif of slate, boulders and limestone forms the western wing of the Rhine slate mountains. To the south Upper Belgium extends to the terraced Lorraine countryside.

Lower Belgium

In Lower Belgium the **coastal strip**, only 67 km (42 mi.) in length and with fine sandy beaches and dunes, has but few openings leading down to the sea, among these being the mouth of the Yser near Nieuwpoort. The lines of sand dunes are as high as 30 m (100 ft) in the great De Panne field. Behind the dunes and along the Westerschelde (the southern bank of which, the Zeeuws Vlaanderen, or Zeeland Flanders, forms part of the Netherlands) lies marshland enclosed with polders, narrower than those in Holland, being only 12 km (7½ mi.) wide near Blankenberge. In the main these marshes are safe, well-cultivated land. The old inlets, which

◀ *The Schipdonk canal in Flanders*

Natural Regions and Waterways

once extended far inland, are now silted up; an example of this is Het Zwin, which at one time led from the mouth of the Scheldt to Bruges. The silting-up of the river led to the decline of Bruges, from one of the wealthiest towns in Europe to a provincial town. Bruges, although pierced by canals, rests on the flat and sandy coastal moorland, in the same way as Ghent and Antwerp. The famous Flanders seaports are therefore not marshland towns like those of the neighbouring Netherlands.

Geest, a sandy fluvial deposit, refers strictly speaking to that area known as Kempen (Campine) east of the Scheldt and Dijle and north of the Demer, the northern part of which forms part of the Netherlands. It is the most thinly populated region of Belgium, with heathland and areas of fluvial sand, patches of pine woods here and there, scattered villages on barren land and just a few small towns. In the Middle Ages monasteries were built in this wilderness, such as those at Westmalle and Tongerlo; one of Belgium's largest military training grounds, Leopoldsburg, was established here in 1850. In recent years environmentally hazardous industries such as lead and zinc foundries or nuclear plants such as the atomic research centre and recycling plant at Mol have been built here. Large coal deposits are mined between Maastricht and Antwerp. This area of Kempen and Limburg, not yet fully developed, with Genk as its centre, is the northern arm of the great European coal seam which divides at Aachen. As this seam runs under a massive mountain the mining has to be carried out by large concerns.

"Geest" in the Kempen region

To the west, in Flanders, the geest is partly a plain formed from comparatively recent deposits and partly hilly land of sand and clay, not very high, between the Scheldt, Leie and the marshland region. Whereas Kempen along the Demer finishes sharply where it meets Central Belgium, to the west, in Brabant and Flanders, roughly on a line from Leuven to Brussels and Kortrijk, there is a more gradual transition to the higher and more fertile land of Central Belgium. Although woodland by nature, and in many places covered in heathland on sandy soil, this area of Flanders has nevertheless been thickly populated and carefully cultivated since medieval times, and is typified by small individual farms in

"Geest" in Flanders

groups and rows, each separated from its neighbour by hedges or poplar trees. In spite of the barren soil the land is cultivated very intensively, some on smallholdings, as in the Waas region around Sint Niklaas, where many vegetables are grown. In addition to agriculture and horticulture, however, homeworkers have always produced traditional cloth goods and the famous pillow lace which was then sold in the streets of Lokeren and Tielt, for example. The banks of the Leie are lined with fields of flax. The larger towns, especially Ghent, are now modern textile centres.

Antwerp

Towards the end of the Middle Ages Antwerp assumed the mantle of Bruges and developed into the most prosperous town in northern Europe, before the damming of the Scheldt by the newly independent Netherlands in 1648 robbed it of its lifeblood for two hundred years. Situated on the higher bank of a meander of the Scheldt, which is some 500 m (1650 ft) wide at this point and affected by strong tides and a rise and fall of 4 m (13 ft), the old trading harbour faces the open river. In the first half of the 20th c. Antwerp once again became an international port. Large harbour basins equipped with locks were built in the river marshes downstream.

Human
geographical
development

From a communications point of view the country is ideally situated as far as the famous medieval ports and trading towns of Flanders are concerned. Trading ships sail to other countries by sea and river. To the south roads lead through flat open country to Picardy and Champagne, and by way of Burgundy to the Alpine passes and the Mediterranean. Flanders provided the link between North Sea and Baltic countries to the far Baltic and southern Europe, until historical events blocked all land and sea routes and caused the country to stagnate. The centre of the town of Ghent, situated at the confluence of the Scheldt and the Leie and

The silhouette of Antwerp

Fertile rolling countryside in Brabant

just above the tidal limit, has retained its old splendour. Modern Ghent is a modest textile centre and even a sea port, being linked by canal to Terneuzen on the Westerschelde.

If the Meuse-Sambre valley between Liège (Luik) and Charleroi is included, Central Belgium with its varied geographical features can be regarded as the very **heartland of the country**. A Tertiary and Cretaceous plateau, it is scarcely 100 m (330 ft) above sea-level in the north, rising gradually to some 200 m (660 ft) in the south. The northern part, although lower, is very hilly and dissected by the rivers Dijle, Senne, Dender and Scheldt, and its border with Flanders is somewhat ill-defined owing to the existence of numerous secondary plateaux which have become separated by erosion from the parent plateau. The more recent, upper strata in the hilly region is formed from conglomerates from the Late Tertiary period and protects the individual hills from being eroded. These include Pellenberg near Leuven, Kemmelberg south of Ypres (Ieper), scene of a famous battle in the First World War, and Mont St Aubert overlooking the countryside of Tournai.

Central Belgium

The Tertiary layer is not very deep, and the valleys which are scarcely 100 m (330 ft) in depth cut their way into the very old Brabant Massif below. The latter is formed partly from crystalline stone which is mined in large quarries at Lessines and Tournai. Layers of clay and sand have formed above the Tertiary stone and these are somewhat more productive than the geest-like sandy soil of northern Flanders. In addition deposits of fertile loess are to be found here and there on the slopes and hills. Small farmsteads on undulating and intensively cultivated land and green stretches dotted with trees give central Brabant its character. In between lie remains of the former vast forests, such as that of Soignes south of Brussels.

Topography

On the Meuse

Hesbaye (Haspengouw) Hainaut

To the south it is a slow climb over broad, open plateaux covered in loess, Hesbaye (Haspengouw) in the east and Hainaut in the south. Large self-contained villages nestle in the valleys. Vast fields of corn and sugar-beet cover the plateaux, rich farmland like that found in the Rhineland or in Picardy.

There are, however, regional differences: if Tertiary clay lies under the loess the land is better irrigated and grass grows in abundance, for example in the damp Hesbaye region north of Sint Truiden and also in parts of Hainaut. If the subsoil is chalk and limestone, however, the character of the land matches that of fertile plains. That is particularly true of the dry Hesbaye region around Tongeren and Waremme.

Brussels

Situated between fertile plains and Lower Belgium, Brussels grew in strength to become the political capital of the Kingdom when Belgium declared its independence in 1830. It is accessible from the sea along the River Senne and is also linked to the naturally richer south. Following the decline of the Flemish towns when they found themselves shut off from the sea as a result of the rivers silting up, Brussels became a Brabant royal seat and the country's chief city. Although situated in the Flemish-speaking region of Brabant Brussels was strongly influenced by the French language, from the royal court down to the man in the street. Large open spaces and boulevards built in the 19th c. gave it something of the appearance of a second Paris, but without entirely losing its Flemish character. Linked to the Scheldt by a maritime canal Brussels has now grown into a community of almost a million inhabitants.

Meuse-Sambre Valley (Vallée de la Meuse)

Forming a natural part of the Ardennes, the Meuse-Sambre valley stretches along the border of Upper Belgium. Along its flanks lie layers of soft coal and it links up with a number of coalfields. In between, layers

14

of limestone under the carboniferous strata produce rocky and narrow stretches of valley, such as that below Namur. West of Charleroi the carboniferous zone merges into the fertile plains of Hainaut. Prior to industrialisation the valley lay in charming countryside, with palaces nesting in parkland, vineyards, hop and fruit fields along its flanks and castles on the spurs of the hills. Although the hard coal was in fact mined many years ago, as it was in the Ruhr valley, there was in fact little demand for it, as the iron industry established itself by the small streams running from the Ardennes rather than near the capital itself. Hard coal forms part of the main carboniferous seam stretching from the Ruhr to England by way of Aachen, Belgium, Northern France. In Belgium it skirts the southern side of the Brabant Massif, which separates it from the coalfields of Kempen. In the tectonic boundary zone of the Brabant and Ardennes Massifs the coal is in marked folds and in part covered by older layers of stone. This results in high mining costs, although these are partially offset by lower wastage. There is a preponderance of lower-quality coal rather than that which can be made into charcoal or coke. Going from east to west, the coalfields are those of Liège, Charleroi, Bassin du Centre and Borinage near Mons, where the coal comes to the surface between chalk hills.

Industrialisation began in the first half of the 19th c. when for the first time on the mainland of Europe the Cockerill works in Seraing developed the system whereby collieries, iron foundries and rolling mills worked in conjunction with one another. This had important technical and economic repercussions on industry throughout the whole of continental Europe. The highly-industrialised Walloon region is very interesting. In the early days of its "industrial revolution" it had to face many problems connected with the living and social conditions of the workers, but on the other hand it has shown itself to be a pioneer in the fields of working conditions and housing for more than a century.

However, the coal-mining industry appears to be under threat in the foreseeable future, as the worldwide steel crisis is affecting the Walloon and the neighbouring Lorraine regions too, bringing closures and unemployment in its wake. However, this is compensated to some degree by glassworks, non-ferrous metal factories, large chemical works and a highly-specialised finished product industry, and the unemployment rate has fallen in recent years. The region's position is safeguarded by means of the Albert Canal between Liège and Antwerp, which will take large ships, as well as the Meuse and Sambre canals, while the important Canal du Centre from Brussels to Charleroi is due for extension. The iron ore comes mainly from Minette in Lorraine. Liège, whose old churches date back to Carolingian and Early Romanesque times, and the fortified town of Charleroi, named after Charles II of Spain, have grown during the last century into conurbations of some half a million inhabitants each, although there are no actual statistics to show this, as in Belgium all such surrounding communities have remained independent.

The importance of the Central Belgian regions in the context of human geographical development has changed many times. From earliest pre-history up to Roman times the fertile plains were centres of settlement, closely linked to the cultures of central Europe. There were barely any links with the country to the north. The great Roman road from Cologne to Rheims stretched from east to west across the fertile plains, from Maastricht via Tongeren-Gembloux to Bavay in France. Tongeren, the Roman civitas of Tongres, is the oldest town in the country.

Towards the end of the period of antiquity the Meuse valley gained in importance. First Maastricht and then the as yet unknown town of Liège succeeded Tongeren as diocesan towns and ruling centres. Although the fertile plains did not deteriorate to any great extent, traffic nevertheless tended to move from the main road to the waterways of the Meuse and

Human
geographical
development

In the lower Ardennes

Sambre. In the west Tournai, situated on the Scheldt, the civitas of Nervier and the first capital city of the Franks, increased in importance. On the Meuse Huy and Dinant developed into major towns. It was not until the early Middle Ages that the Flemish wastes along the waterways were opened up and the coastal regions developed into important economic centres, and have remained so to this day.

Upper Belgium

The Ardennes form Upper Belgium. They are part of the west side of the Rhine range of slate mountains and a continuation of the Eifel. The Signal de Botrange, 694 m (2278 ft) high, is the highest point in Belgium. The Ardennes are an old stretch of mountains the surface of which intersects the folded strata, but are recognisable as mountains only in the deeply slashed valleys.

The Upper Ardennes are to be distinguished from the Lower Ardennes. At one time rather isolated and with few roads, they are now fully developed and a favourite "villégiature", or holiday region, for the towns in the north.

The **Lower Ardennes** reach heights of only 200–500 m (660–1640 ft), and extend south of the Meuse; they are characterised by forest-covered plateaux divided by areas of meadowland, without any heights worthy of mention. The regions of Condroz, Entre-Sambre-et-Meuse, Fagne and Famenne all form part of the Lower Ardennes. The Meuse tributaries of Ourthe and Lesse have dug out giant caves with magnificent limestone stalactite formations (Han-sur-Lesse, Rochefort).

The **Upper Ardennes**, which go up to more than 500 m (1640 ft), boast some scenery which is unique in central Europe. There are the high moors known as the High Fenns (Hohe Venn or Hautes Fagnes), where the geomorphological and climatic conditions – an impermeable layer of clay and slate and high rainfall – are ideal for the formation of moorland. The amount of rainfall exceeds that of the water which flows away, producing the characteristic "hour-glass" moor, with sections filled or saturated with water. The High Fenns today form part of the Belgo-German natural park.

Climate

The climate in Belgium is generally temperate and humid, the result of its position in the temperate latitudes. It is quite strongly influenced by the sea, as it lies very close to the coast and the predominant westerly winds come in off the sea. In more detail, the country can be divided into three climatic zones, i.e. that immediately adjoining the coast, the interior lowlands and the Ardennes range of low mountains.

The climates experienced in the various regions are illustrated in the climatic diagrams of various places showing the annual range of temperature and precipitation. The letters represent the individual months. Temperatures are shown as an orange-red band. The upper edge corresponds to the average maximum day temperature, the lower to the average minimum night temperature. The corresponding temperature figures can be read off the scale at the side. The blue rain/snowfall columns show the average precipitation (in mm) in the month concerned.

Climatic stations (see map and diagrams)

Working from these diagrams, it is possible to estimate the climatic conditions in the intervening areas, while bearing the following rules in mind. Moving inland, the influence of the sea obviously becomes weaker, and variations in temperature between day and night and winter

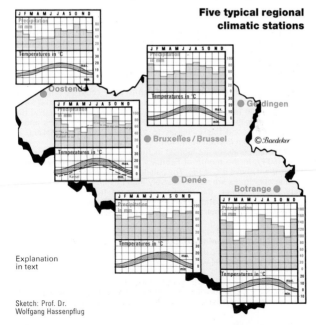

Five typical regional climatic stations

Oostende

Gedingen

Bruxelles / Brussel

© Baedeker

Denée

Botrange

Explanation in text

Sketch: Prof. Dr. Wolfgang Hassenpflug

and summer increase; periods of sunshine, precipitation and other climatic features change accordingly.

The higher above sea-level the more temperatures decrease, roughly at a rate of 0.5°C (1°F) per hundred metres (330 ft). For example, the average annual temperature in Brussels, which is 100 m (330 ft) above sea-level, is 9.9°C (49°F), while that on the Botrange, at 694 m (2278 ft), is 5.7°C (42°F). The number of frosty days and the amount of rainfall also increase accordingly.

The ribbon of land running immediately **along the coast** (Ostend diagram) differs climatically in some important respects from the coastal hinterland.

In the summer months in particular the periods of sunshine are greater and cloud amounts less than those found just a few miles inland. The reason is as follows: as moisture-laden air masses from the North Sea pass over the land on the prevailing westerly air currents they are interrupted by the relatively rough land surface, pile up, climb and produce condensation and cloud-formations. In the coastal hinterland, to where the wind takes the clouds, the tendency towards cloud build-up and rain is much greater, while along the beach it remains sunny with very little cloud. Close to the sea there are more than 1750 hours of sunshine in the course of a year, e.g. Ostend has 1760 hours, the maximum being 230 hours in June. The strong sunshine – aided by the clean air – never becomes unpleasantly hot because of the fresh winds which always blow, mainly from the west, making the days cooler and avoiding risks of sunburn. Inhaling the ozone is also very beneficial to health.

Even in January minimum temperatures lie just above freezing point, and the average maxima are about 5°C (40°F). The highest temperatures are not reached until August, when the average minimum is at least 13°C (55°F) and the maximum just under 20°C (68°F).

The wind always blows on to the coast, being at its strongest during the winter months; the average wind force over the year in Ostend, for example, is 6.5 m per second (15 m.p.h.), increasing to 7.1 m per second (16 m.p.h.) in January. Because of the considerable differences in air pressure wind strengths in winter are about 2–1 (4 to 3 m.p.h.) more than those in summer. Westerlies predominate, with southerlies quite often from October to January and north-easterlies in spring. The annual rainfall in southern Flanders as far as the Lille region remains below 600 mm (24 in.), while in the north-west of Ghent more than 600 mm (24 in.) fall; Ostend has 579 mm (23 in.) The number of days on which rain falls is less than 150 (Ostend 143). From March to June about 30 mm (1¼ in.) falls in a month; from July to November this increases to 60 mm (2½ in.), the most – 70 mm (2¾ in.) – falling in October. During the first of the above periods there are ten days in each month on which it rains, and in the second period this increases to fourteen. Generally speaking, in summer the rain is often in the form of heavy showers.

Water temperatures are highest in July and August, when they reach 16°C (60°F). In the month of February the effects of the Gulf Stream keeps them above 6°C (43°F). The balancing effect of the sea means that land temperatures are not excessively high in summer and are seldom very low in winter; the number of days of frost in winter is 40. Accordingly the temperature band shown in the diagrams is narrow and fairly straight, and generally above freezing point.

There are regular and marked differences in climate between the coastal strip and the **interior of the country**, while variations within the interior are minor (see climatic diagrams for Brussels and Gerdingen).

The daily and annual variations in temperature increase. If the climatic diagrams for Brussels and Gerdingen are compared with those for Ostend, the wider and more curved temperature bands will indicate this. In summer it is considerably warmer during the day than on the coast. The average minima in January lie below freezing point (Brussels minus

1.2°C (30°F), the average maxima between 4° and 5°C (39° and 41°F) (Brussels 4.3°C/39.7°F). The highest temperatures are reached in July, with maxima well above 20°C (68°F) (Brussels 22.7°C (73°F)) and minima 12°C (53.6°F) (Brussels 12.1°C (53.8°F)) or lower. Thus the daily variation of more than 10°C (18°F) clearly exceeds the figures at the coastal situations (e.g., in August the daily variation in Ostend is only 6.3°C (11.3°F)).

Away from the coast the length of the period of the year which is free from frost is shorter, and the number of frosty days increases from about 40 to 60.

Also, away from the coast the number of hours of sunshine each year reduces by more than 100 (Brussels 1585 hours, compared with 1760 in Ostend). Equally, this means an increase in cloud amounts inland; while on the coast 140 to 160 days have a cloud amount of 80 per cent, there are 170 to 180 such days in the eastern inland regions. Cloud amounts are particularly small in September in those areas away from the coast.

As the land rises towards the Ardennes region, so the annual rainfall increases from 700 mm (28 in.) to more than 800 mm (32 in.) Even small hills can result in localised increases in rainfall, in the same way that air, condensation and cloud formation produces precipitation on the coast. From September to November it can usually be assumed that rainfall amounts inland will be less than on the coast. As the relative atmospheric humidity is greatest in the winter months (monthly average just under 90 per cent), this is when most foggy days occur (about 30 to 50 in the course of a year).

Wind strengths slacken noticeably as one moves inland; the average wind strength in Brussels is 3.8 m per second (8½ m.p.h.) compared with 6.5 (15) in Ostend. In winter they are without exception about 0.5 to 1 m per second (1 to 2 m.p.h.) stronger than in summer. South-westerly winds predominate. They influence the nature of the countryside in several ways: they blow away clouds, drive old and new windmills or deform trees by their force and as a result of the salt they contain render it necessary for farmers and others to erect hedgerows as protection.

Because they are higher **the Ardennes** have their own climate, particularly noticeable at the high point of the Botrange (694 m/2278 ft), and progressively less so where the ground is lower (see climatic diagrams for Botrange and Denée-Maredsous).

On the Botrange the average annual temperature is 5.7°C (42°F). On the high ground too the daily maxima in January lie below freezing point, while the night minima sink to below minus 4°C (25°F). In July the daily maxima rise to 17°C (63°F), while the minima remain below the 10°C (50°F) mark (Botrange 9.3°C) (48.7°F)). Thus there are only a few months when the night minima are well above freezing; only the period from the middle of May to early October is frost-free; 120 frosty days are recorded.

As the height above sea-level increases, so does the amount of rainfall. Annual precipitation often exceeds 1500 mm (60 in.) (Botrange 1510 mm) (61 in.)); it increases yet further on the lee side of the mountain. The number of days with rain is not much more than that on the plains (Botrange 213, Brussels 206 per annum), but they are heavier. Thus in autumn it is possible to have 100 mm (4 in.) in a day.

As a result of the lower temperatures a large proportion of the precipitation falls as snow, on 140 to 160 days. The nature of the climate, however, means that it seldom lies for more than 25 days.

Flora and Fauna

Cultivated and arable land Large areas of Belgium have been put to the plough or subjected to planned afforestation, with the result that comparatively little of its native vegetation remains.

Flora

Originally there were extensive forests of birch, oak and other trees to be found in the sandy "geest" region, but over the years cultivation reduced these to vast tracts of heathland which in recent centuries have been planted with pine trees. The natural deciduous forests of the loess and loamy soils of Belgium, comprising mainly oak, hornbeam and beech in the Ardennes, have largely been replaced with coniferous forests of pine and fir, because the latter grow faster and are more profitable. The natural vegetation of the south-eastern parts of the Ardennes, protected from the winds, includes forests of oak and beech. Stands of oak and hornbeam are characteristic of the Pays Gaumais in the south of Belgium, where vineyards are also to be found. Forests of oak and birch are also native to the barren sandstone soil where Belgium borders on Luxembourg, like those in the sandy "geest" region.

The dunes and polders along the North Sea coast and the few remaining moorland regions have some particularly interesting species of plant life. Typical beach plants include halophytes, which need salt to survive and so are found only where the soil contains salt. The best known examples of this genus are samphire and saltwort, which are found growing on strips of the coast which are flooded by the sea as well as on newly reclaimed polderland. To protect them against erosion the dunes are planted with varieties of mat-grass, marram grass and small fir trees. As well as these halophilic plants sea-violets are also found in the dunes. An extensive programme to neutralise the marshland soil has meant that meadows and lush grass have replaced the halophytes to a large degree.

Very characteristic are the **moors** to be found in parts of Peel, with cotton grass, other acid-loving grasses, cranberries and wild rosemary or marsh tea. Heathers and trees such as alder, pine and birch are gradually being added.

Fauna

The **original fauna**, never very varied at the best of times, has been further decimated as the result of man seeking to cultivate every available corner of the countryside. Apart from in the Ardennes there is scarcely any natural habitat left for the larger species of animal. Roe deer are to be found in the Sambre-Meuse valley. Red deer are seen only in the Ardennes, together with wild boar. The very rare wild cat is occasionally seen in the southern Ardennes; they hide by day in deserted foxholes. The tree marten is more common. Among the interesting birds seen here are the hoopoe and the tree-creeper, which frequent only the meadows and arable land to the north of the Sambre-Meuse valley or the dense forests to the south of it. As a result of the increasing pollution the number of fish found in rivers and canals has reduced drastically.

If there is an animal typical of Belgium – apart from the species of rabbit known as the "Belgian Giant" – then it must be the **Belgian carthorse**. These powerful horses were used in agriculture and forestry as draught animals, but rendered obsolete with the arrival of the tractor. However, they are still traditionally reared in the Ardennes and win many prizes at various annual horse-shows. In the Musée de la Vie Rurale en Wallonie near Saint-Hubert (see A to Z) an exhibition is devoted to the Belgian carthouse.

Population

According to the 1991 census, there are 10.02 million people living in Belgium, equivalent to 328 inhabitants per sq. km (850 per sq. mi.), a figure exceeded in Europe only by Monaco and the Netherlands. However, it must be borne in mind that there are marked regional variations in this average figure. At one extreme lie the six most densely populated regions, those of Brussels, Antwerp, Liège, Ghent, Charleroi and Mons. These account for more than one-third of the total population of Belgium, with a density of more than 1000 inhabitants per sq. km (2590 per sq. mi.). The provinces of Antwerp and East and West Flanders are also above average in density, with some 500 per sq. km (1300 per sq. mi.). In contrast, the central mountainous region of the Ardennes can boast only 50 folk per sq. km (130 per sq. mi.), and even fewer in some parts.

57.6 per cent of the total population live in Flanders, 32.5 per cent in Wallonia and 10 per cent in Brussels.

Belgium's dense population is an indication of the extensive degree of **urbanisation** which has taken place. Almost one-half of the people live in towns and cities, with a further 38 per cent in urbanised communities. Only about 13 per cent are to be found in rural districts.

Population changes After the Second World War the rate of population increase reduced markedly. The birth rate is the lowest in Europe, having remained relatively static overall in the 1980s, while the death rate, at 1.2 per cent, is relatively high as a result of the increase in the percentage of old people. However, the birth rate in the Flemish regions is above the average for the country.

Religion Nearly 90 per cent of Belgians are adherents of the Roman Catholic faith, only 0.9 per cent being Protestants. Moslems account for 1.1 per cent, and 7.6 per cent belong to other religious groups or are atheists or agnostics. Finally, 35,000 Jews (0.4 per cent) live in Belgium, mainly in Antwerp, the largest Jewish community in Europe.

Carthorses – the working animals of the Ardennes

''Just'' a dispute about language?

For many years conflicts have existed between Flemings and Walloons which the phrase "linguistic differences" does not really explain adequately. Disputes on the matter of language are but one way of expressing far-reaching cultural and economic differences.

It could be argued that past attempts to link Belgium with France constituted a major stumbling block in the emergence of the Belgian nation. While French had become the official language because the upper classes spoke, dressed and acted like the French, Flemish was considered good enough only for the lower and middle classes. In addition industrialisation and its concomitant prosperity took place in the coal-producing Francophone region of Wallonia, Dutch-speaking Flanders being excluded from these developments and remaining predominantly rural. This situation produced a breeding-ground for the Flemish Movement in its fight for equality for the Flemish people. In 1898 it succeeded in forcing through the Equality Act, which decreed that official texts in French and Flemish were equally valid. However, by 1936 French had again become the only language accepted in Parliament, and it was not until 1962 that a Dutch translation of the criminal code was produced.

Detrimental to the Flemish cause was the fact that, during the German occupation in the Second World War, the Flemish Movement to a large degree co-operated with the occupying forces because they hoped to be granted Flemish autonomy by the Germans, which in fact the latter did do their best to enforce. This background helps the foreigner to understand the disputes in the 1930s over the language laws and why Flemish was made the compulsory language at the University of Ghent; this latter change did much to further the Flemish cause.

After the Second World War these disputes intensified even further. The recession in the Wallonian steel industry, which was particularly noticeable from the early 1970s onwards, coupled with the simultaneous growth of new industries in Flanders shook the Walloons' self-confidence; at the same time the Flemings fought against the non-observance of the language laws. When the language border was fixed in 1962 it was hoped that this would produce a peaceful solution to the problem, but in fact right up to the present day violent disputes still occur between Flemings and Walloons. Thus in October 1991 the last government of Wilfried Martens foundered on a typical Belgian dispute: the Flemish minister refused to support the proposal put forward by Walloon armaments firms to export to the Near East; as a countermove, the Walloons tried to prevent Flemish telephone companies from acquiring a large block of business and also called for payment of the national radio and television fees to be apportioned by regions. The dispute ended with the withdrawal of the Flemish People's Union from the government coalition resulting in new elections, which produced large gains for the radical Flemish Nationalists.

There are hopes that converting Belgium into a federal state will bring about a solution, but already there are complications and doubts as to whether it will be possible to obtain a responsible reaction from the various local governments and councils, cultural bodies and regions as well as signs of an increasingly strained atmosphere in dealings between the various factions. The situation now reflects more than anything else the contrast which exists between the "rich" Flemish north and the "poor" Wallonian south, a fact demonstrated by the resistance shown by the Flemings to a suggestion that there should be a redistribution of taxes to aid the Walloons. The Walloons fear a Flemish "takeover", their economic decline being exacerbated by the fact that a low birth-rate means that the number of French-speaking Belgians is continually on the decline.

Linguistic Regions

— Linguistic boundary
German
Dutch (Flemish)
French
Bilingualism (French and Flemish)

The **employment structure** of the Belgian people reflects the high degree of industrialisation and urbanisation. Agriculture, the most important branch of the economy prior to industrialisation, now employs only 2.6 per cent of the work force. The percentage of those engaged in industry, on the other hand, is now over 27.6 per cent. Even higher, however, is the number of people working in the service sector – currently 69.7 per cent and still growing. After having reached an all-time high of some 15 per cent of the work force in the 1980s, the unemployment rate had sunk to 11.2 per cent by 1992. It is expected to continue to fall.

About 850,000 **foreigners** live in Belgium, of which some 520,000 are from other EU countries. The remainder are guest workers from North Africa and Turkey.

Belgium is divided into areas where either Germanic or Romance ethnic backgrounds and languages predominate. The **Walloons** live in the southern part and speak French, while Walloon, a French dialect differing from the Parisian dialect mainly in being less nasal, now lives on only in certain idiomatic expressions. The **Flemings**, speaking a Dutch dialect, live in the northern regions of the country. Strictly speaking, there are three dialects – the Zeeland dialect spoken at the mouth of the Scheldt and in West Flanders, the Brabant and the Limburg. The dividing line between the two ethnic groups, which has remained almost unchanged since the Middle Ages, is the Flemish-Walloon language border, running roughly from Visé on the Meuse in an east-west direction by way of Waremme, Halle and Ronse to Menen on the French border.

In addition to Flemings and Walloons, **Germans** form a third ethnic and linguistic group around Eupen St.-Vith and Arlon.

Brussels, a Walloon enclave in the Flemish region, is officially bilingual, although it cannot be denied that it is fundamentally French-speaking. Over the years "Brusselese", a dialect which is a mixture of French and Dutch, has developed.

Ethnic Groups
and Language
Areas

23

The Belgian royal couple, Albert and Paola

State and Society

The **flag** of the Kingdom of Belgium is in the form of three vertical stripes of black, yellow and red. They are the Brabant colours, which first appeared in this form in 1797 during an unsuccessful uprising against its Austrian overlords.

The Belgian **coat-of-arms** depicts the Lion of Brabant, with the larger versions also containing the motto "L'Union fait la force" (Unity is Strength) and the banners of the nine Belgian provinces.

Parliament

Under the Constitution of 1831 the Kingdom of Belgium is a **constitutional monarchy** and, according to the constitutional reforms enacted in 1993, Belgium is a "**federal state**, composed of communes and regions". Following the unexpected death in 1993 of King Baudouin I (Boudewijn, Baldwin), who had ruled since 1951 but had remained without issue, his brother Albert II ascended the throne. The new constitution confers executive powers on the king, but in practice his role has now been limited to merely that of a national figurehead.

The constitutional reforms which came into force in 1995 have turned Belgium into a federal state, in which the concept of a unitary state has been foregone in favour of a greater emphasis on the individual regions and communes. Since 1989 Flanders and Wallonia have been largely autonomous in matters involving economic, financial, commercial, labour, environmental and energy policies. The third federal state, The Brussels region, enjoys special status. Flanders and Wallonia now elect their own parliament and can even negotiate internationally binding agreements and treaties. This constitutional reform can be seen as the logical outcome of a developmental process lasting many years, which now recognises the increased self-awareness of the regions and yet in the final analysis aims to strengthen Belgium's national integrity.

The constitutional reforms have given the House of Representatives (Chambre des Représentants, Kamer van Volksvertegenwoordigers) considerably more legislative powers than it had hitherto possessed. The chamber has 150 members who are directly elected by the people, voting being compulsory. It can by a constructive vote of no-confidence bring down the government. Group divisions of the members are determined both by their party-political allegiance and by their linguistic backgrounds, which can in effect bring about electoral coalitions which transcend normal party-political boundaries.

The Senate (Sénat, Senaat) has 71 members, of whom 40 are elected, 10 each are appointed by the Council of Flanders and the French community, one by the German-speaking community, and a further 10 are co-opted. Although the Senate can introduce legislative initiatives by itself, its real function is intended to be that of a deliberating assembly and a "senate of the communes". What is new is its role as mediator in disputes between the country's various federal assemblies. The final decision in legislative matters, however, rests unequivocally with the lower chamber.

The Belgian government is appointed by the King, but must be confirmed by both Houses of Parliament. Leaving aside the Prime Minister, it must be made up of equal numbers of French- and Flemish-speaking ministers.

Government

Belgium's regional and federal structure is extremely confusing. It is mainly the result of disputes between Flemings and Walloons and subsequent concessions made to the popular groups. Since 1971 Belgium has been divided into four linguistic areas, three cultural communes, three regions and now three federal states. Added to this there is the historical sub-division into provinces.

Regionalism and federalism

The division of Belgium into ten provinces (until 1995 nine) is quite simple to explain. Each is administered by a directly elected provincial

Belgien
Koninkrijk België
Royaume de Belgique

council with a governor at its head. The council of state was designed back in 1946 to negotiate between communes and provinces.

The four linguistic areas referred to above are the Flemish-speaking, the French-speaking and the German-speaking areas plus the (officially) bi-lingual city of Brussels.

The communes are the Flemish, French and German-speaking ones. In all three there is an elected community council, each with an executive arm, which deals with cultural matters and subjects affecting the individual such as health and social politics.

The three regions are the Flemish, the Walloon and the Brussels regions. Each has a regional council with an executive arm which inter alia is responsible for environmental matters, nature conservation, administration and regional economic, financial and social policies. In the Flemish council, however, the community council and regional council are combined, but in matters affecting the Flemish region Brussels members may not vote, although they can do so on community matters.

Parties

No less confused is the picture relating to the Belgian political parties, for they too are shaped both by ideological and cultural differences. The language barrier also runs through the main parties.

The most recent elections in June 1999, under the cloud of never-ending scandals – most recently relating to dioxin-contaminated chicken feed –, turned the political landscape upside down. Voters clearly rejected the ruling coalition of the Socialist Party (PS = Parti Socialiste or SP = Socialistische Partij), which leads in Wallonia, and the Christian Democratic Party (CVP = Christelijke Volkspartei or PSC = Parti Social Chrétien), with its major stronghold in Flanders. For the first time since 1875, the strongest party is the Liberal Party (VLD = Vlaamse Liberalen en Demokraten, or PRL–FDF = Parti Réformateur Libéral with the Front Démocratique de Bruxellois Francophones). They provide the President who is the head of a 'rainbow coalition' with the two socialist parties and the Greens of the Walloon Ecolo (Ecologistes) and the Flemish Agalev (Anders gaan leven) who gained the highest number of votes, respectively. Even more successful – at least in Flanders – was right-wing radical and xenophobic Vlaams Blok, which in Antwerp, Mechelen and Ghent even gained the majority. Their Walloon counterpart, the Front National, is far less successful. The PDB, the Partei der Deutschsprachigen Belger (Party of German-speaking Belgians), is of importance only in East Belgium where German is spoken.

Trade unions

The trade unions have avoided being divided into culturally different branches. There are three ideologically different employees' organisations: the Socialist Federation of Trade Unions (FGTB or ABVV), the Christian Federation of Trade Unions (CSC or ACV), and the Federation of Liberal Trade Unions (CGLSB or ACLVB).

Foreign policy

Belgium is a member of the EU and of NATO, and linked to both organisations in a special way, Brussels being the seat of the EU Council of Ministers, the EU Commission and, together with Strasbourg, the seat of the European parliament and thus the effective political capital of Europe. NATO also has its most important divisions in Belgium, namely, the NATO Council in Brussels and its military headquarters in Casteau near Mons.

Education and Science

School system

School attendance is obligatory for all children and young people aged between six and eighteen. This can be at a state school (Athenée, Atheneum) or private school (Collège, College), which may concentrate on providing a general education or technical, artistic or professional

Province Town	Area in km²	Population	Chief town
1 Antwerpen	2 867	1 611 000	Antwerpen
Antwerpen	1 001	919 000	Antwerpen
Mechelen	510	293 000	Mechelen
Turnhout	1 365	375 000	Turnhout
2 Flemish Brabant	1 206	1 951 000	Leuven
Halle-Vilvoorde	943	525 000	Halle/Vilvoorde
Leuven	1 163	423 000	Leuven
3 Wallonian Brabant	1 090	303 000	Nivelles
Nivelles	1 090	303 000	Nivelles
4 Hainaut	3 788	1 283 000	Mons
Ath	487	76 000	Ath
Charleroi	555	429 000	Charleroi
Mons	585	250 000	Mons
Mouscron	101	71 000	Mouscron
Soignies	518	166 000	Soignies
Thuin	934	141 000	Thuin
Tournai	608	140 000	Tournai
5 Liège	3 863	1 006 000	Liège
Huy	659	91 000	Huy
Liège	798	591 000	Liège
Verviers	2 016	249 000	Verviers
Waremme	390	61 000	Waremme
6 Limburg	2 422	755 000	Hasselt
Hasselt	907	361 000	Hasselt
Maaseik	884	197 000	Maaseik
Tongeren	631	179 000	Tongeren
7 Luxembourg	3 755	234 000	Arlon
Arlon	317	47 000	Arlon
Bastogne	1 043	37 000	Bastogne
Marche-en-Famenne	955	45 000	Marche-en-Famenne
Neufchâteau	1 353	52 000	Neufchâteau
Virton	77	45 000	Virton
8 Namur	3 666	426 000	Namur
Dinant	1 592	92 000	Dinant
Namur	1 152	266 000	Namur
Philippeville	909	58 000	Philippeville
9 Oost-Vlaanderen	2 982	1 340 000	Gent
Aalst	469	258 000	Aalst
Dendermonde	343	181 000	Dendermonde
Eeklo	334	79 000	Eeklo
Gent	943	485 000	Gent
Oudenaarde	418	112 000	Oudenaarde
Sint-Niklaas	475	213 000	Sint-Niklaas
10 West-Vlaanderen	3 134	1 111 000	Brugge
Brugge	651	261 000	Brugge
Diksmuide	362	47 000	Diksmuide
Ieper	550	104 000	Ieper
Kortrijk	403	275 000	Kortrijk
Oostende	292	135 000	Oostende
Roeselaere	272	137 000	Roeselaere
Tielt	329	85 000	Tielt
Veurne	275	51 000	Veurne
Region Vlaanderen	13 511	7 070 000	Antwerpen
Region Wallonie	16 848	2 950 000	Namur
Region Bruxelles/Brussel	**162**	**970 000**	
Kingdom Belgium	30 514	Estimate 1991: 10 020 000	Bruxelles/Brussel

qualifications. The private schools are mostly Catholic, as generally speaking the Catholic Church has had a considerable influence on education. The schooling system is divided into voluntary nursery and pre-school instruction for three to six-year-olds, followed by six years in primary school and then six years of secondary education, split into three two-year cycles each with its own final examination.

Universities Belgium's universities are under either state, church or private control. Differences between Flemings and Walloons have led to the universities of Brussels and Leuven (Louvain) each being divided into two independent Flemish and French colleges. In Leuven, founded in 1425 and the Belgian university which is most steeped in tradition, this division has been taken to the point where the French-speaking tutors and students have founded a new model university at Louvain-la-Neuve 30 km (20 mi.) south of Brussels. The way in which the library of Leuven university, so rich in tradition, is split up is really quite incomprehensible: one part contains all the odd shelf-numbers, the other the even ones! There are other full universities in Ghent, Liège and Mons. In addition there are university centres in Antwerp and Limburg as well as nine part-universities, fifteen institutes and technical colleges, five music colleges and five art colleges.

Economy

Because of its lack of raw materials and small indigenous market the country is very export-orientated, and more than 70 per cent of its products go abroad. Belgium, which forms one economic, customs and currency union with Luxembourg, is in tenth position among the world's trading nations. In 1996 goods valued at 140 billion US dollars were imported, mainly machinery, vehicles and foodstuffs. Exports in the same year were 138 billion dollars, mainly machinery and vehicles, chemical products, iron and steel. Its major trading partners for imports are Germany and the Netherlands, and France and Germany for exports.

The gross national product (GNP) in 1996 amounted to 268.6 billion dollars, which statistically speaking means that each Belgian citizen contributed 26.440 dollars. On the other side of the coin, there is an immense national debt, the highest of any EU country, and, in consequence, a heavy burden of interest payments. However, compared to figures for earlier years, these do begin to show signs of the success of the government's stabilisation measures and of an economic upswing, which is reflected in increased investment activity and a very stable inflation rate of under 2 per cent (1.6 per cent in 1998) – prices in Belgium are amongst the most stable in Europe. However, the unemployment rate also remains unchanged, at over 12 per cent.

Industry **Decline of heavy industry** The Belgian economy is supported in the main by the country's highly-developed industry. The industrialisation process started in the early 19th century, thanks to the hard coal and iron-ore deposits found in Wallonia, and then spread from there to the rest of mainland Europe. However, it was this very advantage which proved to be its downfall after the Second World War. Industrial plant quickly became obsolete as the result of lack of investment. This, and the loss of the Belgian Congo from whence much of the raw materials had come, led to an economic crisis which the government tried to meet by means of tax reliefs on investment, but which was made worse by the economic situation within the European Community. With this government aid the Wallonian heavy industry was able to expand until the mid-1970s, but then the worldwide steel crisis hit Belgium harder than most, with the result that Wallonia's once flourishing industries are now in a state of depression, as assembly and production plants have not been

Natural gas liquefaction plant in the port of Antwerp

modernised and in consequence the Belgian coal and steel industry is no longer competitive and relies on support from the state and the EU.

Structural changes and relocation After the Second World War there was a noticeable relocation of the main centres of industry in Belgium, combined with structural changes some of which were far-reaching. Expansion moved away from iron and steel in favour of the petro-chemical and chemical industries. As a result Belgium's two largest companies are now Petrofina (oil) and Solvay S.A. (chemicals); the steel industry can manage only third place, in the shape of the Cockerill-Sambre Works, which can claim only a third of the turnover of Petrofina. In fourth place lies Agfa-Gevaert, another chemical company, with Ford in fifth place.

Increasing imports of raw materials have shown that the favourable situations of the ports make them very cost-effective. Antwerp in particular has profited from this fact, so that it and the surrounding countryside have developed into a giant industrial conglomerate, composed predominantly of huge chemical and petro-chemical plants. In contrast, the capital Brussels is home to much smaller firms, and its share of the country's total industrial production is about one-fifth.

As the Flemish north grew in economic power so the Walloon south declined. Promising new industries such as the chemical, metal-working and service sectors set up mainly in Flanders because of the locational advantages; 60 per cent of Belgium's gross national product now comes from there. This fact also served to exacerbate the long-standing animosity between Flemings and Walloons – the one side has no wish to be the nation's paymaster, while the other resents being its poorhouse.

Belgium's major branch of industry continues to be its export-orientated **metalworking industry**. The most important locations are at Namur,

Liège and Antwerp. The products range from investment plant, machinery, industrial equipment and consumer goods to enamelware and the manufacture of railway coaches, locomotives, textile machinery and sea-going ships. Belgium also manufactures more than one million cars a year, 90 per cent of which are exported, making it one of Europe's major producers. One of the most stable branches of the metal industry is arms production, mainly firearms and munitions made in the Fabriques Nationales (FN), which also has considerable exports.

The future appears rosy for the **chemical and petro-chemical industry** centred in Antwerp. Mile upon mile of tanks and plant belonging to mineral oil and chemical companies lie along the banks of the Scheldt. The major products are paints, dyes, fertilisers, medicines and photochemical materials. However, the growth of the chemical industry has meant that a high price has had to be paid in the shape of contamination of rivers and the atmosphere.

The **textile industry** is traditionally located in Flanders and Brabant. The once-important linen industry is now in a state of stagnation and has been almost completely overshadowed by the cotton and man-made fibre industries. Flax is grown around Ghent, Kortrijk and Aalst, while Antwerp leads in the field of wool-processing.

Just as important is the Belgian **glass industry** in Flanders, Hainaut, Liège and Namur. The main products are mirror and window glass.

About 25 per cent of world requirements are manufactured in the export-orientated factories in these provinces.

Mining and Energy

Hard **coal** is the only important raw material mined in Belgium today. The area along the Sambre-Meuse valley, with the old Wallonian districts of Borinage, Centre, Charleroi and Liège was where the industrialisation of Belgium first began. The stocks of coal and those of iron-ore, now exhausted, were important factors which led the iron and steel industries to establish themselves here as long ago as the early 19th century. However, it was not long before demand for raw materials exceeded local supplies, so that coal and iron-ore had to be imported even in the last century. Competition from cheaper imported coal, mainly from the USA, led in the 1960s to the closure of many large mines, just as it did in other places in Europe, reaching its peak with the final closing of mines in the South Basin in 1984. Today indigenous coal supplies are mined in the Kempen region, where the less complex nature and position of the seams means that considerably less expensive mining methods can be employed than those used in the heavily-folded seams along the Sambre-Meuse valley; in addition, the quality of the Kempen coal is better. However, the amount of foreign coal used continues to increase.

Energy An annual consumption of 5 thousand oil units per head of population puts Belgium at the head of all EU countries. The Belgian state continues to back nuclear energy as the main energy-producer. Seven nuclear power stations, the most productive being that at Mol near the Dutch border, produce nearly two-thirds of Belgium's energy needs, while conventional power stations using fossil fuels account for just under one-third. Water- and solar power privide only a tiny proportion. The bias towards atomic energy is being criticised more and more, particularly because in a densely populated country like Belgium there is no location where the safety of the population can be assured – for example, the Tihange and Doel reactors are on the edges of the Liège and Antwerp conurbations respectively. Also in recent years the atomic research centre at Mol has suffered much adverse press because of its outdated plant, lax use of hazardous materials and questionable business ethics in connection with the recycling of German atomic waste.

Belgian agriculture, working to high technical standards, produces mainly for the home market. Amounts produced per hectare are considerably above the EU average, but this is achieved only by over-fertilisation of the soil. However, demand still cannot be fully met, so 40 per cent of the country's needs have to be imported. The fact that agriculture contributes only two per cent of the GNP shows that it adds little to the total economy. The 1.4 million ha (3.5 million acres) of agricultural land are worked mainly by small farmers owning at the most 50 ha (125 acres) each, for a third of whom it is only a second occupation. As in the rest of Europe, many farmers have been obliged to give up their farms in recent years.

Cattle industry About 60 per cent of the value of agricultural production comes from cattle and dairy farming, the centres of which are found in the Ardennes, the Famenne, Kempen and the polder regions. The breeding of Belgian carthorses in the Ardennes is nowadays carried on mainly for sporting and traditional reasons.

Arable farming and horticulture The main crops grown in Belgium are wheat, barley, sugar-beet and potatoes, together with fruit and vegetables of all kinds, including chicory used in salads or as a vegetable, which is a Belgian speciality. Around Ghent flowers are grown together with industrial crops such as flax and tobacco.

The main centres of agricultural production are determined mainly by the natural conditions prevailing. In addition, however, the proximity of local markets is often a decisive factor, especially when culture is specialised or intensive. They are concentrated mainly in the triangle formed by Mechelen, Leuven and Brussels with its light soil, where vegetables are grown in huge glasshouses. Fruit is extensively grown south-east and south-west of Antwerp in the Kempen and Waas regions as well as near Sint-Truiden, Namur, Liège, Mons and Charleroi. The fertile plains of Hainaut and Hesbaye (Haspengouw) are also extensively cultivated, where wheat and sugar-beet predominate, as well as being grown in the marshy areas. The "geest" soil of Flanders and of the Kempen region is best suited to growing potatoes, wheat and barley. Grassland is found mainly in the Ardennes, in Herver and in Famenne, followed by parts of Kempen, Sietland and the marshes.

Belgian **fishing** is suffering as a result of the EU fishing-quota rules as well as from the trend towards high-tech trawlers and factory ships, which local fishermen seem unable to come to terms with. As a result traditional coastal fishing from the ports of Nieuwpoort and Ostend now plays only a minor role.

In recent years the Belgian service sector has continually increased in importance, and the number of people employed in this sphere now far exceeds that of those in industry. Naturally, it is concentrated in the larger towns, especially Brussels, it being the seat of many EU bodies and institutions as well as of NATO. Being so favourably situated from a communications point of view Belgium is very important to commerce and the transport industry. There is little doubt when the Common Market becomes a total reality the services sector will become even more important.

To the regret of the Belgian tourist authorities, tourism plays only a minor role in the country's economy. In the main Belgium is just a country which travellers pass through, with merely a fleeting glance at any sights they may see along the way. The majority of visitors to Belgium come from the Netherlands, followed by Germany, Great Britain, France and the USA.

The bulk of holidaymakers are concentrated at the seaside resorts along Belgium's coastal strip, especially at Ostend, but in fact it is pre-

The seaside resort of Koksijde

dominantly native visitors who come to the coast, almost the entire length of which is lined with hotels and which is not really very attractive. Far behind it lies the Ardennes holiday region, which is particularly favoured by the Dutch, with its charming river valleys (Semois, Meuse, Ourthe and Lesse) and extensive forests. However, in recent years the spas here, such as that at Spa itself, have shown smaller increases in the number of visitors than the resorts on the North Sea coast have experienced. Historically important towns, such as Brussels, Ghent and Bruges, have become increasingly popular for short-stay breaks.

Communications

As the result of its high concentration of industry and population and its position between the North Sea coast and central Europe, communications within Belgium have been excellent ever since the nineteenth century.

First mention must go to the **rail network**. It was in 1835 that the first train on the mainland of Europe ran between Mechelen and Brussels; now Belgium can boast some 4000 km (2500 mi.) of railway, making it one of the densest networks in the world, even though parts of it are now rather old. Transit traffic acounts for about one-fifth of the total transport capacity.

The **road network** is first-class. The motorways, most of which are lit, are justifiably famous.

The **waterways**, which form a self-contained transport system in themselves, cover a total length of 1569 km (975 mi.). The volume of goods conveyed on inland waterways far exceeds that carried by rail. The major natural waterways are the Meuse and the Scheldt. Of the artificial canals the Albert Canal from Maastricht to Antwerp, the Ghent-Bruges-Ostend Canal, the Canal du Centre and that running from Charleroi to Brussels are of great importance; the latter two canals link the Belgian waterway network with that of France. Of the larger ports particular mention must be made of Antwerp, Brussels, Bruges and Ghent, which are also accessible to sea-going ships. Ostend is one of the major ports linking the continent of Europe with Great Britain.

Air traffic plays little part within Belgium itself. From Brussels-Zaventem airport the state airline Sabena provides good connections to Africa in particular.

History

Strictly speaking, the history of Belgium as such did not commence until 1830, the year in which the State of Belgium was founded. However, the country's name does in fact perpetuate the name of the ancient tribe, the "Belgae", mentioned by Caesar in his "Gallic Wars". Until the Kingdom of Belgium was formed the history of this country was generally speaking merged with that of the Netherlands, with the result that historians often spoke of the Netherlands when they really meant the whole region of Belgium, the Netherlands and Luxembourg. The year 1568 is of decisive importance, for it was then that in the Netherlands as we know them today the War of Independence against Spain began, but those provinces which now comprise Belgium supported Spain.

From Pre-history to the Division of the Carolingian Empire

c. 4000–1500 BC	In the Neolithic Age the loess regions of present-day Belgium are inhabited by Celts. Germanic tribes first emerge from the marshlands c. 1500 BC
58–51 BC	Julius Caesar conquers the whole of Gaul, the northern part of which is inhabited by the Celtic Belgae. These include the Aduatukes, Menapi, Eburons, Trevers, Nervi and Morins.
54–53 BC	The Eburon Prince Ambiorix rises up against the Romans but is decisively defeated.
12–9 BC	The Romans attempt in vain to conquer the Germanic regions on the right bank of the Rhine.
to 400 AD	Until the early 5th c. the area which now forms Belgium, the "Provincia Gallia Belgica", forms part of the Roman Empire. From the 1st to the 3rd c. present-day Tongeren, then known as "Aduatuca Tungrorum", is the most important city in the province.
4th and 5th centuries AD	Salian Franks occupy the region between the Meuse, Scheldt and Lower Rhine. Servatius founds the diocese of Tongeren and commences to convert the region to Christianity with the aid of Irish and Scottish missionaries.
c. 440	Chlodio, progenitor of the Merovingians, makes Tournai his capital.
476	From Tournai Childerich reigns over the whole region between the Scheldt and the Somme.
482–511	Chlodwig extends the rule of the Franks to the whole of Gaul.
7th century	In the course of a second wave of Christianity large monasteries are built.
721	St Hubert moves the seat of his diocese from Maastricht to Liège.
742	Charlemagne is born near Liège.
843	Under the Treaty of Verdun the Carolingian Empire is divided up. The

area west of the Scheldt is ceded to France, ruled by Charles the Bald, while that east of the Scheldt passes to Lother I (hence Lothringia = Lorraine). The region of present-day Belgium is thus divided into two.

Emergence of Earldoms and Dukedoms

Between the 10th and 14th c., following the fall of the Carolingian Empire, large numbers of individual rulers ally themselves with others in various ways in an attempt to increase their power and to weaken the feudal power of the great neighbouring states. In the 11th c. the name "Netherlands" is applied for the first time to this collection of regions; by the end of the 18th c. it also embraces what is now known as Belgium.

In 1006 Count Lambrecht of Leuven raises the region to the status of dukedom, and originally names it Lower Lothringia. In 1248 Brabant becomes the first European state to abolish bondage. Brabant is joined with Limburg in 1288, Luxembourg in 1355 and Burgundy in 1430. The Golden Bull issued by Emperor Charles IV in 1349 grants freedom from any foreign jurisdiction. In the 15th c. Brabant is a major centre of commerce, trade and culture in the Netherlands. In 1648 it is divided into North and South Brabant.
Brabant

Established in 884, during the 14th and 15th c. this dukedom becomes the most powerful state between France and Germany. Between 1384 and 1473 the dukes gain power over almost all the temporal domains in the Netherlands – Flanders, Namur, Brabant, Limburg, Hainaut, Luxembourg, Holland, Zeeland and Picardy. Brussels becomes the glittering centre of the dukedom. After the death of the last duke Charles the Bold, who is slain in 1477, the Burgundian Netherlands pass to the Habsburgs.
Bourgogne (Burgundy)

In the mid-9th c. an earldom is formed to fight the Normans. In the 11th to 13th c. it is several times linked with Flanders, and in 1299 passes to Holland, 1345 to Wittelsbach and 1433 to Burgundy.
Hainaut

Formed as an earldom c. 1060, it becomes a dukedom in the early 12th c. and forms a part of Lower Lorraine (Lothringia). From 1221 to 1226 it is united with Luxembourg, with Brabant from 1288 and then divided up in 1648.
Limburg

In 721 the town becomes a diocese, its land belonging to Germany as a religious principality. During the 15th and 17th c. the citizens fight several times for their freedom. After the town is stormed by Charles the Bold in 1477 the region shares the same fate as Burgundy.
Liège

Having been formed in the 10th c., Luxembourg has links with Namur, Limburg and Brabant until the 13th c. In 1354 it becomes a dukedom, and in 1443 it passes to Burgundy and in 1477 to the Habsburgs.
Luxembourg

Formed in the 10th c., this dukedom passes to Hainaut c. 1200, to Flanders in 1262 and to Burgundy in 1420.
Namur

As a result of continuing Norman attacks the earldom of Flanders is formed in 864. The first Count of Flanders is Baldwin Iron-Arm. His successors extend their sphere of influence north and south. As, following the Treaty of Verdun, the Scheldt divides the area of authority, the Flemish counts are feudal lords of the French king ("Crown Flanders" west of the Scheldt) as well as of the German emperor ("Imperial Flanders" east of the Scheldt).
Vlaanderen (Flanders)

Under Theodoric and Philip of Alsace the rule of the Counts reaches its zenith. In the Crusades Counts of Flanders become "Latin" emperors of Constantinople in the years 1204–61.

The growth of the towns results in serious opposition to the Counts. The citizens of the Flemish towns, particulary Ghent, Ypres (Ieper), Kortrijk and Bruges, acquire considerable economic and political power through trade and the textile industry. In the mid-14th c. Bruges and Ghent, together with Paris, are the largest towns north of the Alps. The towns repulse attacks by the French King Philip the Fair (and with him the Count of Flanders), who had annexed Flanders to France. On May 18th 1302 rebel citizens of Bruges who had been expelled and had now returned, led by Pieter de Coninck and Jan Breydel, butchered the men of France at the "Matines of Bruges"; on July 11th of the same year the Flemish army routed the might of French chivalry at the Battle of the Golden Spurs. This battle is of worldwide significance; the defeat of France means that England now has landing places on the continent which are available to it during the Hundred Years' War. In 1337, with support from England, Ghent under Jacob van Artevelde rises up against the French. However, after Artevelde is murdered the Flemish towns lose their influence, and 45 years later his son is also killed in the Battle of Roosebecke. In 1384 Flanders becomes part of Burgundy.

From the Merger of the Netherlands to the Spanish Conquest

The separation of the Netherlands by the Holy Roman Empire is initiated by the Burgundian Duke Philip the Good, who gains possession of several duchies. A little later the Netherlands fall to the Austrian Habsburgs, who annex other territories. Spain gains power by inheritance.

1384	After the death of Louis, Count of Flanders, the Burgundian Duke Philip the Bold, having married Louis' daughter Margaret in 1369, inherits Flanders together with Antwerp and Mechelen.
1419–67	Philip the Good enlarges his possessions still further. Brussels and Leuven become the centres of the Burgundian dukedom. Under Philip's regency the Netherlands experience their first period of economic prosperity and enjoy wealth and luxury. Painting, architecture and tapestry-making flourish, and the Netherlands are regarded as the "treasure-house of Europe".
1464	The Burgundian General Assemblies meet in Bruges.
1467–77	Duke Charles the Bold, the richest and most ambitious prince of his time, oppresses the nobles and towns (Liège). He dies at the siege of Nancy in 1477.
1477	Mary, the first daughter of Charles the Bold, marries Maximilian, son of Frederick III of Austria and later to be Emperor Maximilian I.
1482	Mary of Burgundy dies. The Netherlands fall to Maximilian and thus to the Habsburgs.
1488	Maximilian is held prisoner in Bruges for eleven weeks.
1496	Philip the Fair, son of Maximilian and Mary, marries in Lier Juana, the daughter of Ferdinand and Isabella, joint sovereigns of Spain. Charles, later Charles V, is born to them in 1500 in Ghent.
1507–17	Margaret of Austria, daughter of Maximilian, reigns over the Netherlands following the death of Philip.
1519–56	Charles, King of Spain since 1516, following the death of Maximilian in 1519 in Brussels is made Emperor of the Holy Roman Empire.

He brings Utrecht (1528) and Geldern (1538), among others, under Habsburg rule. His aim is to combine the whole region into one strong state and to limit the old freedoms, which restrict the power of the crown. After 1520 Luther's teachings gain popularity, but after 1550 Calvinism becomes the prevailing religious belief in the northern provinces. Charles fiercely resists the new teachings and sets up Courts of Inquisition after 1552.

The Netherlands come under Spanish rule when the empire of Charles V is broken up following his abdication. The new ruler is Philip II.

1556

The Partitioning of the Southern Netherlands and the End of Spanish Rule

With the help of political, economic and religious repression Spain tries to enforce its rule upon the Netherlands. This leads to uprisings by the nobles and the estates and finally to war. The Seven Provinces of the northern Netherlands are able to free themselves from Spanish domination and form the Republic of the United Netherlands, while the Catholic Wallonian and Flemish southern provinces swear allegiance to Spain under the Union of Arras. This completes the separation between the two sections of the country and the territorial limits of Belgium and the Netherlands as they are known today are largely laid down.

Philip II of Spain, son of Charles V and the dominant force behind the Counter-Reformation, wants to prevent any break with Catholicism in the Netherlands or any attempts to obtain independence. He sends Spanish troops into the country, disregards the rights of the estates and the nobility and displays fantastic intolerance in seeking to stamp out Protestantism.

As a result of the struggle which lasts for decades the Netherlands are financially ruined; more than 100,000 people flee to the northern provinces.

Under the governorship of Margaret of Parma, daughter of Charles V, riots and resistance grow. Cardinal Granvelle, advisor to the throne, is recalled at the insistence of the Prince of Orange.

1559–67

The Dutch nobles form an alliance in Breda and call themselves "geusen", or beggars, a name derived from a derisive nickname given to them when they hand a petition to the governess – "Comment, Madame, peur de ces gueux?" or "What, madam, are you afraid of these beggars?". Later this term is used to describe their armed resistance, particularly at sea ("sea-beggars"). They are led by William of Orange, Egmont and Hoorn.

1566

In the "Iconoclasm" Catholic churches are laid waste.

Philip II sends the Count of Alba with new troops to quell the uprising.

1567

The struggle for liberation begins in the north of the Low Countries. The Seven Provinces rise up under the leadership of William I, the Silent One. Alba's troops cause havoc; tens of thousands are killed. William flees to Germany. The Counts Egmont and Hoorn are taken prisoner and executed in Brussels.

1568

The unity of the Low Countries falls apart. In the Union of Utrecht the Protestant northern provinces form a protective alliance against Spain which proves to be the forerunner of the Republic of the United Netherlands. In the Union of Arras the pro-Spain provinces in the south unite.

1579

In these years of struggle the Spaniards take one south Netherlands town after another. In 1604, after a three-year siege, they succeed in

1579–1604

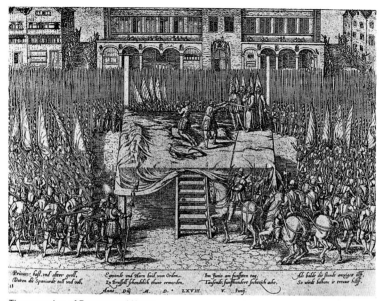

The execution of Egmont and Hoorn

taking the fortress of Ostend, the last surviving Dutch stronghold in the southern provinces. Apart from a brief interlude (1792–1830) this determines the division of the Low Countries into northern and southern parts.

1598–1621
There is an economic recovery under the reign of Archduke Albert of Austria, married to Isabella, daughter of Philip II. Baroque art is at its peak – Rubens, van Dyck, Jordaens, Brouwer.

1648
The Treaty of Westphalia sees the end of the Eighty Years' War in the Low Countries and the Thirty Years' War in Germany. The southern provinces – later to become Belgium – remain under Spanish rule; s'Hertogenbosch, Maastricht, Venlo, Roermond, Breda and Zeeland–Flanders pass to Holland, while France receives Artois, French Flanders, Franche-Comté and French Hainaut.

1667–97
During the wars of conquest waged by Louis XIV French armies fight on several occasions in the Spanish Netherlands.

1695
The French bombard Brussels and destroy over 4000 buildings.

1701–14
In the Wars of the Spanish Succession the French are defeated by the English under Marlborough and the Austrians under Prince Eugen. In the Spanish Low Countries they are defeated at Ramillies (1706), Oudenaarde (1708) and Malplaquet (1709).

1713
Under the Peace of Utrecht the southern Low Countries are promised to Austria. This sees the end of Spanish rule.

Austrian Rule and the Union of Belgium and the Netherlands

In the War of the Austrian Succession the French conquer almost the whole of the Austrian Netherlands (Battle of Fontenoy 1745), but these are returned to Austria under the terms of the peace treaty.

1745–48

Emperor Joseph II rules in an enlightened fashion. His well-meaning but over-zealous reforms offend the traditional religious order of the people.

1780–89

Against the backdrop of the French Revolution the people rise up and the Austrian Netherlands declare themselves to be "The United States of Belgium" (this is the first time the name "Belgium" has been used since Roman times), an independent republic, and they defeat the Austrians in the Battle of Turnhout. The revolutionaries carry the Brabant colours of black, yellow and red.
   The Austrians are able to regain control of the territory by the end of 1790, however, and Leopold II is restored to power.

1789–90

Belgium and the Low Countries are taken by the French. In the First Coalition War the Austrians are defeated at Jemappes (1792) and Fleurus (1794) by a French revolutionary army, but the latter is held up by the Netherlanders.

1792–94

After the conquest of the Low Countries both countries are united in the Batavian Republic. The territory now known as Belgium is divided into nine départements, which remain the provincial borders to this day.
   During almost twenty years of French occupation the Belgian territory becomes the most industrially-rich region in Europe, as there is no competition from England as a result of Napoleon's economic war against that country and the retaliatory English sea blockade.

1795–1813

In the Battle of Waterloo (south of Brussels) Napoleon is decisively beaten by the combined British, Prussian and Dutch armies.

1815

The Congress of Vienna establishes the Kingdom of the United Netherlands under William I of Orange. The Kingdom embraces the northern Netherlands, Belgium and the former diocese of Liège. Eupen and Malmedy are ceded to Prussia. Luxembourg becomes a Grand Duchy and a German federal state; the Kings of the Netherlands are at the same time Grand Dukes of Luxembourg.

1814–15

Universities are founded in Ghent in 1816 and in Liège in 1817.

1816–17

The Kingdom of Belgium until the Second World War

The economic, religious and linguistic differences between the northern and southern parts of the United Netherlands lead to a popular uprising in Belgium; in the struggle against the Dutch troops Belgium gains the upper hand and becomes independent. After overcoming some teething troubles Belgium becomes one of the leading industrial countries on the European mainland and builds a considerable colonial empire (Belgian Congo). In the First World War almost the whole of Belgium is occupied by German troops. In the period between the wars the dispute between Flemings and Walloons intensifies.

Influenced by the July revolution in Paris, the revolution which is to lead to the Kingdom of Belgium begins in Brussels on August 25th. On October 4th Belgium declares its independence from the United Netherlands.

1830

History

1831	A Dutch army defeats the Belgians at Leuven, but retreats before the advancing French. Leopold of Saxe-Coburg-Gotha (an uncle of Queen Victoria) is crowned King of Belgium on July 21st. He reigned until 1865.
1834	Founding of Brussels University.
1835	Opening of the first railway line on the European mainland, between Mechelen and Brussels.
1839	Belgium's neutrality is guaranteed by the major powers. Belgium is given the western part of Limburg and Luxembourg and the southern part of Brabant.
from 1840	The "Flemish Movement", which seeks to promote the equal status of Flemings with Walloons in political and cultural life, attracts more and more adherents.
1863	Abolition of the Scheldt customs duty; the Netherlands receive compensation.
1865–1909	During the reign of Leopold II Belgium becomes the fifth largest industrial state in Europe. Internal development is governed by differences between liberal and clerical forces as well as the ever more urgent social problems. Since the Workers' Congress in Brussels in 1886 socialism gains in importance. At the end of the 19th c., after bloody strikes and riots by workers agreements are formulated on workers' rights and social matters.
1878–1908	For 30 years the Congo, now Zaire, is privately owned by King Leopold II, who exploits it mercilessly, causing thousands of deaths. In 1908, following intervention by an international commission, the Congo becomes a Belgian colony, the Congo Belge.
1893	All adult males have the vote.
1914–18	After a German ultimatum demanding the right of the German army to march through Belgium is rejected, German troops invade Belgium on August 3rd 1914 and occupy the whole country, with much devastation. The government flees to Le Havre in France. Initially the German advance is halted at the Ijzer Canal in Flanders by detonating the dykes near Nieuwpoort and flooding the countryside. The Belgian army, under the command of King Albert I, with its French and British allies, fights a bitter trench war against the Germans and Austrians which lasts four years. During this time Flanders suffers terrible damage; among other places, Ypres and Diksmuide are completely destroyed. In April 1915 poison gas is used for the first time by the German troops at Ypres.
1919	Under the Treaty of Versailles Belgium is granted Eupen-Malmedy, St Vith and Moresnet, as well as the right to reparations.
1921	Equal franchise for male adults.
1922	Creation of the Belgian–Luxembourg Economic Community.
1923	Belgian troops participate in the occupation of the Ruhr.
1930	Ghent University is made Flemish.
1932–38	Language legislation: all central administrative offices will be bi-lingual; administration, lower courts, the law and the army will be monolingual

The centre of Ypres at the end of the First World War

according to which section of the country they apply to. Brussels is officially bi-lingual.

On February 17th King Albert has a fatal accident. He will be succeeded by Leopold III.   1934

Queen Astrid, wife of Leopold III, dies in a motor accident in Switzerland.   1935

In the Second World War German troops occupy Belgium in May 1940, in spite of its neutrality. The Cabinet escapes to England, but King Leopold III stays in Belgium, signs the Capitulation Document and is interned. During the period of occupation the Gestapo and SS terrorise the country. Breendonk concentration camp is set up. Flemish Nationalists and the Fascist Rexists of Léon Degrelle collaborate with the Germans. The Resistance succeeds in helping half the Jews in Belgium to escape abroad. Following the Allied landings in Normandy in June 1944 most of Belgium is liberated by September 1944. A final attempt by the Germans to regain the upper hand fails in the Ardennes offensive 1944–45. This failure signifies the final end of the German occupation. In the years following the liberation over 55,000 trials are held of war criminals and collaborators.   1940–44

Belgium after 1945

After the Second World War Belgium gives up its ineffective neutrality and joins NATO and the European Economic Community (EEC). Since the 1960s there have been marked disputes between Flemings and Walloons, mainly in the linguistic sphere but also on social and cultural grounds.

History

1944	Founding of Benelux Customs Union between Belgium, the Netherlands and Luxembourg, to come into force in stages by 1948.
1948	Franchise for women.
1949	Belgium joins NATO.
1950	After fierce political disputes Leopold III gives up the throne. In 1951 his son Baudouin, born 1930, becomes King.
1957	Belgium is a founder-member of the EEC, and Brussels becomes the headquarters of the EEC bodies.
1958	Under the Treaty of Hague the Customs and Economic Union between the Benelux States is ratified initially for 50 years. The Economic Union comes into force on January 1st 1960.
1960	Congo crisis. On June 29th the Belgian Congo becomes independent. A few days later there is a military uprising leading to the arrival of UN troops. When the rich mining province of Katanga under Moise Tshombe declares itself independent of the new Congo state UN troops act as an emergency government. Following the murder of the prime minister Lumumba open war breaks out between Congolese and UN troops on the one hand and Katanga troops on the other. Tshombe is supported by the Belgian Union Minière which supports him with arms and (mainly Belgian) mercenaries. It is 1964 before the last UN soldiers leave the Congo Republic (known as Zaire after 1971).

In the same year King Baudouin I marries the Spanish aristocrat Fabiola de Mora y Aragøn.

After 1960 the dispute between the Flemish-speaking Flemings and the French-speaking Walloons intensifies.

1963	The Flemish–Walloon language border is laid down.
1967	After France withdraws from the NATO defence organisation the latter moves its headquarters from Paris to Brussels. The military headquarters are set up in Casteau near Mons.
1970	Creation of four language regions: one Flemish, one French, one German and the capital Brussels, which is officially to be bi-lingual (Flemish and French). The Universities of Leuven and Brussels are divided into two independent colleges, one Flemish and one French.
1974	In addition to the Christian churches and Jewish communities, Islam is also given equal religious rights.
1975	The setting up of three regional parliaments in Brussels, Mechelen (for Flanders) and Namur (for Wallonia and the German-speaking regions in east Belgium). Dispute about Brussels.
1978	Agreement in principle on state reform – the Egmont Constitutional Reform – for the regionalisation of the country.

French and Belgian paratroopers intervene in Zaire in support of the authoritarian regime of General Mobutu.

1980	Regionalisation. Two regions – Flanders and Wallonia – are formed with extensive degrees of autonomy. Brussels receives special status.
1981–83	Government crises and strikes are the result of serious economic and financial problems. High rate of unemployment.

The German-speaking minority in eastern Belgium is given its own parliament and local government in Eupen. 1984

In May there is a disaster in the Heysel football stadium before the start of the European Cup match between Liverpool and Juventus of Turin. British "fans" provoke bloody riots with the Italian supporters, and 39 people are crushed fleeing from the rioting. 1985

On March 6th, shortly after leaving Zeebrugge harbour, the British car-ferry "Herald of Free Enterprise" capsizes. 209 people die. 1987

On July 31st the Belgian parliament passes a bill making Belgium a Federal State, with Flanders and Wallonia as autonomous regions and Brussels as a region with special status. 1988

On January 9th the Belgian parliament passes the Finance Bill for the regions of Flanders and Wallonia and the statute for the city of Brussels and its environs. This completes the transition to a Federal State. 1989

On April 28th the courts announce their findings on the Heysel Stadium disaster of May 1985. Fourteen Britons are imprisoned and fined; the president of the Belgian football association and the police officer responsible are also convicted.

On April 4th and 5th King Baudouin declares that he is no longer able to perform his royal duties. He does this in order not to have to sign an Abortion Bill which he disagrees with, and also to enable the government to make the bill law, as in such cases the Belgian constitution provides for the government to take over the authority of the king. 1990

In March parliament passes a law which enables female members of the royal line to accede to the throne. 1991

In October the ninth coalition government led by Wilfried Martens breaks down. The elections held in November are described as a "landslide", as the established parties lose many seats and the right-wing radical party "Vlaams Blok" makes considerable gains, but so do the "Greens".

At the end of February the ruling Christian Democrats, Socialists and People's Union combine to form a new coalition. The Flemish Christian Democrat Jean-Luc Dehaene is made prime minister. However, this does not hide the fact that the Belgian state finds itself in the middle of a serious crisis. 1992

Both chambers of parliament agree to a change in the constitution which paves the way for Belgium to become a federal state by the year 1996. 1993

On July 31st King Baudouin I dies unexpectedly. He is succeeded by his brother Albert as Albert II.

The Belgian foreign minister Willy Claes is appointed Secretary General of NATO in September. 1994

A corruption scandal surrounding the Italian helicopter manufacturer 'Augusta' touches the highest political circles. Despite this, the ruling coalition of Socialists and Christian Democrats holds on to power in the parliamentary elections. In May, however, foreign minister Vandenbroucke resigns, and in September Willy Claes resigns his office with NATO. 1995

In October, Brussels witnesses the largest ever demonstration in the history of Belgium. 200,00 people are taking to the streets because of the events surrounding the arrest of child pornographer and murderer Marc Dutroux, as well as findings about the murder of the Socialist politician 1996

André Cools. Both cases reveal that the highest judicial and political circles are caught in a veritable swamp of corruption, inactivity and incompetence on the part of the investigators as well as criminal activity resembling that of the Mafia. The scandal rocks the Belgian state to its core.

1999

In early summer it becomes public knowledge that chicken feed contaminated with dioxins is in use throughout the country. The scandal has a direct influence on the parliamentary elections: the coalition, in government since 1988, loses; new President is the Liberal Guy Verhofstadt, as the head of a 'rainbow coalition'.

Famous People

The following lists in alphabetical order people who are associated with Belgium through birth, residence or death and have gained national, even international recognition.

Albert I was the son of Count Philip of Flanders and Mary of Hohenzollern-Sigmarinen. On December 23rd 1909 he succeeded his uncle Leopold II to the throne, the latter's son having died young. In 1900 he married the Bavarian duchess Elisabeth von Wittelsbach. After German troops invaded Belgium in 1914 Albert I set himself at the head of the Belgian army and for four years defended the only unoccupied region in Flanders west of the Ijzer. As Belgian commander he played an important part in the decisive battles after September 1918, when he earned the nickname "Koning-Ridder", or "King Knight". After the First World War he applied himself to rebuilding his country and to introducing various reforms, such as overall male franchise (women had to wait until 1948), equality of the two languages and improving the infrastructure. He was killed while climbing in the Meuse valley in 1934.

Albert I (1875–1934)

Jacob van Artevelde, a memorial to whom stands on the Vrijdagsmarkt in Ghent, was a forerunner of Flemish self-awareness. The son of a merchant family, he first of all went about his business without showing any interest in politics, but political events forced him to change his ideas. When Louis of Nevers Count of Flanders, in the conflict leading up to the Hundred Years' War, took the side of the French, England promptly stopped the export of wool to the Flemish towns, which caused much loss of income and distress to the local weavers, clothmakers and traders. This led to uprisings by the trade guilds in which Jacob van Artevelde was elected a leading figure and finally in 1338 made leader of the town of Ghent. He was successful in forming the powerful towns of Bruges, Ghent and Ypres (Ieper) into an alliance and in wringing considerable concessions out of the Count of Flanders, including his agreement to accept only Flemings as advisors. He ensured that the Flemish language, as well as Latin and French, was accepted in legal circles. In the dispute between England and France he remained neutral at first, but after the start of the Hundred Years' War he sided with England, from whom he hoped to obtain guarantees of Flanders' independence. On January 26th 1340 King Edward III of England came to Ghent and was proclaimed King of France. Jacob van Artevelde, who was becoming increasingly high-handed in his official dealings, even thought of disinheriting Louis of Nevers in favour of the Prince of Wales, but before he could put this plan into operation he was murdered by members of the weavers' guild.

Jacob van Artevelde (1290–1345)

When he ascended the Belgian throne in 1951, King Baudouin I had not yet turned twenty-one and could scarcely be said to command the sympathy and support of the people. His father, Leopold III, had brought grave discredit on the Belgian monarchy by his conduct during the Second World War, and as a result abdicated soon after his return to his homeland. His son, Baudouin, who had shared the experience of deportation to Germany with his father, certainly did not seem to be the type to win the hearts of the people, his general demeanour being one of shyness and awkwardness. Yet during the 42 years of his reign he gave lie to all his critics. More than any of his predecessors Baudouin succeeded in making the Belgian throne into a bond which could unite Flemings and Walloons together. People were reassured by his unas-

Baudouin I (1930–93)

suming manner, which at the same time came across as warm and human. He also acquired high moral integrity and authority, and his reputation was enhanced by that of his consort, Queen Fabiola, a Spanish aristocrat. The fact that their marriage was childless undoubtedly earned them popular sympathy. On the morning after King Baudouin died at his Spanish holiday home at Motril, thousands of mourners gathered quite spontaneously in Brussels in order to file past the royal palace, while 100,000 Belgians lined the streets of the capital for his funeral.

Jacques Brel
(1929–78)

Jacques Brel, who became famous in Paris as a poet, a singer of satirical songs and an actor, was a native of Brussels. He had made a name for himself with his songs satirising society and sung in his distinctive voice. His songs "Les Flamandes", "Marieke" and "Ne me quitte pas" are very well-known. As the result of a serious illness he retired to the South Pacific in 1975, returning home only occasionally. He died in Paris in 1978. A cultural centre and youth hostel in Brussels has been named in his honour.

Pieter Breugel the Elder (c. 1525–69)

Pieter Breugel the Elder, also known as "Peasant Breugel", was born about 1525 in Brogel (Kempen) or near Breda. He is one of the most important painters of the 16th c. His extensive works include about 45 paintings as well as drawings and engravings. He is particularly well-known for his paintings of peasant life and his landscapes, scenes which accurately portray his Flemish homeland. What is known of Breugel's life is based on only a few definite dates and other documentary evidence. In 1551 at the latest he was a member of the Antwerp Guild, and as a Master of that guild he undertook a journey to Italy about 1552–54 which is partly chronicled by drawings and engravings. After his marriage to Mayken Coeke, the daughter of his teacher Pieter Coeke of Aelst, he moved to Brussels in 1561. This marriage produced both sons, Pieter Breugel the Younger ("Inferno" Breugel, 1564–1638) and Jan the Elder ("Flower" Breugel or "Velvet" Breugel, 1568–1625).

His most famous works include two engravings, "Seven Virtues" and "Seven Vices", his crowd scenes such as "Children's Games" and "The Battle between Carnival and Lent", as well as "Peasant Wedding", "Peasant Dance", "Land of Milk and Honey", "Hunters in the Snow", "Massacre of the Innocents" and "The Building of the Tower of Babel".

Charles de Coster
(1827–89)

Fame came only posthumously to Charles de Coster, who was born in Munich but lived in Brussels from early childhood. In his lifetime he had many money worries, and it was 1870 before he obtained a post as German teacher at the Brussels Military Academy and was assured of a regular income. In "La légende d'Uilenspiegel", which took him ten years to write, he created in strong and vivid language a literary memorial to the struggle for freedom in the Spanish Netherlands. The central characters of the book are the satirist and enemy of tyranny Uilenspiegel from the Flemish dykes and his friend Lamme Goedzak.

Lamoraal Count of Egmont
(1522–68)

Lamoraal Count of Egmont (Egmond) was the second son of Jan van Egmond, ruler of Egmond op de Hoef near Alkmaar, and Francisca of Luxembourg. He was born in La Hamaide near Ath. At a very young age he came to the court of Emperor Charles V, where he entered on an outstanding military career and carried out several important diplomatic missions. When only 24 he was made a Knight of the Golden Fleece, and in 1554 was entrusted with the arrangements for the marriage by proxy of Philip II and Mary Tudor. In 1555 he was present at the abdication of Charles V, and he defeated the French army at Saint-Quentin in 1557 and at Gravelines in 1558.

The accession to the throne of Philip II was the beginning of a new period for the Count. In 1559 he became a member of the town council and governor of Flanders and Artois. When the Dutch nobles, with

Albert I

Jacques Brel

Lamoraal, Count of Egmont

William of Orange at their head, demanded from the general governess Margaret of Parma tolerance towards those of different religions and more rights for their own representatives in the state assemblies, Egmont originally hesitated but then conveyed these requests when he went on a mission to the Court of Madrid in 1565. However, he was refused an audience by Philip II who adopted a hard line. After the iconoclasm of 1567 Philip sent the Duke of Alba to the Netherlands, where he crushed any resistance in the most cruel fashion. He had Egmont, who had meanwhile sided with the "geusen" party (see History – 1566), and Count Hoorn imprisoned and charged in Brussels with high treason. The trial ended with a sentence of death, which was immediately carried out on the Grand' Place. After some time Egmont's remains were taken to his house at Zottegem and buried in the crypt there. The grave was only re-discovered during restoration work in 1804.

Egmont is remembered in Goethe's drama (although this does not keep to the historical facts) and in Beethoven's "Egmont Overture".

Born in Maaseik, Jan van Eyck had a very marked influence on the development of Western painting. His realistic portrayals of people and landscapes. with freely-expressed religiously symbolic themes harmoniously set out, exemplify the new way of looking at the world which was coming to the fore at the end of the Middle Ages and which attempted to give a deeper meaning to the realities of the universe.

Jan van Eyck (c. 1390–1441)

Van Eyck, initially court painter to John of Bavaria in Den Haag, entered the service of Philip of Burgundy in 1425. After 1430 he lived in Bruges, where he died in 1441. Far and away his best-known work is the "Altar of Ghent" in the cathedral of Sint-Baaf, on which he worked with his brother Hubert.

César Franck was born in Liège but when quite young moved to Paris where from 1843 he worked as organist, and in 1872 became a teacher of the organ in the Paris Conservatory. Franck pioneered the Impressionist movement in France and introduced the cyclical form, the return of a theme in almost all parts of a piece of music. His works embrace both instrumental and vocal music, including opera and oratorios. He made a major contribution to organ music, not only as a composer but also as an improviser.

César Franck (1822–90)

Legend has presented Godfrey of Bouillon as the very ideal of Christian chivalry. In 1089, as the feudal servant of the Duke of Lorraine, he was

Godfrey of Bouillon (c. 1060–1100)

the first imperial knight to answer the call by Pope Urban II to follow the crusades to the Holy Land. In 1096, together with his brothers Baldwin and Eustace, he travelled at the head of an army of 20,000 men down the Danube to Constantinople, where they met the armies of other princes and then marched on into Palestine. In 1098 the armies conquered Antiocheia, and in 1099 Godfrey took part in the storming of Jerusalem after a five-week siege, following which he was granted the title of "Steward and Protector of the Holy Sepulchre". In the same year he defeated the Sultan of Egypt at Askalon; shortly after he died in Jerusalem and was buried in the church there. However, his remains were destroyed in the 13th c. and in 1808 fanatical Greek monks desecrated his grave.

Victor Horta
(1861–1947)

Born in Ghent, Victor Horta was one of the Belgian architects who pointed the way forward at the end of the 19th c. and during the first half of the 20th c. In particular he was an advocate of the Art Nouveau style, as witnessed by such buildings as the Hitel Tassel, Hitel Solvay and the Maison du People in Brussels. After living in the United States of America from 1916 to 1919 his designs again showed Classical influences; this is clearly shown in the Palais des Beaux-Arts in Brussels which was built to Horta's design in the 1920s.

Charles V
(1500–58)

Charles V, grandson of Emperor Maximilian I and son of Philip the Fair and Joanna of Castille, was born in Ghent. In 1506 he inherited from his father the estate of Burgundy and in 1516 was crowned King of Spain in Brussels cathedral. With strong support from Brussels and Brabant Charles V was made German emperor in opposition to Francis I of France. This latter event is widely celebrated in Brussels in the form of the "Ommegang" on the first Thursday in July every year. The foundations of the Spanish colonial empire were laid during the reign of Charles V, and it was during this time, too, that the Reformation took place and with it the beginning of the clashes between Catholicism and Protestantism which were to prove so momentous in the history of Europe. In 1556 Charles V abdicated; the Spanish throne passed to his son Philip II and the German emperorship to his brother Ferdinand I. Charles then entered a monastery in Spain.

Leopold I
(1790–1865)

As the result of his marriage to Charlotte, the heir to the English throne, Leopold, son of Duke Francis of Saxe-Coburg, seemed about to enter on a glittering career. However, Charlotte's early death in 1817 put an end to that. In 1830 Leopold was offered the Greek throne, but withdrew his acceptance. A year later he was chosen as the first King of the Belgians and was crowned on July 21st 1831. As a constitutional monarch he removed himself as far as possible from politics and thus enjoyed the esteem of his people. Under his reign Brussels developed markedly. At times Leopold played a leading role in Europe and frequently acted in an advisory capacity to Queen Victoria. In 1832 he married Louise-Marie, daughter of King Louis Philippe of France.

Leopold II
(1835–1909)

As Crown Prince, Leopold II, son of King Leopold I, bore the title of Duke of Brabant, and on December 10th 1865 he was made king. He proved to be skilled in financial matters, and during his reign Belgium enjoyed an unprecedented economic boom. Markets for Belgian products sprang up in Russia, Asia and Egypt. However, Leopold II proved unpopular, even hated, because of his colonial policies. When in 1878 Henry Morton Stanley offered him his discoveries in the Congo Leopold promptly seized them and in 1885 declared himself sovereign and sole owner of the Congo State which became recognised in that year. By 1908, when an international commission intervened, the Congo – eighty times larger then its Belgian motherland – had been mercilessly and bloodily plundered for

César Franck

Leopold I

Margaret of Parma

Leopold's personal gain, which led to his being described by Mark Twain as "the king with ten million dead on his conscience". On the credit side, however, it must be pointed out that through his policy of strict neutrality he was able to keep Belgium out of the Franco–Prussian War of 1870–71.

In 1934 Leopold III succeeded his father Albert I to the throne. He had married the Swedish Princess Astrid in 1926, but she was killed in an accident in 1935. Under Leopold's reign Belgium cut its ties with the Western Powers and became universally neutral. In spite of that German troops invaded in May 1940. After a war lasting eighteen days the King and his army capitulated but – unlike his government, which fled to London – he remained in Belgium. Until June 1944 he was held prisoner in his palace in Laeken, but then he and his family were transported by the SS to Germany and Austria, where he was freed by American troops in 1945. When Belgium was liberated his brother Charles, Count of Flanders, was made regent. After the end of the war Leopold became the subject of fierce controversy, as it was, and remains to this day, not clear whether and to what extent he had tried to collaborate with Hitler, with whom he had a private conversation. Right up to 1950 he was prevented from returning to Belgium and resuming his position as King, even though a referendum showed that only 58 per cent of the people were in favour. When he did in fact return there was a general strike in Wallonia (which had voted against him) resulting in martial law being imposed. In August 1950 he abdicated and assigned his rights to his son Baudouin. Baudouin adopted the title of Royal Prince until he became the fifth King of the Belgians on July 17th 1951. Leopold retained the title of "king" right up to the time of his death.

Leopold III
(1901–83)

Maurice Maeterlink, born in Ghent, a pioneer of the Surrealist movement in literature, studied law but then changed over to writing. When staying in Paris in 1887 he first made contact with the Symbolists, and in 1896 he finally moved to Paris, but was obliged to leave it in 1940. His dramatic piece "La Princesse Maleine" (1889) brought him instant success; his other dramatic writings are some of the major Symbolic works. He became world-famous, however, through his essays in which he set out to explain how human existence is threatened by the Powers of Darkness. His lyric verse is based on associations and fantastic sequences. In 1911 Maeterlink received the Nobel Prize for Literature; in 1947 he became President of the International PEN Club.

Maurice Maeterlink
(1862–1949)

The artist Magritte, born in Lessines, was the chief initiator of Surrealism in Belgium. After completing his training at the Academy of Art in Brussels he first obtained employment as a commercial artist. He was

René Magritte
(1898–1967)

strongly influenced by the work of Giorgio de Chiricos. After a stay in Paris from 1927 to 1930 he settled in Brussels and founded his own school where the emphasis was on Surrealism. His pictures are detailed paintings of commonplace objects in novel contexts. In addition to large panels he also painted impressive murals, such as those in the Knokke Casino (1953) and in the Palais des Congrès in Brussels (1961).

Margaret of Parma (1522–86)

Margaret of Parma was born in Oudenaarde, the illegitimate daughter of Johanna van der Gheynst. She was taken to Brussels, where she was educated by Margaret of Austria and Mary of Hungary. After a short marriage to the nephew of Pope Clemens VII, Alessandro de Medici, who was murdered, she was married in 1538 for political reasons to Ottavio Farnese, grandson of Pope Paul III, following which she moved first to Rome and then to Parma. In 1559 the Spanish King Philip II appointed her governess of the Spanish Netherlands. Under her rule the attempts by the Netherlands – led by the nobles with whom she initially tried to negotiate – to obtain independence became even stronger. After the iconoclasm of 1567 and the uprising by the "beggar nobles", however, she resorted to force which culminated in her attempting to exile the Duke of Alba who promptly relieved her of her position. She returned to Italy, but was sent back again by Philip II in 1580 with orders to pacify the provinces in the Netherlands, but this she failed to do. She died in Ortona in Italy.

Gerhard Mercator (1512–94)

The famous cartographer and geographer Gerhard Mercator was born in Rupelmonde, south of Brussels. He studied in Leuven and in 1537 produced a map of the Holy Land, followed by his first map of the world in 1538 and a terrestrial and celestial globe in 1541. After moving to Duisburg in Germany he engraved his fifteen-page map of Europe and finally his famous world map which was to prove invaluable to seafarers. Not until after his death did all his work appear together in the form of an atlas.

Eddy Merckx (b. 1945)

Between 1966 and 1973 Eddy Merckx, from the Meenzel–Kiesegem district of Brabant, dominated the world's cycling-tracks. He was the winner in the major cycling classics several times in succession; for example, he won the Milan–San Remo race five times, the Paris–Roubaix three times, the Fléche Wallone three times, the Italian circuit three times and the Tour de France on four consecutive occasions. In 1967 and 1971 he was world champion road-racer, and in 1972 he produced a world speed record. Together with his fellow-countryman Patrick Sercu, Eddy Merckx was also successful in indoor six-day races. He still ranks as one of the best racing cyclists of all time.

Peter Paul Rubens (1577–1640)

Peter Paul Rubens was born in Siegen in Westphalia, the son of an Antwerp lawyer who, being a Protestant, had fled to Germany; however, Rubens and his mother returned to Antwerp, where he attended the Latin School and was educated in the humanities and the classics. In 1598 he was made a Master in the Lucas Guild. In 1600 he travelled to Italy, where he lived in Venice, Florence and Mantua as court painter to Duke Vincenzo Gonzaga. Rome, Spain, back to Mantua and Rome and finally Genoa were his other stops on this "Grand Tour". In 1608 he returned to Antwerp, where he married Isabella Brant in 1609; she died in 1626. He became court painter to Archduke Albert and founded his own workshop in which he employed large numbers of artists. As a diplomat, Rubens also attended the French, English and Spanish courts on several occasions. In 1630 he married the sixteen-year-old Helene Fourment. After 1635 he lived in his country mansion at Steen near Antwerp. His tomb can be seen in St Jacob's Church in Antwerp.

Of the 2000 to 3000 paintings which came out of his studio some 600 are ascribed to him. In addition there are the items he produced when abroad. His works include portraits, nudes, animals, still-lifes and land-

Antoine-Joseph Sax   *Georges Simenon*   *Paul-Henri Spaak*

scapes, battle and hunting scenes and religious and historical subjects. His second wife was often his model for nude drawings and portraits.

Antoine-Joseph Sax, also known as Adolphe, was born in Dinant, the son of a musical instrument maker. He was apprenticed in the same profession, and initially worked in his father's workshop. In 1842 he moved to Paris, where he developed a new instrument, based on the clarinet, which was capable of producing notes beyond the octave; it was the saxophone, which he patented in 1846, and followed it up with the saxhorn, saxtromba and saxtuba. Sax's instruments quickly found acceptance in French military music and later in orchestral music; Sax himself taught the saxophone and his other instruments at the Paris Conservatory, but failed to make his inventions commercially successful. In fact he became so poor that prominent supporters had to ask the Minister of Arts to make maintenance payments to him.

Antoine-Joseph
(Adolphe) Sax
(1814–94)

Born in Liège, Georges Simenon created one of the most famous police characters in criminal literature; this was Commissioner Maigret of the Paris police, who was able to put himself in the place of the criminals and to bring them to justice more by instinct than through tough investigation work. For seventeen years Simenon worked on the "Gazette de Liège". In 1923 he went to Paris, where he wrote his first Maigret novel in 1930, which was to be followed by over a hundred more, bringing their author worldwide fame. Georges Simenon was an extremely productive writer; in addition to the Maigret books he produced psychological novels and over 100 short stories and poems, 21 volumes of his "Dictées" and further novels under the pseudonym "G. Sim". About 60 of his books were made into films, and most have been translated into all the world languages.

Georges Simenon
(1903–89)

The Socialist Paul-Henri Spaak was the most important Belgian politician of the post-war era. With a few intermissions he served his country as Foreign Minister from 1936 to 1966, including the years 1940–44 spent in exile in London, and was Prime Minister in 1938–39, 1946 and 1947–49. During the period spent in London he began to work with others on creating the Benelux Customs Union. In 1945 he helped to formulate the UN Charter and was President of the first full UN Assembly in 1946. Spaak was a decisive influence in the abdication of King Leopold III. In the 1950s he was one of the prime movers in seeking European integration.

Paul-Henri Spaak
(1899–1972)

Montanunion and the founding of the EEC and EURATOM bear the signature of Paul-Henri Spaak who, after having been General Secretary of NATO from 1957–61, finally held office as Foreign Minister in a coalition government until 1966.

Henry van de Velde (1863–1957)

The Antwerp-born Henry van der Velde was one of the major architects to pioneer the Art Nouveau style; he was also influential in the field of arts and crafts. First he studied painting, but then changed over to architecture. He built his first house for his family in Uccle near Brussels in 1892–95; everything, right down to the furniture and the cutlery, was designed by himself. The products of his workshops, the "Ateliers d'Art Industriels", proved very successful in Germany, to where he moved in 1899 and where he did most of his work. Among other things, he fitted out the Folkwang Museum in Hagen and built the School of Applied Art in Weimar and became its principal in 1902. During the First World War he left Germany and went via Switzerland to Holland, where the Kröller-Müller family engaged him to build a new museum in Otterlo which did not finally come to fruition until 1937–54. He returned to Belgium in 1925, where he founded the Institut des Arts Décoratifs in Brussels and became its principal. He also taught architecture at Ghent University, the library of which he designed (1935–40). In 1947 van der Velde returned to Switzerland where he lived until his death in 1957.

Felix Timmermans (1886–1947)

Together with Stijn Streuvels, Felix Timmermans, born in Lier, was one of the major exponents of Belgian regional art and one of the best-known Flemish writers. In his books he idealised life in the countryside and in small towns, and painted a picture of a love of nature and simple piety. In 1916 his novel "Pallieter", whose hero was the archetypal Belgian peasant farmer with a love of life, made him famous almost overnight. His best-known work, "Het kindeken Jezus in Vlaanderen" (The Infant Jesus in Flanders) came out in 1917 and again describes idyllic rural life. Perhaps his best book is "Boerenpsalm" (Peasants' Psalm, 1935), a more thought-provoking work. Timmermans does have his critics. The underlying tone of his books comes near to "blood and soil literature" (the idea that political stability and power depend on unification of race and territory), and after the invasion by German troops in the Second World War he was not afraid to arrange pan-Germanic propaganda events.

Rogier van der Weyden (probably 1400–64)

Rogier van der Weyden was the major Flemish artist of the Renaissance whose first recorded date is 1427, when he completed his apprenticeship in Tournai to Robert Campin, the Master of Flémalle and former pupil of Jan van Eyck. In 1435 van der Weyden became the city artist in Brussels where he achieved a great reputation and solid fortune. He visited Rome, Florence, Ferrara and Venice about 1450 at the invitation of their princes, journeyed to Cologne some ten years later to paint the "Altar of the Magi" (now in Munich) for St Columba, always returning to Brussels, where he died.

Since none of his works was signed, and there are no contemporary sources as to their authorship, it is often difficult to attribute them with absolute certainty. What was new about this artist was above all the dramatic nature of his compositions, compared with the almost wholly static nature of the figures painted by his contemporaries. His most important work is the "Descent from the Cross" (1435–40) in the Escorial in Spain.

Marguerite Yourcenar (1903–87)

Born in Brussels, this writer of psychological novels and short stories, whose real name was Marguerite de Crayencour, was the first woman to be elected to the Académie Française in 1980. Her best-known work is the imaginary "Mémoires d'Hadrien".

Art and Culture

Art History

Strictly speaking, it would only be correct to speak of Belgian art as applying to the period after the founding of the Kingdom of Belgium in 1830. However, in order to obtain a clearer picture of the varied cultural history of this country situated between the North Sea, the Meuse, Scheldt and the Ardennes, it makes more sense to give a resumée of the earlier periods of art in the whole of the area which is now known as Belgium.

Although only covering a small area, divided into regions speaking Flemish and French respectively, Belgian art does in fact reflect the whole history of the subject through all the major European epochs and supplements it with the individual artistic achievements of the Flemish-Walloon region itself.

Information about the hunters and gatherers of the Neolithic and Mesolithic Ages is provided by the few tools and everyday objects made from animal bones and stone which are exhibited in the prehistoric departments of the provincial museums (such as that at Tongeren) and in the Museum of Art and History in Brussels.

Early History

Since about 4000 BC, the beginning of the Neolithic Age, arable farming and cattle-raising developed in the fertile hilly regions. At the same time more refined articles were made, especially pottery vessels showing the influence of those successive civilisations which spread through the whole of Europe, known as the beaker, ribbon-decorated and braid-decorated cultures. After about 1700 BC the use of copper and bronze enabled decorated weapons and jewellery to be made.

The death-cult found expression in a large number of burial-mounds or barrows containing artistically worked burial objects such as bronze weapons and bejewelled pendants. After about 1300 BC cremation came more into vogue; the dead were burned on pyres and their ashes buried in urns in large burial grounds. During the Iron Age, from about 800 BC onwards, the Meuse–Scheldt region came under the influence of the Hallstatt culture. Long iron swords and elaborate clasps were either obtained by trading or made locally, as well as beautifully-shaped vessels of precious metal or pottery, stamped or engraved, filigree gold jewellery and lavish ornaments.

In the centuries which followed and up to the time of the Roman Conquest, that region which was later to become known as Belgium was dominated by Celtic and Germanic cultures. The use of the potter's wheel often led to the mass production of pots of more uniform shape and decoration.

When seeking to extend the Roman Empire north-westward Caesar conquered the Belgae, those North Gallic tribes who had settled between the Seine and the Rhine and who were mostly of Celtic but some of Teutonic descent, such as the Bellovaks, Nervi, Manapi, Eburons, Ambians and others. The regions they inhabited were combined to form the Roman province of Gallia Belgica, ruled by Augustus and administered from the capital Durocortororum (Rheims). The Rhine formed the

Roman Period

frontier of the Roman Empire and also the cultural border with the Teutons. Roman rule brought with it a fresh cultural impetus arising out of the new style of living. In Arlon, the Roman Orolaunum, a row of stone reliefs have been found which superbly illustrate Roman everyday life in the province. In Tongeren, which was probably Aduatuca Tungrorum in Roman Gaul and an important centre and junction of the Roman roads leading from Bavay to Cologne, remains of the Roman town fortifications have been found. In the Gallo-Roman Museum visitors can see various archaeological finds dating from Roman times which provide detailed information about handicrafts and engineering achievements as well as of the cult of the dead and worship of the gods in the oldest Roman town in Belgium.

The top of a Roman standard

From the early 4th c. BC, in the course of the mass migration which took place throughout the whole of Europe, the warlike Germanic tribes from the east of the Rhine suppressed the cultures and way of life left behind by the Romans. Franks settled between the Meuse and the Scheldt basin. Around AD 500 the Merovingian king Chlodwig ruled this region from his capital city Tournai. **Conversion to Christianity** began with the missionary work of St Servatius, who founded the diocese of Tongeren as early as the 4th c. Other Christian centres were Tournai and Arlon, where Early Christian basilicas were built. As Christianity spread through Franconia a large number of churches and monasteries sprang up. In the 7th c. in particular monasticism, in close alliance with the Frankish imperial nobility, was able to carry out a wide programme of instilling the Christian religion into the people. St Amandus (594–684), known as the Apostle of the Belgians, and his pupil, St Bavo (or Baaf; d. 654), patron saint of Ghent, were both of noble descent and typical representatives of this period. The Benedictine abbeys of Sint-Baaf in Ghent (founded 647), Saint-Hubert (687), Stavelot-Malmédy and Nivelles (both c. 650) were centres of teaching and education. The priesthood also remained an important pillar of Carolingian society. Around the year 800, with the help of the clergy, Charlemagne was able to effect the Carolingian cultural renaissance, nurtured on a mixture of ancient bodies of thought and Roman appreciation of art leavened with Christian ideals. The small Carolingian cursive script became the favoured form of writing. Book illumination and work in ivory and gold flourished. Church architecture was based on the T-shaped plan with a nave and transept, somewhat reminiscent of the Roman basilica. The octagonal Palace Chapel in Aachen, the model for similar chapels at Nijmegen and Sint-Donatus in the Meuse region, was a revival of ancient ideas of building round a central hall.

Evidence of Early Christian artistic skills

Unfortunately, few buildings and works of art from this early medieval period have survived. All the original wooden churches have been destroyed, and only fragments of the first stone churches and monastic cells remain to provide any sort of archaeological and documentary evidence, such as the remnants of the 4th c. precursor of the present churches at Tongeren, Tournai and Arlon and the above-mentioned 7th c. abbeys. Only the treasuries of the Church of the Holy Virgin in Tongeren and of Tournai cathedral contain impressive works of art from the early Middle Ages, such as a 6th c. ivory plate with a carving of St Paul the Apostle and a Merovingian gold clasp at Tongeren, a valuable Byzantine reliquary crucifix decorated with ivory (6th–7th c.) and a 9th c. ivory carving of St Nicolas at Tournai. The famous 7th c. ivory diptych from Genoels-Elderen, showing Christ and two angels standing in triumph on the Devil disguised as an animal, is now on display in the Brussels Museum of Art and History.

None of the **wall-paintings** in churches and abbeys has been preserved, apart from the remains of some 12th c. frescoes depicting St Margaret in the transept of Tournai cathedral. It is only the sheer quality of the **book illuminations** that leads experts to think that wall-paintings and the like must have been of an equally high standard. Sumptuously decorated Bibles and Gospels from the Benedictine abbey at Stavelot, the Premonstratensian abbeys at Floreffe and Park near Leuven as well as from Echternach near Luxembourg (codex aureus, 11th c.) have been saved for posterity.

Romanesque

Sculpture In the Ottonian and Early Salian period (10th–11th c.) Byzantine ivory carvings continued to predominate. One outstanding example is the book-cover of the Notker Gospels (c. 980–1000) in the Maison Curtius in Liège.

Few stone sculptures remain. The total range of such artistic development is now limited to an archaically abstract 12th c. tympanum showing the Baptism of St Basil in the undercroft of the Church of the Blood of Christ in Bruges and an emotive and moving relief of the Virgin Mary (c. 1149–58) which is also to be seen in the Maison Curtius in Liège.

There are two fine examples of 11th c. wood-sculpture – the large crucifix in the chapel at Tancrémont with an usual depiction of the crucified Christ in a long, folded robe gazing rapturously up to heaven, as well as the dignified head of Christ in the treasury of the Church of the Holy Virgin at Tongeren.

Skills displayed in metal-working in the Meuse region during the 12th c. made it famous throughout Europe. In addition to bronze-casting and relief engraving, enamelling and artistic work in gold were also carried out. In competition with more ancient sculpture, the art of metal-working first reached its zenith under Renier de Huy with the font (1107–18) ascribed to him and made for the church of Notre-Dame-aux-Fonts in Liège; it is now in the church of Saint-Barthélemy. This brass font is supported by twelve cows (only ten are still the originals) – symbolising the Twelve Apostles and the Twelve Tribes of Israel. Five baptismal scenes in high-relief on the wall of the font illustrate the First Sacrament – the Baptism of Christ in Jordan, the Sermons of John the Baptist, the Baptism of the Newly Converted, the Baptism of the Roman Centurio Cornelius and of the Greek philosopher Crato, so that in the baptismal and salvation ceremonies conversion to Christianity was shown as extending from the Jewish world by way of that of the Greeks and Romans and thus into the present. Finely-modelled figures with restrained gestures and arranged in groups to provide the fullest effect, combined with the way in which trees encompass and provide a frame to the christening scenes, all bear witness to the maker's detailed knowledge of ancient Roman sculpture and to his keen and mature feeling for and understanding of form and composition. Other major works from the Meuse workshops working in gold and brass are in the form of reliquaries, small altars and shrines. Examples are the bust of Pope Alexander, dating from pre-1145 and to be seen in the Royal Museum of Art and History in Brussels, probably by Godfrey de Huy; the gleaming gold relic of the true Cross from c. 1160 in the church of Saint-Croix in Liège, in the form of a small triptych with relief figures of the Apostles around a central cross held by one of two angels; the altar by Stablo, c. 1150–60, also in the Royal Museum of Art and History in Brussels, made from enamel

Metallurgy in the Meuse region

The font by Renier de Huy in Liège

sheets with carvings showing public assemblies and synagogues as well as Jonah and Samson around a central panel of rock-crystal; and the Processional Cross (*c.* 1160–75, also in the above museum) set with precious stones and with dimpled enamelled panels portraying scenes from the Old and New Testaments showing Christ's Passion.

One of the oldest reliquary shrines to survive in the Meuse region is the house-shaped Shrine to St Hadelinus (in Saint-Martin's, Visé), the 11th c. gable-ends of which show a figure of Christ and the crowning of SS Hadelinus and Remaklus, while the eight clearly defined relief panels along the sides probably date from *c.* 1140 and show the influence of Renier de Huy. The shrine to SS Oda and George was built one hundred years later (1230–40, parish church of Amay), as was the shrine to St Remaklus (*c.* 1240–68, church of Saint-Sebastian, Stavelot), and these display a distinctively different and more realistic and captivating portrayal of the human form. Somewhat similar are the works by Hugo of Oignies, dating from around 1230–35 and found in the treasury of the Sœurs de Notre Dame in Namur, the phylactery of St Martin, the two book covers with the Crucifixion and majestas domini, as well as the chalice by Gilles de Walcourt worked in the niello technique of chasing out lines and forms and inlaying a black composition.

Nicolas of Verdun

However, the supreme master of gold and silver work in the 13th c. was undoubtedly Nicolas of Verdun, whose major work, the Shrine to Our Lady of 1205, together with the 1247 Shrine to St Eleutherius which also shows his influence, is housed in the treasury of Tournai cathedral. In spite of numerous restorations, especially in the 19th c., the sculpted figures, spacious areas of relief, enamelled panels and fine engraving on the Shrine to Our Lady reflect an awakened interest in the human form and in nature. Purity of form and freedom of movement are also the hallmarks of this shrine.

In **church architecture** the Romanesque basilica style predominated, as exemplified by the schools of architecture on the Lower Rhine, especially in Cologne. The Romanesque church is recognised by the rectangular shape of the main building, together with twin towers on the west front and a group of towers above the crossing. The choir may be stepped, semi-circular with a triple-domed roof or end in a straight line. Inside, those sections which branch out from the crossing serve to unify the whole structure. The arcades of rounded arches, blind arcades and triforium galleries added a degree of subtle refinement. Barrel-vaulting and groin-vaulting replaced flat roofs.

The 11th c. church of St Gertrude at Nivelles still has the Early Romanesque flat-roof, and so has the church of St Vincent in Soignies, while in Liège the west side of the church of the Holy Cross and the fortified twin towers of the west front of Saint-Barthélemy are examples of a different stage in the development of Romanesque architecture. The most impressive of all is the group of five towers to be seen above the transept of the Cathedral of Notre Dame in Tournai with its 12th c. Late Romanesque nave, providing a better example of a medieval house of worship than any other church anywhere in Belgium.

Secular building Two imposing 12th c. castles have survived. On a rock above Bouillon towers the castle of Godfrey of Bouillon, dating from c. 1100. Even more massive is the Château des Comtes in Ghent, built between 1180 and 1200 on 9th c. foundations. It is a splendid example of medieval fortification techniques, with an encircling wall and battlement-walk and flanked by a number of defensive towers and with a massive keep. The Château de Namur, built c. 1230, has slender towers which give it a less fortified look. On the other hand, the 14th c. brick-built castle built in the water at Beersel near Brussels has two massive keeps which dominate the surrounding countryside.

The greatest Gothic achievements are to be found in the religious and secular architecture of the 14th c. It was not until the 15th c. that panel painting came to the fore, while sculpture remained somewhat mundane and was also seriously decimated by the 16th c. iconoclasts.

Church architecture The re-building of the choir of the Cathedral of Notre Dame in Tournai, which began in 1242 and was influenced by the style of French cathedrals, marked the beginning of Gothic architecture in Belgium. It took until 1325 to complete and is a masterpiece of the Gothic filigree building principle, with load-bearing buttresses supporting the tall and finely-proportioned walls and the groin-vaulted roofs which rest upon them. Brussels Cathedral, too, began in 1220 as the church of Saint-Gudule, with its massive 15th c. twin-towered front and rich tracery, is reminiscent of Notre-Dame in Paris. The building of the seven-aisled Antwerp Cathedral in 1352–56 was the crowning glory of Gothic architecture in the region now known as Belgium. In addition a considerable number of impressive single-towered churches sprang up in the prosperous Flemish textile towns, such as that of Notre Dame in Bruges, the tower of which was finally completed in 1297, and that of St Salvatore in the same town, an Early Gothic brick building with a massive west tower built in various phases during the 12th, 14th and 19th c. Also worthy of mention are the Ghent churches of Sint-Niklaas (13th c.) and Sint-Baafs, a plain granite building. St Peter's in Leuven, with its uncompleted front, its light and high interior and hall-like choir ambulatory, is one of the more important Late Gothic edifices. The richly-traceried walls and magnificent fan-vaulted roof of the church of Saint-Jacques in Liège also belong to this era. The cathedral of St-Rombout (Sint-Romuald) in Mechelen, built in 1342–1487, was originally to have the highest tower of any Christian church, namely 168 m (550 ft), but when finally completed in 1578 it measured only 97 m (318 ft). Nevertheless it is an

St Gertrude in Nivelles

The keep of the Gravensteen in Ghent

important landmark in the town, a symbol both of fear of God and of civic pride.

Little Gothic **architectural sculpture** has survived the ravages of time. In the church of Saint-Jacques in Liège there is a Coronation of the Virgin Mary from c. 1380–90 in the north porch, showing Mary and Christ seated and wearing artistically-draped robes. The tympanum of the late 14th c. Door of Bethlehem in the Collegiate Church of Notre Dame in Huy depicts in carved stone the Birth of Christ, with Mary lying-in after the birth, above the Adoration of the Shepherds and the Magi and the Massacre of the Innocents. In the three pediments above the doors in the portico of Notre-Dame in Tournai sculpture cycles from c. 1400 have been preserved; these show prophets, fathers of the church and a Sculpture: City

Sculpture: City Hall, Leuven

Hall, Leuven portrayal of the Fall of Man and the Expulsion of the Jews. Only the Basilica of Our Lady (St Martinus Basiliek) in Halle and that of St Leonard in Zoutleeuw have retained almost in their entirety their Late Gothic (15th–16th c.) interiors, making them treasure-chambers of sculpture in stone, wood and brass. The figure of the Virgin Mary above the west door and the 14th c. Coronation of the Virgin Mary on the south door of the Halle church, like the apostolic events depicted in the choir

(c. 1400), are all evidence of the high-quality stonemasons' skills displayed in a period when Claus Sluter in Dijon was producing his greatest sculptures for the Dukes of Burgundy. In St Leonard's in Zoutleeuw there are a number of altar-carvings describing the legend of St Leonard, abbot of Nibliac, the childhood and sufferings of Jesus and the life of Mary. In the vaulted roof of the nave hangs a double-sided Madonna, known as a Marianum, as well as a magnificent triumphal cross. To the right and left of the altar are some valuable dinanderies, yellowish-gold brass work from Dinant, a six-armed Easter lantern dated 1483, several hanging lanterns and a superb 1469 lectern. The treasure-chamber of the cathedral of St Paul in Liège houses two further outstanding Late Gothic sculptures in metal – the group of figures carved by Gerard Loyet in 1470, showing Charles the Bald, Duke of Burgundy kneeling with St George before the Virgin Mary, and the silver bust of St Lambert, the patron saint of the town, by the Aachen goldsmith Hans von Reutlingen (c. 1505).

In competition with the church-building, a unique form of **secular architecture** came to the fore in Flanders from about 1300 onwards – town gates, cloth halls, guild buildings, urban residences and town-halls. Public buildings in particular, with their belfries visible from afar, bore witness to the prevailing sense of civic pride and commercial enterprise. Their façades were prime examples of the Late Gothic love of flamboyant decoration. Good instances of this are the town-halls of Bruges (1376–1420), Leuven (1448–63), Brussels (east wing, 15th c.), Ghent (north front, 1518–35) and Oudenaarde (1526–30). The cloth halls, some of which were huge – the one in Ypres is 132 m (433 ft) long – still serve as a reminder of the economic power wielded by the Flemish towns. The same was true of the multi-gabled market halls, such as the meat hall in Ghent (c. 1400) or the corn hall in the same town, a trading centre dating from the early 13th c., making it one of the earliest public buildings. Among the many beautiful palaces and castles are those of Gaasbeek south-west of Brussels and that at Spontin near Dinant, which is surrounded by water.

The rooms of noblemen's houses, guild and court-buildings, town halls and some private houses were bedecked with paintings of all kinds. These included historical pictures, hunting scenes, those portraying rectitude and incorruptibility, and also landscapes. Apart from some portraits most of this rich store of secular paintings have been lost to posterity, although details of their provenance are preserved in the form of documentary evidence. Only the Late Gothic religious paintings from 1400 to 1500 still to be seen on church panels remain as witness to the prodigious output of the Old Dutch and Flemish painters. It originated in the painting of miniatures, colourful illustrations in the "books of hours", intended to assist the nobility in carrying out their devotions. Such miniatures were ordered, for example, by the Dukes of Burgundy, who also ruled over Flanders after 1384. There is evidence to show that Melchior Broederlam from Ypres (Ieper) worked on such miniatures in Dijon from 1381 to 1409 for Duke Philip the Bald, and that the brothers Paul, Jan and Hermann of Limburg did the same. Their paintings which embellished the "Très Riches Heures" (1413–16) for the Duke of Berry show a high degree of realism in the way they depict the lives of the nobility, citizens and peasants as the seasons change in town and countryside.

Painting

The van Eyck brothers worked for a short time as painters of miniatures, for example, on the Turin-Milan "book of hours", but it was in the field of panel-painting that their epoch-making work was done and through which they, together with Italian Renaissance painters, helped to make this form of art finally take precedence over sculpture. Jan van Eyck (c. 1390–1441) in particular was the most notable artist to learn from study-

Hubert and Jan van Eyck

Van Eyck 1432

ing the old pictures which had been painted in Dijon and Paris and then – with the aid of the new techniques using oils – to succeed in producing paintings with an unprecedented degree of realism. The principal work by the van Eyck brothers is the "Altar of Ghent", completed in 1432; nobody can now tell which parts are the work of Hubert, who died in 1426, and which are by Jan van Eyck. This magnificent polyptych of ten sections was donated by the well-to-do patrician and Lord Mayor Joos Vijd and his wife Isabella Boorluut to their chapel in Sint-Baafs (St Bavon) in Ghent. Although researchers differ as to the origin and interpretation of this altar-piece – variations in the manner in which the large figures at the top and the smaller ones engaged in the Adoration of the Lamb of God are painted seem to suggest a "marriage" of the various panels – the Ghent Altar is nevertheless generally regarded as representing the Blessed Sacrament, with the celebration of Holy Communion (symbolised by the Lamb and the Goblet) in the presence of all the major Christian saints, and as having been painted in a more realistically faithful and colourful manner than had ever been achieved before. Another major work by Jan van Eyck, the Madonna of Canon van der Paele, hangs in the Groeninge Museum in Bruges. In a unique manner he succeeded in combining an icon – showing the Enthroned Virgin Mary in the centre flanked by St Donatius and St George on horseback – with a picture of an interior scene, thus merging the worlds of Heaven and Earth in a most magical manner. On the tiled floor a soft, patterned carpet is spread before the Virgin's throne. The bishop's robe is bedecked with precious stones; the surrounding objects and figures are colourfully reflected in the armour worn by St George and his horse. Plagued by gout, the venerable old canon, holding an open book and spectacles, kneels before the Virgin Mary and the child Jesus. When closed the doors reveal a portrait of the donor and his wife, a masterpiece of naturalistic painting portraying age in an uncompromising fashion.

As well as Jan van Eyck there were a number of other excellent painters working in Flanders between 1400 and 1500. The interiors painted by the elder Master of Flémalle, who was probably Robert Campin (d. 1444 in Tournai), show that religious themes were becoming more bourgeois. The realism, vividness and strength of composition shown in his painting contrast with the softer and more delicate style of van Eyck.

Master of Flémalle

Roger van der Weyden (c. 1400–64) was a product of the studio of Robert Campin. He concentrated on painting portraits, often three-quarter face, which is how he painted the dukes of Burgundy as well as members of the nobility and the middle classes. Hung in the Art Museums of Brussels and Antwerp are portraits of Laurant Forimont and Philipp de Croy, as well as panels from two diptychs showing the Adoration of the Magi. His major religious paintings, the "Descent from the Cross" which was originally intended for the church of Notre Dame in Leuven and today hangs in the Prado in Madrid, as well as the Last Judgment altarpiece painted between 1443 and 1450 for the Burgundian Chancellor Rolin and now in the Hitel de Dieu in Beaune, both display perfect line, natural-looking figures and exude a sense of dramatic tension.

Rogier van der Weyden

The painter Dirk Bouts (c. 1415–75) made a great impression through the dignity and solemnity he portrayed together with his effective use of depth of perspective. The vertical pictures he painted c. 1468 depicting justice, which were intended to act as an example to the guardians of the law in the court-room of the Leuven town hall and which now hang in the Musées Royaux des Beaux-Arts in Brussels, are good examples of his skill, as is the altar-piece showing the Last Supper in the church of St Peter in Leuven. The lines and perspective of the room in which the Last Supper took place are so precisely drawn that all the rays emanating

Dirk Bouts

◀ *The central panel of the altar of Ghent*

from the head of Christ converge in front of the cruciform panelling above the fire-place in such a way that not only is Christ the centre of the composition but also appears as the radiant centre of the universe, as indicated by the Old Testament precursors of the Holy Communion which are depicted on the side-panels.

Petrus Christus

The panels painted by Petrus Christus (1410–73), a pupil of Van Eyck and the head of his studio from 1441, initially showed his teacher's influence. Subsequently, however, he progressively simplified the latter's some-what effusive and gushing style to produce a more unified spatial effect which in turn gave a sense of cohesion to his previously isolated figures. The "Mourning of Christ" in the Musées Royaux des Beaux-Arts in Brussels is a good example of this.

Hugo van der Goes

One of the more important members of the Old Dutch school of painting in the second half of the 15th c. was Hugo van der Goes (1440–82). Between 1476 and 1478 he produced his major work, the Portinari Altar, depicting the "Adoration of the Shepherds", which is now housed in the Uffizi in Florence. It was donated by Tommaso Portinari, the manager of the Bruges branch of the Medici Bank. Something of the splendour of this altar-piece can also be found in his "Anna Selbdritt" in the Musées des Beaux-Arts in Brussels. His later work – such as the "Death of the Virgin Mary" in the Groeninge Museum in Bruges – shows signs of the onset of insanity, as reflected in the restless composition and the pain-racked faces of the Apostles painted in flickering and coldly iridescent colours.

Hans Memling

A contemporary of van der Goes was Hans Memling (1430–95), who was actually born in Germany but worked in Bruges after 1465. Some of his major works can be seen in the Hopital St-Jean in Bruges; these include a painted shrine of St Ursula with contemporary views of Cologne, a triptych showing the Adoration of the Magi and a superb two-part pic-ture donated by Martin Niewenhove in 1487. The most outstanding work, however, is the 1479 St-Jean Altar dedicated to the patron saints of the hospital, John the Baptist and John the Evangelist, with the Beheading and Revelation of the latter on the side panels. The centre panel of this triptych shows the mystic marriage of St Catharine in the presence of the two patron saints. In an open columned chancel – with a view of the town of Bruges and a large crane in the distance – the Christ child is shown handing over the ring while to the far right of the Virgin Mary St Barbara appears engrossed in a book. The enchanting fig-ures of St Catharine and St Barbara are also portraits of Mary of Burgundy, later to be the wife of Emperor Maximilian, and of her step-mother Margaret of York; in this way, idealism and mortality are combined. The world of Memling's pictures typically portrayed contem-plative peace, with little in the way of dramatic presentation; he created pictures of situations in which the individual form was of more import-ance than ingenious groups or complex composition. His works are timeless pictures of devotion and meditation, showing a medieval con-servative approach with few signs of a Renaissance awareness.

Gerard David

After Memling's death Gerard David (c. 1460–1523) became head of the Bruges school of painting. A selection of his work can be seen in the Groeninge Museum there. David's art was in the tradition of van Eyck and Memling, but with a truer grasp of perspective he achieved greater spatial clarity in his composition with the naturally-painted figures grouped in such a way as to give a more realistic impression overall.

Quentin Massys

Quentin Massys (1466–1530), a contemporary of David, lived and worked in Antwerp. His works included the Altar of St Anne in 1509 (now in the Musées Royaux des Beaux-Arts in Brussels) for the St Anne Brotherhood, and the Altar of St John for the Guild of Carpenters; this is

Hans Memling: "Christ and Angels"

now to be seen in the Musée Royale des Beaux-Arts in Antwerp. The winged Altar of St Anne shows strong Renaissance influences; the overall impression is one of size, harmony and clarity of composition. While the architectural background to the centre panel emphasises the sense of peace and the balanced placing of the figures, the lines of the composition as they fall on the left side-panel and rise on the right dictate the formal content – the Annunciation and the Death of St Anne.

The transition from the medieval iconic concept of imagery to the authentic Renaissance generic form of portraiture, group portraits, landscapes, still-life and genre pictures took a long time to come to fruition, namely, from the 15th to the 16th c.

Renaissance Painting

Joachim Patinir (c. 1485–1524) may be regarded as the founder of the Flemish–Dutch school of landscape painting. He worked in Antwerp at the same time as Massys and was a personal friend of Dürer. However, Patinir still did not paint pure natural scenes; his idealistic landscapes, mainly painted as if viewed from the air, were somewhat heavy in comparison to the small, often biblical figures they contained. Only a few of his works were signed; those definitely attributed to him include the "Flight into Egypt", which is in the Musée des Beaux-Arts in Antwerp, and the "Preachings of John the Baptist", in the museum of the same name in Brussels.

Joachim Patinir

Influenced by the Roman High Renaissance and Italian painting, a group of painters calling themselves the Romanists introduced into Flanders – albeit in a rather different manner – the style of composition and feeling for colour shown by the somewhat affected Italian painters, particularly in the field of nude painting. This is reflected very strongly in the work of Jan Gossaert, known as Mabuse (1478–1533), who showed the extent

Romanists

to which he had been influenced during his trip to Rome as a student in 1508–09 by the powerful way in which he drew figures and in his work in the field of Renaissance architecture. Another artist working at about this same time was Bernaert van Orley (c. 1488–1541), who had been influenced by Raphael. He was employed as court painter in Brussels for the Stadholder Margaret of Austria and for Mary of Hungary. His monumental style is expressed in the Altar of the Last Judgment of the Givers of Alms, dated 1525 and now housed in the Musée Royale des Beaux-Arts in Antwerp, and especially in his wall-hanging drawings showing scenes from the lives of Abraham and Jacob, as well as in the large stained-glass windows of Brussels Cathedral. Also worthy of mention is Frans Floris (1516–70), who ran a studio of four in Antwerp which produced large compositions containing many human figures.

Pieter Breugel the Elder

The most significant opponent of the Romanists was Pieter Breugel the Elder (1525–69), even though he learned something from them. His major creation was the "peasant picture", and he elevated the art of the rustic landscape so as to make it universally popular as a genre in its own right. Breugel depicted the comedy and tragedy reflected in the lives of the simple peasant folk as they pursued their labours through the changing seasons or followed their customs and traditions. His "Census at Bethlehem" (1566, Musées Royaux des Beaux-Arts, Brussels) is a splendid panorama of Dutch village life in winter-time. Children are shown playing on the frozen lakes, peasants pulling sleds piled with stores for the winter, men are gathered in front of the inn, a pig is being slaughtered, in the twilight figures are grouped around a hollow tree-stump, and in the middle of all this can be seen the unobtrusive forms of Jesus and Mary. Breugel was able successfully to find a synthesis with the event in Christ's life set in a traditional rustic scene; in the middle of winter, in front of a ruined castle, a new house is being built,

Pieter Breugel the Elder: "Census in Bethlehem"

symbolising the House of God being newly built on Earth through the Birth of Christ. Mythologial subjects, such as the "Fall of Icarus", painted in 1558 and also housed in the Brussels museum, are shown by Breugel against the background of a quiet rustic world. The death of Icarus – who considers himself to be godlike, with the result that pride inevitably comes before a fall! – goes almost unnoticed, in the same way that the death of any individual does not shake the world, which still revolves in much the same way as the peasant continues to plough his field, the shepherd still watches his flock and the fisherman and the crew of the ship in the distance still sail the deep. As Breugel saw it, it is not the ordinary, genial and imaginative individual who changes the world, but rather the constant work done to please God by so many anonymous people. However, it was not just the vitality of the peasant which intrigued Breugel – he was equally fascinated by the world of evil. The "Fall of the Angels", in the Brussels museum and "Dulle Griet" (Mean Maggie) in the Museum van den Bergh, Antwerp, both dating from 1562, come close to the demon-world of Hieronymus Bosch. Numerous grotesque and cruel beings, part man, part beast, populate an inferno with renegade angels and "Mean Maggie", the very personification of greed in a devastating world of lust and Satanism. In an enigmatic and sinister way Breugel mirrors the conflict men faces between good and evil, reason and physical desire, at a time when religious struggles were rife between Protestants and Catholics. The sons of Pieter Breugel were also artists, especially Jan Breugel (1568–1625), who made such a name for himself with his still-lifes of flowers and small thematic landscapes that even Rubens took him under his wing. Pieter Breugel the Younger imitated his father, with his ghostly scenes and religious pictures.

Architecturally speaking, the Renaissance primarily affected the interior decoration of buildings. Examples are the alabaster, black marble and oak fire-place in the court buildings in Bruges, designed by L. Blondeel and G. de Beaugrant in 1529–31, as well as the huge alabaster altar made in 1533 by Jean Mone for the church of Notre Dame in Halle. Few castles and palaces, the hallmark of Renaissance secular building elsewhere, were built at this time in the Netherlands.

Renaissance architecture

The only exceptions to this are the residence of the royal bishops of Liège (1526–40) and the palace of the Stadholder Margaret of Austria in Mechelen. The architects Guyot de Beaugrant and Rombout Keldermans were responsible for the Mechelen building (1507–25), with its mélange of flamboyantly Gothic and more balanced Renaissance ornamentation. The latter architect, together with Dominicus de Waghemaker, designed the somewhat similar north front of Ghent Town Hall (1516–38). Cornelius Floris de Vriendt (1514–75), an architect, sculptor and artist all in one, made his mark when he built Antwerp Town Hall between 1561 and 1565. Schooled in designing façades for Italian palaces, he combined this skill with the North European preference for gables and oriel windows to which he added lavish ornamentation and scroll-work. This produced the Floris Style, named after him and which pointed the way ahead for the future. The elegant guild-houses in the Antwerp market-place were built in this elegant style, as were the house built for the mayor and patron of Rubens Nicolas Rockox and the palace belonging to Plantin-Moretus, a famous printer and publisher.

The richly-carved choir-screen of 1570–73 in Tournai Cathedral and the figured, tower-like tabernacle of Sint-Leonardus in Zoutleeuw (1549) are highlights in the sculptural career of Cornelius Floris. The major Renaissance sculptors of the second half of the 16th c., however, worked abroad; these included Jean de Boulogne, known as Giambologna, a pupil of Jacques Dubroeuq from Mons, in Italy, and Adrian de Vries in Germany.

When the political and religious split between the northern and southern provinces took place at the end of the 16th c. this resulted in a simul-

Baroque Painting

Paintings in Cloth

Embroidery and tapestry work is an old art-form going back to pre-Christian times, as shown by finds from ancient Egypt and Greece. Pictures worked in wool are also known from Early Christian times. In Byzantium and in Moorish Spain silk hangings were made to decorate the walls. In the Middle Ages, especially in France, there were periods during which some famous tapestries were made, such as the Bayeux Tapestry in the 11th c. and that portraying the Apocalypse which was made in the workshop of Nicolas Bataille in Paris between 1376 and 1381 and placed in the Cathedral of Angers. Around 1400 first Arras – after which tapestries generally became known in Italy as "arazzi" – and then Tournai became further centres of tapestry-work. The word "tapestry" was derived from "tapis", the French word for carpet.

The boom in Flemish wool and cloth production towards the end of the 15th c. led to further workshops being set up, mainly in Lille, Oudenaarde, Ghent, Bruges and Leuven. However, after the decline of Paris as a centre of tapestry-making it was Brussels which became the new centre of the industry; between 1500 and 1700 the most magnificent tapestries in Europe were produced here – see the collection displayed in the Musées Royaux d'Art et d'Histoire in Brussels. Being a sophisticated court centre under the Dukes of Burgundy and the Spanish and Habsburg rulers, Brussels was also a city of art and culture and closely involved in the fields of painting and tapestry. These wall-hangings were made from a sketch, usually a pen and wash drawing, known as a "petit patron", which was provided by the artist and then used by the pattern-maker – who was often better-paid than the artist – in the form of a mirror image to provide a full-sized pattern for the embroiderers to work from. After Raphael had painted with his own hand the original sketches for the famous series of tapestries depicting the Acts of the Apostles this became the accepted practice, and many famous artists right up to and including Peter Paul Rubens made their own sketches.

The actual embroidering was usually shared out between a number of people employed in central workshops. The width of the loom was sufficient to allow five, sometimes as many as seven weavers to sit side by side. However, because it was necessary constantly to change over to threads of a different colour, it was possible for each worker to produce only a few square inches in the course of a ten-hour day, and it took at least six months to complete a large tapestry, which accounts for the high prices charged.

A large number of linen warp-threads were stretched across the loom – between 3000 and 4000 on a 5 m (17 ft wide loom. When they were stretched vertically it was known as hautelisse work, and as basselisse work when they were horizontal. Products made on the "basselisse" looms were cheaper, as the work went faster because by stepping on the pedals the weaver could raise and lower the warp, whereas when working with the "hautelisse" loom opening up the warp had to be done with one hand, leaving only the other hand to work with. Somewhat differently from normal weaving, where the weft thread passes through the warp from edge to edge of the loom, when embroidering tapestry differently coloured weft threads of wool or silk – later of gold and silver as well – are led over and under as many warp threads as is necessary to produce the required shape and area in that colour. Frequently changing the colours of the threads used results in vertical slits appearing where the different colours meet, and these then have to be sewn together.

Among the major Brussels workshops was that of Pierre van Aelst, where the famous tapestries now in the Vatican and portraying the Acts of the Apostles were woven between 1516 and 1519 on instructions from Pope Leo X and to the designs by Raphael. The many commissions by King Charles V were executed mainly by the Brussels factory of Pieter Pannemaker. The most outstanding designer of patterns for tapestries from this period was the Brussels court painter Bernaert van Orley, who lived from about 1488 to 1541. His designs, based somewhat on those of Raphael, were marked by strict draughtsmanship, monumental configuration and the effect of depth and space – see Scenes from the Life of Jacob in the Brussels Musées Royaux d'Art et d'Histoire. The decorative sparkle of his tapestries was intensified by the use of gold and silver threads. In addition to van Orley, Pieter Coecke van Aelst and Jan Vermeyen were also well-known designers of tapestries. The increasing reputation of the workshops soon led to the tapestries being signed with the workshop's own trade mark, to avoid imitations.

"The Life of Jacob" (16th c.; by Bernaert van Orley)

The themes and motifs used in the tapestries were many and varied. They included tales from olden times, mythological scenes, stories from the Old and New Testaments, allegories, tales of chivalry and hunting and scenes from everyday life. In addition to these where the picture told a story there were also purely decorative "green tapestries" or "tapis de verdures", with leaves and plants and later often whole landscapes. The best quality "green" tapestries were produced in Oudenaarde, where they can be seen today in the local museum. In France in the 16th c. lavish flower patterns "à mille fleurs" were very popular. The decorative borders around the wall-hangings were also very artistically done but sometimes over-decorated to the extent that they tend to divert one's attention from the main centre section.

Tapestry-making in Flanders reached its peak during the Baroque period in the 17th c., and the demands of palaces, mansions and churches could scarcely be met. In the first half of the 17th c. Peter Paul Rubens was the top designer and gave the tapestries their distinctive artistic quality. The Decius-Mus Series in Vienna, the Eucharistic Cycle and the "Vatican Tapestries" constitute the epoch-making products of the Brussels manufacturers. Ruben's successor David Teniers was soon to feel the effects of French competition.

In 1662 King Louis XIV established the first Royal Manufactory in Paris, with the aim of supplying locally the wall-hangings needed for his many castles and palaces, As it was set up in the workshop of the Gobelin family its products were given the name of gobelins, and soon the term was applied generally to all tapestries. The true gobelins were hand-embroidered, while the machine-woven Jacquard tapestries, named after their inventor J. M. Jacquard (1752–1834) were frequently regarded as non-genuine "gobelins". The factories in Beauvais, Aubusson and Paris led in the field of tapestry-making in the 18th c. until the French Revolution caused its rapid demise.

Antwerp Town Hall

taneous divorce between Dutch art in the north and Flemish in the south. Any common factors remaining in the field of painting finally disappeared in the 17th c. when the two major artists from the two regions, Rembrandt and Rubens respectively, went their separate ways with their different interpretations of both form and colour.

Peter Paul Rubens Peter Paul Rubens (1577–1640) set new horizons in Flemish and European painting. Displaying a marked degree of sensuousness together with a Classical and Humanist attitude and an inexhaustible imagination Rubens produced paintings covering many religious and secular subjects, from altar-pieces to allegory, from historical scenes to portraits and landscapes. He soon became rich and famous and in the grand house and studio in Antwerp where he lived and worked in style, assisted by such specialists as F. Snyders, J. Breugel the Younger, van Dyck and others, more than 3000 paintings were produced, of which some 500 to 600 were definitely by him or are attributed to him. Rubens lived in Italy between 1600 and 1608, visiting Mantua, Genoa and Rome, and this had a great bearing on his artistic development. He was particularly influenced by the Early Baroque work of Caravaggio and Caracci and the Renaissance skills of Leonardo da Vinci and Titian, as well as by older paintings. Soon after returning to Antwerp he produced his monumental masterpiece, the triptych in Antwerp Cathedral in 1610. The powerful and muscular figures in the "Raising of the Cross" are reminiscent of the ceiling frescoes in the Sistine Chapel, the use of light and shade being modelled on the style of Carvaggio. The dramatic composition, aided by the diagonal line and colouring used in the centre panel, is typically Romo-Baroque, while the precise and detailed brushwork conforms to traditional Flemish realism. The "Descent from the Cross" (1612) is more restful and formal; the diagonal line is less dynamic and broken, and the contrast between light and dark success-

Peter Paul Rubens: "The crucifixion"...

... and "Descent from the Cross"

fully gives the impression of the body of Christ being raised, while in death it appears as a source of radiant light. The overall coloration differs; in particular, the red of John's robe in the centre panel, that of the priest in the temple in the right-hand panel and of Mary's cloak in the left-hand panel depicting the Visitation all serve to compose the individual panels into one large compositional unit.

Subsequently Rubens concentrated on nudes and figures, dramatic hunting and fighting scenes, pictures illustrating historical tales, and large altar-pieces in a multiplicity of forms – see the Museums of Art in Brussels and Antwerp. The painting above the high altar in the Cathedral of Notre-Dame in Antwerp, the "Assumption of the Virgin Mary" completed in 1626, showed early signs of the lyrical and delicate later style of Rubens as inspired by Titian. During the final decade of his work he produced some idyllic landscapes and portraits.

Anthonis van Dyck

Rubens' most distinguished pupil was Anthonis van Dyck (1599–1641). He too travelled to Italy, primarily in order to study the painting of Titian. After being employed for a short time as court painter to the Archduchess Isabella in Antwerp he went to London in 1632 where he became court painter to King Charles I. His altar-pieces – such as those in Sint-Paul and Sint-Augustinus in Antwerp, the church of Notre-Dame in Kortrijk and Sint-Romuald in Mechelen – give an impression of muted pathos and religious sensitivity. He achieved fame mainly for his portraits, some of which hang in the Art Museums in Antwerp and Brussels. His portrayals of figures are distinguished by keen individual observance, a noble style of composition and balanced use of colour.

Jacob Jordaens

His contemporary Jacob Jordaens (1593–1678) was a master of genre painting, portraying the earthier pleasures of life, such as carousing, eating and so on. His vigorous and muscular characters and sensuous female nudes reflect the influence of Italian Baroque, which he must have received from Rubens, as he never actually visited Italy himself.

Adriaen Brouwer

Adriaen Brouwer (c. 1606–38), actually a Dutchman by birth who lived in Antwerp, painted folksy and graphic everyday scenes – the peasant in the ale-house, at play or involved in a rough and tumble, as well as festivities of all kinds.

David Teniers the Younger

David Teniers the Younger (1610–90) is another 17th c. Antwerp genre painter, who was employed after 1651 as court painter in Brussels and curator of the archduke's art collections. He was a humorous painter of Flemish rustic life and also provides an interesting insight into contemporary art-galleries and collections.

Baroque Sculpture Duquesnoy

Although Baroque sculpture was overshadowed by painting, it nevertheless produced some noteworthy works and artists, such as the Duquesnoy family of Jerôme the Elder and his sons Jerôme the Younger and François. In 1619 the father sculpted the famous bronze fountainstatue of the Manneken-Pis in Brussels as well as the tabernacle of the collegiate church in Aalst in black and white marble. François worked mainly in Rome in a somewhat Neo-Classical variation on the Baroque. The works of his brother Jerôme, who lived from 1602 to 1654, included the monument for Bishop Anton Triest in the Cathédrale St-Bavon in Ghent. The Baroque interior of the church of Notre-Dame-les-Victoires-au-Sablon in Brussels is also his work.

Quellin

The Quellin family of sculptors worked both in Holland and Flanders. Artus the Elder (1609–68) and his pupils were responsible between 1648 and 1655 for all the sculpture-work in Amsterdam City Hall. His nephew and pupil Artus the Younger (1625–1700) copied the Rubens' style of sculpting from his uncle and produced a large number of pulpits and monuments in Flemish churches. Also worthy of mention are the communion rail in Sint-Romuald in Mechelen and the impressive 1682 figure of God the Father on the rood-screen of Sint-Salvator in Bruges.

Pieter Verbruggen the Elder (1615–86) made religious statues and altar-figures for churches in Antwerp, while his son Pieter the Younger (1640–91) was responsible for the marble altar in the church of St Dominic in Antwerp and his other son Hendrik (1654–1724) carved the Baroque pulpits in Leuven and Brussels.

Verbruggen

Mention should be made of the 1673 monument to the Bishop of Allamont by the Liège sculptor Jean Delcour in the church of Sint-Baaf in Ghent, carved on the lines of Italian Baroque à la Bernini.

Jean Delcour

One of the earliest examples of the Baroque style being used in religious buildings was the Carmelite church in Brussels, built between 1607 and 1671, but now destroyed. It was designed by the architect Wenceslas Coeberger. Lavish High Baroque design was used by Jacques Francart in the convent church in Mechelen (1629–47) and the church of St Augustus in Brussels. The church of St Carolus Borromeüs in Antwerp (1614–21) and that of St Peter in Ghent (1629–44) were built by F. Aguillon and P. Huyssens. Huyssens also designed the Église St-Loup in Namur between 1621 and 1645.

Baroque Architecture

The field of secular architecture saw the building of town residences, palaces modelled on those of Italy and France, as well as the magnificent guildhalls on the Grand'Place in Brussels. After most of the buildings on the Grand'Place had been destroyed by the French during the siege of 1695 twenty-nine such guildhalls with slender multi-storey façades were built between 1695 and 1710, using a mélange of decorative styles ranging from the historical to the Renaissance and the Baroque. By thus imitating the feudal image the middle-classes tried to make their buildings the equal in style to the palaces of the nobility.

Painting The period between Rococo and Neo-Classicism had little impact on Belgian art. Painters turned again to the Rubens and French schools without being able seriously to compete with either. Towards the end of the 18th c. Jacques-Louis David from Paris hastened the reaction in favour of Neo-Classicism. In his paintings of the French Revolution and as court painter to Napoleon he portrayed the traumatic events of his time in programmatic pictures; the Brussels Museum of Art owns his oil-painting "The Murder of Marat" (1793).

18th Century

In the field of **sculpture** church interiors continued to be vested with work of high quality. Particular mention should be made of the pulpit by Michiel van der Voort the Elder in the Cathedral of Notre-Dame in Antwerp, decorated with carvings of animals of all kinds, as well as of the Rococo pulpit of marble and oak (1741–45) by Laurent Delvaux which can be seen in Sint-Baaf's in Ghent. In 1740 Josef Couven from Aachen constructed the high-altar framed with clustered columns.

In **architecture** too ideas came from outside the country. In Namur Gaetono Pizzoni from Milan built the Cathedral between 1751 and 1767; the monumental pillars of the curved façade were early precursors of Neo-Classicism. In Liège the main façade of the 1737 Bishop's Residence is powerfully articulated with columns and pilasters, in the French style of the time. In the upper town of Brussels some splendid town-houses were built to the design of the French architect Guimard in the Rue Royale and the Place Royale and surrounded by a large park. Of the many noble mansions built in the countryside particular mention should be made of the Palace and Park of Belöil, seat of the Prince of Ligne.

Painting Nineteenth century Belgian artists followed the styles then current in the rest of Europe. Many of their works are on dispaly in the

19th Century

Musées Royaux des Beaux-Arts in Antwerp and Brussels. Historical art originally followed the precedents set by the French painters Jacques-Louis David and Delacroix; their chief followers in Belgium were Gustav Wappers, L. Gallait and Nicaise de Keyser who, especially after Belgium became independent in 1830, painted national subjects in a romantic manner. Henri Leys – who did the frescoes in the Antwerp Town Hall – painted in a more objective and down-to-earth fashion. Antoine Wiertz concentrated on monumental painting with a moral or philosophical theme, sometimes using effective nightmarish scenes, such as those in the Musée Wiertz in Brussels. F. Courtens and A. Baertson made a name for themselves as landscape painters. Among the Realists mention must be made of François Lamorinière and Hippolyte Boulenger as well as of the socially-biased works of Willem Vogels and Jan Stobbaerts. The lives of the peasants and the underprivileged formed the theme of paintings by E. Laermans, a subject again used in Expressionist form by Charles de Grux towards the end of the century. Impressionism, which was rapidly spreading from France to the rest of Europe, was reflected in the Parisian boudoir themes and still-life of Albert Steven, in the idyllically luminous paintings of Henri de Braekelaar and in the charming society portraits and landscapes of Henri Evenepoel. Another Neo-Impressionist who should be mentioned was Theo van Rysselberghe, a member of the Cercle de Vingts (1884–93), to which Fernand Khnopff also belonged, albeit as an exponent of Symbolism as favoured by the Viennese Secessionists. The works of George Minne, Valerius de Saedeleer, Gustave van de Woestyne and Jakob Smits all reflect in different ways the mystical and religious variations of Symbolism. Mention should also be made of the graphic artist and engraver Félicien Rops, who was close to Gustave Moreau in the style of his Symbolistic paintings and portrayed the darker side of life. His opposite was Rik Wouters, an advocate of Fauvism who painted vital compositions with a strong use of colour.

James Ensor

European recognition came late to James Ensor (1860–1949), but he was a strong influence on Expressionist and Surrealist painters. The stories of Edgar Allan Poe, together with the thousands of objects to be found in the souvenir shop run by his uncle and aunt in Ostend, impelled him to paint his colourful but grotesque, bizarre, even nightmare-impressionistic scenes of people in masks who are caricatures either of themselves or of society. For example, his huge oil-painting called "The Entry of Christ into Brussels" (1888–89) shows an endless, almost carnival-like mass of people surging through the streets, representing various walks of life such as soldiers, priests, judges and so on, with Christ standing on the sidelines and with the features of James Ensor himself. It was in this way that this eccentric artist wrestled with his fantasy world. His pictures "Strange Masks" (1892, Musées Royaux des Beaux-Arts, Brussels) and "The Intrigue" (1890, in the museum of the same name in Antwerp) also convey an eerie and ghostly atmosphere. Instead of a world of outward appearances and phenomena, which so fascinated the Impressionists, Ensor lived in one governed by experiences, emotions and psychological fantasies, and was in some ways well ahead of his time.

Constantin Meunier

In the early 19th c. Belgian **sculpture** was still modelled on that of France and showed a mixture of styles involving Realism and emotional Baroque pathos. Towards the end of the century the naturalistic style of Constantin Meunier (1831–1905) caught on, especially in the shape of monumental, sometimes heroised figures. Much of his work is to be found in the Meunier Museum in Brussels. George Minne (1866–1941) preferred the delicate lyricism of the Art Nouveau style in his figures, for example, in the Fountain of Youth in his home town of Ghent.

Architecture In the early 19th c. the tradition of French Neo-Classicisim was perpetrated in Belgian architecture, together with an increased Baroque impact and perhaps an excessive regard for past styles. The master-builder Jean-Pierre Cluysenaer, for example, worked on the long covered passages in Brussels. In Ghent L. Roelandt built the University and the Palais de Justice, and in Antwerp P. Bourla was the city architect. Brussels, freshly chosen as capital of Belgium in 1831, was the scene of extensive building alterations. Wide boulevards were laid out and large prestigious buildings erected. The economic boom was reflected in the building of the Neo-Classical Stock Exchange (1830–73), the National Bank (1859–64), glass-covered passages such as the Galeries Saint-Hubert (1847) and the temple-like opera house, the Theatre Royal de la Monnaie. The apotheosis of how the upper-classes now saw themselves and of the sovereignty of the rule of law were reflected in the building of the giant Palais de Justice (Law Courts) by J. Poelaert in 1883, with its giant dome which still dominates the city's skyline.

Towards the end of the 19th c. the Art Nouveau style took hold in Brussels; a prime example is the Hôtel Tassel, built in 1892–93 by Victor Horta (1861–1947). His own house and office were richly decorated and furnished in the Art Nouveau style. Paul Hankar, too, was an advocate of the new movement, an example being Klever House in Brussels, 1898); so was Henry van de Velde, but he left Brussels in 1902 to attend the school of art in Weimar, Germany.

Victor Horta
Henry van de Velde

Expressionism played a leading role in Belgian painting at the beginning of the 20th c. Constant Permeke (1886–1952) and Frans Masereel (1889–1972) were its leading lights. From time to time Permeke returned to traditional Flemish styles of painting. His "Winter Landscape" of 1912, now in the Musées des Beaux-Arts in Antwerp, is strongly reminiscent

Modern
Painting
Constant Permeke

In the house of Victor Horta

of Breugel, while his later landscapes and seascapes are more on the lines of French Realism Ö la Gustave Courbet. In between these two extremes he produced many sensitive studies of the lives of ordinary folk, such as "The Sower" (1933) which, together with many others, now hangs in the Constant Permeke Provincial Museum in Jabbeke near Bruges.

Frans Masereel

Masereel, who was born in Ghent and trained there as a painter and graphic artist, lived in Paris from 1921, where his black-and-white wood-cuts denounced the exploitation of the Paris workers and the hedonism of the bourgeoisie. The powerful brush-strokes of his oils vividly portray simple folk, such as fishermen or barmaids. His landscapes are rather sombre, as if reflecting the destructive powers of two world wars.

Other Expressionists worthy of mention are Jean Brusselsmans, some of whose paintings are reminiscent of the early works of Paul Klee, for example, his landscape "In the Country of the Payotte", painted in 1928 and now in the Musées des Beaux-Arts in Antwerp, as well as Gust de Smet, who came close to Cubism, and Fritz van den Berghe, who felt himself to be in empathy with the German Expressionists.

René Magritte

The Belgian Surrealist painters René Magritte and Paul Delvaux (b. 1897) have gained international acclaim. In contrast to Salvador Dali or Max Ernst, Magritte represented the realistic form of Surrealism which, by means of a precise and accurate painting technique, manages to combine various levels of factuality in such a way as to reflect both reality and appearance, fact and fiction. Of one of his major works, "The Constitution of Man", painted in 1939 and now in the Claude Spaak Collection, Magritte himself explained "Before a window of a room through which one looked outside I had placed a picture. The picture was of exactly that section of the landscape which it covered up; thus, the tree in the picture

René Magritte: "This is not a pipe."

concealed the tree which was outside. To the observer, therefore, it (the tree) was both inside on the picture and also – in his imagination – outside, in the landscape itself. This is how we see the world; we see it as something outside, even though we carry a picture of it within ourselves. In the same way we transpose into the past many things which are happening in the present. Time and space thus lose their trivial meaning, the latter being of importance only as an everyday experience."

Also of significance are Magritte's "Talking Pictures", such as that of a pipe with the words underneath informing us that "This is not a pipe". In this way Magritte presents the observer with ambiguities and contradictions, arguing that words are not the things themselves, merely a symbol to represent them, and that pictures are not actuality, only an imaginary presentation of it, and that as they all depend on conventional ways of thinking and recognising they restrict freedom of thought. In addition to framed pictures Magritte also painted murals in public buildings, for example, in the Knokke Casino (1953), in the Palais des Beaux-Arts in Charleroi (1957) and in the Palais des Congrès in Brussels (1961).

The pictures of Paul Delvaux explored much more deeply the Kingdom of the Unconscious, which began to fascinate artists in the early 20th c. as a result of the psychoanalytical theses published by Freud and Jung. These argued that the external world which we know and trust is being increasingly defamiliarised by the dream world or even replaced by it as a form of higher reality. Bringing to the fore this concept of the Forces of the Unconscious led coincidentally to pictures being painted which were psychically associated with and shaped by it. Using precise and realistic draughtsmanship and cold colours, Delvaux painted many female nudes against landscape backgrounds, in murky interiors, on railway stations or in the presence of skeletons reacting as human beings. His statuesque women emit an eerie atmosphere of cold eroticism. Some of the works produced by Delvaux during his long life hang in the Modern departments of the art museums in Brussels and Antwerp and also in the Paul Delvaux Foundation in Sint-Idesbald.

Paul Delvaux

Abstract art in Belgium began with the Constructivist painters Jozef Peeters and Georges Vantongerloo. They were members of the Dutch De Stil-Bewegung, founded in 1917, during the 1920s, and of the Parisian group, the Abstraction-Création (founded 1931) during the 1930s. Constructivism, and Concrete Art which followed it, aimed at creating, by the use of geometrical abstract forms, an aesthetic discipline not dependent on nature and which was also intended to represent universal harmony. Other major exponents of Belgian Constructivism are Victor Servranckx and Félix de Boeck.

Constructivism

After the Second World War abstract art received a further impetus through the work of Corneille (actually Cornelis van Beverloo) and Pierre Alechinsky, members of the international group of artists known as COBRA, formed in 1948–50 from the first two letters of Copenhagen and Brussels and the "A" of Amsterdam. They practised a spontaneous and informal method of painting with naïvely happy elements of popular art combined with the archaically primitive sign language of earlier cultures.

COBRA

In the 1950s Zero Art, with such exponents as Heinz Mack, Otto Piene and Günther Uecker, received an enthusiastic reception in Antwerp, and an exhibition, Vision in Motion, was held in 1959. These artists reduced all figures in both painting and sculpture to mere suggestions of colour and light in space, something which was later to be used again and developed further in Op Art.

From 1958 to 1962 Maurice Wyckaert, an advocate of informal painting, was a member of the International Situationists formed in 1957 who – together with writers – aimed at changing through the medium of art the alienated world in which man found himself.

From the mid-1960s Conceptual Art in Belgium found an enthusiastic advocate in M. Broodthaers.The painter Panamarenko produced a style all of his own with his technically Utopian flying objects, but is better known perhaps, in company with such as Paul Thek and Michael Buthe, under the collective concept of individual mythology. Panamarenko's flying machines portray the dream of a modern-day Icarus setting off to discover the Universe.

In the field of contemporary sculpture mention must be made of Roel d'Haese and his abstractly bizarre metal sculptures, and of P. Bury, known for his kinetic objects. A good overall idea of international trends in modern sculpture can be obtained by visiting the Middelheim Sculpture Park in Antwerp.

Early 20th c. architecture was strongly influenced by the Art Nouveau style. After the First World War the architect V. Bourgeois designed the Cité Moderne in Berchem-Sainte-Agathe near Brussels between 1922 and 1925; this is a town quarter in the International style. L. Stijnen was an exponent of Functionalism, based on practical yet constructively aesthetic concepts.

Of contemporary buildings, special mention should be made of the University Quarter in Woluwé-Saint-Lambert near Brussels, built under the guidance of L. Kroll, and the university town of Louvain-La-Neuve south-east of Brussels, planned after 1970 by Raymond Lemaire and some 80 other architects in individual building styles.

Literature

The border between the Dutch and French-speaking regions runs across Belgium. One consequence of this has been that since the Middle Ages two distinct literary traditions have evolved; that written in the Dutch language is described as Flemish literature, while French-worded books from the Walloon region form a completely separate branch of writing. As a result it is not possible simply to talk of Belgian national literature as such. Flemish authors have always compiled their writings against a background of Dutch tradition, in spite of attempts to distance themselves from it, because they have followed the history and traditions of the Flemings, while many of the French-speaking writers regarded themselves as forming part of the literature of France and frequently chose to live there, especially in Paris.

Flemish Literature

Flemish literature first flowered in the 12th–14th centuries. Henry of Veldeke (c. 1140/50–c. 1210) can be said to have been the founder of the

courtly romance novel with his poem "Eneïde". His minneliederen (courtly love songs) governed the styles of many of his contemporaries and those that came after him.

Jacob van Maerlant (c. 1230–c. 1288) distinguished himself in many literary spheres. His works included the oldest romance about the quest for the Holy Grail written in the Dutch language, a rhyming Bible, a history book and poems. Hadewijch, one of the few renowned female figures of medieval literature, was a mystic who expressed her visions in poetry and letters.

Eneïde manuscript dating from the 13th c.

It was at this time too that the most important work to come from the central Netherlands, the romance of chivalry known as "Karel ende Elegast", was written, together with that famous medieval animal epic "Van den vos Reinaerde" (Reynard the Fox), which has continued to inspire writers up to the present day. Other highlights of the times were the mystical works of Jan van Ruusbroec (1293–1381) and the dialect folk play "Elckerlyc" by Petrus Dorlandus (1454–1507). The "rederij-kerkamers" at the end of the Middle Ages formed a movement similar to the "meistersingers" in Germany.

From the 16th to 19th c. Flemish literature tended to play second fiddle to the French. It was not until 1815, when the northern and southern provinces were united, that it received a fresh impetus. It was only then that – very belatedly – the linguistic transition from Middle to High Dutch reached completion. Jan Frans Willems and the movement he started, the "Vlaamse Beweging" campaigned strongly for Dutch to be the language of the Flemings.

19th Century

The prime mover in the new beginning to Flemish literature was the Romantic writer Hendrik Conscience (1812–83), whose novel "De leeuw van Vlaanderen" (The Lion of Flanders), which took the Battle of the Spurs of 1302 as its subject, became a Flemish national epic. August Snieders (1825–1904) was also one of the major writers of his time.

Hendrik Conscience

The outstanding personality of the second half of the 19th c. was the priest and lyricist Guido Gezelle (1830–99), who used a variety of Flemish dialects in his deeply pious anthologies. His pupil Albrecht Rodenbach (1856–80) was one of the founders of the Flemish popular theatre.

Towards the end of the 19th c. a group of young writers came to the fore and issued a periodical with the name "Van nu en straks" (Here and Now) which deprecated Romanticism and traditional historical awareness. Among those who remained outside this new trend were August Vermeylen (1872–1945), Karel van de Woestijne (1878–1929) and Hermann Teirlinck (1879–1967). Stijn Streuvels, or Frank Lateur (1871–1969), a nephew of Gezelle, described in objective and committed terms the hard lives led by the Flemish peasants. Cyriel Buysse (1859–1932), who initially expressed his support for this same group, later changed direction and became the founder of Flemish Naturalism.

20th Century "Van nu en straks"

The events of the First World War led to the emergence of the "homeland novel", of which Felix Timmermans was one of the principal exponents.

Felix Timmermans

At the same time Expressionism found its way into Flemish literature. However, authors such as Paul André van Ostaijen (1896–1928), Victor J. Brunclair (1899–1944) and Wies Moens (1898–1982) restricted themselves almost entirely to lyric writings, producing hardly any Expressionist novels or stories.

Expressionism

However, it was not until after the Second World War that Belgium entered the international rankings, beginning with Maurice Roelants (1895–1966) with his psychological novels. Flemish Realism flourished through the works of Marcel Matthijs (1899–1964) and Johan Daisne (b. 1912). The latter was inspired by the works of Prandello and E. T. A. Hoffman and was the first to develop a specifically Flemish literary trend. Equally important was Maurice Gilliams (1900–82), the creator of Flemish Individualism. In his novels and stories Louis Paul Boon (1912–1979) takes the side of the socially deprived.
Through his novels "The Book of Alpha" (1963) and "Orclies Militaris"

After 1945

(1968) Ivo Michiels (b. 1923) strives for international recognition of Flemish "nouveau réalisme".

Hugo Claus

In more recent years, however, Michiels has been somewhat overshadowed by Hugo Claus (b. 1929), the successful Flemish contemporary writer. He uses almost exclusively material gleaned from his Belgian homeland and is not afraid to tackle delicate subjects such as that of collaborating with the German occupying forces during the Second World War. Claus writes drama, poems and novels, such as "Het verdriet van Belgie" (The Sorrow of Belgium).

Lyric verse

Lyric verse calls to mind such names as Hubert van Herreweghen (b. 1920), Jan Veulemans (b. 1928), Paul Snoek (b. 1933) and Pieter Aerts (b. 1928). Their work re-awakens the traditions established in the first half of this century.

Literature in the French Language

Medieval chroniclers

For hundreds of years before the Kingdom of Belgium was founded literature of that country written in the French language formed a part of French literature in the widest sense. Chroniclers of the Hundred Years' War who have been remembered include Jean Froissart (1337–1400) and Philippe de Commynes (1447–1511), whose preserved memoirs from 1464–98 entitle him to be considered as the originator of modern French historical narrative.

Charles Joseph de Ligne

Between the medieval chroniclers and the time when Belgium could claim to have established its own independent literary forms there was a large gap, which even Prince Charles Joseph de Ligne (1735–1814) could fill only to a small degree. The Prince, a field-marshal in the Austrian army, wrote letters, essays and polished cameos of the rulers of the time.

19th Century

Even after this two-language country became independent little changed initially; Belgian authors tended to maintain close contacts with France, especially Paris, and at first there was no sign of the emergence of any original and independent literary trends. Even a number of Flemish authors wrote in French.

Charles de Coster

However it was one of those very writers, Charles de Coster (1827–79; see Famous People) who achieved a breakthrough in 1867 with his novel "La légende de Thyl Uilenspiegel". Coster told the tale of Thyl Uilenspiegel in his Flemish home town during the War of Liberation against the Spaniards. In powerful lan-

Thyl Uilenspiegel by Franz Mansereel

guage studded with vivid descriptive passages he describes the cruelty and pitilessness of the struggle, in which Thyl and his friend Lamme Goedzak are the symbols of the Flemings' desire for freedom and love of their homeland.

A contemporary of Coster was Camille Lemonnier (1844–1913), whose realistic novels bring out his love of nature. In works such as "Happe-Chair" he also wrote about the lives of Walloon mineworkers and could see help for them only in a socialist society. In addition to his poems, Georges Rodenbach (1855–98) also produced one novel, "Bruges morte" (Dead Bruges).

The efforts to bring about an original literary form in the French language in Belgium led in 1881 to the launching of the publication called "La jeune Belgique" by Max Waller (1860–89). The best-known members of his circle included Albert Giraud (1860–1929). a lyric poet who lived and worked in Paris, and Emile Verhaeren (1855–1916). | "La jeune Belgique"

In 1881 also, in competition to the above, the magazine "L'Art Moderne", whose allegiance was to France, was founded. | "L'Art Moderne"

A further publication which took up a position between "La jeune Belgique" and "L'Art Moderne" was "La Wallonie"; founded in 1886, it allowed writers of both leanings to express their views. Those who contributed articles included Emile Verhaeren, Charles van Leberghe (1861–1907), Grégoire Le Roy (1862–1941) and Max Elskamp (1862–1931). | "La Wallonie"

The Symbolist Maurice Maeterlinck (1862–1949; see Famous People) was one of the outstanding Belgian literary figures of the 20th century. His lyrical works – such as "Serres Chaudes" and "Douze Chansons" – and his drama and philosophical essays won him the Noble Prize for Literature in 1911. | 20th Century Maurice Maeterlinck

The Surrealist Henri Michaux (1899–1984), who settled in Paris in the 1920s, will be remembered for his absurd poems, novels and descriptions of his travels to imaginary countries. | Henri Michaux

The "Belgian School of the Fantastic" has gained considerable recognition outside Belgium, at least with its afficionados. Writers who belong to it include Jean Ray, Frans Hellens and Mobique Wayyeau. | "School of the Fantastic"

Great stage success was gained by Fernand Crommelynck (1885–1970) and, above all, by Michel de Ghelderode (1898–1962), who deliberately included repulsive and violent themes in his plays in order to provoke criticism and discussion. | Drama

The most popular of all French-speaking Belgian writers must be Georges Simenon (1903–89), but few people will know that he was born in Liège. That is largely due to the fact that his "Inspector Maigret" stories, which have appeared since 1930 and centre around this intelligent and instinctive detective, were set in Paris, where Simenon actually lived. He has left behind a vast range of books and films which have been translated into many languages (see Famous People). | Georges Simenon

Other important contemporary writers include Marcel Moreau, the politically-involved professor of literature and novelist Pierre Mertens, and Marguerite Yourcenar (1903–87; see Famous People).

Music

Evolution in the field of music can be said to have commenced with the merging of most of the individual Dutch domains under the Dukes of | Dutch Music

Music

Burgundy, to have enjoyed its heyday under Charles the Bald and Charles V, and to have come to an end shortly after the northern provinces (now the Netherlands) finally became separated from those in the south which make up Belgium as we know it today. As the original Netherlands comprised roughly the whole region now known as the Benelux states the music of the period is usually described under the general heading of Dutch music; thus this term should not be taken to mean only the work of Dutch composers in the narrower sense, but rather that of Flemish and Walloon masters together with those from the north of France.

Characteristics

About the year 1400 Dutch music developed a highly-perfected style centred on a choir of four or five voices. A form of counterpoint was created in which the individual registers sang the same melody in harmony.

Court music

The earliest epoch of Netherlands' music was closely linked with the court of the 15th c. Dukes of Burgundy, Philip the Good and Charles the Bald. The major composers of that era were Johannes Ciconia (c. 1335–1411), who was employed at the courts of Venice and Padua, among others, and Guillaume Dufay (1400–74), who for a time also went to Italy and whose further elaboration of 14th c. motets and ballads led to the first apotheosis of Dutch music. Gilles Binchois (c. 1400–60), composer at the Burgundian court in Dijon, should also be mentioned.

Franco-Flemish school

Towards the end of the 15th c. it was the famous Cambrai and Antwerp schools (the Franco-Flemish school) which set the tone. Under the latter's guidance the music of the Netherlands was able to hold its own against that of England and to compete on equal terms with that composed by almost all the European master musicians. It maintained this dominant role until the end of the 16th c. The motets, secular songs and masses sung in harmony, by such composers as Pierre de la Rue, Nicolas Gombert, Johannes Ockeghem, Josquin Desprez, Adriaan Willaert, Henri Isaak and Clemens non Papa became widely known, especially after the invention of printed music in the early 16th c. A famous theoretician of his age was Johannes Tinctoris (c. 1435–1511).

Later period

In the later periods of Dutch music names such as Philippe de Monte, Jacob der Kerle and, in particular, Orlando di Lasso from Mons all became known outside the Netherlands. Di Lasso (actually Roland de Lassus, 1532 BC), together with Giovanni Palestrina, is the most respected composer of the 16th c. For a long time he worked in Germany and from 1560 until his death in 1594 was the leader of the court orchestra in Munich.

The work of Jan Pieter Sweelinck (1562–1622) clearly showed the gradual move that was taking place away from the principle of Dutch counterpoint. Although he also was a very important figure in the field of 17th c. organ music he was to prove the last of the great Dutch musicians, and towards the end of the 17th c. the Dutch school, which until then had been universal and European in concept, fell into decline. Various external trends and influences were imported, differing according to region; the composers of the Netherlands increasingly became imitators, after centuries spent improving and developing their own styles.

Walloon Composers French influence

French classical music had a profound influence on the Walloon composers who moved to Paris in increasing numbers, while most of those in what are now the Flemish and Dutch regions stayed at home, with the result that they remained unaffected by the trends sweeping the rest of Europe and so became largely forgotten. It was not until the early 20th c. that the Flemings finally emerged from their long period of lethargy.

18th century

Among the Walloon composers from the present-day Belgium who were able to make their mark in Paris in the 18th c. were Jean-Noël Hamal (oratorio "In Exitu Israel"), Jean-Baptiste Lœillet, Jean-François Gossec ("Messe des Morts"), Pierre van Maldere and André Ernest Modeste Grétry (1742–1813), one of the founders of the French Opéra Comique, who wrote "Zemire et Azor", "Richard Cœur de Lion" and "Céphale et Procis".

André Grétry

In the 19th c. it was only César Franck, a native of Liège (1822–90; see Famous People), who gained international recognition. After adopting French citizenship and settling in Paris, where he became a celebrated organ teacher, he composed his extremely unconventional Symphony in D minor, a number of symphonic poems, an oratorio, a violin sonata and numerous pieces for the organ. Franck successfully strove to revise the French style to accord with German taste, which he taught to his pupils. Among the most talented of these were the Frenchman Vincent d'Indy and the Belgian Guillaume Lekeu, but the latter unfortunately died young before his talents could be developed to the full. He left behind a beautiful violin sonata and a fine adagio for strings.

César Franck

Charles de Bériot (1802–70) and Henri Vieuxtemps (1820–81) founded the Belgian School of Violin Music which has remained famous to this day. Both composed several virtuoso violin concertos, of which the 4th and 5th by Vieuxtemps are still played quite often, especially in French-speaking and Anglo-Saxon countries. Eugène Ysaye (1858–1931), one of the greatest violin virtuosos of all time, continued this tradition into the 20th c. As a composer his six sonatas for solo violin were well received. An important music teacher of the time was Mathieu Crickboom, whose piano-teaching is still recognised as having been of the best.

Belgian Violin School

The Belgian Romantic Benoît (1834–1901) played an important part in his country's music in the years leading up to the 20th c., producing his own unique brand of Flemish music. His works – often popular and folksy, always full of effect and reflecting the national character – included "De Pacificatie van Gent" and "Rubenscantate". At the same time, some of his compositions anticipated new musical trends.

20th Century Peter Benoît

In the early 20th c. Paul Gilson (1865–1942) dominated the Belgian music scene. His many splendidly orchestrated symphonic works include a highly original suite entitled "La Mer". Gilson can be regarded as the founder of the Brabant–Flemish School, which numbered among its members Auguste de Boeck, Gaston Brenta and Marcel Poot (b. 1901). The latter is without doubt the most popular Belgian composer of the 20th c. His exclusively tonal music combines colour, rhythm and melody into a cavalcade which reflects the Belgian's predilection for folk-lore, mass processions, festivals and religious celebrations. Poot's adherents were also known as "Synthesists".

Brabant–Flemish School

The New Antwerp School – much less subject to Latin influences than the Brabant–Flemish School and with strong Romantic characteristics – numbered among its members Marinus de Jong, Karel Candael, Lodewijk Mortelmans, Flor Alpaerts and the famous organist and composer Flor Peeters.

New Antwerp School

Examples of the Liège School are César Franck and Vincent D'Indy, as well as Gabriel Fauré and Gabriel Pierné. Joseph Jomgen, who wrote his sinfonia concertante for organ and orchestra in 1928, and his brother Léon Jongen are the most important adherents of this school. Scarcely known outside Belgium are such composers as Armand Marsick, Jean Rogister and Albert Dupuis.

Liège School

Films

René Bernier

A composer who does not fit into any particular category is René Bernier (b. 1905) whose music displays Mediterranean spirit, elegance and clarity.

The music scene today

Belgium has produced a number of fine interpreters of classical music, one of the best-known being the violinist Arthur Grumiaux (1921–86). The Théâtre Royal de la Monnaie opera house in Brussels has an international reputation and is particulary famous for its "Ballet of the 20th Century" founded by Maurice Béjart.

The Flanders Festival, which is held mainly in Ghent and Bruges, is one of the major European music festivals. One of the most demanding competitions held anywhere in Europe is the "Concours Reine Elisabeth", which takes place every two years and alternates between violin and piano. Previous prizewinners include David Oistrach, Malcolm Frager, Vladimir Ashkenazy and Gidon Kremer.

Popular music Jacques Brel

Belgium has not had much to offer in the field of popular music. However, the singer of satirical songs Jacques Brel (1928–78; see Famous People) did make a considerable contribution. The Belgian Salvatore Adamo, who was born in Italy, and the female singer Tonia are also quite well-known abroad as pop-singers. In the world of jazz the guitarist and harmonica virtuoso Jean "Toots" Thielemans (b. 1928) has made a name for himself as an interpreter of swing, a composer and arranger.

Folk music

Belgian folk music has no particularly distinctive style. In addition to the folk songs, most of which Belgium shares with France and the Netherlands, Wallonia especially has a number of dances which show a strong French influence both in their movements and in the music which accompanies them. The latter is usually characterised by drums and pipes as well as brass bands which play music that is somewhat shrill, loud and high-pitched. In Flanders folk-dancing is often accompanied by the Flemish spinet, fiddle, flute and accordion.

Films

"There is Belgian painting and Belgian literature which stays Belgian even though written in the French language. There are the varied forms of Belgian life embracing Antwerp as well as Charleroi, the fishermen of Ostend as well as the forests of the Ardennes; the country has its unique landscape and its own customs ... Surely there is enough there to form the basis of a good film?" complained Georges Simenon in 1940. In fact little has changed since then, and Belgium is still the poor man of Europe as far as films are concerned.

At best the pre-war Belgian film industry could boast a few notable documentaries produced by such directors as Henri Storck and Charles Dekeukerleire and which dealt mainly with historical and cultural subjects. The best-known film from that era was made by a Dutchman, Joris Ivens, in co-operation with Storck; it was "Misère au Borinage" (1934), which took as its theme the strikes and living conditions then prevailing in the coal-mining region of southern Belgium and was the prototype of the contentious documentary we know today. During the German occupation in the Second World War Storck again emerged as writer, director and cameraman in the film "Symphonie Paysanne", a study of peasant life over the years. The feature films of this period, mainly in Flemish, were undistinguished.

Little has emerged in the post-war years either. Worthy of mention are the directors André Delvaux, the only one to encourage Marguerite Yourcenar to make one of her works, "L'Œuvre au Noir", into a film, and also the younger Chantal Akerman and Marion Hänsel.

While the Belgian film industry has developed very modestly indeed many native Belgian film-makers have tried their luck in France. Outstanding among these was Jacques Feyder, who before his death in 1948 made numerous films and had considerable success with "La Kermesse Héroïque" (1935). This film, for which the Belgian Charles Spaak wrote the script, is set in Flanders at the time of the War of Liberation against the Spaniards and in a congenial way transposes the metaphorical language of Flemish masters into the form of a film.

Jacques Feyder

Comics

In no other European country – with the possible exception of France – are comics (bandes dessinées in French) so popular nor is there such a variety of strip cartoons as in Belgium.

Belgium the Land of Comics

The reasons for this are many. For one thing, Belgium can look back on a long tradition of comic strips which are quite independent of those produced in the "classical" land of comics, the USA. In 1929 appeared the first "Adventures of Tin Tin", undoubtedly the most famous comic figure to come out of Belgium, which soon enjoyed great success and was able to pick up the threads after the war without any trouble. Back in 1946 Raymond Leblanc produced "Tin Tin", a magazine for young people which, under its revised title of "Hello B. D." has remained to this day Belgium's most successful comic publication. Not only does it include comic strips and serials but it also has an excellent editorial section and gives many young artists their first chance of getting something published. Another important factor is the close co-operation which has already developed between publishers of comics and the other media. As well as appearing in newspapers and cheap paperbacks comic strips have been published as "real" books in album form. Many of the adventures of Tin Tin have been produced as animated cartoons or feature films, and the stories centred around the "Schtroumpfs" (The Smurfs), "Lucky Luke" or "Spirou" have been seen in cinemas and on television. Comics have become an accepted feature of Belgian life.

Belgium's chief publishers of comics today are Casterman in Tournai ("Tin Tin"), Dupuis in Charleroi ("Les Schtroumpfs", "Spirou and Fantasio") and Lombard in Brussels ("Cubitus", "Ric Hochet").

Publishers

"Tin Tin" is arguably the most successful of all European comic series. Its creator was Georges Remi, born in Brussels in 1907, who inverted his initials and used them phonetically to form his pseudonym "Hergé". The first Tin Tin story, "Tin Tin in the Land of the Soviets", appeared as a serial in 1929 in the children's supplement "Petit XXième" to the daily newspaper "Le Vingtième Siècle". The hero of the stories is the young and cool-thinking reporter Tin Tin with the unusual blond hair-style who, accompanied by his fox-terrier Milou and assisted by the grumpy Captain Haddock, has adventures all over the world and even on the moon. Apart from the tension and excitement the charm of the stories lies in the simple caricaturised portrayal of the main characters and the detailed background and surroundings, especially the technical equipment, vehicles and buildings. Tin Tin is incredibly popular; there are Tin Tin figures, records, T-shirts, two theatrical plays, feature films and animated cartoons. In 1985 the Belgian astronaut Patrick Boudry even took a replica of his hero with him into space on board an American spacecraft and held it up in front of the camera. In addition to "Tin Tin" Hergé also drew the "Jo et Zette" and "Quick et Fluppke" comic strips.

"Tin Tin"

"Spirou" is the name of a hotel page boy or bellhop and was invented by "Bob Vel" (Robert Velter), although he has been drawn by André Franquin since 1946. Together with his friends, the reporter Fantasio and

"Spirou and Fantasio"

the scientist Comte de Champignac, Spirou enjoys numerous adventures with a humorous side to them. Our heroes are actively supported by Kokomiko, the legendary marsupial from the jungles of South America, an ape-like creature with the skin of a leopard and an incredibly long tail who possesses unbounded strength. As in the case of Tin Tin, Spirou has been the subject of a comic paper of the same name which is still published. In the series the figure of Gaston Lagaffe also comes to life after starting out as a doodle drawn by Franquin, the office junior in the newspaper office where Fantasio works. Gaston thinks of everything except work and causes havoc especially when Monsieur de Mesmaeker is trying to complete important business deals which Gaston inevitably, if unintentionally, sabotages.

"Les Schtroumpfs" (The Smurfs)

Since 1952 Pierre Culliford has been drawing for the "Spirou" magazine the adventures of the knight "Johan" and his squire "Pirlouit". In 1958 small blue dwarfs with bulbous noses, white tights and white pointed caps were also introduced; they lived in toadstool houses and spoke "Smurfish" – in the anglicised version the series was known as "The Smurfs". They soon became more popular than the knight and plastic replicas sold like hot cakes and held pride of place in most children's bedrooms.

"Lucky Luke"

The Wild West comic strip about the cool cowboy "Lucky Luke", who was faster on the draw than his own shadow, also originated in Belgium. He was "born" in 1947, the brainchild of Maurice de Bevere ("Morris"). After 1959 René Goscinny (also the writer of "Asterix"), who died in 1977, wrote the stories about the cowboy who, accompanied by his faithful horse Jolly Jumper, tangled with such people as the Dalton Brothers and Calamity Jane, and even rode for the Belgian mail service.

Adventure comics

As well as the more or less funny comic strips there are a large number of adventure series of various kinds, all drawn in a most realistic way. Most were conceived in the 1950s and 1960s and have remained successful ever since. These "classics" include stories about such figures as the reporter and detective "Ric Hochet" by Gilbert Gascard, the racing-cyclist "Michel Vaillant" (Mike Valiant) by Jean Graton and the agent "Bruno Brazil" by "William Vance" (William van Cutsem), as well as the science fiction series "Luc Orient" by Eddy Paape. One of the best artists in this field is "Hermann" (Hermann Huppen) with the series "Bernard Prince", "Jugurtha" and "Comanche". Edgar P. Jacobs ("Blake and Mortimer"), Jacques Martin ("L. Frank") and Bob de Moor ("Barelli"), together with Hergé, can be considered to be the founders of the Brussels comic tradition.

Younger artists

A new star in the Belgian comic firmament is François Walthéry with a series about a little boy called "Nickel" and his humorous adventure-strip about the stewardess "Natasha". Benoît Sokal ("Canardo"), Eric Warnauts and Guy Raives ("Lou Cale", "Congo 40") are also making a name for themselves.

Brussels Comic Museum

As comics are so many and so popular it will come as no surprise to learn that Brussels has the largest Comic Museum in the world. It is housed in a former department store designed by Victor Horta and owns 25,000 comics and numerous original printing plates of 650 Belgian artists (see Practical Information, Museums).

To celebrate the 100th anniversary of the comic strip – it is said to date back to the strip "The Yellow Kid" which appeared in the "New York Journal" in 1896 – some house façades in Brussels were painted with scenes from Belgian comics in 1996. Thus you can meet Lucky Luke and the four Daltons in the Rue de la Buanderie, Boule takes his dog for a walk in the Rue du Chevreuil, and detective Ric Hochet moves hand over hand along the guttering of a house in the Rue du Bon Secours. The Brussels tourist office (see Practical Information, Information) has a brochure listing the other façades adorned with comics. Further houses are supposed to be painted in the future.

Parcours Bande Dessinée in Brussels

Some sculptures of famous comics heroes can also be found in the streets of Charleroi, for example the much-loved Marsupilami "Kokomiko", faithful companion to Spirou and Fantasio.

Comic Sculptures in Charleroi

Carillon

Everywhere in Belgium can be heard the sound of the carillon, often ringing out across the market-square every quarter of an hour. This custom originated from the clocks which sounded the hour from church towers or belfries and which first appeared in Belgium in 1370. At first it was just a simple bell rung by hand, but as time went by the number of bells was increased so that melodies could be played; with the introduction of the keyboard and pedals in the 16th c. these became more and more complicated and ended in the chimes of the bells being controlled by clockwork. The chimes (Flemish beiaard, French carillon) rung in Belgian towns usually have between 45 and 50 bells and can also be played by hand. Some beautiful chimes can be heard in Antwerp, Bruges, Mechelen, Brussels, Ghent, Hasselt, Hoogstraten, Leuven, Kortrijk (Courtrai), Oudenaarde, Ostend and Tournai.

Bell-ringers learn their art in Mechelen in the province of Antwerp. There can be found the only "carillon school" in the world, founded in 1922 and named after the master bell-ringer from Mechelen, Jef Denyn. The school also has a museum.

Mechelen Carillon school

Folklore

Belgium is steeped in living folklore which finds expression through an almost incredible list of public festivals, processions and fairs, some of them on a very large scale and nearly always boisterous and full of festive spirit. Giants are an important part of many processions and parades. These grand events, organised by various companies or clubs, are held mostly on religious feast-days or historical anniversaries spread throughout the year. In between these many towns hold smaller celebrations at, for instance, race-tracks or when the maypole is erected. Very popular indeed are the "Kermesses aux Boudins", at which many publicans invite their regulars to a huge meal of sausages with plenty of free beer.

The **dates** of the most important festivals will be found under "Events" in the Practical Information section of this book.

The first big festival of the year is the Carnival (Carnaval), which is celebrated in the Walloon region in particular in a most original fashion. The earliest procession is held in January in Ronse south of Oudenaarde, when thousands of folk dressed in costume celebrate "Fools' Monday" on the first Monday after Epiphany.

Carnival

Pious Women

In some of the Flemish towns, you can still find béguinages (Flemish begijn-hof, French béguinage). These enclosed convent-like groups of houses, a town within a town, date back to the Middle Ages and have beguines living in groups in the larger houses or by themselves in the smaller houses.

The system of béguinages originated in the late 12th century. It flourished during the 13th and 14th centuries, particularly in the Netherlands, France and Germany. Arising from the Catholic lay movement, these were initially free communities of working women who joined for economic, but also for religious reasons. They found their purpose in the care of the poor, sick and elderly. The church bestowed order on the communities, and each one was housed in a closed court with a chapel or church. Later they were made into parishes and finally into béguinages. Their vows of obedience to the Church allowed them to escape condemnation by Pope Clemens V in the Netherlands in 1311, while similar communities in Germany were affected.

In Dendermonde Béguinage

Very few béguines are still operating in Belgium today, and only the béguinage of St–Amandsberg near Ghent is of some importance. The modest and isolated life led by béguines is no longer attractive to young women today. Although béguines do not make a vow of chastity for life, they do have to obey their superiors in the community. Only few women leave the communities. Initially, the sisters live and work together in convents (lace-making, sewing of clothes etc.). After six years they are allowed to move into small individual dwellings, each holding between two and four apartments. Two to three times a day they hold a mass together. During the day, béguines are allowed to venture out by themselves, but they have to be back in the béguinage in the evening. When working they wear the traditional grey-brown uniform, with a black Flemish head-dress (Flemish Falie; French faille) on top.

The bishop appoints the leader of the béguinage, a Mother Superior who is addressed as 'Grootjuffrouw' or 'Grande Dame' respectively.

Today the béguinages are mainly let to elderly people or, as in Leuven, to students. They have become popular tourist sights, and some, such as the one in Kortrijk, have set up some of the houses as museums to portray the life and work of the béguines that used to live there. The most beautiful béguinages are at Kortrijk, Bruges, Ghent, Diest, Oudenaarde, Leuven, Lier and Dendermonde.

The traditional home of carnival is **Binche**, between Charleroi and Mons, with its characteristic "gilles". This tradition, going back to the 14th c., literally takes over the town for four whole days and reaches its peak on "Mardi Gras" (Shrove Tuesday), when the "Gilles" make an appearance dressed in their gloriously colourful costumes decorated with twelve heraldic lions, bright ribbons, pointed toes and bells hanging from their belts. To the rhythm of drums and brass bands they dance all day and night, swing bundles of birch-twigs to frighten away evil spirits and throw oranges to (or at!) the onlookers. On their heads they wear eight giant white ostrich-plumes to the final dance held in the market-place. At the end of this dance, in which everybody joins, a huge fire is lit and the "Gilles" dance through the streets, where they are only allowed to drink champagne. As long as four weeks before the carnival processions and dancers can be seen practising for the big day, these rehearsals being known as the "répétitions de batteries".

The **Malmédy** Festival, known as "Cwarmê", is equally famous. On the Saturday the "Trouv'Lê" (ladle or scoop) takes over the town. On the Sunday the "bânes corantes" (roving bands) roam the streets and frolic with passers-by, on the Monday plays are performed based on events which occurred locally during the past year, and finally on the Tuesday the "haguètes", the symbolic carnival figures, are burned. The "haguètes" are the much-feared masks worn by the "bânes corantes", together with ostrich-plumes, horns on their heads, a cowl and the Austrian double eagle on their backs. They perform a huge "conga" through the streets and pull unwilling onlookers into the line with them. Other masks are the "sotê", a goblin with a big top-hat reaching down to the shoulders, the "vèheû" (skunk), which hits people on the head with an inflated pig's bladder, as well as the "sâvadje" (savage).

The "Gilles" are abroad ...   *... in Binche*

Eupen is also renowned for its carnival, with a Carnival Prince and a Council of Eleven.

In the Flemish region of the country the **Aalst** Carnival attracts thousands of spectators every year. Carnival Sunday is the day of the Giants, the Monday sees the Throwing of the Onions, and on the Tuesday the "Vuil Jeannetten" ("dirty aunts") parade through the streets in their curious old costumes.

Spectacular
festivals

In Belgium Ash Wednesday is not the end of things by any means. **During Lent** a number of carnivals and events are held. For example, on the Saturday following Shrove Tuesday (Mardi Gras) the masked ball of the "Rat Mort" (dead rat) is held in Ostend. Mid-Lent processions take place in Hasselt, Tilff, Stavelot and Fosses.

The traditional figure seen in **Stavelot** is the "Blanc Moussis", wearing a long-nosed mask and a white habit who gets up to all sorts of pranks.

In **Fosses** can be seen the "Chinels" (an abbreviation of Polichinelle or Pulcinella), who dance like living dolls.

At the end of February **Geraardsbergen** holds its curious "Cracknel Festival" (Krakelingenworp). A procession of several hundred people climbs the Oudenberg and then throws down to the spectators some 8000 "cracknels" or rusks. Finally the town dignitaries have to drink down small live fish from a silver beaker. In the evening the "Tonnekenbrand" is lit in a barrel.

Processions

Belgium being almost totally Roman Catholic, processions play an important role, especially in **Holy Week**, although not all of them need be taken too seriously. The best-known of the Easter processions take place in Rupelmonde near Antwerp on Maundy Thursday, in Hakendover on Easter Monday and in Veurne during the night of Maundy Thursday to Good Friday.

Veurne offers two impressive processions – one on the Sunday preceding May 3rd, and the famous Procession of the Penitents on the last Sunday in July. Praying and hidden under dark hoods, the penitents walk carrying a Cross weighing 40 kg (70 lb). Reminiscent of Spain, this procession does in fact date from the time when Spain ruled the Netherlands.

Also worth seeing is the Procession of the Penitents in **Lessines** on Good Friday. The disguised and cloaked figures carry torches in their hands, thus giving the whole a ghostly atmosphere.

The Ascension Day Procession of the Holy Blood at **Bruges** is world-famous. Numerous pedestrians and cars pass through the festively decorated town, depicting the Biblical story from the Fall of Man to the Redemption. Members of the clergy bear a reliquary said to contain drops of the Blood of Christ thought to have been given to Theodoric of Alsace, Count of Flanders, by the patriarchy of Jerusalem in 1150.

On Trinity Sunday in **Mons** the reliquary of St Waltraud is carried through the streets in the "Procession of the Golden Carriage". It ends with St George killing the green dragon – a symbol of the victory of Good over Evil.

Typical of the region between Sambre and Meuse are the **Military Processions**, a tradition dating back to the time when the valuable holy relics had to be defended against robbers. The marchers dress in uniform, some dating from the time of Napoleon, and parade through the town in strict order, firing their arms. Among the better-known military processions are those held in Gerpinnes near Charleroi on Whit Monday and in Jumet around July 20th.

Well-known places of pilgrimage include Halle, Hakendover, Scherpenheuvel, St-Hubert and Nivelles.

Children in particular enjoy celebrating the Feast of St Martin in November, when they receive gifts. This tradition lives on in a number of places, including Eupen, Genk, Retie and Visé.

Brussels The most famous non-religious celebration is undoubtedly the "Ommegang", the origin of which dates back to processions held in the Middle Ages seeking protection against plagues of all kinds. The present "Ommegang" copies that held on July 2nd 1549 in the presence of Charles V. On the first Thursday in July over 2000 people wearing costume and carrying some 300 flags, representatives of ancient trade guilds, drummers and numerous vehicles file past characters representing the imperial family on the Grand'Place.

Every year, on its anniversary, the Battle of **Waterloo** is re-enacted in historical costume on the actual battlefield. The "armies" are made up of groups from various countries.

At the end of August the "Kermis of the Giants" ("ducasse") is held in **Ath**. Figures up to 4 m (13 ft) tall parade through the town; they represent Goliath, the four children of Haimon with the horse Bayard, Samson, Ambiorix and "Mam'selle Victoire", who personifies the town. The highlight is the fight between David and Goliath. The festival ends with the wedding of Goliath ("Monsieur et Madame Gouyasse").

Cat festival in Ypres

The **Bruges** "Procession of the Golden Tree" is held only every five years; the next time will be in 2000. It commemorates the glittering times of Burgundian rule.

The Festival of the Cats in **Ypres** (Ieper) is unique. In the Middle Ages cats were often considered to be the Devil incarnate. Count Baudouin III decided to put a stop to this superstition and ordered that all existing cats were to be thrown down from the tower of the town hall in order to prove that they were merely mortal animals. This cruel game was still played right up to the early 19th c. Today only soft toys are thrown down. There is also a large procession portraying the role played by the cat in culture and folklore.

The Flemings remember their famous predecessors in many ways. As an example, the Beer Festival held in **Oudenaarde** in June is in memory of the painter Adriaan Brouwer (1605–38).

Every two years in **Wingene** the good people of the town remember the artist Pieter Breugel the Elder by acting out some of his paintings.

Autumn in Belgium is the time of thanksgiving for beer, hops and harvests. In the little town of **Wieze** near Aalst the "Wieze Oktoberfeesten" have become famous. In a giant marquee holding up to 10,000 people beer from the Wieze brewery flows like water. Entertainment is provided by three bands, usually Bavarian, with a Flemish compère.

Belgium in Quotations

A country belonging to our Allies, and indeed a great deal more, which they who can speak no language but the new French, choose to call Belgium, but which neither by that name, nor with any certain bounds or limits is to be found in any Map ... These new Appelations have been adopted in order to support the new System of giving to modern France the limits of ancient Gaul.

Edmund Burke (1729–97)

"Letter to French Laurence", March 1st 1797

Imagine to yourself a succession of avenues with a Dutch spire at the end of each – and you see the road; – an accompaniment of highly cultivated farms on each side intersected with small canals or ditches – and sprinkled with very neat and clean cottages – a village every two miles – and you see the country – not a rise from Ostend to Antwerp – a molehill would make the inhabitants think that the Alps had come here on a visit – it is a perpetuity of plain & an eternity of pavement (on the road) but it is a country of great apparent comfort – and a singular though tame beauty.

Lord Byron (1788–1824)

"Letter to Augusta Leigh", May 1st 1816

Fine cities – admirable architects, far exceeding ours, both in their old and new buildings – good bakers – very ugly – stink of tobacco – horses all fat – soldiers little – inns dirty and very expensive; – better modern painters than we are ...

I went to the Belgic Parliament. There was a pound short in the public accounts, and they were speaking about it ...

All the great cities of Flanders are underpeopled.

Sydney Smith (1771–1845)

"Letter to Sir George Philips", May 20th 1837

Antwerp

This goodly ancient City methinks looks like a disconsolate Widow, or rather some super-annuated Virgin, that hath lost her Lover, being almost quite bereft of that flourishing Commerce wherewith before the falling off the rest of the Provinces from Spain she abounded to the envy of all other Cities and Marts of Europe. There are few Places this side the Alps better built and so well streeted as this; and none at all so well girt with Bastions and Ramparts, which in some place are so spacious that they usually take the Air in Coaches upon the very Walls, which are beautified with divers rows of Trees and pleasant Walks. The Citadel here, tho' it be an addition to the stateliness and strength of the Town, yet it serves as a shrewd Curb unto her; which makes her chomp upon the Bit, and foam sometimes with anger, but she cannot help it.

James Howell (1593–1666)

"Letter to Sir James Crofts", July 5th 1645

View from the spire of the Vrou-Kirke
It is a very venerable fabrique, built after the Gotik manner, and especially the Tower, which is in truth of an excessive height: This I ascended, that I might the better take a view of the Country about it,

John Evelyn (1620–1706)

which happning on a day when the sunn shone exceedingly hot, and darted the rayes without any interruption, afforded so bright a reflection to us who were above, and had a full prospect of both the Land and Water about it, that I was much confirm'd in my opinion of the Moones being of some such substance as this earthly Globe consists of; perceiving all the subjacent Country (at so smale an horizontal distance) to repercusse such a light as I could hardly looke against; save where the River and other large water within our View appeared of a more darke & uniforme Colour, resembling those spotts in the Moone, attributed to the seas there &c according to our new Philosophy & the Phaenomenas by optical Glasses.

"Diary", October 4th 1641

William Beckford
(1760–1844)

Were any man to ask my advice upon the subject of retirement, I should tell him: By all means repair to Antwerp. No village amongst the Alps, or hermitage upon Mount Lebanon is less disturbed: you may pass your days in this great city without being the least conscious of its sixty thousand inhabitants, unless you visit the churches.

"Dreams, Waking Thoughts and Incidents", 1783

Bruges (Brugge)

Philip Thicknesse
(1720–92)

When you have seen what this town offers to the notice of a stranger, you will be, as I was, glad to quit it, for the inhabitants (quite the reverse of their neighbours the French) are all shut up within their houses, and a stranger is apt at Bruges, to think himself in a city just depopulated by the plague.

"A Journey through the Austrian Netherlands", 1786

Dorothy
Wordsworth
(1771–1855)

One might fancy that as the city had been built so it had remained. ... The general effect upon the mind can never be forgotten. The race of the Great and Powerful by whom the noble public edifices were raised has passed away, yet the attire, the staid motions and demeanour of the present inhabitants are accordant with the stateliness of former ages; and the City remains as if self-sustained – no new houses to be seen, no repairs going on! you might fancy that the sound of the Builder's hammer was never heard in these days!

"Journal", July 14th 1820

William
Wordsworth
(1770–1850)

In Brugès town is many a street
Whence busy life hath fled;
Where, without hurry, noiseless feet
The grass-grown pavement tread
There heard we, halting in the shade
Flung from a Convent-tower,
A harp that tuneful prelude made
To a voice of thrilling power

"Incident at Bruges", 1828

Henry Wadsworth
Longfellow
(1807–82)

In the market-place of Bruges stands the Belfry old and brown;
Thrice consumed and thrive rebuilt, still it watches o'er the town.

As the summer morn was breaking, on that lofty tower I stood,
And the world threw off the darkness, like the weeds of widowhood.

Thick with towns and hamlets studded, and with streams and vapors gray

Like a shield embossed with silver, round and vast the landscape lay.

At my feet the city slumbered. From its chimneys, here and there,
Wreaths of snow-white smoke ascending, vanished ghost-like into air.

Not a sound rose from the city at that early morning hour,
But I heard a heart of iron beating in that ancient tower. ...

Visions of the day departed, snowy phantoms filled my brain;
They who live in history only seemed to walk the earth again.

William
Makepeace
Thackeray
(1811–63)

"The Belfry of Bruges", 1845

Brussels

My impressions of this city are certainly anything but respectful. It
has an absurd kind of Lilliput look with it. There are soldiers, just as
in Paris, better dressed, and doing a vast deal of drumming and
bustle; and yet, somehow, far from being frightened at them, I feel
inclined to laugh in their faces. There are little Ministers, who work
at their little bureaux; and to read the journals, how fierce they are!
A great thundering Times could hardly talk more big ... Think what
a comfort it would be to belong to a little state like this; not to abuse
their privilege, but philosophicaly to use it. If I were a Belgian I
would not care one single fig about politics. I would not read thundering leading articles. I would not have an opinion. What is the use
of an opinion here? Happy fellows! do not the French, the English
and the Prussians spare them the trouble of thinking, and make all
their opinions for them. Think of living in a country, free, easy,
respectable, wealthy, and with the nuisance of talking politics
removed from out of it. All this might the Belgians have, and a part
do they enjoy, but not the best part: no, these people will be brawl-
ing and by the ears, and parties run as high here as at Stoke Pogis
or Little Pedlington.

The Parc
Numbers of statues decorate the place, the very worst I ever saw. These
Cupids must have been erected in the time of the Dutch dynasty, as I
judge from the immense posterior developments.

"From Richmond to Brussels", May 1844

If any person wants to be happy I should advise the Parc. You sit drink-
ing iced drinks and smoking penny cigars under great old trees. The
band place, covered walks, etc. are all lit up. And you can't fancy how
beautiful was the contrast of the great masses of lamplit foliage and the
dark sapphire night sky, with just one blue star set overhead in the
middle of the largest patch. In the dark walks, too, there are crowds of
people whose faces you cannot see, and here and there a colossal white
statue at the corner of an alley that gives the place a nice artificial, eigh-
teenth century sentiment. There was a good deal of summer lightning
blinking overhead, and the black avenues and white statues lean out
every minute into short-lived distinctness.

Robert Louis
Stevenson
(1850–94)

"Letter to his Mother", July 25th 1872

Ghent

Ghendt is an extravagant Citty of so vast a Circumference, that it is
reported to be no lesse than 7 leagues in compasse; but there is not an
halfe part of it now built; much of it remaining in the feilds and desolate
pastures, even within the Wales, which had marvailous strong Gates

John Evelyn

towards the West, and two faire Churches in one of which I heard a Sermon ... The Ley and Scheld, meeting in this vast Citty divide it into 26 Hands which are united togethere by many bridges somewhat resembling Venice.

William Beckford

To one so far gone in the poetic antiquity, Ghent is not the most likely place to recall his attention; and I know nothing more about it, than that it is a large, ill-paved dismal-looking city, with a decent proportion of convents and chapels stuffed with monuments, brazen gates, and glittering marbles.

"Dreams, Waking Thoughts and Incidents", 1783

Dorothy Wordsworth

The buildings, streets and squares, all are picturesque; the houses green, blue, pink, yellow, with richest ornaments still varying. Strange it is that so many and such strongly contrasted colours should compose an undiscordant whole.

"Journal", July 14th 1820

William Makepeace Thackeray

Ghent has, I believe, been called a vulgar Venice. It contains dirty canals and old houses that must satisfy the most eager antiquary, though the buildings are not in quite so good preservation as others that may be seen in the Netherlands. The commercial bustle of the place seems considerable, and it contains more beershops than any city I every saw.

"Little Travels and Roadside Sketches", October 1844

Liège

Martin Farquhar Tupper (1810–89)

Near Liège, the gradient being steep, we are pulled up to Hautpré by a rope; and soon coming to the top, have a grand view of the Belgian Birmingham, nearly as well supplied with tall chimnies, but more countryfied and much prettier. Liège is quite an urbs in rure, – houses and manaufactories dotted about among trees and hills, and winding streams, with turreted and spired and cupola'd churches here and there, picturesque enough. Within, however, most of the streets are narrow wind-about and roughly trottoired – dirty withal and smelly; and the rapid Meuse, from thunder-showers I suppose, a river of mud.

"Diary of Everybody's Tour", 1856

Spa

Philip Thickness

The town of Spa is situated in a stoney, mountainous country, on the banks of what in Summer is a murmuring stream, but in Winter is sometimes a rapid river. The air is good, and the environs, in general are pleasant, though rude, and uncultivated, having much the appearance of a part of the globe which has been broken up by earthquakes, or some violent convulsions of Nature. ...

Having mentioned that the Pohoun is the spring from which the bottled Spa-water is taken, it may be necessary to inform you that there are near Spa, several other mineral springs, viz. the Geronstere, and about two mi. from Spa, the Sauveniere and the Tonnelet, somewhat nearer; and all these waters are used by those who are within the reach of them. I cannot pretend to tell you what the healing powers of the last mentioned springs are; but I suppose there must be some extraordinary virture in the Geronstere water, as it is exceedingly nauseous, and tastes and smells like rotten eggs, but it is perfectly clear.

"A Journey through the Austrian Netherlands", 1786

Waterloo

The Plain at Waterloo is a fine one, but not much after Marathon & Troy – Cheronea – & Platea. Perhaps there is something of prejudice in this, but I detest the cause & the victors – & the victory including Blucher and the Bourbons.

Lord Byron
(1788–1824)

"Letter to John Cam Hobhouse", May 16th 1816

We stood upon grass and cornfields where heaps of our countrymen lay buried beneath our feet. There was little to be seen; but much to be felt; sorrow and sadness, and even something like horror breathed out of the ground as we stood upon it! … The ruins of the severely contested château of Hougamont had been ridded away since the battle, and the injuries done to the farm-house repaired. Even these circumstances, natural and trivial as they were, suggested melancholy thoughts, by furnishing grounds for a charge of ingratitude against the course of things, that was thus hastily removing from the spot all vestiges of so momentous an event.

Dorothy
Wordsworth

"Journal", July 17th 1820

I have seldom been more interested. One has read the account of the battle so often, the area is so limited, and the main points of the battle so simple, that one understands it the moment one sees the place with one's eyes.

Matthew Arnold
(1822–88)

"Letter to Miss Arnold", October 9th 1860

Sights
from A to Z

Suggested Routes

The following two suggested routes through the eastern and western parts of Belgium should give those touring by car some ideas without depriving them of the freedom to make their own plans. In addition, the routes can be combined to form a "Grand Tour" of the whole of Belgium.

The roads to take have been chosen so as to pass close to all the main places of interest to visitors. Nevertheless, not all the places described elsewhere in this guide can be reached without making some detours; details can be found in the suggestions and recommendations for detours, excursions and surrounding places of interest which are given under the individual entries in the main A to Z section and which complement these main routes.

The routes can be followed on the map accompanying this book, thereby facilitating more detailed planning.

Places and regions listed in the A to Z section under a main heading are printed in **bold** type; where there is a French or Flemish alternative name this is added in brackets.

The places of interest, towns, regions, rivers and archaeological sites mentioned are to be found in the index at the end of this guide.

The distances in brackets following the titles of the routes are approximate and refer to direct routes. Distances for the longer recommended diversions or detours are also given.

Tourist Routes

Many of the places mentioned in the following routes are on or form the setting-out point for "Tourist Routes". Most of the latter are along minor roads off the major link-roads, are marked by a distinctive sign and thread through the Belgian countryside for between 50 and 150 km (30 and 90 mi.).

These Tourist Routes, of which there are 63 in all in Belgium, are marked with a hexagonal, bright yellow sign with a blue inscription. Informative leaflets can be obtained from local tourist information offices (see Practical Information, Information).

Cycling
tours

The Tourist Routes are particularly well-suited to **cycling tours** lasting one or several days.

First Circular Tour through Eastern Belgium
(about 330 km/205 mi.)

The setting-out point of this journey, most of which passes through Wallonia, the French-speaking region of Belgium, is **Liège** (Luik). Liège, the capital of Wallonia, is predominantly a heavy-industrial town, but offers the visitor some excellent museums which house treasures from the time when it was an independent principality. The N2 leaves Liège and proceeds west along the right bank of the Meuse. The first stop is **Huy** (Hoei), whose collegiate church is the most important High Gothic church in Belgium. The N2 continues along the river to **Namur** (Namen), which stands at the confluence of the Mass and Sambre and is dominated by its massive citadel. From here take the N92 south and enjoy the picturesque and rocky Meuse Valley (**Vallée de la Meuse**) until you reach **Dinant**. This town too is dominated by a fortress high up on a rock, in the shadow of which stands the Collegiate Church.

Detour from
Dinant

From Dinant it is worth making a detour into the lovely Fagne countryside, with French territory on three sides of it. Take the N96 along the

Meuse and, after passing through Herr-Agimont, continue via Doische and Viroinval through some lovely countryside to Couvin, a little to the north of which lie the caves known as the Grottes de Neptune. From Couvin the N99 leads to **Chimay**, seat of a Trappist monastery, and thence via Rance to Rance with its Marble Museum to **Beaumont**. Here turn east again along the N40, past the holiday region of the Barrages de l'Eau d'Heure near **Walcourt** and then finally, after passing through the fortified town of Philippeville, return to Dinant along the N97 (about 155 km) (97 mi.))

The original main route through eastern Belgium now continues southward on the N95 via Beauring and through forests and fields to **Bouillon**, the massive castle of which towers over the charming Semois Valley (**Vallée de la Semois**). Bouillon is a good starting point for some beautiful walks in the surrounding forests or for an excursion to the very interesting Trappist monastery of **Orval** 45 km (28 mi.) to the south-east. From Bouillon continue north – first on the N89, then on the N899 – deeper and deeper into the Ardennes, making the next stop in **Rochefort** near the Lesse et Lomme Nature Park. A little way from Rochefort lie the caves of **Han-sur-Lesse**, the largest accessible dripstone caves in Europe; a visit is followed by a drive through the forests with their abundance of game and wild-life to **Saint-Hubert**, the home of St Hubert. From this little town the N89 leads to La-Roche-en-Ardenne, the central point of the Ourthe Valley (**Vallée de l'Ourthe**). Continuing now north-east from La-Roche, on the N89 via Vielsam and then on the N68 via **Stavelot** to **Malmédy**, the traveller will finally reach the Upper Ardennes and the Hohe Venn (Hautes Fagnes); the best way to get to know this region is by walking through the **Belgian-German Nature Park**. Finally spend a time in the famous health resort of **Spa** before returning to Liège by way of **Verviers**.

North of Liège lies the Province of Limburg, with a number of towns which are worth a visit. First take the N20 to **Tongeren** (Tongres), the town built by Ambiorix, the father of all Belgium's resistance movements and which claims to be the oldest town in the country. Continue westward via **Sint-Truiden** (Saint-Trond) to **Zoutleeuw** (Léau), where the church is a little gem; it is the only church in Belgium to have withstood the iconoclasm of the 16th c. completely unharmed. From Sint-Truiden the N80 continues to **Hasselt**, where the Bokrik open-air museum a little way to the north is worth a visit. From there return finally to Liège by way of Tongeren (about 100 km/62 mi.).

Detour from Liège

Second Circular Tour through Western Belgium (about 470 km/292 mi.)

This tour takes in the major and most beautiful towns in Flanders and Brabant. It begins in **Brussels**, whose magnificent buildings such as the City Hall on the Grand'Place or the Atomium, together with its world-famous museums make it worth staying there for several days if possible. The tour starts with a visit to the battlefield at **Waterloo**, scene of Napoleon's final defeat. In **Nivelles** (Nijvel) south of Waterloo the Collégiale Sainte-Gertrude is one of the most important Romanesque churches in Belgium. From Nivelles take the N27 south to **Binche**, the true home of Belgian carnival, as will be proved by a visit to the Carnival and Mask Museum (Musée International du Carnaval et du Masque). The technically-minded will benefit from a visit to the nearby old La Louvière shipyards and the new Strépy-Thieu ones. Proceed by way of **Mons** (Bergen) to the west of Binche and thence close to the French border on the N50 to **Tournai** (Doornik), where the cathedral is a masterpiece of Romanesque church architecture in the Scheldt region; even some Romanesque middle-class houses have been preserved. **Kortrijk**

Béguinage cottages in Kortrijk

(Courtrai), the sister town of Tournai to the north, possesses one of the country's most romantic "béguinages" (see entry) and is also a good starting point for an excursion to **Oudenaarde** (Audenarde) with its magnificent town hall (30 km/19 mi. to the east).

In Kortrijk the visitor will find himself in Flanders, in the Middle Ages one of the richest strips of land in Europe with numerous proud towns which had the cloth industry to thank for their prosperity. One of these towns is **Ypres** (Ieper), on the N8. Ypres lies in the centre of the First World War battlefields, by the end of which it had been completely destroyed. The large Cloth Hall and the Town Hall, which can be admired today, were built later. From Ypres the tour continues gradually to the Belgian North Sea coast. Passing through the polder countryside the N8 leads to **Veurne** (Furnes), where the traveller can rest in a café on the picturesque old market place before continuing to **De Panne** (La Panne), the first of the well-known seaside resorts. Then follow one upon the other along the coast road – with many a view of dreary hotel blocks – **Koksijde** (Coxyde), **Nieuwpoort** and then Belgium's best-known resort, **Ostend**, which is more or less exactly in the middle of the Belgian coastal strip, the total length of which is 67 km (42 mi.). Our route continues via **Blankenberge** and the important port of **Zeebrugge** to **Knokke-Heist**, the last of the seaside resorts, known for its casino. From here return inland, turn south near Westkapelle towards Bruges, and then – after crossing the Schipdonk Canal with its seemingly endless rows of poplars – proceed to the charming town of **Damme**, the home of Thyl Uilenspiegel (see Literature, 19th Century – Charles de Coster). **Bruges** (Brugge), a few miles to the south, will probably leave a more lasting impression on the visitor than any other Belgian town. The medieval town centre, completely preserved and pierced with canals, is uniquely beautiful and when the visitor sees the Town Hall (stadhuis) and Cloth-Hall and the Belfry he will soon realise why in the Middle Ages Bruges was the richest and most magnificent town north of the Alps. Almost as splendid is **Ghent**, easily reached from Bruges by the A10/E40 motorway. Here, too, the visitor will be inspired by the great Belfry, the splendid guild-houses and noblemen's dwellings along the canals and the magnificent churches, the largest of which, Sint-Baafskathedraal, contains the "Altar of Ghent", a masterpiece of Late Gothic painting.

The next stop on the tour is also a city – **Antwerp**, best approached along the A14/E17. Antwerp is Belgium's second largest city, the second largest European port after Rotterdam and one of the major diamond-dealing centres on the Continent. Peter Paul Rubens and the famous printing family of Plantin both lived here; their houses and studios have today been converted into museums which are well worth a visit. Two of Rubens' masterpieces, the "Raising of the Cross" and the "Descent from the Cross" are in the Cathedral, the tall, slender tower of which dominates the skyline.

This suggested route then passes through two more places in which to stop. South of Antwerp lies **Mechelen** (Malines), the centre of Belgian campanology, with its very fine Late Gothic Town Hall. To its south – on the N26 from Mechelen – will be found the old university town of **Leuven** (Louvain), with its proud Town Hall surpassed only by that of Brussels. From Leuven it is only 15 km (9 mi.) back along the N2 to Brussels where the tour began.

Sights from A to Z

The first name in each heading of this section is normally the Flemish or French name, depending on the linguistic area concerned. In a few cases where there is a distinct English form of the name, or where the French name is more familiar to English readers, this is given first (see List of Contents, p. 5). In all cases the alternative place name follows.

References to "the Netherlands" are always to the present-day Low Countries as a whole, i.e. the kingdoms of Belgium and the Netherlands (Holland) together with the Grand Duchy of Luxembourg.

Aalst · Alost   F 8

Province: Oost-Vlaanderen
Altitude: 7–29 m (23–95 ft). Population: 76,400
Intercity and Inter-regional Station (bicycle rental at station)

Aalst (French Alost), once the capital of a largely autonomous Flanders, straddles the banks of the river Dender. It is the administrative centre of the arrondisement, with schools which serve a large rural catchment area. Cotton processing, textile manufacture and mechanical engineering are among Aalst's many well-established industries; hops are grown in the surrounding countryside and marketed in the town. Flower-growing is now a particularly important source of employment. Every weekday morning and Wednesday evening wholesalers gather to buy cut flowers at the modern flower market (Bloemenveilingshal) in Albrechtlaan. Since the Belgian capital with its wealth of job opportunities lies only 28 km (17 mi.) to the south-east, many of Aalst's residents are commuters who work in the Brussels area.

History Aalst Castle is mentioned in documents dating from as early as 866. The town itself received its charter in 1164 having previously been granted in fief to the counts of Flanders. In the Middle Ages because of its location on the navigable Dender and the trade route between Bruges and Cologne, Aalst quickly developed into the major centre of the Flemish county of that name. During the Netherlands' long struggle for independence the town was the scene of repeated fighting in which many of its inhabitants were killed and numerous of its buildings destroyed or damaged. The same fate befell it at the time of Louis XIV's wars and again in the two World Wars. A number of buildings of historic interest have nevertheless survived.

The printer Dirk Martens (1446–1534) and the priest Adolf Daens (1839–1907) were both born in Aalst. The Flemish writer Louis Paul Boon also lived there.

One of Aalst's major attractions is its **carnival** which opens on the Sunday before Shrove Tuesday with a "Parade of the Giants", among them Aalst's "own" giant Ross Bayard. The celebrations continue on the Monday with onion throwing from the Belfry and end on Tuesday with the procession of "Vuil Jeannetten" ("Dirty Jeanette").

Begun in 1225 and now the oldest building of its kind in the Netherlands, the Schepenhuis (the original town hall) dominates the Grote Markt. The ★Schepenhuis and Belfry

◀ *Schepenhuis and belfry in Aalst*

entire evolution of Gothic architecture over three centuries can be clearly traced in this ancient sandstone edifice. The rear façade and side facing onto Kattestraat both date from the first half of the 13th c. and are of particular interest. The other side and the main façade were built later, following a fire in 1407. The beautiful Belfry (1470) with its carillon of 52 bells juts out to the right of the main façade. Embellished with Flamboyant Gothic pinnacles (1543–44) the tower bears the town's motto "Nec spe nec metu" ("Neither hope nor fear").

The **Daensmuseum en Archief van de Vlaamse Sociale Strijd** (D.A.V.S., Opening times Wed. and Sat. 9am–noon and 2–5pm) on the second floor of the Belfry is dedicated to the movement for social justice founded by the priest Adolf Daens. Expelled from the Catholic Church because of his political activities Daens established the social-democratic "Christian People's Party" which, after the First World War, was absorbed into the "Vlaamse Beweging".

Dirk Martens Memorial In front of the Schepenhuis a memorial (1856) by Jan Geef commemorates the south Netherland's most famous printer, Dirk Martens. A close friend of Erasmus of Rotterdam, Martens began printing in 1473. He developed his own lettering system and was the first person in the Netherlands to print Greek and Hebrew texts. After spending many years in Antwerp, Louvain and also Spain he eventually returned to his birth-place at Aalst. From his printing press came, for example the first editions of Thomas More's "Utopia", major works by Erasmus, and the first report of Columbus's journey of discovery, the latter appearing little more than a year after the navigator's return.

Borse van Amsterdam

Built between 1630 and 1634 the brick and sandstone Flemish Late Renaissance Borse van Amsterdam (Amsterdam Bourse) on the west side of the Grote Markt was once the site of the Vrije Vleeshuis (Butchers' Hall) and then later the headquarters of the Barbaristes, a literary guild. Above its arcaded lower storey rise four round Baroque gables and a slender central tower (1908).

Stadhuis

The Stadhuis (Town Hall) on the opposite side of the market square was rebuilt in 1830, at which time it acquired its Rococo façade and Late Neo-Classical banqueting hall. The original building, the "Landhuis", constructed between 1643 and 1645, was the meeting place of the Aalst provincial assembly which represented not just Aalst itself but also Geraardsbergen (see entry) and 150 rural parishes.

Sint-Martinus-kerk

A short distance east of the Grote Markt the road opens onto Priester Daensplein with Sint-Martinuskerk in the centre. The church was begun around 1480 under the direction of a little known masterbuilder Jan van der Wouwe. However, the choir and its ring of chapels, much the most interesting part of the building, are the work of more famous architects, in particular Herman and Dominic de Waghemakere who built Antwerp Cathedral, and the great Laurens Keldermans from Mechelen. The religious wars of the 16th c. prevented the church's completion.

The church **interior**, plain in itself, contains some exceptionally fine works of art, outstanding among which is the painting "St Roch and the Plague Sufferers" attributed to Peter Paul **Rubens**. This hangs in the chapel of the brewers' guild located to the left of the right-hand aisle.

On the left of the altar can be seen a stone tabernacle by Jerome Duquesnoy the Elder (1604). Two of the chapels encircling the choir deserve particular mention: the first chapel on the right, in which hangs an especially fine painting by Ambroise Francken entitled "Shepherds Praying"; and the fourth chapel along, containing the tomb of Dirk Martens. Amongst the church's other treasures is a three-part monstrance by the Antwerp goldsmith Lestiens (1631).

In 1224 Joanna of Constantinople, Countess of Flanders, made a gift to the town of a site for a hospital. The present building, situated on the Vismarkt behind Sint-Martinuskerk, dates from the 14th and 16th centuries. Having been restored between 1959 and 1965 it now houses the Academie voor Schone Kunsten (Academy of Fine Art) and the Stedelijk Oudheidkundig Museum. Items on display in the latter include chains of office belonging to the various guilds, mementoes of the Battle of the Golden Spurs, carnival costumes and furniture. (Open Tue.-Fri. 10am-noon and 2–5pm (Wed. till 7pm), Sat., Sun. 2–5pm.)

Oud-Hospitaal

Of the once thriving béguinage in Pontstraat to the south-east of Sint-Martinuskerk only the Neo-Baroque Sint-Antoniuskapel and Neo-Classical Sint-Catherinekerk remain.

Begijnhof

Surroundings

The world famous "Oktoberfeesten", a Munich style beer festival, takes place every autumn in Wieze, 6 km (4 mi.) north-east of Aalst.

Wieze

Gijzegem, 12 km (7 mi.) north-east of Aalst, is noteworthy for a farm dating back to 1688. This originally belonged to Gijzegem Castle of which, with the exception of two pavilions, no trace now remains. Its name, however, lives on as that of the farm, known today as "Hof van Gijzegem" or "Neerhof".
    The parish church of Sint-Martinus (second half of the 18th c.) has a splendid high altar.

Gijzegem

3 km (2 mi.) east lies the Abdij van Affligem, founded by Benedictine monks in 1083 (opening times Sat. 2.30–8pm, Sun. 11am–1pm and 2.30–8pm). The old abbey was largely destroyed in 1797 by French Revolutionary troops. Rebuilding began in 1869 and has continued in a variety of architectural styles. Parts of the original 12th and 13th c. nave can be seen in the garden. There is also a museum in which items of archaeological interest from the abbey grounds are displayed.

Abdij van Affligem

At Moorsel, 5 km (3 mi.) east of Aalst, there is a moated castle (waterkasteel). This Renaissance château, constructed entirely in red brick, was built in 1520 as a summer residence by Charles de Croy, Abbot of Affligem and later Cardinal of Tournai.
    According to tradition Moorsel's 13th–15th c. Sint-Martinuskerk grew out of a 7th c. communion chapel dedicated to St Gudula. The present church contains three Baroque altars by Jacob Ulner.

Moorsel

The original Sint-Margarethakerk in Baardegem (8 km/5 mi.), a three-aisle Late Romanesque church first constructed in 1260, was extensively damaged by fire in 1592. Restored in the 17th c. and partly rebuilt, further restoration work in 1969 revealed the choir to have been part of a 10th c. pre-Romanesque hall church. Above the high altar hangs a painting of "St Veronica" by Gaspar de Crayer (1650).
    Baardegem's imposing Hof ter Linde dates from 1803 and is also well worth a visit.

Baardegem

Aarschot   F 11

Province: Brabant. Altitude: 15 m (50 ft.) Population: 26,000
Inter-regional Station (bicycle rental at station)

The small Hageland town of Aarschot is situated on the river Demer on the border with Kempenland. It is the centre of an asparagus-growing area but also has some industry (batteries, textiles).

History First mentioned in 825 Aarschot became part of Brabant in 1172. In 1212 it joined the Hanseatic League, quickly developing into the principal centre of the Flanders cloth industry. Its heyday period ended with Maximilian I's siege and sacking of the town in 1489, a fate it was to suffer again at the hands of the Spaniards in the 16th c. In 1782 Aarschot was captured by the Austrians and in the First World War it was the scene of a bloody Belgian rearguard action against the Germans. Between 1940 and 1944 the town was several times subject to heavy bombardment.

Aarschot was the birthplace of the artist Pieter Joseph Verhaghen (1728–1811) whose work – contrary to prevailing fashion – was greatly influenced by Rubens. He achieved success as a court painter in Vienna.

★Onze Lieve Vrouwkerk

Begun in 1337 with construction of the choir by the French master-builder Jacques Piccart, the Onze Lieve Vrouwkerk was completed in 1400 when the 85 m (279 ft) high tower was finished. The sandstone church is an outstanding example of Demer Gothic, a regional variation of Brabant High Gothic.

The **interior furnishings** of the church include a number of items of interest, chief among which is the 16th c. Flamboyant choir-screen surmounted by a Late Gothic crucifix. The choir stalls (also 16th c.) are decorated with satirical carvings, e.g. of "The Wolf and the Stork", attributed to Jan Borchman of Eindhoven. A painting "The Disciples of Emmaus" by Verhaghen (1788) hangs in a chapel to the right of the choir.

Begijnhof

Adjacent to the church stands the former béguinage, originally founded

Onze Lieve-Vrouwkerk in Aarschot

in 1251 but rebuilt in 1635. Nos. 15–19 are the only houses surviving from those early days, however. The Stedelijk Museum voor Heemkunde en Folklore in No. 25 offers an evocative insight into everyday life in the 18th and 19th c. (open daily 10am–noon and 2–5pm).

Still standing on the banks of the Demer these brick ducal mills were built between the 13th and 16th c., doubling as part of the town's fortifications.

s'Hertogenmolens

Rising above the Grote Markt the 14th c. tower known as Sint-Rochustoren was originally part of the Weavers' Hall.

Sint-Rochustoren

The Orleanstoren (Aurelianus Tower) on the southern edge of the town offers splendid views over the surrounding countryside.

Orleanstoren

Surroundings

An outing to the Kasteel van Horst at Sint-Pieters-Rhode, 13 km (8 mi.) south of Aarschot, is deservedly popular among local people. Set in delightful parkland, the moated château began life as a medieval castle of which only the magnificent tower escaped destruction at the hands of Maximilian I's troops. The existing brick building, polygonal in shape and with sandstone ornamentation, is largely the product of 16th and 17th c. rebuilding and conversion.

Kasteel van Horst

Amay

See Huy, Surroundings

Amblève valley

See Stavelot, Vallée de l'Amblève

Andenne

See Vallée de la Meuse

Antwerp · Antwerpen · Anvers   D 9/10

Province: Antwerpen
Altitude: 3–9 m (10–30 ft)
Population: 475,000
Intercity and Inter-regional Station

Antwerp (Flemish Antwerpen, French Anvers) is situated on the right bank of the river Scheldt (Flemish Schelde, French Escaut), 88 km (55 mi.) from its mouth in the North Sea. The river at this point is some 500 m (1650 ft) wide and, despite the distance from the sea, still experiences a tidal range of over 4 m (13 ft). Antwerp is the capital of the province of Antwerpen and the second largest seaport in Europe.

Commercial and cultural metropolis

Thanks to its harbour Antwerp was an important **centre of trade and commerce** even before records began. In addition to its long established traditions in banking and insurance, the continual expansion and modernisation of the port has seen the emergence of a multitude of trades and industries processing imported raw materials on the spot. Today Greater Antwerp is the biggest industrial conurbation in Belgium with shipbuilding and ship repair, petro-chemicals, vehicle assembly and food manufacture among its principal activities. The city is also a major port with a freight volume of 110 million tonnes (1998), of great importance, not just for Belgium but for Europe as a whole. Five rail routes and several canals terminate at the Port of Antwerp.

Antwerp is the world centre for diamond trade

Antwerp's international reputation is in part due to the **diamond industry** and the special role the city plays in the diamond trade worldwide. While Amsterdam (Holland) is the diamond cutting capital of the world – although Antwerp has more than 250 diamond cutting firms of its own – Antwerp is the premier marketplace for industrial and ornamental cut diamonds, accounting in fact for almost half of the global trade.

The centre of the diamond trade lies in the district along the Pelikaanstraat, in the Jewish Quarter near the main railway station. There are several showrooms and other diamond trade outlets catering for prospective buyers (Diamondland, Appelmansstraat 33; Dilady, Lange Herentalstraat 29). Further information is available from the Diamond Advisory Council at Hoveniersstraat 22.

The city's remarkable reputation does not rest solely on its trade and industry, however; it is also the **cultural capital** of Flanders. Centuries of prosperity have bequeathed an inheritance which includes the magnificent cathedral, the town hall, many other outstanding historic buildings and, above all, the city's paintings, an incomparable collection of 15th to 17th c. masterpieces from a time when the work of artists of the South Netherlands school attained extraordinary heights. Quentin Massys, the "Velvet" Bruegel, Rubens, van Dyck, Jordaens, Cornelis de Vos and many others all lived and worked in Antwerp. This rich cultural tradition is maintained today by the city's numerous museums, theatres, three universities and several academies and institutes, in recognition of which Antwerp was chosen European City of Culture 1993.

Among the groups contributing to Antwerp's cultural diversity are 20,000 members of the Jewish community, the largest in Europe.

The relocation of port facilities around a newly constructed basin to the north has opened the way for redevelopment of the old wharves close to the city centre. This dockland area is now the focus of Antwerp's most ambitious building project in recent times, known as "the **City on the River**". Architects invited to take part in a design competition submitted outline schemes, three of which have now been selected for further appraisal. Assuming plans come to fruition the old basin north of the Steen will become a residential area incorporating an open-air maritime museum. The embankments on either side will also be redeveloped and a multi-level square with a subterranean arts centre will be built on the site of the former south dock.

Antwerp Cathedral viewed from the Scheldt Quay ▶

Origin of the name Traditionally the name Antwerp originates with a giant, Druon Antigonus, whose castle stood on the site in Roman times. He reputedly cut off the hand of any passing seafarer who refused to pay a toll, throwing the severed hand into the Scheldt. Antigonus is supposed to have been slain by the Roman Silvius Brabo who, it is said, himself hacked off one of the giant's hands and tossed it ("handwerpen") into the river. More mundane is the suggestion that the name is derived from the word "aanworp" or "aanwerpen" (meaning "thrown up ground") – referring to a piece of land which jutted out into the river abreast of the Steen and where there was once a settlement.

Early period Whatever the truth about its name, in the 2nd and 3rd centuries AD a Gallo-Roman settlement most certainly existed on a site now occupied by part of southern Antwerp. This was followed in the 4th and 5th centuries by a Frankish village. Christian missionaries established themselves in the area around Antwerp in the 7th and 8th centuries, during which time St Amand is believed to have founded the "Infra castrum Antwerpis", destroyed by the Normans in 836. Under the Treaty of Verdun of 843 Antwerp became part of Lothringia, and in the 10th c. it was made a margravate of the Holy Roman Empire. The city's emergence as a port began in 1031, the Hansa establishing a presence there in 1313.

Heyday and decline Having earlier, in 1106, passed to the dukes of Brabant, the city on the Scheldt was now transformed into the North Sea's leading trading port, its wealth founded on its wool warehouses. In addition to new fortifications the building of the cathedral reflected growing prosperity, and Antwerp was already thriving when, at the end of the 15th c., the Zwin silted up, bringing even more trade to the city at the expense of its great rival Bruges. Under the protection of the emperor Charles V, Antwerp swiftly developed into the busiest and richest commercial city in Christendom. By the year 1560 the population had risen to around 100,000 inhabitants, 100 ships entered or departed the port every day, and more than 1000 business-houses had become established.

From the 16th c. onwards Antwerp also enjoyed a reputation for high standards of craftsmanship, its products being in demand as far afield as Arabia, Persia and India. This economic success was marked by the building of the old Beurs, the commercial exchange, and numerous artists including the painters Massys, Venius and the Bruegels, the sculptors Coecke van Aelst and de Vriendt, the writers Marnix van Sint-Aldegonde and Anna Bijns and the musicians Ockegem, De Hertogen and Cornet worked in the city, as did scientists such as Mercator, Dodoens, Ortelius and Lipsius and the printer Plantin.

This heydey period was, however, doomed not to last, the seeds of destruction being sown during the reign of Philip II when the Inquisition caused thousands of Antwerp's citizens to flee the port. In 1576 the mutinous Spanish garrison went on the rampage, plundering the city and killing an estimated 7,000 of its inhabitants. Capture by Duke Alexander Farnese in 1585 further hastened its decline. Antwerp's commercial mantle was assumed by Amsterdam and Rotterdam, whence the persecuted Protestants had fled. By 1590 the city's population had more than halved to just 40,000 people.

Many masters Antwerp suffered another mortal blow when, following unification of the seven provinces, control of shipping on the Scheldt fell into Dutch hands, eventually leading to the closure of the river under the terms of the 1648 Treaty of Westphalia. Even so Antwerp still retained its status as the cultural centre of the region. Painters including Rubens, van Dyck, Jordaens and Teniers, and sculptors such as Quellin, were among the artists living and working in the city where, in 1663, Philip IV of Spain founded an Academy of Art modelled on those of Rome and Paris.

It was not until the French conquests at the end of the 18th c. that Antwerp's fortunes revived. The Scheldt was reopened for navigation in 1795 and between 1800 and 1803 Napoleon I laid out the Scheldt quays and old dock. The port assumed a crucial role in the Emperor's blockade of England ("Antwerp is the pistol aimed at the heart of England").

The 1815 Congress of Vienna gave Antwerp to the Kingdom of the Netherlands, bringing a significant boost to the city's prosperity (population 73,500 in 1830). This was mainly the result of trade with the Dutch colonies, trade which Antwerp was soon to lose once more to Rotterdam and Amsterdam. Bombardment of the city during the sieges of 1830 and 1832 caused massive damage. In 1863 Belgium bought back from the Dutch the right to levy dues on shipping in the Scheldt, a right which the Dutch had exercised since 1839. This brought a revitalisation of trade and commerce in the second half of the 19th c., marked by the fact that both the world trade exhibitions of 1885 and 1894 were held in Antwerp. In parallel with its economic growth, after 1859 Antwerp was also transformed into one of Europe's most heavily fortified cities. When the inner defences were finally dismantled, the massive ramparts were replaced by wide boulevards.

First and Second World Wars In the First World War the Germans beseiged Antwerp in September and October 1914, eventually occupying the city. Between the two wars the tonnage of freight passing through the port increased steadily and Antwerp soon regained its former prominence, being the venue of the seventh modern Olympic Games held in 1920 and ten years later of another world trade exhibition. In the Second World War the city was again occupied by the Germans. It continued to suffer heavy bombing even after the Allied liberation, being the target of some 800 German V1 and V2 rockets.

The present Following the Second World War the volume of freight traffic continued to expand. Antwerp's outer fortifications were demolished, the only remaining vestige now being the "Vestingwater", the former moat. An apparently endless series of new tunnels, docks and locks were constructed and in Inner Old City and the Scheldt Embankment 1975 work commenced on the city's underground. Since 1989 Antwerp has boasted the largest sea-lock in the world, the Berendrechtsluis.

Visitors with only a day to spend in Antwerp probably do best to limit themselves to the major city centre sights, principally the Grote Markt with its town hall and numerous guild-houses and, only a short distance away, the cathedral. Both can be viewed without haste in a morning leaving the afternoon free for a visit to one, or perhaps two, of Antwerp's museums. Usually the choice can be narrowed down to either the Plantijn Moretus Museum and Rubens' House, for which an afternoon suffices, or the Museum voor Schone Kunsten, which really requires more time to do it justice. A trip on the Scheldt, or one of the longer tours of the harbour, provides a different kind of alternative to the museums.

What to see

Having two days available for sightseeing means the added options of a visit to the Maritime Museum in the Steen, or a walk through the Jewish Quarter calling in at the Diamond Museum and Antwerp's famous zoo. Also highly recommended are the Museum Mayer van den Bergh and the Sint-Jacobskerk where Peter Paul Rubens lies buried.

Round and guided tours As well as organising coach tours the Antwerp Tourist Office (see Practical Information) publishes brochures detailing

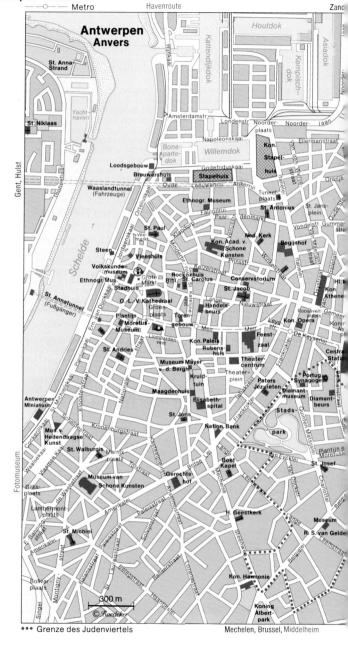

Antwerp · Antwerpen · Anvers

—o— Metro   Havenroute   Zand

**Antwerpen
Anvers**

St. Anna-
Strand

Houtdok

Yacht-
haven

St. Niklaas

Amsterdamstr.

Londenstr.   Noorder-
plaats

Napoleonskaai   Kon.
Stapel-
Bona-   Willemdok   huis
parte-
dok

Loodsgebouw   Godefriduskaai
Brouwershuis
Waaslandtunnel (Fahrzeuge)   Oude   Leeuwenrui   Ankerrui   Tunnel-
plaats   St. Jans-
St. Antonius   plein

Ethnogr. Museum   Falconrui
Paar- denmarkt   Vondelstr. Gummar-
St. Paul   Klapdorp   stra

Vee-   Ned. Kerk
markt   Kon. Acad. v.   Begijnhof
Steen   Schone
Vleeshuis   Kunsten   Prinsstr.
Volkskunde   Keizerstraat   Conservatorium
museum   Rockoxhuis
Ethnogr. Mus. St. Bibl. St. Carolus
Grote   St. Jacob   Hl.
Stadhuis   Markt   Kon.
Nieuwstraat   Athene
St. Annatunnel   O.-L.-V. Kathedraal   Lange
(Fußgänger)   Groen- Handels-
plaats   Toren- beurs   Kon. Opera
Plantijn- gebouw   Leys-   De Keyserlei
Moretus-   Meir   str.   Meir
Museum   Feest-
Lombardenvest   zaal
St. Andries   Kon. Paleis
Rubens-   Theater-
Museum Mayer   huis   centrum
v. d. Bergh   Theater-
Kruid-   plein   Paters   Portug.
tuin   Jezuïeten   Synagoge
Maagdenhuis   Diamant-
Elisabeth-   museum Diamant-
spital   beurs
St. Joris   Stads-
Antwerpen   Nation. Bank   park
Miniatuur
Plantijn e
Mus. v.   Moretus
Hedendaagse
Kunst   St. Walburgis   Boet   St. Josef
Kapel
Museum van   Gerechts-
Schone Kunsten hof
Gillis-
plaats   Museum
Lambermont-   H. Geestkerk   P. S. van Gelde
plaats
St. Michiel

Bolwar-
plaats   **300 m**
©Baedeker   Kon. Harmonie

••• Grenze des Judenviertels   Mechelen, Brussel, Middelheim

Koning
Albert-
park

Gent, Hulst

Schelde

Fotomuseum

gen op Zoom, Breda

Mechelen, Lier, Flughafen

various signposted walks around the city. The Office will also arrange the services of a guide. On Saturdays, Sundays and public holidays between Easter and the end of October (but daily throughout July and August) horse-drawn carriages are available for hire in the Grote Markt.

Scheldt and harbour trips The Flandria Shipping Co. runs boat trips on the Scheldt and tours of the docks, daily from April to September, departing at 10am. Tickets can be obtained from the Flandria office at Vlotbrug. Available excursions include:

Short trip on the Scheldt lasting 50 minutes, from Vlotbrug;

Longer trip on the Scheldt lasting 1 hour 20 minutes, also from Vlotbrug;

Harbour tour lasting 2 hours 20 minutes, from Quay 13 at Londenbrug (courtesy bus from Steenplein).

Public transport Antwerp's Metro links Groenplaats in the city centre via Centraal Station to the terminus at Plantin in the Jewish Quarter. Several tram routes make their way around the narrow streets of the inner city through which also pass all bus services bar one (No. 9 via the Minderbroederrui). Buses Nos. 6 and 34 run from the Scheldt embankment to the districts south of the city centre. Groenplaats is the main city centre tram stop. Most bus lines call at Franklin D. Rooseveltplein, not far from Centraal Station.

The inner city area can easily be explored on foot without the need for any form of transport. In what follows therefore, advice about getting to places is limited to sights further afield.

Inner Old City and the Scheldt Embankment

In the middle of the Grote Markt, the heart of old Antwerp, stands the large **Brabo Fontein** (Brabo Fountain) by Jef Lambeaux. Erected in 1887 it depicts the Roman soldier Silvius Brabo tossing the severed hand of the giant Antigonus into the Scheldt.

★ Grote Markt

The **Stadhuis**, the 78 m (256 ft)-long façade of which forms the western side of the Grote Markt, was built by Cornelis Floris de Vriendt between 1561 and 1565. Beneath the statue of the Virgin which adorns the central gable can be seen, from left to right, the arms of the dukes of

113

Brabant, Philip II and the margravate of Antwerp with, separating them, allegorical figures of Wisdom and Justice. Inside the town hall the rooms are hung with 19th c. paintings by H. Leys illustrating the history of Antwerp (guided tours: Mon.–Thu. 11am, 2pm and 3pm, Sat. 2pm and 3pm).

Apart from the Stadhuis most of the buildings bordering the Grote Markt are former "gildehuizen" (**guild-houses**), originally the headquarters of the city's 16th and 17th c. guilds. Among those on the north side are the Gildehuis der Kuipers (Coopers' House; No. 5), the Huis van de Schutters (Archer's House; No. 7) and the Huis van de Kruideniers (Grocers' House; No. 11), while on the south-east side stand the Huis van de Kleermakers (Tailors' House; No. 38) and the Huis van de Timmerlieden (Carpenters' House; No. 40). The streets behind and to the north of the Stadhuis (Gildekamersstraat, Zilversmid-, Braderij- and Kuipersstraat) offer further glimpses of the beauty that was once old Antwerp.

Folk museum	Immediately behind the town hall, in the Gildekamersstraat, two former guild-houses have been turned into a folk museum devoted to the many traditional arts and crafts found in the Antwerp area. The museum has collections of marionettes and costumes, etc. and a complete chemists shop and pharmacy (open Tue.–Sun. 10am–5pm).
Ethnographic museum	No. 19 Suikerrui – the street leading off from the southern corner of the Grote Markt – is now the home of Antwerp's recently established and extremely interesting ethnographic museum (open Tue.–Sun. 10am–5pm).
North of the Grote Markt	The elegant rooms of the late Gothic Vleeshuis (Butchers' Hall) in the Vleeshouwerstraat include the former council chamber of the butchers' guild. The impressive brick building, built in 1501–04, was deliberately sited close to the Scheldt, allowing the blood of slaughtered animals to run off into the river.
★Vleeshuis	The Vleeshuis is now a museum of applied art and archaeology with collections of pre-historic, Egyptian, Roman and Merovingian artefacts; weapons and armour; ceramics; furniture; sculpture and woodwork; and coins. Among its most prized possessions are a depiction of the conversion of Saul in 16th c. Antwerp tiles, the Averbode Retable by Pieter Coecke van Aelst, and an outstanding collection of **musical instruments** including the remarkable harpsichord from the workshop of Ruckers the instrument-makers (open Tue.–Sun. 10am–5pm).
Poesjenellenkeller	In the Poesjenellenkeller in the little Repenstraat opposite the Vleeshuis puppet shows are perfomed in the Antwerp dialect, maintaining a tradition which goes back to the 18th c.
Sint-Pauluskerk	At its northern end Vleeshouwerstraat opens out into the Veemarkt, the former cattle market. The Late Gothic Sint-Pauluskerk in the north-east corner, begun in 1517, was not completed until 1639. The Baroque clock tower dates from 1680. A fire in 1968 badly damaged the church and only the spirited efforts of local people prevented the loss of valuable interior furnishings. These include the superb Baroque confessionals by Pieter Verbruggen the Elder and three paintings by Rubens: "The Scourging of Christ" (1617) in the left aisle and the "Adoration of the Shepherds" and "Disputation on the Blessed Sacrament" in the left transept (open May–Sep. daily 2–5pm; Oct.–Apr. 9am–noon).
★★Onze Lieve Vrouwekathedraal	The Onze Lieve Vrouwekathedraal, Belgium's largest Gothic church and the largest of its kind in the Netherlands, stands a short distance south-east of the Grote Markt opening times Mon.–Fri. 10am–5pm, Sat. 10am–3pm, Sun. and public holidays 1–4pm, but 10am–3pm on the eve of public holidays).

Brabo Fountain and guild-houses in the Grote Markt

Work was started on the cathedral in 1352, continuing until 1521. Jacob van Thienen, Pieter Appelmans, Jan Tac, Everaert Spoorwater, Hermann and Dominic de Waghemakere and Rombout Keldermans were among the architects and masterbuilders who contributed to its construction.

The church has suffered serious damage on a number of occasions over the years, depriving it of many of its most precious works of art. First came a fire in 1533, then despoliation at the hands of dissident iconoclasts in 1566, Calvinists in 1581 and French Republican troops in 1794 and 1800. Sadly only a few of the lost treasures have since been recovered.

Restoration of the exterior was begun in the 19th c. and all the carved stonework on the outside of the building is therefore recent. Work on the interior began in 1965, starting with the nave where repairs were completed in 1983. Following the completion of restoration work on the choir and transepts in 1993 the light interior of the church can again be seen to its best advantage with the most important works of art having been returned to their original locations. Restoration work is now completed and the Church shines again in its former glory.

The 123 m (404 ft) **North Tower**, radiating lightness, can be seen from miles. away along the Scheldt. No wonder that the tower with its carillon of 47 bells has become the emblem of Antwerp. A memorial plaque at its foot commemorates Quentin Massys. The south tower was never finished.

The **interior** of the cathedral, 117 m (384 ft) long, 55 m (180 ft) wide and 40 m (131 ft) high, is notable for its spaciousness and the perspectival artistry of the nave and six aisles. The Baroque pulpit (1713) is the work of Michel van der Voort.

115

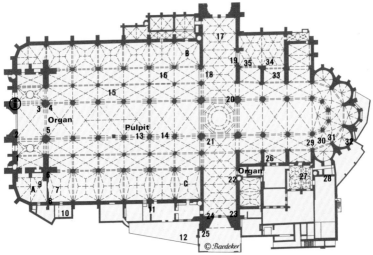

A Baptistery
B Lady Chapel
C Chapel of the Sacrament
D Sacristy

1 H. van Balen: "Madonna with Angels" (17th c.)
2 H. van Balen: "St John and Herod" (17th c.)
3 A. Quellin the Younger: "Immaculate Conception" (marble; 17th c.)
4 P. Scheemaeckers: Tomb of the Kuerlinckx family – Van Delft (1688)
5 H. van Mildert: SS Peter and Paul (Alabaster; 16th c.)
6 H. van de Elsburgh: "The Miraculous Draught of Fishes" (1589)
7 A. Quellin the Younger: "Jonathan" (17th c.)
8 Unknown master: "The Bearer of the Cross" (fresco; 15th c.)
9 J. Cauthals: "Christ on the Cross"
10 Unknown master: "John the Baptist and John the Apostle (window; 1525)
11 J. van Gérinnes (?): Tomb of Isabella of Bourbon (1478)
12 L. van Noort: "The Last Supper" (window; 1566)
13 R. van Olim: "Conversion of St Paul" (window; 1537)
14 Unknown master: "The Adoration of the Magi" (window; 1537)

15 Unknown master: "Madonna of the Meuse" (alabaster; 14th c.)
16 Unknown master: "Our Lady of Antwerp" (wood; 16th c.)
17 C. Cussers: "Archduke and Duchess Albrecht and Isabella kneeling before the Cross" (window; 1616)
18 M. Pepijn: "St Norbert" (1637)
19 F. Francken: "Jesus in the Temple" (1587)
20 P. P. Rubens: "The Raising of the Cross" (1610)
21 C. Schut: "The Assumption" (1647)
22 P. P. Rubens: "Descent from the Cross" (1612)
23 S. Murillo: "St Francis" (17th c.)
24 M. de Vos: "The Wedding at Cana" (1597)
25 O. van Veen: "The Last Supper" (17th c.)
26 P. P. Rubens: "Christ Rising from the Dead" (1612)
27 A. Quellin the Younger: "Tomb of Bishop Capello" (1676)
28 Unknown master: "Calvary with St Sebastian" (fresco; 15th c.)
29 P. P. Rubens: "The Assumption" (1625/1626)
30 A. Mathijssens: "The Death of Mary" (1633)
31 Unknown master: "Philipp II, SS Paul and Andrew with Mary Tudor" (window; 1556/1557)
32 A. Quellin the Younger: "Pietà" (wood; 17th c.)
33 St Anthony's Altar (A. Quellin the Younger; 17th c.)
34 Unknown master: "Henry VII and Elizabeth" (English window; 1503)
35 Unknown master: "Philip the Fair and Joanna with their Patron Saint" (Burgundian window; 1503)

Famous throughout the world and outstanding even among the cathedral's many exceptional works of art are two masterpieces by Peter Paul **Rubens**: "The Elevation of the Cross" to the left and "The Deposition" to the right of the rood screen. Considered among the finest of all Baroque paintings both were executed between 1610 and 1614, shortly after Rubens returned from Italy. While "The Deposition" was commissioned by the Antwerp Guild of Archers, "The Elevation of the Cross" was painted for the high altar of Sint-Walburgakerk. There are in addition two other major works by Rubens to admire: "The Assumption" (1626), the cathedral altar-piece, and perhaps the finest of the ten such works from the artist's brush – and "The Resurrection" (1612), originally painted for the Moretus family, the famous printers, but now hanging on the right side of the ambulatory.

Also displayed in the **treasury** are priceless liturgical accoutrements, vestments and paintings, including a "Pietà" (1556) by Maarten de Vos, a 17th c. "St Francis" by Murillo, and "The Mourning of Christ" by Cornelis de Vos. The marble "Head of Christ" is a gem, possibly by Leonardo da Vinci.

The Put (well) on the **Handschoenmarkt**, the former glove market in front of the cathedral, has a 15th c. wrought-iron canopy adorned by a figure of Silvius Brabo attributed to Quentin Massys.

In the vicinity of the cathedral

The Handschoenmarkt leads into a street known as the Oude Koornmarkt, off which (at the side of No. 16) runs the **Vlaeykensgang**, an alleyway of houses dating back to the 16th c. and altogether typical of old Antwerp.

Immediately south of the cathedral lies the bustling **Groenplaats**, cafés on every side. The statue of Rubens was erected in 1840.

Two Jesuit priests named d'Aguillon and Huyssens were the architects of Sint-Carolus Borromeuskerk, built between 1614 and 1621 on Hendrik Conscienceplein, a couple of minute's walk north-east of the cathedral. A devastating fire in 1718 largely destroyed the church, after which it was rebuilt in a less opulent style. Among the decorations lost for ever were ceiling paintings, 39 in all, by artists from Rubens' workshop and also by van Dyck. The full Baroque splendour of the original church can now only be glimpsed, primarily in the magnificent, clearly articulated main façade the design of which is attributed to Rubens himself. The 58 m (190 ft) bell tower is considered one of the loveliest in Belgium.

Sint-Carolus Borromeuskerk

Specially noteworthy in the interior are the carved Baroque confessionals guarded by angels and, between them, the wood reliefs showing scenes from the lives of St Ignatius and St Francis Xavier. Rubens painted three pictures for the altar but these are now in the Kunsthistorisches Museum in Vienna. The gallery, crypt and sacristy have been turned into a museum displaying, among other things, some exquisite lace. Every Sunday at 11am a High Mass with muscial accompaniment takes place in the church.

In 1576 Christophe Plantin the printer, who hailed originally from France, moved into a house he christened "De gulden Passer" – the Golden Compasses – close by the Vrijdagmarkt (south of the Grote Markt). Thereafter Plantin and his heirs the Moretus family extended the house, ultimately bequeathing to posterity a supreme example of Flemish Renaissance architecture (though the façade facing the Vrijdagmarkt was an 18th c. addition). Today the building is a museum. It incorporates the Old Flemish patrician house, the quiet, vine-covered inner courtyard, and the commercial premises, the latter including an early print-works complete with office and typesetters' room, all in an unparalleled state of preservation. The original furnishings, the wide-ranging exhibits, some of which are unique, but above all the still tangible atmosphere arising from the proximity of home and workplace, enthral every visitor and make the Plantin-Moretus Museum one of Antwerp's premier attractions (opening times 10am–5pm, address Vrijdagmarkt 22).

★★Plantin-Moretus Museum

Having set up as a printer in 1549, Christophe Plantin (1520–89) transferred his **print-works** lock, stock and barrel to his new home when he moved to the Vrijdagmarkt in 1576. After his death the business carried on more or less unchanged under his son-in-law and successor Jan Moerentorf/Moretus, and subsequently the latter's family. The print-

The Plantin printing works

works with its sixteen presses was by far the largest in the Europe of the day. Plantin's greatest masterpiece was the eight-volume "Biblia Regia", or "Biblia Polyglotta", in five languages, Latin, Greek, Hebrew, Syrian and Aramaic, over 1500 copies of which were produced in the workshop. The most distinguished member of the Plantin-Moretus family proved to be Jan's son Balthazar who, on many occasions between 1613 and 1637, employed Rubens as an illustrator. From the mid 17th c. onwards the printing-house concentrated almost exclusively on missals and prayer books, Philip II having earlier granted Plantin a monopoly in the printing of liturgical books throughout the Spanish empire. When in 1800 the Spanish government finally withdrew this privilege, printing operations ceased, resuming only intermittently thereafter.

The **tour of the house** covers 34 rooms. Videos in several different languages recounting the story of the Plantin-Moretus family and the history of printing are shown in one of the ground-floor rooms reached via the courtyard.

Since a short guide to the museum is included in the price of entry, only the items of most interest receive mention below.

Room 3 contains manuscripts from the 9th to the 16th c. including an edition of the Chronicle of Jean Froissart, written in the 15th c., and the Bohemian bible of 1401/02 belonging to King Wenceslas.

Room 7 is devoted to the history of books and the processes involved in their production, from the earliest forms of writing and development of the alphabet – exhibits include important archaeological finds and manuscripts – to Johannes Gutenberg and the invention of letterpress printing using movable type. Later developments in printing technology are also featured, culminating in the phototypesetting of today.

Room 9 The proof-readers' room. Original proof-correction sheets dating back to the 16th and 17th c. can be seen on the desks.

Room 11 The humanist scholar Justus Lipsius (1547–1606) was a close friend of the family, often working in this room. The walls are hung with rare gold 16th c. Spanish leather.

Room 14 The print-works, the core of the old family business, with a total of eight printing presses on display.

Room 16 The "Second Plantin Room". Among the exhibits is an edition of the famous "Biblia Regia".

Room 18 is principally devoted to the Moretus family. One of the books on display contains the earliest known European illustration of a potato plant (1588).

Room 19 Peter Paul Rubens had a close association with the Moretus family. Here his work as an illustrator is recorded.

Room 24 This room is a celebration of the art of printing in Europe as a whole, the jewel in the crown being a 36-line Gutenberg Bible.

Room 30 The type foundry, originally set up in the 17th c. The various processes used in the manufacture of metal printing-types are displayed.

Room 33 A room to delight any bibliophile, housing the Max Horn Collection of rare books from the 16th to 18th c.

Antwerp's civic collection of copperplate engravings (**Prentenkabinet**) is housed next door to the museum at Vrijdagmarkt 23. Access is for purposes of research only.

Riverside terraces To left and right respectively at the western end of Suikerrui, the Ernest van Dijckkaai and the Jordaenskaai separate the Old City from the Scheldt, forming a no-man's-land ripe for redevelopment and a challenge for the architects and planners of the "City on the River" project. Antwerp's 100 m (330 ft)-wide quays, built in the 19th c., extend along the river for 5.5 km (3½ mi.) providing berthing for the largest sea-going ships. Considerable areas of the Old City were ruthlessly demolished to make way for them, including sections of the fortress. Running the length of the two quays, above the warehouses, are pedestrian terraces, complete with cafés, from where excellent views are obtained of the busy river, the Cathedral and the Steen. Midway along is the Vlotbrug (floating bridge), also constructed in the last century, from which the River Scheldt excursion boats depart. *(margin: Scheldt embankment)*

Pedestrian tunnel A tunnel 572 m (1875 ft) long and 31.5 m (103 ft) below the river provides a pedestrian crossing to the west bank of the Scheldt. The entrance (escalator or lift) faces the south end of the southern riverside terrace at Sint-Jansvliet.

A short distance north of the Vlotbrug the road opens out into Steenplein, named after Antwerp's ancient citadel the Steen. The fortress's various phases of construction span a period from the 10th to the 16th c. For much of the time up to 1823 it was used as a prison. Not far from the entrance stands a modern statue of the "Lange Wapper", a notorious figure in Antwerp folklore. *(margin: ★Nationaal Scheepvaart-museum in the Steen)*

Having been restored in both the 19th and the present century, the Steen was converted in 1952 into the Nationaal Scheepvaartsmuseum (National Maritime Museum). The museum occupies twelve rooms, one of the highlights being a marvellous collection of model ships, among them a 15th c. Flemish warship as well as junks and other oriental craft. There are also ships-in-bottles, figure-heads and comprehensive displays of navigational instruments, tools, old maps and charts. One section is devoted to the influence of the sea upon religion, mysticism and art. Temporary exhibitions are held aboard the "Lauranda", a ship which belongs to the museum and is berthed permanently in the river (open Tue.–Sun. 10am–5pm).

More vessels are moored across on the left bank of the river, near the western entrance to the pedestrian tunnel. These make up the Maritim Openlucht Museum (Open-air Maritime Museum). *(margin: Maritiem Openlucht Museum)*

Old City – North-east

The Meir is Antwerp's main shopping street. Meirbrug, in the centre of which stands a modern memorial to Anthonios Van Dyck, links the inner nucleus of the Old City with the eastern part. The Torengebouw, at the western end of the Meir, was Europe's first skyscraper.

Walking east along the Meir, the handsome Rococo façade of No. 50, the former Koninklijke Paleis (Royal Palace), is the first to catch the eye. Having begun life as a patrician mansion in 1745, the house was Napoleon's Antwerp residence during the French occupation. In its latter day role as an international culture centre (I.C.C.), it provides a venue for exhibitions of contemporary art.

Meir No. 85, Osterrieth Huis, another 18th c. Rococo former mansion, is now the headquarters of a bank.

At the eastern end of the Meir a pair of identical department stores in Art Nouveau style face each other across the street.

★ Rubenshuis

Immediately beyond the old Koninklijke Paleis the open Wappersstraat turns south off the Meir. Peter Paul Rubens acquired No. 9 in 1610 – a year after his marriage to Isabella Brant – living there until his death in 1640 (opening times Tue.–Sun. 10am–5pm).

He arranged the house to his own taste and requirements, making his home to the left of the entrance and turning the right wing into his studio. The two parts are joined by an elaborate and much admired portico. In the 18th c. the house was owned for a time by an English aristocrat. Following the French Revolution it was used as a prison, thereafter falling more and more into disrepair. Rubenshuis (Rubens' house) finally came into the possession of the City of Antwerp in 1937 and, between 1939 and 1946, was meticulously restored with the aid of old documents and drawings.

Vlotburg, riverside terraces and the Steen

House and studio of Peter Paul Rubens

Furnishings The ten rooms of the house are furnished in the style of the period and contain numerous original paintings. These include works by Rubens (self-portrait, *c.* 1625/28, in the dining room) as well as by Snyders, Jan Bruegel, Veronese, Jordaens and Otto Venius. The large studio contains several more works by Rubens ("Adam and Eve in Paradise") and others by his pupils.

The Baroque façade of the studio overlooks the **courtyard**, from which three archways lead into the garden. Both portico and garden were designed by Rubens himself.

The Wapper continues at its southern end into Maria Pijpelincxstraat and then Oude Vaartplaats where a Sunday bird market is held. Plants, clothing, food, antiques and junk are among the items sold, as well as birds.

Bird market

Both streets open out onto Theaterplein, a large amphitheatre-like square with, on its north side, the Theatre Centre and Stadsschouwburg (Civic Theatre).

Theaterplein

Off to the left of the Meir coming from Meirbrug the Handelsbeurs (Commercial Exchange) in Twaalfmaandenstraat was erected in 1868–72 as a replacement for Dominic de Waghemakere's original (1531) destroyed by fire in 1858. Jos Schadde's building features a huge glass-covered hall on which a great many other stock exchanges were subsequently modelled. The Exchange is a public thoroughfare with access on all four sides.

Handelsbeurs

Set in a pleasant court at the western end of Lange Nieuwstraat, a few steps north of the Beurs, are the buildings of the former 15th c. Sint-Niklaashospitaal (Nos. 3–5), including a Late Gothic chapel.

Lange
Nieuwstraat

Further along the street the Burgundian Chapel (No. 31) takes its name from the 15th c. heraldic wall-paintings which decorate it.

★Sint-Jacobskerk

The 15th to 17th c. Gothic Sint-Jacobskerk, its exterior at present under restoration, faces onto Sint-Jacobsstraat on the north side of Lange Nieuwstraat (opening times Apr.–Oct. Mon.–Sat. 2–5pm; Nov.–Mar. Mon.–Sat. 9am–noon).

With its sumptuously ornate Baroque interior Sint-Jacobskerk is one of the richest ecclesiastical buildings in Antwerp, blessed with an exceptional endowment of art treasures. It was the church at which the city's patrician families worshipped, and they regularly commissioned leading artists to design their private chapels, altars and tombs. Each family had its own seats in the choir stalls, the twelfth along on the left being that of the Rubens family for instance, marked as are the others with the family arms.

Inevitably the Rubens Chapel provides the chief focus of interest for visitors.

Rubens Chapel

Rubens Chapel Situated behind the high altar it contains the tomb of the artist (1640) and those of other members of his family. The **altar-piece**, "The Virgin and Child with Saints" (1634), was painted by Rubens a few years before his death specifically for his burial chapel. In the painting St George's features are said to be those of Rubens himself while Isabella Brant appears as the Virgin and Hélène Fourment, Rubens' second wife, as Mary Magdalena.

Also to be seen in the church are paintings by, among others, de Vos, Seghers, Jordaens ("Healing of the Plague Sufferers", next to the Rubens Chapel), Venius ("Virgin", left aisle, fourth chapel) and Rockox (triptych "Last Judgment", left aisle, third chapel). On the high altar stands a marble statue by Kerricx and Artus Quellin the Younger, the "Transfiguration of St James" (1685).

Valuable liturgical accoutrements, books and vestments are displayed in the **treasury**.

Rockoxhuis

Nicolaus Rockox, art collector and burgomaster of Antwerp, was a friend and patron of Rubens. In 1603 he acquired Nos. 10–12 Keizerstraat, a street a little to the north of the Sint-Jacobskerk. Rockoxhuis, easily recognised by its white facade, became a museum in 1977. In addition to rare period furniture, porcelain, glass and ceramics, it is endowed with a magnificent collection of paintings. These include two by Rubens, "Mary Worshipping the Sleeping Infant Jesus" and a sketch of the "Crucifixion" which once belonged to George Sand, as well as works by Jordaens, Massys, Teniers, Snyders, van Dyck and others (open Tue.–Sun. 10am–5pm).

Museum voor het Vlaamse Cultuurleven

The Flemish Cultural Museum and Archives at Minderbroedersstraat 22 trace the revival of Flemish culture since the 18th c. (open Tue.–Sat. 10am–5pm).

Koninklijke Academie voor Schone Kunsten

Minderbroedersstraat leads at its eastern end into Mutsaertstraat where, since 1662, the Koninklijke Acadamie voor Schone Kunsten (Royal

Academy of Fine Arts) has occupied the buildings of a former Minorite monastery. Archways and other architectural pieces can be seen in the grounds.

Further east beyond the Academy the Béguinage in Rodestraat dates from 1542–46. The church was restored in the 19th c.

Begijnhof

Anyone with an interest in industrial archaeology should make a detour north from the Academy of Fine Arts, along Mutsaertstraat, across Falconplein and past the International Seamen's House to Adriaan Brouwerstraat. The former gildehuis (No. 20), built by the engineer Gilbert van Schoonbeke in 1553, used not only to be the headquarters of the brewers' guild but a working brewery and pumping station as well, supplying the water for other breweries. It remained in operation until 1930. The pumping mechanism, powered by horses until as short a time ago as 1873, can still be seen, together with rooms containing the paraphernalia of the coopers' and brewers' trades. A portrait of Gilbert van Schoonbeke, who contributed hugely to Antwerp's expansion beyond the confines of the old city, hangs in the council chamber (visits only after prior arrangement, Tel. (03) 232 65 11).

★Brouwershuis
(detour)

City centre – south

Viewing of the Gothic Sint-Andrieskerk in Sint-Andriesstraat is by appointment only (tel. 232 0384). Building started on the church in 1515. The interior boasts a fine choir stall (1821) with a depiction of St Peter's miraculous catch of fishes, a reliquary of "36 saints", and several splendid altars. One of the piers in the south transept bears a memorial to Mary Queen of Scots, erected by two of her exiled ladies-in-waiting.

Sint-Andrieskerk

In the course of only a short period during the 1890s, a connoisseur of the fine arts, Fritz Mayer van den Burgh, assembled a remarkable collection of more than 3,000 items. These are now displayed on four floors of a Neo-Gothic house at Lange Gasthuisstraat 19 (opening times Tue.–Sun. 10am–5pm). The collection includes some superlative works of art, among them paintings by Pieter Bruegel the Elder ("Dulle Griet" and the earliest of the artist's signed works "The Twelve Proverbs", both in Room 26), Rubens, Jordaens, Bouts, van der Weyden, van Ostade, Lucas Cranach and Quentin Massys. Also of great interest are, in Room 20, the Flemish and French religious statues, the outstanding collection of ivories, and a unique 16th c. Flemish breviary, and in Room 14, a polychrome group "Christ with St John" (1300) by Henry of Constance and a Netherlands diptych (c. 1400). The second floor features a collection of porcelain, while 17th c. furniture and paintings occupy the third.

★Museum Mayer
van den Bergh

A few doors further along Lange Gasthuisstraat part of a 17th c. former orphanage for girls known as the Maagdenhuis (the Maidens' House, No. 33) has also been turned into a museum and archive. In addition to tracing the history of the orphanage and its orphans the museum possesses important paintings by Jordaens, Venius and van Dyck and a rare collection of Antwerp faience bowls (open weekdays except Tue. 10am–5pm, Sat., Sun. 1–5pm, closed on public holidays).

Maagdenhuis

The Elisabeth Gasthuis (Lange Gasthuisstraat No. 41) was a hospital founded in the 13th c. Its 16th c. chapel has an ornately carved high altar by A. Quellin the Younger (1682).

Elisabeth
Gasthuis

Antwerp's botanic garden, the Kruidtuin, is situated approximately level with and behind the Maagdenhuis, on Leopoldstraat, which runs parallel to Lange Gasthuisstraat and just to the east (open daily 8am–6pm).

Kruidtuin

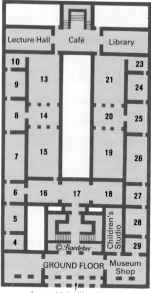

Leopold de Waelplaats

GROUND FLOOR

19th and 20th c.

4–10 Abstract art, Surrealism
13 Gustave van de Woestyne,
Constant Permeke
14 Albert Servaes
15 Gustave de Smet, Frits van den Berghe, Edgard
Tytgard, Jean Brusselmans
16–18 Temporary exhibitions
19 Henry de Braekeleer, Rik Wouters, Jacob Smits
21 James Ensor
24–29 Romanticism, Realism, Impressionism

UPPER FLOOR

Old Masters 14th–17th c.

A Maarten de Voos
B Marinus van Reymerswael

C David Teniers, Adriaan Brouwer
D Ambrosius Francken, Maarten Pepijn
E Franz Hals, Abraham von Beieren,
Rembrandt van Rijn
F Jacon Jordaens
G Jan Fyt, Franz Snyders, Jan Siberechts
GA Abraham Janssens, Theodor Rombouts
H Anton van Dyck, Jacob Jordaens
I–J Pieter Paul Rubens
K Titian
L Lucas Cranach, Jean Clouet, Pieter
Pourbus
M Cornelius de Vos, Erasmus Quellin
N Hans Memling
O Masters of Frankfurt
P Frans Floris de Vriendt
Q Jan van Eyck, Rogier van der Weyden,
Antonella da Messina
R Quinten Metsys, Joachim Patinir,
Barend van Orley
S Simone David
T Bruegel Family

★★ Koninklijk
Museum voor
Schone Kunsten

The Koninklijk Museum voor Schone Kunsten (Royal Museum of Fine Arts) celebrated its centenary in 1990, having opened its doors eleven years after work began on its Neo-Classical building in 1879. The nucleus of the museum's collection belonged originally to the Lucas Guild of Painters and Sculptors, founded in 1442. Following the winding up of the guild in 1773 the works of art accumulated over the years passed into the possession of the Academy of Fine Arts and were housed in the Academy's premises in the old Minorite monastery. In the mid 19th c., however, the collection was swollen by a substantial number of new acquisitions, particularly gifts, mainly of 15th and 16th c. paintings, from Florent van Ertborn, a former burgomaster of Antwerp.

The Academy found itself with insufficient space to accommodate the enlarged collection and the decision was taken to build a new museum.

Address: Leopold deWaelplaats 1–9: Tram Nos. 4, 8: opening times Tue.–Sun. 10am–5pm.

Tour The collection is housed on two floors. The ground floor is largely devoted to modern, i.e. 19th and 20th c. paintings and sculpture, some 1500 items in all, providing among other things an excellent overview of the development of the plastic arts in Belgium since 1830. The exhibition of Old Masters on the first floor comprises more than 1000 works, mostly from the Flemish and Dutch schools. Although visitors wish to be guided by their own preferences aided by the plan of the museum provided here, some of the most important of the works on view are mentioned below:

Specially noteworthy in the exceptionally well represented Old Netherlands school of 15th c. painting are Rogier van der Weyden's triptych with the Seven sacraments, two small pictures (a Madonna and a St Barbara) by Jan van Eyck, and a large triptych and portrait of Jehan de Candida, both by Hans Memling. Quentin Massys triptych with the Entombment, one of the artist's major works, dates from the early 16th c.

Some supreme examples of Rubens' religious paintings hang in the museum, among them his "Last Communion of St Francis", "Adoration of the Magi", "Education of the Virgin" and "Virgin with Parrot". There are also numerous works by the Master's predecessors, pupils and imitators. The paintings by Jordaens and van Dyck are well executed, though perhaps not quite up to the standard of their finest. In addition, be sure not to miss the very typical examples of 16th and 17th c. Flemish sculpture, the animal paintings and still lifes by 17th c. artists such as Snyder and, from the 17th c. Dutch school, the "Young Fisherman" by Frans Hals and a portrait by Rembrandt. Of the Italian paintings three are particularly outstanding: the series of small panels by Simone Martini, Antonello da Messina's "Christ on the Cross", and a Titian.

Old Masters

The pick of the 19th and 20th c. artists exhibited include Henri de Braekeleer, James Ensor, Rik Wouters ("Woman Ironing") and René Magritte.

19th and 20th c.

The area to the west of the Koninklijk Museum voor Schone Kunsten, especially the unprepossessing square bounded by Waalsekaai and Vlaamsekaai, forms one of the major sites for redevelopment under the "City on the River" project. Already two rather unusual museums have been established in waterfront buildings.

Scheldt embankment and quays – south-west

Opened in 1987 the Museum voor Hedendaagse Kunst (Museum of Contemporary Art) occupies an old corn silo with a lovely Art Déco façade at Leuvenstraat No. 32, off the Waalsekaai. The museum promotes the latest in modern art, not just through its own collection but also by inviting artists to exhibit their work. Nor are the works on show the only items of interest; equally worth seeing is the cafeteria wall sprayed by the New York graphic artist Keith Haring (open Tue.–Sun. 10am–5pm).

Museum voor Hedendaagse Kunst

Aficionados of the camera will also find a treat in store at Waalsekaai No. 47, an old warehouse recently given a new and rewarding lease of life as the Provinciaal Museum voor Fotografie. The museum charts the history of photography with the help of an important collection of cameras and old photographs (open Tue.–Sun. 10am–5pm).

Provinciaal Museum voor Fotografie

An old hangar on Cockerillkaai beside the Scheldt is the location of Antwerpen Miniatuurstad, the city in miniature (open daily 10am–8pm).

Antwerpen Miniatuurstad

The Avenues and the New Town

The Avenues

Between 1540 and 1543 massive ramparts incorporating ten bastions and walls up to 10 m (33 ft) high were constructed to form a defensive ring around the city on its eastern side. These have since been replaced by broad avenues (the Flemish for avenue is "lei") which separate Old Antwerp from the New Town. The northernmost of these avenues, Italiëlei, extends from the docks in the north to Franklin Rooseveltplein, passing the entrance to the Scheldt road tunnel at Tunnelplaats en route. On the south side of Franklin Rooseveltplein Italiëlei becomes Frankrijklei, crossed at Tenierplaats by the road linking Centraal Station to the city centre. Near the intersection stands the Koninklijke Vlaamse Opera (Royal Flemish Opera House) built in 1907. Next comes Britselei with the Gerechtshof (Law Courts; 1871–75) at the city end, and then finally the Amerikalei. The latter passes quite close to the Koninklijke Museum voor Schone Kunsten before terminating at Bolivarplaats.

Centraal Station

Keyserlei, a particularly lively place in the evenings, lined with cafés, restaurants, cinemas and hotels, runs from Tenierplaats to Centraal Station, Antwerp's main railway terminal. The "Middenstatie" (the middle section of the station building) with its imposing steps and impressive dome was built between 1895 and 1905. All the materials used in its construction came from Belgium itself. To the north the station opens onto Koningin Astridplein, again a popular focus of city life and site of a branch of the Antwerp Tourist Office.

**The Port
Dierentuin**

Located right in the midst of the city, immediately behind Centraal Station, the 10 ha (25 acre) Antwerp **Zoo** was founded in 1843. Entrance Koningin Astridplein, opening times daily from 9am; closing times vary according to season.

In the Antwerp Zoo

It is widely regarded as one of the finest zoos in Europe on account of its variety of species, its success in breeding, the care bestowed on the animals, kept in the most natural environment possible, and, last but by no means least, its architecture. While the Art Déco façades of the entrance area are the first features to catch the eye, inside the zoo there are several buildings of note, among them the giraffe and elephant house (1855) in the style of an Egyptian temple. More than 6,000 animals of 950 species live in the zoo, including rare breeds such as white rhino, okapi and mountain gorilla. In the cleverly designed aviary occupants and visitors are able to mingle freely. The terrarium and aquarium are filled with many interesting animals, among them the komodo dragon and exotic fish from the Zaïre River. A nocturnal house, a dolphinarium seating over 1000 (performances: summer 11.30am, 2, 3, 4, 5pm; winter 11.30am and 3pm only) and a planetarium (presentations: Wed. and Sun. 2pm) have recently been added.

The zoo also has a natural history museum concentrating mainly on native fauna. One rather unusual section is devoted to a collection of old microscopes and specimens.

Natural history museum

Antwerp's Jewish Quarter, home to the largest and most influential Jewish community in Europe, extends from Frankrijklei south as far as Koning Albertpark and eastwards to beyond the main railway line. Most of the Jews are orthodox and there are several synagogues in the area.

Jewish Quarter

Busiest thoroughfare in the district and centre of the diamond trade, Pelikaanstraat runs south from Centraal Station, alongside the railway line. In addition to the principal Diamantbeurs (Diamond Exchange), numerous jewellers, diamond merchants and cutters have premises on Pelikaanstraat or in the side streets leading off it.

Pelikaanstraat

The Provinciaal Diamantmuseum (Lange Herentalsestraat 31–33) explores all the different aspects of the trade in diamonds, including sections on their extraction, processing and industrial use. Diamond cutters can be seen at work on Saturday afternoons. There is also a display of cut and uncut diamonds (genuine) together with copies of the more famous stones (open Sun.–Fri. 10am–5pm, Sat. 2–5pm; guided tours).

Provinciaal Diamantmuseum

Immediately south of the diamond museum lies the triangular Stadspark (City Park), on the site of one of the Antwerp's old defence works. Stocked with a fine range of plants the park is attractively laid out with an ornamental lake, footpaths, and several monuments.

Stadspark

From the south-east corner of the Stadspark Charlottalei continues to its junction with Belgiëlei, on the opposite side of which No. 91 houses the delightfully unmuseumlike Ridder Smidt van Gelder Museum. With its fine period furniture and collection of fine porcelains the 18th c. mansion retains the atmosphere of a patrician house of the day (visits only after prior arrangement; tel. (03) 230 22 81).

Museum Ridder Smidt van Gelder

★★The port

The Port of Antwerp is second only to Rotterdam among the major seaports of Europe and one of the largest in the world. The harbour installations alone cover an area of more than 10,000 ha (25,000 acres), with a further 3400 ha (9300 acres) of land in industrial use. A total of 124 km (77 mi.) of wharves provide berthing for sea-going ships and inland craft, while 387 quayside cranes, twelve floating cranes, nineteen loading gantries and 20 container hoists handle their cargoes. Access to the harbour basins from the Scheldt is via six sea-locks on the east bank and one on the west, among the former being the 500 × 57 m (1640 × 187 ft)

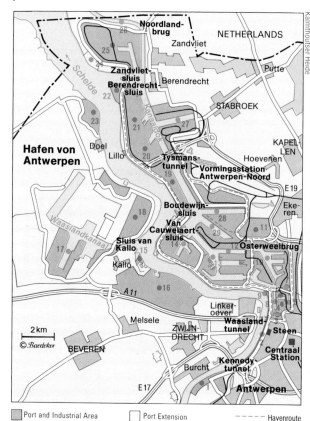

Kalmthoutser Heide

Port and Industrial Area □ Port Extension – – – – – Havenroute

1 Petroleumrichtingen Zuid
2 Vlotbrug (landing-stage for Scheldt trips, quays for visits to the fleet)
3 Bonapartedok and Willemdok
4 Kempschdok
5 Asiadok
6 Houtdok
7 Statsburgdok and Albetkanaal
8 Kattendijkdok
9 Royerssluis (1907) Amerikadok (grain silos, Marine Academy)
10 Albertdok, with 1–3 Havendok
11 Ford works (tractors)
12 Leopolddok
13 Hansadok (Esso Belgium, second largest refinery in Belgium) with 4 and 5 Havendok (chemical products, timber)
14 Marshalldok (Fina, largest refinery in Belgium)

15 Kallo thermal power station
16 Petrochemical plant (BP, Texaco, Fina, Exxon, Ucar)
17 Vrasendok
18 Bayerwerk
19 Bayerwerk
20 Degussa
21 Solvay
22 Container terminal
23 Doel nuclear complex works
24 Planned container terminal
25 BASF
26 Scheldt-Rhine Canal
27 Delwadedok (container, bulk goods, civic towing service)
28 Churchilldok (1967; container, vehicle loading)
29 6 Havendok (grain silos, cold-stores parcel service, timber, General Motors, Opel)

Zandvlietsluis (cubic capacity 613,000 cu. m/733,150 cu. yd) and the Berendrechtsluis (765,000 cu. m/914,940 cu. yd), the largest lock in the world, opened in 1989.

Approximately 20,000 vessels from 70 nations enter the port each year carrying between some 110 million tonnes of freight (1998), mainly oil, foodstuffs, raw materials for the chemical industry, mineral ore and manufactured goods such as vehicles. There are 300 ha (740 acres) of covered storage, including grain silos with a total capacity of 238,000 tonnes. Storage tanks with a combined capacity in excess of 10 million cu. m (350 million cu. ft) hold the oil and oil-based products (about 28 million tonnes annually) which together make up a significant proportion of the goods brought into the port for onward shipment. In recent years the container handling facilities have been steadily enlarged. Efficient modern industries, mainly petro-chemicals, metal (motor car assembly) and food processing, have grown up on sites around the port.

History A flourishing port from the late Middle Ages onwards, Antwerp's earliest harbour installations were built on the city's old waterfront along the Scheldt. The first docks, the Bonapartedok and Willemsdok, were constructed during the period of French occupation, largely for military purposes. Commercially speaking it was only after 1863, when Belgium bought back from the Dutch the right to levy dues on shipping in the Scheldt, that the port took on a new lease of life. Since that time the facilities have been developed systematically and with great success. The initial stage of expansion was accomplished in 1913 with the completion of eighteen docks for sea-going ships and seven for barges. Following the First World War priority was given to improving the storage and loading facilities of the existing port, but in 1956 a huge building programme was embarked upon, bringing the Haven to its present size. The Churchilldok and the 10 km (6 mi.) long Kanaaldok, through which the port is linked to Rotterdam via the Scheldt-Rhine Canal, were among the projects completed at this time. The process of expansion and development is still continuing, concentrated now around Kallo on the river's west bank. Four docks and the Sluis van Kallo are already in operation.

The enormous size of the port rules out any attempt to explore it on foot. This leaves the option of joining one of the boat tours or resorting to bicycle or car.

Docklands tour

Given sufficient time public transport offers another possibility, though not all parts of the port area can be reached in this way. The No. 37 bus goes as far as the Van Cauwelaertsluis and back, the No. 76 much further north to the Zandvlietsluis. But travelling by bus does not always guarantee a close look at the harbour installations.

The Flandria Shipping Co.'s boat tours of the Port of Antwerp depart from Kaai 13 (Londenbrug) on the northern extremity of the Old City. The same company also runs excursions on the Scheldt from the Vlotbrug near the Steen. These, however, are river trips and the entrance to the Sluis van Lallo is as close as they get to the docks themselves.

The **"Havenroute"** is an approximately 50 km (30 mi.) long sightseeing tour of the port area, marked out by the Antwerp Tourist Office. Start from the Loodsgebouw (Pilot House) on the embankment north of the Steen, from where the route heads northwards, passing almost immediately the two oldest docks, the Bonapartedok and Willemsdok, at the far end of which can be seen the massive Koninklijk Stapelhuis. Continue through the Kattendijkdok, built between 1853 and 1860, crossing the Kattendijksluis linking the dock to the river. Adjoining it to the east and north are a number of smaller docks, including the Straatsburgdok – off which leads the Albert Canal – and the Lefebvredok with access to the Scheldt via the Royerssluis. Beyond the Royerssluis the Havenroute turns westwards along the

Outlying places of interest

Havenroute

The Scheldt Quay and pilots office

Scheldelaan, following the river as it makes its way past an apparently end-less series of oil refineries. Eventually it bends rightwards again to the Van Cauwelaertsluis and Boudewijnsluis, continuing past the 17th c. Eenhoorn windmill to **Lillo**, one of the few polder villages to have at all survived engulfment by the port. The Polder Museum and the remains of Lillo's 16th c. fort are both well worth visiting, the latter having been part of the great fortifications which once surrounded Antwerp, the former documenting life as it was on the Antwerp polders prior to their being swallowed up by indus-trial development (open Easter–Oct. Sun. and public holidays noon–6pm).

At Lillo there is a choice between driving on to inspect the huge **Berendrechtsluis**, the world's largest lock, or shortening the tour by turn-ing round and following the Havenroute south again towards Antwerp, via the Frans Tijsmanstunnel beneath the Kanaaldok and then along the Noorderlaan. On the way the vast General Motors plant will be seen at the Churchilldok, beyond which a short detour to the left leads alongside No. 6 Havendok and back, passing the container terminals, the giant grain silos and the UK ferry terminal. From there the city centre can be reached by either of two routes, directly by continuing along the Noorderlaan and across the Albertkanaal or more circuitously via the Oosterweel Steenweg between Albertdok and Leopolddok, thence through No. 5 Havendok and Amerikadok to rejoin the Scheldelaan and so return to the Steen.

Outlying places of interest

★ Nachtegalen-park

Nachtegalenpark (Nightingale Park), on the southern side of the city, was laid out in 1910 on land formerly belonging to three estates: Den Brandt, Vogelenzang and Middelheim (Location South of the motorway ring, Entrance Beukenlaan, Bus No. 17).

The gardens of the Middelheim mansion have been made into an open-air sculpture museum (Openluchtmuseum voor Beeldhouwkunst), a sylvan setting for more than 300 works of art by well-known sculptors including Auguste Rodin, Aristide Maillol, Henry Moore, Rik Wouters, Louise Nevelson and Alexander Caldin. Smaller items are displayed in the pavilion (open daily 10am–dusk). A biennial festival of sculpture is held from July to September every odd-numbered year in the section of the Nachtegalenpark adjoining the Middelheimpark.

Middel-heim
Open-air Sculpture
Museum

Located to the east of Berchem's railway station in Antwerp's south-east suburb of that name, the district known as Zurenborg is something of an architectural curiosity. Built around the turn of the century in a medley of Neo-Classical, Neo-Renaissance and Art Nouveau styles, it was designated a conservation area in 1970 (Location: suburb of Berchem, tram nos. 8, 11).

Cogels-Osylei with its splendid houses is the pick of several very attractive streets.

Zurenborg district

Both these parks, popular recreation areas for the people of Antwerp, are in Borgerhout, a district in the southern part of the suburb of Deurne where, every year in September, the "Parade of the Little Giants" is held, as it has been since 1712. (Location: suburb of Deurne, tram Nos. 8, 11).

Te Bolaerpark is planted with several rare species of tree and also has an arboretum.

The mansion belonging to Boekembergpark has been converted into a home for the elderly. The park itself boasts an intriguing natural history museum complete with fossil and mineral collections, all housed in an artifical grotto (open May–Sep. Sun. and public holidays 2–6pm).

Te Bolaerpark
Boekenbergpark

The 87 ha (215 acre) Rivierenhof, another park also in Deurne, possesses a large lake and open-air theatre. It is also noteworthy for the great size of some its trees. (Location: suburb of Deurne, tram: No. 10).

In the south-west corner of the park stands the Renaissance château Sterckshof, now the Provinciaal Museum voor Kunstambachten (Provincial Craft Museum). Among the items on display are furniture, silver- and glassware, costumes and the fittings from an old apothecary's shop (open Mar.–Nov. Tue.–Sun. 10am–5pm).

Rivierenhof and
Provinciaal
Museum
Sterckshof

Surroundings

Despite being situated in the shadow of a huge nuclear power station Doel (Bus No. 293), on the west bank of the Scheldt opposite Lillo, still retains something of the character of a Zeeland polder village. Protected from the Scheldt by a dyke Doel is the last community on the Belgian side of the border with Holland.

Old milling equipment can be seen in the windmill (1615) on the dyke.

Doel

Also close to the Dutch border, but in this case some 25 km (16 mi.) north of Antwerp near the small town of Kalmthout, the Kalmthoutser Heide nature reserve covers 732 ha (1800 acres) of dunes and heathland. Within the reserve Putse Moer is a breeding ground for gulls, woodcock, curlew and lapwing.

**★Kalmthoutser
Heide nature
reserve**

A great attraction for little travellers is the Children's Museum in Kalmthout. It is housed in the villa of comics artist Willy Vandersteen, the creator of the characters "Suske" and "Wiske".

Children's
Museum
Kalmthout

The Kempenland town of Brecht lies 18 km (11 mi.) north-east of Antwerp. The town's grammar school, founded by Jan de Coster (Johannes Custos) in 1515, grew to be a centre of humanist learning. Among its notable pupils was the Jesuit Lenaart Leys

Brecht

(Leonardus Lessius), a statue of whom stands beside the church. Brecht was also the birthplace of the great Netherlands Renaissance poet Jan Baptista van der Noot (Jonker Jan), born in 1540.

Sint-Michielskerk provides a fine example of Kempenland church architecture in the late Gothic period. Except for some Baroque sculptures, however, all the interior furnishings are modern.

The **Kempen Museum** (Mudaeusstraat 1–2) traces the history of the town and Kempenland, including a section devoted to the humanist tradition (open Apr.–Sep. every 3rd Sun. 2–6pm).

Hoogstraten

Hoogstraten, 6 km (4 mi.) north-east of Brecht, is famous for its vast strawberry fields.

Sint-Catharinenkerk was built in the 16th c. by Rombout Keldermans, its 105 m (345 ft) high tower making it a landmark for mi. around. The sixteen stained glass windows in the choir and transepts are by Bernard van Orley.
    Inside the church the splendid mausoleum of Antoon van Lalaing and his wife Elisabeth van Culembourg, a masterpiece of Renaissance sculpture by Jean Mone, stands out amongst the other tombs. The superb choir stalls with their life-like figures were the work of Albrecht Gelmers and date from between 1532 and 1548.

The small 15th c. **Begijnhof** (béguinage) is a secluded haven of tranquillity. Its Baroque church has a fine portal.
    Works by the Flemish painter Alfred Ost can be seen in the Alfred Ost Museum at No. 21.

Arlon · Aarlen   P 16

Province: Luxembourg
Altitude: 450 m (1475 ft.) Population: 23,000
Intercity Station

Situated in the far south-east corner of Belgium wedged between France and Luxembourg, Arlon (Flemish Aarlen) is one of the country's oldest towns. Now the capital of the Belgian province of Luxembourg, it lies on the plateau of the Ardennes at the intersection of two Roman roads, Reims to Trier and Tongeren to Metz. Having founded the settlement (Orolaunum), the Romans also later fortified it in the 3rd c. AD. The town is built on the slopes of a conical hill once topped by the castle of the counts of Arlon.

Among Arlon's special attractions is a drink called **Maitrank**, a traditional wine cup the origins of which can be traced to medieval Germany – to the monks of PrÅm Abbey in the Eifel who used to sweeten their wine with fruit or aromatic plants. The custom has survived and is celebrated annually at Arlon's Maitrank festival, held on the third or fourth Sunday in May.
    Arlon Maitrank is a Moselle wine flavoured with woodruff buds and fortified with brandy. It is served chilled, garnished with a slice of orange.

Grand'Place

The square known as the Grand'Place with its medieval cross, symbol of civic freedom, is the centre of the old part of Arlon.

Tour romaine

Reached by an alleyway leading off the south-east corner of the square, the Tour romaine (Roman tower) is a relic of the 3rd c. Roman ring walls. Today it is a museum (open daily except Sun. 9am–6pm).

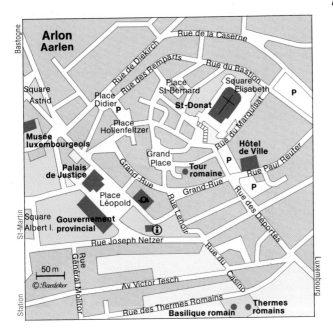

From the Grand'Place the road climbs to the top of the hill, where Saint-Donat's church now occupies the site of the counts of Arlon's medieval stronghold. Capuchin friars built a monastery on the ruins of the old castle in 1626, only for it to be converted into a fortress again by Louis XIV. The erstwhile chapel became a church in 1807, undergoing considerable alteration later in the 19th c.

Saint-Donat

On the west side of the hill stone steps lead up in an impressive arc to the church, and near their foot is a statue (1987) of the "Helleschman", an Arlon carnival figure. The interior of the church is embellished with 17th and 18th c. frescos of the life of St Donatus. There are also a number of other treasures well worth seeing.

The tower affords a splendid **panoramic view** encompassing four countries – France to the south, the Belgian Ardennes to the north and west, and to the east Luxembourg with Germany beyond.

Down the hill from Saint-Donat's, below the Grand'Place, Arlon's provincial government building (1845), Palais de Justice (1864) and main post office stand grouped around Place Léopold. At the southern corner of the square an American tank commemorates the liberation of the town by General Patton's forces in December 1944.

Place Léopold

Beyond Place Léopold, on the far side of Square Albert I, the 97 m (318 ft) tower of Saint-Martin's church (1907) rises high above the roofs of the new town.

Saint-Martin

Leaving the Place Léopold by the Rue des Faubourgs and turning left into the Rue des Martyrs leads us to Arlon's exceptionally interesting Musée Luxembourgeois, three rooms of which are taken up by a collection of Roman tombstones and sarcophagi unique in Belgium. Opening

★Musée Luxembourgeois

133

Saint-Donat and "Helleschman" monument

times Tue.–Sat. 9am–noon and 1.30–6pm; Sun. and public holidays 10am–noon and 2–6pm; closed Sun. and public holidays from 15 April to 15 September.

Particularly noteworthy among the sculptures are a relief showing travellers in the course of their journey (AD 170–180), statues of a divine horseman and various other gods, a satyr-decorated stele, and a large fragment found only recently, in 1980, carved with scenes from ancient mythology.

The room devoted to ceramics and Roman artefacts contains vases, glassware, bronzes, weaponry, etc.

There is much to see apart from the Roman finds. One room concentrates on the Merovingian period with a collection of weapons, Damascene work, glass and items of everyday use.

Folk art is also well represented, with displays of furniture and domestic items such as kitchen utensils and jewellery. Exhibits include some from the Luxembourg Ardennes and range in date from the Middle Ages to the recent past.

Among the museum's many examples of religious art the most notable is the Fisecne retable, made in Antwerp in the 16th c.

Thermal baths

Also part of the museum are the remains of a 1st c. AD Roman bathhouse in the Rue des Thermes Romains.

Basilique romaine

Next to the thermal baths lie the ruins of the oldest Christian church in Belgium, originally a Roman building converted in the 5th and 6th centuries into a basilica and around which, in the 6th and 7th centuries, the Franks buried their dead.

Surroundings

Just outside Arlon, to the south-east, is the little village of Weyler. Here, the Musée de la Bicyclette exhibits about 70 bicycles and other items connected with the history of the bike.

Weyler

Until the late 18th c. demand all over Europe for the iron smelted in its furnaces made Habay-la-Neuve, a small town 14 km (9 mi.) north-west of Arlon on the banks of the Rulles, a place of some importance. An abandoned iron works, the insignia of the master iron workers in the Church of Saint-Nicolas and a few castles in the wooded countryside, houses such as Château Pont d'Oye (1742), 2 km (1¼ mi.) east on the Martelange road, still testify to the prosperity of those days. Later, in the 19th c., the château was the meeting place of an intellectual circle which formed around the writer Pierre Nothomb. A good restaurant is based at the château.

Habay-la-Neuve

Ath · Aat   H 6/7

Province: Hainaut
Altitude: 30–75 m (98–246 ft)
Population: 24,000
Intercity and Inter-regional Station (bicycle rental at station)

The little town of Ath (Flemish Aat) situated at the confluence of the two rivers Dender (East and West), boasts some modest industry, mainly furniture manufacture and silk processing. In addition it serves as a market town for the surrounding villages. Ath's Parade of Giants – with the Wedding of Goliath one of the highlights – is among the oldest manifestations of this folk tradition in Belgium.

History The town was founded in the 12th c. when Baldwin IV, Count of Hainaut, purchased the title to the area. Because of its strategic importance he fortified it by building several castles, including one at Ath. War has principally shaped Ath's history ever since. Following capture by Louis XIV in 1667 it became the site of one of Vauban's earliest exercises in military engineering. Ironically enough it was the French who also later razed Vauban's fortifications during the War of Austrian Succession.
    The humanist scholar Justus Lipsius (1547–1606) was brought up in Ath.

In addition to the 17th c. town hall, built between 1614 and 1624 by Wenceslas Cobergher, a number of fine 18th c. houses line Ath's central Grand'Place. These include the Maison Espagnole, a reconstruction of an earlier house dating from 1564.

Grand'Place

The 23 m (75 ft) high Tour de Burbant (Burbant Tower) is a relic of Baldwin IV's original stronghold, built in 1168. Walls up to 3.7 m (12 ft) thick leave little room actually inside the tower. The rest of the castle was demolished in the 16th c., to be replaced by another in the 17th c.

Tour de Burbant

Reached via the main thoroughfare running through the market-place, the 12th c. church of Saint-Julien had to be substantially rebuilt after a fire. Standing out from the rest of the church today the sturdy tower (1462) with its four turrets and carillon of bells was one part of the building to survive.

Saint-Julien

The Musée du cercle royal d'histoire et d'archéologie in the Rue Bouchain is dedicated to the history of the region. Well worth seeing are

Museum

two paintings from the 14th and 16th c. respectively, both showing scenes of the Entombment.

Surroundings

Maffle

An old quarry near Maffle, 3 km (2 mi.) south-east of Ath, has been turned into the rather unusual Musée de la Pierre (open July and Aug. daily 2–5pm; Apr.–Jun. and Sep.–Oct. weekends 2.30–6.30pm).

★Château d'Attre

Built in the 18th c. for the Comte de Gomegnies, replacing a medieval castle, the Louis XV style Château d'Attre, situated 5 km (3 mi.) south-east of Ath, was a favourite with Maria Christina, daughter of Empress Maria Theresa of Austria and Governor of the South (Austrian) Netherlands. The château's interior furnishings are almost entirely original, providing a unique glimpse into the life of the aristocracy in the 18th c. The fine parquet floors are by Dewez and the stucco work in the great salon by the Italian Ferrari. The paintings include works by Snyders, Hubert Robert and Watteau ("Les plaisirs d'été"). The wall-coverings are a particularly noteworthy feature of the house. They exemplify the many different materials in vogue at the time, from rice-paper and Chinese silk to the painted wallpaper (1760) of the Archduke's salon, the first such paper to be used in Belgium (open Easter-end of June and Sep.-end of Oct. Sat., Sun. 10am–noon and 2–6pm; July and Aug. daily except Wed. 10am–noon and 2–6pm).

The château overlooks a **park** laid out in the English manner, through which flows the river Dender. In addition to ruins and e.g. a dovecot and bathing pavilions in the style of the period, there is also a curious 24 m (80 ft) high artificial hillock complete with grottoes and caves. This

Ath: Apse and tower of Saint-Julien

Gardens of the Château d'Attre

seems to have been intended partly as a vantage point for the Archduchess Maria Christina when out hunting.

Chièvres

Chièvres, another small town, 6 km (4 mi.) south-east of Ath, began as a Roman settlement, later being a possession of, among others, the Counts of Gavre, Egmont and Croy. In the Middle Ages Chièvres grew to some importance on account of its manufacturing but subsequently proved unable to compete with Ath. The late Gothic church beside the Tour de Gavre dates from this period of prosperity, as does the Hotel de Croy or "Maison Espagnole" (1560) in the Grand'Place, the residence at one time of Count Lamoraal van Egmont. The tombs of the Gavre, Croy and Egmont families can be seen in Saint-Martin's church, built in the 14th c. and renovated in the 16th c.

Not far outside Chièvres, on a farm estate in the valley of the Hunnelle, stands the even older Romanesque chapel of La Ladrerie. In the 12th c. it belonged to a hospice for lepers.

The airfield serving SHAPE, the NATO headquarters in nearby Casteau (see Mons), lies to the south-east of Chièvres.

Cambron-Casteau

Ruins are all that remain of the 12th c. abbey at Cambron-Casteau, 12 km (7½ mi.) south-east of Ath. The adjacent land on the banks of the Dender has been turned into a leisure park. "Paradiso", its main attraction being an ornithological park with more than 2500 species of birds. (Open Easter to November 10am–6pm)

Tongre-Notre-Dame

The church at Tongre-Notre-Dame, 6 km (4 mi.) south of Ath, owes its status as a pilgrim church to a Romanesque statue of the Virgin, said to have undergone a miraculous transformation in 1081.

See entry

Belœil

Bastogne · Bastenaken   N 16

Province: Luxembourg
Altitude: 515 m (1690 ft)
Population: 12,000
Local Rail Station (bicycle rental at station)

The small town of Bastogne (Flemish Bastenaken), known for its tasty smoked ham and its nuts, is situated on the plateau of the Ardennes not far from the Luxembourg border. Today the town's name is inseparably linked with the Battle of the Ardennes, the final German counter-offensive of the Second World War mounted late in 1944 and early 1945. The "Road to Freedom" (French "Voie de la Liberté") which, with its kilometre-stones, marks the route of the 1944 Allied advance from Normandy to near Bastogne, passes through the town.

History Bastogne's medieval fortress, strategically sited at the intersection of two great military roads (Reims to Cologne and Arlon to Tongeren), caught fire in the 13th c. and was eventually destroyed by the French in 1688.

On December 16th 1944 German forces launched their last great offensive of the Second World War in the Ardennes, with the intention of advancing on Antwerp. The initial swift German push succeeded in surrounding Bastogne, trapping US troops commanded by General McAuliffe. Called upon to surrender McAuliffe refused, holding out for a further four days. General Patton's tanks finally broke the German siege, so liberating Bastogne for the second time. The Battle of the Ardennes ended on January 25th 1945 with the Allies poised to advance into Germany.

Bastogne's town centre, the old Grand'Place, is now called **Place McAuliffe** in honour of the man who ended the German occupation. The events of those days are further commemorated by a US Sherman tank and a monument to the general, both of which stand in the southern corner of the square.

Musée original au pays d'Ardenne

The Musée original au pays d'Ardenne, just off the square, about 50 m (165 ft) along the Route de Neufchâteau, focuses on all the multifarious aspects of life in the Ardennes. As well as displays of farm implements and stuffed animals, etc. there are weapons and other equipment from the Battle of the Ardennes (open daily 10am–5pm; Jul. and Aug. 9am–6pm).

Monument Patton

A monument in the form of a relief dedicated to the US General Patton can be seen in the Rue Joseph Renquin, also quite near the square.

Saint-Pierre

The founding of the church of Saint-Pierre (Place Saint-Pierre) can be traced back to the 7th c., though nothing from that time survives. The tower of the present church dates from the 12th c. while the nave, damaged by fire in the 13th c., was later completed in the Meuse Gothic style in the 15th c.

The church interior has several interesting features, chief among which is the nave vaulting, colourfully decorated with scenes from the Old and New Testaments by Renadin de Wicourt. Also noteworthy are the Romanesque fonts, the 12th c. altar, and the Baroque pulpit by Georges Scholtus from Bastogne.

Porte de Trèves

The Porte de Trèves (Trèves Gate), a massive, square, sandstone tower near the church, is all that remains of Bastogne's late medieval ramparts razed by the French in 1688 (open Jul. and Aug. daily 9am–6pm).

Only a short distance from the church and gate, archaeological finds and other artefacts can be seen displayed in the Maison Mathelin, the town's historical and archaeological museum. Spanning a period from Gallo-Roman times, through the Middle Ages up to the Second World War, the collection covers the early as well as the modern history of Bastogne and the surrounding region. One section is specifically devoted to the rural life of the Ardennes (open Jul. and Aug. daily 9am–6pm).

Maison Mathelin

Housed in fifteen rooms of a 17th c. Bethlehemite monastery at Place Saint-Pierre 24, the rather unusual Musée en Piconrue is a celebration of popular religion in its various forms, including its expression in folk art (open: Mon.–Fri. 1.30–6pm, Sat., Sun. 10am–noon and 1.30–6pm).

Musée en Piconrue

American Memorial From Bastogne the kilometre-stones of the "Road to Freedom" lead 3 km (2 mi.) north-east to Mardasson Hill with its broad vista over the countryside around. Here in 1950 an impressive memorial was erected in honour of the US soldiers who lost their lives during the Battle of the Ardennes. Built in the shape of a five-pointed star the monument bears the names of the units which took part in the battle, as well as recording details of the principal events. The crypt, decorated with mosaics by Fernand Léger, contains three altars, one Catholic, one Protestant and one Jewish.

★Mardasson Hill

The Bastogne Historical Center describes itself as "the finest war museum in the world", a claim which some might feel to be somewhat less than justified. Like the nearby American Memorial, the Center is built in the shape of a five-pointed star. Presentation takes three different forms. The central display consists of an amphitheatre-like model of the battle illustrating the different phases of the action. This is surrounded by screens featuring authentic still photographs with

Bastogne Historical Center

Mardasson Hill: Monument for over 76,000 US soldiers

commentaries in six languages. Next come collections of weaponry, tanks, military vehicles and uniforms, all fully authentic, together with groups of uniformed figures representing the main protagonists.

Finally there is a cinema which shows films of the Ardennes offensive made by the two sides (open mid Feb.–May and Sep. daily 9.30am–5pm; Oct. daily 10am–4pm; Jul. and Aug. daily 9am–6pm).

Surroundings

The 6,785 German soldiers killed in the Ardennes lie buried in the German War Cemetery at **Recogne**, 6 km (4 mi.) north of Bastogne (see Practical Information, Military Cemeteries).

Beaumont   L 9

Province: Hainaut.
Altitude: 230 m (755 ft.) Population: 6000

Beaumont lies surrounded by woods on a hill above the river Hantes, close to the French border. As early as the 12th c. it was defended by a 2.4 km (1½ mi.) long wall with 30 towers, later demolished in the 16th c. During the 18th and 19th centuries the town experienced a modest upturn in fortune, boosted by its cloth industry.

The **Tour Salamandre** (Salamander Tower) on the southern edge of the hill is the main survival from the old ramparts. Built in the 16th c. it is now a museum, its five floors given over to documents and other items of local history as well as a display of regional arts and crafts. The former include memorabilia of Napoleon I (who made a stop here en route to Waterloo).

The top of the tower affords a lovely view of the Hainaut countryside. (Open May, June and Sep. daily 9am–5pm; Jul. and Aug. daily 10am–7pm; Oct. Sun. 10am–5pm.)

Montignies-Saint-Christophe

In Montignies-Saint-Christophe, 5 km (3 mi.) to the north-west, the Hantes is spanned by a 25 m (82 ft) bridge with thirteen arches. Lying as it does on the route of the Roman road to Trêves, the bridge is often referred to as a "pont romaine" (Roman bridge) but in fact almost certainly dates from the 15th c.

Solre-sur-sambre

Some 10 km (6 mi.) north-west of Beaumont, just off the road to Merbes-le-Château (which bypasses the village), the moated château at Solre-sur-Sambre is one of the less well-preserved of Hainaut's feudal castles. It is entered through the 13th–14th c. keep on either side of which high walls extend in a square with two round corner towers. The right-hand tower and knights' hall, the latter with a magnificent fireplace, are open to visitors (open daily 10am–noon and 2–6pm).

Sivry

Sivry's natural history and toy museum boasts a collection of more than 5,000 animal specimens, 11 km (7 mi.) south-west of Beaumont; open Mon.–Fri. 10am–5pm; Easter–Sep. also Sat., Sun. 2–6pm).

Rance

The area around Rance, a small town 12 km (7½ mi.) south of Beaumont, is noted for its red marble, Rance itself being the location of the **Musée National du Marbre** (National Marble Museum, Place Albert I).

Despite the dust and the appearance of chaos, the museum is unique and utterly fascinating, demonstrating the techniques of marble extraction and processing. The museum also maintains a collection of all the different kinds of marble found anywhere in the world (open Apr.–Oct. Mon.–Fri. 9.30am–6pm, Sun. and public holidays 2–6pm; Nov.–mid-Dec. and mid-Jan.–March Mon.–Fri. 8.30am–5pm).

Beaumont: Tour Salamandre   *Solre-sur-Sambre: the castle tower*

Beauraing

See Dinant, Surroundings

Belœil   J 6

Province: Hainaut
Altitude: 28 m (92 ft.) Population: 13,500

The little town of Belœil is situated about 30 km (19 mi.) north-west of
Mons (see entry). Belœil's Baroque château and park have the reputation
of being the finest of their kind in Belgium.

For almost seven hundred years the Château de Belœil (opening times   ★★Château de
Apr.–Nov. daily 10am–6pm) has been in the possession of the aristo-   Belœil
cratic de Ligne family. The most brilliant member of this noble line was
Charles-Joseph Lamoral, Prince de Ligne (1735–1814), diplomat, officer
in the Austrian army, writer, and friend of many of the great figures of
his time including Marie-Antoinette and Catherine the Great. Such was
his character he earned himself the sobriquet "Prince Charming".

In the 16th c., and in the 17th and 18th centuries in particular, the small
12th c. castle which originally stood on the site was progressively
altered to the taste of successive generations of the de Ligne family until
finally completely transformed. The main house burnt down in 1900,
being rebuilt in its present 18th c. style in 1920. Only the two free standing wings and the entrance pavilions survive substantially unchanged
from 1682. The latest in the long and distinguished line of the princes of
Ligne lives with his family in the left-hand wing.

The rooms of the château are **superbly furnished** with a wealth of period furniture, Gobelin tapestries, glass and porcelain, etc. belonging to the de Ligne family. Especially noteworthy are Prince Charles-Joseph's apartment with its series of paintings depicting episodes in his life, the Salle des Médailles with its valuable coin collection, the library which has over 20,000 volumes (including an hour-book dated 1532 and said to have belonged to Charles V), the dining-room hung with superb Gobelins, the Salon des Ambassadeurs with its magnificent painting by Canaletto ("Canale Grande in Venice"), and the Tour Maria-Antoinette where some locks of hair from the head of the French queen, executed in 1793, are preserved in a pouch knitted from gold yarn.

Precious items of religious art, e.g. coral sculptures and enamel work from Limoges, can be seen in the **chapel** created in 1950 in the right-hand wing.

The 120 ha (296 acre) **park** of Belgium's "Little Versailles" (opening times Apr.–Nov. daily 10am–6pm) was designed and laid out in the 18th c. by Prince Claude Lamoral II, with the aid of the French architect Chevotet. A series of small hedged gardens, several with pools, are arranged in typical Rococo fashion around the 460 m (1500 ft) long ornamental lake known as Le Grand Pièce d'Eau, at the far end of which stands a Neptune group by Henrion. The splendid 5 km (3 mi.) Allée Grande Vue extends beyond the boundaries of the park itself.

Jardins Anglais With English-style gardens very much in fashion at the end of the 18th c., Prince Charles-Joseph had one laid out to the side and rear of the left-hand wing. This part of the park remains private and is not open to the public.

In the park of the Château de Belœil

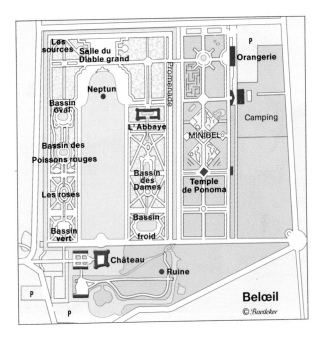

Beloeil
© Baedeker

Parcs des Attractions Some years ago various attractions were added, utilising land on the west side of the estate (orangery and kitchen garden). They include a restaurant, a children's playground, and "Park Minibel", a 1:25 scale reconstruction of some of Belgium's most famous sights and buildings – the Huy Collégiale, Liége railway station, Brussels Town Hall, the Bruges Belfry, Zeebrugge harbour, and much more. A miniature train ferries tourists between château and amusement area.

Beveren

See Sint-Niklaas, Surroundings

Binche   K 6

Province: Hainaut. Altitude: 110 m (360 ft)
Population: 32,600. Inter-regional Station

Situated between Charleroi and Mons (see entries) not far from the French border, Binche takes great pride in being the only town in Belgium – and indeed in the Netherlands – to retain intact a substantial proportion of its medieval ramparts including 27 towers. Now serving primarily as the market town for the surrounding region, little remains of Binche's once quite considerable textile industry apart from the manufacture of carnival costumes.

Throughout its long **history** those who have held the fate of Binche in

Carnival figures greet the visitor to Binche

their hands have frequently been women – Joanna of Constantinople, Margaret of York, and especially Mary of Hungary under whom the town enjoyed its heydey. Mary, sister of the Emperor Charles V, played host to her brother, his son Philip and the flower of Europe's nobility at a great celebration held at her Renaissance palace in 1549. Only five years later Binche was occupied by troops of the French King Henry II and the palace was destroyed. Apart from the 19th c. when it had a thriving textile industry, the town has remained something of a backwater ever since.

Once a year, however, Binche reclaims its place in the national limelight with the holding of its **carnival**, probably the most famous event of its kind in Belgium. Hundreds of "Gilles" (carnival jesters) in brightly coloured costumes dance in the streets. This custom may in part have originated with the great fête organised by Mary of Hungary in 1549 for Charles V in celebration of Pizarro's conquest of Peru, when many of those attending were dressed as Incas. The carnival itself is older, however, being mentioned in documents from as early as the 14th c., while the figure of the "Gille" goes back only to the 18th c.

Hôtel de Ville

The Hôtel de Ville (Town Hall) in the Grand'Place is emblazoned with the coats of arms of Charles V and Mary of Hungary as well as those of the town itself. The belfry has a carillon of 27 bells.

Town walls

To the right of the town hall a narrow alleyway joins a path running along the old town walls as far as Rue de Posty. This latter in turn leads up to the Rue Haute.

Chapelle Saint-André

On the left-hand side of the Rue Haute stands the Chapelle Saint-André

(1537). Inside the chapel the heads of the rafters are interestingly carved, two with scenes from a Dance of Death.

At the end of the street the large votive church of Saint-Ursmer (12th–15th c.) has a very fine Renaissance gallery directly behind the main portal. Noteworthy in the interior are a wooden pietà dated 1511 and a 15th c. polychrome Entombment.

Chapelle Saint-Ursmer

Mary of Hungary's palace once occupied the site behind the church, now a park. The bronze statue at the entrance is of a carnival "Gille".

Housed in a former Augustinian monastery immediately adjacent to the church, the Musée international du Carnaval et du Masque (International Museum of Carnival and Mask) is surely unrivalled anywhere. Its collection comprises some 15,000 costumes, masks and other carnival items, and the museum features carnival customs from all over the world.

★ Musée international du Carnaval et du Masque

The first floor concentrates on costumes and masks from European countries, ranging from Russia to Italy and from the Balkans to the extreme north. The comprehensiveness of the collection can be judged from its inclusion of, e.g. masks from the Swabian–Alemannic shrovetide carnival. The second floor focuses on the carnival traditions of Africa, America, Asia and Oceania, many of whose customs are quite different from those of Europe. The story of Binche's own carnival is told on film in a special display hall (open Mon.–Thu. and Sun. 9.30am–12.30pm and 1.30–6pm; Sat. 1.30–6pm only).

Surroundings

About 12 km (7½ mi.) north of Binche the Canal du Centre passes by the industrial town of La Louvière. Although the town itself has little to offer in the way of sights, anyone with an interest in industrial archaeology should make a point of visiting it, if only to see the four ★ hydraulic barge lifts on the canal at Houdeng Goegnies and Bracquenies on the outskirts. These steel monsters were constructed between 1888 and 1917 to overcome a height difference of 68 m (225 ft) in the space of just 7 km (4 mi.). Although the four lifts have been replaced by the modern hydraulic-lift locks at Strépy-Thieu, but they have been declared a World Cultural Heritage Sight by UNESCO and are therefore saved.

La Louvière

One of the best ways of seeing the locks in operation is by taking a **boat trip** on the canal (from Bracquenies, Rue Noulet). If a more leisurely kind of canal excursion is prefered, there are also rides aboard an old horse-drawn barge (from the "Cantine italien").

Museums Near lock No. 1 (Houdeng Goegnies, Rue Tout-y-Faut) an exhibition of models and photographs has been set up under the title "Ship-lifts of the World", illustrating the history of these and other similar installations around the world.

The industrial history of the area more generally is also explained in the "Cantine italien" close by. Lastly, all the different kinds of craft used on the inland waters of Wallonia can be seen in the open-air museum on the Canal du Centre quay at 120 Rue G. Boel (opening times for all the museums: May–Jun., Sep. daily 10am–4pm; Jul. and Aug. until 6pm).

In the suburb of Bois-du-Lac, south of Houdeng-Goignies, the Mining Museum highlights the life of the miners of the region (open Mon.–Fri. 9am–noon and 1–5pm; Sat., Sun. and public holidays 2–5pm).

A detour west of La Louvière to the enormous, modern ★ **hydraulic-lift locks** at Strépy-Thieu provides an interesting comparison with the old barge locks. The new locks overcome a difference in level of 73 m (240 ft) (open daily 10am–6pm).

Strépy-Thieu

★★Domaine de Mariemont

Situated near the village of Morlanwelz about 8 km (5 mi.) from Binche, the Domaine de Mariemont is named after Mary of Hungary who built a hunting lodge there in 1546. Eight years later the lodge was to suffer the same fate at the hands of the French as Mary's palace in Binche. The Austrian Archdukes Albert and Isabella rebuilt and enlarged it, only for French revolutionaries to set fire to the palace again in 1794. Later, one of the administrators of Mariemont, Nicolas Warocqué, acquired part of the estate, and in 1831 built himself a small château. This was subsequently expanded by Warocqué's grandson Raoul in order to house his extensive private art collection. In 1960, however, the greater part of this château was also burnt down and since 1975 the art collection has occupied a modern purpose-built museum.

The museum and palace ruins are set in an English-style **park** adorned with some very fine sculptures. These include several works by the Belgian sculptor Victor Rousseau, as well as Auguste Rodin's "The Burghers of Calais".

The first floor of the new **museum** building designed by Roger Bastin contains extensive collections of Egyptian, Greek and Roman antiquities as well as precious jade and lacquer work from China and Japan. On the lower ground floor there are archaeological finds from Gallo-Roman and Merovingian times, although the most exciting section here is the extraordinary collection of Tournai porcelain with pieces representing four stylistic periods from between 1750 and 1799 (open Tue.–Sun. 10am–6pm).

The museum also has a library with some very valuable manuscripts and other items.

Abbaye de Bonne-Espérance

The Abbaye de Bonne-Espérance, just 4 km (2½ mi.) south of Binche near the village of Vellereille-les-Brayeux, was founded in the 12th c. by Premonstatensian friars. Apart from its 15th c. Gothic tower, however, the present church is largely 18th c., the work of Laurent Dewez. Many visitors are drawn to the Abbaye by a reputedly miraculous statue of the smiling Madonna and Child (stone, 14th c.). The cloisters adjacent to the church also date principally from the 18th c., though one or two arches are survivals from the 13th c.

Blankenberge

C 4

Province: West-Vlaanderen. Altitude: sea level
Population: 17,000. Intercity Station

Seaside resort Blankenberge, with its 3 km (2 mi.) stretch of beach on Belgium's North Sea coast, first began to attract holidaymakers as long ago as 1860. Despite having been somewhat eclipsed of late by Knokke-Heist (see entry), it remains one of the country's best known seaside resorts, popular especially with families and offering a wide range of sporting and leisure activities. Today the tourists who throng the town in summer are the primary source of income, the small fishing fleet contributing only modestly to the economy; the old fishing harbour has been converted to a marina.

The very colourful **flower parade** held annually on the last Sunday in August always attracts many visitors.

Kerkstraat, Blankenberge's main thoroughfare, runs past the station, lined with shops and restaurants. Steps at its northern end lead up to the Zeedijk. No. 31 Kerkstraat, the former town hall built in 1680, is used for art exhibitions.

Blankenberge: the beach

Opposite the station stands the Gothic Sint-Antoniuskerk, first consecrated in 1358. Restored in the 17th c. its furnishings are mainly 18th c. pieces.

Sint-Antoniuskerk

Majuttehuis, in the Breydelstraat, a little to the west of Casinoplein, is now the only survivor from among Blankenberge's once numerous fishermans' cottages.

Majuttehuis

Two monuments adorn the **Grote Markt**, one a memorial to the writer Hendrik Conscience, the other a war memorial.

Further west lies a modern yacht **marina**, its entrance protected from silting by a 300 m (990 ft) long pile breakwater. There are berths for 900 boats.

Blankenberge's promenade, the more than 2 km (1¼ mi.)-long Zeedijk, runs along the seafront 10 m (30 ft) above the level of the beach. Interspersed with somewhat unattractive modern hotels, restaurants, cafés and shops, are one or two pleasing older buildings from the town's early days, as well as a number of villas.

★Zeedijk

Ever since its opening in 1933 the "Lustige Velodroom", a "fun" cycling track at the eastern end of the promenade, has been one of the resort's most popular attractions.

Also at the eastern end of the Zeedijk is a 350 m (1140 ft) long seaside pier with an excellent "Aquarama" spotlighting the coast's marine life.

The cinema, located just before the steps up from Kerkstraat, was built in 1932; the Kursaal, just after the steps, once housed Blankenberge's first casino. This is also where you can find the most recent addition to Blankenberge's attractions: Reptile Land, opened in 1998.

4 km (2½ mi.) east of Blankenberge, is a small seaside resort, considerably more sedate in atmosphere than its larger neighbour.

Wenduine

Extending all the way along the coast between Blankenberge and Zeebrugge (see entry), the **Fonteintjes dunes** offer excellent walking.

Bokrijk (Provincial)

See Hasselt, Surroundings

Bouillon   O 13

Province: Luxembourg. Altitude: 221 m (725 ft.) Population: 5,000

Location In the south of the Belgian province of Luxembourg, close to the French border, Bouillon nestles prettily in a loop of the River Semois, encircled by the wooded heights of the southern Ardennes. Dominated by its imposing castle, the small town is a popular summer resort and makes a lively centre for excursions into the surrounding countryside.

Bouillon is closely linked in name and by history with Godfrey of Bouillon (Godefroy de Bouillon), the "most Christian of all knights".

Because of its favoured location Bouillon, principal town of the old Duchy of Lower Lotharingia, was for hundreds of years an important link between the Eifel and Champagne. It began life as a village which grew up in the shadow of Godfrey the Bearded's castle (started 1050). When, almost half a century later, the famous Godfrey of Bouillon left home to lead the First Crusade (1095), he mortgaged the castle to the Prince-Bishops of Liège who retained it, with one or two interruptions and in the face of challenges to their title by local noblemen, until the 17th c. After the French took over the region in 1676, Louis XIV gave the castle to the La Tour d'Auvergne family. Under their liberal patronage Bouillon developed in the 18th c. into a centre of Enlightenment where the printer Pierre Rousseau was able to publish numerous avant-garde journals, as well as works by Mirabeau and Diderot which had been banned in France. The town eventually became part of Belgium in 1830.

Bouillon

100 m

© Baedeker

Dinant

Rue G. Lorand

Blvd Heynen

Rue des Augustins

Blvd Heynen

Semois

Rue du Château

Hôtel de Ville

Pt. de Liège

Musée Ducal

Pt. de la Poulie

Château Fort

Rue du Moulin

Semois

Quai du Hennart

Quai des Saulx

Rue de Collège

Porte de France

Pt. de France

Arlon

★★Château Fort
Starting at the lower bridge, the Pont de Liège or Vieux-Pont, go along the left bank of the river past the church and up to the castle square from where there are some fine views. To the right is the entrance to the Château Fort (Fortified Castle), enthroned on its elevated "island" of rock overlooking the looping Semois on two sides. Built by Godfrey the Bearded between 1050 and 1067 on the remains of a still older fortress, the

148

Approaching the Château Fort of Bouillon

Château is the earliest and best preserved example of medieval feudal architecture in Belgium. After Louis XIV's troops had taken over the castle, the fortifications were strengthened by Vauban. Further alterations were also made during the Dutch period.

Tour The castle, which contains some fine paintings, is entered over three drawbridges. The main courtyard then leads to the ducal palace with its 13th c. Salle Godefroy de Bouillon. From there visitors climb up to the top of the 16th c. Tour d'Autriche for a breathtaking panorama of the town and river, before making their way back via the torture chamber, cisterns and dungeons, and past the 65 m (213 ft) deep well shaft (open Jan., Feb. and Dec. Mon.–Fri. 1–5pm; Sat. and Sun. 10am–5pm; Mar., Oct., Nov. daily 10am–5pm; Apr.–Jun., Sep. daily 10am–6pm; Jul., Aug. Mon. and Thu. 9.30am–7pm; other days 9.30am–10pm).

The Musée Ducal (Ducal Museum), in a delightful 18th c. town house below the north side of the castle square, has a refreshingly old-fashioned charm. The section on local history and folklore includes displays of craftwork, old furniture and kitchen fittings as well as memorabilia relating to Bouillon's noble families and the printer Pierre Rousseau. There is also a section entitled "Godefroy de Bouillon" which, being devoted principally to the First Crusade, has among its exhibits some exceptionally lovely examples of Islamic craftsmanship. Works by the painter Albert Raty are exhibited in two side rooms (open Apr.–Jun. daily 10am–6pm; Jul., Aug. daily 9.30am–7pm; Oct. daily 10am–5pm; Nov., Dec. Sat. and Sun. 10am–5pm).

Musée Ducal

An attractive **riverside promenade** with a good selection of restaurants, cafés and shops follows the bend in the River Semois. Several establishments have rowing boats and pedallos for rental.

Archéoscope
Godefroy de
Bouillon

On the other side of the river, in a former monastery of the 17th c., the Archéoscope Godefroy de Bouillon has been erected. Great technological wizardry, including the sudden appearance from the mists of a model of the fortress, the time of the first crusade is brought to life (open Jan. Sat. and Sun. 10am–4pm; Feb. and Dec. additionally Tue.–Fri. 1–4pm; Mar./Apr. daily 10am–4pm; May/Jun. and Sep. until 5pm; Jul./Aug. until 6pm; Oct./Nov. daily except Mon. until 4pm).

Surroundings

Picturesquely situated on the right bank of the Semois, the **Abbaye de Cordemoy** (Notre-Dame de Clairefontaine) is reached by taking the tunnel under the castle hill from the Porte de France, crossing the old Pont de Poulie and continuing westwards for about 3 km (2 mi.). Founded in the 13th c. the abbey was burned down in 1794 and acquired its present Neo-Gothic character when last rebuilt in 1935.

More trips around
Bouillon

See Vallée de la Semois

Brecht

See Antwerp, Surroundings

Breendonk (Fort)

See Mechelen, Surroundings

Bruges · Brugge   D 4

Province: West-Vlaanderen
Altitude: 9 m (30 ft). Population: 116,500
Intercity Station (bicycle rental at station)

Bruges (Flemish Brugge, French Bruges), the old capital of Flanders and an archbishopric since 1559, is located on the little river Reie 12 km (7½ mi.) south of the port of Zeebrugge (see entry) to which it is linked by the Boudewijn-Kanaal. Other canals connect Bruges with Ostende, Nieuwpoort, Veurne, Ghent (see entries) and Sluis (Holland).
  Despite the addition of new building and the loss of its old town walls (all but four towers having been demolished since the mid 19th c. to make way for traffic), Bruges with its perfectly preserved medieval town centre remains a tourist dream, a magnet drawing more than two million visitors a year. But the town does have thriving industries as well – steel works, calico mills, furniture factories, breweries, gin (jenever) distilleries, prefabricated cement works and yeast, paint, television set and outboard engine manufacturers. Bobbin lace, for which Bruges has long been famous, continues to be important. Complementing all this industry is a strong service sector which makes a significant contribution to the local economy. The chief commodities passing through the port of Zeebrugge – the second largest fishing port in Belgium – are crude oil, coal, iron ore, packaged goods and meat.
  In addition to its Academy of Fine Arts and its Chamber of Commerce and Industry, Bruges is also proud to play host to the College of Europe.

Festivals Bruges's major festival is the annual Procession of the Holy Blood, celebrated in May. The superb historical Pageant of the Golden Tree which commemorates the marriage in 1468 of Charles the Bold and Margaret of York takes place every fifth year (the next being in 1996).

Every 3 years in August (the next time is 1998) the Canal Festival features historical scenes acted out against the backdrop of Bruges' illuminated canals.

History Surprisingly little is known about the early history of Bruges. There is mention of a "Municipium Brugense" in documents dating from the 7th c. but the name itself seems to have originated with the Vikings who landed at the mouth of the Reie ("bruggja" = place of embarkation). Rather more certain is that Baldwin I (Iron Arm), who died about 879 and who was the founder of the powerful dynasty of Flemish counts and a son-in-law of Charles the Bald of France, built himself a castle here. Trade gradually flourished until Robert the Frisian (died 1093) made the town his capital.

Cosmopolitan medieval city During the 12th and 13th centuries, when still linked by the Reie to the North Sea via the inlet known as the Zwin, Bruges evolved into one of the principal trading cities of the medieval world. Banking and commercial houses representing seventeen different nations became established in the city, trading in commodities as various as fabrics from Italy and the Orient, fish from Scandinavia, furs from Russia, wine from Spain and spices from Arabia. As the headquarters of the "Flemish Hanse in London" Bruges held a virtual monopoly of trade with England, including the wool trade so vital to the Flemish cloth industry. At the same time it served as the commercial entrepot for the cities of the German Hanseatic League. The city reached a pinnacle of prosperity in the 14th c. when work began on building the town walls. Its wealth at that time can be judged from the remark attributed to Joanna of Navarre, wife of Philip the Fair of France. Arriving in Bruges in 1301 and catching sight of the burghers' wives with their sumptuous clothes and unmistakable trappings of luxury, she is said to have exclaimed indignantly: "I thought I was the only queen, but here I am surrounded by hundreds".

"Bruges Matins" In the 13th c. passions in the rich Flemish cities were inflamed by disputes between the francophile "Leliaerts" (so-called after the French Lily) and the "Clauwaerts" (after the claws of the Flemish lion), the latter being determined to maintain their traditional independence from France. Exploiting this dissension the French king Philip the Fair seized control of Flanders, appointing Jacques de Châtillon governor. Châtillon's suppression of the Bruges guilds was so harsh that on the night of May 17th-18th 1302 the inhabitants rose up in a revolt known as "the Bruges Matins". Led by Pieter de Coninck and Jan Breydel they put to the sword anyone suspected of being French. In the same year an army of Flemish burghers triumphed over the French nobility at the Battle of the Golden Spurs near Kortrijk, ensuring thereby the continued independence and success of the Flemish cities.

Decline The fruits of victory over the French were dissipated, however, by growing rivalry between Bruges and Ghent. Partly for this reason, but mainly due to the silting up of the Zwin, in the 15th c. Bruges's fortunes fell into decline. At first the signs of impending disaster remained obscured by the outward brilliance of the city under by the Dukes of Burgundy, rulers of the County of Flanders since 1384. The marriages of Philip the Good to Isabella of Portugal in 1430 and of Charles the Bold to Margaret of York in 1468 were both celebrated with great splendour in Bruges. But from 1500 onwards the city's wealthy merchants gradually forsook Bruges for Antwerp and the religious turmoil of the second half of the 16th c. finally brought the era of prosperity to an end.

Recent revival It was only in the 19th c. that the city roused itself again from the long period of dormancy vividly described by Georges Rodenbach in his melancholy novel "Bruges la Morte". The construction

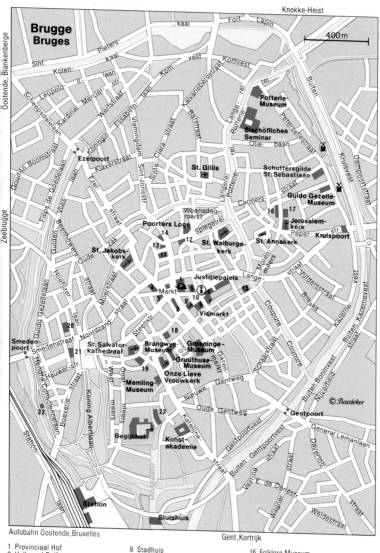

Bruges · Brugge

1 Provinciaal Hof	8 Stadhuis	16 Folklore Museum
2 Halls and Belfry	9 Heiligbloedkapel	17 Kantcentrum
3 Huis Bouchoute	10 Burg	18 Hof van Watervliet
4 Craenenburg	11 Schouwburg	19 Bisschopspaleis
5 Former Provost's House	12 Oud Tolhuis	20 Blindenkapel
6 Oude Griffie	13 Geneose Lodge	21 Waterhuis
7 Paleis van het	14 Huis ter Beurze	22 "Straffe Hendrik" Brewery
Brugse Vrije	15 Pelicaanhuis	

of the Boudewijn-Kanaal in 1907 gave renewed access to the sea, leading, especially after the Second World War, to the siting of major industries along the waterway. Then an ambitious restoration programme was undertaken, rescuing much of the town centre from dereliction.

Old Flemish paintings in Bruges Bruges was the centre of the Old Flemish School of painters. Here Jan van Eyck painted his famous "Adoration of the Mystic Lamb", the centrepiece of the polyptych for Sint-Baafskathedraal in Ghent, and near here Hugo van der Goes (1440–82), a native of Ghent, lived and died, leaving one of his most famous works "The Death of the Virgin" to the city. Together with van Eyck's "Madonna and the donor, Canon van der Paele", it now hangs in the Groeninge Museum.

The painter most closely associated with Bruges, however, is Hans Memling (1435–94). Born in Seligenstadt he settled in the town from 1465 onwards. Some of his greatest works can be seen in the Memling Museum housed in the 12th c. Sint-Jansspitaal. Gerard David (1460–1523), a pupil of Memling's, came to Bruges in 1483. Fine pictures by him and by Pieter Pourbus from Gouda can also be seen in the Groeninge Museum.

Townscape With its wealth of interesting old buildings and its canals Bruges still retains a medieval air, more so perhaps than anywhere else in Belgium. Anyone taking a walk through the narrow streets or a boat trip on the canals falls immediately under its spell, charmed by the atmosphere of what is for many the most delightful of all the cities of Flanders. This together with its remarkable state of preservation makes Bruges a tourist destination almost without rival in Europe.

The style of the medieval brick houses is thoroughly distinctive. Above many of the windows are recessed shallow arches, and the windows themselves are often found bracketed together by a continuous sill running the length of the frontage.

Equally distinctive of Bruges are the godshuizen, almhouses for the elderly and infirm paid for by the guilds or in some cases prosperous burghers. Most are groups of whitewashed brick houses with a communal entrance gate and janitor's window. Examples can be seen in e.g. Gloeribusstraat, Moerstraat, Zwarte Leertouwersstraat, Sint-Katelijnstraat and Nieuwe Gentweg. The Folklore Museum, the Kant Centre (Lace Centre) and the Pelicaanhuis are also former godshuizen.

The loveliness of Bruges today is the result of a massive **programme of restoration**. The first and most pressing problem was to deal with the sewage and other effluent which flowed untreated into the canals, creating a smell obnoxious enough to spoil any stay.

Thanks to the construction of a proper sewage system and efficient purification plant the canals are now clean and free of smell. The task of saving the houses from crumbling into ruin also called for radical measures. Most of the 8000 buildings in the city centre were taken into civic ownership, responsibility for their restoration being placed on the shoulders of the municipal authorities. Few houses now remain in private hands, the vast majority being leased to their occupants.

What to see Because the centre of Bruges is comparatively small, even those with only a day to spend looking around can expect to take away a good idea of all the major sights. Essential viewing includes the Markt with the Belfry, the Burg and Stadhuis, Onze Lieve Vrouwekerk, the Memling Museum, the picturesque Minnewater, and the Béguinage. A trip on the grachten (canals) is a never-to-be-forgotten experience.

Having two days available for sightseeing allows the pleasures of the city to be complemented by those of its museums, with visits to, for example, the Gruuthusemuseum, the Groeninge Museum, the Chapel of

Bruges: one of the canals in the city

the Holy Blood, or any of several more. The descriptions below are intended to be of help in making a choice.

The **tours of the grachten** (canals) last half an hour, passing under bridges so low that passengers must duck their heads and with one delightful view following another. Boats leave from the landing stages at Huidenvetterplein, Rozenhoedkaai and at the Dijver (Gruuthuse Palace).

Town tours and guided walks The Bruges Tourist Office organises minibus tours but it is more fun to take one of the horse-drawn carriages starting from the Burg (except on Wed. morning from the Markt). Tours last ½ hr and include a short stop at the Béguinage.

Parking Avoid driving right into the centre of Bruges unless it is absolutely essential. Park your car off the Ringlaan (Ring Road) near the railway station or in one of the underground car parks in the town. The underground car park below t'Zand on the south-western perimeter of the city centre is a convenient place to leave a car.

An ideal way of seeing the town is by **bicycle**. You can hire a bicycle at the railway station or from one of the cycle rental companies in the town.

Between the Markt and the Burg

★★Markt

The Markt is Bruges's main square and traffic hub at the very heart of the city. Surrounded on all sides by fine buildings from a variety of different periods it also boasts a large monument erected in 1887 to the guildmasters Jan Breydel and Pieter de Coninck who led the rebellion against the French in 1302.

The Halle, begun in 1248 and twice enlarged, first in the 14th c. and then again in the 16th c., occupies the south side of the Markt, a large rectangular brick building 85 m (278 ft) long and 43.5 m (142 ft) wide enclosing a picturesque courtyard. It was once Bruges's main market and the city fathers used to promulgate their statutes from the balcony above the entrance, reading them out to the populace assembled beneath.

★Halle and
★★Belfry

Above the Halle soars Bruges's most distinctive landmark the Belfry, 83 m (272 ft) high and with a slight lean towards the south-east. It is one of the finest bell towers in Belgium and there can surely be few more impressive symbols of civic pride. Work started on the tower in 1282, the crowning octagonal upper section being completed two centuries later (in 1482). A carillon of 47 bells hangs in the tower (chimes: mid Jun.–Sep. Mon., Wed. and Sat. 9–10am, Sun. 2.15–3pm; Oct.–mid Jun. Wed., Sat. and Sun. 2.15–3pm). The tower is entered from the inner courtyard of the Halle and the top (366 steps) affords a superb panorama of the town and surrounding countryside. On the way up the old Treasure Room where civic documents are kept behind wrought-iron grills can be visited on the second floor (open Apr.–Sep. daily 9.30am–5pm; Oct.–Mar. daily 9.30am–12.30pm and 1.30–5pm).

The east side of the Markt is dominated by the Neo-Gothic Provinciaal Hof (1887–1921), seat of the West-Vlaanderen provincial government. Adjacent to it on the south side is the post office. Until the end of the 18th c. cloth halls dating back to the 13th c. stood on both sites. The cloth stored in them was brought into the city by water, the Reie at that time flowing close by.

Provinciaal Hof

Over on the west side of the Markt the attractive brick 15th c. Huis Bouchoute occupies the left-hand corner of Sint-Amandstraat. On the opposite corner stands the Craenenburg where, in 1488, at the instiga-

Craenenburg and
Huis Bouchoute

Huis Bouchoute and the Craenenburg

tion of Ghent, the burghers of Bruges kept the future Habsburg Emperor Maximilian imprisoned for eleven weeks. He was freed only after agreeing to respect the authority of the ruling Regency Council and to order the withdrawal of all foreign troops.

★★Burg

From beside the Halle Breidelstraat leads eastwards to the square known as the Burg. Encircled by some of the finest buildings in Bruges it takes its name from the former Grafenburg, the original seat of the Counts of Flanders built by Baldwin Iron Arm but demolished in 1434.

Proosdij

The corner of the Burg and Breidelstraat was once the site of Sint-Donaas, a cathedral church of Carolingian origin, built in 900. The lovely Baroque building standing there today is the former Provost's House (1665–66), the cathedral itself having been demolished in 1799. A few remnants of the walls of the choir are still visible in the garden adjacent to the house.

Paleis van het Brugse Vrije

Across on the east side of the square the Bruges Tourist Office occupies part of what was, up until 1984, the Law Courts, built between 1722 and 1727 on the site of the former Paleis van het Brugse Vrije (Liberty of Bruges) from where independent magistrates exercised jurisdiction over the country area around Bruges. Some fragments of the older building have survived, including the pretty 16th c. façade overlooking the canal at the rear. One or two of the more historic rooms now make up the Brugse Vrije Museum (open Apr.–Sep. daily 9.30am–12.30pm and 1.15–5pm; Oct.–Mar. daily 9.30am–12.30pm and 1.15–2pm.).

In the Schepenzaal ("vierschaar" or lay magistrates court) can be seen the famous **chimneypiece** (1529) designed by the painter Lanceloot Blondeel and executed in black marble and oak by Guyot de Beaugrant and others, a magnificent piece of Renaissance craftsmanship which in the imaginative quality of its ornamentation anticipates Baroque art. Above an alabaster frieze depicting the story of Suzanna and the Elders are carved oak figures of the Emperor Charles V and his parents, Ferdinand and Isabella of Castille, Mary of Burgundy and Maximilian. The hand holds were for the magistrates' use while drying their boots.

★Civiele Griffie

To the right of the Paleis van het Brugse Vrije stands the Civiele Griffie (Old Recorder's House). Richly decorated in gold and adorned with statues it was built between 1534–37 in typical Renaissance style.

★Stadhuis

On the south-east side of the square the Stadhuis is one of the oldest town halls in the Netherlands, having been constructed between 1376 and 1420. The façade of the delicate Gothic building displays the strong vertical emphasis characteristic of the style, with tall Gothic arched windows and pointed towers. Statues of the counts of Flanders from Baldwin Iron Arm onwards fill the 49 niches.

Inside are two rooms which should not be missed: the great Gothic Hall on the first floor with its beauti-

The City Hall

ful timber vaulting (1402) and its murals recording events in the town's history by A. and J. de Vriendt (1895–1900); and the Historical Room containing documents which again relate to the history of Bruges (open Apr.–Sep. daily 9.30am–5pm; Oct.–Mar. 9.30am–12.30pm and 2–5pm).

In the southern corner of the square, to the right of the town hall and adjacent to it, stands the two-storeyed Heiligbloedbasiliek (Basilica of the Holy Blood). Kept inside the church is a crystal phial reputed to contain a drop of Christ's blood brought back from the Holy Land by Dietrich of Alsace in 1149 on his return from the Second Crusade. From this has originated the traditional Procession of the Holy Blood when each year in May the sacred relic is carried through the streets of Bruges.

★ Heiligbloed-basiliek

The façade of the basilica with its three Flamboyant-style arches and gilded statues was erected between 1529 and 1534. The basilica itself consists of a Romanesque lower chapel and late Gothic upper chapel. The lower chapel (1149) houses relics of St Basil brought from Palestine by Robert II, Count of Flanders. A Romanesque tympanum depicts the saint's baptism. An elegant spiral staircase leads to the upper chapel (1480) where every Friday the phial containing the Holy Blood is brought out and shown to the faithful. The windows, copies of the originals from the 15th c., show the Counts of Flanders. Next to the upper chapel a small museum has been established, its most precious possession being the reliquary (1614–17) in which the Holy Blood is borne through the streets. Among the 15th and 16th c. paintings beside the reliquary are two wings of a triptych by Pieter Pourbus showing members of the Brotherhood of the Holy Blood (open Apr.–Sep. daily 9.30am–noon and 2–6pm; Oct–Mar. daily, except Wed. afternoon, 10am–noon and 2–4pm).

To the left of the Stadhuis **Blinde Ezelstraat** passes under a pretty Renaissance arch between the town hall and the Civiele Griffie before crossing Blinde Ezelbrug to the **Vismarkt** (1821). Here each morning (6am–1pm) from Tuesday to Saturday fishmongers sell their wares laid out on stone counters.

Running alongside the Reie are Steenhouwersdijk and Groene Rei, two streets lined with picturesque buildings. Note in particular the rear façade of the Palais de Justice and also Pelicaanhuis.

Pelicaanhuis

From the Vismarkt cross Huidenvetterplaats (Tanners' Square) with its guild-house dating from 1630, to Rozenhoedkaai, one of the departure points for boat trips on the canals. From Rozenhoedkaai an exceptionally **fine view** is obtained of the old houses bordering the canal, with the Belfry rising high above the rooftops in the background.

Rozenhoedkaai

Dijver to Minnewater

Skirting the south bank of the canal beyond Rozenhoedkaai is the tree-lined quay known as the **Dijver**. One of the row of superb old patrician houses (No. 11) is now occupied by the College of Europe, a post-graduate institute for the study of greater European integration.

To the left of No. 12 Dijver an entrance leads from the quay to the Groeninge Museum (Stedelijk Museum voor Schone Kunst) tucked away behind. In addition to its excellent endowment of Old Flemish paintings the museum incorporates a gallery of modern art and a superb collection of views of old Bruges. Open Apr.–Sep. daily 9.30am–5pm; Oct.–Mar. daily except Tue. 9.30am–12.30pm and 2–5pm.

★★ Groeninge Museum

The first five rooms of the museum are the ones most likely to claim the visitor's attention, however, containing as they do some quite exceptional paintings by **Old Flemish masters**.

Groeninge Museum

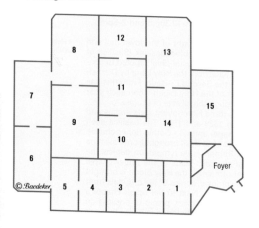

1–5 Flemish painting 15th c.

6 Mannerism, Jan Provoost, Lancelot Blondeel, south Netherlands painting 16th c.

7 Pieter and Frans Pourbus, Marcus Gerards

8 Jacob van Oost, 17th c. painting in Brugge

9 Flemish and Dutch historical painting, 17th and 18th c. chef d'œuvres

10 Classicism in Brugge

11 Romantic and Realist genre painting, Symbolism

12 19th c. landscape painting

13–14 Fauvism, Flemish Expressionism, Surrealism

15 Art since 1945

In Room 1 hang two major works by Jan van Eyck: "Madonna and the donor, Canon van der Paele" (1436) and the portrait of Margarete van Eyck, the artist's wife, painted when she was 33 years of age (1439). Both illustrate the extraordinary realism of his style. Room 3 has paintings by Hugo van der Goes ("Death of the Virgin"), Petrus Christus ("Annunciation and Birth of Christ"; altar wing depicting Isabella of Portugal), panels illustrating the legend of St Ursula and a portrait of Luis Gruuthuse, both famous works by unknown Bruges masters. Hans Memling's Moreel Triptych, 1484, is in Room 4. Hanging in Room 5 are two large pictures entitled the "Judgment of Cambyses" (1498) and a triptych showing the Baptism of Christ, all by David Gerard, while the "Last Judgment" by Hieronymus Bosch is among the paintings in Room 6.

t'Leerhuys

Over in the Arentspark adjacent to the museum an art gallery (t'Leerhuys) has been established in the intriguing surroundings of an old tannery.

★Gruuthuse-museum

On the left at the far end of the Dijver at No. 17 stands an attractive ensemble of 15th c. buildings comprising what was once the mansion of the "Heren van Gruuthuse". Here in 1471 the fugitive English king Edward IV took shelter. The original "heren" were not noblemen at all but merchants with a monopoly on the trade in "gruut", the dried herbs, etc. used to flavour beer before the introduction of hops. In summer the charming courtyard with its vine covered colonnades and neighbouring Onze-Lieve-Vrouwekerk for a backcloth, becomes the venue for an atmospheric son-et-lumière show. The courtyard can also be reached direct from the Groeninge Museum by first crossing Arentspark and then the picturesque Bonifatiusbrug, beside which can be seen a bust of Juan Luis Vivés, the Spanish humanist.

The mansion itself, beautifully furnished in different period styles, now houses the quite exceptional Gruuthusemuseum, a superb collection of antiques and applied art occupying in all 22 rooms. Particularly eye-catching are the lace-work, carvings, tapestries and weaponry, also the delightfully restored and completely authentic old Flemish kitchen and the dispensary. Open Apr.–Sep. daily except Tue. 9.30am–5pm; Oct.–Mar. daily except Tue. 9.30am–12.00pm and 2–5pm.

Brangwyn-museum

The Brangwyn Museum, in the 18th c. Arentshuis next door to the Gruuthusemuseum, has porcelains, pewterware, ceramics, mother-ofpearlware and a charming collection of views of old Bruges as well as an exhibition of paintings and drawings, etc. by the Bruges-born English artist Frank Brangwyn (1867–1956) (opening times as for the Gruuthusemuseum except closed in Jan. and early Feb.).

Immediately south of the Gruuthusemuseum towers the 122 m (400 ft) spire of the Onze-Lieve-Vrouwekerk (Church of Our Lady), the tallest in Belgium. Work began on the nave and aisles around 1230, the outermost aisles and chapels being added in the 14th and 15th c.

★ Onze-Lieve-Vrouwekerk

The church is of interest chiefly for its wealth of art treasures, among which is a sublime **sculpture by Michelangelo**, "Virgin and Child" (1503–04). The sculpture stands on the altar of the chapel at the end of the south aisle and was a gift from the Bruges merchant Jan Moscroen who personally acquired it from the master in 1506. Dürer, who visited the church in 1521, was filled with admiration.

Choir and ambulatory The Calvary on the high altar is by Bernaert van Orley (16th c.), the triptych "Adoration of the Shepherds" is by Pieter Pourbus and the "Transfiguration of Christ" is by Gerard David.

Positioned adjacent to one another in the choir are the **tombs of Mary of Burgundy** (who married Maximilian, later Holy Roman Emperor; died 1482) and her father **Charles the Bold** (died 1477). Mary's tomb (1502) by Jan Borman is pure Gothic in style and of considerably greater interest from an artistic point of view than her father's, which dates from 1559. The black sarcophagi on which the copper gilt figures of father and daughter lie are colourfully emblazoned with coats of arms (viewing: Apr.–Sep. Mon.–Fri. 10–11.30am and 2.30–5pm, Sat. 10–11.30am, Sun. and public holidays 2.30–5pm; Oct.–Mar. Mon.–Fri. 10–11.30am and

The courtyard of the Gruuthusemuseum   *A Michelangelo sculpture*

Sint-Jansspitaal

2.30–4.30pm, Sat. 10–11.30am and 2.30–4pm, Sun. and public holidays 2.30–4.30pm).

Mary of Burgundy's actual burial place is now believed to be one of a group of tombs discovered in the choir in 1979. All are notable for their mural decoration and can been seen behind a protective glass screen.

Pieter Lanchals, an adviser to Maximilian of Austria, lies buried in the Lanchals chapel off the south ambulatory. He was murdered in Bruges in 1488 at the time of Maximilian's "imprisonment". A number of fine paintings hang in the chapel including Adriaan Isenbrant's "Mater Dolorosa" (1530), a "Last Supper" by Pieter Pourbus and two panels by the Cologne artist Stefan Lochner ("Birth of Christ" and "Adoration of the Magi"). From the north ambulatory an elegant wooden gallery (15th c.) links the church to the Gruuthuse.

★★Memling-museum in the Sint-Jansspitaal

Immediately opposite the west door of the Onze-Lieve-Vrouwekerk stands the oldest building in Bruges, the **Sint-Jansspitaal** founded in the 12th c. The tympanum over the bricked up gate to the left of the Mariastraat entrance, embellished with reliefs showing the Virgin, bears the date 1270. Inside the ancient building, in what were once wards, an exhibition of documents, surgical instruments, etc. charts the hospital's history. The old dispensary adjacent to the wards has also been preserved. Open Apr.–Sep. daily 9.30am–5pm; Oct.–Mar. daily except Wed. 9.30am–12.30 and 2–5pm.

Occupying the former chapel is the **Memlingmuseum** where six exquisite masterpieces by Hans Memling (c. 1430–94) are on view, each a pearl of Old Flemish art. Outstanding even among these is the "Reliquary of St Ursula" (1489), recognised to be one of the master's most important works. Six scenes from the legend of the saint decorate the reliquary: the arrival in Cologne; the entry into Basle prior to crossing the Alps; the

Pope's welcome in Rome with the baptism of Ursula's companions; the re-embarkation at Basle for the return to Cologne; the massacre of the 11,000 virgins by the Huns; the Hun chieftain's proposal of marriage and Ursula's death. Scarcely less famous is the "Mystic Marriage of St Catherine", painted for the so-called St John altar. Completed in 1479 it depicts Saints Barbara and Catherine (portraits it is thought of Mary of Burgundy and Margaret of York) flanked by St John the Baptist and St John the Evangelist.

The four other works by Memling in the museum are the Maarten van Nieuwenhove diptych of 1487 (with on one wing the Virgin handing the Christ child an apple and on the other a superb portrait of the donor), a triptych (1479) with the "Adoration of the Magi" and the donor Jan Floreins, another triptych with the "Descent from the Cross" (1480) and finally the portrait of Sibylla Zambetha (1480).

The museum also contains works by other Old Flemish masters (e.g. Blondeel and Van Oost) as well as items of applied art (antique).

To **Minnewater** South of Sint-Jansspitaal, along Katelijnestraat, **Walstraat** branches off to the right, a street of tiny, exceptionally pretty, gabled 16th and 17th c. houses which today house mainly souvenir shops.

South again, beyond the bustling Walplein, the **"Straffe Hendrik" brewery** has been producing its fairly strong light beer in Bruges since 1546 (guided tours: Apr.–Sep. daily 10am–5pm; Oct.–Mar. daily 11am–3pm).

★Minnewater

In medieval times Minnewater (the "Lake of Love"), on the far side of Wijngaardplein, was part of Bruges's busy outer harbour. Nowadays only the Gothic sluishuis (lockhouse) at the north end provides a clue to

Minnewater, a rendezvous for lovers

The Béguinage

its far from tranquil past and few of today's visitors think twice about how this enchanting little stretch of water came by its romantic name.

From the bridge which crosses the southern end of the basin delightful waterside paths follow the line of the old town moat. The Poedertoren to the right of the bridge was built in 1398.

★Begijnhof

Standing by the lockhouse there is a lovely view of the bridge over to the Béguinage.

The Prinselijk Beguijnhof ten Wijngaarde, its white 17th c. houses grouped around a grassy, tree-shaded court, was founded in 1245 by Margaret of Constantinople. Today the Béguinage is the home of Benedictine nuns.

No. 30 was the Grootjuffrouw's house. To the left, between the entrance gate and church (founded 1245, restored 1605), one of the former béguine houses has been turned into a museum. It offers a fascinating insight into life in the béguinage as well as providing an outlet for the sale of lace (museum open: Apr.–Sep. Mon.–Sat. 10am–noon and 1.45–5.30pm, Sun. and public holidays 10am–noon and 1.45–6pm; Mar., Oct. and Nov. daily 10.30am–noon and 1.45–5pm; Dec.–Feb. Wed., Thu., Sat., Sun. 2.45–4.15pm, Fri. 1.45–6pm).

Town centre – south-west

Sint-Salvatorskathedraal

From the Onze-Lieve-Vrouwekerk the short Heilige Geeststraat makes its way past the Bishop's Palace (16th-18th c.) to Sint-Salvatorskathedraal, the oldest parish church in Bruges and a cathedral since 1834. First founded in the 10th c. most parts of the present building date from the 12th and 13th centuries. The fortress-like 99 m (325 ft)-high west tower was constructed in several phases, the lower Romanesque portion between 1116 and 1227 and the brick section between 1183 and 1228. Building continued in the 15th c. and again in the 19th c., the Neo-Romanesque upper part being added between 1844 and 1846 and the steeple in 1871. Over the centuries the cathedral has survived four fires as well as the iconoclastic fury. Restoration work is not yet complete so only parts of church are open to visitors.

The 101 m (331 ft)-long **interior**, distinguished by its harmonious proportions, contains some noteworthy furnishings. Outstanding are the Baroque rood-screen with a figure of God the Father by Artus Quellin the Younger, the 15th c. choir stalls embellished with the coats of arms of Knights of the Golden Fleece and, above the stalls, Brussels tapestries made in 1731.
   The cathedral organ is famous for its magnificent case.

Even more priceless, however, are the art treasures in the **cathedral museum** off the right transept. In the cloister are six fine brass 14th–16th c. tomb plates. Displayed in the various rooms are liturgical accoutrements and several superb Old Flemish paintings including a polyptych by Pieter Pourbus with a Last Supper on the centre panel (open Apr.–Sep. Mon., Tue. and Thu.–Sat. 10–11.30am and 2–5pm, Sun. and public holidays 3–5pm; Oct.–Mar. Mon., Tues., and Thu.–Sat. 2–5pm).

Running between the cathedral and the Markt, **Steenstraat** with its row of typical Bruges gable gildehuizen is one of the loveliest of the city's streets.

Around Sint-Salvatorskathedraal

About halfway along towards the Markt Steenstraat opens onto Simon Stevinplein, named after the mathematician Stevinus, born in Bruges in 1548 and sometime adviser to Maurice of Nassau. Branching off from the south side of the square is Oude Burg, at the near end of which stands the **Hof van Watervliet**, a complex of restored old buildings dating from the 16th c. Over the years the Hof's illustrious residents have included Erasmus of Rotterdam and the exiled Charles II.

Hanseatic Bruges 1548

West of the cathedral lies the large square known as t'Zand with, a short distance north, the **Blindenkapel**. Erected in the 14th c. the chapel boasts a magnificent pulpit (1659) and a gilded statue of Our Lady of the Blind.

The 14th c. **Smedenpoort** was medieval Bruges's south-west town gate. The bell would be rung when the gate was to be shut.

Following the moat south from the Smedenpoort leads to the 14th c. **Waterhuis** on which the town used to rely for its water supplies.

Hanseatic Bruges

The districts north of the Markt and to the north-east of the city centre were the commercial heart of Hanseatic Bruges where the city's merchants lived and carried on their business.

From the north-west corner of the Markt Sint-Jacobstraat continues beyond the Eiermarkt to the Gothic Sint-Jacobskerk, passing on its way the 18th c. Musical Academy (left) and Boterhuis (Cultural Centre; right). Gifts from the dukes of Burgundy, whose palace was near by, transformed the 13th–15th c. church from its relatively modest beginnings to its present size. The richly ornamented interior contains a number of fine 16th–18th c. paintings by local artists as well as some interesting tombs. Among the latter, to the right of the choir, is the twin-tiered tomb of Ferry de Gros (a treasurer of the Order of the Golden Fleece; died 1544) and his two wives.

Sint-Jacobskerk

Bruges · Brugge

Hof Bladelin

In 1440 Pieter Bladelin, also a treasurer of the Order of the Golden Fleece, built himself a house in Naaldenstraat, which branches right off Sint-Jacobsstraat. In addition to its exceptionally picturesque courtyard Hof Bladelin is distinguished by the portraits of subsequent owners embellishing the façade, among them Lorenzo di Medici who gave the house to his Bruges agent and banker Tommaso di Portinari.

Huis ter Beurze

Naaldenstraat terminates in Grauwwerkersstraat, at the east end of which stands the Huis ter Beurze, now a bank. In the 15th c. when the house was built it was common practice for merchants to do business in their lodgings. Many took rooms here in the home of the van der Beurze family, as a result of which the word "beurs" or "bourse" has found its way into numerous languages as the term for a commercial exchange.

Natiehuis van Genua

The Natiehuis van Genua (1399–1441) opposite the Huis ter Beurze was where Bruges's Genoese merchants carried on their business.

★Jan van Eyckplein

Not far from the Huis ter Beurze the delightful Jan van Eyckplein adjoins the Spiegelrei, Bruges's busy inner harbour during the city's heyday. A statue of Van Eyck adorns the square.

Poorters Loge

Dominating Jan van Eyckplein is the Poorters Loge, a striking 14th c. building with a slender tower. Once a sort of club for the merchant burghers of Bruges it now houses the city archives. Several figures decorate the façade, most notably that of the bear, "Beertje van de Logie", which dates from 1417. (A bear also appears on Bruges's coat of arms.)

Oud Tolhuis

Across the Academiestraat stands the Oud Tolhuis (customs house; 1477) where merchandise was inspected. It now houses the city's library of 100,000 volumes and 600 manuscripts, the latter including 13th and 14th c. missals.

Woensdagmarkt

Oosterlingenplein

In the Woensdagmarkt, just to the north of Jan van Eyckplein, are a statue of Hans Memling and, near by, the Convent of the Black Sisters founded in 1561. The Oosterlingenplein beyond owes its name to the fact that the German Hanse had premises there (oosterling 5 easterling).

Sint-Gilliskerk

Sint-Gilliskerk, a hall church (1275) across on the north side of the canal from Oosterlingenplein, has a number of excellent paintings. Hans Memling and Lanceloot Blondeel are among those buried in the churchyard.

Church of Sint-Walburga

In the opposite direction from Sint-Gilliskerk, a little to the south of the Spiegelrei, stands the magnificent Baroque church of Sint-Walburga (1619–42). Built by Pieter Huyssens, a Jesuit from Bruges, its furnishings include a superb pulpit by Artus Quellin the Younger and a similarly fine marble communion rail.

Sint-Annakerk

Sint-Annakerk, a short way east of Jan van Eyckplein, was erected in 1624 in place of an earlier Gothic church demolished in 1561. The Baroque choir stalls, rood-screen and pulpit are notable for their unity of style.

Jeruzalemkerk

The distinctive oriental-looking tower visible behind Sint-Annakerk belongs to the Late Gothic Jeruzalemkerk in Peperstraat. Dating from 1428 it was modelled on the Church of the Holy Sepulchre in Jerusalem, the builders, members of the Adorne family, having made a pilgrimage there. The church boasts very fine 15th–16th c. stained glass windows and a copy of Christ's tomb (church open: same hours as Kantcentrum, see below).

View of the Poorters Loge from the Spiegelrei ▶

Kantcentrum

The 15th c. "Jeruzalemgodshuizen" adjoining the church is now the Kantcentrum (Lace Centre), a museum cum studio/workshop where the art of bobbin lace making is preserved and handed on. In the afternoons the skilled craftswomen and their young pupils can be watched at work (open: Mon.–Fri. 10am–noon and 2–6pm, Sat. until 5pm).

Stedelijk Museum voor Volkskunde

The Stedelijk Museum voor Volkskunde occupies a group of 17th c. houses opposite the Kantcentrum. It comprises a collection of West Flemish folk art, costumes and items of an everyday kind, as well as interiors furnished in contemporary style. These include a hatter's workshop, a grocer's, a confectioner's, a kitchen, and an ale house known as the "Zwarte Kat" (open Apr.–Sep. daily 9.30am–5pm; Oct.–Mar. daily except Tue. 9.30am–12.30pm and 2–5pm).

Gouden Boom brewery

Spurred on by their visit to the "Zwarte Kat" (see above) beer drinkers may care to make a short detour south from the Jeruzalemkerk to see the 1902 maltings at the Gouden Boom brewery in Langestraat which houses a museum of brewery (entrance at Verbrand Nieuwland 10) with brewing exhibits from the turn-of-the-century (open Jun.–Sep. Wed.–Sun. 2–5pm).

Kruispoort

Kruisvest

The white limestone Kruispoort (town gate) at the end of Peperstraat dates from 1402. Running north from the gate, Kruisvest follows the line of the old ramparts. On the canal side are three windmills one of which, the Sint-Janshuysmolen (1770), can sometimes be seen working (open Apr.–Sep. daily 9.30am–noon and 12.45–5pm).

Sint-Joris

The guild-house of the Sint-Joris **Guild of Archers** opposite the first windmill contains a collection of crossbows, paintings and documents (open Mon., Tue., Thu., Fri. 2–6pm).

Guido Gezelle-museum

Guido Gezelle-museum The Flemish poet Guido Gezelle was born in a house in Rolweg which runs citywards off Kruisvest. The house is now a museum (open Apr.–Sep. daily except Tue. 9.30am–noon and 1.15–5pm; Oct.–Mar. 9.30am–12.30pm and 2–5pm).

Sint-Sebastian

The Sint-Sebastian **Guild of Archers**, which counted English royalty among its members, used to meet in the delightful turreted house (1562) in the Carmersstraat. Inside the house the history of the guild and its illustrious membership is documented and there are displays of weaponry and gold and silver work (open Mon., Wed., Fri., Sat. 10am–noon and 2–5pm).

Engels Klooster

The lovely domed chapel (1736–39) on the right-hand side a little further up Carmersstraat belongs to the Engels Klooster, an English nunnery.

Potteriespitaal

The Potteriespitaal, on the extreme northern edge of the city centre near the Episcopal Seminary on the Potterierei, was founded in 1276, though most of the present buildings date from the 15th c. Today it is still in use as a pleasant home for the elderly. The interesting Baroque chapel of Onze-Lieve-Vrouw van de Potterie and the even more interesting **Museum Onze-Lieve-Vrouw ter Potterie** in the old building are open to visitors, the latter comprising various items of ecclesiastical art including furniture, Gobelins, gold and ivory work and paintings (open Apr.–Sep. daily except Wed. 9.30am–noon and 1.15–5pm; Oct.–Mar. 9.30am–12.30pm and 2–5pm.).

Surroundings

Tillegembos estate

The Tillegembos estate 2 km (1¼ mi.) south of the city centre in suburb of Sint-Michiels comprises 83 ha (205 acre) woodland park with footpaths and bridleways, lake with mill and 14th c. moated château which is the headquarters of West Flanders Provincial Tourist Board (see Practical Information).

See Practical Information, Leisure Parks

The church in Zedelgem, 8 km (5 mi.) south-west, is justifiably proud of its extremely rare 11th–12th c. Romanesque font in the style of the Tournai school with reliefs illustrating the legend of St Nicholas of Myra.

Zedelgem

Jabbeke (11 km) (7 mi.) west of Bruges was for 20 years the home of the painter and sculptor Constant Permeke (1868–1952). His house and studio in Bruggerstraat, designed by the artist himself, have been turned into a museum containing fine examples of his work from various creative periods. These include sculptures in the garden studio (open May–Sep. daily 10am–6pm; Nov.–Apr. until 4pm only).

Jabbeke

Children in particular will enjoy a visit to "Zeven Torenjes", a farm at Assebroek 5 km (3 mi.) east of Bruges. Here there is a chance to experience life on the farm and to encounter the various animals.

Assebroek

Bruges offers several opportunities for **boat trips**. All are a delight, particularly the excursion aboard the "Lamme Goedzak" along the Brugge-Sluis-Kanaal to Damme (see entry; daily from Easter–Sep.; from the Noorwegse Kaai). Excursion launches also run to Ghent (see entry; every Thu. in Jul. and Aug.; from Bargeweg) and Ostende (see entry; every Tue. and Wed. in Jul. and Aug.; from Houtkaai). Further information from the Benelux-Damme-Rederij, Sint-Salvatorstraat 6, B–9000 Ghent; tel. 350285 (Bruges).

See Zeebrugge

Lisseweg

See entry

Zeebrugge

Brussels · Bruxelles · Brussel   F/G 9/10

Province: Brabant. Altitude: 15–100 m (50–330 ft)
Population: 970,000 of whom some 140,000 live in the inner city
Intercity and Inter-regional Station

The Baedeker AA series already includes a separate, fully comprehensive guide to Brussels. The descriptions given below are therefore somewhat abbreviated.

Where appropriate, names are given first in French and then in Flemish.

Brussels, **capital** of Belgium and principal **seat of the Belgian Royal Family**, is situated at the geographical centre of the country. It occupies rising ground on the edge of the valley of the Senne, a tributary of the Scheldt, at a point where the hills drop away to the plain of Flanders. The city is capital of the province of Brabant, and Greater Brussels ("L'Agglomération de Bruxelles") forms one of the country's three autonomous regions, the others being Flanders and Wallonia. Brussels is part of an archbishopric which also includes Mechelen (see entry).

Numerous international organisations and authorities are based in Brussels, in particular the European Union (EU). As the home of the EU Ministry and the EU Commission, the city prides itself on being the de facto capital of Europe. Since 1967 it has also been the headquarters of NATO, the western defence alliance (General Secretariat and NATO Council; military supreme command headquarters SHAPE at Casteau near Mons (see entry)). The European space agency ESA also has its base here.

Urban district and administration The municipality of Brussels proper comprises only the area formerly enclosed by the old ramparts – long since replaced by the broad boulevards of the so-called "Pentagon". It is made up of the Lower Town, through which flow several branches of the Senne (now canalised underground), and the smaller Upper Town on a ridge to the east. Clustered around the city centre and today continuous with it are eighteen separately administered suburban districts. Thus Brussels as a whole is an agglomeration of nineteen different municipalities, each with its own local government. That this has been an obstacle to the coherent development of the city is all too obvious from the many dilapidated areas and failed or poorly executed building projects.

Population Nowhere in Belgium do Flemings and Walloons live in quite such close proximity as in Brussels, the linguistic frontier running only a few kilometres south of the city. While Brussels itself is officially bilingual, Francophones in fact predominate (80 per cent) in the central district and Flemish speakers in the suburbs. It is Brussels' fate therefore to be at the mercy of often opposing ethnic group interests, the paralysing effects of which have frequently proved to the city's disadvantage.
Nevertheless, few if any European cities have such an international feel as Brussels. A quarter of the approximately one million inhabitants are foreigners and they could hardly be a more varied mixture. On the one hand there are the army of people employed by the international organisations, and on the other hand guest workers and immigrants from North and sub-Saharan Africa, many of whom live in the country illegally.

Architecture Brussels is an entirely modern city, extensive replanning and redevelopment since the early part of the century having profoundly altered the character of the old Brabant capital except in one or two places. Even now several major projects are in progress. Work is complete on reshaping the area in front of the Gare Centrale to create a more fitting "entrée" to the historic heart of the city. And an ambitious plan to redevelop the area around the headquarters of the EU Commission in the Palais Berlaymont (closed because of the asbestos risk) is well underway. Amid all this redevelopment those with an eye for such things will spot many an architectural disaster, as well as districts still badly in need of revitalisation. At the same time, speculative fever combined with the already mentioned ethnic rivalry and fragmented administrative responsibility threatens to destroy the vernacular character of attractive quarters like Les Marolles.

Culture, Science, Economy As Belgium's main cultural and scientific centre Brussels is home to the Belgian Royal Academy as well as to a university, a polytechnic, numerous technical colleges and art schools and a variety of other cultural institutions. It is also the country's financial capital (National Bank) and economic hub, lying as it does at the intersection of some of western Europe's primary transport routes. Second only to Antwerp (see entry) as the largest industrialised area in Belgium light industry predominates, in particular the manufacture of "Brussels lace", woollen, cotton and silk goods, carpets and porcelain. The metal, automobile and chemical industries are also well represented, as too is brewing. Even so, the commercial and service sectors outweigh manufacturing in importance to the economy, owing in no small measure to the presence of the big international organisations employing about 100,000 people. The EU alone has a staff of 14,000.

Brussels: a floral carpet in the Grand'Place outside the Maison du Roi ▶

Most of the latter however are nationals of other EU countries who not only earn considerably more than local people but also pay no tax.

Food Not surprisingly Brussels is also the country's gastronomic capital, plentifully provided with restaurants of high repute catering for a discriminating clientèle. Brussels chocolates are famous and, as is only to be expected in the city where Gambrinus was born, the art of brewing is cherished and cultivated.

Festivals and events The city's foremost festival, the marvellously colourful parade known as the "Ommegang", is celebrated in July on the Grand'Place where it was held for the first time in 1549 in the presence of Charles V. The prestigious "Concours Reine Elisabeth", an international music competition, takes place in the spring. The ambitious biennial "Europalia" festival, held in June, takes each European country in turn as its theme.

Art Nouveau in Brussels At the beginning of this century Brussels became a focal point for the Art Nouveau movement, Victor Horta, Henry van de Velde and Philippe Wolfers being among the architects and artists whose genius enriched the city with houses and objets d'art. The Brussels Tourist Office (see Practical Information, Information) arranges tours of the most beautiful Art Nouveau buildings, as does the Organisation ARAU (Atelier de Recherche et d'Action Urbaines, tel. 2193345).

History

Modest beginnings The founding of Brussels is usually attributed to St Goorik (or Géry), Bishop of Cambrai, also credited with introducing Christianity into Belgium. He is thought to have established the original settlement here in about 580, on an island in the Senne. In 977 Charles, Duke of Lower Lotharingia, took up residence on the island, thereby attracting craftsmen and tradespeople to it. As a result the name "Bruocsella" (from "broec" = breach or marsh and "sele" = village) appears for the first time in 979 in a document of Otto the Great. Later, in the 12th c., the counts of Louvain, forerunners of the dukes of Brabant, built anew on the more elevated site of the Coudenberg. Standing as it did at an important crossing on the great trade route between Bruges and Cologne, subsequent expansion was rapid, and between 1357 and 1379 new ramparts were built around the much enlarged town. Brussels then ceased to be in the shadow of the hitherto more powerful Louvain.

Heyday At the end of the 14th c. Brussels became the capital of Brabant, consequently falling in 1430 into Burgundian hands. By 1455 the population had reached 43,500 inhabitants. The dukes of Burgundy occasionally held court in Brussels and the French nobility who gathered there and who were already making the French language fashionable among their Netherlands counterparts, were responsible for a first flowering of the arts and sciences. At the same time

Metro

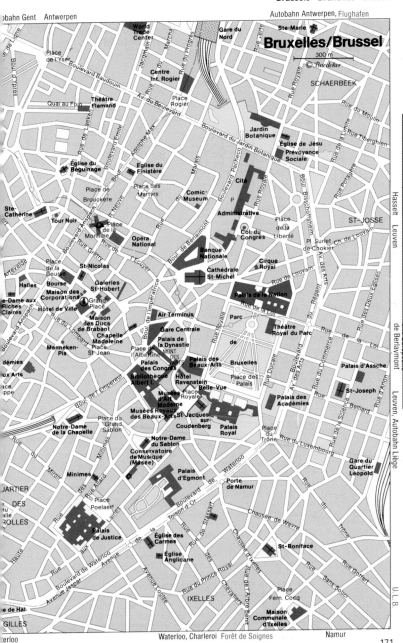

Brussels · Bruxelles · Brussel

171

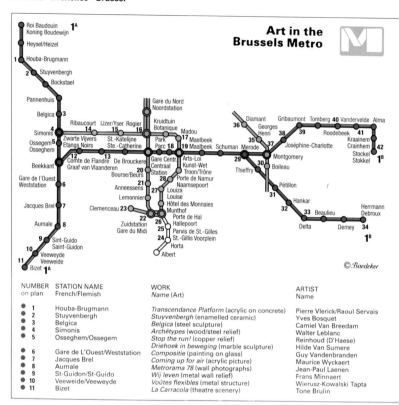

Art in the Brussels Metro

© *Baedeker*

NUMBER on plan	STATION NAME French/Flemish	WORK *Name* (Art)	ARTIST Name
● 1	Houba-Brugmann	*Transcendance Platform* (acrylic on concrete)	Pierre Vlerick/Raoul Servais
● 2	Stuyvenbergh	*Stuyvenbergh* (enamelled ceramic)	Yves Bosquet
● 3	Belgica	*Belgica* (steel sculpture)	Camiel Van Breedam
● 4	Simonis	*Archétypes* (wood/steel relief)	Walter Leblanc
● 5	Osseghem/Ossegem	*Stop the run!* (copper relief)	Reinhoud (D'Haese)
		Driehoek in beweging (marble sculpture)	Hilde Van Sumere
● 6	Gare de L'Ouest/Weststation	*Compositie* (painting on glass)	Guy Vandenbranden
● 7	Jacques Brel	*Coming up for air* (acrylic picture)	Maurice Wyckaert
● 8	Aumale	*Metrorama 78* (wall photographs)	Jean-Paul Laenen
● 9	St-Guidon/St-Guido	*Wij leven* (metal wall relief)	Frans Minnaert
● 10	Veeweide/Veeweyde	*Voûtes flexibles* (metal structure)	Wierusz-Kowalski Tapta
● 11	Bizet	*La Carracola* (theatre scenery)	Tone Brulin

trades and crafts increasingly flourished, leading to the emergence of a prosperous middle class and a new pride and self-confidence which soon found expression in the building of the splendid guild-houses and town hall on the Grand'Place.

When the country became a Habsburg possession in 1477, and especially following Charles V's accession in 1515 and the elevation of Brusselsto capital of the Spanish Netherlands in 1531, a brilliant court life evolved in the city attracting a bevy of artists. It was during this time also that, in 1490, Franz von Taxis organised a permanent postal link between Brussels and Innsbruck. Charles V's abdication in 1555 however presaged the ending of Spanish rule.

Many masters The year 1566 saw the first rebellion in the Netherlands against Spanish oppression, culminating in the execution of Counts Egmont and Hoorn on the Grand'Place. For the time being the Spanish hold remained unbroken, but economically the city was weakened by an exodus of its citizens to the free Netherlands. In 1695, during Louis XIV's wars, Marshal DeVilleroy's bombardment set fire to the Lower Town, destroying more than 4000 houses including the magnificent buildings around the Grand'Place. Although with the end of the War of Spanish Succession the Spanish Netherlands and with them Brussels passed to Austria, the struggle of the people of Brussels for their freedom con-

No.	Location	Work	Artist
12	Etangs Noirs/Zwarte Vijvers	De Zwarte Vijvers (wall pictures in oil colours)	Jan Burssens
13	Comte de Flandre/Graaf van Vlaanderen	16 × Icarus (hanging bronze figures and plaster ceiling relief)	Paul Van Hoeydonck
14	Ribaucourt	Le Feu de Néron (canvas hanging)	Fernand Flausch
15	Yser/IJzer	La Piëta-Yser (steel reliefs)	Antoine Mortier
16	Rogier	The fall of Troy (wall pictures in oil)	Jan Cox
17	Botanique/Kruidtuin	Les Voyageurs (21 coloured wooden figures)	Pierre Caille
		The last migration (copper sculpture)	Jean-Pierre Ghysels
		Tramification fluide – Tramification syncopée (coloured steel tubes)	Emile Souply
18	Parc/Park	La ville (wall mosaic)	Roger Dudant
		Happy metro to you (coloured wooden figures)	Marc Mendelson
19	Arts-Loi/Kunst-Wet	Isjtar (lacquered wooden reliefs)	Gilbert Decock
		Ortem (coloured ceramic tiles)	Jean Rets
20	Bourse/Beurs	Moving ceiling (steel cylinder)	Pol Bury
		Nos vieux trams bruxellois (oil picture)	Paul Delvaux
21	Anneessens	Sept écritures (word painting)	Pierre Aléchinsky and Christian Dotremont
22	Gare du Midi/Zuidstation	Structures rythmées (ceiling and wall frescos)	Jacques Moeschal
23	Clemenceau	Promenade (oil on canvas)	Joseph Willaert
24	Horta	Maison du Peuple/Hôtel Aubecq	Victor Horta
25	Parvis de St-Gilles/St-Gillis Voorplein	Dyade (ceramic)	Françoise Schein
26	Porte de Hal/Hallepoort	Le passage inconnu (wall installation)	François Schuiten
		Halleport (oil on canvas)	Raoul de Keyser
27	Louise/Louiza	La Terre en fleur (tapestry, ceramic)	Edmond Durunfaut
28	Porte de Namur/Naamse Poort	Het uiteindelijk verkeer (four round enamelled ceramic reliefs)	Octave Landuyt
29	Mérode	Carrelage cinq (coloured ceramic tiles)	Jean Glibert
		Ensor: "Vive la Sociale (?)" (oil picture)	Roger Raveel
		Aequus Nox (tinted mirror glass)	Vic Gentils
30	Thieffry	Sculptures (bronze and steel)	Félix Roulin
31	Pétillon	Que la mer épargne (aluminium chrome relief)	Lismonde
32	Hankar	Notre temps (acrylic on concrete)	Roger Somville
33	Delta	Delta Mouvement (wall installation)	Jan Van den Abeel
34	Herrmann-Debroux	L'aviateur (bronze sculpture)	Roel D'Haese
		Ode aan een bergrivier (bronze)	Rik Poot
35	Georges-Henri	t' Is de Wind (porcelain)	Piet Stockmans
36	Diamant	Diamant (wall mirror)	Michel Martens
37	Montgomery	Rythme bruxellois (coloured ceramic tiles)	Jo Delahaut
		Magic city (wall pictures in oil colours)	Jean-Michel Folon
		Thema's (seven oil pictures)	Pol Mara
38	Joséphine-Charlotte	La fleur unique ou les oiseaux émerveillés (coloured wooden reliefs)	Serge Vandercam
39	Gribaumont	Le Tropolitain (wall pictures in oil colours)	Frans Nellens
40	Roodebeek	Intégration-Roodebeek (steel and glass)	Luc Peire
41	Vandervelde	La grande taupe et le petit peintre (large wall painting in acrylic colour)	Paul de Gobert
42	Stocke/Stokkel	Comic pictures from Tintin	Atelier Hergé

tinued. In 1719 Frans Anneessens, leader of the Brussels guilds, was beheaded on the orders of the Austrian-appointed Governor, Prince Eugène.

Under Maria Theresa and her Governor Charles of Lorraine (1744–80) more peaceful times ensued, the population rising again to reach 74,000. Then came the French Revolution, Brabantine supporters of which led a new revolt against the Austrians. In 1794 the French themselves marched in, Brussels remaining in French hands until 1814. Possession then passed to the Dutch under whom Brussels became the Netherlands' second city. Finally a popular riot in Theatre Square on August 25th 1830 was the signal for the start of the revolution out of which Brussels was to emerge as the capital of the newly created Kingdom of the Belgians.

The Belgian capital The new capital now developed rapidly. In 1834 the university was founded, and a year later continental Europe's first rail service began operating between Brussels and Mechelen. Subsequently, under King Leopold II and Burgomaster Ansprach, the great boulevards were built. Although occupied in both World Wars the city was fortunately spared the worst destruction. The 1958 World Exhibition brought a new landmark in the form of the Atomium while the arrival of the EEC (now the EU) and EURATOM in 1959 followed by NATO in 1967 marked

Brussels' elevation to unofficial "Capital of Europe". The 1980s saw the first steps towards the city's becoming an autonomous region alongside Flanders and Wallonia, a process which should come to fruition in the 1990s. Sadly, in 1985, the Heysel Stadium was brought to the attention of the world when, before the European Cup Final between Liverpool FC and Juventus of Turin, British football hooligans caused panic in the course of which 38 spectators were killed.

Famous people Brussels was the birthplace of, among others, the painters Bernard van Orley, Pieter Breugel the Elder and René Magritte, the Art Nouveau architect Victor Horta and the cabaret singer Jacques Brel.

Sightseeing

All the most important sights in Brussels are comfortably within the scope of a single day's sightseeing on foot. The best place to start is at the Grand'Place with its Hôtel de Ville, guild-houses, and the Maison du Roi. Then the part of the Old Town around the Place can be explored, including the mandatory visit to the world-famous Manneken Pis and a tour of the shopping arcades of the Galéries Saint-Hubert. From there it is only a short step uphill to the venerable old Saint-Michel Cathedral, to be followed by a walk through the green Parc de Bruxelles to the Palais Royale. Next stop should be at the Place Royale to the right of the palace, from where the Mont des Art (literally Hill of the Arts) descends to the Lower Town and where the Royal Museums of Fine Arts beckon those equipped with both time and patience. Afterwards the Place du Grand Sablon demands inclusion in the route back to the Lower Town.

Visitors with more time to spend in Brussels should be sure to visit the Atomium located in the north of the city. The next priority should be the museums, the main ones, apart from those on the Mont des Arts, being located in the Parc du Cinquantenaire – Autoworld, the Military Museum, and the Museum of Art and History. Any visits further afield should certainly include Waterloo (see entry) and the Central Africa Museum.

Guided walks and tours For information about guided tours apply to the Brussels Tourist Office in the Grand'Place. Horse-drawn cabs are available for hire in the Place and the taxis marked "Taxi-Tour" likewise undertake city tours. The "Rose des Vents" ("Compass Card") is a list of suggested excursions by public transport compiled by the Brussels transport authority (information from e.g. the Midi, Porte de Namur and Rogier Metro Stations).

Traffic In Brussels as in all major cities visitors are well advised to dispense with their own cars. The city's extensive and dependable public transport system brings everything of interest within easy reach.

Art in the Metro The 33 km (20 mi.) combined network of the Metro and Prémétro provides the quickest and most convenient method of transport, trains running from 6am to midnight. The Brussels Metro is quite exceptional. Many of the stations have been decorated by well-known contemporary artists, the most recent being Bockstael, now enlivened with characters from "Tin Tin" by Hergé. In addition to the Metro there is a tram service operating mainly outside the "Pentagon" and a very extensive bus network. Tram stops have red and white signs, bus stops blue and white ones. "Request only" stops are marked "Sur demande". Tickets can be obtained from the above mentioned information offices, at Metro stations (at the counter or from machines), from the tourist information office and from numerous newspaper kiosks. There are single tickets, five or ten trip tickets and a 24 hour ticket for the city centre. An additional "Z" ticket is necessary for the outer zones. For a longer stay it is advisable to purchase a monthly ticket.

City centre

Many of Brussels' chief sights are located within the comparatively
small area enclosed by the "Pentagon", the ring of great boulevards
following the line of the old 14th c. walls (Metro Gare Centrale/De
Brouckère).

The 110 m (360 ft) by 68 m (225 ft) Grand'Place (Grote Markt) lies at the
very heart of Brussels Old Town, its sublime stylistic unity making it one
of the loveliest squares in the world. Delightful at any time it is especially
so when lit up in the evening and when filled with the additonal colour
of the Sunday bird market and daily flower markets. First established on
a marsh in the 11th c. the market soon evolved to become the city's political, economic and social nerve centre. The bombardment by the
French on August 13th–14th 1695 wrought havoc with its buildings,
nearly all of which were subsequently rebuilt. The Place has thus preserved all its old magnificence and its original happy blend of Gothic
and Baroque. Across the years, from the 14th and 15th centuries to the
revolution of 1830, the square has witnessed many a dramatic political
moment, including in 1568 the execution of Counts Egmont and Hoorn,
beheaded in front of the Maison du Roi. It has also been the scene of
much celebration and a stage for the city's major festivals. The
"Ommegang" is held here every year and every second August the
square is carpeted with flowers.

★★ Grand'Place ·
Grote Markt

The Place is dominated by the Hôtel de Ville (Town Hall), one of the
biggest and finest buildings of its kind in Belgium (Tours in English:
Tue. 11.30am and 3.15pm; Wed. 3.15pm; Sun. and public holidays
12.15pm Apr.–Oct. only). It was begun in 1450 with the intention of
upstaging the Stadhuis in the rival city of Bruges (see entry). At first the
plan was to build only what is now the left wing (1402–10); but in 1444
the right wing was also completed, followed in 1455 by Jan van
Ruysbroek's 96 m (315 ft) high belfry surmounted by the figure of St
Michael. Although the French bombardment left only the walls and
tower standing, rebuilding started almost at once. Both wings are
embellished with very fine Gothic sculptures beneath which, under the
arcades on the right, are the signs of inns demolished to make way for
the town hall.

★★ Hôtel de Ville ·
Stadhuis

Inside are several magnificent rooms. Among the most impressive are
the Maximilian Chamber hung with Brussels tapestries (historical
scenes from the life of Clovis), the large Council Chamber with a superb
ceiling by Victor Janssens and tapestries to his designs, the great banqueting hall and the Marriage Chamber, both beautifully panelled, and
the Escalier d'Honneur with murals by Lalaing (1893) illustrating the history of Brussels.

Opposite the Hôtel de Ville stands the Maison du Roi which, despite its
name, was never a royal residence. The king in question was the king of
Spain and the "maison" was in fact the law courts. Directly in front is the
spot where executions were carried out. The Maison's 13th c. predecessor was a building known as the **Broodhuis** (Bread House), appropriately
enough since bread was indeed sold there for a time. Later it became a
ducal law court before being replaced in 1515. By now rechristened the
Maison du Roi, it was destroyed in 1695. The post-bombardment reconstruction was never very satisfactory and in 1873 rebuilding started yet
again, based this time on the 1515 plans. The house as seen today was
completed in 1895. The statues above the central arcade are those of
Mary of Burgundy, Charles V and Duke Henry I.

★ Maison du Roi

Communal Stadmuseum The Maison du Roi is now Brussels' civic
museum. The ground floor rooms to the left of the entrance contain
14th–18th c. sculptures, including some of the original ones from the

Musée

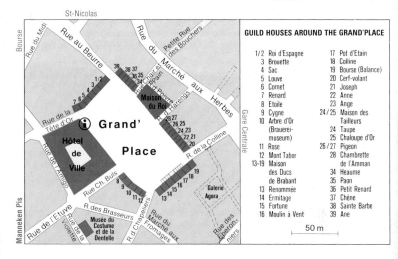

GUILD HOUSES AROUND THE GRAND'PLACE

1/2	Roi d'Espagne	17	Pot d'Etain
3	Brouette	18	Colline
4	Sac	19	Bourse (Balance)
5	Louve	20	Cerf-volant
6	Cornet	21	Joseph
7	Renard	22	Anne
8	Etoile	23	Ange
9	Cygne	24/25	Maison des
10	Arbre d'Or		Tailleurs
	(Brauerei-	24	Taupe
	museum)	25	Chaloupe d'Or
11	Rose	26/27	Pigeon
12	Mont Tabor	28	Chambrette
13-19	Maison		de l'Amman
	des Ducs	34	Heaume
	de Brabant	35	Paon
13	Renommée	36	Petit Renard
14	Ermitage	37	Chêne
15	Fortune	38	Sainte Barbe
16	Moulin à Vent	39	Ane

50 m

Hôtel de Ville. In the rooms to the right of the entrance are 15th and 16th c. paintings, Brussels tapestries, porcelain and faience. The city's own development is the subject of a display on the first floor while on the second floor the emphasis is on social history – popular art, religion and other social themes. Also on the second floor is the wardrobe of Manneken Pis, a collection of costumes presented to "Petit Julien" by the rich and famous over the centuries, among them the French King Louis XIV (open Apr.–Sep. Mon.–Fri. 10am–12.30pm and 1.30–5pm (until 4pm Oct.–Mar.); Sat., Sun. and public holidays 10am–1pm; Oct.–Mar. until 4pm).

Grand'Place owes much of its character to its elegant gildehuizen, with their magnificent gables, pilasters and balustrades, their ornately carved stonework and rich gold decoration. Most were built between 1696 and 1700 in the style of the Italian Baroque but with some Flemish influences. As well as bearing the name of the guilds, all the houses have individual names – see the map above. Only some of the most splendid are mentioned below.

.Guild-houses

The row of houses on the **north-west side** of the square are the most elegant of all. No. 1–2, known as "Au Roi d'Espagne" and now the premises of a famous café of that name, belonged to the bakers' guild. Then, from right to left, come No. 3 "La Brouette" ("The Wheelbarrow"; the grocers' house), No. 4 "Le Sac" ("The Sack"; the joiners and coopers' house), No. 5 "La Louve" ("The She-Wolf"; the archers' house), No. 6 "Le Cornet" ("The Cornucopia"; the bargees' house) and No. 7 "Le Renard" ("The Fox"; the shopkeepers' house).

South-west side The five houses to the left of the Hôtel de Ville are also very splendid. No. 8, "L'Étoile" ("The Star"), was not a guild-house but seat of the ducal judiciary. No. 10, "L'Arbre d'Or" ("The Golden Tree"), was the brewers' house and now contains a small brewing museum (open daily 10am–5pm).

◀ *The imposing City Hall of Brussels*

Making up the **south-east side** of the Place is the large building known as the Maison des Ducs de Brabant, its façade reminiscent of an Italian palazzo. It is adorned with the busts of nineteen dukes of Brabant – hence the name. Also here is the new Cocoa and Chocolate Museum (open Tue.–Sun. 10am–5pm).

South-west side Of the houses on either side of the Maison du Roi the most interesting is No. 24–25, "La Chaloupe d'Or" ("The Golden Sloop") which belonged to the tailors' guild.

Musée du Costume et de la Dentelle

A narrow street off the south side of the Grand'Place just to the left of the Hôtel de Ville leads in a few steps to the Musée du Costume et de la Dentelle (Museum voor de Kleederdracht en de Kant) on the left-hand side a short way down the hill. As well as documenting the history of fashion from the 17th to the 19th c. the museum is a shrine to the art of Brussels lace making (open Apr.–Sep. Mon.–Tue. and Thu.–Fri. 10am–12.30pm and 1.30–5pm; Oct.–March until 4pm; Sat., Sun. and public holidays 2–4.30pm).

★★Manneken Pis

Along the Rue de l'Etuve (Stoofstraat) from the Musée du Costume is by far the best-known landmark in Brussels, the Manneken Pis, usually besieged by a throng of tourists. Although he can be traced back to at least 1388, nothing much is known about the origin of the figure of a little boy urinating, popularly referred to as "the oldest citizen of Brussels". The Manneken is however surrounded by various legends. According to one the fountain is a memorial to a courageous infant who averted a conflagration, according to another it commemorates the son of a count who succumbed to a pressing urge while taking part in a procession. The present statue was made in 1619 by Jérome Duquesnoy the Elder and has been stolen on several occasions though always recov-

Guild-houses on the north-west side of the Grand'Place

Manneken Pis, the best-known monument in Brussels

ered. During the War of Austrian Succession (1741–48) it was removed and smashed. Found in pieces it was restored and replaced. Even in recent times attempts have been made to steal it. During major Brussels festivals wine or beer spurts from the fountain instead of the usual 70 litres (15 galls) of water per hour. The Manneken has been presented with more than 450 costumes, which he wears on certain appointed days (see above, Maison du Roi).

Ilôt Sacré, the district extending north of the Grand'Place as far as the Place de la Monnaie, was the original Senne island on which St Géry founded his chapel. Nowadays it is known for its numerous, always busy, restaurants and bars in the Rue des Bouchers (Beenhouwerstraat) and the streets round about. Tucked away in a narrow cul-de-sac called the Impasse Schuddeveld is one of Brussels' oldest institutions, the **"Royal Toone Theatre"**, a puppet theatre carried on by the Toone family for seven generations; it has a museum (open daily noon–midnight with puppet shows at 8.30pm daily except Sun. and Mon.).

Ilôt Sacré

Situated only a short distance from the north-east corner of the Grand'Place is one of the first covered shopping arcades to be built in Europe, the Galéries Saint-Hubert completed in 1846. There are two main arcades, one either side of the Rue des Bouchers, the nearer of the two being the Galérie de la Reine (Queen's Gallery) with, on the other side of the road, the Galérie du Roi (King's Gallery). Off the latter runs the little Galérie des Princes (Princes' Gallery). The motto "Omnibus omnia" ("Everything for everyone") above the entrance is all that remains of the silversmiths' guild-house demolished when the Galéries were built. The three-storeyed arcade is a shoppers' delight with luxury boutiques, cafés, restaurants and chocolate shops.

★ Galéries Saint-Hubert

Turning left at the end of the Galéries leads to the Place de la Monnaie and the Théâtre Royal de la Monnaie, both of which take their name from the 15th c. Hôtel de la Monnaie, the Duchy of Brabant's mint, which originally stood there. Designed by the architect Damesme the Neo-Classical theatre, its façade embellished with Ionic columns and gable relief, was built in 1819 to replace an earlier building, also a theatre. It

Théâtre Royal de la Monnaie ˘ Muntschouwburg

Places of Temptation

For many inhabitants of Brussels, the entrance to Paradise can be found in the centre of town, and it is even got an address: 25–27, Galerie de la Reine. For this is the headquarters of the chocolate manufacturers Neuhaus. Chocolates, however, seems much too mundane a name to call these small, exquisite and transitory works of art. They are hand-made and beautifully wrapped in the so-called ballotins, those green-golden boxes which signal to chocoholics around the world: attention, Neuhaus! Only to be eaten with respect!

The Swiss pharmacist Jean Neuhaus and his son Frédéric, however, had a long way to go, and pass many a test, before they actually succeeded in creating their very first genuine chocolate. It all began with a pharmaceutic sweet shop which father Jean opened in the Galerie de la Reine. Not contented with this, his son Frédéric experimented with caramel sweets and fruit jellies, until, in 1912, he finally created his first chocolate. Today, Neuhaus produces 65 different kinds, and sells them throughout Belgium and all over the world.

Behind these windows those with a sweet tooth are in heaven

Neuhaus is the best, and certainly also the most exclusive of chocolate manufacturers in Belgium. Buying something here almost takes on a ritual character as you see the white-gloved hands of the assistant flitting over the delicacies and hear the cognescenti expertly discuss the quality of the Armagnac in the truffle cream and the flavour nuances of the almond cream covered in brown – or should it be black? – chocolate. Neuhaus, however, is certainly not the only chocolate manufacturer in the country – it couldn't be: Belgians eat 12.5 kg (27 lb) per year which makes them the European champions of chocolate consumption. Apart from Neuhaus, and forgetting about mass-produced chocolates, they like to shop at Godiva which is almost as exclusive (in Brussels at 22, Grand' Place, and at other addresses), in one of the branches of Corné de la Toison d'Or (in the Galerie de la Reine, immediately opposite Neuhaus) or, at more affordable prices, at Leonidas (for example at 46, Boulevard Anspach). Another address for fine chocolates, but even more renowned for its excellent cakes and tarts (including chocolate cakes!) is Wittamer at the Place du Grand Sablon. But wherever you buy or try, you'll never be disappointed, because the Belgians follow very strict quality laws in the manufacture of their chocolates.

was here on August 25th 1830 that the Belgian Revolution began. During a performance of the opera "La Muette de Portici" (by D. F. Auber) the audience, stirred by the duet "Sacred Love of the Fatherland", rushed out onto the streets sparking off the rebellion against the Netherlands. The theatre burned down in 1855 and was then rebuilt with the original façade. It was here also that Maurice Béjart founded his world-famous ballet company "Ballet du XXme Siècle" (now based in Lausanne).

Across the square towers the Centre Monnaie (Muntcentrum), a shopping precinct and office block facing onto the large and busy Place de Brouckère (Brouckèreplaats) with its restaurants, cinemas and shops.

Place de Brouckère · Brouckèreplaats

A block or two south of the theatre, hidden away behind the Bourse, stands one of the city's oldest churches, Saint-Nicolas, built originally by merchants in the 11th or 12th c. in honour of their patron saint, and from which, as was the custom, they marketed their wares. Inside the church, which has since undergone alteration several times, is an interesting 15th c. Madonna.

Saint-Nicolas · Sint-Niklaas

Saint-Nicholas faces the rear of the Bourse (1871), the country's leading stock exchange. The main façade, overlooking the Place de la Bourse, has wonderfully rich figurative ornamentation with a crowning figure symbolising Belgium itself.

Bourse · Beurs

Not far west of the Théâtre Royal lies the majestically proportioned church of Sainte-Catherine, built in 1850 in a blend of Romanesque, Gothic and Renaissance styles to replace an earlier building. Of particular interest in the interior are the 14th or 15th c. figure of a black Madonna and a painting by de Crayer. The Tour Noire (11th–12th c.) which stands behind the church is a remnant of the old city wall while, on the west side, the delightful fish market is a reminder that this was once one of the old town quays.

Sainte-Catherine · Sint-Katelijne

Even when seen at a distance along the Rue du Peuplier (Populierstraat) from the fish market, the magnificent façade of Saint-Jean-Baptiste au Béguinage is an impressive sight. The church, all that remains of a Béguine convent founded in the 13th c., was built between 1657 and 1676. Designed by Luc Fayd'herbe it is one of the finest Flemish–Italian Baroque churches in Belgium. Among the items of note in the light and spacious interior are the beautiful pulpit and the many paintings, including seven by the Brussels artist Van Loon.

★Saint-Jean · Sint-Jans

The dilapidated state of the Place des Martyrs, situated to the east of the pedestrianised Rue Neuve (Nieuwstraat) running north from the Théâtre Royal, is a sad commentary on the inactivity of the Brussels city council. The square, encircled by buildings dating from 1775, has in its centre a monument to the martyrs of the 1830 rebellion.

Place des Martyrs · Martelaarsplein

Lovers of comics should not miss out on a visit to the Comic Museum or Belgian Centre for Comic Strip Art (Centre Belge de la Bande Dessinée/Belgisch Centrum van het Beeldverhaal). It is housed in a building which is well worth seeing in its own right – the Maison Waucquez in the Rue de Sable (Zandstraat), a 1906 department store designed by Victor Horta. Here, the visitor finds out about the development of the comic strip and animation, and can admire a is a constantly rotated exhibition of 200 original drawings by Belgian and French comic artists. The history of Belgian and French comic strips follows, with a collection of many original manuscripts, draft sketches, and imaginatively reconstructed sets – of which Gaston Lagaffe's office, Lucky Luke's saloon and Tim, Struppi and Captain Haddock's moon rocket are only three (open Tue.–Sun. 10am–6pm).

★Comic Museum

Half way up the hill on the way from the Grand'Place to the Upper Town

★Saint-Michel · Sint-Michiel

stands the Cathédral Saint-Michel (Sint-Michielskathedraal). Dedicated to St Michael and St Gudula, the patron saints of Brussels, it has been the episcopal church of the Mechelen-Brussels diocese since 1962. First founded in 1225 the white building in plain Brabant Gothic style was to all intents and purposes complete by the end of the 15th c. The façade is impressive, rising majestically above a broad flight of steps and crowned with twin 69 m (226 ft) high towers designed by Jan van Ruysbroeck.

The beautifully proportioned **interior** (108 m (354 ft) by 50 m (164 ft)) is exceptionally pleasing to the eye. As well as being lavishly furnished the church has some outstanding 16th–17th c. stained glass windows, the finest – all by Bernard van Orley – being those in the transepts (1537–38) depicting Charles V and Isabella of Portugal (south) and the Hungarian royal pair Louis II and Mary (north), and in the Chapel of the Holy Sacrament to the right of the choir illustrating the story of the "Miracle of the Host" (1534–39). The piers of the nave are adorned with figures of the Twelve Apostles by Fayd'herbe and Duquesnoy the Younger while towards the right aisle is a projecting carved wooden pulpit by Verbruggen (1669). Under the very beautiful triforium in the choir (1215–65) are the tombs of John, Duke of Brabant and his wife Margaret of York (left), and of Archduke Ernst of Austria. During July and August six magnificent tapestries by van der Borght (1785) are usually hung in the choir. In the ambulatory to the right of the choir there is a statue of the Virgin by Quellin the Elder (1645), and to the left of the choir, beside the Chapel of the Redeemer, a memorial tablet to the Brussels artist Roger van der Weyden who is buried here.

Colonne du Congrès · Kongreszuil

Behind the cathedral the Treurenberg (Hill of Mourning) ascends to the Rue Royal (Koningstraat) in the Upper Town. To the left, a little way along the Rue, the Colonne du Congrès (1859), surmounted by a statue of Leopold I, commemorates the National Congress of 1831. At its foot an eternal flame burns on the Grave of the Unknown Soldier. A good view of the Lower Town can be had from the esplanade around the column.

Botanique · Kruidtuin

Beyond the Colonne, across the boulevard at the north-east extremity of the city centre, the conservatories of the former botanic garden (1826–29) have been put to new use as a cultural centre for the city's French-speaking community.

Quartier Royal

On the way up from the cathedral to the Rue Royal the west elevation of the 18th c. **Palais de la Nation** (Paleis der Natie) can be seen ahead. The façade of the Neo-Classical building, seat of the Belgian Senate and Chamber of Deputies, overlooks the Parc de Bruxelles.

The **Parc de Bruxelles**, one time hunting preserve of the dukes of Brabant and the scene in 1830 of much bloodshed during the rebellion against the Dutch, is laid out geometrically with its main axis towards the Palais Royal at the southern end. In the north-east corner stands the Royal Park Theatre built in 1872.

★Palais Royal · Koninklijk Paleis

In the place of the original seat of the dukes of Brabant, destroyed by fire in 1731, stands the present Palais Royal. It is not the home of the Belgian Royal Familt, but only used for state occasions. The Belgian flag, flown from the roof, signals the sovereign's presence. A ceremonial Changing of the Guard takes place every day at 2.30pm. The palace originally comprised two separate buildings which were made into one in 1827–29. Further alterations continued until 1904. (The state apartments are opened to the public in late July and August; further information from tourist offices.)

The **Musée Bellevue** in the west wing of the palace contains 18th and 19th c. furniture, glass and other objets d'art.

A square extends in front of the palace, on its east side being the Palais des Académies, home of the Royal Academy of Sciences and once the residence of the Crown Prince of Orange.

Palais des Académies

The Palais des Beaux-Arts (Paleis voor Schone Kunste) on the opposite (west) side of the square was designed and built in the 1920s by Victor Horta. Cleverly integrated into its sloping site the Palais houses several cultural institutes, a concert hall and theatre and cinema museum.

Palais des Beaux-Arts

Behind and to the west of the palace stand an exceptionally attractive ensemble of Neo-Classical buildings grouped around the Place Royale. In the 18th c. the French architect Barnabé Guimard was commissioned to produce a design for this important site on the Coudenberg, resulting in the construction of the Place between 1773 and 1780. The principal building in the square is the **church of Saint-Jacques-sur-Coudenberg** – the Chapel Royal – with its imposingly spacious interior.

★Place Royale · Koningsplein

The spring of the year 2000 will see the opening of the redesigned Museum of Musical Instruments in the Magasin Old England, on the town-facing side of the Place. It possesses one of the richest collections of its kind. There are more than 6000 exhibits from around the world and from all periods demonstrating the manifold possibilities of creating sound.

Musée Instrumental Instrumenten-museum

The Mont des Arts was created between 1956 and 1958, occupying the elevated site between the Place Royale (above) and the Place de l'Albertine (lower down). The architecturally imposing complex of large buildings includes the Bibliothèque Albert I and the strikingly modern Palais de la Dynastie and Palais de Congrès. From the square between them a fine view can be obtained of the Lower Town.

★Mont des Arts · Kunstberg

Although named after King Albert I the library is actually of much older origin, having been founded during the period of Burgundian rule. Its stock now comprises more than three million volumes together with a valuable collection of manuscripts. The library incorporates several interesting museums; also the Chapelle St Georges (1520), part of an earlier mansion belonging to the Nassau family.

Bibliothèque Albert I · Bibliotheek Albert I

The museums are: the Musée du Livre (Book Museum) which, in addition to outlining the history of books from Antiquity to the present day, has exhibitions of manuscripts, reconstructed interiors of the studies used by e.g. Emile Verhaeren and Michel de Ghelderode, and several very fine private collections built up by the Van de Velde family among others (open by prior arrangement, tel. 5195357); the Musée de l'Imprimerie (Printing Museum) illustrating the history of printing and bookbinding (open daily 9am–5pm); the Musée de la Littérature (Literature Museum) containing literary manuscripts by mainly French-speaking authors; and the Graphics Room with a collection of more than 5,000 engraving plates, etc. (open Mon.–Fri. 9am–12.45pm and 2–4.45pm).

Museums

Just up the hill from the Palais de la Dynastie, at the end of the Rue Ravenstein in what was once the Jewish Quarter, the 15th c. Hôtel Ravenstein is the city's sole building of any size surviving from the Burgundian period.

Hôtel Ravenstein

Belgium's Royal Museum of Fine Arts (1875–81), one of the largest and best art galleries in the world, extends for some distance along the Rue de la Régence (Regentschapsstraat) from the west side of the Place Royale. The museum grew out of a collection first set up in 1797 and originally housed in the former palace of Charles of Lorraine. This was

★★Musées Royaux des Beaux-Arts en Belgique · Koninklijk Museum voor Schone Kunsten van België

transferred to the newly established Musées Royaux in 1846. In 1978 a major programme of modernisation was undertaken involving enlargement of the museum by the addition of an underground extension. The entire collection was reorganised and divided into two parts, the Musée d'art ancien (15th to 18th c.) occupying the old building, and the Musée d'art moderne (mainly 19th and 20th c. Belgian works) in the new section lit by a shaft opening onto the Place du Musée. The main entrance is in the Rue de la Régence.

Musée d'art ancien

The museum (opening times Tue.–Sun. 10am–5pm) is world famous for its collection of Flemish and Dutch Old Masters. This includes works by Petrus Christus ("Pietà"), Rogier van der Weyden ("The Mourning of Christ"), Dirk Bouts ("Judgment of the Emperor Otto"), Hans Memling, and a fine "Adoration of the Magi" by Gerard David. Also on view are Quentin Massys' triptych with the Life of St Anne (one of the best examples of the work of the man regarded by many as the supreme artist of the transitional period from the 15th to the 16th c.), a triptych with the Trials of Job by Bernard van Orley, an "Entombment" by the same artist, and a portrait by Lucas Cranach. Among the highpoints of the collection are two works by Pieter Breugel the Elder, "Census at Bethlehem" and "The Fall of Icarus". Among paintings of the 17th c. Flemish school are a number by Rubens himself ("Adoration of the Magi", "Calvary", and an unusual landscape painting) and several large altar pictures from his workshop. Jordaens is represented by a number of his very best works of which the finest is his "Allegory of Fertility". There are also paintings by van Dyck and by David Teniers, the latter's "Flemish Fair" being outstanding. Although the quality of the paintings from the 17th c. Dutch school is generally speaking not so high, among the more notable are pictures by Frans Hals, Rembrandt, van der Helst, Thomas de Keyzer and Nicolaus Maes, also the genre paintings by Jan Steen and Gabriel Metsu and a number of delightful landscapes.

The collection also includes other works mainly of the Italian, Spanish and French schools.

The **museum of modern art** (Musée d'art moderne: opening times Tue.–Sun. 10am–1pm and 2–5pm) occupies the ground floor of the old building and the new below ground extension contoured into the slope of the hill. Most of the works displayed are by Belgian artists. Neo-Classicism (Navez) and Romanticism (Wappers) are well represented, while among other 19th c. works on view is the very famous "Assassination of Marat" by the French artist Jacques-Louis David. The collection of 20th c. painting includes works by James Ensor, Paul Delvaux, René Magritte, Fernande Khnopff, Rik Wouters, Frits van den Berghe and the non-Belgian Henri Matisse, Paul Gauguin and Salvador Dali.

Palais de Charles de Lorraine

The former palace of Charles of Lorraine abuts the north-west side of the Place du Musée as it runs down to the Mont des Arts. Parts of the 18th c. residence of the governor of the Austrian Netherlands are open to the public.

Sablon · Zavel

The area to the south-west of the Place Royale, the Sablon (Sands), was originally a barren and desolate piece of ground used as a cemetery for the poor. In the 16th c. members of the Brussels aristocracy began to settle there, with the result that it gradually developed into an elegant residential district.

Walking along the Rue de la Régence from the Place Royale, you will get to the Place du **Petit Sablon** (Kleine Zavel, Little Sand) which is surrounded by 48 small columns, each topped by a statuette representing

15th and 16th c.
(First floor)

- 10–17 Flemish primitives
- 11 Van der Weyden
- 13 Bouts
- 14 Memling
- 17 Bosch
- 21–33 Flemish school of the 16th c.
- 22 Metsys
- 24 Mostaert
- 25 Gossart
- 26 Van Orley
- 31 Bruegel
- 32 Moro
- 34 Heulen bequest
- 17, 24, 25 North dutch school
- 18, 19 German school
- 11, 12, 15, 16 French school
- 37–45 Delporte legacy

© Baedeker

Art from 15th to 19th c.

17th and 18th c.
(Second floor)

- 52–54
- 57, 60, 62 } Flemish school
- 62 Rubens
- 50 Spanish school
- 61 French school
- 60 Dutch school
- 50–51 Italian school (14th–18th c.)
- 55–56 Faille bequest

Musées Royaux des Beaux-Arts en Belgique

Koninklijke Musea voor Schoone Kunsten van België

19th c. (ground floor)

- 68–70 Neo-Classicism, Romanticism
- 71 Changing exhibitions
- 72, 75–78, 80 Realism
- 79 Meunier
- 82–84 Watercolours, drawings
- 80–85 Symbolism
- 87 Luminism
- 88 Evenepoel
- 89 Ensor
- 90–91 Impressionism
- 91 Hess-Vandenbroeck legacy

20th c. Art
(basement)

- –2 New publicity
- –3 New publicity, small format drawings, paintings and sculpture
- –4 Fauvism, Cubism, Futurism, abstract art, Expressionism
- –5 Delvaux, Surrealism
- –6 Magritte, Surrealism, recent Belgian painting, Cobra, lyric abstraction, group "Phases"
- –7 Group "Zero", geometric abstraction
- –8 Contemporary trends

20th c. Art

© Baedeker

Temporary exhibitions

Entrance

185

Notre Dame du Sablon, seen from the Petit Sablon

one of the Brussels guilds. Statues of Counts Egmont and Hoorn and some of the humanist scholars adorn the centre of the Place.

Palais d'Egmont · Egmontpaleis

South-east of the Place stands the Palais d'Egmont (Palais Arenberg), now used for state receptions.

★Église du Sablon · Zavelkerk

The 15th–16th c. church of Notre-Dame du Sablon (Onze Lieve Vrouw op de Zavel), generally considered one of the loveliest Late Gothic churches in Belgium, was built as a replacement for a small chapel first erected on the sandy expanse of the Sablon by the Crossbowmen's Guild in 1304. The interior of the church is breathtaking, in particular because of its marvellous stained glass. Also of interest is the burial chapel of the Tourn und Taxis family, partly the work of Luc Fayd'herbe. Kept in the sacrarium built in 1549 is a figure of the Virgin, a copy, so legend has it, of a Madonna brought to the chapel in 1348 by an Antwerp woman, Baet Soetens, to whom the Virgin had appeared.

Grand Sablon · Grote Zavel

Below the church the Place du Grand Sablon (Grote Zavel) slopes down to the Lower Town. The area is dotted with antique shops and antiquarian bookshops. Brussels' best-known flea market is held on the square itself every Saturday.

★Quartier des Marolles

The Quartier des Marolles (Metro Porte de Hal) occupies a triangular area on the south side of the city centre between the Gare du Midi, Porte de Hal and, towering high above everything, the Palais de Justice. Up to now the district has always been the preserve of the under-privileged, living by their wits and deeply distrustful of "the authorities". This distrust has been fuelled anew now that the very survival of the quarter is threatened by a wave of speculative building and an influx of EU employees for whom the Marolles is the "smart" place to have an apartment – after it has been luxuriously restored that is! About 10,000 people live in the area, mainly low wage earners, Eastern districts shopkeepers and tradespeople, often speaking a patois incomprehensible to outsiders by whom they tend to be regarded as loud-mouthed and uncouth. Even in the Middle Ages the Marolles was a refuge for the persecuted and today as many as a third of its inhabitants are thought to be illegal immigrants. The quarter's most famous son was Pieter Breugel the Elder whose house stands in the Rue Haute (Hoogstraat; No. 132).

The **Place du Jeu de Balle** (Vossenplein) at the heart of the Marolles has a very colourful street market selling all kinds of merchandise. It is most attractive on Saturdays.

The modest houses of the Quartier des Marolles cower in the shadow of the huge Palais de Justice (1866–83), designed by Joseph Poelaert and built on the Galgenberg, the hill where the gallows stood in medieval times. Its massive dimensions, 104 m (341 ft) high and 26,000 sq. m (279,864 sq. ft) in area, make it the largest building to be erected in Brussels in the 19th c.

★Palais de Justice · Justitiepaleis

This gate at the southern extremity of the city centre is the sole remnant of the 14th c. ring walls.

Porte de Hal · Hallepoort

Except for the west tower which was completed in 1699, the Brabant Gothic church of Notre-Dame de la Chapelle on the northern edge of the Marolles dates from the 13th–15th c. Inside are figures of the apostles by Duquesnoy and Fayd'herbe, but the church is best known as the **burial place of Pieter Breugel the Elder** whose tomb can be seen in the fourth chapel along on the right from the main door. The black marble memo-

N.-D. de la Chapelle · Kapellekerk

Colourful Saturday market on the Place du Jeu de Balle

187

rial with a painting by Rubens (now a copy) was erected by the artist's younger son Jan, known as "Velvet". The frame and inscription were added later by Breugel's grandson David Tenier III. To the right of the choir is the burial chapel of the Spinola family.

Eastern districts

Cité
Européenne

The Rue de la Loi (Wetstraat), running east from the city centre towards the Parc du Cinquantenaire, terminates at the Rond Point Schuman (Schumanplein, Metro Schuman) around which is grouped the Cité Européenne, the "EU City" consisting of 43 buildings. The main building was the Palais Berlaymont, headquarters of the EU and its administration. The irregular cross-shaped building is currently undergoing renovation because of the asbestos used in its construction between 1963–69. Opposite are the new EU buildings built in post-Modernist style: the Ministers Council building and behind it the 72 m (236 ft) high glass dome of the European Parliament, already referred to locally as "Caprice des Dieux" (Whim of the Gods), because to some people it resembles the box which contains the French soft cheese of the same name, and to others, because of its size, it may well have arisen from a whim of the (European) gods.

Musée de
l'Institut Royal
des Sciences
Naturelles de
Belgique

One street south of the EU building lies the attractive Parc Léopold, at the southern end of which is the Museum of the Royal Institute of Natural Sciences (Musée de l'Institut Royal des Sciences Naturelles de Belgique/Museum van het Koninklijk Belgisch Instituut voor Natuurwetenschapen).

Dinosaur skeletons The biggest attraction in the museums are the partially reconstructed skeletons of 29 iguanodons discovered in 1878 at Bernissart in western Belgium (opening times Tue.–Sat. 9.30am–4.45pm, Sun. until 6pm).

Musée Wiertz

The Musée Wiertz immediately next to the Natural Sciences Museum contains a large number of paintings by the Belgian Romantic painter Antoine Wiertz.

★Parc du
Cinquantenaire ·
Jubelpark

The Parc du Cinquantenaire (Metro Schuman, Merode), was established in 1880 to commemorate the country's 50th anniversary. Its centrepiece is the monumental Palais du Cinquantenaire, the two wings of which, linked in 1905 by a massive triumphal arch designed by the French architect Charles Girault, house two of Brussels' most interesting museums.

★★Musées
Royaux d'Art et
d'Histoire

The Royal Museums of Art and History (Musées Royaux d'Art et d'Histoire/Koninklijk Musea voor Kunst en Geschiedenis, open Tue.–Fri. 9.30am–5pm) occupying the south wing of the Palais is split into two main sections: Mediterranean culture from early history to Antiquity (in the new Kennedy Wing) and Belgian pre- and early history, the history of Christian Europe from the Middle Ages, and Asian and American culture (in the older Nerviens Wing).

Kennedy Wing Ground floor: archaeological finds from, e.g. Luristan and Jericho. First floor: Etruscan, Greek and Roman cultures including a 2nd c. AD street and very large 5th c. AD mosaic from the town of Apamea in Syria. Second floor: Egyptian artefacts.

Nerviens Wing Only the most interesting rooms can be listed. Rooms 1–6: Belgian settlement up to Roman times; Rooms 16–31: art and applied art from the 14th to 17th c., including Paris, Tournai and Brussels tapestries (legend of the Sablon Virgin, Battle of Roncevaux) and, in pride of place, a carved altarpiece of St George by Jan Borman; Room 36: large narthex with eight Brussels Gobelins from cartoons by Bernard

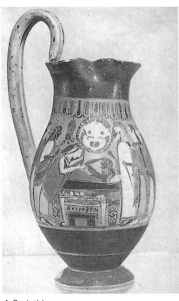

A Corinthian vase

Stained glass: William II, Count of Namur

van Orley illustrating the story of Jacob; Rooms 45–46: Oriental and Islamic art; Rooms 48–53: European applied art from the 17th to 20th c. including, Room 51, Art Nouveau; Rooms 55–67: South-east Asia, America and Oceania; Rooms 76–83: 15th to 20th c. European costume and lace; delftware; Room 96: China.

The Belgian Army Museum and Museum of Military History (Musée Royal de l'Armée et d'Histoire Militaire/Koninklijk Museum van het Leger en van de Militaire Geschiedenis) occupies the north wing of the Palais Cinquantenaire (opening times Tue.–Sun. 9am–noon and 1–4.45pm). It provides an overview of the development of military technology and of the major campaigns fought on Belgian soil.

★Musée Royal de l'Armée et d'Histoire Militaire

The museum has three **principal sections**: Belgian military history (documents, uniforms and weaponry from the Middle Ages to the present day, including a most comprehensive collection of medieval arms and armour); the Armoured Vehicle Hall with artillery, tanks, etc. from the two World Wars; and the Air Section with a collection of aircraft from the First World War onwards.

Established in 1986 and housed in the imposing Palais Mondial (1880) where, between 1902 and 1934, the famous Brussels motor car and motor cycle exhibitions were held, Autoworld (opening times daily 10am–6pm, Oct.–Mar. only until 5pm) comprises a display of some 950 vintage cars and other vehicles. Most come from private collections and span the whole range of marquees starting from the very earliest days of motoring. Among them are all the best known names including Mercedes-Benz, Horch, Opel, Minerva, Cadillac, Rolls Royce, Hispano Suiza, Ford, Humber, Bentley, Packard and Oldsmobile. A collection of

★Autoworld

American presidential limousines is one of Autoworld's special attractions.

Northern districts

Laeken

Although the **Château Royal**, home of the Belgian Royal Family, is not itself open to the public, the park surrounding it at Laeken is (Metro to Bockstael, then bus No. 53). There are delightful footpaths and a number of things worth seeing such as the monument to Leopold I at the centre of the circular flowerbed in front of the palace. The Japanese Tower in the northernmost corner of the park was originally built for the Paris Exhibition of 1900.

The **hothouses**, erected in Leopold II's time, are the highlight of the gardens and open to the public for 10 days during late April and early May when many of the plants are in flower.

The **Chinese Pavilion**, facing the Japanese Tower, on the opposite side of the road, was likewise brought to the park from the Paris Exhibition. It now houses a good collection of Chinese and Japanese porcelain (open Tue.–Sun. 10am–5pm).

Notre-Dame de Laeken

On the far side of the wide avenue skirting the western edge of the park stands the extremely large church of Notre-Dame de Laeken (Onze Lieve Vrouw te Laeken), burial place of Belgium's kings and queens. Commissioned in 1851 by Leopold I following the death of his wife Louise-Marie, the building was designed by Josef Poelaert, architect of the Palais de Justice. It was completed in 1872. Inside the church a much revered 13th c. Madonna adorns the high altar and behind the choir can be seen the entrance to the royal crypt. The graves of many an important Belgian public figure are to be found in the churchyard.

★★Atomium

Apart from Manneken Pis the Atomium is Brussels' best-known landmark (Metro: Heysel; opening times Apr.–Aug. 9am–8pm; Sep.–Mar. 9am–6pm). Designed by the architect André Waterkeyn for the 1958 Brussels World Exhibition, the 102 m (326 ft)-high steel and aluminium structure represents a molecule of iron magnified 165 million times. The spheres are used for the presentation of a show called "Biogenium" about the developments in science and medicine over the last forty years. The topmost sphere contains a viewing platform which offers an excellent panorama of Brussels.

Bruparck

Bruparck, a popular leisure park immediately adjacent to the Atomium, incorporates four principal attractions: "Mini-Europe", a collection of 1:25 scale models of the continent's most famous historic and modern monuments; the "Océade" in the Parc Aquatique, a 7000 sq. m (75,375 sq. ft) swimming pool with all kinds of additional features; the "Kinepolis", a 24-auditorium cinema complex; and "Le Village", with restaurants, bars, etc. and a place to sit down! (See Practical Information, Leisure Parks for opening times.).

Heysel Stadium

A short distance beyond Bruparck lies the Heysel Stadium, made tragically familiar by the events of May 1985.

Palais du Centenaire

The Palais du Centenaire (Paleis van het Eeuwfestwijk) north of the Atomium was completed for Belgium's centenary celebrations in 1930. It now forms part of the Brussels trade fair and exhibition centre also incorporating the big International Trade Mart (1975).

Western districts

Koekelberg

The Koekelberg (Metro Simonis) district is dominated by the massive

The Atomium, an iron molecule exaggerated 165 thousand million times ▶

Basilique National du Sacré Cöur (Nationale Basiliek van het Heilig Hart), the brainchild of Leopold II and begun in 1905 to mark the country's 75th anniversary. The building was only completed in 1970. Not surprisingly therefore it displays something of a mixture of styles, impressing nevertheless by its sheer size (141 m/463 ft × 107 m/351 ft). The picture of Christ giving His blessing which hangs above the altar is by Georges Minne. The dome affords a magnificent view over the city (access to dome: Jul. and Aug. Sat., Sun. and public holidays 2–5.45pm; May, Jun. and Sep.–mid Oct. Sun. and public holidays 2–5.45pm).

Anderlecht	The Anderlecht district to the west of the city centre (Metro: Gare du Midi, St Guidon) is the home of Brussels' most famous football club, RSC Anderlecht.
Musée de la Gueuze	A short distance north of the Gare du Midi Metro station, in the Rue Gheude (Gheudestraat), one of the most unusual of all the city's museums, the Musée de la Gueuze (Gueuzemuseum), can be visited in the only Brussels brewery still producing this bitter-sweet speciality beer of the Payotte region (open: all year Mon.–Fri. 8.30am–5pm).
★Maison d'Erasme · Erasmushuis	In 1521 the humanist scholar Erasmus of Rotterdam (1469–1536) lodged for five months in the early 16th c. house still standing today in what is now the Rue du Chapitre (Kapiteelstraat) near the Metro station St-Guidon. In addition to Gothic and Renaissance furnishings the rooms of Maison d'Erasme contain a number of items belonging to the great man. Visitors can see his study and his bedroom, in the latter a first edition of "In Praise of Folly" is displayed. On the ground floor are several interesting paintings, including one by Hieronymus Bosch (open Mon., Wed., Thur., Sat., Sun., 10am–noon and 2–5pm).
Saints Pierre et Guidon · Sint-Pieter en Guido	The fine Gothic building seen not far from the Maison d'Erasme is the 14th–16th c. collegiate church of St Peter and St Guido, the distinctive spire of which is a 19th c. addition. As well as a 14th c. arch and some reasonably well preserved medieval wall paintings, the interior boasts an 11th c. five-aisled crypt below the choir, probably originally part of a church above ground. The crypt contains a stone sarcophagus, the tomb of St Guido, patron saint of horses.
Béguinage	Anderlecht's béguinage, founded in 1252, used to be situated near the church. Four surviving 17th c. buildings have been converted into a museum (open Mon., Wed., Thu., Sat., Sun., 10am–noon and 2–5pm).

Southern districts

Forest · Vorst	The suburb of Forest (Tram 19, 52) lies sprawled across the slope of the Senne valley 3 km (2 mi.) south of the city centre. The Parc de Forest and Parc Duden are the remains of a large forest which was once Charles V's hunting preserve.
Saint-Denis · Sint-Denijs	Built in 1250 on the site of an earlier (7th c.) chapel, the small church of Saint-Denis (Square Omer Denis) contains the 11th c. tomb of Alène, daughter of a non-Christian nobleman from Dilbeek. Incensed by learning of his daughter's secret baptism he is said to have beaten her to death, only to become a convert to Christianity himself as a result of miracles witnessed at her grave.
Saint Gilles · Sint-Gillis	**Musée Horta,** (Tram: 92) Victor Horta's house (Rue Américaine /Amerikaansestraat), itself a masterpiece of Art Nouveau architecture (1898–1901), has been turned into a museum celebrating the life and work of the movement's leading Belgian exponent. The staircase is magnificent (open: Tue.–Sun. 2–5.30pm).

The suburb of Ixelles (Tram 81, 93, 94) extends south of the ring boulevard, its main shopping street being the Chaussée d'Ixelles (Elsenesteenweg), a busy thoroughfare.

Ixelles · Elsene

The **Musée communal des Beaux-Arts** (Gemeentemuseum voor Schone Kunsten) in the Rue Jean van Volsem off the east side of the Chaussée possesses an excellent collection of Belgian and French paintings and of Belgian Impressionist paintings in particular.

Abbaye de la Cambre · Abdij ter Kameren In 1200, in what was then a small valley between the Etangs d'Ixelles (the little lakes now situated at the end of the Chaussée d'Ixelles) and the Bois de la Cambre which today forms an oasis of tranquillity amidst the city traffic, Cistercian nuns founded an abbey. It was destroyed in the 16th c. but then rebuilt. Now, set in lovely French gardens, it houses the National Geographical Institute and an art college.

The former abbey church (14th c.) is a slender, elegant building with Baroque vaulting. Inside can be seen a painting by Albert Bouts ("The Mocking of Christ") and the shrine of St Boniface, a 13th c. Bishop of Brussels. The windows of the cloister are decorated with the coats of arms of over 40 abbesses and nuns.

The **Bois de la Cambre** (Kamerenbos) in the very south of Ixelles is one of the favourite recreation areas close to Greater Brussels. The 24 ha (59 acre) park has a lake, restaurants and broad expanses of grass for games or merely for resting.

The wide and splendid Avenue Louise (Louizalaan) links the park directly with the city centre.

University Located at the east edge of the park are administrative buildings and lecture halls belonging to the Université Libre de Bruxelles (Free University of Brussels), the larger and more modern part of which occupies a site a little further east still, in Etterbeek.

Charles de Coster (see Famous People) lies buried in the **cemetery** on Ixelles' boundary with Etterbeek. A figure of Till Eulenspiegel decorates his grave.

Musée van Buuren The museum at Avenue Léo Errera No. 41 (Tram 92), home of art collectors David and Alice van Buuren, is of great interest on two counts, the first being the house itself with its genuine Art Déco furnishings. The second of course is the superb art collection complementing the furniture. Among the finest items are Pieter Breugel the Elder's "The Fall of Icarus", paintings by Patinir, Fantin-Latour, Permeke, and van de Woestyne, sculptures by Minne and the collection of delftware (opening times Mon. 2–4pm, Sun. 1–5.30pm).

Uccle · Ukkel

This south-eastern district of Brussels (Tram 44) borders the Forêt de Soignes (see below). The Etangs de Rouge Cloître (Rood Klooster) are a reminder of the priory which once stood here, where in 1482 the painter Hugo van der Goes died. The Château de Val Duchesse in the large park just to the north is best known for being the place where the original Treaty of Rome setting up the EEC (now the EU) was made ready for signing.

Anderghem · Oudergem

Surroundings

Beyond the Bois de la Cambre south-east of Brussels stretches one of the finest woodlands in Belgium, the 4000 ha (9900 acre) Forêt de Soignes (Tram 44). With its magnificent beech groves the Forêt is a popular recreation area for the capital and in summer old trams from the

★**Forêt de Soignes ·**
Zoniënwoud

urban transport museum (Musée du Transport Urbain Bruxellois/Museum voor Het Stedleijk Vervoer te Brussel) in Woluwe-Sint-Pieter (364b Avenue de Tervueren) trundle through the woods (open early Apr.–early Sep. Sat. and Sun. 1.30–7pm).

Groenendael

Some 13 km (8 mi.) south-east of the city centre, tucked away in a pretty valley in the midst of the forest, the little hamlet of Groenendael was once the site of a famous Augustinian abbey founded in 1343 by the mystic Jan van Ruysbroek. The only abbey building to survive (18th c.) is now in use as a high-class restaurant. The interesting Groenendael arboretum on the valley's south-facing slope has over 500 exotic tree and shrub species as well as a forest museum.

Tervuren

A visit to Tervuren (Tram 44), 12 km (7½ mi.) east of Brussels, should be high on any list of excursions outside the capital simply on account of its quite exceptional museum.

The **Musée Royal de l'Afrique Central** is housed in a palatial building designed by the French architect Charles Girault. Completed in 1910 the project was yet another brainchild of King Léopold II. The museum's extremely comprehensive collection, deriving mainly from the former Belgian Congo, embraces the wildlife, archaeology, minerology, ethnography and art of the peoples of Central Africa. The minerals section in particular, and also the collection of masks and carved wood and ivory figures, are unique (open Tue.–Fri. 10am–5pm, Sat. and Sun. 10am–6pm).

Well stocked with fine old trees, the large and pleasant Tervuren Park extends south from the museum.

More inviting even than the Park is a stroll through the Tervuren **arbore-**

The Kasteel van Gaasbeek, popular for outings with the people of Brussels

tum in the delightful woodland setting of the Bois de Capuchins (Kapucijnenbos).

Plentifully supplied with restaurants, including many which serve the local cherry-flavoured beer called kriek, **Jezus Eik**, a small commune immediately south of the Arboretum, offers welcome respite for tired legs.

Ensconced in a charming park 14 km (8½ mi.) south-west of Brussels (leave by Anderlechtsepoort, thence via Viezenbeek) stands the medieval Kasteel van Gaasbeek (Bus LK). Parts of the château are 13th c. but the main Renaissance-style building dates from the 16th c.

★**Kasteel van Gaasbeek**

The magnificent interior contains superb furniture, carpets, glass, porcelain, paintings, gold and silverware and armour. Most remarkable of all however are the priceless 15th–17th c. Brussels and Tournai tapestries. Rubens' will can also be seen, on display in the archive room.

The terrace has a lovely view of the gently undulating countryside which Bruegel so often captured in his paintings and which today remains a delightful place to walk (open Apr.–Oct. Tue.–Thu., Sat. and Sun. 10am–5pm; Jul./Aug. also open Mon.).

★**Nationaal Plantentium van Bouchout** Belgium's national botanic garden in the suburb of Meise 14 km (8½ mi.) north of Brussels (Bus L to Meise) opened in 1958. The nurseries and hothouses are grouped around the castle (12th c.) and lake of the Domaine Bouchout, where Leopold II's sister the Empress Charlotte of Mexico lived after fleeing the Mexican Revolution. More than 10,000 plants are arranged according to geographical origin. Among the highlights are the collection of water and wetland plants in the "Victoria" hothouse and the tropical and subtropical plants in the so-called "Palais des Plantes" (open: park daily 9am–6.30pm; hothouses and herbarium Apr.–Oct. Mon.–Thu. and Sat. 9am–4pm, Sun until 5pm).

Meise

Grimbergen, 12 km (7½ mi.) north of the city centre (Bus G, H), could once lay claim to an abbey founded in the 12th c. It still takes pride in its impressive abbey church (1660–1700), the Baroque interior of which is one of the most sumptuously ornate in Belgium. Particularly noteworthy are the four confessionals by Verbruggen.

Grimbergen

See Halle, Surroundings

See entry

Beersel

Waterloo

Charleroi

K 10

Province: Hainaut
Altitude: 40–200 m (130–656 ft). Population: 220,000
Intercity and Inter-regional Station

The modern industrial city of Charleroi and its environs lie at the heart of one of Europe's oldest industrial regions. This part of southern Belgium is almost synonymous with coal and steel production, both of which industries have been in crisis in recent years but now show signs of recovery. Such is the scale of industrialisation hereabouts that the area is known as the Pays Noir (the Black Country). More than 450,000 people live in the conurbation around Charleroi, a pool of skilled labour for the 200 companies engaged in iron and steel (Cockerill-Sambre) or chemical production, various types of manufacturing (farm machinery, electrical goods, medical appliances), aircraft assembly and publishing (Dupois). Charleroi is famous too for its glassworks, carrying on a tradition going back more than 400 years. The city is an important crossroads served by the Charleroi–Bruxelles Canal which forms a vital link between the Sambre and the Scheldt. It has a technological university (Université de Travail) and a number of other scientific institutes. Even though separated from the industry dominated lower town, the upper town with its pedestrian zone has little in the way of sights apart from one or two interesting museums. Charleroi however is a big, lively, enterprising city. Every year thousands of visitors are attracted to its various trade fairs, one of which, the Salon de la Bande Dessinée (Comic Strips), is unique in Europe.

History Charleroi began as an ordinary medieval rural village called Charnoy the inhabitants of which also engaged in a little mining. This changed in 1659 when much of Hainaut was captured by the French and

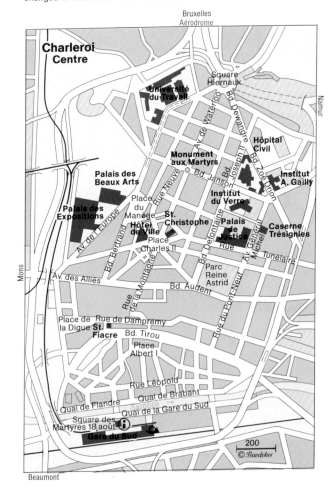

Charnoy suddenly found itself a Spanish frontier post. As a check on the ambitions of the French King Louis XIV, Charles II of Spain expanded the village into a fortress, renaming it at the same time. For the next 30 years Charleroi lay at the centre of a battlefield, being taken by the French in 1667 – after which Vauban strengthened the fortifications – and recovered by Spain in 1679. The Peace of Rujswijk in 1697 brought a period of respite, which ended when hostilities were renewed following the French Revolution. Industrialisation proper began in the first half of the 19th c., accompanied by the construction of a canal link with Brussels in 1832. The old walls were demolished in 1868 being replaced by boulevards which can still be seen today. In the First World War, after heavy fighting, German troops occupied the city in August 1914.

Military processions The region around Charleroi is unique in Belgium for its tradition of "marches militaires", a form of religious cum military festival in which the members of various local societies and brotherhoods don colourful military uniforms and parade to the music of brass bands and the noise of guns. One of the best-known is the Marche de la Madeleine (end of July) when 1500 "infantry", 150 horsemen and 30 bands set off from Jumet on a 20 km (12 mi.) "march".

The heart of Charleroi's upper town is the Place Charles II, dominated by the Hôtel de Ville (Town Hall; 1936) and its towering 70 m (230 ft-high) belfry with a carillon of 47 bells.

Hôtel de Ville

Housed in the Hôtel de Ville the Musée des Beaux-Arts (Museum of Fine Arts) consists primarily of a collection of works by Hainaut artists. Another whole section (Musée Jules Destrée) is devoted to the lawyer, statesman and writer Jules Destrée (1863–1936; open Tue.–Sun. 9am–5pm).

Musée des Beaux-Arts

Across the square from the Hôtel de Ville can be seen the cupola of the Basilique Sainte-Christophe (1801; fine mosaic in the choir).

Sainte-Christophe

The Palais des Beaux-Arts in the Avenue de l'Europe (west of the Hôtel de Ville on the far side of the Place de la Manège) is the home of the well-known Ballet Royal de Wallonie.

Palais des Beaux-Arts

The Musée du Verre (Glass Museum) occupies part of the Institut National du Verre on the Boulevard Defontaine to the east of the Hôtel de Ville. The museum comprises two large departments, one concerned with the history and production of glass throughout the world, the other with the development of the Belgium glass industry in particular. On display are some quite exceptional examples of the glass-maker's art from Antiquity to the present day. A permanent exhibition on the ground floor provides a showcase for the glassware manufactured in Belgium today (open Tue.–Sun. 9am–5pm).

★Musée du Verre

The **Musée Archéologique** occupies the basement of the Institute National du Verre. As well as archaeological finds mainly from the Roman and Merovingian periods there are interesting exhibits from the early modern and industrial eras (open Tue.–Sun. 9am–5pm).

Surroundings

In the western suburb of Marchienne-au-Pont, part of an old ironworks (134, Rue de la Providence) has been converted into the **Musée de l'Industrie**. Sections of an old rolling mill, forges, a machine workshop and a print-works are among the many intriguing exhibits (open daily 9am–4pm. Sat. on request).

Marchienne-au-Pont

Also in Marchienne-au-Pont (Place des Martyrs) the **Musée d'Histoire, de Folklore et d'Archéologie Industrielle** (Museum of Local History and Industrial Archaeology) traces the history of industrial development in and around Charleroi (open Wed. and Fri. 5–7pm).

Marchienne-au-Pont's 17th c. **château** was the family seat of the writer Marguerite Yourcenar.

The south-western suburb of **Mont-sur-Marchienne** also has a surprise in store in the shape of its remarkable Musée de la Photographie in the former Carmelite convent. Here, in one of the best museums of its kind, there are excellent displays explaining the development of photography as well as collections of cameras and photographs old and new (open Tue.–Sun. 10am–6pm).

Gerpinnes

Gerpinnes, 8 km (5 mi.) south of Charleroi, is a traditional stronghold of the marche militaire, well-known for its big Easter Monday Marche de Saint-Roland.

★Abbaye d'Aulne

Some 12 km (7½ mi.) west of Charleroi stand the impressive ruins of the Abbaye d'Aulne, founded in the 7th c. by St Landelin of Lobbes. It was taken over by the Cistercians in 1147 and burnt down by French revolutionaries in 1794.
 The abbey remains are well worth seeing. They include the great court and Prince-Bishops' reception hall, also the 14th–15th c. choir and transepts of the ruined abbey church.

Claire-Fontaine

The Claire-Fontaine leisure centre in the small town of Chapelle-lez-Herlaimont, 11 km (7 mi.) north-west of Charleroi, offers an extensive range of amusements including boating, swimming, dry tobogganing and mini-golf.

Chimay N 9

Province: Hainaut
Altitude: 100–270 m (328–885 ft.) Population: 10,000

Surrounded by extensive woods the small town of Chimay is situated in the province of Hainaut, near the French border. Jean Froissart, chronicler of the Hundred Years' War, spent his last years in Chimay; another famous inhabitant of the town was Thérése Tallien (1773–1835), an enigmatic personality, who went down in history as "Notre-Dame de Thermidor". As the wife of the proconsul of the French republic, Tallien, she encouraged him to resist the tyrant Robespierre, which later led to his downfall. Following her divorce from Tallien she married François-Joseph de Caraman, Prince of Chimay, and turned the château at Chimay into a meeting place for lovers of music and theatre.

Grand-Place

The attractive small Grand-Place is surrounded by several old manor houses and the 17th c. town hall.

The collegiate church of **Saints-Pierre-et-Paul** stands directly in the centre of the Grand-Place. Building of the choir started in the 13th c. but the tower was not completed until the 18th c.
 The church interior contains Baroque choir stalls (1702) and the tombs of Charles de Croy, the chamberlain of Charles V, Madame Tallien and Jean Froissart. Among the church treasure is a small chest decorated with Byzantine mosaics which belonged to Philippe de Croy.

★Château

A few yards to the west of the Grand-Place is Chimay Château, built on a rocky promontory over the Eau Blanche River by the Croy family in the 16th c. Madame Tallien commissioned the construction of a theatre in the courtyard but it was partly burnt down in 1935 together with the château.

The tour leads through rooms furnished in contemporary style to the Grand Hall with an interesting 14th c. fireplace and into various drawing rooms where keepsakes of Madame Tallien and her visitors can be seen, including a portrait of Princess Gérard; in the Napoleon Room the christening dress of Eugène, son of Napoleon III is displayed.

Surroundings

Founded in 1850 the Trappist monastery of Scourmont is idyllically situated in the forest of Chimay 9 km (6 mi.) south of the town. The monastery is widely known for its own beer, "Trappiste de Chimay", brewed in three different strengths, and its cheese.

Abbaye de Scourmont

In the small town of Couvin 11 km (7 mi.) to the east the first coking plant in Europe was erected. The Cavernes d'Abîme, inhabited in prehistoric times, as illustrated by a slide show on early history, are worth visiting as are the Grottes de Neptun, cut into the limestone rocks by the Eau Noire river. The tour finishes with an underground boat trip (open Apr.–Sep. daily 9.30am–noon and 1.30–6pm; in Jul. and Aug. all day; Oct. at weekends).

Couvin

Nismes, 15 km (9 mi.) east of Chimay, is a popular venue for summer holidays. A small tourist train calls at the sights: the ruins of the magnificent castle, the Neo-Gothic town hall and the Museum of Folklore and History.

Nismes

The cloister garth of Scourmont, near Chimay

Mariembourg

On the instructions of Charles V Mariembourg, 16 km (10 mi.) north-east of Chimay, was fortified in 1546 in the shape of a star. The town gets its name from Maria of Hungary. Mariembourg is the departure point of the nostalgic steam railway "Trois Vallées", which chugs through the protected area of Viroin via Chimay to Momignies (Apr.–Sep. Sat., Sun., public holidays; Jul. and Aug. also Tue., Wed., Thu.). There is a 600 m-long go-karting track, the "Karting des Fagnes" with go-karts available for hire in Mariembourg.

★Étang de Virelles

The êtang de Virelles, 3 km (2 mi.) north of Chimay, is a popular venue for excursions.

Damme   D 4

Province: West-Vlaanderen
Altitude: 8 m (26 ft.) Population: 10,500

The charming little Flemish town of Damme lies about 7 km (4 mi.) north-east of Bruges (see Bruges). Up until the silting of the Zwin inlet it served as the customs point and outer port of Bruges, in which capacity it enjoyed great importance and prosperity. Its heyday only lasted about 200 years but several significant buildings still remain from this period which give the town a contented atmosphere and have kept the image of a **medieval Flemish town** alive. In addition its highly-praised and excellent restaurants make Damme a popular destination for many gourmets while the antiquarian bookshops attract many friends of the book.

The Stadhuis in Damme

In the second half of the 13th c. the "Vader der Dietsche Dichters" (Father of Dutch poets) Jacob van Maerlant lived in Damme where he wrote his most significant works. However, the town was immortalised as the home town of Thyl Ullenspiegel and Lamme Goedzak, the famous characters in the novel by Charles De Coster (see Introduction, Famous People).

History 850 years ago, when the Zwin, a wide inlet, penetrated far into the coastal plain Bruges began to gain importance as a port. A terminal dyke was built up at the end of the Zwin on which a small town, which is now Damme, developed. It became the outer port of Bruges and received its town charter in 1180 but was burnt down in 1213 together with its fleet of 400 ships by the troops of the French king. Undeterred the citizens of Damme set about rebuilding so that it retained its function as port and commercial centre with important nations and trading companies being represented here until the beginning of the 15th c.; in its heyday Damme was the chief trade centre in northern Europe for wine and the most important market in Europe for Swedish herring. Silting up of Bruges harbour was already noticeable by the end of the 13th c. finally reaching the harbour basin at Damme. A final high point before its eventual decline was the marriage of Charles the Bold with Margaretha of York.

The central point of Damme is the **Grote Markt** surrounded by some interesting buildings. A monument to Jacob van Maerlant stands in the centre of the square.

The magnificent Gothic town hall (Stadhuis) built by Gottfried von Bosschere in 1464–68 has six statues of Flemish counts and countesses decorating its façade: Philip of Alsace, Johanna and Margaretha of Constantinople, Philipp of Thiette, Charles the Bold and Margaretha of York. The entrance loggia was added in 1860. The interior houses original doorways carved with historic scenes. | Stadhuis

To the right of the town hall stands the "De Grote Sterre" (Great Star) House, a 15th c. patrician's house and later seat of the Spanish governor. It also houses the Ullenspiegel Museum and the Jacob-van-Maerlant Museum. | "De Grote Sterre"

The semi-detached house next to the Grote Sterre was where the wedding party of Charles the Bold and Margaretha of York took place in 1468. | Sint-Janshuis and Weytshuis

Not far from the Grote Markt in the Kerkstraat, Damme's main street, is the Sint-Janshospitaal. It was founded in 1249 by Margaretha of Constantinople and has been a home for the elderly since the 19th c. Part of it, however, serves as a museum with exhibitions of paintings, enamel, silver and books from the monastery library (open Apr.–Sep. Tue.–Thu. and Sat. 11am–noon and 2–6pm; Oct.–Mar. Sat. and Sun. 2–4.30pm). | Sint-Janshospitaal

The impressive 45 m (147 ft)-high tower of the Onze-Lieve-Vrouwkerk (Church of Our Lady) is visible from afar, a brick building begun in 1230 in the Schelde Gothic style. At the beginning of the 14th c. the choir which was completed in 1250 was converted into an interesting hall choir. In 1578 the church was set on fire by troops belonging to the Prince of Orange; in 1725 when Damme was becoming increasingly impoverished the top of the tower, the transept and parts of the nave were demolished. The interior houses valuable figures of the apostles carved in oak from 1400, the St Anne altar dated 1555 and the Baroque Holy Cross altar of 1636. Jacob van Maerlant is buried under the former main portal below the tower. From the top of the tower there is | Onze-Lieve-Vrouwkerk a marvellous view of the Flemish countryside, sometimes as far as the coast.

Museum Delporte

In the nearby Burgstraat the Museum Delporte was opened in 1990 in the pretty whitewashed old school-house. Modern paintings and sculptures by the Belgian artist Charles Delporte are on display (open Easter–Autumn daily 2–6pm).

Charles Deporte is both painter and sculptor, known primarily for his portraits. He uses a variety of material in his work. Typical of his sculpture are heads looking into the light as in this example.

Uilenspiegel Monument

Erected in 1979 the Uilenspiegel monument on the canal bridge commemorates the 100th anniversary of the death of Charles de Coster.

Schellemolen

On the other side of the canal, to the east of the town centre, stands the Schellemolen, erected in 1867, a popular subject for photographs.

Museum Frans Wiro van Hinsberg

In a typical Flemish house near the mill copper casting in an artist's forge can be seen at the Frans Wiro van Hinsberg Museum (open Sat. and Sun. 2–5pm; Jun.–Sep. also Wed. 2–5pm).

Surroundings

Schipdonkkanaal

In 1846 work commenced on the branch canal for the Leie (Afleidingkanaal van de Leie), also known as Schipdonkkanaal. It leads north of Damme in a north-west direction to Zeebrugge. Road 374 crosses the canal at Oostkerke where there is a small guest house with a terrace. The two straight courses of the canal flowing past with the apparently endless rows of poplars provide a wonderful scene of peace and tranquillity.

In summer there are daily **boat trips** from Damme to Bruges (see Bruges) on the "Lamme Goedzak" (Information: Benelux-Damme Shipping Company, Stadhuis Damme, tel. (050) 353319).

Dendermonde · Termonde   E 8

Province: Oost-Vlaanderen
Altitude: 25 m (82 ft) Population: 42,000
Inter-regional Station (bicycle rental at station)

On the right bank of the Scheldt, which joins the Dender lies Dendermonde (French Termonde; mouth of the Dender). The town's prosperity, still apparent from the magnificent buildings, stems from the textile industry. A large number of interesting historical monuments and art treasures have been preserved from its long history.

History The first building on this site at the mouth of the river was a castle in the 10th c. under the protection of which a small town developed and received its charter in 1233. Owing to its strategic position Dendermonde was fortified and often besieged, as in 1667 when the 50,000 soldiers of Louis XIV had to retreat when the townspeople opened the locks thereby flooding the land. Parts of the town were badly damaged in 1914 when it was captured by German troops.

Festivals On the last Sunday in August a giant procession takes place

Dendermonde: the Vleeshuis in the Grote Markt

annually in Dendermonde where the giants Indiaan, Mars and Goliath dance. A more unusual event is the procession of the Bayard steed with the four children of Haimon on its back. This takes place every ten years (next date: 2000). Every year at the beginning of September Dendermonde stages a busy international jazz festival.

The buildings of the Grote Markt in the centre of the town provide the picture of an attractive enclosed Flemish market square towards the end of the Middle Ages.

★Grote Markt

The **stadhuis** (town hall) was built between 1336–50 as a textile hall and converted in 1600. It was almost competely destroyed by fire in 1914, only the belfry (1378) with its carillon remained undamaged. Rebuilding took place in the Twenties. The rooms contain some interesting paintings among which are works by the painter Jan Verhas (1834–96) who came from this town.

The former **Vleeshuis** (meat market) is another notable building in the market square, easily recognisable by its octagonal tower. This Gothic hall was built in 1460–62. Until 1862 the benches still stood on the ground floor where the butchers offered their products for sale. The Sint-Joris-Gilde used to meet on the first floor and under the roof the rhetoric guild "De Leeuwerckenaers". From 1715 both these rooms were used as the main police station. Since its restoration in 1899 the Vleeshuis houses the Stedelijk Oudheidkundig Museum (Municipal Museum) of the town's history (open April–Oct. Tue.–Sun. 9.30am–12.30pm and 1.30–6pm).

From the market square the Kerkstraat leads west to the Kerkplein where stands the Gothic 14/15th c. Onze-Lieve-Vrouwkerk (Church of Our Dear Lady); the octagonal crossing tower was completed in 1388.

Onze-Lieve-Vrouwkerk

Viewing of the church **interior** is highly recommended. The Romanesque limestone font from the first half of the 12th c. was made in Tournai and depicts the Last Supper together with the Vision of SS Paul and Peter before Paradise. Among the many paintings are two noteworthy works by van Dyck ("Crucifixion", 1630; "Adoration of the Shepherds", around 1632), three by Gaspar de Crayer ("Virgin of the Canon van Calandries", 1634; "St Roch and the Plague Victims", 1650; Virgin of the main altar, 1634–36) and an "Adoration of the Shepherds" credited to Blès.

The magnificent high altar with marble columns is the work of Hubert van den Eynde from 1683. The church also possesses many works of sculpture by A. Fayd'herbe (the figure of the Madonna in the west door-way) and Artus Quellin (parts of the choir screen) among others.

Vlasmarkt

To the south of the market square over the Dender is the Vlasmarkt where the Benediktijnabdij (Benedectine Abbey), destroyed in 1914 and rebuilt in Flemish style 1919–24, and the Neo-Gothic church Sint-Pieters-en Pauluskerk (1901/1902) are situated.

Begijnhof

Not far from the Vlasmarkt an alley in the Brusselsestraat turns off right to the Sint-Alexiusbegijnhof, where the last béguines lived until 1975. The béguinage was established in 1250; in 1597 the buildings were devastated by the Geuzen. Most of the 61 brick houses now grouped around the peaceful courtyard were rebuilt at the beginning of the 17th c. House No. 11 is today the Béguinage Museum and a small béguine house equipped in the original 19th c. style with furniture and two bedrooms containing typical béguine beds is on display. In No. 25, the former house of the Grootjuffrouw (oldest béguine) the Museum voor Volkskunde (local museum) has been set up. The institution dates back to the 17th and 18th c.; the brewery is of particular interest (open Apr.–Oct. first Saturday in the month 10am–noon and 2–6pm).

Sint-Amands

Sint-Amands, 15 km (9 mi.) north-east of Dendermonde, is the birthplace of the great Flemish poet Emile Verhaeren (1855–1916). The town is situated on the Scheldt, which is 225 m (738 ft) wide at this point and can be seen from the riverside promenade. The marble tombstone of the poet and his wife stands behind the church on the bank of the Scheldt.

Emile-Verhaeren-Museum The poet's birthplace at Verhaerenstraat 69 is open to the public as a museum (open Tue.–Sun. 10am–noon and 2–6pm).

Molenmuseum The Molenmuseum (Mill Museum) at Verhaerenstraat 7 has everything there is to know about wind mills (open Mon.–Fri. 8am–noon and 1–6pm).

Diest   F 12

Province: Brabant. Altitude: 23 m (75 ft)
Population: 21,600. Inter-regional Station

Diest, situated on both banks of the Demer in the transition zone between the fertile and hilly Hageland and the wooded Kempenland, is the market centre of an intensively farmed area. The main products grown here are asparagus, early potatoes and vegetables. Diest, which received its charter in the second half of the 13th c., ranked among the most important towns in Brabant because of its famous cloth-making, but which has long since disappeared. It has been replaced by flour-milling and other branches of the food industry. Diest is also well known for its special beers (gildebier). From its rich history remarkable buildings and parts of the fortifications have been preserved. Diest is closely associated with the House of Orange-Nassau, to which the present day Queen of the Netherlands belongs. Like Breda in the Netherlands, Dillenburg in Germany and Orange in France Diest was the seat of the royal house. Its most important representative was Prince William I of Orange-Nassau, called William the Silent, who led the Dutch revolts against Spanish domination.

St Jan Berchmans (1599–1621), patron saint of youth, is a native of Diest. The room in which he was born in the "Gulden Maan" house in Sint Jan Berchmanstraat near the Grote Markt has remained unchanged and is open to visitors.

The Grote Markt, the picturesque centre of the Old Town, is framed by several beautiful patrician houses of the 16–18th c. In the south-west of the square is the pre-Classical Stadhuis (town hall) built in 1728.

★Grote Markt

The cellars of the town hall house the **Stedelijk Museum** (municipal museum) which is impressive not only because of its valuable collections but also because of its medieval premises. The Gothic hall has a collection of weapons, a fine painting on wood of the "Last Supper" (around 1450) and goldsmiths' work belonging to the guilds. In the Romanesque room are paintings depicting scenes from the life of William the Silent's son, Prince Philipp of Orange-Nassau, who was born in Diest. The Van der Linden room is named after the museum's founder and contains prehistoric finds from the surrounding area of Diest (open daily 10am–noon and 1–5pm).

In the Demerstraat which leads away from the right of the town hall are the refuges of the abbeys of von Tongerlo ("Het Spiker"; 16th c.) and von Averbode (15th c.)

Refuges

In the midst of the market stands the noteworthy collegiate church of Sint Sulpitius, one of the finest examples of Brabant Gothic (Demer Gothic). It was built mainly in 1417–1534 using the characteristic reddish brown brick. The choir dates from 1320. The small tower, known as "mostaardpot" (mustard pot), has a carillon with 43 bells.

Sint-Sulpitiuskerk

Interior The church houses interesting works of art including superb carvings on the pulpit, altars and confessionals. In the choir can be seen magnificent Late-Gothic choir stalls dated 1491 and the tomb of Philip of Orange-Nassau, who died in 1618; the font of St Jan Berchmann in the right side aisle and the treasure in a room adjoining the choir also warrant close examination. The main altar (18th c.) is by Michael van der Vorst; before it on the right is a work of the Antwerp school "Worship of the Kings".

Behind the church to the right in Ketelstraat is the Lakenhalle (cloth hall) from 1346, where the products of the Diest cloth industry were traded. Next to the hall stands the "Holle Griet", a 15th c. catapult.

Lakenhalle

Also behind the church Koning Albertstraat heads north, off which branches Schaffensestraat where the 16th c. Watermolen van Oranje (water mill) presents a charming scene by the canal.

Watermolen van Oranje

In Begijnenstraat is the begijnhof founded in 1252 together with the Gothic Sint Katharinakerk. The béguinage of Diest is one of the oldest and most important in Belgium. Its well-preserved 17th c. houses stand around a square and in five small streets. The houses are separated from the street by a magnificent Baroque portal with a likeness of the Madonna and Child. Today the béguinage is used chiefly as a youth and cultural centre; house No. 5 in the Engelen Conventstraat is still furnished in keeping with the béguinage period.

★Begijnhof

Sint-Katharinakerk	The Sint-Katharinakerk (14th c.) in Brabant Gothic style has a brilliantly carved pulpit dating from 1671. Former monasteries, spitals and a hospital surround the church, all built between the 16th and 18th c.
Town fortifications	Behind the béguinage extend the former 19th c. double fortifications of Brialmont with the Schaffense Post gate on the left. Leopoldsvest street follows the line of the fortifications with a good view of the béguinage. To the south it leads to the 18th c. Lindenmolen.
Warandepark	Within the ring of the Leopoldsvest lies the Warandepark, part of the former hunting lodge of the Princes of Orange-Nassau. Opposite the main entrance of the park stands the Nassau residence (1516), a brick building with a typical gable and octagonal tower.
★Abdij Averbode	An excursion to the picturesque Premonstratensian Abdij Averbode (Abbey of Averbode), 6 km (4 mi.) north-west of Diest, is well worth while. The monastery was founded in 1134. The oldest part of the building, which dates from the 14th–18th c., is the entrance gate which stands at the point where the three provinces of Brabant, Limburg and Antwerp meet. A large number of monks still live in the abbey and their activities include the operation of a large printing press for daily newspapers.
	The Baroque **abbey church** built by Jan van Eynde in 1664 has rich interior furnishing (pews from 1672, high altar from 1758, beautiful organ) and noteworthy paintings by P. J. Verhaghen. The size of the interior is surprising. The monastery building, which was set on fire in 1942, cannot be visited. The 18th c. cloisters, chapter house and sacristy survived the fire.
Scherpenheuvel	Scherpenheuvel, 6 km (4 mi.) west of Diest is a popular place of pilgrimage. Seven paths lead to the Onze-Lieve-Vrouwkerk (Church of Our Lady) standing on high ground. This Baroque building shows strong Italian influence with an oriental cupola. It was built in 1609–27 according to plans by W. Coebergher and marks the beginning of the Baroque style in present day Belgium. The interior houses beautiful paintings by Th. van Loon, a marble relief by F. Duquesnoy and a rich treasury.

Diksmuide · Dixmude   E 2

Province: West-Vlaanderen. Altitude: 0–10 m (0–32 ft)
Population: 15,000. Inter-regional Station

The small Flemish town of Diksmuide (French Dixmude), 20 km (12 mi.) inland from the coast on the IJser, was flattened to ground level by week-long German artillery fire during the First World War. Like Ypres (see entry) the town has been rebuilt in the old Flemish style and is now an important market centre for intensive dairy farming. The fact that the ordinary soldiers who died along the IJzerfront on the Belgian side were chiefly Flemish – whereas the officer corps was made up primarily of Walloons and French was the language of command – makes Diksmuide with the IJzer monument a place of great symbolic importance for Flemish political consciousness.

History Diksmuide grew up in the 9th c. around a wooden castle built to combat the threat of Norman invasion. In 985 Count Balduin III awarded the town its charter and market rights. In the Middle Ages Diksmuide was a sea port and achieved considerable prosperity through its cloth trade with England. With the silting up of the IJser and sea-going vessels no longer able to reach the town Diksmuide declined.

From October 10th to November 10th 1914 6000 Belgian and 5000 French soldiers defended the town, then withdrew over the IJser and abandoned the totally destroyed town to the German troops. Following its rebuilding Diksmuide was bombed again in 1940.

At the Grote Markt stand the Sint-Niklaaskerk, which was rebuilt in 1940 in accordance with 12th c. plans, the town hall with a belfry and carillon dated 1923 and the butter hall.

Grote Markt

There is a monument to General Baron Jacques, commander of the Belgian army.

North of the market across the Handzamekanaal is a béguinage originating from the 12th c. with houses which were rebuilt in the Twenties in 17th c. style. In the entrance can be seen a small figure of Thomas Becket who is said to have taken refuge here when fleeing from Henry II. Some of the treasures which survived the destruction are in the Godelieve chapel.

Béguinage

IJzertoren Monument

To the west of the market in the General Baron Jacquesstraat is the handsome building of the Stedelijk Museum (municipal museum). Together with works of art and documents relating to the history of the town there is a room dedicated to the First World War on the IJser (open Easter–Oct. daily 10am–noon and 2–6pm).

Stedelijk Museum

The IJzerlaan leads a short distance out of the town to the IJzertoren Monument (IJzer gate memorial), clearly visible on the left bank of the river. The 84 m (275 ft)-high memorial commemorates the 40,000 Flemish soldiers killed during the First World War. At the same time it is a peace memorial with its appeal "No more war". It also symbolises the pride of the Flemish people who made up nearly 90 per cent of the ordinary soldiers in the First World War and had to bear the brunt of the fighting. Today many Flemish still see the letters A.V.V. and V.V.K. (Alles voor Vlaanderen and Vlaanderen voor Kristus) inscribed on the memorial as a symbol of resistance and the struggle against the cultural and linguistic domination of the Walloons at the beginning of this century, which also finds expression in the added French inscription "Et pour les Flamands la même chose". There is an annual remembrance service every August at the foot of the memorial which in recent years has been accompanied by right-wing extremist marches. The first memorial, erected in 1928, was blown up by unknown persons with only the Paxpoort (peace gate) remaining. The present tower was completed in 1965. The first floor houses a commemorative museum; from the tower there are far-reaching views over the Flemish battlefields (open Easter–May and Sep.–mid-Nov. 9am–noon and 1–5pm; Jun. until 6p, Jul. and Aug. 9am–6pm).

★IJzer gate

About 2 km (1 mi.) north-west of Diksmuide the Dodengang runs along the left bank of the IJser. This trench with numerous dugouts was part of the front line of the fighting in the Battle of Flanders. The German

Dodengang

"Grieving Parents", created by Käthe Kollwitz in memory of her son

lines lay just a few yards away on the opposite bank. Visitors can enter the reconstructed trenches; a pavilion houses an information centre (open Apr.–Sep. daily from 9am–noon and 1–5pm).

Vladslo

Around 4 km (2½ mi.) north-east of Diksmuide 25,644 German soldiers are buried in the Vladslo **military cemetery**. Among them is Peter Kollwitz, killed in 1914, son of the sculptress Käthe Kollwitz, whose gripping work "Trauernde Eltern" (Grieving Parents) was exhibited here in 1932.

Castle Esen, 2 km (1 mi.) east of the town, contains the **IJser museum** with documents and items from the First World War.

Torhout

Torhout, 23 km (14 mi.) north-east of Diksmuide, was an important market town in the Middle Ages. Sint Petersbandkerk with its typical octagonal tower, blown up in 1918 and again destroyed in 1940, has been rebuilt. The Kasteel Ravenhod houses a museum of ceramics and faïences.

Kasteel van Wijnendale

Kasteel van Wijnendale, a moated castle surrounded by splendid parkland, situated 3 km (2 mi.) west of Torhout by a town of the same name, was the favourite retreat of the Counts of Flanders. In 1482 Maria of Burgundy died in a riding accident nearby.

Dinant   L 12

Province: Namur
Altitude: 90m (295 ft) Population: 12,000
Intercity Station (bicycle rental at station)

Dinant is the second largest town in the Belgian region of Condroz and one of the most important tourist centres in the Ardennes. Thanks to its delightful situation in the Upper Meuse valley (see Vallée de la Meuse) below precipitous limestone rocks, crowned by a mighty citadel, Dinant has become a very lively tourist resort, especially at weekends when the Meuse is dotted with pleasure boats and canoeists.

The town's culinary specialities are "coques", shaped biscuits made with honey, and "flamiches", a spiced cake made from bread, eggs and cheese. The painter Joachim Patinier (1485–1524) and Adolphe Sax (see Introduction, Famous People), the inventor of the saxaphone, were born in Dinant.

History From the time of the Hohenstaufen dynasty the town belonged to the diocese of Liège and was highly prosperous as early as the 13th–15th c. It was famous throughout the Middle Ages for its brass and copperware, the so-called dinanderies.

Unlike any other town in Belgium Dinant has been destroyed by war throughout its history. The town was conquered and burnt by Charles the Bold in 1466; Philip the Good had 800 townspeople tied together in pairs and drowned in the Meuse. In 1554 the French laid siege to the town and destroyed it; under Louis XIV they conquered the town and fortress occupying it until 1703.

In the First World War Dinant was an important bridgehead on the Meuse and, therefore, the focus of heavy fighting, in which 674 of its citizens lost their lives. In the Second World War the Meuse Bridge was bombed in the 1940 air raids and the town suffered heavy damage in 1944, so that hardly anything remains of old Dinant.

The famous medieval **art of dinanderies** has been revived in recent years and can be observed in two workshops:

Monsieur de Marco, 64, Rue Grande (daily by appointment) and Dinanderie Mecap, 13, Rue de Moulin (Mon.–Thu. 3pm, Fri. 10am).

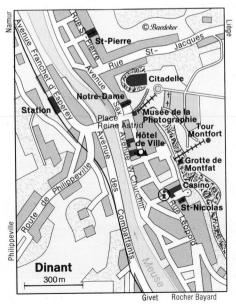

© Baedeker

Dinant
300 m

The museum of Dinanderie has many examples of old and modern items including the largest collection of church weathercocks in Europe (open Easter–Sep. daily except Mon. 1.30–6pm).

Trips on the Meuse Pleasure boats depart from Dinant to Anseremme, Freÿr (see Vallée de la Meuse), Hastière, Namur and the French border.

Collégiale Notre-Dame

In the Place Reine Astrid at the foot of the citadel hill the collegiate church of Notre-Dame stands at the end of the Meuse bridge. It is a beautiful early Gothic building from the 13th c. standing on the sight of a Romanesque basilica which was destroyed by falling rocks in 1227. Following the devastation of 1466 the arches had to be reconstructed. The central tower with a pear-shaped dome (1566) provides a harmonious contrast to the dominating citadel high above the town.

The only remains of the Romanesque church is the sandstone doorway on the north side. Inside the church examples of dinanderies can be seen in the form of the font, the Easter candles and the lectern. In the left transept is the tomb of Gérard de Blanmostier dated 1356. The light shines through a beautiful Gothic arched stained window above the south doorway.

Musée de la Photographie

The Musée de la Photographie is situated directly next to the church at the valley station of the cable railway up to the citadel. It contains over 300 old cameras and a reconstructed dark room from 1920 (open mid-Mar.–Apr. Sat. and Sun. 10am–6pm).

Rue Grande

The busy main street in the elongated town, the Rue Grande, runs parallel to the right bank of the Meuse from the Place Reine Astrid to the

Dinant: Above the Collégiale Notre-Dame towers the Citadel

Rocher Bayard

bridge heading south. Through traffic is concentrated on the left bank.

Further south of the Place Reine Astrid is the Hitel de Ville (town hall) with a monument to the citizens who lost their lives in 1914. Continuing south Dinant casino is on the left.

Behind the casino a narrow path leads up to the cableway to Mont-Fat. This ascends to the Mont-Fat viewing tower and children's playground. Prehistoric discoveries were made in the Grotte de Mont-Fat; it was a Roman temple to the goddess Diana (open Apr.–Aug. daily 10.30am–7pm; Sep. and Oct. Sat. and Sun. 11am–6pm).

Grotte et Tour de Mont-Fat

The Rue Grande continues southwards as the Rue Léopold and, at the end of the town, passes between the rocks of the high plateau and the famous Rocher Bayard, a rocky needle some 40 m (131 ft) high, rising steeply up from the river. Bayard was the name of the horse of the legendary four sons of Haimon. Fleeing from Charlemagne they all crossed the river in one mighty jump, thereby splitting the rocky needle with its hooves. In fact a thoroughfare was blown through the rocks in 1698.

★Rocher Bayard

The northern continuation of the Rue Grande from the Place Reine Astrid is the Rue Adolphe Sax, named after the inventor of the saxaphone who was born here. A window in the house (No. 31) commemorates the instrument maker.

Birthplace of Adolphe Sax

Further north in the suburb of Leffe at the entrance to the rocky cleft Fonds de Leffe is a former Premonstratensian abbey. It was founded in 1152 and suffered during the besieging of Dinant. Only the guest house, prior's house and refectory, all from the 17th and 18th c. remain.

Abbaye de Leffe

The suburb of Saint-Médard which includes the railway station and numerous hotels extends along the left bank of the Meuse. West of the bridge, 500 m from the railway station on the Route de Philippeville, is the entrance to the Grotte de Raimpaine ("La Merveilleuse"). The 500 m-long cave has beautiful stalactite formations (open Apr.–Jun. and Sep.–mid-Nov. daily 11am–5pm; Jul. and Aug. 10am–6pm).

Grotte "La Merveilleuse"

The citadel of Dinant towers high above the town (opening times Apr.–Oct. daily 10am–6pm; Nov.–Mar. daily except Fri. 10am–4pm; closed in Jan). There are four ways up to it: the cabin cable railway (télépherique) behind the collegiate church, a difficult route consisting of 400 steps next to the cableway, the chair-lift to Mont-Fat and a short walk or via the Rue Adolphe Sax and then to the right by the Rue de Saint Jacques. The present-day citadel was built by the Dutch government in 1821 on the site of the episcopal fortresses which had often been destroyed. A tour through the citadel leads along battlements heavily contested by the Germans and French in 1914, through a bakery and a weapons museum. There is a reconstructed dugout, riddled with bullets, from the First World War. From the ramparts projecting over the town there is a magnificent **view** over the Meuse. At the top are a cemetery for French soldiers (see Practical Information, Military Cemeteries) killed in action and a monument to the German soldiers.

★Citadel

Surroundings

Bouvignes

Situated 2 km (1 mi.) north of Dinant on the left bank of the Meuse, Bouvignes, dating back to the 7th c., was a former rival of Dinant but is now incorporated. The fortifications of the 15th c. Château de Crèvecoeur used to tower above the town but today only the ruins remain. There is a splendid view from the top. The remains of Poilvache and Géronsart castles (see Vallée de la Meuse) are visible to the north high up on the opposite bank.

Built in the Meuse Gothic style the church of **Saint-Lambert** has two choirs: the east one dated 1247 and the 16th c. west choir.

The Renaissance building "Maison Espagnole" in the market place of Bouvignes houses the **Musée de l'Eclairage** (Museum of Lighting), which describes mankind's technical efforts to create light (open May–Sep. Tue.–Sun. 1–6pm).

Spontin

The Château de Spontin, an impressive moated castle, one of the finest in Belgium, is situated in the Bocq valley near the small town of Spontin 11 km (7 mi.) north of Dinant. It was built on the site of 12th c. keep which was extended into a fortified castle in the 14th c. and rebuilt in Renaissance style in the 16th c. In 1622 the working quarters were added adjoining the courtyard in which there are beautiful 19th c. wrought-iron fountains.
  A tour through the castle rooms shows how styles have changed with time. The keep has two bare rooms with Gothic chimneys, the library a chequered floor, the Renaissance salon and the Neo-Gothic south wing with the dining room and staircase (open Jul. and Aug. daily 10am–5pm).

Spontin Castle

The village of Anseremme, not far south of Dinant where the Lesse enters the Meuse, is a good place for walking and hill-climbing. Both train and bus operate to the village of Houyet on the Lesse, the starting point of a boat trip along the scenically beautiful ★**lower reaches of the Lesse** (Descente de la Lesse). It is possible to hire canoes or take a guided boat tour along the 21 km (13 mi.) stretch through the Furfooz nature reserve, past Walzin (13th c.) and Pont-à-Lesse castles back to Anseremme with its 16th c. bridge Pont Saint-Jean across the river (departures daily between 9 and 11.30am; journey time about 4½ hours).

The Furfooz nature reserve (Parc Naturel de Furfooz) extends around the lower reaches of the Lesse. In the caves of this limestone plateau above the meandering river Stone Age relics such as tools and bones have been found together with remains of Roman baths.

At Falmignoul, 8 km (5 mi.) south of Dinant, centre for climbing in the nearby cliffs at Freÿr, there is an interesting bicycle, motorcycle and poster museum (Musée du Cycle et de la Moto et de l'Affiche). Its exhibits range from the 1818 dandy horse to the racing bike on which Eddy Merckx won the Tour de France, old motorcycles and posters from before 1914.

The village of Celles, 10 km (6 mi.) south-east of Dinant, is famous for its Church of St Hadelinus, built in the Mosan Romanesque style with a beautiful 9th c. crypt and squat fortress-like towers. The triple-naved interior houses a stone pulpit, a beautiful marble memorial slab for Louis de Beaufort and his wife and early Gothic 13th c. choir stalls, the oldest in Belgium (open Easter–Nov. daily 10am–6pm).
   At the entrance to Celles a German tank marks the furthest point reached by the German troops during the Ardennes offensive.

Not far south-west of Celles stands the Château de Veves, seat of the Lords of Beaufort, a fine 15th c. building with a large keep and smaller side towers with pointed roofs. The rooms are furnished with family heirlooms from various periods.

Situated almost 10 km (6 mi.) east of Dinant Foy-Notre-Dame is a popular place of pilgrimage. The object of veneration is a miracle-working Madonna figure which was reputedly found in an oak tree in 1609. It is now housed in an outwardly apparently unassuming church but which has a splendid interior: outstanding wood carving and a highly impressive coffered ceiling with 145 biblical scenes, painted in the 17th c. by the Goblet brothers from Dinant.

20 km (12 mi.) south of Dinant the small town of Beauraing became famous in 1932 and 1933 for several alleged appearances of Mary before five children. These events dominate the character of the town. Various consecrated shrines, the chapel built in 1954 and a large pilgrimage church with over 7000 seats (1968) are frequented by believers and those seeking cures.

For other places in the surroundings see Vallée de la Meuse

Anseremme

Houyet

★**Parc Naturel de Furfooz**

Falmignoul

Celles

★**Château de Veves**

Foy-Notre-Dame

Beauraing

Ecaussinnes   J 8

Province: Hainaut
Altitude: 40–159 m (131–521 ft) Population: 9500
Inter-regional Station

Château d'en Haut in Ecaussinnes-Lalaing

The twin parish of Ecaussinnes, about 45 km (28 mi.) south of Brussels, consists of both towns of Ecaussinnes-Lalaing and Ecaussinnes-d'Enghien. The names originate from the noble lines to which the town belonged in the Middle Ages.

Ecaussinnes-d'Enghien

The castle of the Enghiens, the Château de la Folie, dates back to a 13th c. building, which was demolished in 1506. The new building of 1528 was enlarged by a late-Gothic chapel. This was again converted in the 18th c. to the country house which the visitor can see today (visits only by arrangement). Some of the chapel windows are the work of Bernard van Orley who is buried together with his wife in the church of Saint-Remy.

Ecaussinnes-Lalaing

Ecaussinnes-Lalaing is situated in a region rich in granite quarries. On Easter Monday every year it is the scene of a marriage market where those wanting to marry are fed in the Grand-Place. In the local church Blandine Rubens, the sister of the great painter and Michel de Croy (fine reclining figure) are buried.

★Château d'en Haut

The first building of Château d'en Haut on a rocky promontory not far from the Grand-Place originates from the 12th c. In the 14th c. a new, larger construction followed which has remained almost unchanged to the present day and is one of the best preserved medieval castles in Belgium. The gate tower of 1372 was altered in the 17th c., other alterations have not made such an impression on the overall picture such as the extension of the castle chapel around 1600. Under the French (around 1800) and in the 19th c. when the building was being used among other things as a factory, it collapsed. Restoration work began at the beginning of this century; since 1928 the château has been under the ownership of the Counts van der Burch, who inherited it in the 17th c.

Lower lock of the ship-lift of Ronquières

The tour of the rooms takes in the weapons hall, kitchen, sick room, state room and dungeon; some rooms have exhibitions of glass, sculpture, ceramics and porcelain (open Apr.–Jun., Sep., Oct. Sat., Sun. and public holidays, Jul./Aug. daily except Tue. and Wed. 10am–noon and 2–6pm).

Surroundings

Just 4 km (2½ mi.) north-east of Ecaussinnes is the technical spectacle of the ★**sloping lock of Ronquières** (Plan incliné de Ronquières), a gigantic

Ronquières

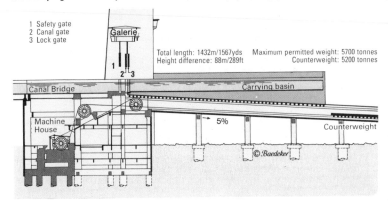

215

barge lift on the canal from Charleroi to Brussels (opening times Tower: May–Aug. daily 10am–6pm). The difference in height between the Sambre Valley at Charleroi and the Senne south of Brussels was for a long time an insuperable obstacle to linking the canal network between north and south Belgium. The first canal project completed in 1832 involved 55 locks over a distance of 60 km (37 mi.). This canal soon proved to be too small and following further enlargements in the 19th c. it was decided to modernise the waterway in 1937. The work lasted from 1947 to 1968 and reduced the number of locks to ten. The centrepiece of the canal is the sloping lock of Ronquières. Barges up to a total of 1350 tonnes enter one of two tanks up to 91 m (298 ft) long and 12 m (39 ft) wide (water depth 3.7 m (12 ft); max. weight 5700 tonnes), which are pulled or lowered on rails on 59 axles with 236 rollers by 8 steel cables (55 mm diameter). The basins are moved independently of each other as they are counterbalanced by 5200 tonne weights. The height difference of 68 m (223 ft) is resolved over a distance of 1432 m (4698 ft) in about 90 minutes. The entire complex is dominated by a 154 m (505 ft)-high control tower with a viewing platform at 139 m (456 ft). The technology is explained in an exhibition (open Apr.–Oct. daily 10am–7pm). There are boat excursions to the lock (departures: Jun.–Sep. Tue., Thu., Fri., Sat. and Sun. noon, 2pm, 3.30pm and 5.30pm).

Eeklo

See Ghent, Surroundings

Eupen · Néau   H 17

Province: Liège
Altitude: 300 m (984 ft) Population: 17,500
Intercity Station (bicycle rental at station)

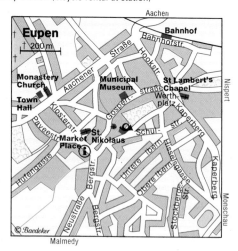

Eupen (French Néau), the largest town in the German-speaking part of Belgium, lies at the confluence of the Vesdre (Weser) and the Helle (Hill). In the south and south-west the wooded hills of the Hohe Venn (see German-Belgian Nature Park) reach almost to the edge of the town, whereas in the north and west the green carpet of a continuous belt of meadow and pasture stretches from the hills of the Aachener Wald to the banks of the Meuse. Eupen has, despite its modest altitude of 300 m (984 ft), a cool highland climate which has contributed to its reputation as a popular health resort. Visitors can among other things enjoy the Kneipp water cure. Most of the inhabitants of the town are employed in the textile industry and manufacture of man-made fibres, with 25 per cent of the workforce commuting from the surrounding countryside. Eupen is the headquarters of the council, the executive and administration of the German-speaking part of Belgium and the German language Belgian radio station is here.

History Eupen, which once belonged to the Duchy of Limburg, is first mentioned in the Chronicles in 1213. The Duchy's location proved to be a frequent drawback for the town. As a result of the Battle of Worringen (1288) Limburg, and therefore Eupen, became part of the Duchy of Brabant. But in 1387 Joanna of Brabant handed over Limburg to Burgundy. Only 90 years later (1477) the Duchy of Limburg was acquired by the Austrian Habsburgs, but their domination only lasted until 1555. The Duchies of Limburg and Brabant were then taken over by Spain. In 1674 Eupen received its town charter. After the Peace Treaty of Utrecht (1713) the Austrian Habsburgs became its rulers for the second time. Eupen became prosperous during this period and by 1721 had a population 13,000. The famous cloth industry of Eupen exported its products to the whole world. In 1795 the district of Eupen was annexed by France, but after the defeat of Napoleon it became part of Prussia (Congress of Vienna 1815). Until 1920 Eupen was the westernmost district of Germany. In the Treaty of Versailles the town was given to the Kingdom of Belgium, but was again part of Germany between 1940 and 1945.

Eupen is famous for its **Carnival** which is similar to those in the Rhineland.

Eupen is clearly divided into the more industrial lower town and the upper town characterised by buildings from its period of prosperity (18th c.). Superb patrician houses stand in the market place, Gospertstrasse and in the Werthplatz. | ★Patrician houses

The Church of Saint-Nicholas in the market square was built between 1724–29 according to plans by the city architect of Aachen, Mefferdatis as a triple-aisled hall church; the towers were completed in 1898. Of interest inside are a Baroque high altar by Couven (1750), pulpit of 1730, confessionals and apostle figures from the Minorite church in Cologne.
    In the market place is the Column of St Mary, 1857. | Saint-Nicholas

Until the French Revolution the town hall in Aachener Strasse was part of a Capuchin monastery. The former Baroque church of this monastery is worth visiting. | Town hall

The municipal museum is at 52 Gospertstrasse. It is housed in the former house of a cloth handler (1697) and documents the changing history of the Eupen region. It contains a clock collection, Raeren stoneware, clothing and a completely equipped goldsmith's forge (open: Tue.–Fri. 9.30–noon and 2–5pm, Sat. 2–5pm, Sun. 10am–noon and 2–5pm). | Municipal museum

The surrounding countryside is ideal for **walking** in the Hertogenwald, around the Barrage de la Gileppe dam (8 km (5 mi). south-west) and in the Hohe Venn nature reserve (see German–Belgian Nature Park). | Surroundings

The Gileppe Dam

A nostalgic and peaceful way to get to know the surroundings of Eupen and the Hohe Venn (see German–Belgian Nature Park) is a trip on the **Venn railway** established in 1886. A train departs at 10am every Sunday between May and October from Eupen and puffs past Raeren into Roetgen in Germany, continues to Monschau through the border town of Kalterherberg in the Hohe Venn and back into Büllingen in Belgium, near the Bütgenbach dam (see Malmédy, Surroundings).

★Barrage de Vesdre

It is worth a visit to the Vesdre dam (Barrage d'Eupen), 5 km (3 mi.) east, with a capacity of 25 million cu. m and an area of 126 ha. (311 acres) the largest reservoir in Belgium. The wall is 58 m (190 ft) high and 410 m (1345 ft) long; the base of the wall is 55 m (180 ft) wide. The reservoir serves the Herver Land and the surroundings of Liège. There is sailing on the lake.

Raeren

9 km (5 mi.) to the north Raeren is a centre of pottery and stoneware, with a tradition stretching back to 1400. Pottery from Raeren was valued throughout the world. A pottery museum in the magnificent château shows the development of Raeren pottery in seven rooms (open Tue.–Sun. 10am–5pm).

Henri-Chapelle

In the military cemetery at Henri-Chapelle (5 km/3 mi. north-west) are buried 7989 American soldiers who died in 1944/45.

Kelmis

Kelmis, 12 km (8 mi.) north of Eupen, is an ideal starting-out point for walks, but is more interesting for its curious history: at the Congress of Vienna agreement could not be reached over which country Kelmis belonged to. Moresnet became Dutch (then Belgian), Neu-Moresnet German, and the zinc-quarrying area in between neutral under joint administration. Out of this Kelmis developed but did not become Belgian until 1919.

A few kilometres north of Kelmis the borders of Belgium, Holland and Germany meet. In clear weather the Eifel, Aachen and Maastricht can be seen from the 321 m (1053 ft)-high Drielandenpunt. Just inside the Dutch border is the highest point in Holland.

Gaasbeek (Château)

See Brussels, Surroundings

Geel   D 12

Province: Antwerp. Altitude: 20 m (66 ft)
Population: 32,000. Inter-regional Station

The town of Geel is situated in the centre of an agricultural region in Kempenland in the eastern part of the province of Antwerp. It is well known for its pioneering method of treating psychiatric patients and the mentally ill. They receive treatment at a large psychiatric hospital but live in the community with families, taking part in everyday life. There are about 1400 patients living in Geel.

This tradition is derived from the legend of St Dymphna or Dimpna, the patron saint of the possessed and insane. Dymphna was an Irish princess from the 6th c. who fled from her father who wanted to marry her after the death of his wife. With her confessor Gerebernus Dymphna sought refuge in Geel, but she was discovered by her father who, in a frenzy, is supposed to have decapitated her. The town soon became a place of pilgrimage for the mentally ill. The pilgrims who came to visit the tomb were accommodated by the townspeople, a custom which has remained, although in a different form, until the present day. An annual fair, the oldest in Belgium, resulted from the pilgrimages.

Situated on the road to Mol, Sint-Dimpnakerk is late Gothic, built 1349–1479. The massive tower (16th c.) made of alternating white sandstone and brown ironstone was never finished. The church's art treasures include the Sint-Dimpna retable of 1515 on the main altar with fine wood carving, a Brabant retable of the Passion in the right transept (wood; 1490), a stone retable depicting the twelve apostles (14th c.) and the silver reliquaries of St Dymphna and her confessor, Gerebernus. In the choir the Renaissance mauseoleum in marble and alabaster of Jan III de Merode and his wife was the work of Cornelis Floris de Vriendt in 1554. From 1484–1601 Geel was owned by the de Merode family. The so-called "sick room" built against the church tower housed the sick during the nine day pilgrimage and from here they were carried into the church three times a day to pray.

The first hospital was founded in Geel in 1280; the present day buildings are primarily from the 17th c. and have been converted into a local museum with collections of furniture, paintings and church exhibits (open mid May–Aug. Wed., Thu. and Sun 2–5.30pm).

Surroundings

14 km (9 mi.) west of Geel is Herentals which was awarded its town charter in 1209 and was a flourishing cloth-making town in the 14th and 15th c. During this period the town walls were built, of which two towers remain.

The **Stadhuis** (town hall) in the centre of Herentals is the former cloth hall dating from the beginning of the 15th c. and rebuilt in 1534 following a fire. A niche on the north faáade houses a Madonna statue from 1616. The narrow belfry contains a carillon with 50 bells (1590). On the top floor is a museum in honour of the sculptor Karel August Fraikin who was born in the town (open Jun.–Sep. daily 10am–noon and 2–5pm).

Sint-Waldetrudiskerk is a fine example of Brabant High Gothic, its oldest parts being the lower part of the tower and the transept (14th c.). The choir and nave were built in the 15th c.

Inside is the retable depicting the martyrdom of Sts Crispinus and Crispianus, the patron saints of shoemakers and tanners, an outstanding work by Pasquier Borreman (16th c.). Among the numerous paintings are works by Frans Francken the Elder of Herentals; choir stalls and confessionals survived the iconoclastic fury.

The **Begijnhof** (béguinage) was founded in 1266 and is the oldest in Kempenland. It was destroyed by the Geuzen in 1578, but rebuilt in 1590; in 1614 the late Gothic béguinage church, Sint Catherinakerk, was completed. Other interesting buildings around the landscaped inner courtyard are the fondatiehuis (1647) and the sick hall (1715).

Grobbendonk

At Grobbendonk, 6 km (4 mi.) west of Herentals, a diamond museum informs the visitor of all there is to know about the mining and working of these precious stones. Reproductions of the most famous diamonds are on display (open Mon.–Fri. 10am–4pm, Sat. 10am–1.30pm and Sun. 10am–noon).

Abdij van Tongerlo

The abbey of Tongerlo, 9 km (5 mi.) south-west of Tongerlo, was founded by the Premonstratensians of Sint-Michielsabdij of Antwerp in 1130, who set about converting the heathens. Following the French Revolution the abbey was abandoned and only reinhabited and restored in 1840. The oldest parts of the building are the 14th c. tower and a barn dating from the 15th c.; the remaining buildings originate from various later epochs to the Neo-Gothic Onze-Lieve-Vrouwkerk (1851–58). A splendid avenue of lime trees, planted in 1676, leads up to the entrance.

In the abbey is the **Museum da Vinci**, which has a remarkable copy of "The Last Supper", painted barely 20 years after Leonardo had finished the original for the Santa Marie delle Grazie church in Milan. The copy in Tongerlo was acquired for the abbey church in 1545. Other paintings include a small Pietà by Roger van der Weyden (open Sun. 2–5pm).

Kasteel van Westerlo

The small town of Westerlo, situated in woodland only 2 km (1¼ mi.) south of Tongerlo, is famous for the two châteaux of the van Merode family, who lived here from the 14th c. and were engaged in Belgian politics from time to time.

The right-angled keep of the château surrounded by parkland belonged to the van Merode princes and was built around 1300 as part of the new château, which replaced the first 11th c. house. Further extension and conversion work took place from the 16th c. and during the next two centuries. A second château was built along the Boerenkrijglan in 1910. Since 1972 the Neo-Gothic building has been the parish house of Westerlo.

Lommel

German military cemetery South of Lommel which lies 30 km (18 mi.) north-west of Geel is a military cemetery where all the German soldiers killed in Belgium during the Second World War are buried. 20,000 crosses represent the 40,000 graves.

Kasteel van Westerlo

Gembloux-sur-Orneau · Gembloers   J 11

Province: Namur. Altitude: 230 m (143 ft)
Population: 18,000. Intercity Station

Situated between Brussels and Namur the small town of Gembloux
(Flemish Gembloers), which dates back to a Roman settlement on the
military road from Bavai to Cologne, received its town charter in the
12th c. The town walls, parts of which are still standing, were constructed in the same period. From the 17th to the 19th c. Gembloux was
famous for its steelware but this was only small scale and was superseded by other metal-working industries. Together with several surrounding districts Gembloux forms the administative district of
Gembloux-sur-Orneau.

Sigisbert of Gembloux (1030–1112) wrote a world chronicle of the
years 381–1111 in the Benedictine abbey.

During the Dutch Wars of Independence the Spanish commander Don
Juan d'Austria defeated a Spanish army here in 1578.

The abbey was founded in the 10th c. by St Guibert but the buildings
from this period were demolished between 1762 and 1779. The new
building including restoration of the old cloisters began in 1779 according to plans by the architect Dewez on a rocky outcrop above the
Orneau. The former abbot's palace with an Ionic portal with columns
stands in the impressive courtyard. The former abbey church, a parish
church from 1812, is built above a 12th c. Romanesque crypt. Since 1861
the monastery buildings have been occupied by the National

Benedictine abbey

221

Agricultural Institute – The Faculty of Agronomical Sciences (visits by groups only).

Maison du Bailli

The Maison du Bailli (Bailif's house) is known to date back to the 12th c. The present day building is 16th c. and is used as a town hall; it houses a small museum about the production of steelware.

★ Corroy-le-
Château

Corroy-le-Château 6 km (4 mi.) south-west owes its name to the 13th c. **castle**, one of the best preserved medieval castles in Belgium. This moated fortification with its massive gate building, drawbridge and seven massive round towers was commissioned by Philipp of Vianden and was part of a defensive ring around Brabant. The 18th c. conversions have not had a major effect on the overall appearance.

A visit to the castle, which is still inhabited, passes through the 13th c. chapel, refurbished in the 19th c. The remaining rooms contain furniture and paintings from the 16–18th c.; one hall has a collection of old-fashioned clothing (open May–Sep. daily 10am–noon and 2–6pm).

Château de
Mielmont

Near Onoz, 8 km (5 mi.) south of Gembloux, the 12th c. Château de Mielmont towers over the Orneau on a steep cliff.

Ligny

Ligny, 12 km (7 mi.) south-west, is the site of Napoleon I's last victory, where two days before the Battle of Waterloo he defeated a Prussian unit. The battlefields of Waterloo are visible from a viewing platform.

Grand-Leez

In Grand-Leez, 6 km (4 mi.) east of Gembloux, numerous Roman finds were made. The Moulin Defrenne from 1830 is still in use today but driven by electricity.

Genk

See Hasselt, Surroundings

Geraardsbergen · Grammont   G 7

Province: Oost-Vlaanderen
Altitude: 14–110 m (45–360 ft). Population: 30,000
Inter-regional Station (bicycle rental at station)

Geraardsbergen (French Grammont) lies in the hilly countryside of the Flemish Ardennes on the Dender, close to the border. The town, which received its charter as early as 1068, had a flourishing textile industry. The highest point of Geraardsberg is the 110 m (360 ft)-high Oudenberg, which, on account of its steep cobblestone incline, is known to cyclists as "The Geraardsberg Wall" and is the most difficult stretch of the Tour de Flandres.

Grote Markt

By the steps of the stadhuis (town hall), which is of 15th c. origin and was rebuilt in Neo-Gothic style at the end of the 19th c., is a fountain with a Manneken Pis from 1455 making it the oldest monument of its kind in Belgium. The "Marbol" stands in front of the town hall, an octagonal Gothic fountain (1495), the only Gothic fountain in East Flanders.

In the square is the Church of Sint-Bartholomeus (15th/19th c.). Interesting features include a stone font (1620), a wrought-iron communion rail, choir stalls, 18th c. confessionals and the choir lectern.

The Onze-Lieve-Vrouwhospitaal in Gasthuisstraat is one of the oldest hospitals in Belgium. It was founded in 1100, but the monastery wing with the bishop's room, refectory and council chamber are from 1763. A small museum with objets d'art and paintings has been set up in the hospital.

Onze-Lieve-Vrouwhospitaal

In Abdijstraat is the site of former Sint-Adriaans-abdij, a Benedictine monastery founded in 1100 but of which only a few 18th c. buildings have been preserved. These house a small museum with craftwork and paintings. The rest of the site is a recreational park with a small zoo.

Sint-Adriaans-abdij

Every year the famous Oudenberg is the destination of the "Krakelingenworp" pilgrimage, a curious custom which finishes at the Onze-Lieve-Vrouwkapel on the hill.

Oudenberg

Extensive **views** of the countryside are to be had from the top. An information board explains the view.

Across the linguistic divide 8 km (5 mi.) south of Geraardsbergen in Lessines, known for its porphyry quarries, the surrealist painter René Magritte (see Facts and Figures, Famous People) was born.
    The Hôpital Notre-Dame à la Rose was founded in 1242 by Alix de Rosoit, widow of the Lord of Lessines, Arnold IV of Oudenaarde. The first floor of the monastery is now a museum with furniture, paintings, old instruments and household goods. The Musée Communal in the hospital documents the history of the quarrying of porphyry.

Lessines

German-Belgian Nature Park   H–K 17/18

Province: Liège

The German-Belgian Nature Park was created in 1971 by the amalgamation of the Belgian Parc Naturel Hautes Fagnes with the German Nordeifel nature reserve. The area which comprises 2,485 sq. km (959 sq. mi.) stretches east of the Eupen–Malmédy line between the North Rhine Westphalian town of Aachen and the Luxembourg border to Euskirchen in Rheinland Pfalz in Germany. 722 sq. km (278 sq. mi.) are in Belgium, 1359 sq. km (524 sq. mi.) are in North Rhine Westphalia and 404 sq. km (156 sq. mi.) in Rheinland Pfalz.

The characteristic landscape of this sparsely inhabited, undulating range of rounded hills is that of the Hohe Venn (corresponding to the Dutch "Fehn" = fenland; French Hautes Fagnes). Its average altitude is around 400 m (1312 ft) with the highest point being the Signal de Botrange at 694 m (2277 ft), which is also the highest point in Belgium. This region consists of extensive moor and heath, which gives it its name and forms a giant natural reservoir of water providing the source of several rivers, which have in turn been dammed to create large lakes. This remote moor with its flora provides unique evidence of the preglacial climate and is crossed only by very few footpaths.

★★Landscape

There are impressive all-round views from the tower on the Signal de Botrange, to the north of Malmédy (see Malmédy), and from Mont Rigi (672 m/2205 ft) near Baraque-Michel.
    About 1 km (½ mi.) east of Baraque Michel is the Fontaine Périgny,

★★Viewpoints

Dead trees on the moor

The Helle stream

Peat-digging

where the Helle (Hill) has its source. Here, too, there are fine views of the surroundings.

A few hundred yards from the source remains of the **Via Mansuerica** were discovered, according to recent research a 7th c. military road.

On the Belgian side comprehensive information about the Hohe Venn nature reserve is available from the **Botrange Nature Park Centre**. A permanent exhibition features a relief model of the moor landscape and a slide show of the most beautiful views. A 5 km (3 mi.) long educational nature walk leads through the countryside and is marked with seven observation posts giving facts about the flora and fauna. The centre also organises walks, photography courses and introductions to herbal medicine (open daily 10am–6pm; Nov./Dec. closed for two weeks).

A total of 4000 km (2485 ft) of **footpaths and walkways** cross the reserve; citizens of EU countries may, if necessary, cross the green border. Main footpaths are marked by a red and a white post; double horizontal stripes indicate a change of direction, crossed stripes inform the walker that he/she has taken the wrong direction. Minor walks are marked by numbers, letters or symbols (see Practical Information, Sport).

Horse riding is permitted in Belgium only in the Eupen area on clearly marked bridleways. In winter 23 long-distance **ski runs** (13 in Belgium) are marked out (see Practical Information, Sport).

A trip on the **Venn railway** is a pleasant way to explore the high Venn (see Practical Information, Railways)

Behaviour in the nature reserve The visitor to the protected nature reserve should not interfere with the animals and plants in their habitat and should enjoy nature quietly. Under no circumstances should the marked paths and trails be left. Litter must not be thrown away but taken home; dogs must be kept on a lead. The picking of wild flowers is not allowed, neither are camping, radios, walking at night nor camp fires.

Fire is a particular threat to the ecologically sensitive moorland so that in the warmer months it may not permitted to enter certain areas including signposted footpaths. These areas are marked by by red warning flags.

Ghent · Gent · Gand   E 6/7

Province: Oost-Vlaanderen
Altitude: 5–29 m (16–95 ft) Population: 250,000
Intercity and Inter-regional Station (bicycle rental at Sint-Pieter station)

The old city of Ghent (Flemish Gent; French Gand), capital of the province of Oost-Vlaanderen and seat of the university, is situated on the confluence of the Scheldt and the Leie, the many branches of which intersect the city. With the surrounding communities Ghent is the third largest urban region in Belgium.

Economic centre Ghent is the largest industrial conurbation in West Belgium. For centuries the most important industry was textiles which made Ghent into a "Manchester of the European mainland". Today the city still has large cotton spinning mills and linen weaving mills where the world famous Flemish cloth is produced, but the decline of the textile industry has forced the establishment of new areas of economic activity. Thus today factories in and around Ghent produce paper, chemicals, cars, optical, engineering, electrical and electronic components with a large steelworks being the major industry. Many of these

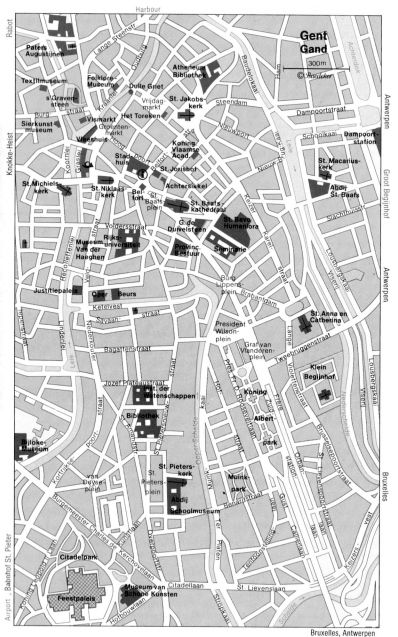

Gent
Gand

300m

© Baedeker

Harbour

Rabot

Knokke-Heist

Antwerpen

Groot Begijnhof

Antwerpen

Bruxelles

Airport · Bahnhof St. Pieter

Paters Augustijnen
Textilmuseum
s'Gravensteen
Folklore-Museum
Sierkunst museum
Dulle Griet
Vismarkt
Vleeshuis
Groentenmarkt
St. Michielskerk
St. Niklaaskerk
Belfort
Atheneum Bibliotheek
St. Jakobskerk
Vrijdagmarkt
Het Toreken
Steendam
Nieuwpoort
Dampoortstraat
Schoolkaai
Dampoort-station
St. Macarius-kerk
Abdij St. Baafs
Slachthuisstr
Koning. Vlaamse Acad.
Stadhuis
St. Jorishof
Achtersikkel
St. Baafs-plein
St. Baafs-kathedraal
St. Bavo Humaniora
Volderssraat
Rijksuniversiteit
Museum Van der Haeghen
G. de Duivelsteen
Provinc. Besfuur
Seminarie
Burg Lippensplein
Brabantdam
Justitiepaleis
Opera
Beurs
Ketelvest
Savaanstraat
Bagattenstraat
President Wilsonplein
Graf van Vlanderenplein
St. Anna en Catherina
Twseebruggenstraat
Klein Begijnhof
Jozef Plateaustraat
Inst. der Wetenschappen
Bibliotheek
Bijloke-Museum
van Duyseplein
St. Pieterskerk
St. Pietersplein
Abdij
Schoolmuseum
Koning Albert park
Muinkpark
Benardstraat
Citadelpark
Feestpaleis
Museum van Schone Kunsten
Citadellaan
St. Lievenslaan

Bruxelles, Antwerpen

companies are on the Ghent-Terneuzen canal, exploiting the advantages of the waterway network.

Together with Antwerp and Zeebrugge (see entries) Ghent is one of the three most important sea ports in Belgium. The harbour is linked by various canals with the Westerschelde (Gent–Terneuzen canal) and with the North Sea (Bruges–Ghent canal, Bruges–Zeebrugge canal and Bruges–Ostend canal) and can accommodate vessels up to 60,000 tonnes. The annual turnover of goods handled amounts to about 25 million tonnes; Ghent being an important trade centre, especially for the import and export of cereals. In addition the city and its environs are the heart of the garden and cut flower growing area: 80 per cent of all foliage plants in Belgium are grown here, chiefly for export. The ultra-modern exhibition site "Flanders Expo" in Sint-Denijs-Westrem has been instrumental in gaining Ghent prestige as a venue for trade fairs and exhibitions.

Festivals Every five years (next in 2000) in late April the Ghent Floralién is held at "Flanders Expo" with the gardeners of the region showing their produce. The Ghent Festival Week takes place in mid-July with music and theatre literally on every street corner and stands selling food and drink set up everywhere. The Flanders' Festival (series of concerts of predominantly Baroque music) which is celebrated throughout Flanders focuses on Ghent.

Beginnings As far back as the Romans a settlement had been established on the small island at the confluence of the Scheldt and the Leie. In the 7th c. the missionary St Amandus, together with his pupil, St Bavon, patron saint of Ghent, came to this area and founded two abbeys dedicated to St Petrus, in between which Ghent itself developed. The Norman threat led to the first fortifications being built, with the Gravensteen around 1000.   History

Powerful guilds Around 1000 a council of 11 jurors governed the city, where the cloth industry was gaining more and more in importance. After Paris Ghent became the most powerful city north of the Alps. In 1228 34 patricians took over the further fate of the town. The oligarchical rule of their successors, who together with the Counts of Flanders followed the French king, increasingly aroused the anger of the powerful guilds that were seeking independence.

When the import of English wool, upon which the Ghent cloth industry depended, was stopped, the citizens of Ghent united in 1337 behind Jacob van Artevelde with England and led other Flemish towns in opposing France. Artevelde ruled for years with dictatorial powers until he was murdered in 1345 by the head of the weavers' guild. The defeat of the Flemish army under Artevelde's son Philip near Rozebeke put a temporary stop to the Ghent citizens' desire for self-government.

Burgundian rule The marriage of the heiress of Count Louis II of Flanders to Duke Philip the Bold brought Flanders under Burgundian domination. His attempts to curb the power of the guilds again led to resistance. After the Battle of Gavere on the Scheldt on the July 23rd 1453, when thousands of Ghent citizens lost their lives, the most prominent burghers and the Council had to come out beyond the town gates wearing only their shirts and beg the victor for mercy. Following the death of the Duke in 1477 his daughter Maria of Burgundy was forced to grant the citizens of Ghent greater rights. The Burgundian period of the 15th c. was a time of prosperity for Ghent when culture and the arts flourished. The van Eyck brothers (Altar of Ghent) were active here at this time.

Habsburg rule Ghent fell to the Habsburgs on Maria of Burgundy's marriage to the future Emperor Maximilian. In the 16th c. under the govern-

ment of Emperor Charles V (born 1500 in the Prinsenhof in Ghent) Ghent tried to make up for the decline of the cloth industry as river navigation developed. Time and again the citizens of Ghent opposed the ruling dynasty; the climax was reached when the Protestant Geuzen rose up against the Spanish who reacted by sending troops in 1567, commanded by the Duke of Alba who exacted terrible revenge. In 1576 the "Pacification of Ghent" was signed in the city, a peace and friendship league between the general states and the southern provinces of the Spanish Netherlands. After Alexander Farnese, the Spanish governor of the Netherlands, had finally subjected Ghent to Spanish rule again in 1584, the town's downfall was sealed.

Revival The establishment of the cotton industry brought a new revival in the 18th c. under Austrian rule; in 1800, under French occupation, Lieven Bauwens brought in English cotton looms and revolutinised the trade. In the course of the 19th c. the town experienced real prosperity with the rapid growth of industry and trade.

Ghent was occupied by German troops in both World Wars but mostly escaped damage.

The Belgian-French poet and Nobel prize winner Maurice Maeterlinck (see Facts and Figures, Famous People) was born in Ghent in 1862.

Townscape Ghent's historic inner city offers a superb collection of splendid buildings along picturesque canals, only superseded by Bruges. A walk through the town on a summer's evening, when the most important buildings are illuminated, is a particularly unforgettable experience. In high summer the canals, almost at a standstill, have their own distinctive aroma which permeates the city in the heat. However, this hardly mars the overall impression of this unique city.

Tour of the town

Programme As the historic Old Town is quite compact it can be taken in on one day and still include a detailed visit to the Sint-Baafskathedraal, the Gravensteen and the Museum of Ethnography. A visit to the Museum voor Schone Kunsten requires more time.

Round trips and tours Two organisations offer guided tours around the city on foot: Gidsenbond van Gent en Oost-Vlaanderen (tel. 258302) and Sightseeing Service (tel. 235226). Boats depart continually from berths on the Korenlei and the Graslei from April to the beginning of November for canal trips through the centre. Horse-drawn carriages depart from Sint-Baafsplein from Easter to October. It is also possible to tour the city by minibus (departing from the Belfry) or by taxi.

Car parks Cars should not be driven into the city centre. There are car parks at Vrijdagmarkt, at Wilsonplein (underground) at the University, at Kouter Square, at Sint-Pieterskerk and at Sint-Pieter station (tram to the city centre).

Historic Inner Town

The Inner Town is encircled by the Leie and the western branch of the Scheldt, the Opper Schelde. The central point of Old Ghent is Sint-Baafsplein.

On the eastern side of Sint-Baafsplein stands Sint-Baafskathedraal (Cathedral of St Bavon), a majestic building of brick and granite (opening times Apr.–Oct. Mon.–Sat. 9.30am–noon and 2–6pm, Sun. 1–6pm; Nov.–Mar. Mon.–Sat. 10am–noon and 2.30–4pm, Sun. 2–5pm).

★★Sint-Baafskathedraal

◀ *The towers of Ghent: Sint-Niklaas, Belfry and Sint-Baaf*

Sint-Baafskathedraal

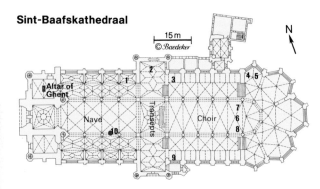

1 Gaspar de Crayer
  "Assumption"
2 Maarten de Vos: "Ecce Homo"
3 Frans Pourbus or Michiel or
  Rafael Coxie: "The Seven
  Works of Mercy"
4 Peter Paul Rubens:
  "The Summoning of St Bavo"

5 Otto Venius:
  "Raising of Lazarus"
6 High Altar
7 Tomb of Bishop Antonius Triest
8 Tomb of the Bishop d'Allamont
9 Frans Pourbus: "Christ among the
  Scribes"
10 Baroque pulpit

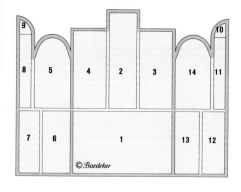

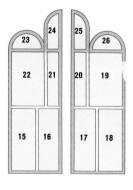

OPEN

1 Adoration of the
  Lamb of God
2 Christ
3 John the Baptist
4 Mary
5 Singers
6 Knights
7 Righteous knights (copy)
8 Adam
9 Abel's sacrifice

10 Cain slays Abel
11 Eve
12 St Christopher and pilgrim
13 Hermits
14 Music-playing angel

CLOSED

15 Josse Vijd
   (donor of the altar)
16 John the Baptist

17 John the Evangelist
18 Elizabeth Boorlut
   (wife of Josse Vijd)
19 The Annunciation
20 Room with washbasin
21 Room with a view of the town
   through the window
22 The Archangel Gabriel
23 Zacharias
24 Sibyl of Eritrea
25 Sibyl of Cuma
26 Micheas

Charles V gave the cathedral its present name after he destroyed the old Sint-Baafsabdij (see p. 229) to build a fortress.

The High Gothic cathedral choir is 13/14th c., the late Gothic tower and the main nave are 15/16th c., whereas the transept and the nave were only completed in 1539–59. The Romanesque crypt of its predecessor, Sint Jans Church, has been preserved.

The tower, which lost its roof in a fire in 1602, has a carillon and there is a good view from its platform.

The light interior of the cathedral is richly decorated with some unique **paintings**. These include "The Conversion of St Baaf" by Peter Paul Rubens (1624) and "Christ among the Doctors" by Frans Pourbus (1571), in which the artist painted well known people of his time such as Philip II, the Duke of Alba, Thomas Calvin, Pieter Breugel the Elder and Charles V, who can be seen in the bottom left corner. There are other important works by Gaspar de Crayer, Maarten de Vos and Otto Venius.

The **Altar of Ghent**, also known as "The Adoration of the Mystic Lamb" after the centre panel, is by far the greatest masterpiece of old Flemish painting.

The panels, commissioned by the Ghent patrician Josse Vijd for an ambulatory chapel, were allegedly begun about 1420 by Hubert van Eyck (around 1370–1426) and completed by his brother Jan (around 1390–1441) in 1431/32. It has never been known to what extent each of the brothers was involved in the genesis of the painting. It is generally accepted that in the representation of the Knights of Christ the fourth rider has the features of Jan and the front rider those of Hubert van Eyck.

The large winged altar, which is regarded as the most monumental example of medieval altar painting and as the most important step away from the iconic painting of the Middle Ages towards a realistic style, illustrates in vivid sequential panels the story of Salvation from the Fall of Man to the Redemption (see diagram of panels below). Albrecht Dürer on visiting the altar during his travels through Flanders called it "a magnificent realistic painting".

The work became famous shortly after its completion and had a chequered history. After Philip II coveted it, in 1566, it narrowly escaped destruction by the iconoclasts and was saved from a fire in 1640. The Austrian Emperor Joseph II had the panels with Adam and Eve removed in 1794, objecting to their nakedness – an illustration of the work's striking realism. They were replaced by "clothed" copies. In 1794 the centre panels were taken to Paris and exhibited in the Louvre; six panels found their way onto the art market and were bought by the Prussian king, who displayed them in the Berlin Museum. In 1815 the centre panels were returned from France, in 1861 the panels of Adam and Eve were acquired by the Brussels Museum. Under the Treaty Of Versailles Germany had to return the wings from Berlin and in 1920 the entire work, with the exception of the Predella (socle) lost in 1550, was put on display again in the cathedral. In 1934 two panels of the left wing were stolen. "John the Baptist" was returned but the inner panel ("The Righteous Judges") was never rediscovered and was replaced by a copy by van der Veken. During the Second World War the altarpiece was hidden in Pau, in southern France, but it was found by German troops and stored in a salt mine near Lake Altau in Styria, Austria. Here it was discovered by American troops and returned to the cathedral. Since 1986 it has been housed in its own room on the left side of Sint-Baafskathedraal and can be seen from all sides.

Worth mentioning among the splendid works of **sculpture** in the cathedral are the pulpit by Laurent Delvaux (1741), the tomb of Bishop A.

Triest by Jerome Duquesnoy (1652), the Baroque organ case (1653) and the bronze door (1633) of the chapel of Bishop A. Triest.

The extensive **crypt** contains numerous 15th and 16th c. tombs of bishops, a rich treasury including a 9th c. gospel and the shrine of St Macarius by Hugo de la Vigne (1616).

The outstanding **Calvarian triptych** of 1464 by Joos van Wassenhove (Justus van Ghent) is shown in one of the chapels. To the left of the choir steps lead down to the crypt of the earlier 10th c. church.

Sint-Baafsplein

Sint-Baafsplein, which has been re-designed in the past few years, opens out in front of the cathedral with the Koninklijk Vlaams Theater (Royal Flemish Theatre) on the north side and the memorial to Jan Frans Willems (1793–1846), the founder of the Flemish movement, integrated into a modern fountain on the south side.

Hotel van Branteghem/Hamelinck Among the surrounding houses No. 10 stands out, a very handsome patrician house of 1739 with a bust of the goddess Juno in the gable. It is the house of the Hamelinck family, who built the house on the site of the "Roosecransche" guest house which belonged to the van Branteghem family. It once housed the oldest theatre in Ghent.

Belfry (opening times mid-Mar.–mid-Nov. daily 10am–12.30pm and 2–5.30pm) On the west side of Sint-Baafsplein stands the 91 m (298 ft)-high belfry, symbol of the city's independence, where the charters of the privileges of Ghent were kept. The tower was begun about 1300 and by 1338 was mainly completed. The present-day spire was restored to its original 14th c. form at the beginning of this century and replaced the wooden bell tower of 1380. It is crowned by a gilded copper dragon, which was first installed in 1377. Today it is a replica as are the four armed figures at the corners of the platform. Only one of the originals of these survives and can be seen on the ground floor.

The **Roeland bell** was cast in 1315 and installed ten years later in the tower. It has often called the population of Ghent to arms; in 1659 it was melted down and from the metal Peter Hemony cast a carillon of 37 bells. At the same time three large bells, the Triomfanten, were made, the largest of which, again being called Roeland, cracked in 1914 and was removed in 1950. It now stands again in the belfry on the Sint-Baafsplein. The new Roeland weighing 5000 kg was put in place in 1948.

Interior At the entrance to the tower platform, from where there are good views of Ghent, on the ground floor is the room, called "Secreet", where the privileges of the city were kept in an iron chest. On the fourth floor the workings of the clock (1670), the oldest in Belgium, and the 52-bell carillon can be seen.

★Lakenhalle

The splendid Cloth Hall directly adjoins the Belfry. This building (1426–41) by Simon van Assche, restored in 1900–03 was the meeting place of the wool and cloth traders, the "Halleheeren". The Gothic ground floor, partly below ground, is divided into three by 20 columns. In 1741 it housed the town prison, today it has a café-restaurant which is popular with tourists.

"Multivision" An audio-visual display about Ghent of 30 minutes duration is held in the Cloth Hall (performances: Apr.–Nov. from 9.30–11.30am and 2–5.20pm every 40 minutes).

The Louis XIV style gaoler's house of the former prison is built on to the north side of the Belfry. There is a relief known as **"Mammelokker"** above the doorway. It depicts the old man Cimon, who has been condemned to death by starvation, being suckled by his daughter.

North of the Lakenhalle on the Botermarkt stands the magnificent Stadhuis (town hall). Tours: Apr.–Oct. Mon.–Thu. 2–5pm 2pm Dutch; 2.20pm French; 3.20pm German; 4pm English.

★Stadhuis

It combines a variety of architectural styles, having been built over a long period of time. On the oldest parts of the building on the Hoogpoort, completed in the style of Bruges City Hall in 1482 and containing the council chambers, the architects Rombout Keldermans and Dominik de Waghemakere built a new wing in the finest late Gothic form richly decorated with statues. However, building work on this part, which is best seen from the corner of Hoogpoort and Belfortstraat, was suspended because of religious disputes in 1539. Only a quarter of the original plan was realised and only the Pacificatiezaal (Peace Hall; actually the court room for the Keure, the protectors of the town constitution) and the Marriage Chapel, both 1535, were built. Work only resumed at the end of the 16th c. so that the wing facing the Botermarkt is in Renaissance style as is the Throne Room on the upper floor (1635). Further building was carried out in the 18th c. on the Conciergerie (Flemish Baroque; corner of Hoogpoort/Stadhuissteeg) and the Armenkamer (Rococo, 1750; at the Poeljemarkt).

Directly opposite the town hall on the corner of Hoogpoort stands the former house of the Guild of Crossbowmen, Sint-Jorishof of 1477, where Maria of Burgundy granted greater freedom to the Flemish towns.

Sint-Jorishof

There are many fine old houses in Hoogpoort which runs north of the Stadhuis.

★Hoogpoort

Ghent: Stadhuis

Groot Vleeshuis

On the Sint-Jorishof are No. 50 "Grote" or "Witte Moor" (15th c.) and No. 52 "Zwarte Moor" (15th c.), both fine examples of Brabant Gothic with typical stepped gables. No. 54 "De Grote Sikkel" (14th c.) adjoins, once owned by the van Sikkeln family; today it houses the Academy of Music. Off the Biezekapelstraat is the "De Achtersikkel" (16th c.) with an attractive courtyard and small tower.

In Hoogpoort heading west are No. 33 "De Samson" (1481; the guild house of the Ghent goldsmiths until 1540), No. 15, "De Draecke" (15th c.) and finally house No. 10 (1732). It is called "De Ram" and was originally occupied by an apothecary. On the façade are an apothecary sign and a bust of the botanist Carolus Clusius, founder of the botanical gardens in Leiden, Holland.

Groentenmarkt

At the western end of the Hoogpoort is the Groentenmarkt, originally a fish market and since the 18th c. a vegetable market. In the Middle Ages the pillory stood here. A mustard factory and shop are in one of the surrounding houses.

★Groot Vleeshuis

On the west side of the market is the long Groot Vleeshuis, a medieval covered meat market with a guild house, chapel and numerous gables in the roof. The building originated in 1406–10 and was restored in 1912. At the south end of the Vleeshuis is the "Penshuizeken" (entrails cottage) where the poor were given the entrails of slaughtered animals.

Klein Turkije

At the south end of the Korenmarkt (corn market), surrounded by 16–18th c. buildings, the business centre of old Ghent, the lane known as Klein Turkije branches off. The oldest house is "De rode Hoed" (red hat) from the 13th c., where Albrecht Dürer lived during his stay in the town in 1523. The "Huis der Kruideniers", the guild house of the grocers, is in the same street.

The tower of the Sint-Niklaaskerk dominates the Korenmarkt, an excellent example of Scheldt Gothic. The first work began in the 13th c. and continued with interruptions until the 18th c. The Baroque west gateway to the Korenmarkt dates from 1681. The guilds of businessmen and the chamber of rhetoric "De Fonteyne" had a chapel in the church. The house of the orators is in the Goudenleeuwplein No. 7 (1539) behind the church and is the oldest voluted building of its kind in Ghent with a Renaissance façade.

Sint-Niklaaskerk

Opposite the church doorway the architects Cloquet and Mortier attempted to harmonise the Postgebouw, completed in 1903, with the Neo-Gothic style of the neighbouring historic gables.

Postgebouw

The Sint-Michielsbrug crosses the Leie. From the bridge there is a wonderful **view** of Sint-Niklaas, the Belfry and Sint-Baafs together with the Korenlei and the Graslei with the Gravensteen in the background.

Sint-Michielsbrug

At the far end of the bridge stands the Sint-Michielskerk. Work started on it in 1440 and reached the tower by 1648. It has a rich interior with paintings (de Crayer, van Oost, Otto Venius), the most impressive being "Crucifixion" (1629) by **Anton van Dyck**.

Sint-Michielskerk

Along the Leie a group of buildings next to the church to the south in Onderbergen street are known as "Het Pand". This is a former 13th c. Dominican monastery and is one of the oldest buildings in Ghent. Today it is used by the university.

Het Pand

This part of the town from the Sint-Michielsberg northwards along the Korenlei and Graslei was Ghent's oldest harbour where many of the guilds built their splendid, now famous, houses.

★Korenlei and ★★Graslei

View of the Graslei from the Korenlei

The Sint-Michielsbrug leads down to the **Korenlei**, itself lined by splendid façades but which offers the best view of the even finer houses on the opposite bank of the Graslei. No. 7 along the Korenlei, the "Gildehuis der Onvrije Schippers" (House of the Tied Boatmen), is a Baroque building from 1739. No. 9 is "De Zwane", a former brewery with beautiful swan motifs on the gable (16th c.). No. 15 is the site of the former "Hof van Gruuthuse", House of Duke Egmont (1352), now replaced by a building with a Neo-Classical faáade, which also encompasses Nos. 17–19, the "Hotel de Ghellink". Finally No. 24, "Lintworm en Krocht", was a Romanesque château from the 12th c., rebuilt at the beginning of this century.

Some of Belgium's finest guild houses are to be found along the **Graslei**. Next to the rear façade of the post building is the "Gildehuis der Vrije Schippers" (House of the Free Boatmen), built in 1531 in the Brabant Gothic style. Adjoining it is the second "Gildehuis der Graanmeters" (House of the Grain Weighers), from 1698, a late Baroque building with a stepped gable. Almost squeezed in is the tiny "Tolhuisje" (Customs House), a Flemish Renaissance building of 1682, followed by the Romanesque "Spijker" or "Koornstapelhuis" (around 1200). The first "Korenmetershuis" (House of the Grain Weighers) was built in 1435; finally the "Gildehuis der Metselaars" (House of the Masons) from 1527 in Brabant Gothic style completes this unique row of guild houses.

★Museum voor
Sierkunst

At the end of the Korenlei, where the Lieve, the first sea canal of the 13th c., branches off from the Leie, Jan Breydelstraat turns off to the left. The splendid house, No. 5 dated 1754, was the town house of the de Coninck family who furnished it in grand style. The individual rooms of the house are open as a museum (Museum voor Sierkunst = Museum of Decorative Arts) and contain some later works of art, furniture, (including a sofa and two armchairs which belonged to the Tsarina Catherine II), porcelain, glass and paintings. The writing desk of the French king Louis XVIII, who had fled to Ghent in 1815 from Napoleon I, returned from Elba, is on display (open Tue.–Sun. 9.30am–5pm).

'Huis der
Gekroonde
Hoofden"

On the corner of Gewad/Burgstraat stands the "Huis der Gekroonde Hoofden" (House of the Crowned Heads) with a Renaissance façade of scrolled gables and portraits of the Counts of Flanders.

Museum voor
Industrieële
Archeologie en
Textiel

House No. 14 in the Gewad is the Museum voor Industrieële Archeologie en Textiel (Museum of Industrial Archaeology and Textiles). As well as many tools and documents there is a Mule Jenny (spinning Jenny), one of the oldest still functioning spinning machines in the world that Lieven Bauwens introduced to Ghent at the beginning of the 19th c., thereby revitalising the textile industry (open Tue.–Sun. 9.30am–5pm).

Detour

Gewad street comes to the Prinsenhofplein with the Donkere Poort (Dark Tower), remains of the Prinsenhof palace, inhabited by the Counts of Flanders from 1353, birthplace of Charles V, in 1500.

Further north-west is the **Rabot**, a lockhouse built in 1489 on the Lieve with stepped gables, flanked by two mighty round towers. On this spot the citizens of Ghent resisted the army of the German Emperor Friedrich III.

Rabotstraat leads back to Burgstraat, past the ruins of the **Sint-Elisabeth Béguinage** (16th/17th c.). A monument to the poet Georges Rodenbach (1855–98) stands next to Sint-Elisabeth church.

From the Rabot there is a footpath along the Lieve back to Burgstraat. It passes the **Lievekaai**, a romantic spot with small gabled houses.

Missing out the detour, on the right past Jan Breydelstraat is the rear façade of the castle of the Counts of Flanders, the Gravensteen, one of the strongest moated fortresses in Western Europe, surrounded by the River Lieve. Opening times Apr.–Sep. 9am–6pm; Oct.–Mar. 9am–5pm.

★★Gravensteen

It was built 1180–1200 on the orders of Philipp of Alsace, the former count of Flanders, on the foundation of a 9th c. structure in the style of Syrian crusader castles. Together with Bruges Castle it was the residence of the Flemish counts and still remains a unique example of the medieval art of fortification. In the 14th c. it ceased to have a military function and was used by the counts for administration of the land. In 1800 it came into private ownership and was converted into a cotton mill and flats for the workers; between 1894 and 1913 comprehensive restoration took place.

The **tour** of the castle and a recently extensively renovated museum, leaves from the gatehouse into a large courtyard surrounded by a circular wall with 24 half towers and a defence gallery which encircles the main castle. This is dominated by a massive keep or "Meestentoren", its platform being reached by a narrow spiral staircase. Outstanding views of the castle and town are to be had from here. The tour continues through the palace (living quarters of the lords of the castle), where instruments of torture and court documents are now displayed, through the Great Hall, where Philipp the Good gave a huge banquet for the knights of the Golden Fleece in 1445, then through the torture chamber, finishing with the hole down to the dungeons.

In front of the castle extends the ancient Sint-Veerleplein, possibly the oldest square in Ghent, although the neighbouring façades are of 17th c. origin at the earliest. This square was a market place but also the site of executions and burnings of the victims of the Inquisition.

Sint-Veerleplein

The superb Baroque building at Sint-Veerleplein No. 5 is the old fish market, built in 1689 according to plans by Artus Quellin. Following a fire in 1872 it was extended and connected to the new meat market in Rekelingestraat. The gateway depicts Neptune and allegorical representations of the Scheldt (male) and Leie (female).

Oude Vismarkt

To the north-east the Kraanlei adjoins Sint-Veerleplein, also lined with elegant houses. Immediately on the left is No. 1, the "Craenenburgh", then the row of houses "De Lelye" (Nos. 3–11), built around 1500 in Brabant Gothic style. No. 13, "In den Bliekenmarkt" (15th/16th c.) is a former fish shop.

★Kraanlei

No. 65, immaculately restored in 1962, Alijns Godhuis, a children's hospital founded in 1363 and one of the last remaining Godshuizen. These houses were founded by well-off families for the needy.

★Museum voor Volkskunde

In a picturesque courtyard are eighteen typical Flemish cottages, all interconnected. They house the extremely comprehensive Museum voor Volkskunde, which with its notable collection of equipment, documents and everyday objects provides a vivid picture of Flemish folk life around 1900. Of particular interest are the restored workshops and living rooms, a dining room, a barber's shop, a cobbler's workshop, an apothecary's shop, a confectioner's, bakery and a candlestick-maker's workshop.

The museum also has a puppet theatre with performances on Wednesday afternoons at 2.30pm and Saturday afternoons at 3pm (open Apr.–Oct. daily 9am–12.30pm and 1.30–5.30pm; Nov.–Mar. Tue.–Sun. 10am–noon and 1.30–5pm).

Further along the Kraanlei is house No. 75, "De Klok", dating from the 17th c. with a spiral staircase and decorated with numerous allegorical reliefs. On the ground floor are care and temperance, love, faith and hope in the first floor with justice and strength above the roof window. No. 77, "De Zeven Werken van Barmhartigheid", and No. 79, "Het Vliegend Hert", are Baroque 17th c. town houses, decorated with exquisite reliefs.

Dulle Griet

From Kraanlei the Zuivelbrug crosses the Leie to Grootkanonplein, where stands the 5 metre-long and 16 tonne cast iron canon "Dulle Griet" (Mad Meg). It dates from the mid-15th c. and could fire, not very accurately, 340 kg of cannonballs.

Vrijdagmarkt

Next is the Vrijdagmarkt (Friday Market), centre of political life in medieval Ghent. It was in this square that the Flemish counts had to swear their observance of the freedoms accorded to the citizens of Ghent. The guilds also fought each other here and in 1477 two advisers and envoys of the stadholder (governess) Maria of Burgundy were executed.

Artevelde-monument In the centre of the square stands the monument to the hero of Ghent Jacob van Artevelds (see Facts and Figures, Famous People), by Petrus de Vigne-Quyo in 1863.

Several **guild houses** surround the market: the House of the Tanners "Het Toreken", 1460, "Den Bonten Mantel" (No. 45) the furrier, 1675 and the "Lakenmetershuis" (No. 22) which was built on the site of the former tanners' guild house in the 18th c. The Art Nouveau "Ons Huis", belonging to the socialist workers' associations, was built about 1900.

East and Southeast Ghent
Sint-Jacobskerk

To the east of the Vrijdagmarkt Sint-Jacobskerk stands in the Bij Sant-Jacobs square, one of the oldest religious buildings in Ghent. The crossing tower and both west towers are of the Romanesque period; the rest

The dark towers of Gravensteen rise above the roofs of Ghent

The cannon known as "Dulle Griet"

was finished between the 13th and 15th c. The church contains tombs and some fine paintings, especially in the ambulatory (Coxie, de Crayer, van Cleef).

A colourful flower market takes place at weekends in the square in front of the church.

The Hoogpoort is continued by the Nederpolder. No. 1 is the twin-gabled Palais Vanden Meersche dated 1547, an attractive inner courtyard with Rococo façades being added in the 18th c. No. 2 is "De kleine Sikkel", a Romanesque 13th c. patrician's house, which also belonged to the Van der Sickelen family.

Nederpolder

The Nederpolder ends at Bisdomplein. On the right on the bank of the Scheldt is the castle of the steward of the Flemish dukes, Geraard de Duivel. Over the centuries it has served many purposes – as a prison, a lunatic asylum and an arsenal – and it now houses the East Flemish State Archives.

Geraard de Duivelsteen

There is a memorial to the brothers Hubert and Jan van Eyck in the park.

East and South-East Ghent

In the east part of the city, across the Slachthuisbrug over the Leie, are the ruins of Sint-Baafsadbdij, one of the two abbeys still standing from the beginning of Ghent's development. Opening times Apr.–Oct. Tue.–Sun. 9.30am–5pm; Jan.–Mar. by prior arrangement, tel. (09) 2251106.

★Ruins of Sint-Baafsabdij

It was founded in 630 by St Amandus and rebuilt after being destroyed by the Normans in the 10th c. Following the suppression of the revolt by the citizens of Ghent against Charles V. He dissolved the abbey and had a fortress built in its place in 1540, the Spanjards Kasteel, which was in turn destroyed in the 19th c.

A gallery of the late Gothic cloisters, the octagonal lavatorium and parts of the chapter house and the refectory still remain from the original abbey.

The refectory with its beautiful Romanesque frescoes (12th c.) has been the **Museum voor Steenen Voorwerpen** (Museum for Stonecutting and Sculpture) since 1882. It has an extraordinary collection of medieval tombstones, Ghent sculpture and architectural artefacts from the 12th–18th c. as well as mosaics.

Klein Begijnhof

The smaller Béguinage (Klein Begijnhof van Onze-Lieve-Vrouw ter Hoyen) in Violettenstraat in the south-east part of the city dates back to 1234, when it was founded by Johanna of Constantinople and her sister Maria. The present day site with its cottages around a large tree-lined lawn has remained unchanged since the 17th c.

The Onze-Lieve-Vrouw ter Hoyen church which belongs to the béguinage was begun in 1658 and completed in 1720. It has a captivating Baroque doorway. In the interior are valuable paintings (de Crayer, van Cleef, polyptych by Horenbaut).

South City

The area south of the historic inner city, chiefly built in the 18th and 19th c., is, with its pedestrianised areas, the commercial and shopping centre of Ghent.

Kouter

This square has played a major role over the centuries in the history of Ghent. It has been the site of meetings, festivals, tournaments, troop inspections and a shooting range. Since the 18th c. a flower and bird market is held every Sunday. Some of the old buildings have been preserved: the exchange built in 1738 as the main police station, the Hotel Faligan (1775) in French Rococo and the Koninklijke Opera (Royal Opera) (1837–40).

The Municipal Library is on the southern side of the square.

Museum voor de Geschiednis van de Wetenschappen

North of the Kouter in Korte Meer is the Museum coor de Geschiednis van de Wetenschapen (Museum of the History of the Sciences), dedicated to the inventions and discoveries of scientists from Ghent and Flanders. Among these are Jan Palfijn, a famous Flemish surgeon, inventor of birth forceps and founder of anatomy, and Leo Baekeland, the inventor of bakelite. There is an unrivalled collection of surgical instruments from all periods (open Tue.–Fri. 10am–noon and 2–5pm).

The museum is housed in the buildings of the university, founded by King Willem I in 1816.

Veldstraat

The Veldstraat, the oldest and best known shopping street, now pedestrianised, runs parallel to the Korte Meer in a westerly direction. The most striking building is the large 18th c. Palais D'Hane-Steenhuyse with a magnificent Rococo façade and an equally intact Classical façade facing the garden, where concerts are held. The French king Louis XVIII lived in the house in 1815 during the "Hundred Days" of further Napoleonic rule. Other guests included the King of Westphalia, Talleyrand, the Tsar of Russia and the Prince of Orange. Today the house is the information centre on restoration in the city.

In the houses opposite (today C&A department store) the American negotiators stayed who signed the Ghent Peace Treaty with the British in 1814, ending the war between the USA and Great Britain.

The Museum Arnold van der Haeghen is to be found at Veldstraat No. 82. The building dates from 1741 and was first the residence of an industrialist; in 1815 the Duke of Wellington lived here. From 1836 it housed the printing press of the van der Haeghen family.

The Arnold van der Haeghen Museum comprises the Maeterlinck cabinet and the Stuyvaert cabinet. The Maeterlinck cabinet contains personal artefacts, the library and a manuscript collection of the writer and Nobel prize winner Maurice Maeterlinck (1862–1949). Victor Stuyvaert was a graphic artist from Ghent, part of his work is on show in a cabinet named after him (open Tue.–Sun. 9.30am–5pm).

The route along the Bartsoenkaai to the Bijlokemuseum to the south passes the Apotheekstraat. There is an interesting collection of original exhibits relating to school history (Historische Onderwijscollectie; open Wed. 2–4pm).

The Bijlokemuseum is situated on the other side of the Leie in the Godshuizenlaan (opening times Tue. 10am–1pm and 1.30–5.30pm; Sun. 1.30–5.30pm). It occupies the mainly brick buildings of the Cistercian abbey of Bijloke, founded at the same time as the hospital. The museum (Museum van Oudheden) is one of the richest of its kind in Belgium and shows remarkable ancient pieces in a unique historical setting. The numerous rooms contain works in glass, metal, pottery, leather, together with jewellery, weapons and paintings.
Some of the rooms are particularly noteworthy:

The **Armenkamer** is a reproduction, true to the original, of the meeting room of this society (Governors of the Poor House), founded in 1531 by Charles V in the town hall. A painting by Jan van Cleef depicts the ruler at the founding ceremony.

Outstanding centrepoint is the 14th c. **refectory**, 31 m (101 ft) long and almost 14 m (46 ft) high, with an exceptional brick gable. The interior walls are painted with frescoes (around 1325), among which is a 10 m-long painting of the "Last Supper". In the centre of the room is the tomb of the castellan Hugo II of Ghent, who died in 1232.

Gildenzaal The former dormitory contains mainly artefacts of the Ghent guilds: coats-of-arms, insignia and procession lanterns.
The House of the Abbess is beautifully furnished with historic furniture. It contains the Ghent communal hall with the attractive silver insignia of Ghent music societies from the 15th–18th c.

From the Bijlokemuseum the Charles de Kerchovelaan leads south-east to the De Liemaeckerplein, where the Museum voor Schone Kunsten (Museum of Fine Arts) is situated. The museum building with staircase and colonnaded doorway is dated 1904 and was enlarged in 1913. The main emphasis of the collections is painting covering the 15th–20th c. (opening times daily except Mon. 9am–5pm)

The central hall adjoining the entrance hall has eight fine Brussels wall **tapestries**: three with motifs from the story of Darius (17th c.) and five with the theme "Triumph of the Gods" (1717).

Left of this hall are to be found the **Old Masters**. Prominent are two works by Hieronymus Bosch in Room B: "Bearing of the Cross" and "St Hieronymus". Other works are by Flemish and old Dutch masters such as Adriaan Isenbrant ("Seated Madonna and Child"), the Ghent miniaturist Gerard Horenbaut, Frans Pourbus the elder (Room D), Rubens ("Scourging of Christ"; Room E), van Dyck, Jacob Jordaens (Room G) and Frans Hals ("Portrait of an Elderly Lady"; Room L). Representatives of Italian painters are Tintoretto and Magnasco (Room

Hieronymus Bosch: "Christ carrying the Cross"

F); the English department has two paintings by Hogarth and one by Reynolds.

To the right of the Tapestry Room are **paintings of the 19th and 20th c.**, especially Belgian artists. In Room 4 are Henri Evenepoel ("Spaniard in Paris"), Emi. Claus and James Ensor; also Constant Permeke (Room 5) and among others the Sint-Martens-Latern group with Gustave de Smet (Room 13). In Room 6 there is a painting by Oskar Kokoschka; Camille Corot and Théodore Géricault represent the French school (Room 1).

Modern Art Since 1976 the Museum voor Hedendagse Kunst (Museum for Contemporary Art) has been an independent museum under the same roof. It shows modern art post-1945 with the main emphasis on the development of Belgian painting. The rooms of this museum in the left wing adjoin the Old Masters.

On display are the movements and schools COBRA, Hyperrealism. Minimal Art, Concept Art and Pop Art artists such as Andy Warhol, Frances Bacon, David Hockney, Panamarenko and Joseph Beuys; Belgian artists include René Magritte, Paul Delvaux, Karel Appel and Marcel Broodthaers.

Citadel Park

To the west of the museum the Citadel Park is laid out on the site of the citadel commissioned by Wellington. With its ponds and flower beds it is popular with Ghent citizens for taking a walk. Within the park is the Floraliapaleis (Feestpaleis), an exhibition and trade fair complex, which has now partly been replaced by the new trade fair "Flanders Expo" in Sint-Denijs-Westrem.

Stedelijk Museum voor actuele Kunst

Since the spring of 1999, the Stedelijk Museum voor actuele Kunst (Municipal Museum of Modern Art) has been showing its collections in new halls, in the former Ghent Casino. One of the best museums of its kind, it is already known as the "Louvre of Modern Art". Here you will find modern art since 1945, with an emphasis on Belgian artists, for example the movements and schools of COBRA, hyper-realism, minimalist art, concept art and pop art, represented by artists such as Andy Warhol, Francis Bacon, David Hockney, Panamarenko and Joseph Beuys, and including Belgian artists such as René Magritte, Paul Delvaux, Karel Appel and Marcel Broodthaers (open daily except Mon. 9.30am–7pm).

On the other side of the Clauslaan, which borders the park in the southeast, Ghent University maintains botanical gardens (Plantentuin) with an exceptional collection of exotic plants (open Mon.–Thu. 2–5pm; Sat., Sun. and public holidays 9am–noon).

Plantentuin

North-east of Citadel Park is Sint-Pietersplein with Sint-Pietersabdij on its western side. It was probably founded in the 7th c. and dissolved under the government of the French Revolution. Nowadays it is the Centrum voor Kunst en Kultuur, which organises regular art exhibitions.

Sint-Pietersabdij

The Schoolmuseum Michel Thiery is housed in the former sick room and reception hall of the abbey. Contrary to its name its emphasis is not on school, but on school science subjects and displays fossils, stuffed birds and geological collections as well as computer technology (open Mon.–Thu., and Sat. 9am–12.15pm and 1.30–5.15pm; Fri. 9am–12.15pm).

Schoolmuseum Michel Thiery

Sint-Pieterskerk on the north side of the square was built in the 17th and 18th c. by the Huyssens brothers; it was based on St Peter's Cathedral in Rome and has an impressive 57 m (187 ft)-high cupola. Inside are notable paintings by van Dyck and de Crayer.

Sint-Pieterskerk

Surroundings

As well as boat trips along the canals through the city centre there are boat excursions in the vicinity and further afield, for example return trips to Deurle and Sint-Martens-Latem.The boats offer refreshments and leave from the Recollettenlei at the Law Courts. During July and August night trips with dinner are also available (Benelux Rederij, tel. 2303233).

Boat trips

Nieuw Begijnhof 9 km (5 mi.) north-east of the city centre the successor to the abandoned béguinage of Sint-Elisabeth was constructed in an open field in 1873/74. The large, walled béguinage which attempts to recreate the medieval atmosphere is completely enclosed by the houses of the suburb of Sint-Amandsberg. The eighty cottages are still inhabited by béguines who earn their living by lace-making.

Sint-Amandsberg

The béguinage has a museum with religious objects and household goods showing the lifestyle and development of a béguine (open Apr.–Oct. Wed., Thu., Sat., Sun., public holidays 10–11am and 2–5pm).

Sint-Amandsberg is well placed for a visit to the **harbour** (boat trips tel. 218451; bus tours tel. 510550).

Leaving Sint-Amandsberg in an easterly direction the N70 reaches Lochristi, a flower-growing centre, specialising in begonias. The begonia festival takes place during the last week in August.

Lochristi

The Park of Beervelde, built in the English style for the counts of Kerchove in 1873, is another example of the art of horticulture in this region. Its collection of azaleas is one of the largest in Europe. Belgian

Park of Beervelde

gardeners demonstrate their art every year during the "tuindagen", on the second weekend in May and in October.

★Kasteel van Laarne

Laarne castle is situated 11 km (7 mi.) east of Ghent (opening times Easter-Oct. Sun. 2–5.30pm; Jul. and Aug. also Tue.–Thu., Sat.) The 11th/12th c. pentagonal fortress was built to defend Ghent and rebuilt in the 17th c. Today it has two inner courtyards and a large keep on the right-hand façade and is surrounded by a moat. A stone arcaded bridge leads to the entrance.

The interior is furnished in the French and Antwerp styles; with exceptionally beautiful Brussels tapestries (16th c.) depicting the Emperor Maximilian hunting, after cartoons by Bernard van Orley. On the first floor is a collection of silverwork of European class. It is the Claude Dallemagne Kollektion, which comprises chiefly French and Belgian silver from the 15th–18th c., including a plate designed by Rubens in 1628 which belonged to the Tsarina Catherine II and several splendid tankards.

Leiestrek

The Leie meanders south-west of Ghent through delightful verdant countryside. There are numerous places of interest along its banks.

Sint-Martens-Latem

About 8 km (5 mi.) south-west of Ghent is the town of Sint-Martens-Latem, the patron saint of one of the most important schools of Belgian fine arts. In 1897 a group of artists settled in the town around the sculptor George Minne, among whom were Gustav van de Woestijne and Valerius de Saedeleer. Their work was stopped by the First World War; during the Twenties a second group became known, including Albert Servaes, Constant Permeke, Gust de Smet and Frits van den Berghe, all of whom lived in the town or nearby.

A large number of galleries still have collections of this period; the town church has many paintings by the above artists.

Deurle

The small village of Deurle on the Leie, 12 km (8 mi.) south-west of Ghent, consists of villas in the middle of gardens and parks. There are three interesting art museums dedicated to the various members of the Sint-Martens-Latem School:

Museum Gust de Smet The Ghent painter Gust de Smet (1877–1943) lived in Deurle from 1935 onwards. His house and studio have been maintained in their original condition (open Mon. and Wed. 2–6pm).

Museum Léon de Smet Léon, the brother of Gust de Smet (1881–1966), also lived in Deurle. His house has been reconstructed with his furniture and possessions (open Tue.–Thu. and Sat. 2–6pm; Sun. also 10am–noon).

Museum Mevrouw Jules Dhondt-Daenans Built on the Leie in 1969 this museum exhibits important works of the Sint-Martens-Latem School and 19th and 20th c. Belgian art in general, in chronological order.

Artists represented include Servaes, de Smet, Permeke, van den Berghe, Claus, Minne, de Saedeleer, Meunier, Evenepoel and Rik Wouters (open Sat., Sun. and public holidays 10am–noon and 2–5pm, Jun.–Sep. until 6pm; Thu.–Fri. only 10am–noon; closed Dec.–Feb.).

★Kasteel van Ooidonk

To the south, past Bachte Maria-Leerne, Deurle borders the park of the Château of Ooidonk. The original château was built in the 13th c. and burnt down in the 15th. The new building of 1595 was in Flemish-Spanish style with stepped gables and small towers finished with onion-shaped pinnacles. There are two wings off the main building, each ending in a side tower. The house, redesigned in the 19th c., is still inhabited by the Baron de Nevele but is open to visitors. Of interest are the paintings, including portraits of the Counts Hoorn and Egmont, and items belonging to the Royal Family (open every Sun. from Jul.–mid Sep.).

The château stands in beautiful **parkland** which nestles in a bow in the Leie (open daily 10am–noon and 2–6pm).

The end of the Leiestrek is Deinze, 18 km (11 mi.) from Ghent. It has a Gothic church with a painting by de Crayer and a local museum housing archaeological finds, exhibits from the town's history and paintings of the Sint-Marten-Latem School.

Deinze

Eeklo is situated 20 km (12 mi.) north-west of Ghent. The tower, over 100 m (328 ft) high, of the Neo-Gothic **Sint-Vincentiuskerk** from the end of the 19th c. is one of the highest church towers in Flanders.

Eeklo

Jeneverhuis van Hoorebeke This traditional Genever distillery illustrates the history and production of juniper gin (open Tue.–Fri. 10am–6pm, Sat., Sun. and public holidays 11am–6pm).

Maldegem, 10 km (6 mi.) west of Eeklo, provides an interesting diversion. The "Steam Centre" has a number of steam locomotives (every Sun. during the season a museum railway to Eeklo), steam rollers, steam tractors and industrial steam machines (open May–Sep. daily 10am–6pm).

Maldegem

Sint-Vincentiuskerk in Eeklo

Halle · Hal

G/H 9

Province: Brabant
Altitude: 35 m (115 ft) Population: 32,300
Intercity and Inter-regional Station

The neat town of Halle (French Hal) is 15 km (9 mi.) from Brussels, not far from the linguistic border, on the Senne and on the canal which links Brussels with Charleroi. Blast furnaces, textile, leather and food processing plants make up the industrial base.

Halle is an important place of pilgrimage on account of its wonder-working black Madonna statue; donated by Aleydis of Avesnes, wife of the Duke of Hennegau in 1267.

★Onze-Lieve-Vrouw-Basiliek

North-west of the market is the Onze-Lieve-Vrouw-Basiliek (Basilica of Our Lady), also known as Sint-Martinuskerk or Sint-Martinusbasiliek. It is a notable building in Brabant Gothic, its elegant architecture showing French influence. Work began on the church in 1341; it was consecrated in 1410. The baptistery with its sturdy tower (around 1440) was the first onion-shaped roof in the Netherlands. The tower with its four Gothic spires was also started in the mid-15th c.; the Baroque lantern was not added until 1776. The tower houses a carillon with 54 bells. The large southern lateral aisle, next to the baptistery, is decorated with a row of simple wall formations, projecting columns and triangular gables in typical Brabant style and embellished with rich sculpture. There is a beautiful work of Mary with child, surrounded by angel musicians (14th c.) in the tympanum of the south portal; in the small south portal, which creates the impression of a transept, is the coronation of Mary. The north side portal has a Brabant picture of Madonna.

Interior Inside the church the sculptured decoration is remarkable. The Trazegnies chapel, added in 1467, has a beautiful alabaster altar by Jean Mone (1533), sculptor for Charles V, a Renaissance work with reliefs depicting the Seven Sacraments, together with statues of the four evangelists, the Church Fathers and the pelican motif.

In the chapel on the right is the marble memorial of the Dauphin Joachim, son of Louis XI of France, who died in 1460.

Particularly beautiful is the row of apostles over the arches of the choir, probably 14th c. and revealing similarities with the work of Claus Sluter. In the choir itself above the modern altar stands the 95 cm-high Gothic Black Madonna, showing Mary seated on the Throne of Wisdom. It is thought to be from around 1200 and belonged to St Elisabeth of Hungary. The blackness is caused by oxidisation and not, as legend has it, from the gunpowder smoke of the 32 cannon balls which the

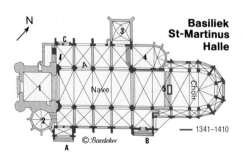

**Basiliek
St-Martinus
Halle**

A Great South Doorway
B Small South Doorway
C North Doorway

1 Bell-tower (pre-1300; Carillon and Museum of bells)
2 Baptistery (c. 1440; font of 1461)
3 Trazegnies Chapel (1467; alabaster altar by J. Mone 1533)
4 Lady Chapel (pre-1335; marble tomb of the Dauphin Joachim, died 1460)
5 High Altar (above – the "Black Madonna" of Halle)

— 1341–1410

© Baedeker

Sint-Martinuskerk

The moated castle of Beersel

Madonna caught during the siege of Halle in 1580 and which can be seen on the north wall.

The baptistery next to the tower has an impressive font, a Tournai work of 1446, with a brass cover depicting the apostles and other saints.

The crypt houses the rich **treasury**; among which are gifts consecrated to the Black Madonna, a reliquary of Louis XI of France and a monstrance of Henry VIII of England.

In the market is the **stadhuis** (town hall) from 1616, restored in the 19th c. Both statues "Truth" and "Justice" are copies of original works by Jerome Duquesnoy.
    In the middle of the square in front of the town hall is a memorial to the violinist Adrien Servais (1807–70), who came from Halle.

Grote Markt

The former **Jesuit college** houses a music academy and the Zuidwestbrabants Museum (local history and art; open May–Aug. Sat., Sun. and public holidays 10am–noon and 2–5pm).

The 91 ha (225 acre) Provinciaal Domein Huizingen, 4 km (2 mi.) northeast of Halle, is a popular recreational area near Brussels with a wide variety of attractions. The main attraction is the Botanical Garden with 1200 different species of plants. There is a also a garden for the blind (open daily 9am–sunset).

Provinciaal Domein Huizingen

Beersel, 7 km (4 mi.) north-east of Halle, is already a suburb of Brussels. It is famous for its brick **moated castle**, built around 1300, on a triangular base. The three 17th c. towers, rounded on the outside but gabled on the side facing the inner courtyard, are linked by defensive walled walk-

Beersel

ways. One of the towers has a torture chamber (open Mar.–Nov. Tue.–Fri. 10am–noon and 2–6pm; Dec. and Feb. Sat. and Sun. 10.30am–5pm).

Braine-le-Château

It is worth visiting Braine-le Château, 6½ km (4 mi.) to the south-east, to see the tasteful castle built by the counts of Hoorn in the 17th and 18th c.

A pillory decorated with ironwork, erected in 1521, stands in the market square. The grand tomb (1542) of Maximilian Hoorns, Charles V's chamberlain, in the local church is by Jean Mone.

Rebecq

The small town of Rebecq, 10 km (6 mi.) south-west in the Senne valley, is the birthplace of the Solvay brothers, the founders of one of the largest industrial companies in Belgium. From Rebecq a small steam train operates along the 7 km (4 mi.)-long route through the picturesque "Vallée des Oiseaux" (Valley of the Birds) to Rognon and back (departs May-Sep. Sun. and public holidays 2.30pm).

Moulin d'Arenberg These 18th and 19th c. buildings were part of an old industrial site from the 19th c. The machine room and forge are open to visitors. One of the rooms contains the porphyry museum, another is fitted out as a tavern.

Enghien

Enghien is situated about 18 km (11 mi.) south-west of Halle on the linguistic border. For a long time the town belonged to the Arenberg family, of whose estate only 342 ha (845 acres) of parkland remain.

Saint Nicholas This large Gothic church on the Grand-Place has a beautiful font (15th c.) and modern church windows by Max Ingrand.

Eglise des Capucins The Renaissance alabaster tomb of Guillaume de Croy, archbishop of Toledo, was crafted by Jean Mone for the church of the former Capuchin convent. On the main altar is a sculptured group "Worship of the Kings" by Servay de Couls, its 51 figures representing members of the Arenberg family.

Han-sur-Lesse   M 13

Province: Namur. Altitude: 120 m (393 ft) Population: 800

The village of Han-sur-Lesse in the south-east of the province of Namur is world-famous for its caverns and at weekends is overrun with tourists. The River Lesse flows through the stalactite caverns which have an amazing variety of rock formations caused by the porosity of the limestone found in this region.

★★**Grottes de Han**

The caverns were inhabited as far back as the Stone Age by people seeking refuge. Not until 1804 did four young men dare to venture further into the caves. During subsequent explorations over the following years the larger caverns with their stalagmites and stalactites were discovered: the grottoes have been open to the public since 1856.

The system as it is known today consists of a series of intricate caverns with a total length of 10 km (6 mi.), only 3 km (2 mi.) of which are accessible, some only since 1962. The dirt left on the ceiling in the oldest caves by the smoke and soot from torches is clearly visible but they remain extremely impressive thanks to the skilful illumination. Especially striking are the Salle des Scarabées, the Salle des Renards, the Salle du Vigneron, the Grotte du Précipice, Le Trophée, Le Styx, the Salle des Mystérieuses and the Salle des Draperies, all with superb stalactite formations. In the Salle d'Armes, a beautiful round cave where the Lesse reappears, a son-et-lumière show highlights the most

© Baedeker

PARC ... NATIONAL
DE LESSE
ET LOMME

Entrance

Grottes de Han
Stalactitic caves
near Han-sur-Lesse

Constant temperature
in the caves 12°C/54°F

1 Salle des Scarabées	8 Salle Blanche	15 Salle des Mamelons	23 Salle des Draperies
2 Salle des Renards	9 Grotte du Cocyte	16 Grotte Centrale	24 Embarquement
3 Grotte	10 Grotte du Précipice	17 Le Trophée	(boat departure)
de la Grenouille	11 Salle d'Antiparos	18 Salle des Mystérieuses	25 Grotte des Petites Fontaines
4 Salle du Vigneron	12 Salle des Priapes	19 Grotte des Aventuriers	26 Grotte
5 Grande Rue	13 Grotte de	20 Le Capitole	de la Grande Fontaine
6 Petite Rue	l'Hirondelle	21 Le Styx	27 Débarquement
7 Salle de l'Escarpement	14 Labyrinthe	22 La Tamise	(boat arrival)

impressive formations. The highpoint is the last cavern, the Salle du Dome, its vastness (length 154 m/505 ft, width 140 m/459 ft, height 129 m/423 ft) can be appreciated by the torchlight provided by an attendant. The exit to the Grottoes is reached by boat where a cannon is fired. It is just a few minutes' walk back to the village.

A **tour** of the grottoes takes about two hours. The temperature in the caverns is a constant 12°C (53°F) and so warm clothing is recommended as are strong shoes.

The only access to the grottoes is by the train which runs through the beautiful Ardennes countryside and departs from the information and ticket office opposite the local church.

Departure times: May–Jun. every 30 mins. from 10am–noon and 1–4.30pm, and till 5.30 on weekends; Jul. and Aug. every 30 mins. from 10am–noon and 1–6pm; Apr., Sep., Oct. hourly from 10am–noon and 1.30–4.30pm; Mar., Nov., Dec. 11.30am, 1pm, 2.30pm and 4pm.

At the exit to the caverns there is the **Musée du Monde Souterrain** (Museum of the Underground World) which explains the origin of the caverns and shows archaeological finds from the various expeditions ranging from the Stone Age to the Merovingian period (open: mid-Mar.–early Nov. daily 11.30am–6pm; Jul. and Aug. noon–7.30pm).

The walk back to the village leads through grounds with a playground and restaurant and around a farm. Here an audio-visual show "**Spéléothème**" presents fantastic insights into the world of the Grottoes of Han (open end Mar.–Nov. daily noon–6pm, Jul. and Aug. until 8pm).

★Wildlife reserve

The Grottes de Han are surrounded by a wildlife park which belongs to the Lesse et Lomme National Park. In the beautiful countryside indigenous animals such as stags and wild boars can be observed together with strains bred from extinct animals including bison, aurochs and tarpans in enclosures. The drive in the "safari car" passes by the Gouffre de Belvaux, where the Lesse disappears roaring into the mountain and does not reappear until Han.

Han-sur-Lesse: Leaving the "Underworld"

Tour The safari cars depart from opposite the local church.

Departure times: May–Jun. every 30 mins. 10am–noon and 1–4.30pm, and until 5.30 on weekends; Jul. and Aug. every 30 minutes from 10am–noon and 1–6pm; Apr., Sep., Oct. hourly 10am–noon and 1.30–4.30pm; Mar., Nov., Dec. at 11.30am, 1pm, 2.30pm and 4pm.

A **combined ticket** can be purchased for a visit to the grottoes, the wildlife park and the museums.

Lavaux-Sainte-Anne

Close to the E411 motorway Namur-Arlon, 6 km (4 mi.) south-west of Han-sur-Lesse, is the village of Lavaux-Sainte-Anne. It has an interesting moated castle from the 14th and 15th c. with three corner towers and a keep, which replaced its predecessor from 1190. New Renaissance style residential wings were built between the towers in the 17th c. The castle which is partly furnished with contemporary furniture houses a hunting and conservation museum; agricultural equipment is displayed in the adjoining buildings. A film shows the reconstruction of the castle which was destroyed in 1795 (open Mar.–Oct. daily 9am–6pm; Jul. and Aug. until 7pm; Dec.–Feb. until 5pm).

Lessive

Near Lessive, 4 km (2 mi.) north-west of Han-sur-Lesse at the confluence of the Lesse and Lomme, the satellite transmission station Belgacom became operational in 1972. The giant 30m (98 ft)-high parabolic antennae weighs 53 tonnes. A tour lasts around 1½ hours (open mid Apr.–mid Oct. daily 9.30am–5pm, last tour 4pm; Jul. and Aug. tours at 9.45am, 11am, 2pm and 4pm).

Hasselt F 14

Province: Limburg
Altitude: 39 m (128 ft) Population: 66,900
Intercity and Inter-regional Station (bicycle rental at station)

Hasselt, the lively capital of the province of Limburg, is situated between Liège and Antwerp on the Demer, a tributary of the Dijle. To the south extend fertile fields and orchards, in the north is the Limburg coal basin. Hasselt, as well as being a market and commercial centre for the region, a role which was acknowledged by the establishment of the Economics Institute in 1968, is an important industrial town; its chief industries being food processing, chemical and electronics. The construction of the modern cultural centre in 1959, the biggest in Flanders, brought the town considerable cultural significance. Hasselt is known for the production of good quality Genever gin.

History Hasselt was already a market town in the Middle Ages in the county of Loon. In the 12th c. it received its town charter. In 1356 Hasselt was acquired together with County Loon by the Diocese of Liège and became the seat of local administration. In 1795 it was annexed by France and became capital of the Département of Meuse-Inférieure, and later, in 1813 capital of the Dutch province of Limburg. On August 8th 1831 a battle took place to the west of the town between Dutch troops

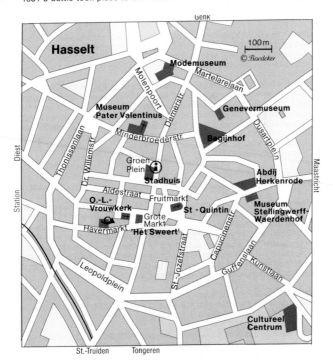

under Crown Prince Wilhelm and the Belgian army of the Meuse. In 1839 Limburg was divided between Belgium and the Netherlands and Hasselt became capital of the Belgian province of Limburg.

Festivals Every seven years in August a procession for the Madonna Virga Jesse is held in Hasselt. The statue is kept in the Onze-Lieve-Vrouwkerk. On this occasion the "Langeman" is also carried, a 7 m (23 ft) high figure in Spanish uniform, which goes back to the 15th c. (next date 1996).

On April 30th the "Meiavond" takes place, whereby a may tree is set up and the "Meiliedeken", known to date from the 17th c., is sung

Grote Markt

The busy Grote Markt is surrounded by several old patrician houses, the most attractive being the chemist shop "Het Sweert", built in 1659 in place of a guest house from 1452. A masked head with an arm holding a raised sword decorates the corner of the house.

Sint-Quintinus-kathedraal

Through the Kortstraat heading north-east is the Vismarkt with the 15th–16th c. Gothic Sint-Quintinuskathedraal, built on Roman foundations. Its 63 m (206 ft)-high west tower (base 12th/13th c.) has one of the most attractive sounding carillons in Belgium with 47 bells; there is a small carillon museum (Beiardmuseum; open Jun.–Sep. Sat. and Sun. 2–6pm). The interior of the church contains Gothic frescoes on the columns of the main nave, fine Renaissance choir stalls from 1549, the pulpit and a Gothic triumphal cross below the crossing.

The church was elevated to the status of cathedral in 1967 when Belgian Limburg became a diocese and Hasselt the seat of the bishopric.

Onze-Lieve-Vrouwkerk

The Onze-Lieve-Vrouwkerk a short distance west of the market is as far as its art treasures are concerned, of greater importance than the Sint-Quintinuskathedraal. It was built betwen 1728 and 1740 in a transitionary style between Baroque and Classicism and rebuilt true to the original in 1950–52 following its bombardment in 1944.

In the interior some notable works of art from the former Cistercian abbey of Herkenkode near Hasselt have been preserved. The **high altar** (with the 14th c. Virga Jesse-Madonna statue) is an important work by Jean Delcour of Liège. In the transepts are the Baroque tomb of Anna-Catharina de Lamboy, abbess of Herkenrode 1653–75, by A. Quellin the Younger (1675) and the marble Rococo tomb of Barbara de Rivière d'Arschot, abbess of Herkenrode 1738–44, with the bas relief "Resurrection" by L. Delvaux (1744).

Stadhuis

North of the Grote Markt on Groenplaats is the stadhuis (town hall), an attractive patrician house from 1630, later converted in Classical style.

Begijnhof

The Sint-Katharina béguinage north of Sint-Quintinuskathedraal was originally built 1245–1567 beyond the town wall south of the town as it was at that time and was called "Extra Muros". In 1567 it was completely destroyed; in 1571 work began on a new béguinage, this time within the town walls. At the beginning of the 18th c. the premises were extended and underwent conversion. The buildings from this later period stand in the southern part of the grounds. The Classical church was destroyed during air raids in 1944; the only evidence of it are some ruins.

Museum Pater Valentinus

In Minderbroederstraat leading from the béguinage is the Museum Pater Valentinus which documents the life and work of Father Valentin Paquay (1828–1905; open daily 9am–5.30pm).

Stedelijk Modemuseum

The attractive and original Stedelijk Modemuseum (Municipal Fashion Museum) is situated on the north side of the Inner Town. It has numerous examples of 19th and 20th c. fashion and is arranged not only chronologically but also thematically, for example, bridal dresses;

underwear (open Tue.–Fri. 10am–5pm; Sat., Sun. and public holidays 1–5pm and Apr.–Oct. 10am–5pm).

In a town renowned for its genever it is fitting that there should be a museum dedicated to gin. It is in an old 19th c. steam distillery, not far from the béguinage, that the production of this noble drink can be followed and the beneficial juniper gin sampled (open Tue.–Fri. 10am–5pm; Sat., Sun. and public holidays 1–5pm and Apr.–Oct 10am–5pm).

National Jenever Museum

On the east side of the Inner Town is the beautifully painted Maastrichterstraat with the Museum Stellingwerff-Waerdenhof, devoted to local and town history. The most outstanding exhibit is the oldest known monstrance in the world dating from 1286 (opening times see Genevermuseum). Opposite the museum is the refuge of the Abbey of Herkenrode from the 16th c.

Museum Stellingwerff-Waerdenhof

Opened in 1993 the Japanese Garden at Hasselt is the largest of its kind in Europe (open Apr.–Oct. Tue.–Fri. 10am–5pm, Sat., Sun. 2–6pm).

Japanese Garden

Surroundings

Across the Albertskanaal, 8 km (5 mi.) north-east of Hasselt, the 540 ha (1334 acres) of heath and woodland of the Domain Bokrijk offers a wide choice of leisure activities (opening times Open-air museum: Apr.-Sep. daily 10am–6pm). There is an enormous play area with roundabouts and pony rides for children together with facilities for various sports. Nature lovers can stroll through the arboretum, rose and herb garden. For variety the extensive open-air museum comes first with reconstructions of farmhouses and farmsteads from individual regions of the country. Old crafts such as milling, baking and lace making are demonstrated. A recent addition is a small town with a beer cellar where beer is served that has been brewed in Bokrijk. A total of seven cafés and restaurants cater for the visitor.

★**Provinciaal Domein Bokrijk**

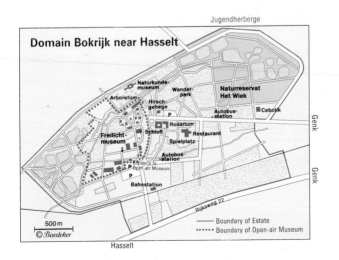

Domain Bokrijk near Hasselt

Jugendherberge

Naturkunde-museum
Wander-park
Naturreservat Het Wiek
Arboretum
Hirsch-gehege
Cebolik
Autobus-station
Rosarium
Schloß
Restaurant
Freilicht-museum
Spielplatz
Autobus-station
Entrance to Open-air Museum
Bahnstation
Rijksweg 22
Genk
Genk

500 m
© Baedeker

—— Boundary of Estate
•••••• Boundary of Open-air Museum

Hasselt

Farmhouses in ...

... Bokrijk Open-Air Museum

The industrial town of Genk lies on the edge of the Kempenland coal mine 12 km (8 mi.) north-east of Hasselt.

Genk

Genk's town park known as the **"Molenvijver"** is a 21 ha (52 acre) walker's paradise by a lake.

Museum v. Doren The painter Emi. van Doren (1865–1949) settled in a villa in Genk. It is now a museum displaying some of his works in an unaltered setting.

The Genk **police museum** has over 1000 police hats, 300 uniforms and numerous pieces of equipment.

The **Europlanetarium** is the most modern planetarium in Belgium with an audio-visual show followed by a visit to the Limburg Observatory (open Tue.–Fri. 10am–5pm, Sun. 2–6pm).

6 km (4 mi.) north of Genk the largest zoo in the province of Limburg is laid out on the site of the old coal mine Zwartberg. It has a remarkable bear collection (open Easter–Oct. daily 9am–7pm).

Limburgse Zoo

Unspoilt heathland can be found on the Mechelse Heide nature reserve 7 km (4 mi.) north-east of Genk.

★Mechelse Heide

A **railway museum** has been set up in the 1930s station of the district of As, 10 km (6 mi.) north-east of Genk. It focuses on the history of Belgian Railways in general and coal transport on narrow gauge railways in particular.

As

In the area around the twin community of Houthalen-Helchteren (13 km/ 8 mi. north of Genk) there are **three leisure parks** offering a variety of entertainment. The Domein Molenheide has water slides, swimming pools, sports grounds, a Robinson park and wildlife park and the Domein Hengelhoef and Kelchterhoef each with a zoo and numerous attractions.

Houthalen-Helchteren

The 4½ km (3 mi.) Zolder **race track** (Omloop van Terlamen) is famous outside of Belgium, 11 km (7 mi.) north-west of Hasselt. The Formula I Grand Prix takes place alternating between here and Francorchamps (see Stavelot); other motor car and motorcycle races also take place.

Zolder

Herentals

See Geel, Surroundings

Hoogstraten

See Antwerp, Surroundings

Huy · Hoei   J 13

Province: Liège. Altitude: 77 m (252 ft)
Population: 17,000
Intercity and Inter-regional Station (bicycle rental at station)

The town of Huy (Flemish Hoei) is pleasantly set in an undulating landscape at the confluence of the Meuse and the Hoyoux, approximately

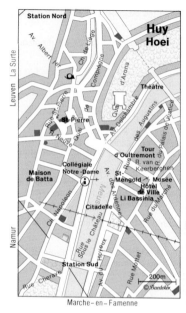

Marche–en–Famenne

half-way between Namur and Liège. Sugar refineries, paper industry and the Tihange atomic power station situated upstream make up the economic base of the town, which is dominated by the powerful citadel. The town's most important buildings are known as the "four wonders": Li Tchestia (the castle, destroyed 1717), Li Pontia (the bridge, its successor is the Pont Roi-Baudouin), Li Rondia (the window rose) and Li Bassinia (the fountain); only the last two still exist in their original form. The two best known masters of metal casting in the Meuse region Renier de Huy and Godefroid de Claire, the latter also known as Godefroid de Huy, came from Huy. Father Dominique Georges Pire (1910–69), the founder of European Villages and winner of the Nobel Peace Prize in 1958, lived and worked in Huy.

History Huy is one of the oldest towns in Belgium. It was mentioned in documents as far back as 636. It received its freedom charter from Prince Bishop Theoduin in 1066. During the High and late Middle Ages it achieved considerable prosperity because of its famous brassworks and wool industry and became a thriving market centre for wine, pewter and copperware. However, as a result of the numerous wars between the prince bishops of Liège and the dukes of Burgundy it gradually declined in importance.

The tourist office in Huy organises boat trips on the Meuse.

★Collégiale
Notre-Dame

On the right bank of the Meuse stands the handsome Collégiale Notre-Dame, the most important High Gothic church in Belgium. Work began on the foundations of a Romanesque basilica in 1311 and was completed in 1377. The church has an unusual exterior with two towers flanking the crossing tower ("Hemony" carillon in the north tower) and the massive west tower, its spire being destroyed by lightning in 1803. The superb rose window "Li Rondia" is on this tower, diameter 9 m (29 ft).

The 72 m (236 ft)-long church **interior** receives its light chiefly through the large rosette and the 20 m (65 ft)-high lancet windows in the apse. The fan ribbed vaulting of the polychromic painted crossing is particularly beautiful. In the right-hand side aisle is the 12th c. entrance to the crypt, its floor covered in tiles decorated with coats-of-arms.

Behind the choir screen (1728) is the **treasury** with four exceptionally splendid shrines beautifully crafted in metalwork of the Meuse region. The most sumptuous are the shrines of St Mengold and St Domitian, both probably the work of Godefroid de Huy from around 1176; the shrine of Our Lady is from about 1260 and the shrine of St Mark with its rich enamelling from about 1200.

Other treasures include the remains of the Holy Cross, brought back by Peter the Hermit from the first crusade, and a chalice and cross from the grave of Prince Bishop Theoduin of Bavaria.

Especially worth seeing is the tympanum (14th c.) of the **Portail de Bethléem** (Bethlehem portal) on the east side of the church, where the entrance to the cloister once was. The splendid sculpture depicts the birth of Christ, the worship of the Kings and Shepherds and the murder of the children in Bethlehem, framed by some lively folk scenes.

Not far to the east of the church is the Grand-Place with the copper fountain "Li Bassinia" from 1406, the only surviving Gothic bronze fountain in Belgium. The town hall (hôtel de ville) is here, a splendid Louis XV building from 1766. Inside is a small collection of paintings.

Grand-Place

From the Place Verte behind the town hall a narrow street passes St Mengold church, founded 1244, in its present form the 17th c. Couvent des Frères Mineurs (Franciscan monastery). It accommodates the Musée communal (district museum) which has twelve rooms displaying pewter, glass, porcelain, coins and medals, faiences, guild signs, archaeological finds, paintings and religious art.

★Musée communal

Particularly interesting are three rooms completely furnished with old Walloon furniture and household objects, the moving figure of Christ "Beau Dieu de Huy" in oak (13th c.) and a cast of the font from St Barthélemy in Liège by Renier de Huy (open Apr.–Oct. daily 2–6pm).

View of Huy from the Meuse

Diagonally opposite the museum is the 16th c. **Tour d'Oultremont**.

On the **left bank of the Meuse** approximately at the same height as the Collégiale Notre-Dame is the Maison de Batta from 1575, former refugium of the Abbey Val-Saint-Lambert. To the north is the church of St-Pierre with a 12th c. Meuse font.

A cableway from the left bank and a lift on the Chaussée Napoléon at the base of the fortress on the right bank ascend to the **citadel** which was built by the Dutch in 1818 and later captured by the Belgians. During the Second World War it was used by the German occupying forces as a prison, with many of the 7000 prisoners being dragged off to concentration camps. On the tour of the fortress old guns, weapons and casemates can be seen and also the interrogation and torture rooms used by the Gestapo (open Apr.–Jun. and Sep. Tue.–Fri. 10am–5pm; Sat., Sun. until 6pm; Jul./Aug. daily until 7pm).

The cableway, built in 1957, continues up to **La Sarte** and the lesiure park Mont Mosan.

Surroundings

Amay

On the left bank of the Meuse, on the edge of the Hesbaye, is situated the little town of Amay 8 km (5 mi.) north-east of Huy. A visit to the church of Saint-George-et-Saintr Ode is highly recommended. It was begun in 1089 in Mosan Romanesque; the nave and west porch are still from that period, with the other parts being 16th–18th c. additions. During restoration work a 7th c. sarcophagus was found below the choir with the inscription "Santa Chrodoara", possibly the coffin of Saint Ode. Also worth seeing are the magnificent high altar (17th–18th c.) and the treasury.

The **reliquary** shrine of Saints Ode and George constitute a masterpiece of Mosan goldwork. The shrine (around 1230) made of gold-hammered copper has pictures of the two saints on its end wall and on its side walls the 12 apostles. The depiction of St George idealised as a medieval knight is particularly impressive. Below the sacristy, where further valuable religious works of art are on show, the remains of Roman building were found.

★Château de
Jehay

The château of Jehay, 10 km (6 mi.) north-east of Huy, has under its roof one of the most interesting archaeological collections in Belgium, in addition to noteworthy paintings (opening times: May–Sep. Sat., Sun. public holidays 2–6pm).

On the site of a Romanesque castle the present day château was built in the 16th c. in an L-shape with characteristic chequered façade, surrounded by parkland with ponds and lakes.

The extensive **art collection** of the present owner Guy van den Steen is displayed in some rooms of the house. It includes tapestries (Brussels, Aubusson), paintings (Tintoretto, Bruegel, Murillo, Peter Lely), Mosan goldwork and much more; notable individual pieces are a clock by Porlaine, commisioned by Marie-Antoinette and the lace bridal veil of the wife of the Duke of Marlborough in a room devoted to this English commander.

In the Gothic vaults of the château alongside a speleological collection is the impressive **archaeological collection** which features a unique bone ice-skate and a prehistoric pipe made of human bone.

12 km (8 mi.) south of Huy high above the Hoyoux is the Château de Mondave with its striking flecked main tower (opening times: daily 9am–6pm, tours on the hour). Onto the part of the building projecting over the river the French architect Jean Goujon built a château in the most attractive Louis XIV style with numerous water games.

These are supplied by a hydraulic machine, invented by the carpenter Rennequin Sualem from Liège, which pumps up water from the Hoyoux. In 1669 Sualem constructed similar grounds for Louis XIV's château in Marly, near Versailles. Picnics are allowed in the park.

The grand **rooms** of the château, twenty of which are included in the tour, are richly appointed with 17th and 18th c. furniture. The architect and sculptor Jean-Christian Haensche designed the multi-coloured stucco ceilings in the vestibule (heraldic family tree of the owners Comtes de Marchin) and in the Hercules room. The alcoves of the Duchess de Montmorency, the cousin of the French king, are especially splendid.

Bois-et-Borsu

The church of Saint-Lambert in Bois-et-Borsu, 7 km (4 mi.) south-east of the château, contains beautiful 15th c. frescoes representing scenes from the life of Christ and the Saints Lambert and Hubert. The small church was built in 911 and altered around 200 years later.

Jehay (Château)

See Huy, Surroundings

Château de Jehay

Knokke-Heist   C 4

Province: West-Vlaanderen
Altitude: sea level. Population: 32,000
Intercity Station (bicycle rental at Knokke station)

Together with Ostend, Knokke-Heist, situated near the Dutch border in
an attractive landscape of dunes, is probably the most elegant **seaside
resort** in Belgium. The broad beach is 12 km (8mi.) long and comprises
approximately one fifth of the Belgian coastline.

Since 1880 the present tourist resort has developed very rapidly from
the small fishing village of Knokke to merge with the residential suburb
Het Zoute and the newer suburb of Albertstrand, and until the Thirties
was one of the leading seaside resorts in Europe, patronised by the
British. In recent years the coastal towns of Heist and Duinbergen have
been absorbed into the growing built-up area. The entire agglomeration
can accommodate five times its population in several thousand apartments, 120 hotels and guest houses and five campsites, which, during
the high season, is not unproblematic. To the large amount of accommodation available in the town can be added an unusually wide range
of entertainment and recreational facilities, with something to offer
every visitor.

Walks and cycle tours Among the best walks in and around Knokke-
Heist are the "Bloemenwandeling" through the residential suburb of Het
Zoute, the "Landelijke Knokke" and the "Polderwandeling" through the
attractive dune landscape. The 7 km (4 mi.) long Zeedijk which stretches
from Heist past Duinbergen to Het Zoute across the wide beach, is lined
with numerous hotels and villas. The tourist information office has
brochures with a total of ten cycle tours in the surroundings of Knokke-
Heist.

Festivals As well as the permanent choice of entertainment there are
occasional important fairs and festivals which are mainly held in
the Scharpoord cultural centre or in the casino. These include the
"Humorfoto" (Internaional Humour Photo Festival) in April, the
International Cartoon Festival from mid-June to mid-September and
the International Fireworks Festival in mid-August. All these events take
place in Duinbergen.

Heist

The western part of this agglomeration is Heist which is increasingly in
danger of being swallowed up by the expanding town of Zeebrugge (see
entry). The Polder-en Visserijmuseum Sincfala is dedicated to the traditions of sea-faring, crafts and everyday life along the coast and in the
hinterland.

Visitors can get in trim at the "Meer van Heist", an indoor swimming
pool with sea water and artificial waves, and the "Fit-o-meter" keep fit
park.

Albertstrand

Knokke's busy main street is the Lippenslaan, which, near the railway
station, adjoins the Verweeplein with the town hall and monument to the
animal painter A. Verwee.

To the west of Knokke is the new quarter of Albertstrand with the
famous Casino situated alongside the dike. It is worth a look as it contains some fine works of art as well as offering roulette and other gam-
bling games. The sculpture "Le poète" by Ossip Zadkine stands in front
of the building. In the foyer hangs a 7 tonne chandelier made from
22,000 pieces of glass, considered to be the largest in Europe. The walls
are hung with works by famous painters including René Magritte's "Le
Domaine enchanté". The changing art exhibitions in the casino have a
very good reputation.

Knokke-Heist: the Casino

The Zegemeer is an artificial lake in the dunes. On its south bank was built the Scharpoord cultural centre with the modern Institute for Thalasso therapy.

Het Zoute, with its elegant villas set back in the dunes and the evening meeting place of Albertplein, owes its reputation as a fashionable sea-side resort to Knokke-Heist. The Royal Golf Club de Zoute, with two 18-hole courses, one of the largest in Europe, and the grounds of the Riding Club add to this.

Het Zoute

A more recent attraction is the butterfly garden ("Tropisch Vlinderparadijs") in the Bronlaan with exotic and indigenous butterflies under 425 sq. m (4575 sq. ft) of glass (open: mid March–mid Oct. daily 10am–5.30pm).

The Het Zwin nature reserve stretches from the end of Het Zoute over the Belgian-Dutch border. Some two fifths of the 150 ha (370 acres) are accessible to walkers. Opening times Easter–Sep. daily 9am–7pm; Oct.–Easter daily except Wed. 9am–5pm. Guided walks Apr.–Sep. Thu. and Sun. 10am, other months Sun. 10 am).

★★'t Zwin Nature Reserve

Het Zwin is now the silted inlet that once made Bruges (see Bruges) one of the richest harbours in Europe. Today the countryside, bordered by dunes and the sea dyke and criss-crossed by rivulets subject to the tides, provides a unique habitat for plants and animals. Over 100 species of bird nest in Zwin, among which are waders, ducks, the silver plover and snipe. At the entrance to the nature reserve the indigenous species are kept on several ponds and in aviaries so that the visitor can see many of the birds at close hand without disturbing those in the wild. The best times to visit are in Spring, to see the birds, and in July and August when the ground is covered with sea of blossom, the "Zwinneblomme".

Koksijde · Coxyde   E 1

Province: West-Vlaanderen
Altitude: sea level. Population: 19,000

The seaside resort of Koksijde (French Coxyde), especially popular with
families, developed from a small fishing village at the beginning of this
century. Today the resort consists of Koksijde-Dorp, Koksijde-Bad and
the residential suburb Sint-Idesbald to the south-west and caters for a
wide range of leisure activities.

Koksijde

Festivals is famous for its flower market on Easter Sat., the flower
ball in the summer season and the flower-covered artists' procession.

Natural
Monuments

The highest and longest dune on the Belgian coast, the 33 m (108 ft)
high and 42 ha (103 acre) "Hoge Blekker", is here in Koksijde. Guided
walks are organised through the Schipgat dunes with its flora and
fauna, the north dunes and the "Doornpanne" and "Kerkepanne"
nature reserves.

Duinenabdij

The ruins of the Duinenabdij of Koksijde are among the most notable
sacral buildings on the Belgian coast. The abbey was founded in 1107
by the Benedictines and taken over by the Cistercians in 1138 who built
dykes to reclaim sizeable strips of land from the sea and farmed large
areas. The monks were driven away when the monastery was
destroyed in 1578. The ruins of the building give an idea of the size of
the abbey. The narthex, the 129 m (423 ft)-long nave of the church of

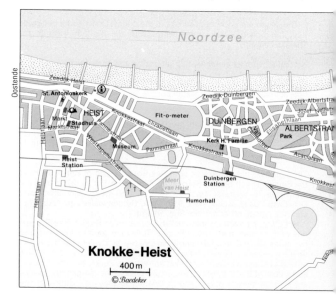

1214, the cloisters, the refectory and parts of the monastery kitchen can still be seen.

Excavated finds on display in the museum comprise ceramics, architectural remains, glass, coins and documents on the history of the monastery (open daily 10am–noon and 1.30–5pm, in Jul./Aug. until 6pm).

The Onze-Lieve-Vrouw-ter-Duinen church is a remarkable modern creation by the Bruges architect Langsoght from 1965. Its wavy roof and blue paint express the sea, whereas the beige bricks symbolise the dunes formed by the wind. The light interior houses in the crypt the tomb of St Iselbald, 12th c. abbot of the abbey. The statue of Onze-Lieve-Vrouw-ter-Duinen weighing 2.8 tonnes is by Brigitte Loire.

Onze-Lieve-Vrouw-ter-Duinenkerk

Paul Delvaux, after René Magritte the most well known Belgian Surrealist, spent a lot of time in Koksijde and painted many of his paintings here. An extensive collection of paintings and drawings by the artist, who died in 1994, are displayed in the museum dedicated to him in a villa in Sint-Idesbald (open Apr.–Jun. and Sep. Tue.–Sun. 10.30am–6.30pm; Jul. and Aug. also Mon.; Oct.–Dec. Thu.–Sun. 10.30am–5.30pm).

Paul Delvaux Museum

Surroundings

Shrimp fishing on horseback Oostduinkerke, 3 km (2 mi.) east of Koksijde, used to be a quiet fishing town and seaside resort. A type of shrimp fishing, which is unique in Europe, is practised here. At the ebb tide the fishermen ride through the shallow water on sturdy cart-horses. The animals trail large nets behind them at a leisurely pace and

Oostduinkerke

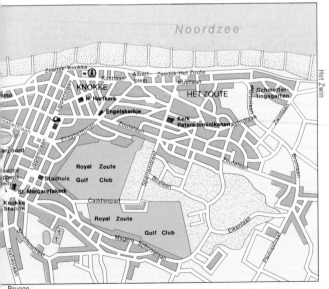

Brugge

Fishing for shrimps on the beach at Oostduinkerke

from time to time the rider empties the catch into the baskets on the horse's back. This custom is celebrated in the annual shrimp festival held at the end of June, when a "Mieke Garnaal", a shrimp queen is chosen.

The **National Visserijmuseum** (National Fishing Museum) is dedicated to the history and technology of fishing and has a collection of model fishing boats, instruments and tools. There are even reconstructions of a fishermen's tavern and cottage (open Tue.–Sun. 10am–noon and 2–6pm; Jul./Aug. also Mon.).

The **Florishof** is a restored group of buildings which is now a folklore museum with exhibitions of furniture, lace and everyday objects (open Easter–mid-Sep. Wed.–Mon. 10am–noon and 1–6pm; mid-Sep.–Easter Sat. and Sun. only).

Sint-Niklaaskerk is an original building from 1954 with its pointed roofs and massive tower. Unusual are the absence of a choir and the columns in the yellowish interior which seem to sprout out of the ground.

The **SunPark Groendyk** is a spacious swimming paradise (see Practical Information, Leisure Parks).

Hof Ten Bogaerde   4 km (2 mi.) to the south of Koksijde, Hof Ten Bogaerde was the refuge of the monks who fled the destruction of the Duinenabdij. It was laid out as long ago as 1184 but today only ruins remain, the most noteworthy being the large 13th c. barn.

Kortrijk · Courtrai G 4

Province: West-Vlaanderen
Altitude: 19 m (62 ft) Population: 76, 500
Intercity and Inter-regional Station (bicycle rental at station)

The town of Kortrijk (French Cortrai) is situated on the River Leie
(French Lys), which is connected to the Scheldt by a canal. The economy of Kortrijk has been based on the textile industry which has its
beginnings in the 14th c. The raw material flax is grown in the surrounding area of Flanders and is processed in several spinning, weaving and finishing mills. Kortrijk is also important for man-made fibres
and has large flax treatment plants and other textile processing concerns (clothing, linen, carpets, canvas). In recent years efforts have
been made to diversify from concentration on the single crisis-prone
textile industry. New industries introduced include engineering, building materials, electronics, jewellery, rubber, furniture and printing.
Polishing of precious stones is also a well known and economically
important activity. In addition Kortrijk is the economic and cultural
centre of an area encompassing 300,000 people and with a department
of the Catholic University of Louvain (see Louvain) is also a university
town. In the "Hallen" built in 1967 important trade fairs and congresses
take place.

History Kortrijk was already an important junction of two roads in
Roman times when it was known as Cortoriacum. In Merovingian times
it had the right to mint coins. It became the seat of a Flemish burgrave
and in 1189 was elevated to the status of town. Its period of prosperity
was in the late Middle Ages, when it developed into a centre of the
Flemish cloth industry. When this declined in the 16th c. it was replaced
by linen weaving based on the local cultivation of flax, which is still
dominant today. The prosperous trading and industrial town was badly

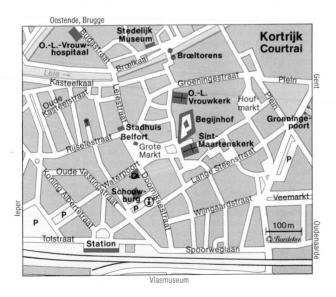

damaged during the wars of Louis XIV and in both world wars. Rebuilding radically altered the townscape, however, some architectural monuments have remained intact.

On July 11th 1302 close to Kortrijk the **Battle of the Golden Spurs** took place on the battlefield on the Groeningekouter. Here the Flemish, mainly armed men on foot from the towns of Bruges and Ypres, routed an army of French knights under the command of Robert, Count of Artois. This battle was of international importance for two reasons: firstly, this victory assured the English allied to the Flemish towns important landing places in the Hundred Years' War; secondly, it was the first time in history that an army of knights had been conquered by foot soldiers, thereby severely deflating the myth attached to the knights – their downfall had begun. After the battle the victorious Flemish weavers collected over 700 knights' spurs and hung them as a symbol of their triumph in the nave of the Onze-Lieve-Vrouwkerk in Kortrijk. They remained there until 1382 when the French inflicted a crushing defeat on the Flemish near Rozebeke, and one of their first acts after the victory was to expunge the humiliation of 1302 and remove the spurs from the church.

However, July 11th remained the most important day in Flemish history and has been a national public holiday since the 19th c.

Grote Markt

The Grote Markt is in the centre of Kortrijk. Standing in the middle is the **belfry** with five small towers, the only remains of the cloth halls built in 1307. Two copper figures "Manten"' and "Kalle" strike the hour. On the reverse of the tower is a memorial to those who died in the First World War.

In the north-west corner of the market is the Gothic **stadhuis** (town hall), built 1418–20, enlarged in the 16th and 19th c. and restored in 1962. The façade is decorated with statues of the Counts of Flanders. In the historic Schepenzal on the ground floor is a magnificent Gothic fireplace (1527) with statues of the Virgin, local saints and allegorical scenes of justice. A similar fine fireplace adorns the old council chamber upstairs; depicted are Charles V in the centre, the Vices and expressive scenes on the theme "The unholy influence of women on men" with a representation of Aristotle and a woman riding on his back. Two maps of Kortrijk and the surroundings from 1641 hang on the walls of the hall (open Mon.–Fri. 9am–noon. and 2–5pm).

Sint-Maartens-hoofdkerk

Not far to the east of the market is Sint-Maartenshoofdkerk dating from the second half of the 13th c.; it was destroyed by the French in 1382 and later rebuilt. The original tower in Brabant Gothic with a carillon with 49 bells was rebuilt following a fire in 1862. In the main nave of the triple-aisled interior the main features are a carved late Renaissance pulpit and in the choir a 6½ m (21 ft)–high hexagonal tabernacle by Henrik Mauris (1585) together with fine goldwork and paintings (de Crayer, Karel van Mander, J. Ykens, F. Francken among others) of the 16-18th c. (open daily except during religious ceremonies 8am–noon and 2–6pm; earlier closing in winter).

★★Begijnhof

Immediately adjoining the church is the picturesque béguinage founded by Joanna of Constantinople in 1242. With its 42 whitewashed cottages closely grouped around the landscaped courtyard, an oasis of tranquillity, it is possibly the most attractive béguinage in Belgium. A stroll through the narrow lanes leads to the chapel of 1465, the bleachery and the Chapel of the Virgin of the Snow. The last béguine in Kortrijk died a few years ago. Her memory and that of all other béguines is preserved in the house of the Grootjuffrouw (oldest béguine). It differs from all other cottages in its size and the double stepped gable and is now a museum. Some of the rooms have been kept in their original condition; other rooms are filled with memorabilia on the history of the béguinage in Kortrijk (Beguinage open daily sunrise to sunset; Beguinage Museum open Sat.–Mon., Wed. and Thu. 2–5pm).

Further north in Begijnhofstraat in a quarter with narrow lanes stands the Onze-Lieve-Vrouwkerk founded by Baldwin IX. Its façade and towers are 13th c. and the choir was completed around 1300. The Flemish poet Guido Gezelle was chaplain of this church for a long time; he is commemorated by a memorial in front of the church (open: as Sint Maartens-hoofdkerk).

Onze-Lieve-Vrouwerk

In the left transept is the outstanding work "The Raising of the Cross" by **Anton van Dyck** in the style of Rubens. Another notable work of art is a statue of St Catherine wearing a martyr's crown (around 1380) by André Beauneveu in the Chapel of the Counts which was founded by Louis de Male, built in the shape of a parallelogram and decorated with the portraits of Flemish counts. The first 32 of these frescoes were completed in 1378 and are by Johann van der Asselt; the remainder by various artists were added later.

From the church Guido Gezellestraat leads to the Broeltorens, two massive towers of a former fortification of the town of the 12th c. (south "Speyertoren") and 13th c. (north "Ingelborchtoren").

Broeltorens

The Municipal Museum of Fine Arts presents its collections in two places: on the opposite bank of the River Leie, at Broelkaai 6, stands one of the finest patrician houses in the town (17th c.). It holds an art collection consisting primarily of Kortrijk painters, among them Roeland Savery (1576–1639), and a good ceramics department. The

Stedelijk Museum

The beautiful béguinage at Kortrijk

267

Groeningeabtei on the Houtmarkt has displays documenting the town's history, especially the Battle of the Golden Spurs, as well as a collection, unique in Europe, of 17th and 18th c. damask (open Tue.–Sat. 10am–noon and 2–5pm).

Nationaal Vlasmuseum

Some distance from the centre the Nationaal Vlasmuseum (National Flax Museum) is housed in a 19th c. flax farmhouse at Etienne Sabbelaan 4. It illustrates the cultivation and processing of flax with 26 slides using life-size figures. There is an inn "In de Vlasblomme" providing refreshments (open Mar.–Nov. Tues.–Fri. 9.30am–12.30pm and 1.30–6pm; Sat. and Sun. 2–6pm).

Battle of the Golden Spurs Memorial To the east outside the town centre can be seen a memorial erected in 1906 in memory of the Battle of the Golden Spurs; it is reached from the Onze-Lieve-Vrouwkerk along Groeningstraat.

Menen

The industrial and commercial border town of Menen, 10 km (6 mi.) south-west of Kortrijk, often changed hands between French and Dutch rulers and suffered many sieges. The town hall in the market was built in 1784 in Classical style; the adjacent octagonal belfry with a carillon of 47 bells is of 16th/17th c. origin.

Wervik

Wervik, 7 km (4 mi.) west of Menen, has a tobacco museum documenting the history of snuff, smoking and chewing tobacco (open Apr.–Oct., Tue.–Sun. 1.30–5.30pm).

Mouscron

In the French-speaking area directly on the border with France is the town of Mouscron, situated on a hill, 7 km (4 mi.) to the south. It is dominated by the 13th c. castle of the Counts of Mouscron.

The Grote Markt of Tielt

25 km (15 mi.) north of Kortrijk is the small town of Tielt. The ruins of the **Tielt**
cloth hall, the belfry and the town hall (stadhuis) together with the other
buildings of the Grote Markt make a handsome scene. There is a small
museum in the town hall chronicling the everyday life of the countryside
around Tielt, the Hageland.

Ingelmunster, 11 km (7 mi.) north of Kortrijk, once possessed a mighty **Ingelmunster**
fortress and was "the key to Flanders" of great strategic importance. The
fortress was replaced in the 18th c. by a splendid château, but is not
open to visitors.

Izegem is only 3 km (2 mi.) west of Ingelmunster. The National Shoe and **Izegem**
Brush Museum in the stadhuis is worth a visit.

The Flemish poet Stijn Streuvels (1871–1969) was born in Ingooigem, 10 **Ingooigem**
km (6 mi.) to the west. His birthplace in the street named after him is
today a museum.

Roeslare, 21 km (13 mi.) north-west of Kortrijk, is home of the poet **Roeslare**
Albrecht Rodenbach and the blind statesman Alexander Rodenbach.
These and other sons of the town are commemorated in the arsenal
building on Polenplein. Even the beer brewed here, a bitter "red" beer,
is called Rodenbach. The main attraction on the Polenplein however is
the National Bicycle Museum (open Apr.–Oct. Tue.–Sat. 2–5pm).

The Roeslare suburb of **Rumbeke** has a fine moated castle (16/18th c.)
with seven octagonal towers. The Sint-Pieter-Paulskerk contains a
Romanesque font of 1200.

At **Westrozebeke**, 8 km (5 mi.) west of Roeslare, the Flemish were
heavily defeated in the battle of Rozebeke in 1382.

Leuven · Louvain   F/G 11

Province: Brabant
Altitude: 20–40 m (65–131 ft) Population: 85,000
Intercity and Inter-regional Station (bicycle hire at station)

Leuven (French Louvain) lies on both banks of the Dijle east of
Brussels. Together with the suburbs, which were incorporated in 1977,
the town is a conglomeration of over 85,000 inhabitants and is the
commercial, cultural and administrative centre of East Brabant and
southern Kempenland. The many different industries are based
mainly in the north of the town along the canal which links the Dijle
with the Rupel. Brewing is the chief industry and headquarters of the
Stella Artois brewery, with an annual output of over 5 million hec-
tolitres, the largest in Belgium. Despite heavy bombardment in both
world wars the university buildings, which are dispersed throughout
the town, provide a good impression of architecture from the 15th c.
onwards.

University town The Catholic university, which was founded in 1425 and
rapidly became one of the most highly regarded universities in Europe,
is world famous. Once the great humanist Erasmus of Rotterdam and
Justus Lipsius taught here. The geographer Gerhard Mercator studied
here and one of its chancellors was elected Pope Adrian VI in 1459. The
university library was unparalleled yet was set on fire by the German
occupying forces in 1914 and again in 1940 with the irretrievable loss of
over a million volumes. Many regard the division of the university in
1968, following linguistic quarrels between the Flemish and Walloons,

269

as the "Third Destruction": the Francophile teachers and students broke away and established the "Université Catholique de Louvain" in the new university town of Louvain-la-Neuve (see Louvain-la-Neuve). The books were divided between them on the basis of odd and even shelf-marks – a really insane initiative. Today 24,000 students are matriculated at the university to soak up knowledge as amusingly demonstrated by the statue on the fountain "Fons Sapientiae", known as "Fonske", in the Grote Markt.

History The first settlement to develop around the castle derived its name from the Low German Loo (bushy hill) and Veen (swamp). It was taken by the Normans, who were in turn driven away at the end of the 9th c., and from the 11th c. onwards a town grew up around the castle of the counts of Leuven. In 1106 the counts became dukes of Lower Lothringia and from 1190 called themselves the Dukes of Brabant. Owing to its position on the main trading route from Cologne to Brussels the town underwent rapid expansion and became the capital of Brabant and centre of cloth-making. Fortified walls were built; their course still visible where the ring-road encircles the inner city. In the 14th c. Leuven with over 100,000 inhabitants was one of the largest cities in Europe and is said to have had 2500 looms. Internal

Leuven: the Fonske Fountain

disputes, in the form of the uprising of the guilds against the patricians in 1379 and resulting in the leaders of the patricians being thrown out of the town hall windows onto upright pikes ending with severe punishment by the Duke of Brabant, the gradual shifting of trade routes and the transfer of the Brabant court to Brussels all led to a decline in trade and crafts. However, at this very time the greatest manifestation of bourgeois pride in the Netherlands took shape in the form of the town hall. In the 15th and 16th c. the university, founded in 1425, a bulwark of Catholic orthodoxy, brought a new impetus for revival. A new period of growth took place in the 19th c. under the Kingdom of Belgium. The town was heavily damaged in both world wars, yet the destruction of the Second World War caused by the German troops and British bombing in 1944 has been rectified. From 1450 onwards Dirk Bouts, one of the greatest late-Gothic painters of the Netherlands, worked in Leuven. His major work "The Last Supper" can be seen in Sint-Pieterskerk. The painter Quentin Massys was born here in 1466.

★★Stadhuis

The south side of the Grote Markt, a traffic junction where all the main streets converge in the middle of the town, is dominated by the stadhuis (city hall), built to plans by Sulpitius van Horst, begun by Jan Keldermans II and completed by Matthaeus de Rayens 1448–63. **Tours**: Mar.–Oct. Mon.–Fri. 11am and 3pm; Sat., Sun., public holidays 3pm only; Nov.–Feb. only Sat., Sun, public holidays 3pm.

It is one of the most magnificent secular buildings of late Gothic style in Europe and is decorated more lavishly than the city halls of Bruges, Brussels, Ghent and Oudenaarde (see entries). The building, which resembles a shrine, bears De Layens' distinctive architectonic trademark in the form of three narrow smaller towers at each gable end instead of a single tall central tower. Three rows of sculpture adorn the main façade and both side façades. The 236 figures which were only installed at the end of the 19th c. represent eminent personalities from the history of the

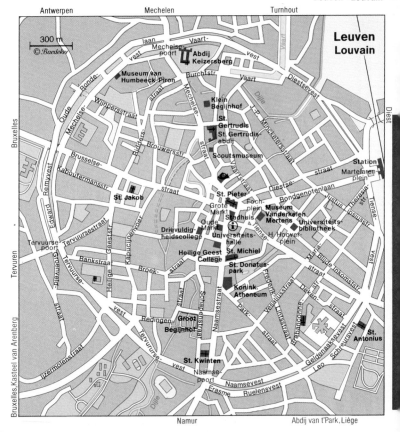

town, whereas the consoles and bases of the niches were carved with
reliefs from the Old and New Testament, some of them with medieval
coarseness, when the stadhuis was built. Even the roof is richly decorated with small turrets.

Inside the entrance hall are flags of the seven noble families of Leuven.
This leads to three rooms newly furnished in the 18th and 19th c. The
Great Gothic Council Chamber with its carved beamed ceiling (15th c.)
and Gothic fireplace and the Small Gothic Hall with a Gothic vaulted
wooden ceiling are noteworthy. In the Great Gothic Chamber, two "justice plaques" by Dirk Bouts can be seen.

The building to the left of the town hall is a reconstruction of 1921. **Tafelrond**
Named the Tafelrond, it is the meeting house of the rhetoricians' guild,
built at the end of the 15th c. by de Layens.

Standing in the middle of the Grote Markt Sint-Pieterskerk is a prime **★★Sint-**
example of Brabant Gothic. Begun in the 15th c. by van Vorst, continued **Pieterskerk**

271

by Keldermans and de Layens, it was more or less completed by Joost Massys. Original plans envisaged three towers on the west side and a main tower of 170 m (557 ft). This work was abandoned as the foundations were on sand and previous buildings had collapsed. After a 400-year absence, the gilded figure of "Meister Jan," who announces the hours with his hammer, has been re-positioned on top of the foundations of the tower that wasn't to be. Today, the Pieterskerk gaain shines in its former glory.

The Romanesque "Head of Christ"

Interior The main nave's notable features are its straight line of sheaf pillars and high pointed arch windows. Among the treasures in this part of the church are the late Gothic brass font in the chapel to the left of west gate and the splendidly carved Baroque pulpit of 1742. In the left transept is a Madonna "Sedes Sapientiae" (1441), the patron saint of the Catholic University. The choir is separated from the nave by a richly decorated late Gothic rood screen (1488) depicting a crucifixion scene by Jan Borreman (around 1500). During restoration work the octagonal Romanesque crypt of the original 10th c. church was discovered below the choir.

Museum of Religious Art (Treasure Chamber) The choir and ambulatory have been converted into the Stedelijk Museum voor Religieuze Kunst (Museum of Religious Art). (Opening times Tue.–Fri. 10am–5pm, Sat. until 4.30pm, Sun. 2–5pm; Mar.–Oct. also open Mon.)

The late Gothic choir stalls have the original carvings; to the left is the impressive 13 m (41 ft)-high stone tabernacle by de Layens (1450). In the chapels to the right and left of the choir are the tombs of Duke Henry I of Brabant (d. 1235), his wife Mathilde (d. 1211) and his daughter Maria (d. 1260). All that remains of a 12th c. wooden cross, burnt in 1914, is a head of Christ with a pitiful expression. Outstanding is the "Last Supper" the chief work of Dirk Bouts, painted 1464–68 and still well preserved. The supper takes place in a Gothic hall and the figures are arranged around Christ; unlike many representations the betrayal of Judas is not in the foreground, instead it is the symbolic Eucharist, as also portrayed in the side panels. The triptych with the "Martyrdom of St Erasmus" as the centre panel (1465) is also by Bouts; the "Descent from the Cross" is a copy of a masterpiece by his teacher, Rogier van der Weyden.

To the right of the town hall is Naamsestraat where many university buildings are to be found either in this street or nearby, in particular the college buildings funded by various patrons in the 15th–18th c. to accommodate students and institutes.

Along Naamsestraat

Just to the right are the main buildings of the Catholic University, formerly the Lakenhalle (Cloth Hall) built in 1317–45, which became the seat of the university following the decline of the cloth industry. An

Lakenhalle/Universiteitshalle

◄ *The magnificent Stadhuis of Leuven*

upper storey was added in the 18th c. and it housed the university library until it was set on fire by the German occupying forces in 1914 destroying the most valuable books. Today it serves as the administrative centre of the university. Items from the university's art collection are exhibited in the Jubilee Hall (visits by request).

★Oude Markt

Not far to the west of Naamsestraat is the Oude Markt, the bustling centre of Leuven, especially on summer evenings. Although its historic brick gabled houses were almost completely burnt down in 1914, they have been beautifully rebuilt and now accommodate many pubs and restaurants. A bronze sculpture commemorates the "Kottmadams" of Leuven, the landladies of the student rooms. On the narrow south side of the square is the Collegium Vauxianum (Heilig Drievuldigheidscollege; Holy Trinity College) with a Baroque façade of 1657.

★Sint-Michielskerk

Where Naamsestraat widens, diagonally opposite the Heilig Geest College (founded 1442, 18th c. building), stands Sint-Michielskerk, built 1650–66 by Willem Hesius. It has a splendid Baroque faáade, one of the finest of its kind in Belgium. The lane in front of the church off to the left leads to Hogescholplein with the Pauscollege (Papal College), founded by Pope Adrian IV in 1523 and rebuilt in the 18th c.

Colleges

Beyond Sint-Michielskerk more colleges line both sides of Naamsestraat, many of which were built in the 18th c.: Koningcolleg (King's College, No. 59) founded by Philipp II of Spain in 1579; the College van Promonstreit (Premonstratensian College, No. 61), founded in 1571; Arras College (No. 63) founded in 1508 by the future Bishop of Arras; the Huis Van 't Sestich (No. 69, Gothic) with the adjacent College van de Hoge Heuvel; the College van Dale (No. 80), founded in 1579 and the oldest, since wonderfully restored, Renaissance building in Leuven; finally the American College (No. 100), founded in 1659 for Cistercians and occupied by American students since 1857.

★Groot Begijnhof

From Naamsestraat head west through the Karmelietenberg and left into Schapenstraat to the picturesque Groot Begijnhof. This romantic complex, traversed by a tributary of the Dijle, was founded in the 13th c. and today comprises over 1000 houses and a church; earlier it encompassed a hospital and a farmhouse. In the 18th c., when 300 béguines were still living in the béguinage, the houses were renovated with stepped gables, mullions and transoms, but the French Revolution brought a temporary halt. Only a few béguines returned afterwards. In 1962 the site was bought by the university and underwent extensive restoration to create student residences and lecture halls. Only the second cottage on the right past the entrance is still furnished as it was when the last béguine died in 1988. The early Gothic béguinage church Sint-Jan-de-Doper, built in the 13/14th c., serves the university community as a place of worship.

Sint-Kwintenkerk

At the end of Naamsestraat is Sint-Kwintenkerk, its towers begun around 1200 and only completed in the 16th c. The choir – possibly by de Layens – and transept were added in the 15th c. The interior houses some notable paintings of the Rubens School.

Vlaams Filmmuseum

For the visitor interested in Flemish films there is the Vlaams Filmmuseum in Boekhandelstraat, a short street to left of the town hall from the market (open Wed. 9am–noon and 1.30–10pm).

★Vander Kelen-Mertens Museum

Leaving the Grote Markt in the direction of the railway station and turning right into Vanderkelenstraat the Vander Kelen-Mertens Museum, which has the Municipal Museum Collections, is on the right (Savoyestraat 6). It is in three departments: painting with good pictures from the Leuven School (Quentin Massys: "Mourning over Christ"; Pieter Coecke van Aalst "Holy Family"; Michiel Coxie) and other paintings from different periods up to the present; sculpture including a 12th c. Madonna "Sedes Sapientiae", an outstanding alabaster relief (16th c.) and a section of a Passion relief from Antwerp (around 1525); finally craftwork including glass painting from the 16th–20th c., ceramics, faãences from Delft, porcelain from China and Japan, engravings, coins, goldwork and textiles (open Tue.–Sat. 10am–5pm, Sun. and public holidays 2–5pm).

Further along the Vanderkelenstraat is the Mgr. Ladeuzeplein. The Universiteits-bibliotheek (University Library) stands here, designed by the American architect Whitney Warren and built with American donations 1921–28 in Dutch Renaissance style. Above the belfry soars the 85 m (278 ft)-high tower with a carillon worth listening to.

Universiteits-bibliotheek

The library's most valuable collections were destroyed in 1914 in the fire and again in 1940, yet it still contains over a million books. The archive and Museum of Flemish Student Life can be found in the library and illustrate the efforts of students in Leuven (visit by request). There is a very original memorial to a balloonist on the neighbouring Hooverplein.

To the north of Grote Markt, between Mechelstraat and the Dijle, set back is the 14th and 15th c. Gothic Sint-Gertrudiskerk. The tower and a chapel were destroyed in the 1944 air raids and the superb choir stalls, of a transitional style between Gothic and Renaissance, were buried under the rubble. They have been restored and are now in the new church built in 1953.

Sint-Gertrudiskerk

Sint-Gertrudiskerk belongs to the Benedictine Abbey of Sint-Gertrudis, which also suffered heavy damage in the Second World War. The former chapel houses the Scouts Museum, which illustrates the history of the Scouting Movement (open May–Oct. Sun. 2–6pm).

Scouts Museum

North of the church stands the Klein Begijnhof (Smaller Béguinage), founded in the 13th c. The present day houses in traditional brick and sandstone were built in the 17th and 18th c.

Klein Begijnhof

The Antwerp Retable of the Passion in the Vander Kelen-Mertens Museum

275

The **Keizersberg** at the end of Mechelsestraat is crowned by the Keizersberg Abbey, built in Neo-Romantic style in the last century on the site of the former castle of the Dukes of Brabant.

Other museums Friends of the age of steam can admire Belgian loco-motives in the station museum Diestsesteenweg 1 – open only to groups and by prior arrangement (tel. 211540). Visits to the gas museum (in the gas works Wilsele, tel. see above) are also only open to groups after agreement.

Abdij van 't Park   South-east of the town lies the Premonstratensian Abdij van 't Park, founded by Gottfried the Bearded in 1129; today most of the buildings date from the 16th and 18th c. The visitor is taken through two gateways and a long entrance, past the watermill and the estate to the courtyard of the prelate's house. The tour continues to the former abbots' palace, the chap-terhouse with its mixture of Gothic and Renaissance styles, the library and the refectory, which both have fine stucco reliefs. The monastery church is of 12/13th c. origin, being redesigned in the 17/18th c.

Kessel-Lo   The town of Kessel-Lo is situated 4 km (2 mi.) east of Leuven. The **Abdij van Vlierbeek** was founded here in 1127 and inhabited by the Benedictines. The troops of William of Orange destroyed the site in 1572 and it was several decades later before it was rebuilt. The main and adjoining buildings were built 1642–1730, the abbey church followed later in 1776–94.

The **provinciaal domein** of Kessel-Lo offers numerous sporting and recreational facilities.

Kasteel van   2 km (1 mi.) south-west of Leuven at Heverlee the Kasteel van Arenberg
Arenberg   (16th c.) on the Dijle has fine grounds and is well worth a visit. The château with its two striking corner towers with gabled roofs was built in traditional late Gothic style with Renaissance features and today is the property of the Catholic University, which maintains several institutes here and in the grounds.

IJse Valley   The IJse, a tributary of the Dijle, flows through peaceful green country-side to the south-west of Leuven, where vegetables, especially chicory, are grown and grapes are pressed.

The church of **Korbeek-Dijle** has an outstanding carved altar represent-ing the life of St Stephan from 1522.

Only a few kilometres east of Korbeek-Dijle are the five lakes of the recreation area and park **t' Zoet Water** (Gentle Water).

The IJse continues to the town of **Overijse**, the birthplace of the human-ist Justus Lipsius (1547–1606).

Liège · Luik   H 15

Province: Liège. Altitude: 70 m (230 ft)
Population: 205,000, with suburbs 490,000
Intercity and Inter-regional Station

Liège (Flemish Luik), the third largest town in Belgium, is situated on the confluence of the Meuse (Maas) and the Ourthe. It is the capital of the province of the same name and of French-speaking Wallonia, seat of a university and of a bishop, and owing to its locational advantages and long tradition an important industrial centre with one of the largest inland ports in Europe. Liège was one of the first places on the continent to start mining coal, thereby creating the base for the coal and steel industry, to which has been added a range of other manufacturing industries. Today more than 200,000 workers are employed in mining, blast furnaces, steel (40 per cent of Belgian steel production), textiles, food, electrical equipment, chemical products, glassware (famous glass production in Val Saint-Lambert), not forgetting weapons manufacture ("FN" small arms from the Fabrique Nationale in Herstal). Liège is the home of the author Georges Simenon (see Introduction, Famous People), who immortalised the town in his work, and enjoys increasing importance as a place of research and science (university, technical colleges and institutes). Liège is at the junction of important international roads and railway lines and an important trade centre for inland river traffic, which in recent years has suffered considerable losses: the waterways of the Rhine and Ruhr, the Albert Canal, which links the Scheldt with the Meuse, and canals crossing the Hainaut from France, unite in Liège and continue into the Netherlands. The inland port covers 97 ha (239 acres) and can accommodate ships up to 2500 tonnes. There is also a yachting marina. Liège is not a particularly attractive town, considering the devastation it has suffered throughout its history and only has a few buildings of historic interest. However, the town's long history is documented in the many churches which avoided destruction and in its many museums, which range among the best in the country.

History According to legend Liège developed around a chapel which St Hubert, Bishop of Tongeren-Maastricht, had built in 705 on the spot where his predecessor, St Lambert, was murdered. In 721 Hubert moved the seat of his bishopric from Tongeen to Liège, but it was under Bishop Notker (972–1008), who elevated the bishopric to the status of a principality, that the town and region began to prosper. In contrast to the Flemish towns the citizens of the Prince-Bishopric, which belonged to the Holy Roman Empire of the German Nation, were involved in bitter quarrels with the bishop over their freedom, as his first allegiance was to the Catholic church. The internal feuds of the 13th and 14th c. were characterised by revolts against the rulers who tried to compromise and called for calm; as did Johann of Bavaria, appointed bishop in 1390, leader of a ruthless régime until 1417. At this time of turmoil the metallurgical industry was beginning to develop. Catastrophe befell Liège when in the 15th c. the Dukes of Burgundy, who had already acquired the rest of Belgium, attempted to take the principality, but came up against heavy opposition from the population. In 1467 the troops of Charles the Bold took the city and its fortifications were razed. The city rose again, but not even the efforts of 600 Franchimontois to break the siege could prevent the town being stormed, plundered and set ablaze again. The city burned for seven weeks and Charles the Bold ordered that only the churches and monasteries should survive the fire. It was not until 1475 that the citizens of Liège received permission to rebuild their town. With his death in 1477 they regained their independence which they again had to defend against Guillaume de la Marck. Under the prince bishop, Erard de la Marck (1505–38), a new period of prosperity began coinciding with the work of Liège's greatest painter, Lambert Lombard (1505–66). In the same century, as well as later, there was new progress as a result of coal mining and weapons manufacture. Repeated power struggles between the guilds, made powerful by industry, and the prince bishops ended this time with the victory of the bishops; several mayors were sent to the scaffold in the 17th c. One of the most important sculptors of the 17th c., Jean Delcour (1631–1701), lived here at this time. Only 100 years later the French Revolution put an end to the ecclesiastical domination and for a short time Liège was the capital of the French département of Ourthe. In the 19th c., in particular since the founding of Belgium as an independent country, Liège began to develop into an important industrial city which found expression in its urban architecture. In 1889 the Fabrique Nationale was founded.

In the First World War Belgian regiments in Liège held off the advance

Liège: Market on the Quai de la Batte

of the German army long enough for the French and remaining Belgian troops to form. In 1939 the Albert Canal was opened. At first Liège sustained little damage during the Second World War, but following the withdrawal of the German occupying forces between November 1944 and January 1945 it was the target of over 1500 V2 rockets which damaged or destroyed over 23,000 buildings. In recent times Liège has been affected by the crisis in the steel industry; since the end of the Eighties the city has an enormous debt problem and is more or less bankrupt. Local government employees fearful of their salaries sought to bring attention to their demands by drastic action: firemen occupied public buildings and did not put out fires, civil servants threw mountains of files out of the offices onto the streets and the police supported it all by benevolent non-intervention.

Tour of the city The sights of Liège are not very far apart so that the most important – Palais des Princes-Evàques, Musée Curtius, Musée de la Vie Wallone and the Church Saint-Barthélemy – can easily be visited on foot in one day. The museums on the right bank of the Meuse can be reached by bus (departure from Place Saint-Lambert).

Guided tours are organised by the tourist office (see Practical Information, Information). A brochure is available here with a city walk following the steps of Georges Simenon and information on **boat trips on the Meuse**, including Visé (see entry).

The best **views** over the city are from the Citadel and the Parc de Cointe to the south, where the Basilique du Sacré-Coeur (1936) and the immense Monument Interallié (Monument to the Allies in the First World War; 1937) can be seen.

Citadelle

Place Hocheporte
Rue de L'Académie
R Sainte Marguerite

Académie des Beaux-Arts
Gare du Palais
Rue de Bruxelles

Musée de la Vie Wallonne
R. du Palais
Palais des Princes-Évêques
Ste-Croix
Place du Marché
St-Lambert
Place Maréchal Foch

St-Antoine
Place Paul Janson
Féronstrée
En
La Batte Quai de Maestricht

St-Barthélemy
Quai St-Léonard
Pont St-Léonard
Quai Godefroid Kurth

Hôtel de Ville
Rue Léopold
Musée d'Art Wallon
Quai des Tanneurs

Aachen

St-Martin
Mont Saint-Martin
VIEILLE

Théâtre Royal
Place de la République Française

Place des Arches
Pont
St-Pholien
Boulevard de la Constitution
Bonnes Villes
Place du Congrès

St-Jean
R. de la Casquette
St-Denis

VILLE
Rue de la Cathédrale

Place Cockerill
Passerelle Saucy

Théâtre de la Place
St-Nicolas
Rue St-Nicolas
Maison Grétry

St-Cristophe
R. sur-la-Fontaine
Boulevard de la Sauvenière
R. Jonfosse
R. Pont d'Avroy

Place du Roi Albert
St-Paul
Université
Musée Préhistoire

Musée Tchantchès
Rue Jean d'Outremeuse
Rue Entre 2 Ponts
Quai de la Dérivation

Abbaye Bénédictine de la Paix N.-D.
Rue Darchis
Place St-Jacques
St-Jacques

Musée de Zoologie
Quai Ed. Van Beneden
Pont J.F. Kennedy
Rue Pitteurs
Rue I. Jamme

R. Méan
Quai de l'Ourthe
Quai de Longdoz
St-Remacle

Fort de la Chartreuse

Jardin Botanique
Rue Fabry
Rue Darchis
Boulevard d'Avroy

Conservatoire

Parc d'Avroy

Rue Roger
Boulevard Frère Orban

Pont Albert Ier

Quai Marcellis
Quai de la Meuse

Meuse

Rue de la Boverie
Grétry
Rue d'Harscamp
Rue Natalis

Rue Grétry
Rue Lairesse
Rue des Champs
Basse
Wez
Rue du Beau Mur

Place de Bronckart

Av. Blonden
Boulevard Frère Orban
Rue de Serbie

Jardin d'Acclimatation
Rue du Parc
Quai Mozart
Boulevard R. Poincaré

Musée du Fer et du Charbon

Namur, Flughafen, Bruxelles

Rue du Plan Incliné
R. Darlois
Rue des Guillemins

Palais des Congrès
Tour
Parc de la Boverie

Musée des Transports

Avenue de l'Observatoire
Rue Mandeville
Rue Fabry

Place de Batty

Guillemins Gare
Point de Vue
Rue de Serbie
Rue Paradis
R. Rue Sclessin
Rue St-Léonard

Musée d'Art moderne

Rue de Fétinne

Rue de Rome
Quai de Rome
Varin
R. de Kinkempois

Dérivation
Quai Mativa

Boulevard Emile de Laveleye
St-Vincent
Bd de Froidmont
Vennes

Liège
Luik
300 m

Basilique du Sacré-Cœur
Monument Interallié
Av. E. Digneffe
Pont de Fragnée

Quai des Ardennes
Quai du Condroz
Ourthe

Luxembourg

© Baedeker

1 Musée d'Ansembourg   2 Musée d'Armes   3 Musée Curtius   4 Fontaine du Perron

Palais des Princes Evêques: the main façade ...

Left Bank of the Meuse

The central area of the city is formed by Place Saint-Lambert and the adjoining squares Place du Marché (Market Place) in the north-east and the Place de la République Française in the south-west. The Place du Maréchal de Foch joins the Boulevard de la Sauvenière. As all four squares are choked by traffic a new road system is being introduced. The district east of the Place Saint-Lambert is the oldest part of the city.

Place Saint-Lambert

Until 1796 the Cathédrale Saint-Lambert, the largest cathedral in the Netherlands at that time, stood in the Place Saint-Lambert. It was destroyed by the French revolutionaries and their supporters in Liège and the ruins moved in 1808. The excavations of the church foundations and the hypocaust of a Roman villa below the square are accessible by a staircase. Georges Simenon was born at No. 24 Rue Léopold which leads from the square to the Meuse.

★Palais des Princes-Evêques

On the north side of the Place Saint-Lambert stands the Palais des Princes-Evàques, the former palace of the prince-bishops. Notker had the first modest bishop's seat built here, which – after being extended – was destroyed at the end of the 15th c. Erard de la Marck was responsible for the rebuilding, which was completed 1526–40 according to plans by Arnold van Mulckens in the transition style betwen Gothic and Renaissance. 1734–40 the new (south) main façade was added. Today the building houses the Law Courts and is the seat of the Walloon government.

There are two picturesque courtyards with arcaded walkways and columns. The artists who carved the columns with fools' masks and grotesque faces were inspired by Sebastian Brants and Erasmus and news from the New World. The second courtyard is more peaceful with a fountain. The palace interior is not open to visitors.

South-east of the palace of the prince-bishops stretches the tree-lined Place du Marché, the market square surrounded by Baroque houses. From here the narrow street En Neuvice, once the street of goldsmiths and today a pedestrian zone, leads down to the Meuse.

Place du Marché

In the middle of the market square stands the **Perron**, which to the communities of the former prince-bishopric symbolised their much-fought for and documented liberty. The Perron, erected in 1697 on the site of a much older predecessor, stands in the centre of the fountain created by Jean Delcour and is crowned by the Three Graces.

The Baroque Hôtel de Ville (town hall), built 1714–18, stands on the south side of the market square, still referred to as "La Violette" after the first meeting hall of the town council. It was destroyed in 1468 by Charles the Bold, again in 1691 by the French. In the interior there is an interesting foyer.

Hôtel de Ville

The onion-shaped cupola of the former church of **Saint-André** (1772), now a concert hall, dominates the market square.

The north-east corner of the palace of the prince-bishops overlooks the Court des Mineurs, the former Minorite monastery built in the 17th c. in the style of the Meuse Renaissance. It houses the Musée de la Vie Wallonne, where 350,000 exhibits and documents illustrate life and culture in the Walloon part of Belgium. The most modern technology and a presentation in four languages make it one of the best museums to visit in Belgium. (Opening times Tue.–Sat. 10am–5pm, Sun. and public holidays 10am–4pm)

★★Musée de la Vie Wallonne

... and the second courtyard

In the former chapterhouse on the ground floor there are temporary exhibitions. The rooms on the first floor are each dedicated to a different theme, for example, national religion, magic, festivals, housework, heating and lighting and craftwork. On display are puppets, various workshops (chandlers, pipemakers, coopers, pewterers) and an unusual collection of old sundials. The upper floor is devoted to agricultural crafts such as cheese-making and basketmaking and to coal mining in Wallonia; in the basement there is a reproduction of a coal mine tunnel around 1900. Traditional puppet shows using old puppets are performed in the adjoining Maison Chamart. A branch of the museum is the Musée du Fer et du Charbon (see p. 275).

Musée d'Art Religieux

Adjoining the Musée de la Vie Wallonne in the Rue Mère-Dieu is the Musée d'Art Religeux (Museum of Religious and Mosan Art). It was the former Diocesan museum and exhibits in nine rooms religious works from the churches of Liège and the Meuse region (open Tue.–Sat. 11am–6pm, Sun. 11am–4pm).

Musée d'Architecture

From En Hors Château, which runs south of the above-mentioned museum complex, a short way on the left the Montagne de Bueren steps climb up to the Citadel. At the beginning of the steps the narrow alley Impasse des Ursulines leads into the quiet former monastery of the Holy Spirit and the adjacent postal station which now accommmodate the Museum of Architecture. There are examples of Liège architecture but it is primarily a document centre for the history of building in the town. In the postal station the study of the Liège violinist Eugène Isaye (1859–1931) can be seen (open daily except Tue. and Thu. 1–6pm).

Detour to the citadel

The climb up the 374 steps of the Montagne du Bueren up to the Parc de la Citadelle (158 m/518 ft) is rewarded with a fine view of the city. The park incorporates the grounds and bastions of the 18th c. citadel (now a barracks). Either return the same way or continue along the path already started, which finally leads back down to the church of Saint-Barthélemy.

Along the Féronstrée

This street runs from the east side of the market square through the heart of the Old Town to the church of Saint-Barthélemy. Its name is a reminder that in the Middle Ages the forges, iron foundries and the offices of the metal merchants together with the guilds' meeting houses were found here. Most of the buildings which escaped demolition are from the 18th c.

Musée de l'Art Wallon

About halfway along this street is the Ilot Saint-Georges Complex with the Musée de l'Art Wallon which houses paintings, sculptures and drawings by Walloon artists such as Joachim Patinir, Lambert Lombard, Henri Blès and Jean Delcour (open Tue.–Sat. 1–6pm, Sun. 11am–4.30pm).

★Musée Ansembourg

A short distance past the Ilot Saint-Georges is the beautiful façade of the house built 1735–40 for Michel Willems, a patrician whose granddaughter married a Count Ansembourg. Converted into a museum (opening times Thu.–Sun. 1–5pm) it is an eloquent example of the bourgeois lifestyle of the nobility in the 18th c. It contains a wooden Madonna from Delcour in the entrance hall, leather wall hangings from Córdoba, a stucco ceiling and an exemplary china cabinet in the dining room, tapestries in the Salon des Tapisseries from Oudenaarde (see Oudenaarde) and a magnificent inlaid table from the Prince-Bishop's palace as well as a huge fireplace on the upper floor with the portrait of the head of the house hanging above it and a large inlaid table from Liège.

Saint-Barthélemy

The second street on the left past the museum leads to the church of Saint-Barthélemy (opening times Mon.–Sat. 10am–noon and 2–5pm, Sun. 2–5pm). It was built in the 11th–12th c. with three aisles and extended in the 18th c. by two main aisles and a side aisle. The west front with its two towers is characteristic of Rhine and Mosan Romanesque church architecture. The late 11th c. choir is also of interest. The interior houses paintings by Bertholet Flémalle (1614–75) and Englebert Fisen (1655–1733), both from Liège; the most valuable treasure is the **bronze font** cast by Renier de Huy between 1107 and 1118. It rests on twelve bulls, symbolising the Apostles, and is splendidly decorated with five baptismal reliefs (see p. 56 for a more detailed description). Originally the font stood in the Notre-Dame-aux-Fonts church which was destroyed during the French Revolution; it was brought to its present location for safety.

On the Meuse

The return from Saint-Barthélemy and around the block of houses between En Féronstrée and the Meuse leads to the quays Quai de Maestricht, **Quai de la Batte**, Quai de la Goffe and Quai sur la Meuse. A market is held here every Sunday at 9am offering everything from a flea market to food and vegetables.

Two buildings on the Quai de Maestricht house three very interesting museums.

★Musée d'Armes

First at No. 8 Quai de Maestricht is the Musée d'Armes (Arms Museum). It has a magnificent collection of small arms (12,500 exhibits) documenting the tradition of weapons manufacture in Liège dating back to the 14th c. Worth particular mention is a room containing splendid ornate weapons and a collection of hunting and blank guns (open Tue.–Sat. 10am–1pm and 2–5pm, Sun only 10am–1pm).

★★Musée Curtius

The Musée Curtius (13, Quai de Maestricht) is in the former mansion of Jean Curtius (1551–1628), once supplier to the Spanish army. Between

Bishop Notker's Gospel ...　　　*... in the Musée Curtius*

1600 and 1610 he had this exemplary red brick house built on the river bank in the style of the Mosan Renaissance. The museum which now occupies the house contains in two departments exhibits from prehistoric, Roman and Frankish-Medieval periods together with furniture and decorative art collections from the Middle Ages to the French Revolution. Only the most notable pieces from its valuable collections are listed: on the ground floor Roman bronzes, a Roman ceramic mask and a unique Roman glass service, Merovingian everyday objects, wonderful early Romanesque ivory carvings including a figure of Christ from Amay and Bishop Notker's Evangelistery (around 1100), the museum's pièce de résistance; on the first floor the finely worked Madonna by Dom Rupert (around 1140), the wooden tympanum with the "Mystery of Apollo" (around 1150), lavishly decorated Renaissance rooms; finally on the second floor a collection of coins from Liège (open Mon. and Wed.–Sat. 10am–1pm and 2–5pm, Sun. 10am–1pm).

★Musée du Verre
In an annexe of the Musée Curtius the Musée du Verre (Glass Museum) has a collection of over 10,000 glass exhibits from the 5th c. BC to the present, among them highly original Art Nouveau glasses and vases (opening times as for the Musée Curtius).

Return to Féronstrée
Further along the river bank, with a view of the Pont des Arches, which was built 1858–62 to replace the oldest bridge (11th c.) over the Meuse, between the Rue du Pont and the Rue de la Halle aux Viandes stands the Meat Hall, built 1544–46. Behind it on the right on the corner of Rue de la Boucherie/Potiérue is Maison Havart, a historic inn from 1594, dominated by the Cité Administrative, the City Administration building. From here it is a short distance back to Féronstrée.

Place de la République
Built 1818–22 and modelled on the Odéon in Paris the **Théâtre Royal** on the south-west side of the Place de la République is home to the Opéra Royal de la Wallonie.

Sainte-Croix
North of the square on the corner of the Rue Haute Sauvenière/Rue Sainte-Croix stands the church of Sainte-Croix (Church of the Holy Cross), consecrated in 979 by Bishop Notker and rebuilt several times. It is one of the few churches in Belgium with two apses: the Romanesque west choir is from 1175, the Gothic east choir (and the nave) are from the 14th c. The west choir contains the notable tomb of Canon Milleman, decorated with hieroglyphics (1558).

The **treasury** contains two exceptional pieces: one is the "Triptych of the True Cross", probably by Godefroid de Huy, into which four fragments of Christ's cross, a piece of John the Baptist's skull and a tooth of St Vincent were worked; the other is a 37 cm (15 in.) long "Clef de Saint-Hubert" (St Hubert's key) which Pope Gregory II gave to St Hubert in 722 in accordance with a custom of giving great churchmen a key to St Peter's tomb in Rome, into which a piece of Peter's chain had been inserted. The only other such key in Europe is in St Servatius' church in Maastricht.

Basilique Saint-Martin
From Sainte-Croix the Rue Mont Saint-Martin climbs up to the Basilique Saint-Martin, visible from afar, founded in the 10th c. and destroyed by fire in 1312 in disputes between the guilds and the nobility. It was rebuilt in its present form at the beginning of the 16th c. with a large star-covered choir. The church has stained glass windows dating from 1526–36, paintings by Englebert Fiesen together with 14 marble plaques in the first side chapel on the right by Delcour commemorating the initiation of the feast of Corpus Christi (Fàte-Dieu). This was first celebrated in 1246 following a vision by St Juliana, a Liège nun, and was proclaimed by Pope Urban IV (former Archdeacon of Liège Cathedral Church) a church holiday throughout Christendom.

Théâtre Royal

Not far beyond the Théâtre Royal stands the Eglise Saint-Jean, founded in 980 by Bishop Notker. It was modelled on the Pfalz chapel in Aachen as can be seen from the octagonal outline of the central building. In the 18th c. it fell into disrepair and was partly demolished, being rebuilt according to the original plans in 1754–60. It contains two beautiful sculptures, a Madonna "Sedes Sapientiae" (around 1230) in oak and from the same period "Mary and John the Baptist".

Saint-Jean

A second pedestrianised area lies to the south of the theatre around the triangular square Vinâve d'Ile (fountain by Delcour), off which leads the Passage Lemonnier, the first covered shopping arcade in Belgium (1839).

Vinâve d'Ile

The Vinâve d'Ile opens out onto the Place de la Cathédrale. Here stands the former Convent Church of Saint-Paul, founded by Bishop Heraclius in 971; since 1801 it has been the successor to the Cathedral of Saint-Lambert in the diocese. The 90 m (295 ft-high) tower has a carillon from the old cathedral which plays the Walloon hymn "li Chant dès Wallons". The original Romanesque church was destroyed at the beginning of the 13th c. and replaced by the early Gothic church of 1232–89, which later underwent further expansion. The decoration of the expansive interior (85 m/278 ft long, 34 m/111 ft wide, 24 m/78 ft high) took place between the 16th and 19th c. and encompasses works such as the marble sculpture of the burial of Christ by Delcour in the left side aisle, a large glass window by Hans of Cologne (1530) in the right hand aisle and other examples of artistic stained glass from 1557–87 in the choir apse. The **Treasury** in the adjoining cloisters possesses two outstanding works together with two 11th c. ivory pieces. The 1.5 m (5 ft)-high reliquary of St Lambert was made in 1506–12 by Hans von Reutlingen, the goldsmith of Emperor Maximilian and Charles V, resident in Aachen, and

★Cathédrale
Saint-Paul

commissioned by Erards de la Marck. The gold reliquary of Charles the Bold depicts the Duke of Burgundy kneeling with St Lambert's reliquary, while St George standing behind him is also portrayed with the face of the Duke. This work of art by Gérard Loyet in 1467 was allegedly a gift to the city of Liège from Charles the Bold in 1471 as an expression of regret at the destruction of the city which he had ordered.

Saint-Denis

In a street running parallel to the Rue de la Régence from the theatre to the Meuse stands the Church of Saint-Denis, founded by Bishop Notker in 987 and consecrated in 1011. The tower is of 11th c. origin, the choir was built in the 14th c. In the right side aisle there is a fine carved Gothic altar with a representation of the Passion of Christ.

Right Bank of the Meuse Université

At the end of the Rue de la Régence is the Place Cockerill with the Neo-Gothic main post office and the state university founded in 1817. As well as lecture halls the university building houses a library containing over a million volumes and a natural science museum with an important palaeontology department.

Southern parts of the city

South of the cathedral the Rue St-Remy comes to the church of **Saint-Jacques** (St Jacob's Church), founded in the 11th c. and converted to a splendid example of late Gothic architecture in 1513–38. The Romanesque portico of 1170 on the west side has been preserved; the magnificent north portal was remodelled by Lambert Lombard in Renaissance style in 1558–60, but leaving the relief below the arch of the Coronation of the Virgin (1380), a masterpiece of Mosan Gothic sculpture. Worth seeing inside the church are the superb vaulting, the rood-screen (17th c.) and the stained glass (1520–40).

Further south the **Parc d'Avroy** is laid out on the site of an old harbour. In the north of the park is a massive statue of Charlemagne on horseback (1868), a few yards to the east, on the Boulevard Piercot, stands the Royal Conservatory of Music (1881–86). Alongside the Meuse is an elevated terrace surrounded by a wall with four groups of bronze statues, among them the Bulltamer by L. Mignon and the Monument National de la Résistance (National Monument to the Resistance Fighters in the Second World War).

Right Bank of the Meuse

Outre-Meuse

The Pont des Arches links the Old Town with the district of Outre-Meuse lying between the Meuse and a canal of the Ourthe. It is the most colourful and extrovert quarter of the city where in 1927 the not entirely serious République Outre-Meuse and the Commune de Saint-Pholien proclaimed themselves "free states", thereby keeping the custom alive. Pure dialect is still spoken here and this is the home of **"Tchantchès"** (Walloon for François), the hard-drinking symbolic figure of the population of Liège, allegedly born in 760, adviser to Charlemagne and companion of Roland, who first appeared as a marionette in 1836 together with "Polichinelle" and "Guignol" in the puppet theatre. A monument to him was placed at the Place d'Yser in 1936.

Maison Grétry

Not far from the site of the monument the composer André-Ernest-Modeste Grétry was born (1741–1813). His birthplace is open to visitors.

Musée Tchantchès

To the south in Rue Surelet the Musée Tchantchès documents the history of this popular figure with over 200 of its costumes and a notable collection of puppets (open Wed. and Thu. 2–4pm, puppet shows Sep.–Easter Sun. 10.30am).

Musée de Zoologie with Aquarium

On the Meuse near the Pont John F. Kennedy the Musée de Zoologie with an aquarium is part of the Zoological Institute of the University.

There is a coral collection, a zoological collection and 26 ponds containing exotic fish (open Tue.–Fri. 10.30am–12.30pm and 1.30–5.30pm, Sat., Sun. and public holidays 10.30am–12.30pm and 2–6pm).

South of the Pont Albert I (Pont de Commerce) is the Parc de Boverie with the Palais de Justice (1952–58) and the Tour spatio-dynamique et cybernétique, a 52 m (170 ft)-high bizarre steel construction.

Parc de Boverie

In the southern tip of the park the Musée d'Art Moderne (Museum of Modern Art) awaits the visitor, an impressive collection of 19–20th c. paintings, including Picasso, Pissarro, Monet, Kokoschka, Chagall and primarily Belgian artists such as Evenepoel, de Smet and Delvaux. Adjoining it is the Cabinet des Estampes (copper engraving gallery), which has 26,000 items from all periods since the 19th c. (open Tue.–Sat. 1–6pm, Sun. 11am–4.30pm).

Musée d'Art moderne

On the other side of the Ourthe canal the Musée du Fer et du Charbon, a branch of the Musée de la Vie Wallone on the Blvd. Poincaré, specialises in mining and metal working in Wallonia and has a 17th c. melting furnace and 18th c. blacksmiths' hammers (open Mon.–Fri. 9am–5pm; mid-Mar.–Oct. also Sat. and Sun. 2–6pm).

Musée du Fer et du Charbon

Further along the same road the Musée des Transports exhibits vehicles and documents of the city's transport system.

Musée des Transports

The Château d'Aigremont lies on the left bank of the Meuse 16 km (10 mi.) south-west of Liège and according to legend was built by the four children of Haimon. The present day château is of 15th c. origin and was rebuilt in the 18th c. The tour takes in the kitchen with over 1000 Delft tiles. It has a beautiful staircase with Italian idyllic landscape paintings in a trompe-l'oeil style.

Château d'Aigremont

The Fort de Loncin 8 km (5 mi.) to the north played an important role in the resistance against the advance of the German troops in 1914. After incessant artillery fire it was destroyed when its magazine exploded.

Fort de Loncin

Domäne Sart Tilman (740 ha/1829 acres), part of the university, extends along the right bank of the Meuse to the south of the city. There are Botanical Gardens, the Château de Colonster (17th c.) with the Georges Simenon Foundation and an open air museum with over 70 sculptures and works by Belgian sculptors.

Sart Tilman

In the south-west suburb of Seraing the visitor can watch the famous glass being blown as it is manufactured in Val Saint-Lambert, purchase one of the beautiful crystal glasses on sale and visit the splendid glass collection (open: Tue.–Sun. 9.30am–5pm).

Val Saint-Lambert

At Neuville-en-Condruz, 20 km (12 mi.) south-west, the largest American cemetery of the Second World War is situated (see Practical Information, Military Cemeteries).

Neuville-en-Condruz

From Neuville it is another 3 km (2 mi.) (branch off to the right) to Saint-Séverin-en-Condroz, where there is a notable Romanesque church (12th c.), the former priory of the Cluny Convent. It is notable for its octagonal tower and a fine Romanesque font, formed by twelve lion-shaped figures.

Saint-Séverin-en-Condroz

Chaudfontaine, 10 km (6 mi.) south, is an attractive thermal spa resort on the Vesdre.

Chaudfontaine

Blégny, 20 km (12 mi.) north-east of Liège, is a traditional small mining town. There are guided tours of the old coal mines in Blégny-Trembleur

Blégny-Trembleur

287

(open Apr. and Oct. weekends only; May–Sep. daiily 9.30am–5pm). A small old-time railway runs through the Herver Land to Montroux and back (departures daily between 10am and 3.30pm, Jul. and Aug. also Sun. and public holidays until 4.30pm).

Montroux

The old railway station at Montroux houses a museum with agricultural equipment and horse-drawn carts.

Lier · Lierre

D/E 10

Province: Antwerp
Altitude: 4–13 m (13–43 ft) Population: 31,000
Interregional Station (bicycle rental at station)

The town of Lier (French Lierre), birthplace of the popular Flemish author Felix Timmermans (1886–1947) and other well known artists including the painter Isidoor Opsomer, is situated 17 km (11 mi.) south-east of Antwerp at the confluence of the Grote and Kleine Nete. Lier is the gateway to the region of Kempen and is nicknamed "Lierke Plezierke" (Lively Lier), on account of its colourful folklore.

The economy of the town is based on the textile industry with its old and famous traditions of silk spinning, lace making and embroidery. Also important are some recently introduced industries including brewing, the manufacture of synthetic fibres and the production of building materials near the Nete canal, which provides a waterway between Lier and Antwerp for vessels up to 1350 tonnes. Many people commute daily between Lier and Antwerp.

Culinary specialities of the town are Lierse Vlaaikes (sweet tarts with candy) and the light "Caves" beer.

History The origins of the town can be traced back to a hermitage founded in 760. In the early Middle Ages the town was known for its cloth making and received its town charter as early as 1212. It was fortified in the late Middle Ages and its fortifications resisted all enemy attacks until 1784 when they were razed but rebuilt in 1830. During the First World War the town held a key strategic position and was often heavily shelled.

★Sint-Gummaruskerk

East of the Kleine Nete stands Sint-Gummaruskerk, a masterpiece of Brabant late Gothic, built in 1425–1540 by Keldermans and de Waghemakere. The octagonal tower with its carillon of 45 bells was begun in 1377 but only completed in 1702.

Philipp the Handsome married Johanna the Mad of Castille here in 1496.

The church contains some outstanding art treasures. Among them is the late Gothic **choir screen** carved out of light sandstone by the Mechelen sculptors Mynsheeren and Wischavens (1536–39) depicting the story of the Passion, evangelists and churchmen. The small turret was added in 1850.

The late Gothic **stained glass** is of outstanding beauty: in the right side aisle the "Coronation of the Virgin" (15th c.), in the choir apse three windows presented by the Emperor Maximilian in 1516 representing himself and his wife Maria of Burgundy and in the same place a window of Sts Gummarus and Rumoldus (1475).

Of the numerous **paintings** the most impressive are a triptych in the first ambulatory chapel, its side panels probably painted by Rubens; in the fourth chapel the Colibrant triptych (1517) representing the marriage of the Virgin in the centre and the Annunciation and Circumcision on the side panels, probably by Goswyn van der Weyden, the grandson of Rogier van der Weyden; finally in the right aisle a triptych by Otto Venius ("Coming of the Holy Spirit"; 1612).

The Baroque pulpit of 1642 by Artus Quellin is also noteworthy. The most important of the church treasures is the 800 kg silver shrine of St. Gummarus which is carried through the streets in processions.

Opposite the church of St Gommarus stands the Romanesque Sint-Pieters-kapel, the oldest building in the town (1225).

Sint-Pieterskapel

In the centre of the town is the Grote Markt, which was badly damaged during the German shelling of Antwerp, but its most important buildings survived.

Grote Markt

In Sint-Gummaruskerk

On the east side of the square is the 18th c. **stadhuis** (town hall) with an attractive Rococo staircase and beautifully decorated rooms. The adjoining Gothic **belfry** (1369) is all that remains of the medieval cloth hall.

North of the stadhuis stands the **Vleeshuis** (meat hall) built in 1418, today an exhibition hall, and some notable **guild houses** such as the bakkerhuis (1717) and the Huis d'Eyckenboom (1721).

Sint-Jacobskapel

Sint-Jacobskapel behind the town hall is also called the "Spanish Chapel" and originates from 1383.

Museum Wuyts van Campen en Baron Caroly

Not far to the west of the market No. 14 Cauwenberghstraat houses the Museum Wuyts van Campen en Baron Caroly (Stedelijk Museum) which has a notable collection not only of Dutch and Flemish, but also of French and Spanish masters as well as contemporary works. Among the artists represented are Jan and Peter Bruegel the Younger, Rubens, van Dyck, Floris ("Berchem family"), Poussin, Lorrain and Murillo; the Modernists are represented by Permeke, de Vlaminck, de Braekeleer and Opsomer and de la Haye from Lier (open Easter–Nov. Mon., Tue., Thu., Sat, Sun. 10am–noon and 1.30–5.30pm).

★Begijnhof

From the Grote Markt Eikelstraat leads south through Gevangenpoort (1375) by the wall promenade (former moat) to the adjoining begijnhof (béguinage), one of the most picturesque in Belgium. With its low cottages, narrow alleys and crossroads it resembles a small town within a town. The béguinage was founded in the 13th c. and, together with most of the others, destroyed in the 16th c. The church dedicated to St Margaret is 17th c. and has a pulpit by Schneemaeckers.

★Zimmertoren

The Zimmerplein extends south-east of the Gevangenpoort. Here stands the Zimmertoren, once part of the town's defences and called the Corneliusturm, named after the astronomer and watchmaker Louis Zimmer (1880–1970). On its façade is his centenary clock from 1930 with 13 dials and scales: Greenwich Mean Time, day and night, zodiac, solar cycle, week days, the earth's meridian, months, date, seasons, tides, ages of the moon, phases of the moon and the metonic cycle. Every day at noon figures appear on the right façade. Inside the tower the clock mechanism and an astronomic studio with 57 dials can be seen.

In a pavilion near the tower is the clock which Zimmer featured in the 1939 World Exhibition in New York. It has 93 dials and made Zimmer world famous (open daily 9am–noon and 1–6pm; in winter 9am–noon and 2–4pm).

Between the pavilion and the tower there is a wrought iron sculpture "Eagle and Chamois" by the Lier artist van Boeckel.

Museum Timmermans-Opsomer

The Timmermans-Opsomer Museum, situated to the right of the bridge over the Nete next to the Zimmertoren, commemorates four artists born in Lier. The first is the author Felix Timmermans, who was also active as a musician and painter; several rooms are dedicated to him and his works such as "Pallieter".

Also on view is the studio of the painter Baron Opsomer, van Boeckel's forge and memorabalia of the Flemish composer Renaat Veremans, who also composed texts for Felix Timmermans (open Apr.–Oct. Mon., Tue., Thu., Sat., Sun. 10am–noon and 1.30–5.30pm; Nov.–Mar. Sun. 10am–noon and 1.30–4pm).

Lokeren

See Sint-Niklaas, Surroundings

Lommel

See Geel, Surroundings

Louvain-la-Neuve

H 10

Province: Brabant. Altitude: 70 m (230 ft)
Population: 4500 (permanent).
Local Rail Station

The university town of Louvain-la-Neuve is a product of the conflict between the Walloons and the Flemish. When this confrontation reached another zenith in 1968 the Flemish expelled their Walloon colleagues from the Catholic University of Leuven (see entry) founded in 1425. The Walloons looked for a fresh place and found it 30 km (19 mi.) south-east of Brussels in the French part of Belgium and Louvain-la-Neuve, "New Leuven", was founded; it was the first newly set up town in Belgium since the foundation of Charleroi in 1666. Building went on from 1971, and between 1972 and 1979 all the French-speaking faculties moved out of Leuven with the exception of the medical faculty which was accommodated in the Brussels suburb of Woluwe-Saint-Lambert. Today in this town, which was conceived for 35,000 people, about 4500 permanent residents and 18,000 students live. It can be seen that the aim of a homogeneous structure of residence has not been achieved and as a consequence at weekends and in the university holidays it can be very quiet in the town.

In Louvain-la-Neuve it was intended to try out new forms of residence and living. More than 80 architects wanted to turn away from the idea of a large town and to recreate the intimate character of small areas as they were in a medieval town; therefore around the urban centre brick was the preferred material for the buildings in the narrow little streets. Here pedestrians have priority; the station access roads and car parks are sited underground and from them a system of passages, branching out in all directions, leads into the open air. The centre of the town is the main square with the concrete university hall, the Church of Saint-François d'Assise and the Museum of the Archaeological and Art History Institute in which sculpture from the 12th to the 18th c. is displayed. Around the centre are grouped the residential buildings of the parts of the town called Bruyères, Hocaille, Lauzelle and Biéreau; to the east towards the motorway lie the science park and the large buildings of the cyclotron. Relaxation from studies can be enjoyed in the provincial estate the "Bois des Rêves".

★Townscape

5 km (3 mi.) west lies Céroux-Mousty where in May a festival of hot air ballooning is held, attracting many visitors.

Céroux-Mousty

In the township of Rixensart, 8 km (5 mi.) north-west, the pretty red brick Château de Mérode was built between 1631 and 1632. It is square with four corner towers and many windows and is open to the public. It is impressive because of its tasteful furnishings which include Gobelin tapestries, Louis XV pieces, pictures (including some by Nattier and Tischbein) as well as a collection of weapons which the French mathematician Monge brought back from Napoleon's Egyptian campaign. (Open Easter–Oct. Sat., Sun. and public holidays 2–6pm; Jul. Tue.–Sun. 2–6pm.)

Rixensart

A little outside Rixensart lies the Lac de Genval which is a favourite rendezvous at weekends for the people of nearby Brussels; the original water and fountain museum is one of the attractions here.

Lac de Genval

291

La Hulpe A little further to the west of Rixensart lies La Hulpe where the Belgian paper industry had its beginnings. Today it is an elegant residential quarter of Brussels with eight little châteaux. A walk in the Domaine Solvay, named after the industrial family, who in the 19th c. owned the château in the middle of the park, is well worth while. Today the château is a culture centre.

Wavre Wavre, 6 km (4 mi.) to the north, has three attractions: the unusual open-air museum of living water plants in the suburb of Limal, with over 800 species of plants (open Apr.–Oct. daily 10am–5pm); the Walibi Adventure Park and the Aqualibi aquapark (see Practical Information, Leisure Parks).

La Louvière (ship lift)

See Binche, Surroundings

Maaseik H 4

Province: Brabant
Altitude: 70 m (230 ft) Population: 21,000

In the extreme north-east of Belgium right on the frontier with the Netherlands lies Maaseik, the birthplace of the Flemish painters Hubert and Jan van Eyck. There was a monastery here as early as the 8th c. around which arose a village which was later destroyed; a new village grew up around the castle, built in the 11th c., and from this developed Maaseik. Thanks to its favourable position on the Meuse the town had some importance as a commercial centre, but after the separation of Belgium from the Netherlands Maaseik became remote. However, the town has always been interesting because of its many examples of the Renaissance architecture of the Meuse area.

★Grote Markt The extensive Grote Markt with its four fountains, a double row of lime trees and in the middle a monument to the van Eyck brothers, is surrounded by a number of examples of this architecture of which the houses "Stad Amsterdam" (1686) and "Drie Lelieën" (1715) are the finest. In the Town Hall of 1827 is the only copy of the "Lamb of God" by the brothers van Eyck 1923 and also a collection of church-tower cockerels.

Bosstraat Along Bosstraat are other examples of Mosan Renaissance architecture, including the brick built house "Verkeerde Wereld" (No. 7), the half-timbered house No. 17 dating from 1600, No. 19 dating from 1620 and the "Stenenhuis" or "Drossaardhuis" (an official house; No. 21).

Museactron At No. 5 Lekkerstraat, in the very fine building of 1704 and also in a new building are housed three museums under the futuristic name of Museactron. They are the Apothecaries' Museum with the oldest apothecary's shop in Belgium (17th c.), the regional Archaeological Museum with historic and Roman exhibits, an impressive ivory collection and many different examples of handwork, a herb garden, and finally in the cellar can be found a bakery museum with an old bakery (open Apr.–Sep. Tue.–Sun. 10am–5pm; Oct.–Mar. 10am–noon and 2–5pm.)

Sint-Catharinakerk The 19th c. Sint-Catharinakerk has little of architectural merit, but possesses an extraordinary treasury, the masterpiece of which is the "Codex Eyckensis" – a gospel dating from the 8th c. (the Gospel of St

Harlinde), which is the oldest book in Belgium – as well as a satin reliquary of the 10th c.

An exhibition in the monastery of the Minderbroeders is devoted to the works of the artist brothers Jan and Hubert van Eyck. A model of the town is also exhibited here.

Minderbroeders-klooster

Sint-Annakerk in the north-west suburb of Aldeneik goes back to a former 8th c. monastic church. The present building is a pillared basilica of the 12th c. which has Merovingian stone sarcophagi, among which beneath the altar are those of the saints Harlinde and Relinde who founded the monastery.

Sint-Annakerk

Bree is situated 16 km (10 mi.) from Maaseik on the Willems Vaart canal. The little town belonged for a long time to the bishopric of Liège. Of interest are the five-aisled Sint-Michielskerk, the fine tombstones and especially a 15th c. calvary and a 16th c. burial group. The Stadhuis of 1754 also houses a local museum.

Bree

Bocholt, 4 km (2½ mi.) north of Bree, has a 15th c. church with an interesting interior; of special note is a Christophorus statue of the 15th c. The Goolderheide Leisure Park with a camping site has an open-air swimming pool with water-chutes.

Bocholt

Maas Valley

See Vallée de la Meuse

Malmédy · Malmedy   K 17

Province: Liège
Altitude: 330 m (1083 ft). Population: 7000

The little town of Malmédy (Latin "malmundarium" = cleansed from evil ones) is in the province of Liège at the confluence of the Warche and Warchenne on the southern slope of the thickly wooded and scenically very charming Hohe Venn. About 90 per cent of the inhabitants are Walloons who speak French or the local Walloon dialect; about 10 per cent are German speakers. The varied history of Malmédy has for a long time led to economic disadvantage of the area. This could only be improved after the Second World War. Several new industries arose so that today canneries, a paper factory, and a dairy are the most important industrial concerns of Malmédy. The well-tended town and the wooded surroundings have also contributed to the prosperity of the place and tourism is now an important economic factor.

History For a long time Malmédy was a source of dispute between France, the Netherlands and the German kingdom, and has changed its national allegiance several times in the last 200 years. The town developed from an abbey founded in 648 by St Remaclus, the Bishop of Maastricht, and from the ecclesiastical town of Malmédy-Stavelot. Malmédy lived in constant rivalry with neighbouring Stavelot (see entry) for pre-eminence in this independent and self-governing principality. In 1690 French troops almost completely destroyed the town and in 1795 it was incorporated into France. After the defeat of Napoleon I it was annexed in 1815 to Prussia and not until 1925 did it become Belgian. In 1940 the town was occupied by German troops and in 1944 was attacked in error by US bombers when parts were destroyed, although it had by then been occupied by American forces.

Carnival "Cwarmê" (carnival) is renowned. For four riotous days known as "Grandes Haguètes" there are large processions and traditional figures, such as the "Haguètes" and the "Sotà", appear (see page 87).

Houses with slate facing

The townscape of Malmédy is characterised by houses with slates decorating their fronts. The slates are so arranged that on close inspection patterns and even inscriptions can be discerned. There are good examples in the street called Rue devant les Religieuses, in the Rue de la Tannerie and in the Place de la Fraternité.

Maisons de Cavens

The centre of Malmédy is the Place de Rome. The most important building in the square is the Maisons de Cavens erected in 1830 as an orphanage. Today it houses the tourist office, the national paper museum (Musée National du Papier) and the carnival museum (Musée du Cwarmê; both museums open Tue.–Sun. 2–5pm).

Cathédrale Saints-Pierre, Paul et Quirin

In the Place du Châtelet, not far east from the Place du Rome, rise the plain towers of the Cathedral of Saints-Pierre, Paul et Quirin. It was built between 1775 and 1784 as an abbey church and in 1921, when Malmédy became a bishopric (until 1925), it was raised to the status of a cathedral. The quite simple interior, designed by the architect Galhausen, has 18th c. choir stalls, a "Virgin with Child" ascribed to Delcour, and the reliquary of St Quirinus as well as a silver reliquary bust of St Gereon and his companion (18th c.).

The **abbey** gardens and the abbey buildings (now a grammar school and law courts) adjoin the cathedral.

To the south of the cathedral in the Ruelle des Capucins can be found the **êglise des Capucins** (Capuchin church) dedicated in 1631; the interior mostly dates from the 17th and 18th centuries.

Pouhon des Iles

The Pouhon des Iles in the north-west on the far side of the Warche is a mineral spring rich in iron. On the bridge over the Warche which leads to the spring stands the oldest chapel in Malmédy, dedicated in 1544.

Walks

Malmédy is surrounded by beautiful woods and is an excellent place for invigorating walks. Almost adjoining the town lies the German-Belgium Nature Park (see entry) with its centre at Botrange. A short walk in the direction of Stavelot leads to the Rocher de Falize, an impressive rock pinnacle towering up over the Warche.

Bütgenbach

15 km (9½ mi.) east of Malmédy lies the village of Bütgenbach once part of the dukedom of Limburg and the property of the Herren von Valkenburg. The fortress and the castle were destroyed in 1689 by the French; still to be seen is a fine estate which dates from the 18th c.

Barrage In 1932 near Bütgenbach the Warche was dammed by a 23 m (75 ft)–high wall and turned into a lake of 120 ha (297 acres) containing 11 million cu.m of water (approx. 14 million cu.yd). Since the completion of the leisure centre of Worriken in 1979 the reservoir annually attracts numerous proponents of water sports and campers. The power station produces 2 million kwh of electricity.

Robertville

Robertville, 10 km (6 mi.) north-east of Malmédy, is another popular holiday and leisure centre thanks to its reservoir, the Lac de Robertville, its close proximity to the German-Belgium Nature Park as well as to the skiing district of Ovifat. The lake which has an area of 63 ha (156 acres) contains 8 million cu.m of water (approx. 10 million cu.yd) was dammed between 1925 and 1919 by a wall 54 m (177 ft) high and 120 m (394 ft) long; it provides electricity and water for Malmédy. Less than a kilometre from the reservoir rises the mighty and picturesque **Burg Reinhardstein**,

Winter around Burg Reinhardstein

surrounded by a park in the valley of the Warche into which a waterfall plunges down 50 m (164 ft). The castle was built in 1354 for Wenzel von Luxemburg and was for a long time owned by the dukes of Nassau until it came into the ownership of the ancestor of the Austrian statesman Klemens Wenzel, Prince of Metternich, through the marriage of Anna von Naussau with William von Metternich. In the 19th c. the castle fell into disrepair but was restored from 1969 according to the old plans.

The interior of the castle is open to the public; the first room to be seen is the Knight's Hall in which there is a remarkable collection of weapons; in the castle chapel are religious works of art dating from the 14th to the 18th c. (open mid Jun.–mid Sep. Sun. and public holidays 2.15–5.15pm; Jul. and Aug. also Tue., Thu. and Sat. 3.30pm).

Saint-Vith

Right on the German border, 22 km (14 mi.) south of Malmédy, lies Saint-Vith (Sankt Vith). Founded in the 12th c., it was Prussian from 1815 to 1919 and almost completely destroyed in 1944 by an Allied bombing attack. The only remnant of the old buildings is the Büchelturn dating from 1350. The local museum in the Heckingstrasse has exhibits about the history and character of the countryside "between the Venn and Schneifel".

Burg Reuland

Another 12 km (7½ mi.) south from Sankt Vith is Burg Reuland; it owes its name to the castle from which the surrounding territory was controlled during the Middle Ages. The Paul-Gerardy Museum documents the life of this 19th c. author and painter.

Mechelen · Malines   E 10

Province: Antwerp

Altitude: 7 m (23 ft) Population: 75,800
Intercity and Inter-regional Station

The impressive town of Mechelen (French Malines) is situated between Brussels and Antwerp on the Dijle which here is still tidal. Since the 16th c. it has been the spiritual capital of the region as the seat of the Archbishop Primas (in common with Brussels) as well as the headquarters of an archipiscopal seminar; it has the only carillon school in the world. Industry includes furniture and canning factories, a brewery, a railway workshop as well as many factories founded within the framework of the European Union by the countries of the Community. The products of lace, carpet and woollen concerns enjoy an excellent reputation. In addition Mechelen is a centre of market gardening (asparagus, peas, etc.).

History There was a settlement on the right bank of the Dijle as early as the 6th c. BC In the 8th c. an Irishman named Rombout brought Christianity to Mechelen, which in the Middle Ages was called Machlina (Latin Mechlinia). In 915 it belonged to the bishopric of Liège and from 1213, thanks to its favourable situation from the point of view of communications, it gained almost complete independence. Bishop Adolf van der Marck sold it in 1332 to the dukes of Flanders. From 1369 it belonged to Burgundy and in 1473 it became the seat of the Great Council, the highest court in the Netherlands. After the death of Charles the Bold his widow Margarete of York chose Mechelen as her residence. From 1507 to 1530 Mechelen was ruled as Stadholder by Margarete of Austria, the aunt of Charles V. The town blossomed as a residence and many scientists and artists, such as Eramus of Rotterdam and Albrecht Dürer, came to stay for a time. After Margarete's successor Maria of Hungary moved her seat in 1546 to Brussels, Mechelen was compensated by the gift of the archbishopric with primacy over the whole of the Netherlands. The first archbishop was Antoine Perrenot de Granville, the confessor of Charles V and Philipp II. At this time lace, carpets and particularly gilded leather tapestry were especially prized. The War of Independence in the Netherlands brought destruction, yet the town flourished again in the Baroque era. In 1835 the first railway on the European continent ran from Mechelen to Brussels. Damage done in the First and Second World Wars has long been made good.

★★Grote Markt

Near the centre of the old town, which was laid out in an almost circular manner with broad boulevards replacing the former surrounding ramparts, and which has in some respects well preserved its medieval appearance, lies the Grote Markt. Here can still be seen some fine gabled houses of the 16th to 18th c. and in the centre the statue of Margarete of Austria. In the pavement around the monument the sizes of the dials of Sint-Rombouts Cathedral have been introduced.

The south-east of the market is occupied by the **Stadhuis** which consists of two parts. On the right is the Lakenhalle (cloth hall), built in 1320–26 according to the models of the halls of Bruges and renewed after a fire in 1342. The central building is flanked by two turrets and over the Gothic doorway is the base of a belltower which, however, was never completed. The left part of the building was presented by Charles V to the seat of the Great Council and designed by Rombout Kelderman in 1529. In his time the building remained incomplete and was only finished in the 20th century.

The **Schepenhuis** on the southern edge of the market was erected in 1374 and until 1618 was the seat of the Great Council. Today it is the municipal library and archive.

On the north-east side of the square stands the **Postgebouw** (post office)

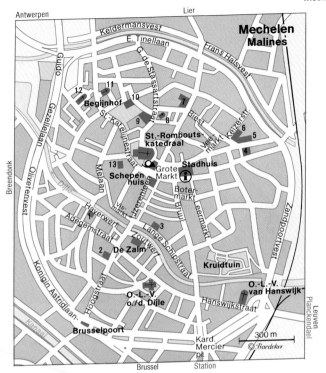

1 Paradijs, Duivelshuis
  St-Josefhuis
2 Klokkengietersmuseum
  (bell-foundry museum)
3 Horlogerie en -klokkenmuseum
  (clock and bell museum)
4 Gerechtshof (Palais van
  Margareta van Ostenrijk)

5 Palais van
  Margareta van York
6 St-Pieter en Pauluskerk
7 Hof van Busleyden
  (museum)
  and Beiaardschool
  (carillon school)
8 St-Janskerk

9 Refugie van de Abdij
  van Sint-Truiden
  (refuge)
10 Refugie van de Abdij
   van Tongerlo
11 St-Katelijnekerk
12 Begijnhofkerk
13 E. Wynants Museum

which was once the town hall (14th/18th c.) and has a restored Gothic façade.

Behind the post office rises the metropolitan Sint-Rombouts Cathedral, begun in the 13th c. and completed as far as the choir in 1342 when a fire broke out. In 1375 reconstruction was finished. The beginning of the building of the **clock tower** was made in 1452 which was intended to be 167 m (580 ft) and the highest tower in Christendom. However, when William of Orange required building material for the fortress of Willemstad in 1546, work was stopped and never again restarted. However, the form of the tower which is only 97 m (318 ft) high is imposing on account of its clear vertical lines and Gothic decoration. The dials of the tower clock (1708) have a diameter of 13.7 m (45 ft). There are two carillons each with 49 bells, one dating from the 17th c., the other from 1981 and altogether weighing 17 tonnes. They are played in summer on Mondays from 8.30pm.

★ Sint-Rombouts
Cathedral

The Stadhuis of Mechelen

The **interior** of this spacious church has important works of art, including statues of the Apostles dating from 1774 on the pillars of the nave and the grave of Cardinal Mercier (1851–1926), who opposed German occupation forces in the First World War, which can be seen in the left aisle near the Lady Chapel. In the Chapel of the Sacrament at the base of the tower is a communion bench by Artus Quellin the Younger and in the second chapel on the left weapons of the Knights of the Golden Fleece who in 1491 maintained a chapter of their order in Sint-Rombouts. In the transepts are several pictures dating from the 15th–16th c. including, on the right, the remarkable painting "Christ on the Cross" by Anton van Dyck (1627). The Baroque high altar (1665) of white marble was created by Luc Fayd'herbe, a citizen of Mechelen. In the choir ambulatory are four Baroque tombs of archbishops, including von Granville, and pictures from the life of St Rombout.

There is a small **archaeological museum** in the churchyard open from Easter to October at weekends.

E-Wynants
Museum

Not far from Sint-Rombouts can be found E-Wynants Museum dedicated to the works of this Mechelen sculptor. (Open Apr.–Sep. Sat., Sun. and public holidays 10am–noon and 2–5pm; in Jul. also on Mon.)

Sint-Katelijnekerk

Sint-Katelijnestraat leads from the cathedral to the Gothic Sint-Katelijnekerk north-west of the market. This church, which was created in the style of the Scheldt and Dender Gothic mainly between the 13th and 15th c., has a Joseph altar by Fayd'herbe and Baroque choirstalls.

Begijnhof

Sint-Katelijnekerk is situated between the Smaller and the Greater Béguinages. The Greater Béguinage was set up in 1350 and the present houses along the narrow streets date from the 16th and 18th c. In the

Baroque Béguinage church (1629–47) can be seen pictures by De Crayer, the Baroque high altar by Jan van der Steen (17th c.) and two statues by Fayd'herbe.

To the east of the Smaller Béguinage we pass the Refuge of the Abbey of Tongerlo and shortly afterwards on the right come to the Refuge of the Abbey of Sint-Truiden. Just to the right of the Wool Market there is the most secluded little square in the town, from which there is an attractive view of the buildings of the refuges on the edge of a little canal.

Refuges

Just right of the Refuge of Sint-Truiden stands the Gothic Sint-Janskerk (15th c.) which also houses notable works of art. Among these pride of place goes to a winged altar by Rubens ("The Adoration of the Kings") painted in 1617–19, one of his most beautiful works and for which his wife Isabella Brant sat as the model for the Virgin Mary. Also of note are various woodcarvings by Theodoor Verhaegen (17th c.) on the pulpit, in the choir and on the pews in the transepts, as well as a wall shrine for the Reliquary of St John by Fayd'herbe.

Sint-Janskerk

Not far from the church we come to the Hof van Busleyden, an attractive Gothic brick building of 1507 with a flower-decked inner courtyard and a belfry. The buildings, which were renovated after the First World War, house the Town Museum of Mechelen. It is currently being renovated and will probably re-open in the year 2000. Part of the collections will then also be exhibited in the Schepenhuis and in the Brusselspoort. The little house in the corner is the carillon school.

Hof van Busleyden

The Biest road leading eastwards from the museum finishes at the Veemarkt. Here stands the Sint-Pieter-en-Pauluskerk the former monastic church of the Jesuits, who came to Mechelen at the beginning of the 17th c. and built their church between 1670 and 1677. The final portion of the façade was only added in the 18th c.

Sint-Pieter-en-Pauluskerk

To the right can be seen the Late-Gothic former palace of Margareta van York, the widow of Charles the Bold. It was erected in 1480 and later became the residence of Philip II and Charles V until 1516. It is now a theatre.

Paleis van Margareta van York

Opposite this palace extends a complex of buildings with a large arcaded courtyard which was once the Hof van Savoye, the palace of the Stadholder (governor) Margareta of Austria, then of the Cardinal de Granville. From 1616–1794 it was the seat of the Great Council and from 1796 onwards a Palace of Justice.
   Around the courtyard the oldest parts were built between 1503 and 1507 by Rombout Kelderman; the part along Keizerstraat was also the work of Kelderman and of Guyot de Beaugrant and is one of the earliest examples of Belgian Renaissance.

★Paleis van Margareta van Oostenrijk

Further east on the far side of the railway line, the Speelgoedmuseum (Nekkerspoelstraat 21) exhibits old and new toys and objects of folk-art (open Tue.–Sun. 2–5pm). On the arterial road to Leuven is a little regional railway museum (open third Sat. in the month 1–5pm).

Other museums

Behind the Schepenhuis extends the long **IJzerenleen Square**. Its name comes from the iron railings (1531–34) which flanked a canal, now filled in, which flowed into the Dijle between the three-arched Grootbrug (13th and 16th c.) and the middle bridge over the river. Just before the bridge there lies on the right the little idyllic Vismarkt; to the left is the Clock and Bell Museum (open Mon.–Sat. 10am–noon and 2–6pm).

Over the Dijle

On the left over the bridge stands the Huis de Zalm (the House of

★De Zalm

The Dijle at the Vismarkt

Salmon, No. 5), the former guildhouse of the fishmongers, with a beautiful Renaissance façade (1530–1534).

★Houses on the Haverwerf

To the right of the bridge by the Haverwerf on the corner of Kraanstraat, stand several houses with very fine façades partly made of wood. Particularly attractive are the so-called Paradies (16th c.) with the representation of Adam and Eve on the arch of the door and nearby on the left the Duivelshuis (a 16th c. timber house) and at No. 20 the Huis Sint-Josef (1669).

Brusselpoort

From the Dijle bridge we go straight ahead across the Korenmarkt (bell-foundry museum in Edwin-Michiels-Moeremanhuis; open Mon., Tue., Thu. 6–8pm, Fri. 2–8pm., Sat. 2–6pm) and through Hoogstraat to the twin-towered Brusselpoort (rebuilt in the 18th c.), the only one of the twelve medieval town gates still remaining.

Onze-Lieve-Vrouw over de Dijle

The foundation stone of the church Onze-Lieve-Vrouw over de Dijle, to the east of Hoogstraat, was laid in 1255; in its present form the church dates mainly from the 14th and 15th c. Inside the left side aisle can be seen Rubens painting "The Miraculous Draught of Fishes" which was a commission from the Fishmongers' Guild (1618–19).

Onze-Lieve-Vrouw van Hanswijk

Further east stands the Baroque basilica of Onze-Lieve-Vrouw van Hanswijk, designed by Luc Fayd'herbe between 1663 and 1678, who was also responsible for the large frescoes on the central dome. Inside the church a miracle-working statue of Mary, dated 986, is much venerated.

Kazerne Dossin

These barracks (153, de Stassartstraat) house a museum which commemorates the Jews, Sinti and political prisoners held here in a concentration camp established by the Germans (open: daily except Sat. 10am–5pm).

Technopolis, Flanders' first interactive centre of science and technology in Flanders, opened here in the autumn of 1999.

Technopolis

Surroundings

In 1956 the Royal Zoological Society of Antwerp bought the Planckendael estate which lies 5 km (3 mi.) south-east of Mechelen near the village of Muizen.

★**Dierenpark Planckendael**

Here the society wanted to set up a breeding station for endangered species for Antwerp Zoo (see entry). Now Planckendael has become a real zoo with over 1000 animals which live in open-air compounds in an attractive park. (Opening times Summer: daily 9am–6.30pm; Winter: daily 9am–5pm)

Only a short way south of Planckendael a typical Belgian recreation centre has arisen around two lakes.

Domein van Hofstade

To the south of the village of Willebroek, 12 km (7½ mi.) from Mechelen, stands Fort Breendonk (Opening times Apr.–Sep. daily 9 am–5pm; Oct.–Mar. daily 10am–6pm), the name of which many Belgians associate with the terror of the German occupation in the Second World War. The fort was built between 1906 and 1914 and was the last defensive position of Antwerp to surrender in October 1914. In the Second World War, when the German army moved in, the SS set up a concentration camp here which up to 1944 held about 4000 prisoners of war, of whom 370 died or were executed. An impressive tour of the fort leads first to the cells and torture chambers and is accompanied by recorded evidence from former detainees. Of the working areas it should be remembered that the walls of the fort were first blown up and the debris then shovelled away by the prisoners. In the former printing press ("Studio") a film is shown about the history of the camp, and this is complemented by the museum in the Saal Jacques Ochs where can be seen drawings by this Belgian painter who was incarcerated in Fort Breendonk from 1941–42.

★**Fort Breendonk**

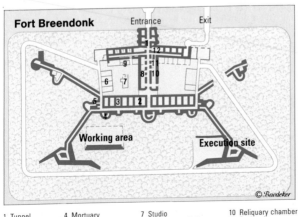

1 Tunnel	4 Mortuary	7 Studio
2 Cells	5 Torture chamber	8 Sal Jacques Ochs
3 Dormitories	6 Barracks	9 Museum

10 Reliquary chamber
11 Dark cells
12 Meditation room

Modave (castle)

See Huy, Surroundings

Mons · Bergen   J/K 7

Province: Hainaut
Altitude: 29–105 m (95–345 ft). Population: 91,600
Intercity and Inter-regional Station

Mons (Flemish Bergen) stands on a ridge between the two rivers Haine and Trouille and owes its name to this situation. It is the administrative seat of the province as well as a commercial and supply centre of the Borinage, one of the largest mining and industrial regions of Belgium. Mons is also an important junction on the railway between Brussels and Paris, and has considerable cultural and scientific institutions including the University Centre, founded in 1965, the Royal Music Conservatory, an academy of fine arts, a mining academy and a research institute for nuclear technology. There are also a number of interesting museums and several large libraries.

Industry plays only a minor role in the economic life of Mons. There are factories producing textiles and leather goods and some smaller pharmaceutical and metal-working concerns. In the inland harbour of the town, which is linked with the Scheldt and the Charleroi–Brussels canal by a branch canal, the principal traffic is coal from the Borinage.

History Mons owes its origin to a castle first mentioned in 642 and to the monastery founded a little later by the patroness of the town, St Waltrud (French Waudru). At this time it was called "Castri Locus" and kept this name until the 12th c. when the first town wall was built. After a period of great prosperity in the 13th–15th c. – in 1295 Mons became the capital of the county of Hennegau – the town suffered considerably in the wars of the 17th and 18th c. From the end of the 17th c. it came in succession under the domination of France, Spain and Austria and endured several sieges including one in 1691 by 80,000 French under Louis XV who, after his victory, gave Mons its present-day aspect. In nearby Jemappes the French revolutionaries beat the Austrians in 1792 and once more gained domination over the country. During both World Wars the town was on many occasions the target for heavy bombing attacks which caused great destruction. It was the first large Belgian town to be freed by the Allies in 1944.

The best known citizen of the town is the composer Orlando di Lasso (1532–94), who became director of music in the court of Munich.

Le "Lumeçon" On the Sunday after Whitsun this strange festival takes place in Mons; it has its origins in a processional game which dates from the end of the 14th c. and which is associated with St George. The participants are St George in the uniform of a cuirassier and a dragon called "Doudou", ten so-called "Chinchins" who carry St George, as well as eight "devils", seven "wild men" and twelve "white men". They all form up in a procession which punctually at 12.30pm leaves the Collégiale Ste-Waudru for the Grand-Place to the sounds of the "doudou" folk song. The dragon, over 9 m (30 ft) long, is carried by the "white men" and moves its tail over the spectators with the help of the "wild men". The fight between St George and the dragon begins when they reach the Grand-Place and the "Chinchins" also fight each other. Finally the saint is declared the winner by two pistol shots and the "Chinchins" drag the "dead" dragon into the courtyard of the city hall.

On the morning of the same day there is also a procession of the "Car

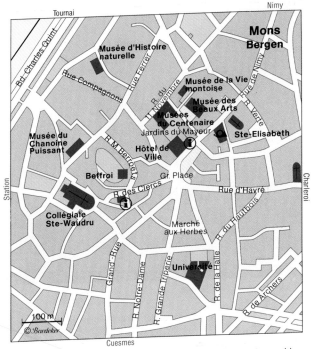

Tournai

Nimy

**Mons
Bergen**

Bd. Charles Quint

Musée d'Histoire
naturelle

Rue Compagnons

Rue Ferrer

Rue du 11 Novembre

Rue de Nimy

R. Verte

Musée de la Vie
montoise

Musée des
Beaux Arts

Musées
du Centenaire

Jardins du Mayeur

Ste-Elisabeth

Musée du
Chanoine
Puissant

R. M. Berliots

Hôtel de
Ville

Beffroi

Gr. Place

Station

Collégiale
Ste-Waudru

R. des Clercs

Rue d'Havre

Charleroi

Grand-Rue

R. Notre-Dame

R. Grande Triperie

Marché
aux Herbes

R. du Hautbois

R. de la Halle

Université

R. de Archers

100 m

© Baedeker

Cuesmes

d'Or" when the relics of St Waltrud are taken in procession in a golden
coach.

In the centre of the town which is surrounded by a ring of wide boulevards is the Grand-Place. On the west side, where it is still flanked by
some old houses, stands the impressive Hôtel de Ville, the façade of
which was designed by Mattheus de Layens in 1458; the rest of the
buildings which are grouped around the courtyard date from the 15th to
18th centuries. The City Hall is framed by the "Toison d'Or" house (1615)
and the Chapel of St George (1604). To the left of the main entrance can
be seen a bronze sculpture of a monkey with a polished head – stroking
it is said to bring good fortune. Among the rooms of the City Hall (which
can be seen on application at the door) should be mentioned the Salle
des Commissions with Brussels tapestries of 1707, the Salle des
Mariages with old wooden panelling, the Gothic Salle des Sacquiaux, so
called because every evening the keys of the town are placed in a leather
purse and guarded, as well as the Neo-Gothic Cabinet du Bourgmestre.

Hôtel de Ville

Through the courtyard of the City Hall can be found the Jardins du
Mayeur, the Burgomaster's garden which has a fountain representing a
street urchin of Mons. On the left is the Conciergerie, the old civic prison
of 1512 with a torture chamber.

*Jardins du
Mayeur*

The landmark of Mons is the bell tower (French Beffroi) which stands on
the former castle hill above the town. The 87 m (285 ft) high tower built
in 1661 is the only purely Baroque belfry in Belgium and contains a car-

★Beffroi

303

The Belfry, landmark of Mons

illon of 47 bells. From the observation platform there is an extensive view over the Hennegau; plaques explain the battle scenes of the First and Second World Wars.

There are only a few remains of the old feudal castle, but the Romanesque Chapel of Saint-Calixte (11th c.) with a few frescoes of this time is better preserved.

★Collégiale
Sainte-Waudru

The Collegiate Church of Sainte-Waudru below the castle hill was built in 1450 to plans by Mattheus de Layens. The building was several times interrupted, but in spite of this the church reveals a remarkable unity of style in Brabant Gothic. The oldest part is the choir of four bays (1450–1502); the transepts date from 1535–37 and the three-aisled nave with its bays was built between 1529 and 1589. A tower was also planned which was to be 187 m (614 ft) high, but building was suspended in 1689 and consequently the roof of the nave is not over-powered. Altogether there are 29 chapels around this fine church.

The first thing to strike the visitor in the **interior**, which is 115 m (377 ft) long, 32 m (105 ft) wide and 24 m (79 ft) high, are the pillars of the central nave which reach up into the vault of the roof without any capitals. Near the main door on the left stands the "Car d'Or", a processional carriage built in 1780 for the shrine of St Waltrude. The shrine can be found near the High Altar and was constructed in 1887 of gilded copper. It holds the body of the saint who died in 682 and was sewn up in a skin of a stag. Her head is kept in one of the chapels in a casket. At various points in the church (transept, choir, chapels 11, 14, 20, 24 and 28) are distributed the remains (reliefs and statues) of the choir screen which were made by Jacques Dubroecq of Mons between 1535 and 1548. This is one of the most important of Renaissance works in Belgium with a strong Italian influence. It was destroyed in 1792 by the French. Many other sculptures by the same artist include those in the right aisle (chapel 6) of "Christ on the Cross", an Annunciation group made of alabaster in the transept, in the choir ambulatory (chapel 12) an altar, and eight fine statues in the choir. Of note also are the ancient windows in the choir and transepts (16th c.) and in the nave (17th c.), as well as the considerable number of wall hangings.

In the **Treasury** can be seen a number of valuable reliquaries including that of St Vincent by the school of Hugo d'Oignies (13th c.), as well as gold and silver work from Mons and district. A 15th c. book of hours has some fine miniature paintings.

Mons has several interesting **museums** most of which can be found near the City Hall. Unless otherwise indicated they have the same opening times: Tue.–Sat. noon–6pm, Sun. 10am–noon and 2–6pm.

The Jardins du Mayeur which adjoin the City Hall have at their end a former pawnshop which now contains the Musées du Centenaire (civic museums) housing three museums under one roof.

Musées du Centenaire

The **Musée de Guerre** (War Museum) occupies two storeys. On the ground floor the First World War is commemorated, especially the British regiments which near Mons on the August 23rd and 24th 1914 stopped the Germans who were proceeding in the direction of Paris. The museum on the third floor is dedicated to the Second World War and the liberation of Mons by American troops on September 2nd 1944.

The **Musée de Céramique** (Ceramic Museum) on the first floor has more than 3500 exhibits from all important European faience and porcelain manufactories such as Delft, Sèvres, Meissen, Ludwigsburg and local products from Mons and Nimy, dating from the 18th c. to the present day.

Almost 20,000 coins and medals from all epochs and countries fill the showcases of the **Musée de Numismatique** (Numismatic Museum) on the second floor.

The Archeological Museum deals with the history of the region, from the Stone Age up to the time of the Merovingians.

Musée Archéologique

Not far away from the Musées du Centenaire is the Musée des Beaux Arts where there is a collection of pictures primarily by French and Belgian artists from the 16th to 18th c., but there are no particularly fine works.

Musée des Beaux Arts

The Musée de la Vie montoise on the left of the Museum of Art is a very beautiful museum which in a very vivid way describes the life of the people in Mons. It is housed in the Maison Jean Lescarts, a convent building of 1632 and in three rooms exhibits everyday objects and objets d'art.

★Musée de la Vie Montoise

This museum is situated a little north of the Collégiale Ste-Waudru and is in two buildings: the so-called "Vieux Logis" a brick building of 1550, and the Chapelle Ste-Marguerite (13th c.). On display is the art collection of Canon Edmont Puissant, who made this over to the town in 1930, with pictures, furniture and other interior items as well as the canon's library which includes a Gutenberg bible.

Musée du Chanoine Puissant

The Natural History Museum is situated north-west of the City Hall in the Rue des Gaillers. Here can be seen numerous articles of geology, zoology, botany and other scientific disciplines (open Mon.–Fri. 8.30am–noon).

Musée d'Histoire Naturelle

Surroundings

Casteau

Casteau, 10 km (6 mi.) north-east of Mons, has a 13th c. church and the remains of a castle. The place is well known as the seat of the headquarters of NATO in Europe, SHAPE (Supreme Headquarters of the Allied Powers in Europe).

Mons · Bergen Belœil

See entry

Binche

See entry

Strépy Thieu

See Binche, Surroundings

Soignes · Zinnik

Soignes, 19 km (12 mi.) north-east of Mons, arose around an abbey founded in 650 by St Vincentius. Its heavy reliquary, weighing 250 kg (551 lb), is carried every Whitsun in a great procession through the town.

Collégiale Saint-Vincent The building of this massive church dedicated to St Vincent and in the style of Scheldt Romanesque was begun in 965 and completed in the 13th c. Both bays of the choir contain the oldest cross-ribbed vault in Belgium (believed 11th c.). The interior of the church with its two rows of arcades and its gallery is similar to that of the cathedral at Tounai (see entry). The most impressive items are undoubtedly the sculpture, the Renaissance choir screen made of marble and stucco, an interment scene in the ambulatory (15th c.), a "Nursing Virgin" (14th c.), and the Baroque choirstalls and pulpit. The great 19th c. shrine of the saint stands in the choir. In the Chapel of St Hubert in the south wall is kept the treasury.

The old cemetery, not far from the church, is a public park in which can be seen a Romanesque chapel which is now an archaeological museum.

Museums In the Culture House of Soignes is an apothecary museum and a photography museum.

La Borinage

To the south and south-west of Mons stretches the coalfield of the Borinage. In spite of the decline of Belgian mining, there are still winding towers and a workers' settlement to be seen amid the high slag heaps, the so-called "terils".

Cuesmes

Vincent van Gogh lived in Cuesmes, 3 km (2 mi.) south, as a worker-priest among the miners of the Borinage from the summer of 1879 to the autumn of 1880 before he finally turned to painting.

Van Gogh house On the edge of the forest stands a little mining cottage where he occupied a room; this is filled with documents and reproductions of his paintings (no originals; open: daily except Monday 10am–6pm).

Hornu

Hornu lies 10 km (6 mi.) to the west and is the oldest mining village of the Borinage. Here between 1814 and 1832 the industrialist Henri de Gorge put into operation his ideas, which were revolutionary for that time, for the unity of work and residence. The working complex of "Grand Hornu", now a protected monument, consisted of the mine, iron foundry, engineering offices, schools, a hospital, public squares, and 400 houses for workers. with an elliptical central square, around which were grouped the offices. Each worker's house had its own garden and even their local currency has been found. In 1829 there were 2500 people in "Grand Hornu"; consideration is being given to a new purpose for the settlement. (Open Mar.–Sep. Tue.–Sun. 10am–6pm; Oct.–Feb. only until 4pm.)

Right in the south-western tip of the Borinage lies the village of Roisin and nearby in a house by the rock "Caillou-qui-bique" the poet Emi. Verhaeren spent the last 15 years of his life. Mementoes of the poet can be seen in the house.

The finds in the "Camp à Cayaux", 6 km (3¾) mi. from Mons near Spiennes, which can be seen in the little museum, prove that coal was being dug in the Borinage as long ago as the Stone Age.

Namur · Namen J/K 12

Province: Namur
Altitude: 83 m (272 ft). Population: 103,000
Intercity and Inter-regional Station (bicycle rental at station)

Namur (Flemish Namen) is situated at the confluence of the Sambre and the Meuse and is the ideal base for visiting the picturesque Upper Meuse Valley. It is the capital of the province of the same name, the seat of a bishop, a university town and an important communications junction for railway, inland shipping and road transport. Industries include glass, porcelain, paper and steel factories which are principally located in the suburb of Jambes. Because of its strategic position Namur has had to suffer a number of sieges in the course of its history. During these large parts of the town were destroyed again and again, so that a coherent and attractive townscape no longer exists. However, the citadel is well worth a visit on account of its excellent museums.

History The hill on which stands the citadel of Namur was already of military importance in Roman times and was fortified at a very early date. Many historians presume that this was the seat of the Germanic Aduatuker, of whom Caesar speaks in the "Gallic Wars". Below the hill a settlement arose on the banks of the Sambre which from the 10th c. was the chief place of the county. This was seized by Burgundy in 1421 and in 1559 was raised to the status of a bishopric. From the 15th c. the history of Namur consists of a sequence of sieges and destruction in war. The most famous siege occurred in 1692 under Louis XIV and Vauban and ended with the entry of the French; in 1695, however, they had to give way to William III of Orange. In 1746 the French were once again in Namur but were driven out two years later by the Austrians, who for their part had to withdraw in 1792 in the face of the French revolutionaries who won back the city in the same year and two years later surrendered it to the Austrians. The latter were succeeded in 1816 by the Netherlanders who extended the citadel. In the Kingdom of Belgium the advance forts which had been erected in 1889–1902 were strong points of the Belgian line from the Meuse which, however, was taken in 1914 and again in 1940 by German troops.

Trips on the Meuse as far as Dinant (see entry) and on the Sambre are organised from Namur. The landing stage is on the Pointe de Grognon, the tongue of land at the estuary of the Sambre.

Inner City

If the Pointe de Grognon is chosen as a starting point for a walk of discovery around the inner city, the Sambre must first be crossed on the Pont de France and on the right will be seen the stately brick front of the former meat hall (1590). This now houses the Archaeological Museum which has a comprehensive collection of antiquities from the

★Musée
Archéologique

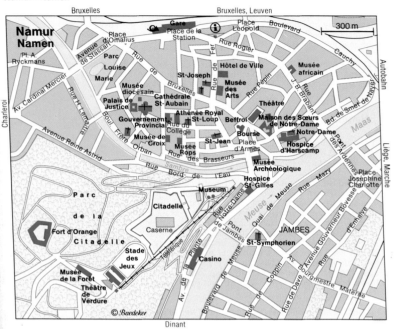

Namur
Namen

Province of Namur from Roman, Frankish, Merovingian periods (1st–7th c.); it is one of the best in Belgium. The goldsmith's work and glass work are valuable and unique. (Open daily except Fri. 10am–5pm.)

Bourse A short way from the museum is the Place d'Armes, the busiest square in the town, the north side of which includes the former exchange. To the rear rises the **Beffroi** (bell-tower), the foundations of which are a remnant of the Tour Saint-Jacques which was part of the second city wall in the 14th c.

Maisons des
Sœurs de Notre-
Dame

The road in front of the exchange leading to the right comes into the square in front of the theatre. On the right in the Rue J. Billart lies the former Convent of the Sisters of Notre-Dame, in which one of the finest ecclesiastical treasuries in the country is kept. It consists of the **treasure from the monastery of Oignies** which came into the possession of the convent in 1818; its finest pieces were the work of the goldsmith Pater Hugo von Oignies. Hugo lived in the 12th/13th c. in the monastery of Oignies, and his work is in the tradition of the great masters of the Meuse district, Renier and Godefroid de Huy and Nikolaus of Verdun. Characteristic of his work is the extremely delicate chasing with foliage and sometimes little hunting scenes. There are two magnificent pieces exhibited in Namur: a cover of a gospel of 1230 from Trier decorated with enamel work, and the goblet of Gilles de Walcourt of 1238. (Open Tue.-Sat. 10am–noon and 2–5pm, Sun. only 2–5pm.)

The Church of Notre-Dame belonging to the convent lies further east. This Baroque church, restored between 1750 and 1756, contains in the crypt the funerary monuments of Counts Wilhelm I and Wilhelm II of Namur (died 1391 and 1418).

Returning and passing the theatre we come to Rue E. Cuvelier which leads into the Rue de Fer where can be seen the fine patrician residence the Hitel de Gaiffier d'Hestroy dating from the 17th/18th c. It contains the Musée des Arts anciens du Namurois which exhibits artistic artefacts of the Middle Ages and the Renaissance from the region of Namur, especially goldsmiths' work, sculptures, copper utensils and ivory pieces. The department of painting contains four works by the painter Henri Bläs (1510-50) who came from Bouvignes on the Meuse. (Open daily except Mon. 10am-5pm; until 6pm Easter-Oct.)

★Musée des Arts anciens du Namurois

On the far side of the Rue du Bruxelles the Rue d'Angle and the Rue de Fer continue. From here there is a turn to the right to the Baroque Church of Saint-Loup, architecturally the most interesting church in Namur because of its stucco façade with 12 Doric pillars. Peter Huyssens designed the plans for the church which was built in 1621-45; the College of Jesuits which now serves as a grammar school is richly furnished.

★Saint-Loup

Straight ahead the Place Saint Aubain opens out with the seat of the provincial government on its right side; this is the white shining former bishops' palace. In the middle of the square rises the Cathedral of Saint Aubain, a stately Classical domed building dating from 1751-67 which was built by Gaetano Pizzoni from Milan on the site of a previous 11th c. church. Particular features of the spacious interior are statues from Florette Abbey by Lauarent Delvaux, a choir screen of 1744, and behind the high altar a memorial plaque to Don Juan of Austria. who died in 1578 near Namur and whose body was taken in 1579 to the Escorial near

Saint Aubain

Namur, where the Sambre joins the Meuse

The belfry

The moat and Saint-Aubain

Madrid. In the plaque a container was incorporated containing the heart of the victor of Lepanto.

Musée diocesain et trésor de la cathédrale

On the right near the choir of Saint Aubain is the Renaissance building of the Diocesan Museum with the cathedral treasury. On display are liturgical vessels, vestments, sculpture and goldsmiths' work. Of special note are a portable altar of the Counts of Namur (12th c.) with ivory decoration, a Merovingian reliquary (8th c.) from Andenne and the reliquary crown of Philip the Noble of Namur which, it is said, bears thorns from Christ's passion crown; it was a gift from Philip's brother Henry of Constantinople. (Open Easter–Oct. Tue.–Sat. 10am–noon and 2.30–6pm, Sun. and Nov.–Easter 2.30–6pm.)

★Musée de Croix

Going south from Saint-Aubain in the direction of the Sambre we come to the Musée de Croix. It is housed in the imposing town palace of the Groesbeck-Croix family which was built in the 18th c. in Louis XV style. In the interior the rooms are decorated in the fashion of the time, including hand-painted wallpaper, and contain magnificent objets d'art such as Chinese porcelain, paintings and sculptures. The kitchen, which has a huge chimney, is full of old household implements (guided tours daily except Tue. 10 and 11am, 2, 3 and 4pm).

Musée Felicien Rops

Leaving the museum we turn right into the Rue des Brasseurs and immediately into a narrow street to the Musée Felicien Rops. Rops (1833-98), who was born in Namur, worked as a illustrator of literary and political books which had a satirical element. He was notorious as his works consisted, in the opinion of many of his contemporaries, of pure pornography. A selection can be seen in the museum (open daily except Mon. 10am–5pm; Easter–Oct. until 6pm.).

To the north-east just outside the inner city is the Musée africain which exhibits artistic objects of art and everyday life from the former Belgium colony of the Congo. (Open Sun., Tue. and Thu. 2–5pm.)

Citadelle de Namur

History The citadel above the town, one of the mightiest fortresses of Europe can look back on a history of 2000 years. As early as Roman times the rocky outcrop between the Sambre and the Meuse was fortified, and the Counts of Namur chose this as the site for their castle. The extension of the citadel began in the 15th c. with subterranean defence passages which were completed in the 17th and 18th c. by Vauban and the Dutchman Coehoorn.

Access There are several ways of reaching the citadel hill: by cable-way (téléphérique; lower station not far from the Pont de France near the Rue Notre-Dame; Apr.–mid Sept. daily 10am–6pm; Sat. and Sun. only rest of year); by bus from the station; by car along the Route Merveilleuse behind the casino, over the steep bank of the Meuse or along the Route Panoramas through the citadel park; on foot on one of the paths along the bank of the Sambre also through the park. The entrance to the citadel is situated opposite the horseshoe-shaped stadium.

Tour Easter–May Sat., Sun. and public holidays 11am–5pm; Jun.–Sep. daily 11am–5pm; Oct.–Easter tour at 2.30pm Sun.

A fine tourist trail leads through the citadel complex and this includes the subterranean passages. From the barracks a light railway covers the major attractions; there is also a film about the history of the fortress. The citadel can be clearly divided into four sections. Nearest the entrance is the "ouvrage à cornes" (earthworks in the shape of horns) and the powder magazine built by the Dutch. The path leads down to the Dutch barracks (which can also be reached along the subterranean

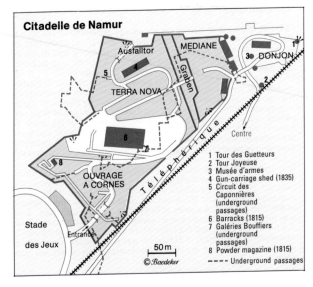

Citadelle de Namur

Ausfalltor
MEDIANE
DONJON
Graben
TERRA NOVA
Centre
OUVRAGE A CORNES
Téléphérique
Stade des Jeux
Entrance

50 m
© Baedeker

1 Tour des Guetteurs
2 Tour Joyeuse
3 Musée d'armes
4 Gun-carriage shed (1835)
5 Circuit des Caponnières (underground passages)
6 Barracks (1815)
7 Galéries Bouffiers (underground passages)
8 Powder magazine (1815)
---- Underground passages

"Galéries Boufflers"), the central point of the section called "terra nova", the "New Fortress" built by Vauban and Coehoorn.

Below the barracks the bridge, from which there is an impressive view of the town, leads across a deep ditch and links the "terra nova" with the section of the fortress called "Médiane" dating from the 16th c. From here the visitor can look down onto the bend of the Route Merveilleuse around the "donjon" (the site of the medieval castle). Only the detached Tour Joyeuse and two other towers (in one of which a military museum is housed) have remained from the fortress. A good view of the town can be enjoyed from a little platform near a halt on the way down from the citadel.

Parc de la Citadelle

From the top of the citadel hill extends the 65 ha (160 acres) wooded Parc de la Citadelle, a favourite rendezvous for the inhabitants of Namur at weekends. The attractions include the "Reine Fabiola" nature park and the Fort d'Orange, built in 1691 to protect the "terra nova". There are sports events in the stadium and performances in the open-air theatre. The **Musée de la Foràt** (forestry museum, open Apr.–Oct. daily except Fri. 9 am–noon and 2–5pm; closed first week in Oct.) is devoted to the flora and fauna of the Ardennes forest; its principal attraction is a very fine large diorama with animals of the forest and a comprehensive collection of insects.

Below the citadel on the left bank of the Meuse extends the oldest part of the town, of which, however, very little has remained. At the confluence of the Sambre and the Meuse, on a spit of land called Pointe de Grognon, stands an equestrian monument to King Albert (1955). To the right is the Hospice Saint-Gilles (16/17th c.) in the chapel of which can be seen the interesting tomb of the sculptor Colard Jacoris of 1395. Further downstream the Pont de Jambes (restored after war damage) links Namur with the suburb of Jambes. Still further to the south in the Avenue Baron de Moareau can be found the casino built in 1911 and the gardens called La Plante.

Surroundings

Floreffe

10 km (6 mi.) west of Namur lies the village of Floreffe where on a hill stands the great former Premonstratensian **abbey**, one of the best preserved examples of this order in Belgium. The abbey was founded in 1121 by St Norbert and extended in the 17th and 18th c. to its present size. The French Revolution put a stop to monastic life, but it is continued today in the form of a little seminar. Of the 90 m (295 ft) abbey church only the transepts and sacristy still remain from the initial phase; the interior was restored at the end of the 18th c. by Dewez. Of particular interest are the choirstalls by Peter Enderlin. There are 74 seats richly carved including some with effigies of the founders of the order. The brewery which served also as a mill dates from the 13th c. and from it the light and sweet monastery beer which is highly prized throughout Belgium can be obtained. The grottoes of Floreffe are also worth seeing.

Fosses-la-Ville

It is another 10 km (6 mi.) from Floreffe to Fosses-la-Ville which was already settled by the Celts and which in Roman times was called "Fossa". The Irish missionary Feuillen (or Follianus) founded a monastery here around 650 which was destroyed in the 10th c. However in the 11th c., when the relics of St Feuillen were brought here, a start was made with the building of a new church. Of this there remain only the tower, the choir and the crypt which is the oldest in Belgium. The remainder of the Church of St Feuillen was rebuilt in the 18th c. The oak choirstalls (1524) and the 16th c. reliquary of the saints are worth seeing.

Highly unusual is the **Musée "Le Petit Chapitre"** in which more than 850 handmade puppets are exhibited representing the various type of Belgian people (open: Jul. and Aug. daily 2-6pm; Sat. and Sun and holidays rest of year). Fosses-la-Ville is also well known for its **carnival**, in which the "Chinels" dance like marionettes, and for its military procession "Marche de Saint-Feuillen" which takes place every seven years (next in 2005).

Franc-Waret

Near Franc-Waret, 13 km (8 mi.) north-east, stands the imposing castle of the same name dating from the 17th c. but which was considerably extended in the 18th c. in the style of Louis XV. The buildings are grouped around an inner courtyard reached across a drawbridge. During the guided tour visitors see the priceless furnished rooms with beautiful Brussels tapestries, a porcelain collection and Dutch–Flemish paintings. Around the castle extend a 17th c. French garden and an 18th c. English garden (open Jun.–Sep. Sat., Sun. and public holidays 2–5.30pm).

Marche-les-Dames

2 km (1¼) mi. before reaching Franc-Waret we pass through Gelbressée where Juan of Austria set up his headquarters during the siege of Namur in 1578. A narrow road leads south from here to Marche-les-Dames on the Meuse where a Cistercian abbey was founded in the 13th c. It is possible to return to Namur on the road along the bank of the river from Marche-les-Dames. Shortly after leaving the village can be seen the 70 m (230 ft) high-rock, the Rocher du Roi Albert, or "Rocher Fatale", from which King Albert I fell to his death on February 17th 1934.

Caves of Goyet

About 10 km (6 mi.) east of Namur, south of the Maas, the life of prehistoric hunters is documented in the Caves of Goyet (open Mar.-Nov. daily 10am–5pm).

Nieuwpoort · Nieuport   D 2

Province: West Vlaanderen
Altitude: Sea level. Population: 9000

The town of Nieuwpoort (French Nieuport) lies on the IJzer 3 km (2 mi.) from where it flows into the North Sea. It is divided into Nieuwpoort Bad and Nieuwpoort Stad lying a little further inland, and is an important fishing port as well as the location of a fish processing industry. Other firms specialise in metalworking and chemicals which play an important part in the economy. The importance of tourism, which is concentrated in Nieuwpoort Bad, can be seen from the extensive yacht harbour (Nieuwpoort Europoort), one of the largest in the North Sea with a capacity of 2000 moorings.

History In the 12th c. when the IJzer had altered its course, Nieuwpoort was founded by Count Philip of Flanders as a fortified new harbour ("Nieuwpoort") for Ypres in place of Lombardsijde and in the course of time suffered seven sieges. In 1383 it was completely destroyed by the English. In July 1600 Mortiz of Orange defeated the Spanish on the dunes between Nieuwpoort and Middelkerke, but this victory was of minor importance in the War of Independence of the Netherlands. In the First World War Nieuwpoort formed the key to the position on the IJzer to which the Allied armies withdrew. On October 29th 1914 the sluices on the IJzer were opened and the polders were flooded in order to prevent the advance of the German troops. However that did not prevent Nieuwpoort being almost completely destroyed in 1918. After the war the town was rebuilt according to the old plans.

On the mole at Nieuwpoort

Boat excursions can be made on the Ijzer as far as Diksmuide and Veurne (see entries) and on the sea as far as Ostend (see entry) (weekends at 2pm; information tel. 232425). Deep-sea fishing is also on offer.

Grote Markt

Nieuwpoort Stad is a tranquil place and an attractive picture is presented by its extensive Grote Markt with its belfry, an old Renaissance house (rebuilt 1924; containing a small ornithological museum) and the corn hall, originally Late-Gothic of 1218 and rebuilt in 1923. The first storey of the hall houses the interesting K. R. Berquin Museum of History and Local History, in which can be seen among other things two views of Nieuwpoort which are attributed to Lancelot Blondeel.

Onze-Lieve-
Vrouwkerk

Behind the town hall stands the Onze-Lieve-Vrouwkerk which was destroyed in both World Wars but rebuilt in 1922 and 1946 in its original Gothic style. In the detached tower there is a carillon of 67 bells.

★IJzer sluices
see IJzermonding

Six canals, which are regulated by many sluices, join the IJzer in Nieuwpoort. These are situated a little north of the Grote Markt near the IJzer bridge and are an interesting sight.

Koning Albert I
Monument

Near the bridge a large equestrian statue was erected in honour of the Belgian King Albert I; it is surrounded by a rondel supported by 20 pillars. From the top of the monument there is good view over the town and its surroundings.

Fishing and yacht
harbour

In the fishing harbour on the Vismijnkaai the daily catch is still auctioned. A little to the north lie the basins of the yacht harbour.

IJzermonding
Nature Reserve

In the area of the IJzer estuary stretches the large Ijzermonding Nature Reserve (16 ha/40 acres). Here many aquatic birds and waders have their nests. The reserve can only be visited on a guided tour (July and August on Sundays at 10.30am).

The little village of Lombardsijde has no attractions apart from the figure of the Madonna which was found on the beach and is now in the village church. The village is interesting on account of its history. In the 5th c. there was a large Anglo-Saxon settlement here which grew in the 11th c. into an important town with a large harbour. Storm floods in 1116 and 1134 devastated the town almost completely and altered the course of the IJzer so that Lombardsijde was divided from Nieuwpoort.

Lombardsijde

Halfway towards Ostend (see entry) lies the quiet resort of Middelkerke which has a casino in addition to the leisure pursuits of water-sports, walking, riding and cycling.

Middelkerke

See Koksijde, Surroundings.

Oostduinkerke

Nivelles · Nijvel

H 9

Province: Brabant
Altitude: 99 m (325 ft.) Population: 22,000
Intercity and Inter-regional Station (bicycle rental at station)

Nivelles (Flemish Nijvel) lies in the middle of an extensive fertile landscape south of Brussels. Although during the heavy bombing in the Second World War a great part of the town and buildings fell in rubble and ashes, including historical treasures of incalculable worth, the town very quickly recovered. Developed from a former agricultural centre to a modern industrial town the most important branches of industry, in addition to metal processing (railway equipment works, machine tools), is the production of paper.

History The origins of the present town go right back to the early Christian centuries. Pippin the Elder, the chamberlain of the Merovingian king Dagobert I, owned considerable estates in this area. After his death his widow Itta and her daughter Gertrude moved here and founded a Benedictine convent around 650, the first convent on what is now Belgium territory. The first abbess was Gertrude, patroness of numerous medieval hospitals. She died in 659 and her grave soon became the object of pilgrimages around which the town developed. In the 11th c. the town had reached the height of its prosperity and this manifested itself in the building of the collegiate church. In the 12th c. Nivelles was surrounded by a wall 12 km (7½ mi.) in length; at the beginning of the 16th c. it developed into a prosperous town with 20,000 inhabitants and eight guilds. Decline set in in 1789 with the dissolution of the convent with which the history of the town had always been connected. In 1815 Nivelles was besieged by Dutch troops. During the First World War the town was spared, but a German bombing attack in May 1940 destroyed 50 per cent of the old town and 20 per cent of all the buildings.

Every year on the Sunday after St Michael's day a large **procession** attended by crowds of people takes place in honour of St Gertrude. The faithful, dressed in historical costumes, accompany the processional chariot which dates from the 15th c. and which is drawn by six horses carrying the reliquary of St Gertrude. During the 14 km (9 mi.) tour around the town two meal breaks are taken. In addition to the faithful the giants Argayon and Argayonne accompany the procession, as well as their son Lolo and his horse Godet.

★Collégiale
Sainte-Gertrude

The former Collégiale Sainte-Gertrude
(guided tours daily 2pm Sat. and Sun. also
3.30pm), a collegiate church dedicated in
1046 in the presence of the German
emperor Heinrich III and which dominates
the Grand-Place of Nivelles, is one of
the most sumptuous examples of
Romanesque architecture in Belgium. The
origin of the church, built in Ottoman
Romanesque style, was the monastic
Church of Saint-Pierre dating from about
650 and rebuilt in four phases until the
10th c. The last church was burnt down at
the beginning of the 11th c., and it was
resolved to erect a new one, but this was
badly damaged in the bombing attacks of
1940. The church treasury and two-thirds
of the sumptuous shrine of St Gertrude
were lost for ever. Rebuilding of the church
was only decided upon in 1984. Today the
Church of St Gertrude appears largely in
the form in which it was conceived in the

11th c. The special nature of its architecture lies in the plan of two
transepts and two choirs opposite one another. The huge west front with
its octagonal belfry and two 12th c. side doors is probably reminiscent
of its Ottonian predecessor. In the right-hand tower a copper figure of
Jean de Nivelles dating from the 15th c. strikes the hours with a
hammer. Of the sculptures on the door of the west front only a doorpost
with scenes of the legend of Sampson (north doorway) and the
Archangel Michael (south doorway) survive; the southern gable of the
east transept is also artistically interesting.

The **interior** of the church is impressive, mainly because of its size (102
m/335 ft long, 20 m/66 ft high) but as a result of losses during the war,
the simplicity of its decoration does not immediately strike the eye. Of
note are the Baroque oak and marble pulpit by Laurent Delvaux with rich
figurative decoration portraying the story of Jesus and the Samaritan, as
well as Renaissance choir stalls in the northern part of the east transept.
The famous shrine of St Gertrude, which was considered among the
most valuable works of the Gothic goldsmith's art, was largely
destroyed in a bombing attack of 1940. In the church can be seen a
replica by Félix Roulina and a Late-Gothic brass container for the
reliquary.

Above the choir at the west end of the church is the 19 m (62 ft)-high
Salle impériale, reached by a flight of 132 steps. It served the abbess for
official receptions.

The three-aisled **crypt**, c. 1100, is situated below the east choir. With an
area of 230 sq. m (2476 sq. ft) it is the largest in Belgium. From it the visitor can reach the excavations in which fragments of the predecessors
of the present-day church were found in 1941–52, as well as the grave of
Ermentrude (1001), the granddaughter of Hugo Capet, the first king of
France.

The beautiful **cloister** of the church is a transitional work of the beginning of the 13th c.; only the north gallery in its original condition dates
from this time. In the passages and in the courtyard gravestones and
parts of the old bells are displayed.

Fontaine du
Perron

At the junction of roads opposite the west front of the church can be
seen the Fontaine du Perron, a fountain donated by the abbot Adrienne

de Moerbeke in 1523 on which can be seen the effigy of the Archangel Michael (replica of 1922).

From the fountain we pass along the Rue Seutin to the Tour Simone the last remaining of the 12 towers of the medieval town fortifications.

Tour Simone

The Museum of Archaeology, Art and History (Musée d'Archéologie, d'Art et d'Histoire) is housed in the vine-clad former refuge of the Trinity Brothers of Orval dating from 1763 (27 Rue de Bruxelles).

Musée d'Archéologie, d'Art et d'Histoire

In ten rooms on two floors are art treasures saved from the Church of St Gertrude, including remains of the saints reliquary, Brussels wall-hangings, tombstones, sculptures, paintings, furniture and instruments of the 18th c., as well as finds from Gallo-Roman times. (Open Mon., Thu., Fri., Sat., Sun. 9.30am–noon and 2–5pm, Wed. 9am–5pm.)

The most important sacred building in Nivelles, apart from St Gertrude, is the Chapelle de Recollets in the Place de l'Abreuvoir, a beautiful Late-Gothic building in which the shrine of St Marie de Nivelles (Marie d'Ottignies) dating from the 17th c. is kept.

Chapelle de Recollets

In the Avenue de la Tour de Guet, which passes the Parc de la Dodaine, stands "La Tourette", an original 17th c. brick tower.

La Tourette

Surroundings

17 km (11 mi.) east of Nivelles lies Villers-la-Ville where the most impressive **ruins of the Cistercian abbey**, the largest monastic ruins in Belgium, can be visited. The complex, founded in 1146 by Bernhard von Clairvaux after the model of the mother house in Citeaux, arose princi-

Villers-la-Ville

Cloister of the Collégiale Sainte-Gertrude

Fontaine du Perron

pally in the 12th and 13th c. and during its history was laid waste on several occasions, but until the 18th c. was again and again restored. Finally the French revolutionary troops destroyed the building which was then used as a quarry and was even further plundered. In the middle of the 19th c. a railway viaduct crossed the area.

The visit to the abbey, which, apart from a few local variations was erected in the Classical style of the Cistercians, follows a signposted route. In the court of honour opposite the entrance is a 13th c. watermill, now used as a restaurant, which is surrounded by 18th c. buildings among which on the right stands the monastery palace. Grouped around the large cloister, built in the 14th c. and restored in the 16th, are the Chapter House, with the dormitory of the monks over it, and in the south a thermal room, refectory and a kitchen. On the west are the dormitories of the lay brothers. The restored gallery of the cloister is now a lapidarium; among the remains can be seen the grave of Gobert d'Aspermont who died in 1263. The 13th c. monastery church follows the French model with the exception of the semi-circular apse which in Cistercian churches is usually straight, and the round window in the roof. The best preserved of the working quarters is the large 13th c. brewery.

In the **parish church** of Villers-la-Ville are two magnificent altar pieces from Brussels' workshops; both portray scenes from the life of Mary; the lower one was made in 1450 and the upper in 1538.

Ophain-Bois-Seigneur-Isaac

Ophain-Bois-Seigneur-Isaac, 6 km (4 mi.) north of Brussels, has a charming group of monastic buildings dating from the 14th-16th c. In the monastery church, which has an altar sculpture by Laurent Delvaux, can be seen a reliquary of 1555 containing a piece of linen said to be stained with the blood of Christ. The other monastery buildings, including the cloister of 1613 and the imposing monastery farm, are also well worth seeing. Opposite the abbey the lords of Ittre built a prestigious castle in Louis XVI style.

Ruins of the Abbey of Villers-la-Ville

9 km (5½ mi.) south of Nivelles stands the three-winged castle of Seneffe also in the style of Louis XVI and surrounded by a very fine park.

See entry

See Ecausinnes

Seneffe

Ecausinnes

The sloping
lock of
Ronquières

Oostduinkerke

See Koksijde, Surroundings

Orval (Abbey)   P 14

Province: Luxembourg. Altitude: 280 m (919 ft)

Amid the quiet and picturesque forest of the Gaume, right on the French border, lies the most extensive and most beautiful monastery in Belgium, the Trappist abbey of Notre Dame d'Orval which has had a moving history. There is a legend about the name "Orval" (from the French "val d'or" = golden valley). It tells that Countess Mathilde of Chiny, Duchess of Lower Lorraine, was one day resting near a spring and lost her ring which fell into the water. Saddened she prayed in a nearby chapel and a miracle occurred: a trout brought the ring back to her at which she cried out "this place must really be a golden valley"; the Romans had already described it as such. The arms of the monastery depict this legend by showing a blue stream on which the trout rises with the ring in its mouth.

The monks run a flourishing farm and the monastery is famous for its beer and its cheese.

The first monastery in the "golden valley" is said to have been founded in 1070 by Benedictines from Calabria in southern Italy. They were followed in 1132 by Cistercians who began building the Church of Notre-Dame. After a fire in 1251 it was rebuilt in the 15th and 16th c. and was extended around the monastery buildings. However in 1637 soldiers of the French Marshall Châtillon set fire to the complex. The monks began again and the building was successfully restored. Around 1700 the Abbey of Orval, which had adopted in 1683 the strict observance of the Trappist order, was one of the most prosperous monasteries in Europe. The architect Benoît Dewez was instructed to plan new buildings which were consecrated in 1732. However, once again it was French soldiers, this time the revolutionary troops of General Loison, who destroyed the monastery in 1793, and in 1797 the grounds were finally sold. It was not until 1926 that a new beginning was made and this on the foundations of Dewez' building. Finally in 1948 the present new monastery, planned by Henri Vaes, conforming to the architectural practices of the Cistercians but with Romanesque and Gothic elements, could be consecrated.

History

The new monastery buildings can only be visited by previous arrangement and accompanied by a monk. From a little tower in the wall just behind the Court of Charity there is a fine view of the extensive complex. In the middle is the Court of Honour with a trapeze-shaped pond; from here a broad flight of steps leads up to the new monastery church, the

★New monastery
buildings

façade of which is dominated by a monumental 17 m (56 ft)-high statue of the Virgin Mary by Lode Vleeshouwers. Near the left aisle rises the 60 m (197 ft) high belfry. On enquiring at the door visitors can attend services (Mon.–Sat. 11am, Sun. 9.30am), Vespers (daily 5.40pm) and Compline (daily 7.30pm).

★Abbey ruins

Opening times Jun.–Sep. daily 9.30am–12.30pm and 1.30–6.30pm; Apr., May, Oct. daily 9.30am–12.30pm and 1.30–6pm; Nov.–Feb. daily 10.30am–12.30pm and 1.30–5.30pm.

Visit From the entrance to the abbey grounds the Court of Charity and the guesthouse can be seen. Visitors pass through the shop where souvenirs, beer, cheese and bread are sold, and arrive in the old reception house where an audio-visual show (in French and Dutch) gives information about the life of the monks. From the ruins looking left is an equipment barn which was once the studio of the lay brother Jean-Henri-Gilson (1741–1809) known as the painter-monk Abraham of Orval; many churches in the vicinity possess one of his paintings. Nearby is the Mathilde Fountain about which is woven the legend of the lost ring. Next can be seen the remains of the early Gothic monastery church; the parts which have survived are the walls and arches of the nave, the choir and the apse, as well as the transepts; the great rose window in the left transept and the slender window arches are striking. Also noteworthy are the Gothic and Romanesque capitals of the pillars. In the choir stands the replica of the tomb of Wenceslas, the first duke of Luxemburg who died in 1383. The monastery buildings adjoin the right side aisle and are entered by way of a flight of steps, at the foot of which the best known abbot of Orval, Bernard de Montgaillard, was buried in 1628. Remains of his grave inscription can be seen on a pillar. The extremely long room was the reading room in which 15,000 books were available;

The picturesque monastery ruins of Orval

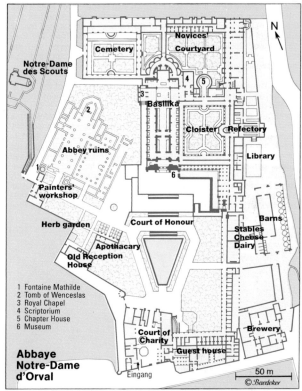

Abbaye Notre-Dame d'Orval

1 Fontaine Mathilde
2 Tomb of Wenceslas
3 Royal Chapel
4 Scriptorium
5 Chapter House
6 Museum

Notre-Dame des Scouts

Cemetery

Novices' Courtyard

Basilika

Cloister · Refectory

Library

Abbey ruins

Painters' workshop

Herb garden

Court of Honour

Barns

Stables Cheese Dairy

Apothacary

Old Reception House

Court of Charity

Brewery

Guest house

Eingang

50 m

© Baedeker

Florenville, Virton

from here we reach the arches of the ancient 18th c. vaulted cellar below the steps which now houses a museum on the history of the monastery. Returning to the entrance building a look should be taken at the herb garden and the old apothecary in which a museum of medicine has been set up.

Ostend · Oostende · Ostende   D 3

Province: West-Vlaanderen
Altitude: Sea level. Population: 69,000
Intercity Station (bicycle rental at station)

Ostend (Flemish Oostende, French Ostende) on the North Sea coast is the home of the largest high seas fishing fleet in Belgium and the location of three technical schools of fishing. It is the most important ocean and ferry harbour in the country and deals with a large part of the ferry traffic to Great Britain. In addition Ostend is the largest Belgium **seaside resort** and one of the most popular in Europe and can look back

321

on a fashionable past; since 1933 the town also is able to call itself a spa. Foreign trade is the lifeblood of Ostend, especially as fishing has suffered a decline, and the economy of the harbour is threatened by the building of the Channel Tunnel and with competition from the very modern port facilities of Zeebrugge (see entry). However, you are advised not to expect an elegant seaside resort; Ostend can hardly be considered attractive and is visited mainly by the mass tourism.

History The town was originally a village at the east end of the spit of land Ter Streep which has meanwhile silted up. It is first mentioned in 814 and received its charter in 1267. A new harbour was built in the 15th c. and new defences in 1583. At the end of the 16th c. Ostend was the last bastion of the Dutch in the southern Netherlands and was violently attacked by the Spaniards. The archduchess Isabella vowed in 1601 to change her shirt only if this bastion fell. One can only hope that she did not comply with her vow for the siege lasted three years and caused 72,000 deaths. In the following centuries the town had various masters, Spanish, French and Austrian until it finally became Belgian. Shortly after that the first British arrived for a seaside holiday and Ostend began to develop into an extensive seaside resort of the Belle Epoque. In 1834 Queen Victoria and later the Belgian rulers also visited it. In the First

"Strongholds for tourists" along Ostend beach

World War Ostend like Zeebrugge was a German U-boat base and suffered greatly from the effects of the conflict; the Second World War brought several bombardments during which almost all the important buildings were damaged. The flood of 1953 also caused considerable damage when the dyke between Ostend and Knokke-Heist (see entry) gave way.

Festivals The most celebrated festival in Ostend is the "Bal Rat Mort" ("Dead Rat Ball") which takes place during the carnival in early March. It was created by Ostend's greatest son, the painter James Ensor (1860–1949) and his friends who had seen it in Paris in the cabaret "Au Rat Mort" in Montmartre. In addition the carnival-like prawn and shrimp festival and the Blessing of the Sea in May attract many visitors.

Beaches and sports facilities Ostend has five bathing beaches with all facilities such as showers, cabins, deck-chairs, etc.: the small beach is known as "Klein Strand", the western beach or big beach is known as "Groot Strand", the beaches of Mariakerke and Raversijde west of the racecourse, and the beach to the east of the harbour. The facilities for sport are so comprehensive (including archery, sailing, riding) that almost every activity is catered for.

A good survey of beach activities can be had from Albert I promenade which is lined with restaurants and a few villas. Here is the **casino**, originally dating from 1745 and re-opened in 1953 after destruction in the Second World War. The first floor is decorated with frescoes by Paul Delvaux. The road continues on the 10 m (33 ft)-high and 30 m (98 ft)-wide Zeedijk which extends as far as the dunes near Westende, 15 km (9½ mi.). Here can be seen the royal residence, the spa complex and the Wellington racecourse.

★Beach promenade

323

Ostend · Oostende · Ostende

★Harbour

Two so-called sea landing stages (Flemish Staketsel) extend out for a long way into the sea to protect the entrance of the harbour. The western breakwater, 625 m (2052 ft) long, is popular as a viewpoint. The harbour installations include several large and small basins and extend 2 km (1¼ mi.) inland as far as the mouth of the Ostende–Brugge canal. The old fishing harbour is at Visserskaai. On the breakwater the – albeit rather modest – North Seas Aquarium can be visited. From the ferry terminal, where the first ferry to England left in 1846, ferries and jetfoils ply to Dover. In the yacht harbour the former training ship of the Belgian maritime marine the "Mercator" lies at anchor. This three-masted schooner is now a museum in which souvenirs of the 41 trips that the ship made are displayed (open Apr.–Jun. and Sep.–Nov. daily 10am–1pm and 2–6pm; Jul. and Aug. 9am–6pm; otherwise only at weekends).

The new fishing harbour is located on the far side of the harbour basin by the Visserijdok. In the fish hall (vismijn) every weekday except Thursdays the fish auction begins at 7am. From 9am prawns and shrimps are auctioned. To the east, on the far side of the harbour entrance and the fishing harbour, rises the 56 m (184 ft)-high Nieuwe Vuurtoren (new lighthouse). Further on stretch dunes with remains of defence works of both World Wars and the Fort Napoléon which dates from Napoleonic times. There are trips round the harbour and to sea on the "Franlis" (west mole) from 10.45am (Easter–May at weekends; Jun.–mid Sep. daily).

Feestpalais

In the centre of old Ostend on the Wapenplein stands the Feestpalais which was built in 1957 in place of the old town hall of 1711 destroyed in the Second World War. On the first floor is the local museum "De Plate" where a great deal of interesting material about the resort and the fishing at Ostend can be seen. On the second floor is the Museum of Fine Art which has a good collection of works by James Ensor, Constant Permeke and other Belgian artists (open daily except Tue. 10am–noon and 2–5pm).

James Ensorhuis

North of the Wapenplein in Vlaanderenstrat No. 27 James Ensor was born. The house is now furnished as a museum, in which the old shop of his uncle and aunt, personal belongings and sketches, as well as the living-room and studio of the painter can be seen (open Jun.–Sep. and holidays daily except Tue. 10am–noon and 2–5pm).

Museum voor Religieuze Kunst

All the exhibits here also concern James Ensor but are about his religious themes (open Jul.–Sep. Wed.–Sun. 3–6pm).

Sint-Petrus-en-Pauluskerk

In Kapellestraat, leading south from the Wapenplein, stands the three-aisled Gothic Sint-Petrus-en-Pauluskerk (1905). Only the brick tower "Peperbus" from the first half of the 18th c. with relics of the 15th c. remains from the old church. The funeral chapel of the Belgian Queen Louise-Marie, who died in Ostend in 1850, was built on to the choir.

Provinciaal Museum voor Moderne Kunst

The Provinciaal Museum voor Moderne Kunst in Romestraat is devoted to contemporary Belgian art (open Apr.–Oct. daily except Mon. 10am–6pm).

Maria-Hendrike-Park

South of the centre extends Maria-Hendrika-Park with a prominent water-tower. Here visitors can walk or take boat trips.

Raversijde

Remains of the Atlantic rampart can be seen in the suburb of Raversijde situated to the south-west of Ostend.

Gistel

In Gistel, 10 km (6 mi.) to the south, the saint Godelieve was born in 1045. Her husband had her strangled in 1070 and threw the body into a pond; from then on the water was thought to have miraculous powers.

The church and the museum are dedicated to the legend of St Godelieve.

The pretty whitewashed Abdij Ten Putte (abbey of Ten Putte) to the west outside Gistel was laid out around the wonder-working pond. Here can be seen the cellar where Godelieve was incarcerated, as well as the chapel on the spot of her first miracle.

Abdij Ten Putte

Situated in the dunes, 6 km (3¾ mi.) to the north-east, is De Haan (Le Coq) which is more tranquil than Ostend. Strict building regulations ensure that no concrete tower blocks are erected but only pleasant looking houses and villas in green surroundings. De Haan has today, therefore, something of the look of the Belle Epoque.

De Haan

Oudenaarde · Audenarde   G 6

Province: Oost-Vlaanderen
Altitude: 14 m (46 ft). Population: 27,000
Intercity Station (bicycle rental at station)

Oudenaarde (French Audenarde), in the south of East Flanders where the Flemish Ardennes give way to the coastal moorland (geest) and which is traversed by the Scheldt, is a quiet township which possesses a con- siderable textile industry and is known for its exceptional beer

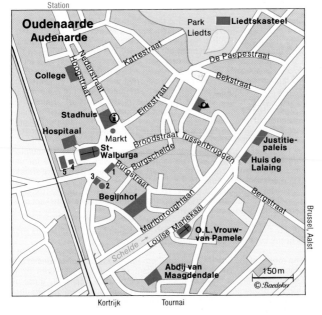

1 Vleeshuis
2 Boudewijntoren
3 Huis van Margaretha van Parma
4 Bisschopskwartier
5 O.-L.-Vrouweziekenhuis

from Liefmans Brewery. For art lovers Oudenaarde is, after Ghent and Tournai (see entries), of the greatest interest because of its impressive buildings in the Scheldt Gothic style and its magnificent town hall. The town was once famous for its wall tapestries, the so-called Verduren, which differed by the colouring of their floral motifs from examples in Brussels where pictorial motifs were preferred. Oudenaarde is the birthplace of Margarethe of Parma (see Introduction, Famous People) the Stadholder of the Spanish Netherlands from 1559–67, and of the painter Adriaan Brouwer (1605–38) in whose honour an annual beer festival is celebrated.

History Oudenaarde was first mentioned in the 11th c. when Count Balduin of Flanders built a fortress here. Around this a linen-weavers' town developed which, in the 13th c., was besieged and attacked on several occasions by the men of Ghent. After the decline of the linen industry in the 15th c. the people of Oudenaarde turned to the production of their celebrated Verduren which continued for some 300 years. Meanwhile Oudenaarde several times suffered destruction and siege during the quarrels of the Flemish towns, the Dutch War of Liberation and the campaigns of conquest of Louis XIV. Oudenaarde intervened conclusively in history in the battle of July 11th 1708 when troops of the Duke of Marlborough, supported by Prince Eugen, defeated the French under the Duke of Vendîme and the Duke of Bourgogne in the Spanish War of Succession.

Market

The market, which is surrounded by an impressive ensemble of historic buildings, is the centre of the life of the town. The most striking edifice is the Stadhuis in front of which can be seen a fountain adorned with dolphins, a present from Louis XIV in 1671.

★★Stadhuis

The wonderful Stadhuis (opening times Apr.–Oct. Tue.–Sun. 10am–6pm) was built between 1526 and 1537 according to plans by the Brussels' civic architect Hendrik van Pede on the site of the courthouse (Schepenhuis) which had been pulled down. The architect followed the Late-Gothic city halls of Brussels and Leuven (see entries) and introduced Renaissance elements. Above an arcaded passage rises the 25 m (82 ft)-high elaborate main façade adorned with figures, pilasters and arches, and separated harmoniously by the introduction of a 40 m (131 ft)-high clock-tower. On the top of this is the figure of "Hanske de Krijger" (Henry the victor) the symbolic protector of the city. The magnificence of the exterior is complemented by the interior. Passing through the vaulted halls on the ground floor we enter the Great Hall (Volkszaal) with a balcony overlooking the market, and which is heated by means of a great Late-Gothic fireplace by the Oudenaarde sculptor Pauwel van der Schelden. The same sculptor was responsible for the porch at the entrance door of the courtroom (Schepenzaal); here should be noted the original oak floor and the pictures: Charles VI, Louis XIV on horseback, Oudenaarde in the 18th c., and some examples from the school of Adriaan Brouwers. In the archive hall documents are kept concerning the history of the town.

Lakenhalle

Next to the City Hall stands the Cloth Hall dating from the 13th c. Its roof is borne by an unusual construction of beams.

Stedelijke Musea

The rooms of the City Hall and the Cloth Hall house the collections of the civic museums. These include excellent examples of Verduren from Oudenaarde on the walls of the Cloth Hall, pictures, especially those of Adriaan Brouwer, Gaspard Heuvick, Jan van Ruysdael and Jan Breugel the Elder, as well as historic documents and objects including cross-

The Stadhuis of Oudenaarde ▶

bows of the Sint-Joris riflemen's guild which had been known from the 12th c., and the famous twelve pewter "presentation tankards" which were filled with wine in honour of an important visitor: two for a prince, six for a king and all twelve for the emperor.

★Sint-
Walburgakerk

The second building which dominates the square is Sint-Walburgakerk with its east end facing the market. It is easy to recognise that it consists of two different parts. First the somewhat slender three-aisled choir with corner towers (the side choirs dating from about 1150, the choir apses from 1406) typical of Scheldt Gothic, and the massive main nave over which rises the mighty 90 m (295 ft)-high tower. This was begun in 1498 and completed in 1620. It houses a carillon with 47 bells. Inside the church can be seen the figures of the apostles on the pillars on the nave, as well a number of beautiful Verduren.

Bisschopspaleis

Behind the church stands the Bishop's Palace built about 1600, one of the finest Renaissance buildings in Belgium. The main part, however, dates from 1722 and is also furnished with beautiful Oudenaarde tapestries.

Immediately adjacent is the Onze-Lieve-Vrouw-Ziekenhuis (Hospital of Our Lady) which was built in 1382.

Vleeshuis

Returning to the market we see on the right the former Vleeshuis. The first meat-hall was built in 1338, a new building followed in 1584 and the present Neo-Classical building, which now houses the town library, in 1779.

Huis van
Margaretha van
Parma

In the nearby Late-Gothic house it is said that Margaretha van Parma was born. Immediately adjacent arises the Boudewijntoren dating from the 12th c., probably a remnant of the town fortifications.

Béguinage

Leaving the market along Burgstraat in the direction of the Scheldt we come to the Béguinage which dates from 1367. The original buildings however were destroyed by the Iconoclasts. The 32 cottages which are here today were built in the 17th c.

★Onze-Lieve-
Vrouw-van-
Pamele

The Tussenbruggen leads across the river to the district of Pamele. On the right stands the church of Onze-Lieve-Vrouw-van-Pamele another example of Scheldt-Gothic architecture in Oudenaarde built by Arnulf von Binche, the first Flanders' builder to be known by name; a replica of a bronze plaque on the outside wall of the choir indicates this with the date 1234. The church is distinctive for its tall narrow choir windows, the corner towers of the choir and the octagonal crossing tower; the northern transept was rebuilt in the 14th c. and both side chapels on the south were added in 1524. Inside can be seen the tomb of Philipp de Locquenghien, Baron of Pamele and Lord of Oudenaarde who died in 1620, as well as a triptych with panels by Jan Snellinck.

Zwartsuisterhuis

By the churchyard stands the Zwartsuisterhuis, once the house of the black sisters who devoted their lives to looking after the sick. After the destruction of the old building by the French it was restored in the 17th c.

Abdij van
Maagdendale

In 1232 Cistercians settled on the right bank of the Scheldt and soon their community became one of the richest in Flanders. As time went on the convent buildings were destroyed on several occasions and rebuilt; the present building dates from the 17th and 18th c. and only the Gothic chapel has survived the storms.

Huis de Laiaing

To the left of the Tussenbruggen can be found the Huis de Laiaing, a pretty Rococo dwelling. As well as an exhibition of works by

Oudenaarde artists it houses a wall-hangings centre where the production of Verdüren is taught, as well as a workshop for restoring old tapestries, etc. (open Apr.–Oct. Mon.–Fri. 9am–4pm).

The Park Liedts is reached by recrossing the Scheldt and continuing north past the post office. In the middle of the park stands the Liedtskasteel built in 1883 in Neo-Renaissance style. The four rooms contain the Folk Art Museum (open Apr.–Oct. Mon–Fri. 9am–noon and 2–5pm, Sun. 2–6pm).

Liedtskasteel

Surroundings

8 km (5 mi.) north-west lies Kruishoutem with a museum which was the gift of Veranneman and contains an important collection of modern art, including works by Permeke, Vasarely and Niki de Saint-Phall. Here also can be seen a little 17th c. castle in the middle of a large park.

Kruishoutem

7 km (4-1/2 mi.) east lies Waregem known for its annual equestrian jumping championship. The local museum has some works by well-known Belgian artists.

Waregem

Maarkedal, 7 km (4-1/2 mi.) south of Oudenaarde, is the heart of the Flemish Ardennes and an excellent place for walking tours.

Maarkedal

The Zwalmstrek in the Flemish Ardennes is an attractive stretch of land to the east of Oudenaarde characterised by the valley of the little river Zwalm, a tributary of the Scheldt. There are excellent opportunities for walking in the area, a number of water-mills and neat little villages such as Brakel, Horebeke and Kortsele, the so-called "Geuzenecke".

★Zwalmstrek

On the extreme eastern edge of the Zwalmstrek lies Zottegem where Lamoraal, Count of Egmont (see Introduction, Famous People) is buried in the former estate of his family. His tomb and that of his wife Sabina of Beierens can be seen in the crypt of the church. Egmont's castle lies in a park with fine trees; in its present form it dates predominantly from the 19th c. The local museum has mementoes of the duke.

Zottegem

There is another château in the suburb of Grotenberge in which a folk art and folklore museum is housed.

Grotenberge

Leeuwergem, 3 km (2 mi.) to the north, also has a castle. It was built in place of a moated castle of 1724 and is surrounded by a park laid out by Le Nôtre.

Leeuwergem

The Romans settled near Velzeke, 4 km (2-1/2 mi.) north of Zottegem. The Archaeological Museum has numerous finds of this and other epochs.

Velzeke

11 km (7 mi.) south of Oudenaarde on the linguistic border is the town of Ronse (French Renaix) where a lively carnival "Bummelfeesten" takes place, and on the first Sunday after Whitsun the "Fiertelommegan" procession is held. In the procession the relics of St Hermes, a Roman martyr, are carried through the surrounding villages. They are kept in the Collegiate Church of Sint-Hermes which primarily dates from the 15th and 16th c. and has a notable large crypt. There is also an interesting local museum in the former house of the chief provost with a historical department and an exhibition concerning the history of textile production in Ronse, as well as the Art-Nouveau house "La Bruyäre" built by Victor Horta.

Ronse

A few kilometres further west rises the 141 m (463 ft) high **Kluisberg** on the border between Hainaut and East Flanders and therefore on the linguistic border. The viewing tower of the Hotond Mill, 150 m (492 ft) high, is the highest point in East Flanders with an extensive panorama of the region.

Ourthedal

See Vallée de l'Ourthe

De Panne · La Panne   E 1

Province: West Vlaanderen. Altitude: Sea level
Population: 9500. Inter-regional Station

De Panne (French La Panne) is attractively situated in a sandy valley near the French frontier. It was originally a fishing village, very popular with artists, which quickly developed into a modern holiday centre. It is much favoured by the French, and has many attractions and all kinds of leisure activities. The township and its surroundings became famous during the First World War as being the only unoccupied part of Belgium and the residence of King Albert and Queen Elizabeth whose government had moved to Le Havre. The king's military headquarters was in Veurne (see entry).

★Beach

At low tide De Panne has the broadest beach of the entire Belgian coast some 400 m (1320 ft) wide. This extends 12 km (7½ mi.) to Nieuwpoort (see entry) and in the other direction to Dunkerque in France, 17 km (11 mi.) distant. It is not surprising that the brothers Dumont constructed their first sailplane here more than 80 years ago. In doing so they instigated a sport which is ideally suited to the beach of De Panne. From time to time a spectacular sailplane race takes place here in November.

★Dunes of Westhoek

To the west of De Panne extends the 340 ha (840-acre) national nature reserve of the Dunes of Westhoek, probably the finest dune landscape in Belgium, in which live ermine, martens, owls and rabbits, and the central part of which is reminiscent of the Sahara. The nature reserve is crossed by six signposted paths.

Dunes of Oosthoek

To the south-east stretch the 61 ha (150 acres) of dunes of Oosthoek, which are adjoined by the wooded area of Calmeynbos, planted in 1903. In this area too there are well signposted walks to be enjoyed.

Adinkerke

3 km (2 mi.) south of De Panne on the French frontier near Adinkerke lies the "Meli Park" amusement park. Here is a fairytale garden, animal enclosures and, as the principal attraction, "Splash" the tallest waterchute in Europe (see Practical Information, Leisure Parks for opening times).

Sint Idesbald

Not far to the east at Sint Idesbald there is a museum exhibiting the works of the Surrealist painter Paul Delvaux (Kabouterweg 42).

Veurne

See entry

Poperinge   G 2

Province: West-Vlaanderen

Strolling the dunes of Westhoek

Altitude: 2–6 m (6½–20 ft). Population: 28,000
Inter-regional Station (bicycle rental at station)

Poperinge, in the south-west of West Flanders a few kilometres from the French border, is the chief place of the "Hoppelandes", the most important Belgian hop-growing area. This is the excuse for an annual "Hoppenfeesten" (third weekend in September) with the election of a hop queen and once every three years (next in 2002) is the "Hoppestoet" (Hops Parade). In the Middle Ages Poperinge was a member of the Hanseatic League and an important cloth-trading town. Although situated in the main battle area Poperinge was largely spared destruction during the First World War. It was the most important base for supplies for the Allied troops in the Battle of Flanders.

Hoofdkerk Sint-Bertinus near the Grote Markt is a 15th c. hall church built on the site of a Romanesque predecessor. It was rebuilt in 1436 after destruction by the English. Features of the interior are a 17th c. rood screen, the choir screen and the Baroque pulpit. | Hoofdkerk Sint-Bertinus

The Onze-Lieve-Vrouwkerk (14th c.) in Casselstraat is also a Gothic church with a massive west tower crowned with a spire. Striking features are the Renaissance west door, the choirstalls, and a very fine sculptured communion bench. | Onze-Lieve-Vrouwkerk

A third hall church and the oldest in Poperinge is Sint-Janskerk (c. 1300) in Sint-Janskruisstraat. It houses a figure of the Madonna believed to be wonder-working, which forms the central point of a procession in July. The interior of the church has beautiful 18th c. panelling. | Sint-Janskerk

In the market stands the Stadhuis (town hall) of 1911 with a fine belfry. | Stadhuis

The Stadhuis of Poperinge, built in 1911

Talbot House	In 1915 the British army chaplain Philip "Tubby" Clayton founded Talbot House in Gasthuisstraat as a meeting place for soldiers from the nearby front at Ypres.
Nationaal Hopmuseum	The old weighbridge (Stadsschaal) of 1579 in Gasthuisstraat, in which hops and other produce used to be weighed, now houses the National Hop Museum. It exhibits the history, tools and techniques of hop-growing in "Hoppeland", and of course beer from Poperinge can also be sampled here. (Open May, Jun. and Sep. Sun. and public holidays 2.30–6pm; Jul. and Aug. daily 2.30–6pm.)
Weeuwhof	Nearby in Sint-Annastraat a small doorway gives access to the Weeuwhof, a picturesque ensemble of 18th c. cottages which served as a hospital.
Lijssenthoek	Lijssenthoek 3 km (2 mi.) south is a **military cemetery** where more than 10,000 Allied soldiers from the First World War are buried.
Westvleteren	In the Abbey of Sint-Sixtus of Westvleteren, 10 km (6 mi.) north of Poperinge, one of the five genuine Trappist beers of Belgium is brewed, the "Abbot", the strongest beer of the country.

Rochefort   M 13

Province: Namur
Altitude: 120–190 m (394–624 ft). Population: 11,000

The pretty little town of Rochefort, about 30 km (19 mi.) south-east of Dinant (see entry) near the Lesse and Lomme National Park (see Han-sur-Lesse), was once the capital of a county the only witness to which are the ruins of a 12th c. castle; now it is a summer resort visited especially by walkers and anglers. In the Abbey of Saint-Rémy, just outside the town, another one of the five genuine Trappist beers of Belgium is brewed. A marble quarry in the immediate vicinity once provided marble for St Peter's in Rome. History touched Rochefort in 1792 when in Rue Jacquet No. 8 the Marquis de La Fayette and Châteaubriand, both fleeing from Jacobin terror, were arrested by Austrian troops.

Apart from its charming scenery Rochefort only has two small **museums** to attract tourists: in one tower of the castle ruins can be found a historical exhibition, and the Musée du Pays de Rochefort et de la Famenne in the Avenue d'Alost has exhibits about the scenery of Famenne.

Rochefort is the base for visiting the grottoes which were carved out by the waters of the Lomme thousands of years ago; they were discovered in 1865 and investigated throughout 1870. They rank almost equal to the grottoes of Han-sur-Lesse as far as their beauty and the number of visitors is concerned. Their stalactite formations are bizarre, the temperature of 8°C (46°F) is less than that in Han so that warm clothing is necessary for the visit which takes about an hour. **Guided tours** Apr., Sep.–mid-Nov. every 90 minutes 10am–4.30pm; May–Aug. daily every 45 minutes 9.45am–5.15pm; Apr.–Jun. and Sep.–Nov. closed Wed.

⋆Grottes de Rochefort

The most impressive caverns and formations are those of the Val d'Enfer (valley of hell), the almost 90 m (295 ft) high Salle du Sabbat – in which there is an impressive son et lumière show – the Salle aux

Grottes de Rochefort
Stalactitic caves near Rochefort
(up to 180m/590ft below ground level)

1 Grotte aux Fontaines
2 Palais de Bagdad
3 Passage des Soupirs
4 Cordillières
5 Obélisques
6 Passage de la Jonction
7 Passage du Lac
8 Marbres Coquillers
9 Cataclysme
10 Passage des Gros Blocs
11 Arcades
12 Salle aux Merveilles

© Baedeker

50 m

Entrance

The ruined castle of Rochefort

Merveilles and the Les Arcades galleries which are located directly below the castle of Beauregard. Above the grottoes stands the Loreto Chapel built in 1620, a copy of the chapel of the same name near Ancona.

Surroundings

Chevetonge

Chevetonge, 15 km (9½ mi.) north-west of Rochefort, lies on the border between the regions of Condroz and Famenne. This village is the head-quarters of the Benedictine monastic brotherhood "Exaltation de la Sainte-Croix" (raising of the cross), founded in 1926 by Lambert Baudouin in Amay (see Huy, Surroundings), the main principles of which are the rapprochement between the Catholic and the Russian orthodox churches. In 1939 the monks moved to Chevetonge where they occupied the buildings of a monastery which had been abandoned in 1902. Here in 1957 they built the oriental church after the pattern of the 11th c. Russian-Byzantine church in Novgorod which is a rectangular brick building with a large narthex, a central dome and a crypt. All the walls of the interior are decorated with frescoes by Greek artists, the religious representation of which corresponds to orthodox beliefs.

Domaine provincial Valéry Cousin

The Valéry Cousin provincial estate, a large area of 500 ha (1235 acres) with forests and lakes situated around a 19th c. castle, offers numerous leisure activities such as an Olympic-sized open-air swimming pool, water slides and mini-golf (open Easter–Sep. hours according to activity and season).

Château de Jannée

About 18 km (11 mi.) north of Rochefort near the N4 stands the Château de Jannée surrounded by a fine game park. It can be traced back to a 12th c. defence building which about 1600 was enlarged, and extended in 1850 to its present size. Grouped around a large courtyard bordered by towers are new buildings and the farm buildings which are of older date. Visitors are conducted through the kitchen with its old utensils, the bedrooms and bathroom as well as several reception rooms on the ground floor, all tastefully furnished and containing fine Louis XV furniture and porcelain (open Jul. and Aug. daily 10am–6pm; Apr.–Jun. and Sep. only Sat., Sun. and public holidays).

Marche-en-Famenne

Marche-en-Famenne, 13 km (8 mi.) to the north-east, is the chief place in Famenne and a centre of Wallonian pillow lace, the production of which is carried on in the village. It was here in 1577 that Don Juan of Austria signed the edict confirming the Peace of Ghent, which had been concluded a year before, and by which the Spanish left the provinces of the Netherlands. Features worth seeing in the village are the Musée de la Tourelle with a collection of lace work, the Musée de la Famenne, as well as the 14th c. Church of Saint-Remacle with its very fine font of the same date.

The Church of Saint-Etienne in the suburb of **Waha** possess the oldest dedication stone of all Belgian churches. It can be seen on a pillar at the entrance to the choir, and states that on June 23rd 1050 the Bishop of Liège dedicated the church. The present building dates from the 16th c. and only the tower is still Romanesque. On the tower is a royal tablet with the arms of the Spanish king Philip II which is a memorial to the edict of 1577. In the three-aisled interior can be seen fine funerary monuments, a 13th c. reliquary, a 16th c. font, as well as fine statues of St Barbara and St Nicholas.

Nassogne

In the church of Nassogne which is situated on the Wamme, 13 km (8 mi.) east of Rochefort, is buried St Monon, a Scottish missionary murdered here in 636. The present-day church, dating from the 18th c., stands on the site of a chapel erected in 661.

Malagne, which has been incorporated into Rochfort, has one of Belgium's largest Gallo-Roman excavation sites. An educational trail leads through the gardens and to the remains of a Roman villa which has been brought back to life with the help of multi-media installations (open Easter–Nov. daily 10am–5pm, Jul. and Aug. 11am–6pm).

See entry

Ronquières

See Ecaussinnes, Surroundings

Ronse · Renaix

See Oudenaarde, Surroundings

Saint-Hubert   N 14

Province: Luxembourg. Altitude: 436 m (1431 ft). Population: 5600

The little town of Saint-Hubert, which is visited by many pilgrims, lies in the centre of the Ardennes amid a wooded region full of game. According to legend Prince Hubert of Aquitaine was hunting in the surrounding forests in 683 when he saw a stag with a shining cross between its antlers, and a voice demanding that he dress as a priest and take up missionary work. Hubert became the first Bishop of Liège after he had renounced the bishopric of Tongeren on the Meuse. He died in 727 in Tervuren and his remains were brought in 825 to Andage which from that day was called Saint-Hubert. The painter and botanist Pierre-Joseph Redouté was born in Saint-Hubert in 1759.

Processions and feast As the place of pilgrimage for the patron saint of huntsmen Saint-Hubert has several processions in the time around Easter. On the Monday before Easter a procession of hunters, which had its origin in 1720 in Lendersdorf in the Eifel, enters the town. On Easter Sunday in even years an Ardennes pilgrimage takes place. The first Sunday in September is the International Day of Hunting which is marked by the traditional hunters' mass at 11 o'clock and a historical

Saint-Hubert   **Basilica**

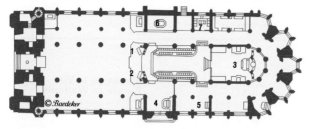

© Baedeker

1 Rosary Altar	3 Main altar	6 Mausoleum of
2 Altar of St Agatha's	4 Altar of St Hubert	St Hubert
martyrdom	5 Altar of St Laurent	7 Church treasury

procession; and on the last Sunday of the year the Brotherhood of Butchers honours St Hubert as their patron saint for he also protects them. Annually in July the "Juillet musical" takes place under the aegis of the Festival du Wallonie.

★Basilique Saint-Hubert

In the Grand-Place, the centre of the town which is situated on a slope, stands the Basilica of Saint-Hubert with its 60 m (197 ft) high towers. It has its origins in a Benedictine abbey church founded in the 7th c. which was destroyed by fire on several occasions. The present basilica was rebuilt between 1526 and 1564 and is a good example of Late-Gothic church architecture. However the façade, renewed in the 18th c., is in a mixture of Renaissance and Baroque work and shows the legend of St Hubert.

The almost 25 m (82 ft)-high light **interior** of the basilica is magnificently adorned with works of art principally of the 17th and 18th c. On either side of the entrance to the choir stand fine altars of Humain (Rochefort) marble. The choir stalls have scenes from the life of St Benedict and St Hubert

Saint Hubert's Altar

(1733). The statue of Mary on the high altar is probably by the sculptor Delcour from Liège. In the choir ambulatory in the Chapelle Saint-Laurent are 24 enamelled paintings in the style of Dürer by M. Didier (c. 1560). In the crypt underneath the choir a few remnants of the 11th c. building can still be seen. Notable in the right aisle are the lavish altars of St Hubert and St Lambert; the left aisle houses the mausoleum of St Hubert whose remains, however, disappeared after the French Revolution. Nearby is the church treasury which includes the saint's

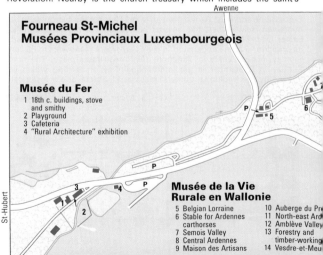

Fourneau St-Michel
Musées Provinciaux Luxembourgeois

Awenne

Musée du Fer
1 18th c. buildings, stove and smithy
2 Playground
3 Cafeteria
4 "Rural Architecture" exhibition

Musée de la Vie Rurale en Wallonie
5 Belgian Lorraine
6 Stable for Ardennes carthorses
7 Semois Valley
8 Central Ardennes
9 Maison des Artisans
10 Auberge du Pre
11 North-east Ard
12 Amblève Valley
13 Forestry and timber-working
14 Vesdre-et-Meu

St-Hubert

stole and his hunting horn, as well as relics of the maidens Hostia, Grata and Areapalis.

On leaving the church the imposing buildings of the former Benedictine abbey, which was rebuilt in 1729, can be seen on the right. They are now used for art exhibitions. Opposite in the square is the local tourist bureau.

Palais Abbatial

The church of Saint-Gilles-au-Pré was built in the 11th c. and the four-cornered tower of the sanctuary still remains from this period. The choir and the ceiling date from 1567. After the Second World War the church was massively restored. On the high altar stands the figure of the saint who is accompanied by his hind.

Saint-Gilles-au-Pré

Surroundings

2 km (1¼ mi.) to the north on the road to Fourneau Saint-Michel we come to a 15 ha (37 acre) game park (Parc à gibier) which is attractive for walking. In the woods live stags, deer, mufflon and wild boar.

★ Game park

In a sparsely wooded depression in the middle of the forest, 7 km (4½ mi.) from Saint-Hubert, can be found the Musées Provinciaux Luxembourgeois (Museum of the Province of Luxembourg). It consists of two open-air museums: the Musée du Fer/Fourneau Saint-Michel with the Musée P.-J. Redouté (open Mar.–beginning Jan. daily 9am–5pm) and the Musée de la Vie Rurale en Wallonie (open Apr.–mid Sep. daily 9am–5pm).

★ Musées Provinciaux Luxembourgeois

The Musée du Fer is concerned with the former monastery smithy of Fourneau Saint-Michel of the 18th c. which was founded by Nicolas Spirlet, the last abbot of Saint-Hubert. Several buildings house tools, examples of forging, the smithy, the stove and the foundry. Adjoining are the exhibitions of rural architecture, the Museum of the Ardennes Forest and the Museum P. J. Redouté which is devoted to the life and works of the botanist.

Fourneau Saint-Michel

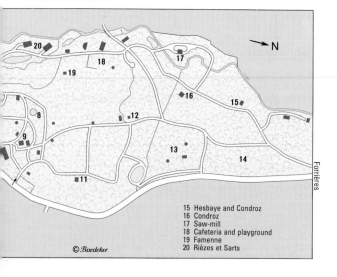

15 Hesbaye and Condroz
16 Condroz
17 Saw-mill
18 Cafeteria and playground
19 Famenne
20 Rièzes et Sarts

© Baedeker

Musée de la Vie Rurale en Wallonie	This museum is laid out on a large scale. Over an extensive area are various farmhouses and farms, a washing place, tobacco stores, a rural chapel and also a saw-mill. One of the most interesting buildings is the Maison du cheval du trait ardennais (house of the Ardennes cart horses), which documents the race of heavy cart horses from the Ardennes. Also available are a large playground with a cafeteria and the Auberge du Prévost restaurant in historic surroundings.
Mirwart	Mirwart, 12 km (7½ mi.) north-west of Saint-Hubert, has a large estate with a château begun in the 12th c. and extended in the 14th.
Redu	The village of Redu, about 18 km (11 mi.) west of Saint-Hubert on the far side of the A4, is a mecca for bibliophiles. In 1984 a collector and a journalist set up the only book village on the continent of Europe in accordance with the predecessor at Hay-on-Wye in Wales. Nearly 30 antiquarians as well as bookbinders, a cooper and craftsmen offer their services. The books are chiefly of French literature and often quantity rather than quality prevails. The shops are open from Mar.–Dec. from time to time; at Easter a large boo kmarket is held.
	Redu is also the home of a satellite communications base.
Euro Space Center Transinne	A full sized model of the European space glider can be seen from the motorway near the Euro Space Center in Transinne. Here all information about space travel, space science and the training of astronauts is available and there are models of various space vehicles. (Open daily 10am–5pm.)
Libramont	Belgium's only Celtic Museum can be found at Libramont, 13 km (8 mi.) south of Saint-Hubert. On show are genuine finds such as a necklace of glass pearls from Le Sart or a sword from Warmifontaine as well as reconstructions like for example a fighting chariot in its orginal size (open Tue.–Fri. 9.30am–5pm., Sun. 2–6pm).

Sint-Amandsberg

See Ghent, Surroundings

Sint-Niklaas   D 8

Province: Oost-Vlaaderen
Altitude: 5–30 m (16–98 ft). Population: 68,200
Intercity and Inter-regional Station (bicycle rental at station)

Sint-Niklaas, situated in the province of East Flanders between the rivers Scheldt and Durme, is the centre of the Waasland, the agricultural region to the north-east of Ghent. The town has important industrial and trading concerns and is a notable administration centre. The largest branch of industry is textiles (weaving, knitwear and the production of carpets). Metal, wood and tobacco also play a part in its economy.

History Sint-Niklaas lies at the crossing of two old trade routes, one led from Brabant to Zeeland, and the other linked Antwerp with Ghent and Bruges. In 1217 the former trading place was raised to an independent parish with St Nicolas as its patron saint. In 1248 Margarete of Constantinople, Duchess of Flanders, gave the area of the present-day market place to the newly formed parish with the instruction that the huge area should be free of building for all time. In the 17th c. Sint-Niklaas grew to be an important centre of textile working and extended

House of the Ardennes cart horses in the Musée de la Vie Rurale en Wallonie

its position in the following century. In 1804 it was raised to the status of a town under Napoleon I. By reason of its favourable position in the European economic area Sint-Niklaas developed in the 20th c. to one of the most important cities of Belgium.

Vredefeesten Annually on the first Saturday in September balloonists from all parts of Europe meet in Sint-Niklaas to start a race from the Grote Markt.

The imposing centre of Sint-Niklaas is the Grote Markt which has an area of 3.2 ha (8 acres), the largest municipal town square in Belgium. Its north-west end is dominated by the Neo-Gothic Stadhuis (town hall) of 1878, the tower of which houses a carillon of 35 bells. Behind the Town Hall rises the tower of Onze-Lieve-Vrouwkerk of 1841 with a gilded dome and a statue (6 m/20 ft high) of Mary.

★Grote Markt

    Opposite on the south-east end stand the Parochiehuis, a priest's house of 1663 later the town hall and now a commercial court, the Cipierage, originally a prison of 1662 and now a library, and the Landhuis, former law courts of 1637.

Behind these three houses rises Sint-Niklaaskerk, the church of the patron of the town, dedicated in 1238 and extended on several occasions in the 16th c. Notable features of the interior include the Baroque side altars of Hubert and Norbert van de Eynden as well as sculptures by Luc Fay'dherbe and a figure of Christ by Duquesnoy. The church museum can be visited only by arrangement (tel. 7763718).

Sint-Niklaaskerk

Zamanstraat branches off Statioonsstraat. Along it can be found the museum of the town and the Waasland (Museum van de Stad en van de Oudheidkundig Kring van het Land van Waas). It is divided into the

Museum

Sint-Niklaas: the Grote Markt

Department of Fine Art (primarily Dutch and Flemish paintings of the 17–19th c.), the Archaeological Section (prehistoric and Frankish finds), the Folklore Section, the Mathys-Vanneste Collection (furniture, porcelain, silver, a painting by Rubens, Belgian paintings of the 19th c.) and of special interest the room devoted to the great geographer Geradus Mercator (see Introduction, Famous People). Mercator was born in Rupelmonde not far east. (Open daily except Mon. 2–5pm, Sun. 10am–5pm.)

Branches Three other collections belong to the museum and these are all housed in a building at Regentiestraat 65 (a little north of the museum). The collections include those concerned with the International Exhibition Centre with 90,000 exhibits and 150 relief plates, the "Barbierama", a collection of toilet articles and hairdressers' implements, and a collection of musical automata such as phonographs and gramophones (opening times as above).

Walburg

The Castle of Walburg in the middle of the town park east of the Grote Markt was built in 1553 and considerably altered in the 19th c. The 5 m (17 ft)-high and 3.8m (13 ft)-wide astronomical clock (Heirmanklok) adjoins the castle.

Organ museum

In Oostjachtpark 15 can be found an organ museum with fair organs, barrel-organs and street organs (open only for groups, tel. (7) 769471).

Surroundings

Waasland

The Waasland along the old Scheldt is a pleasant stretch of country crossed by canals and typical rows of poplar trees. Recently more modern industries have joined the old-established agricultural pursuits (including asparagus), traditional brickworks and cloth manufacturers.

The parish of Beveren lies in the centre of the Waasland about 10 km (6 mi.) east of Sint-Niklaas. This area with its little undulating fields, many lakes and poplar trees is a favourite place for walking.

In the Grote Markt stands the **Sint-Martinuskerk** (c. 1200), of which only the Late-Romanesque crossing-tower remains of the original building phase. The other parts of the church were added in the 15th c. (nave) and the 16th c. (choir). The interesting interior of the church has a high altar by Fay'dherbe (1622).
Around 1840 the three-aisled nave was extended by two additional aisles.

Kasteel Cortewalle, a fine moated castle, dates from about 1600. The building in Flemish Renaissance style will serve after restoration as a culture centre and museum. Inside can be found 19th c. furniture and pictures (open May–Sep. Sun. 2–6pm).

The **Hof Ter Saksen**, now a ruined château was built in 1770 in a fine park. The moated castle **Oud Geestelijk Hof** or Hof Ter Welle (16th/17th c.) is now used as an orphanage.

Temse, 5 km (3 mi.) south of Sint-Niklaas on the Scheldt, is known for its shipbuilding. The town was once a centre of the cloth industry particularly sail-cloth.

In the market stands **Onze-Lieve-Vrouwkerk** a Gothic 16th c. hall church which can look back to a predecessor dating from 770. In the church is

Kasteel Cortewalle in Beveren

the 16th c. tomb of the benefactors of the town, Roeland Lefebure and Hadewigis van Heemstede.

The **Stadhuis** was erected between 1903 and 1906 in Neo-Renaissance style; it now houses the local museum (open Sat. 1–7pm, Sun. 10am–noon and 2–7pm).

Lokeren

Lokeren lies 16 km (10 mi.) from Sint-Niklaas on the Durme. The most important branch of industry in the town is textiles, especially the production of linen.

Some typically fine Flemish houses of the 17th and 18th c. flank the **Grote Markt**; the elegant Stadhuis in Flemish Rococo style was designed by David t'Kindt the architect from Ghent.

The most striking feature of **Sint-Laurentiuskerk** is its white tower crowned by a dome. The church dates from the 16th and 17th c. and was destroyed in 1719 by fire. The reconstruction was in Baroque style. From this time dates the beautiful pulpit by the Mechelen artist Verhaegen. Also noteworthy are the confessionals (1655) and the Late-Gothic font.

The **Stedelijk Museum** (municipal museum) in the old cloth hall on the Grote Kaai exhibits pre-historic finds, furniture and folk art.

Sint-Truiden · Saint-Trond

G 13

Province: Limburg
Altitude: 34–106 m (112–348 ft). Population: 36,800
Intercity Station (bicycle rental at station)

Sint-Truiden (French Saint-Trond) is the chief town of the Haspengouw (French Hesbaye), the market centre of an extensive fruit-growing area (principally cherries), and at the same time an important industrial base with a sugar refinery, distilleries, breweries and various other industries. The cherry blossom and the harvest are an excuse for lively festivals.

History Sint-Truiden developed around an abbey which St Trudo had founded in 657. The town received a charter in the 11th c. and was surrounded by fortifications in 1086. At first the Benedictine abbey came under the jurisdiction of the abbot and bishop of Metz, whose place was taken in the 13th c. by the prince-bishop of Liège. In this period Sint-Truiden developed into an important centre of cloth production on the trade routes between Bruges and Cologne. After the town had fallen to the French in 1795 the monastery was suppressed. From 1814 Sint-Truiden belonged to the Netherlands until the founding of the Belgian kingdom.

★Grote Markt

In the centre of the town lies the Grote Markt, after Sint-Niklaas (see entry) the largest in Belgium, in the middle of which stands the Classical 18th c. **Stadhuis** (town hall). It was built on to the belfry (lower part 12th c.) which had been erected in 1606 which rises above a side gable. The tower, in front of which is a platform dating from 1596, houses a fine carillon of 41 bells.

Onze-Lieve-Vrouwkerk

Near the Town Hall can be found the Onze-Lieve-Vrouwkerk, the choir of which dates from the 14th c. The nave of the church was completed in the 15th c. but the tower was only erected in 1847. The most valuable treasures are a "Last Judgment" by van den Eenheu and the reliquary shrine of St Trudo.

North of the Grote Markt are the buildings of the abbey founded in the 7th c. by St Trudo. It was one of the largest monastic complexes in the Netherlands – the church alone was over 100 m (328 ft) long and 24 m (79 ft) wide – but during the French occupation almost everything was destroyed. The building to be seen today dates mainly from the 18th c.; notable are the archway and the Keizersaal on the left side of the courtyard which has fresco decoration. One part of the building serves as the Hoevemuseum where rural implements and machines can be seen.

Abdij

Further north is the Begijnhof (béguinage), founded in 1258, the cottages of which are grouped around a rectangular open space. The church is now the Provincial Museum of Religious Art (open Tue.–Fri. 10am–noon and 1.30–5pm, Sat. and Sun. 1.30–5pm).

Begijnhof

The Festraetsstudio opposite should be visited. It contains an astronomical clock assembled by Kamiel Festraets (1904–74) from over 20,000 individual parts. It is 6 m (20 ft) high and the largest of its kind in the world. Also to be seen are other exceptionally fine examples of mechanical apparatus (open Easter–Oct. Tue.–Fri. 9.45–11.45am and 1.45–4.45pm, Sat., Sun. and public holidays 1.45–4.45pm).

Festraets-studio

Not far west of the market place stands Sint-Maartenkerk the tower (1550) of which is one of the jewels of early Renaissance architecture. The nave was constructed in the 19th c. in Neo-Romanesque style.

Sint-Maartenkerk

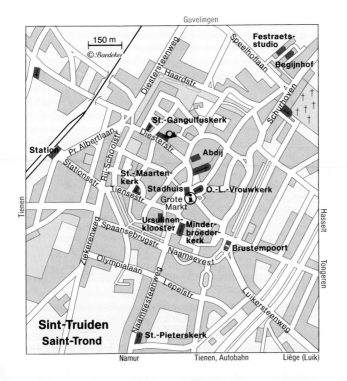

343

Ursulinenklooster	The former Ursuline convent, south of the Grote Markt, now houses an interesting museum of pillow lace, a craft once traditional in Sint-Truiden (open: Sun. and public holidays 10am–noon and 2–6pm). Opposite the convent is the **Minderbroederkerk** built in 1731, the interior of which is impressive because of its size (100 m (328 ft) long, 16 m (53 ft) wide and 26 m (85 ft) high).
Sint Pieterskerk	Sint Pieterskerk (12th c.) in the south of the old town is notable for its Romanesque architecture without any ribs.
Brustempoort	The Brustempoort at the end of Luikerstraat is a subterranean fortification dating from the 15th c. which was slighted under Louis XIV.
Guvelingen	In the north of the town the little Romanesque-Gothic church of Guvelingen occupies a lonely position. Here during the cherry blossom festival the orchards are blessed.
Zepperen	3 km (2 mi.) north-east of Sint-Truiden lies Zepperen where the church of Sint-Genoveva (15th and 16th c.) has an interior which was painted in 1509 with frescoes illustrating the legend of St Genoveva and the Last Judgment. The tower dates from the 12th c.
Kortenbos	A visit should be paid to Kortenbos, 6.5 km (4 mi.) east, to see the Basilica of Onze-Lieve-Vrouw, the interior of which retains its rich Baroque decoration.
Klooster van Kolen	12 km (7½ mi.) to the east we come to Borgloon, once the chief town of the county of Loon, where just outside to the north lies the Klooster van Kolen (monastery of Kolen). It was founded in the 13th c. by Crusaders and then taken over by the Cistercians. The reliquary of St Odile which was made in 1292 is kept in the sacristy; scenes from the life of the saint are painted on the wooden sides.
Zoutleeuw	See entry

Spa   J 16

Province: Liège. Altitude: 260 m (853 ft)
Population: 9700. Local Rail Station ((bicycle rental at station)

The health resort of Spa lies 35 km (22 mi.) south of Liège on the wooded slopes of the northern Ardennes in the charming valley of the Wayai or Spabach, which here is joined by the Picherotte. Within the town boundary are two springs and in the surroundings another seven which are alkaline and contain iron. It is to these springs that Spa owes its fame as the "town of waters" ("Ville d'Eaux") and it was for a long time an elegant health resort attracting visitors from all over Europe for the relief of circulatory diseases, stomach and intestinal disorders as well as gout and rheumatism. The word "spa" became synonymous for health resort in English. Now only the old baths and pump room and a few hotels remain. Today Spa gets its living from patients taking the cure, from individual visitors and coach tours, and offers its guests facilities for sports and for relaxing in the very pleasant surroundings.

History Although the efficacious springs of Spa were already known to the Romans it was not until the 16th c. that a kind of tourism grew up which brought such illustrious guests as Christine of Sweden, Charles II of England, Peter the Great, Joseph II, Giacomo Meyerbeer and Victor Hugo to the little town. In the First World War Spa was occupied by

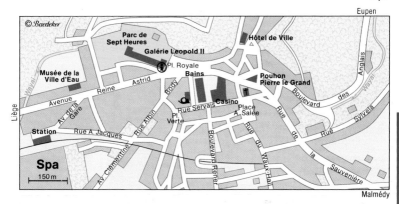

German troops and served as a convalescent centre behind the lines. From March to November 1918 Kaiser Wilhelm II set up his headquarters with his General Staff in nearby Neubois. It was here on November 9th 1918 that he heard by telephone from Chancellor Max von Baden of his enforced abdication. In Spa there were conferences between the victors and vanquished of the First World War about disarmament and questions of reparation.

The life of the spa is principally concentrated in the Place Royale around the **baths** and the **assembly rooms** built by Léon Suys in 1862–68. The baths are provided with water from the Marie-Henriette Spring outside the town. Adjoining is the building of the **casino**, first constructed in 1903–08 and renewed between 1919 and 1921 after a fire. When it was founded in the 18th c. by the prince-bishop of Liège it was the first gaming casino in the world combining the attractive with the useful.

Pouhon Pierre le Grand Just east of the casino in a pump room is the most efficacious of the springs of Spa named after Peter the Great.

Along the Avenue Reine Astrid to the west of the spa extends the Galérie Léopold II, a pump room built in 1878. Behind it lies the Parc de Sept Heures, a memorial to the composer Giacomo Meyerbeer and an armistice memorial.

Galérie Léopold II

Continuing along the Avenue Reine Astrid we come to a villa where Queen Marie-Henriette lived at the end of the 19th c. and where two museums are now housed. The Musée de la Ville d'Eaux is concerned with the history of the town and exhibits so-called "jolités", decorated wooden objects typical of Spa including boxes for various purposes, the oldest of which dates from the 16th c. The second museum is dedicated to horses and horse riding and includes the former royal riding school. (Both museums open mid Jun.–mid Sep. daily 2–5.30pm; mid Apr.–mid Jun. and mid Sep.–Dec. Sat., Sun. and public holidays 2–5.30pm.)

Museums

Further to the south is the factory complex of Spa monopole where visitors can see bottles being filled with the famous water (Rue Auguste Laporte; open Mon.–Fri. 9am–5pm).

Spa monopole

This museum in the Rue de la Géronstère revolves entirely around laundry, from antiquated washing machines to methods of ironing clothes

Musée de la lessive

Spa: the Casino

and the history of soap (open Jul./Aug. daily 2–6pm; rest of the year only Sun. 2–6pm).

There are many fine **walks** to be had in the immediate vicinity of Spa, including the Promenade des Artistes along the Picherotte stream, paths along the Lac de Warfaaz and to the various springs.

Berinzenne

Musée de la Forêt A forest museum documenting plants and animals of the Ardennes has been set up in a farmhouse in Berinzenne 4 km (2½ mi.) south of Spa.

La Reid

In the game park of **La Reid**, 8 km (5 mi.) west of Spa, deer, wild boar and mufflon live in an area of 40 ha (99 acres)

★Theux

7 km (4½ mi.) along the N62 leading north-east lies the little town of Theux which is characterised by 17th and 18th c. town houses. The perron (raised platform) of 1768, the symbol of independence of the town, can be seen in the Place du Perron; outstanding, however, is the Church of Saints – Hermès-et-Alexandre which stands on the site of a Merovingian and Carolingian church. In its present form it goes back to the year 1091 and with its three aisles of equal height it is the only Romanaesque hall church between and Loire and the Rhine. The roof of the central aisle was provided in the 17th c. with 110 coffers with biblical scenes and personalities. The wooden figure of the Virgin of Theux on the left of the choir was created in the 15th c.

To the right of the road to Theux just before reaching the town can be seen the ruins of the **Château de Franchimont** above the valley of the Hoëgne. It belonged to the prince-bishops of Liège and has witnessed numerous wars and sieges, including a massacre in 1468 in which 600 inhabitants of Franchimont, who had taken refuge here, were slain by the soldiers of Charles the Bold. During the course of the French Revolution the castle was destroyed. Visitors can see the remains and a small museum (open Apr.–Sep. daily 9am–7pm; Oct.–Mar. Sat. and Sun. 9am–7pm).

Not far north-west of Theux in the little pilgrimage chapel of **Tancrémont** is kept one of the best restored of early Romanesque wooden sculptures. The polychrome sculpture of "Christ on the Cross" was probably made in the 10th and certainly by the 11th c.

The N62 leads south-east to **Francorchamps** famous for its racecourse which runs through the forests (see Stavelot).

See entry

Verviers

Stavelot   K 16

Province: Liège. Population: 6200. Altitude: 320–430 m (1050–1411 ft)

The little town of Stavelot, 9 km (5½ mi.) south-west of Malmédy on the Amblève, can look back on a great history as an independent princely abbey. The surroundings, especially the valley of the Amblève, are ideal for excursions on foot in the quiet woods on the southern edge of the Hohe Venn.

History In 648 and 650 St Remaclus founded in Stavelot and in Malmédy two abbeys which soon adopted the Benedictine rule, and from which the princely abbey of Stavelot-Malmédy was formed. Under the direct authority of the kingdom they experienced, between the 10th and 13th c. in the time of the prince-abbots Poppo and Wibald, the zenith of their spiritual and cultural development, and they produced unique articles of Maasland metal- and goldsmiths' work which can be seen today in many museums all over the world. Their decline was instigated by the destructive Normans, and in the 17th c. the soldiers of Louis XIV, and in 1794 French revolutionaries continued the destruction. The Second World War added to the tribulations of Stavelot

The **carnival** activities of Stavelot take place in mid Lent (Wednesday or Thursday before Mothering Sunday) in the form of a procession with more than 1000 participants. Several hundred "Blanc Moussis" in white hooded cloaks and masks with long red noses accompany the procession and pummel the spectators with blown-up sheep's bladders.

The Abbey of Stavelot was in existence until the French Revolution when it was dissolved. Afterwards the buildings had various functions and in the First World War were used as a military hospital. Today the premises, principally of the 18th c., house the town administration and three museums. Remaining from the 16th c. are parts of the belfry, a beautiful spiral staircase and the doorway. In some of the rooms of the abbey a festival of concerts and plays takes place.

★Ancient Abbey

Musée d'Art religieux régional et de l'Ancienne Abbey The Regional Museum of Religious Art and of the Old Abbey is accommodated in the west wing which was built in 1714 (opening times Easter–Nov. daily 10am–12.30pm and 2–5.30pm; Nov.–Easter only until 4.30pm).

The museum is divided into four parts. The Department of Local History shows the development of the princely abbey and the life of some of the great abbots by means of documents, paintings, etchings, sculpture and models of the abbey buildings, as well as a replica of the shrine of St Remaclus. A second section is devoted to craft work and especially to tanning, which was carried on in Stavelot from the 16th c. until the end of the 19th c.

The third and probably the most important part exhibits religious articles (14th–19th c.) from the church treasury, and is especially worth seeing for the many examples of goldsmiths' work. The Department of Art is especially concerned with Belgian painters including Degouve de Nuncques, and also with ceramic artists.

Musée Guillaume Apollinaire

In 1899 the French poet Guillaume Apollinaire (1880–1918) spent three months in Stavelot where he fell in love with Marie Dubois to whom he dedicated a number of poems. One night he left the town without paying his hotel bill; it was thought by the citizens of the town that this event justified a museum and this can be found on the first floor of the town hall (the east wing of the abbey) where notable documents and objects from the poet's property as well as a replica of his room can be seen. (Open Jul.–Aug. daily 10.30am–noon and 2.30–5.30pm.)

Musée du circuit National de Spa-Francorchamps

The Romanesque vaulted cellars of the abbey are an extraordinary place for a motor-car museum. Here more than 80 vintage vehicles and racing cars of more recent date, motor-cycles, documents, posters, etc., which illustrate the history of the celebrated motor-racing circuit of Francorchamps, are on show. (Open Easter–Nov. daily 10am–12.30pm and 2–5.30pm; Nov.–Easter only until 4.30pm.)

Saint-Sébastien

Crossing the Place Saint-Remacle, where a platform (1769) typical of the former bishopric of Liège stands, we reach the 18th c. Church of Saint-Sébastien. In the **shrine of St Remaclus** it possesses a unique example of Mosan metal work. The 2.7 m (9 ft)-long and almost 1 m (3½ ft)-high shrine was worked from gilded metal with enamel inlay; it received in

The Shrine of St Remaclus, "Mary and the Child Jesus"

1268 the remains of St Remaclus which had been preserved since the 7th c. On the front are depicted Jesus giving a Blessing and Mary with the Child; on the long side on the left is a representation of Jesus and St Remaclus surrounded by six Apostles and on the right St Lambertus surrounded by another six Apostles. The lid bears another scene from the New Testament. The reliquary bust (17th c.) of St Poppo reveals the great artistry of its creator Jean Geosin. (Open only mid-Jul.–Aug. daily 3–5pm and during the Easter holidays 3–4pm; at other times of year only by appointment tel. (080) 864113.)

Surroundings

Not far east of Stavelot lies the Circuit National de Spa-Francorchamps one of the finest and most famous motor-racing circuits in the world. The circuit traverses the woods of the Ardennes with numerous curves and gradients. Every year international motor sports events are held here including Formula I meetings and motor-cycle master championships. Part of the circuit is on a public road and ordinary motorists can in fact drive on it. The stands for spectators are at the starting and finishing points.

Circuit National de Spa-Francorchamps

Vielsalm, 24 km (15 mi.) south of Stavelot, is a resort for walking in summer and for skiing in winter.
    Not far to the south lies Salmchâteau with the ruins of the princely castle. In the vicinity the so-called "razor stone" was mined which was used as a whetstone and grindstone. A little museum in the village documents the history and use of this stone.

Vielsalm

The river Amblève rises in the Hohe Venn in the German-Belgium Nature Park (see entry). Its lower course winds its way through a pleasant and quiet valley towards the Ourthe (see Vallée de l'Ourthe). On its course it receives the little rivers Warche, Salm, Baleur, Lienne and Ninglinspo. There are picturesque walks in the valley and on its slopes, and in many places canoes can be rented for trips on the river.

★ Vallée de l'Amblève

On the right bank of the river from Stavelot lies Trois-Ponts where the Salm flows into the Amblève. The village is a centre for walks and canoe trips in summer and in winter for skiing and skating (Wanne and Saint-Jacques). Trois-Ponts is also the starting point for two scenic drives by car: to the east along the stretch called "Boucle de Wanne", partly along the Salm and through the area of the old principality of Salm; to the west on the "Boucle de Basse-Bodeux" between the valleys of the Salm and the Baleur.

Trois-Ponts

Until the 18th c. the Amblève formed an enormous curve near the next village of Coo, where the arms of the river almost touched. The monks of Stavelot without ado pierced through this narrow place and there appeared two raging picturesque waterfalls which have become a major tourist attraction. People come every year to see the illuminations of the cascades and to enjoy the restaurants, the canoe trips and the amusement park "Télécoo" with a chair-lift to the viewpoint of the Montagne de Lancre.

★ Coo

Only a little way away lies La Gleize which arouses memories of the Ardennes offensive. In December 1944 an SS Panzer group, stopped because of lack of fuel, drew the population into the bloody fights between Stavelot and Stoumont with over 2500 victims; 100 of the civilians were shot by the SS. The "king's tiger" German armoured car which was left behind and the museum "December 1944" are souvenirs of these events.

La Gleize

The waterfalls of Coo

★"Le Congo"	There are several viewpoints on the road between La Gleize and the little town of Stoumont. The finest is "Le Congo", so-called because after Stanley discovered the river Congo at the end of the 19th c. the surrounding forests reminded the local people of the African jungle which had become popular. Above the right-hand bank of the river rises Froidecœur castle.
★Vallée de la Lienne	From Targnon onwards the road accompanies the river. Here the Lienne flows in, and in its picturesque valley are numerous springs such as those near Chevron; at the end of the valley, near Lienne, an extensive view of the Ardennes appears.
Fonds de Quareux	After passing through Lorcé the road bears sharply right and crosses the railway. Below the lines a footpath leads right down to the bank of the Amblève which here flows along in a particularly romantic reach.
Nonceveux	Near the holiday village of Nonceveux, where the Amblève begins a great curve, the Ninglinspo tributary joins the river. By following this defile on foot we reach in a quarter of an hour the sandstone basin called "La Chaudiäre" from which flow two waterfalls.
★Grottes de Remouchamps	After the bend in the river the road runs below the A6 motorway; on the left stands the Château Mon Jardin and soon we are in Sougné-Remouchamps. Here the visitor should see the grottoes of Remouchamps, discovered in 1828 and open to the public since 1912. They were inhabited in the Stone Age by hunters. In the upper parts of the caves can be seen fantastic dripstone and crystal formations. The lower part is watered by the Rubicon, a tributary of the Amblève. High points of the visit are the 100 m (328 ft)-long and 40 m (131 ft)-high "Cathedral" and the exit from the cave along the Rubicon. (Open Feb.–Nov. daily 9am–6pm; Sep.–Apr. 10am–5pm.)

North of Sougné-Remouchamps lies the **safari park** of Deigné-Aywaille where large African animals live freely in 150 ha (370 acres) of grounds around which runs a tourist train.

5 km (3 mi.) south from Aywaille, beyond Sougné-Remouchamps lies Harzé with a 17th c. castle which has a very fine Renaissance façade and an impressive staircase. In the old mill in the castle park a milling museum has been established.

Near Comblain-au-Pont (see Vallée de l'Ourthe) the Amblève finally joins the Ourthe.

Temse

See Sint-Niklaas, Surroundings

Tienen · Tirlemont   G 12

Province: Brabant
Altitude: 35–89 m (115–292 ft). Population: 31,700
Intercity Station

Half way between Liège and Brussels, right on the linguistic border, lies the town of Tienen (French Tirlemont), centre of the fertile Hageland. The principal agricultural crop of the surroundings is sugar beet which is processed in Tienen, the town being the centre of the Belgian sugar industry.

History The former settlement on a Roman road, which in parts has been well maintained, was first mentioned in a charter of Charles the Bold in 872. As early as 1015 the counts of Leuven granted rights to the town, and a little later the first fortifications were erected. In the Middle Ages the skill of the cloth-makers assumed importance far beyond the town and helped it to gain prosperity and respect. The sugar industry developed in the 19th c. Towards the end of the war in 1944 the town suffered greatly from German bombing attacks.

Tienen: Doorway to the Poelkerk

The Stadhuis on the extensive Grote Markt was built in 1635 in Renaissance style; in 1836 it was partially demolished and afterwards provided with a Neo-Classical façade.

Stadhuis

The neighbouring Gothic Church of Our Lady was never finished; it has a choir and transepts completed in 1345, above which rises the mighty tower of 1660. 300 years before this Jean d'Oisy built the three excellent doorways with their fine figurative decoration. The Baroque choirstalls and the rich panelling are striking, as is the magnificent figure of the Madonna (1362) by Wouter Paus above the high altar. In the right side aisle can be seen a representation of St Anne by Verhaegen.

Onze-Lieve-Vrouw-ten-Poelkerk

Stedelijk Museum Het Toreke	In the courtyard of the Palace of Justice, built as a cloth hall, is the 16th c. prison in which the municipal museum is now housed.
★Sint-Germanuskerk	With an elevated situation near the Veemarkt stands the Church of Sint-Germanuskerk founded in the 9th c. Its impressive western part, dating from the first half of the 13th c., is considered to be one of the most recent Mosan Romanesque architectural features. Extensions including the choir and the nave were carried out in the 14th and 15th c.; the Romanesque tower was rebuilt in 1550 and in the 18th c. received a carillon of 54 bells which is played from July to August every Monday at about 8.30pm. Of particular merit in the church is a copy of a font of 1149, the original of which can be seen in the Musées Royaux d'Art et d'Histoire in Brussels (see entry).
Hakendover	3 km (2 mi.) east on the far side of the Gete lies Hakendover, a well-known place of pilgrimage, where annually in January a procession in memory of the wondrous building of Sint-Salvatorskerk in 630 is held. The present church dates from the 13th c. and has a fine carved altar of 1430 and Baroque choirstalls from the abbey at Oplinter.
Hoegaarden	Barely 5 km (3 mi.) south-west of Tienen we reach Hoegaarden which is famous for its white beer. The brewery museum, based in the oldest house in town, explains how it is made. A Gallo-Roman well and a Roman dining room are also on show.
Jodoigne	In the 12th c. church of Saint-Médard in Jodoigne, 12 km (7½ mi.) to the south, the jaw of St Médardus is kept in a silver shrine.

Tongeren · Tongres   G 14

Province: Limburg. Altitude: 75–108 m (246–354 ft). Population: 29,600
Inter-regional Station

The rural market town of Tongeren (French Tongres), which is also a local administrative centre, lies on the little river Jeker and is surrounded by the fertile fields of the Hesbaye (Hasbengouw). The town has considerable economic importance for the extensive region around it because of the number and variety of jobs available in many small industrial concerns. The sights of cultural and historical interest of the town mirror its long history and are attractions for the tourist.

History Tongeren is proud of its claim to be the oldest town in Belgium. It has its origins in the Roman military camp of Atuatuca which Julius Ceasar mentions in the "Gallic War"; the Roman occupation was lifted by by Ambiorix, prince of the Eburon in 54 BC. Under the Emperor Augustus, Germanic Tongerens settled here and there arose the Roman Civitas Atuatuca Tungrorum which became an important station on the road between Cologne and Bavay; in the 2nd c. AD it was provided with a great encircling wall. In the same period it is said that Saint Maturnus conducted a mission here. Tongeren was raised to be a bishopric around 315 but, however, soon this was removed to Maastricht and in the 8th c. to Liège. As a consequence the town became the property of the prince-bishop. Towards the end of the 4th c. the Salian Franks had destroyed Tongeren; the removal of the bishop's see brought a further decline, so that in the Middle Ages the town had a more modest position than in Roman times and this is clearly shown by smaller encircling fortifications. From now on Tongeren shared the fate of the estates of the prince-bishops and in 1677 was once again bombarded by the troops of Louis XIV. Industrialisation began about 1830 and, together with its function as a market and administrative centre for the surrounding district of rural Hesbaye, helped Tongeren to its present importance.

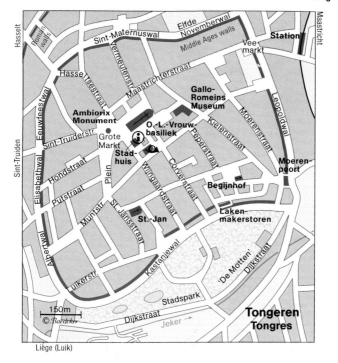

Liège (Luik)

Concerts are given in the basilica every year during the Flemish festival.

Towering over the Grote Markt of Tongeren is the 64 m (210 ft) high basilica of Onze-Lieve-Vrouw which is considered one of the most impressive Gothic church buildings in Belgium. The present church was begun in 1240 on the remains of several previous buildings and was the site where the first stone church north of the Alps was erected in the 4th c. The choir, the transepts and the eastern part of the nave of the present church date from the 13th c., the apse was added a century later and the side aisles in the 15th c. Work was completed in 1541 with the tower, the top of which however has been damaged on several occasions.

★Onze-Lieve-Vrouwbasiliek

The spacious and clearly articulated **interior** with its notable triforium is borne on tall round pillars. Tall windows from the Renaissance allow light to fall on to the choir in which the most valuable art treasures are the Gothic carved altar (first half 16th c.) from Antwerp with 23 detailed scenes from the life of Mary, two pascal candles of 1372 by the masters Jehan Josés of Dinant, and an eagle-lectern. The garlanded sculpture of Mary, the patron saint of the basilica, in the left side aisle, was carved in 1479 from walnut wood. From the right side aisle the visitor passes through a vestibule, in which hangs a huge 11th c. crucifix, into the cloisters.

The Romanesque **cloisters** are situated unusually on the east side of the church and not as normal on the south, because the Roman town wall allowed for no extension. The cloisters are the remains of a monastic

353

complex of the 12th and 13th c. and are notable for their simplicity and for the side chapels, the most beautiful of which can be seen at the entrance. Around the cloisters more than 60 tombstones have been let into the walls.

The **treasury** in the former chapter house is one of richest in Belgium and possesses more than 100 works of art from the Merovingian epoque up to the 18th c. (opening times May–Sep. daily 9am–noon and 2–5pm).

Outstanding is the famous 11th c. Head of Christ a wooden sculpture of the greatest quality which seizes the moment of passing from life into death. Also notable is the Mosan metal work, including the reliquary of St Ursula made of silver-gilt with enamel inlay (about 1350). The oldest pieces include a Merovingian golden clasp of the 6th c. and an ivory diptych of St Paul which dates from about 500. The manuscripts include a specimen from the 10th/11th c. with ivory carvings on the cover and a 9th c. manuscript which was rebound in the 14th c. Every seven years (next in 1995) the crowning of the figure of Mary is the occasion for the most valuable relics to be carried in procession through the town.

Tongeren: Ambiorix monument

Opposite the church tower in the middle of the Grote Markt stands the monument to the Eburon prince Ambiorix who in 54 BC defeated the Roman legions of Sabinus and Cotta.

Ambiorix Monument

The monument was created in 1866 by the sculptor Jules Bertin.

On the ground floor of the City Hall, also in the Grote Markt, can be found the Civic Museum which exhibits documents and objects concerning the history of Tongeren (open daily 10am–noon and 2–4.30pm).

Stedelijk Museum

The most interesting sight in Tongeren apart from the basilica is the Gallo-Roman Museum, which has recently been comprehensively renovated. Its collections are among the most valuable of their kind in Belgium.

Provinciaal Gallo-Romeins Museum

North-west of the centre a considerable part of the Roman town wall dating from the 2nd c., which was once 4½ km (nearly 3 mi.) long, still remains. Near the south door of the basilica remains of a fortress tower of the second Roman wall, dating from the 4th c., were discovered. The third medieval town wall built from 1257–64 almost completely surrounds the town centre. Especially attractive is the section around Leopoldwal which ends at the Moerenpoort, the only one of the six town gates which has survived. It was built in 1379 and now contains a small museum of weapons (admission on enquiry at the tourist bureau). To the east by the wall of the béguinage stands the defensive tower Lakenmakerstoren.

Remains of the town walls

Like almost all Belgian béguinages, that of Tongeren was founded in the 13th c., destroyed by iconoclasts and rebuilt again, until the French

Begijnhof

◀ *The Basilica of Tongeren*

Revolution ended the Beguine communities here in Belgium. The 13th c. church is dedicated to St Catherine and has beautiful Baroque fittings and a crucifixion scene by Gaspar de Crayer. St Luitgard, the protective saint of Flanders, is said to have been born just outside the béguinage.

Kasteel Betho

Outside the town centre to the north-west near the Beukenberg, an earthwork constructed by the Romans, is the great castle of Betho built in the 17th c. and extended in the 18th. To the north in a park is the Pliniusbron, a spring rich in iron which was praised by Plinius the Elder.

Kasteel van Alden-Biesen

11 km (7 mi.) north-east of Tongeren lies the Kasteel van Alden-Biesen (1220) which was the headquarters of the German order of chivalry. The largest part of the recently restored building dates from the 18th c. and is now used as a cultural centre of the Flemish community. As well as the great moated castle, with four corner towers and a main tower, there are extensive gardens, stables, a hospital and a pilgrims' hostel in the complex. The chapel of 1638 contains among other items a picture by de Crayer. A Natural History Museum has been installed in the main entrance.

Rutten

Every year on May 1st many spectators come to Rutten, 4 km (2½ mi.) north of Tongeren, to see the graphic mystery play about the death of St Emervarus who was murdered by a certain Hacco as he returned from a pilgrimage to Santiago de Compostela in northern Spain.

Kasteel van Kolmont

On a hill 4 km (2½ mi.) north-west of Tongeren stands the ruined Kasteel van Kolmont (castle of Kolmont). From the keep there is an extensive view into the Hesbaye.

Tongerlo (Abbey)

See Geel, Surroundings

Tournai · Doornik   H 5

Province: Hainaut. Altitude: 29–147 m (95–482 ft). Population: 67,700
Intercity Station

Tournai (Flemish Doornik) lies on both banks of the Scheldt (French Escaut) near the Belgian/French border. As the administrative capital of an arrondissement, a seat of a bishop and of a Chamber of Industry and Trade and of a law court, Tournai is of more than administrative and cultural importance and possesses major industries. Several attractive but mostly reconstructed buildings testify to the prosperity of the old princely residence and episcopal town. Most of the works of the celebrated medieval school of painting were however destroyed by the iconoclasts in 1566. Cement works, engineering, food processing and a traditional textile industry, especially carpet weaving, form the basis of the town's economy. Tournai has always been the most important market for the surrounding agricultural area.

History Tournai is after Tongeren (see entry) the oldest town in the country. Its origin was a settlement, Christianised by St Piat in the 3rd c., on the Roman road between Cologne and Boulogne and by the 4th c. it was already a considerable fortress. In the mid-15th c. Frankish Salians arrived and made Tournai the capital of their kingdom. In 482 King Childerich, whose son Chlodwig was born here in 465, died in Tournai. Chlodwig moved the royal residence to Soissons, but elevated Tournai

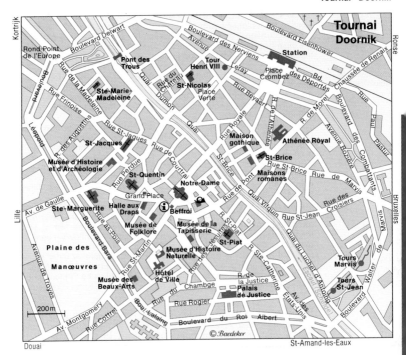

Tournai · Doornik

under St Eleutherius to the status of a bishopric which soon fell to the county of Flanders and which from 1188 was French. When the cathedral and several churches were built in the 12th and 13th c. the prosperity of the town began to increase and it became the centre of stonemasonry, drawing its material from nearby quarries. In the Hundred Years' War Tournai remained the only large town in Flanders on the side of France and withstood the siege in 1340 by the English king Edward III. In the 15th c., thanks to its celebrated carpet making, the town experienced a flowering and its school of painting (Robert Campin, Rogier van der Weyden) achieved international fame. In 1521 Charles V was the new ruler and he ceded Tournai to the Spanish Netherlands, the varied fate of which it shared from then on. Conquered by Louis XIV in 1667 and subsequently fortified by Vauban, Tournai fell to the Austrian Netherlands in 1714. In 1750 a new period of considerable artistic achievement began with the manufacture of porcelain, but this ceased in 1891 with the closing of the factory. In 1794 Tournai belonged once more to France and in 1814 it became part of the United Netherlands until 1830 when it was finally Belgian. The First World War left the town virtually intact but on May 16th 1940 a violent bombing attack destroyed the greater part of the historic buildings but not the cathedral; however, much was capable of restoration.

Festivals After a terrible epidemic of plague in 1092 Bishop Radbod inaugurated the great procession of Mary which henceforth has been held every year on the second Sunday in September. During the procession the shrine of St Eleutherius and other items from the church treasury are carried through the streets.

Fine secular festivals are the "Fàte des Rois" on the Monday after the feast of the Epiphany with a procession and rabbit feasting, and the "Quatre Cortèges" on the second weekend in June, the climax of which is a gigantic procession of historical figures. A colourful flower market is held along the Scheldt on Good Friday.

★★Cathédrale
Notre-Dame

The five towers of the Cathédrale Notre-Dame are visible from afar above the roofs of Tournai. The cathedral is the jewel of the town, the most important ecclesiastical building in Belgium and one of the best examples of Romanesque in western Europe, the epitome of church architecture in the area of the Scheldt.

The present cathedral, a cruciform pillared basilica – the nave and choir are almost equal in length – has a ring of chapels and five towers. It occupies the site of Merovingian and Carolingian predecessors and was dedicated in 1171. At this time the Romanesque nave, the transepts and the 83 m (272 ft)-high central tower resting on its pillars were finished. The remainder of the building, the four other towers, the conclusion of the transepts and especially the huge Gothic choir which dates from 1243–56, were added by 1325.

A narthex was built in front of the 14th main façade in the 16th c. also in Gothic style. Of the beautiful relief figures seen here the lower row (prophets, church teachers, Adam and Eve) date from the 14th c., and the upper row (processional scenes and the battle of Chilperich against his brother Sigbert) from the 16th and 17th c.; the central pillar bears the figure of Notre-Dame des Malades (14th c.). Considerably older is the figurative decoration on both side doors: on the north the Porte Manile has a representation of the Healing of Blind Mantilius by St Eleutherius (12th c.); on the south the sculpture on the Porte du Capitol is considerably damaged.

The three-aisled **interior** of the cathedral, 134 m (340 ft) long, 66 m (217 ft) wide and 22–23 m (72–75 ft) high, shows most clearly the architectural development from Romanesque to Gothic. The dark, purely Romanesque **nave** rises in four distinct zones (arcades, balcony level, blind triforium and rose windows) on tall pillars finished with capitals showing human and floral motifs and is, except for the crucifixion scenes by Jordaens in the Chapel of Saint-Louis completed in 1299, relatively simply decorated. The adjoining **transept** (1140–60), which reaches a height of 48 m (156 ft) at the crossing, shows in the finer detailed working and in the slender lines of the pillars the transition to Gothic. The transept ends unusually in semi-circular fashion as a kind of two additional choir ambulatories beneath the galleries. Remains of 12th c. frescoes show, on the right, the Heavenly Jerusalem, on the left the Martyrdom of St Margaret. The glass pictures (15th–16th c.) mostly by Arnold of Nijmegen draw their motifs from the history of the bishopric of Tournai. A magnificent marble Renaissance **rood screen** separates the transepts and nave from the choir. It is one of the most important works of Cornelis Floris de Vriendt, made in the years 1570–73. Representation of biblical scenes is crowned by sculptures of the Virgin, St Eleutherius and St Piat. The three-aisled **choir** is pure Gothic with light falling on it from the high windows with 19th c. glass. The chapels of the choir ambulatory house valuable paintings of the Dutch–Flemish school; the finest are a purgatory scene by Rubens in the Chapelle-du-Saint-Sacrement, the "Raising of Lazarus" by Pourbus the Elder in the chapel before the entrance to the treasury, and in the central chapel the "Virgin" by Maarten de Vos. Also of interest are a number of tombstones which were damaged by the iconoclasts but all are good examples of the school of sculpture of Tournai. Behind the high altar of 1727 a large marble memorial bears the names of all the bishops and canons of Tournai.

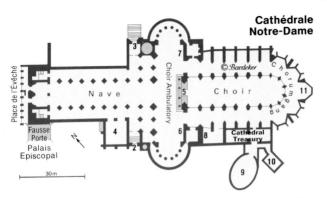

Cathédrale Notre-Dame

1 Narthex
2 Porte du Capitole
3 Porte Mantile
   (Romanesque sculptures)
4 Chapelle de St-Louis
   ("Crucifixion" by Jordaens)

5 Renaissance rood screen
6 Frescoes
7 Remains of frescoes
8 Chapelle du St-Sacrement
   (Chapel of the Sacrament)
   "Purgatory" by Rubens

9 Chapelle du St-Esprit:
   Gobelin tapestry "Sts
   Piat and Eleutherius"
10 Chapter House
11 Maarten de Vos:
   "The Virgin"

The **cathedral treasury** (opening times daily 10–11.45am and 2–4pm; Apr.–Oct. to 5pm), housed in rooms to the right of the choir ambulatory, contains a number of pieces of the first order, the finest of which are two Late-Romanesque reliquary shrines: the shrine of the Virgin (Châsse de Notre-Dame), worked by Nikolaus of Verdun in silver and copper in 1205 and restored in the 19th c., and the shrine of St Eleutherius (Châsse de Saint-Eleuthère) of 1247, a work by Hugo von Oignies created most beautifully with the figures of the apostles, the saint with a model of the cathedral in his hand, and a likeness of Christ in metal. Also very valuable is a Byzantine reliquary cross (6th/7th c.) and the manuscript of the Messe de Tournai (1247) the oldest multi-voiced mass of the west. Adjoining the Chapelle du Saint-Esprit is a magnificent pictorial tapestry from Arras (1402) which tells the legend of St Piat and St Eleutherius in fourteen scenes.

The large triangular Grand'Place is lined by gabled houses most of which are restored. In the centre stands the bronze statue of Christine de Lalaing (Princess d'Espinoy) under whose leadership the town was defended during the siege of 1581. On the north-west side of the square is the Église Saint-Quentin, originally a Romanesque building of the 12th c., which was burnt down during the Second World War and has been restored. On the south side of the square stands the former Hall aux Draps (cloth hall) which replaces a wooden predecessor blown away in 1601 in a storm. The hall was begun in 1610 but part of it fell down in 1881 and three years later it was rebuilt. It now serves as an exhibition and function centre. | *Grand'Place and Surroundings*

On the west side of the square rises the 72 m (236 ft)-high belfry, the oldest bell-tower in Belgium. The first four storeys were built in 1200 and completed in 1294 with the topmost storey and the spire. After a fire in 1391 the tower was rebuilt; the first carillon was mounted in 1392 of which five of the 43 bells of the present ring remain. (Open daily except Tue. 10am–noon and 2–5.30pm.) | *★Belfry*

North of the market can be seen the slender tower of the Eglise Saint-Jacques which, after the cathedral, is the finest church in the town. It dates from the 12th c. and has a Romanesque tower, an early Gothic | *Saint-Jacques*

The towers of the Cathedral above the roofs of Tournai

nave and transepts. The choir which was added in 1368 shows all the features of Scheldt-Gothic: the outer gallery, the triple windows, the side turrets and the triforium with alternate columns and pillars.

Museums

All museums in Tournai can be reached easily on foot from the Grand-Place. They are open daily except Tue. 10am–noon and 2–5.30pm.

Musée de Folklore

The Musée de Folklore is accommodated in a house with twin gables dating from 1673 (Maison Tournaissienne) not far from the cloth hall; it is devoted to customs and handicrafts of the town and its rural surroundings. Particularly charming are the many rooms reminiscent of the past with puppets and original features, such as a shoemaker's workshop, a woolworkers' workshop (so-called "baloitil"), a farm kitchen and a printing press. On the second floor there is a large model of Tournai in the year 1701.

Musée de la Tapisserie

The most recent museum in the town, opened in 1990, can be found in the Place Reine Astrid; it is concerned with carpet weaving which has been carried on in Tournai since the 15th c. It not only tells the story of the craft and exhibits old examples, but visitors can also watch a carpet being made in the workshop.

Musée d'Histoire Naturelle in the Abbaye Saint-Martin

From the belfry Rue Saint-Martin leads west and from it an archway opens into the courtyard of the Abbey of Saint-Martin (1642–1701), founded in the 11th c., the largest Benedictine abbey in Belgium before the French Revolution. In one wing is accommodated the Musée d'Histoire Naturelle (Natural History Museum) which is principally notable for a fine collection of birds; the palace of the abbots, a work of Dewez from 1743, is now the headquarters of the town administration.

Opposite the town hall stands the star-shaped building of the Musée des Beaux Arts, built in 1928 according to plans by Victor Horta Its principal collection is that of the Tournai burgher Henry van Cutsem. Fine paintings of all epoques are displayed in fourteen rooms. Mention must be made of the pictures by the old masters: Roger van der Weyden ("Virgin with Child"), Jan Gossaert ("Saint-Donatien"), the Bruegel family who are represented with various works as are Jordaens and Rubens. A whole room is devoted to the Belgian romantic Louis Gallait and another to the Impressionists including Monet, Seurat, and Ensor, with two masterpieces by Manet: "Chez le Père Lathuille" and "Argenteuil". Also of interest are the drawings by van Gogh and Toulouse-Lautrec.

★ Musée des Beaux Arts

North-west of the Grand'Place behind the Church of Saint-Quentin can be found the former pawnbroker's shop (Mont de Pitié) built by Coebergher in 1622. It now contains the historical museum which until 1940 was housed in the cloth hall. It illustrates the history of the town with numerous exhibits from churches and other buildings which were saved from destruction in 1940. Of exceptional merit are a great collection of porcelain from the Tournai manufactory and fine pieces of local carpet weaving.

Musée d'Histoire et d'Archéologie

On the upper floor is the Musée de Paléontologie et de Préhistoire where prehistoric finds especially from the quarries round about Tournai can be seen.

From the Grand'Place it is downhill and across the Scheldt straight along to the **Church of Saint-Brice**. Building of this church went on from the 12th c. into the 18th c. and in 1940 it was burned down. It was one of the first three-aisled hall churches in the west of the territory of present-day Belgium. In the Chapel of the Sacrament hangs a picture by de Crayer, and the crypt still remains of the original building. In 1653 when exca-

On the right of the Scheldt

View of the choir of Tournai Cathedral

The Belfry

361

Romanesque houses in Tournai

vations were being made for the present day houses Nos. 7 and 8 in Place Clovis, which lies around the church, the grave of the Frankish king Childerich was discovered and the burial gifts were taken to Paris.

★Maisons romanes

Obliquely opposite the main front of Saint-Brice stand two three-storeyed houses, the windows of which are divided by small central pillars. They were built about 1175 and are the oldest remaining Romanesque domestic houses in western Europe. A little way up the street can be seen another citizen's house, this time in Gothic style (14th c.).

Remains of the town fortifications

In the south-east of this part of the town can be found the best preserved parts of the medieval town wall (13th c.) with the towers called Tours Marvis and Tours Saint-Jean.

Tour Henri VIII

The north-west part of the town is also called the Quartier du Château (castle quarter) since in the Middle Ages the castle stood here. During the English occupation under Henry VIII (1513–18) the castle was constructed, of which only the Tour Henri VIII remains. It is a massive structure with two vaulted halls in which is housed a museum of weapons.

★Pont des Trous

At the extreme north end of the old town centre the Pont des Trous spans the Scheldt; it is an impressive example of medieval defence architecture. The two towers (the one on the left dating from 1250/1281, the one on the right from 1304) were linked in 1329 by a three-arched bridge. When they were restored after the Second World War, both towers were raised by 2.4 m (8 ft) in order allow the passage of ships.

Surroundings

Agriculture is the principal occupation of the country around Tournai. There are many old farms and at the end of long drives and hidden behind hedges are fine country houses. Particularly in the east and south-east cement and building stone industries have arisen around numerous quarries.

In the castle in the little town of Antoing, 7 km (4½ mi.) to the south, Philip IV of France and Edward III of England met in 1340 for peace talks. The castle was rebuilt in the 19th c. and only the great 15th c. keep remains from earlier times. The tombs of the Melun family in the chapel are fine examples of the skill of the stonemasons of Tournai.

Antoing

Just beyond the village of Hollain, 9 km (5½ mi.) south, a narrow little road branches off to the right. By a road crossing stands the 4.5 m (15 ft)-high menhir called "Pierre Brunehault" in the form of a trapezium. In the immediate vicinity there once ran the Roman road from Cologne to Bavai.

"Pierre Brunehault"

13 km (8 mi.) to the east of Tournai we reach Leuze where the Church of Saint-Pierre (1745) stands on the site of a Romanesque predecessor. The exterior is uninteresting but the furnishing are far more worth while: wall panelling in the style of Louis XV with fine carving, a magnificent pulpit (1790), a 9th c. reliquary, and two brass desks in the choir (15th c.).

Leuze

Situated 6 km (3¾ mi.) to the north, Mont Saint-Aubert, 147 m (482 ft) high, is the only hill for miles; it is also called Mont Ste-Trinité because of the little church which was built on its summit. From the top there is a fine distant view of the plains of Flanders in the north, the French town of Roubaix in the west and back to Tournai in the south.

Mont Saint-Aubert

Turnhout

D 12

Province: Antwerpen
Altitude: 25 m (82 ft). Population: 37,600
Inter-regional Station (bicycle rental at station)

In the north of Kempenland near the Dutch border lies the little town of Turnhout, a centre of the Belgian paper industry since the early 19th c. when the production of playing cards was begun; these are now exported all over the world. Meanwhile metal, chemical and electronics factories have been established.

History Turnhout, part of Brabant from the 12th to the 16th c. was once popular with the Burgundian dukes, who found that hunting in the surrounding forest was very good, and they indulged principally in falconry. Charles V bequeathed the town to Maria of Hungary; after the Thirty Years' War the princes of Orange-Nassau became the new overlords and they were followed in 1753 by the king of Prussia.
In 1789 history was made in Turnhout when the revolutionaries of Brabant defeated the Austrians and banished them at least until 1790.

Sint-Pieterskerk stands in the Grote Markt and its oldest parts date from the 13th c.; however from the 15th to the 18th c. it was rebuilt and enlarged on several occasions, especially around the remarkable ring of chapels surrounding the choir (1484). Notable in the interior are an "Ecce Homo" (early 15th c.), the confessionals, the high altar of 1740 by Walter Pompe and an artistic choir screen. The tower contains a carillon of 50 bells.

Sint-Pieterskerk

The former moated castle of the dukes of Brabant, not far from the Grote Markt and now used as a law court, once served as a hunting lodge. Maria of Hungary had the first building remodelled by Rombout Keldermans and Dominikus de Waghemakere in the first half

Kasteel

of the 16th c. into a fine residence; there were other alterations in the 17th c.

Begijnhof

The béguinage, north of the castle was gifted in 1372 by Maria, Duchess of Brabant. Most of the houses of the present attractive complex were built after a fire in the 17th c.; the pretty Baroque Heilige-Kruiskerk (Church of the Holy Cross) dates from 1665. Begijnhof No. 56 is a museum illustrating life in the béguinage.

★Nationaal Museum van de Speelkaart

House No. 28 "Metten Toren" in the Begijnhof was built in 17th c. for a patrician. It now contains the Nationaal Museum van de Speelkaart (playing card museum). The first playing cards of Turnhout were printed in 1826 and in 1900 there were six factories producing them in the town; in 1971 they were combined to form the Carta Mundi playing card factory which is today the only one in the Benelux countries. The museum is devoted to the history of playing cards from all over the world in documents which go back to 1100 BC and also exhibits a great number of original cards, of which the oldest date from the 16th c. (Open Tue.–Sat. 2–5pm, Sun. 11am–5pm.)

Museum Taxandria

The Romans called Kempenland "Taxandria" a name which is also borne by the museum in Mermansstraat, south of the Grote Markt, which on the one hand exhibits archaeological finds including Merovingian shields, and on the other is concerned with the popular culture of the Kempenland. (Open Tue.–Sat. 2–5pm, Sun. 11am–5pm.)

Museum "De Wielewaal"

This museum in house Gratakker 13 is devoted to the ornithology of the Kempenland.

Surroundings

The countryside around Turnhout, the **Kempenland** (French Campine)

The castle of the dukes of Brabant

was for a long time under the domination of the Romans until they were replaced by the Teutons. In AD 358 this area fell to the Salien Franks.

Oud Turnhout

Oud Turnhout, 3 km (2 mi.) to the east, was once the seat of the priory of Corsendonk whose comprehensive library was used by Erasmus of Rotterdam for his studies. In the numerous rooms of the restored 15th c. building the Albert van Dijck (1902–51) museum is now located. This painter, who came from Turnhout, was the leading representative in the 30s of the animists and often chose subjects for his paintings from the Kempenland.

Retie

Passing through Oud Turnhout we reach Retie where the church contains furniture and objects d'art from the priory of Corsendonk. A little outside the village by the Witte Nete river stands a stone mill in which corn in still ground on Sundays. The "Prinsenpark" provincial estate nearby is ideal for walks. Originally this area was owned by the royal family but was inherited by the province of Antwerp in 1952. The estate is especially rich in bird and wildlife and is a popular excursion and holiday destination.

Kasterlee

There is good walking country also around Kasterlee, 9 km (5½ mi.) south of Turnhout in the heath and moorland of the provincial estate of Hoge Mouw.

Baarle-Hertog

The enclave of Baarle-Hertog, 14 km (8½ mi.) north of Turnhout, is a curiosity as it is a Belgian enclave completely surrounded by Dutch territory. In the 12th c. the village was divided between the dukes of Brabant and the lords of Breda. Each part has a school, a town hall, a post office and a police station. The market, however, is in Holland, while the inn by the market stands on Belgian territory. Sometimes the frontier goes right through the houses; the nationality can be seen by the house numbers which are painted in national colours. The confusion is completed by the sister parish of Baarle-Nassau; this is a Dutch enclave surrounded by Belgian territory, and thus an enclave within an enclave.

Baarle-Nassau

Moi

The parish of Moi, 23 km (14 mi.) south-east of Turnhout, made headline news at the beginning of 1990 as here there was a recycling plant for nuclear fuel rods. The plant belongs to the Centre d'études de l'énergie nucléaire (centre for research into nuclear energy: CEN/SNK) which has headquarters in Brussels and runs the laboratories in Moi.

Vallée de la Meuse (Meuse Valley)   H-M 11–15

Province: Namur and Liège

The Meuse (Flemish Maas) rises at an altitude of 456 m (1497 ft) in the French plateau of Langres in Champagne. It has a course of 450 km (280 mi.) in French territory and after crossing into Belgium near Givet – from here it is navigable – it flows for 192 km (120 mi.) through Belgium until it reaches the Netherlands near Maastricht, where after a further 250 km (155 mi.) it reaches the North Sea. Between Givet and Namur (see entry) the Meuse has cut a deep valley in the Ardennes plateau and flows northwards, sometimes between fine wooded slopes and sometimes between bare slopes. In the shadow of the steep ridges nestle pretty villages, with hotels and villa settlements in the valley of the river, which are popular summer resorts. The valley has always been of great attraction. As long ago as the Stone Age hunters and gatherers lived in caves along the river, and much later monks chose the lower reaches of the river to build their monasteries, while the secular lords erected imposing castles and fortresses on the heights. Some of these were rebuilt in the 17th and 18th c. and converted into fine châteaux. Thus the upper Meuse valley can claim to be one of the finest **cultural landscapes** in Europe. Yet from Namur where the river turns to the east, and finally beyond Huy (see entry) in the direction of Liège (see entry) the scene changes. The broad Meuse now flows through the heavily industrialised lower Meuse valley past numerous blast furnaces, engineering works and factories, and only isolated ruined castles and rocky sections give the scenery a certain charm. The Meuse became one of the European rivers most heavily polluted with chemicals and for this reason the neighbouring states are insisting on the construction of purification plants and the subsidising of more ecologically favourable technology.

River trips From Namur and Dinant (see entries) trips up and down the Meuse are available. Those with sporting proclivities can undertake canoe trips on the lower course of the Lesse (see Dinant, Surroundings).

The Meuse valley is one of the settings for the series of legends concerning the **Haimon children** which has as its subject the quarrels between Charles the Great and Renaut de Montauban, but historically is more concerned with the events about Charles Martell. Renaut was one of the four sons of Aymon (Haimon) of Dordogne and lived with his brothers Allard, Guiscard and Richard at the court of Charles the Great. When in a quarrel he killed Charles' nephew he fled with his brothers on the back of the mighty horse Bayard, which had been reared on an island in the Meuse, along the valley and into the Ardennes. From there they continued their flight to Gascony where Renaut founded the fortress of Montauban. Finally he was reconciled with Charles and undertook a pilgrimage to the Holy Land. He came back, settled in Cologne and worked as a mason on the cathedral. Jealous fellow workers murdered him and threw his body into the Rhine where, according to the legend, the fish brought his body again to the surface.

★★Upper Meuse Valley: from Hastière to Namur

Grottes du Pont d'Arcole

A trip along the Meuse, which is also very pleasant by bicycle as there are few gradients, begins in the double parish of Hastière near the French border. A little further on is the part of the village called Hastière-Lavaux where are the grottoes of Pont d'Arcole through which flows a subterranean spring.

Hastière-par-Delà

On the far side of the bridge over the Meuse lies Hastière-par-Delà where at the beginning of the 11th c. Irish monks founded a monastery. The purely Romanesque parish church with its massive tower remains from that time; the choir, however, was added in 1264. The choirstalls date from the same period and are some of the oldest in Belgium. In the crypt can be found two Merovingian sarcophagi.

Waulsourt

Remaining on the left bank we come to Waulsourt on a bend in the river. The fine castle was originally the palace of the abbots of the convent founded in the 10th c. A little way downstream on the other bank rises the ruins of Château-Thierry, picturesquely situated on the Rocher du Chien (dog crag).

★Château de Freÿr

Further on is Freÿr where the castle and its wonderful gardens should be visited (guided tours only Apr. and Oct. Sun. 3pm; Apr.–Oct. Tue. 3pm and Sat., Sun. and public holidays 2–6pm; Jul./Aug. also Tue. 3pm). The castle was built between the 16th and 18th c. and unites the style of Mosan Renaissance with the Rococo of Louis XV. In 1675 Louis XIV used the castle as his headquarters during the siege of Dinant. The rooms which he used have been kept in their original condition as have the other salons, among which the dining room, with its Renaissance furniture and leather tapestry from Córdoba, as well as the vestibule with hunting scenes take a special place. A large balcony surrounded by an artistic wrought-iron balustrade looks out over the gardens.

The **gardens** lie along the Meuse on three levels. They were laid out according to the principles of Le Nitre from 1760 onwards under the jurisdiction of the dukes of Beaufort-Spontin. On the lowest level 33 orange trees in containers are set out and some of these are more than 300 years old. On the two levels above is a maze comprised of hedges, and to conclude the gardens there is a small hunting lodge.

The imposing background to the castle and park is formed on the right bank of the Meuse by the towering **Rocher de Freÿr** (rock of Freÿr) which the Belgian Alpine Club uses as a training ground.

The Meuse now describes another curve at the vertex of which lies Anseremme at the mouth of the Lesse (see Dinant, Surroundings).

Anseremme

Now comes Dinant (see entry) the exceptionally picturesquely situated capital of the upper Meuse valley, and a little further on the suburb of Bouvignes with the Château of Crèvecœur (see Dinant, Surroundings).

Dinant

In Dinant our route crosses the Meuse and continues along the right bank of the river. High above the village of Houx are the overgrown ruins of the Tour de Géronsart and the Château de Poilvache, built, according to legend, by the Haimon children. Actually it dates from the 10th c. and was destroyed in 1430 by the soldiers of the Bishop of Liège. Its name "castle cowhide" refers to another legend, according to which the beleaguered inhabitants dressed themselves in cowhide in order to slip away. They were however discovered and the besiegers of Dinant donned the

Château de Poilvache

Château de Freÿr

Vallée de la Meuse (Meuse Valley)

cowhide and were able to get into the castle which they quickly subdued.

Yvoir

A few kilometres past the castle we reach Yvoir, a popular holiday resort particularly for its island in the Meuse. Just south of the village lies the "Oasis nature" a 10 ha (25 acre) park. Signposted paths lead through botanical gardens, educational plantations, and past an old castle and a farm where visitors can study the flora and fauna of Belgium.

★ Vallée de la Molignée

For the detour through the green valley of the Molignée it is necessary to cross the Meuse between Houx and Yvoir after reaching Anhée. Here the Molignée flows from the west into the Meuse. By following its course we reach in 9 km (5½ mi.) the ruins of the **Château du Montaigle** on a crag; built in the 13th c., it was destroyed in 1554 by the French.

Just beyond the castle a narrow road leads off to **Falaën**. Visitors to the 17th c. castle estate there can see a small historical exhibition and try the local specialities, bread and dark beer.

Abbaye de Maredsous

Back on the main road the Benedictine Abbey of Maredsous is soon reached. It was founded in 1872 by a Belgian monk from the monastery at Beuron who wanted to recreate the life style and architecture of the medieval abbeys. Building went on until the 1950s in Neo-Gothic style. The abbey has a small art collection, a library, a publishing house and a pedagogic centre.

Maredsous is also known for its Trappist cheese, its bread and its beer; The beer, however, is not brewed in the monastery but in the Duvel brewery in Breendonk.

Maredret

The Benedictines also built an abbey in 1893 in nearby Maredret. A little museum in the village shows varieties of timber, woodworking and rural life in the region between the Sambre and the Meuse.

Furnaux

Furnaux is the terminus of the excursion into the valley of the Molignée. Here the local church is worth visiting, for it has an extremely artistic font of black marble. This was created around 1135 and shows the Baptism of Christ on the basin which is borne by four lions.

★ Château d'Annevoie

On the left bank of the Meuse lies the castle of Annevoie, the building of which was begun in 1627. In 1775 Charles Alexis de Montpellier had the brick building enlarged with a Rococo wing. The furnishings and equipment of the castle rooms date from this time; particularly fine are the music room and the chapel with stucco work by the Italian brothers Moretti.

However, the actual attraction of Annevoie is the **gardens** which were laid out at the same time as the castle was being extended. The principles of French horticultural layout are here integrated in the most harmonious manner – as can be seen in the geometric form and the many water features such as the cascade called "Buffet d'Eau" – with English and Italian garden layouts, the latter including statues of Carrara marble. The floral displays – in spring daffodils, hyacinths and tulips, in summer roses and begonias – are a first class attraction in the Meuse valley. (Open: castle tours mid Apr.–Jun. and Sep., Sat, Sun. and public holidays 9.30am–1pm and 1.30–6.30pm; Jul. and Aug. daily at the same times; gardens Apr.–Nov. 1st daily 9.30am–6.30pm.)

Godinne

Godinne on the right bank of the Meuse is linked to Annevoie by a bridge. It possesses a beautiful priory of the 16–17th c.

Rochers de Frênes

Remaining on the right bank we soon see the massive formations of the Rochers de Frênes which are pierced by grottoes in which Stone Age men have left their traces. From the viewpoint on the top of the rock an extensive view over the Meuse can be enjoyed; on the opposite bank can be seen Profondeville, one of the most important holiday places in the valley.

Leaving the rock the Meuse is crossed for the last time; in Wépion, the centre of a large strawberry growing area, is a very original strawberry museum. **Wépion**

The trip through the Upper Meuse Valley ends in Namur (see entry). Namur

Lower Meuse Valley: from Namur to Huy

This trip leaves Namur on the right bank of the river following the N90. In a short distance the rock called Albert I (see Namur, Surroundings) can be seen on the far bank. The Meuse describes a broad loop to the south at the vertex of which the little river Samson joins the main stream. In its picturesque valley can be found the grottoes of Goyet with impressive dripstone formations. In one part of the caves, which were inhabited by pre-historic men, there is a representation of their way of life. A little further upstream lies Faulx-les-Tombes with an 18th c. castle. **Vallée du Samson**

Andenne, approximately halfway between Namur and Huy, lies on the border of the Condroz. The little town arose near a monastery which was founded about 700 by St Begga but of this nothing remains. Begga was the daughter of Pippin I, the sister of St Gertrude of Nivelles (see entry), and mother of Pippin II and therefore the progenitrix of the Carolingians. Her grandson Carl Martell is believed to have been born in Andenne; the bear fountain commemorates him and illustrates one of his first heroic **Andenne**

In the gardens of Annevoie

deeds when, at the age of nine, he slew a wild bear with a hammer. For this reason a "bear carnival" is held annually in Andenne, at the climax of which little teddy bears are thrown from the town hall.

In 1273 the "battle of the cow" began in Andenne. It was caused by a farmer who had stolen a cow from a citizen of Ciney but was recognised in Andenne market. However, he refused to return the cow and was immediately hanged in Ciney. His master the Count of Namur besieged Ciney with the help of the Luxemburgers. The owner of Ciney, the prince-archbishop of Liège hurried from Dinant with his supporters and there followed a two-year war at the end of which the Condroz was laid waste.

Collégiale Sainte-Begge The parish church of Sainte-Begge, dedicated to St Begga, was built between 1770 and 1775 on the site of seven monastic chapels (Encloîtres), the model of which can be seen in the church. Also in the church is the black marble tomb of St Begga and her reliquary shrine (16th c.). The Porte Sainte-Etienne (18th c.), the last remainder of the seven chapels, is preserved in the Place Sainte-Begge.

Musée de la Céramique In the 18th and 19th c. Andenne has a flourishing porcelain and ceramic industry which is commemorated in the Musée de la Céramique (open May–Sep. Tue., Fri., Sat. and Sun. 2.30–5.30pm).

Huy

The trip ends at Huy (see entry) where the Meuse begins to widen out considerably and becomes more and more characterised by industrial complexes.

Vallée de l'Ourthe

H-M 14–16

Province: Luxembourg, Namur and Liège

The Ourthe is a 130 km (427 mi.)-long river in east Belgium. Its source is two streams in the Ardennes, the eastern Ourthe and the western Ourthe which unite near the village of Engreux. In a deeply cut winding valley the Ourthe flows in a north-west and later north direction through the plateau of the Ardennes and the districts of Famenne and Condroz, often called the pre-Ardennes region, and enters the Meuse near Liège. The breach valley of the Ourthe is one of the most charming and picturesque scenic regions of Belgium. On the banks of this river, which is rich in fish, are a series of holiday resorts which are ideal bases for walks in the forest and for trips in boats and canoes on the Ourthe and its tributaries. These resorts are provided with excellent hotels and restaurants. The long-distance footpath GR57 accompanies the valley of the Ourthe from Angleur in the vicinity of Liège as far as Houfflaize.

★★Upper Ourthe Valley: from La Roche to Houffalize

In the upper valley of the Ourthe to the south of La Roche-en-Ardennes the river describes narrow bends through steep rock formations so that this section of the valley is the most wildly romantic. This region, as far as Bastogne (see entry) to the south, was one of the most violently disputed areas during the Ardennes offensive in December 1944 and January 1945, and there were many victims, especially among the civil population, caused by the atrocities of the SS and by bombardment; these events still remain vivid in the memory of the local people.

★**La Roche-en-Ardennes**

La Roche-en-Ardennes, the "Pearl of the Ardennes", has an extremely picturesque situation surrounded by forests at the junction of several lateral valleys; with barely 4300 inhabitants it is the largest and most important tourist resort of the Ourthe Valley. There are many hotels, restaurants, facilities for renting boats, and more than 100 km (62 mi.) of footpaths for the enjoyment of visitors. La Roche-en-Ardennes was almost completely destroyed in 1944 by an Allied bombing attack. The Musée de la bataille des Ardennes documents the fighting (open: daily 10am–6pm).

The little town is dominated by the **ruins** on a rocky spur. The castle was begun in the 10th c., rebuilt several times and destroyed in the 18th c., the material being used by the citizens of the town to build their own houses. In 1852 the remains were restored and can now be reached from the market place by a stepped path. In fine weather the ghost of the maiden Berthe appears (provided by the tourist office); according to legend she was killed by the devil although she was innocent. Just above the ruins stands the 16th c. Chapelle Ste-Marguerite which is linked to the castle by a subterranean passage constructed by the French in the 17th c. From here there is a good view of the town and the valleys.

A speciality of local craft is the grey stoneware with cobalt blue salt glaze introduced in 1872. In the craft centre **"Les Grès de La Roche"** the production method is explained, an old kiln can be visited and, of course, stoneware can be purchased.

Parc de Deister Beyond the Chapelle Ste-Marguerite a path leads to the Deister plateau above the river bank where a 15 ha (37 acre) nature park with a little game park has been laid out. This can also be reached by the tourist train which leaves the "Pavillon des Deux Parcs" in the valley, one kilometre outside the town.

La Roche-en-Ardennes, chief town of the Ourthe Valley

Ortho

The route now follows the N384 and comes to Ortho on the plateau where a fortified Celto-Roman camp was found.

Barrage de l'Ourthe

To the east of Ortho near Nisramont the Ourthe is dammed to form a reservoir, the Barrage de l'Ourthe, which encloses 2.5 milliard cu. m of water. From the car park north of Misramont on the right of the road is a wonderful **view** over the lake into which flow the two source streams of the Ourthe, and across to the rock called "Le Hérou".

★★Belvédère des Six Ourthes

Beyond Nisramont the road winds down into the valley, crosses the Ourthe and joins the N860 to Nadrin. From there there is a walk on a 2.2 km (1½ mi.)-long path to the fissured rock "Le Hérou" which is 1400 m (4595 ft) long on two sides and falls steeply into the Ourthe; from the Belvédère des Six Ourthes viewpoint there is an extensive panorama embracing the six narrow loops which the river forms around the rock, the reservoir and the confluence of the two sources of the Ourthe. The last named can be reached from the observation point on the footpath which leads up through the forest on the right bank of the river.

Houffalize

A detour leads east from Nadrin for 12 km (7½ mi.) to Houffalize on the east Ourthe, a pretty summer resort known as the "Heart of the Ardennes". In 1944 the little town was completely laid waste in ashes and rubble by Allied aircraft who stopped a German armoured advance here. In the Place Albert can be seen a memento of this event – a German Panther tank which was left behind. Houffalize possesses two museums: the town museum with a "Paul Verheggen" department concerned with the flora and fauna of the Ardennes and an archaeological section, and the museum of country life "Li Vi Forni". Shortly before reaching the village the road passes under the motorway viaduct over the Ourthe which is 65 m (213 ft) high and 369 m (1211 ft) long and is the largest in Belgium.

Petites Tailles

A diversion north from Houffalize reaches in 15 km (9½ mi.) a marshy plateau the Petites Tailles, where the landscape anticipates that of the Hohe Venn which adjoins it to the north.

★Lower Ourthe Valley: from La Roche to Liège

The lower course of the Ourthe is quieter and flows along in broad curves only occasionally interrupted by narrows caused by the rocks. In several places underground watercourses have dug caves into the limestone; there are ruined castles, fortifications and old watermills to be seen.

Marcourt

From La Roche the road follows the river. In 7.5 km (4¾ mi.) there can be seen on a hilltop on the left the little pilgrimage chapel of Saint-Thibaut, built in 1639. It belongs to the family resort of Marcourt once the seat of the counts of Montaigu whose castle (1050) ruins can still be seen.

Hotton

On the border between the Ardennes and the Famenne lies Hotton, a place which has long been inhabited, for in the vicinity were found relics of the Neolithic and Roman ages. From a steep cliff which dominates the village there is a fine view of the Ardennes and the Famenne: forested hillsides on one side and extensive meadows and pastures on the other.

Grottes de Hotton The dripstone cave "Grotte des Mille et une Nuits" (grotto of the thousand-and-one nights) impresses especially because of its bizarre rock forms and play of light caused by crystal formations (open: Apr.–Oct. daily 10am–5pm; Jul. and Aug. until 6pm).

Durbuy has an exceptionally charming townscape; although it has few more than 350 inhabitants it nevertheless has had the title of a town since 1331 and can call itself "the smallest town in the world". The narrow streets and the old houses, as well as the remains of the town wall, give the impression that here time stands still. In the summer, Durbuy is very overrun with tourists, but it offers a sophisticated cuisine, a chocolate market in March and – from July to September – the largest maze in Belgium, entirely planted with corn.

Beyond Durbuy the road leaves the Ourthe Valley and meets it again near Barvaux, an important tourist resort with a large water-sports complex at the foot of the Rocher de Glawans. Easily reached from here are the villages of Tohogne in the north with its beautifully furnished Romanesque church, and Wéris in the east with the Church of Ste-Walburge (11th c.). In the vicinity of this village the great dolmen Nord and many smaller druidical stones have been discovered.

Bomal which follows also earns its living from tourism. Here the **Aisne** coming from the south joins the Ourthe. The Aisne flows through a pretty valley which is excellent for walking and where there is an imposing view of the rocky walls of the Roche à Frêne.

The Château de Logne is one of the finest castles in the Ourthe Valley. It was built in the 11th c. and in the 15th came into the possession of the quarrelsome de la Marck family who bore the scarcely flattering nickname of "Sangliers des Ardennes" (wild boar of the Ardennes). The castle, destroyed on the order of Charles V, was rebuilt in more recent times and can be visited. Finds from the castle are on show in nearby Vieuxville in the Ferme de la Bouverie.

The road now turns away from the river and returns to it in Hamoir. Here the celebrated sculptor Jean Delcour (1627–1707) and his son and painter Jean-Gilles (1632–95) were born; the latter carried out the painting on the high altar of the village church, whereas the father was responsible for the altar sculpture and part of the tabernacle in the Romanesque church of Saint-Pierre in nearby Xhignesse; this church is notable for the blind arcades in the apse.

In Hamoir the little river Néblon joins the Ourthe. This stream winds for 14 km (8½ mi.) through wild vegetation to the pretty village of Ocquier, in the vicinity of which, near Vervoz, remains of Roman villas and 3rd c. graves have been found.

The next stage is to Comblain-au-Pont at the confluence of the Ourthe and the Amblève (see Stavelot, Vallée de l'Amblève) which is surrounded by impressive rocks such as the Rocher des Tartines, the name of which is due to its tart-like form.
   Just outside the village a grotto with 20 chambers and a deep chasm was found in 1909.

Between Comblain-au-Pont and Poulseur to the north the first nature park in Belgium was created on the bank of the Ourthe in 1946; this is the Parc naturelle des Roches-Noires, du Chession et du Vignoble.

Near Esneux the Ourthe makes another large bend and forms a peninsula. Interesting rock formations, a few ruined castles in the surroundings and the Parc du Mary with its arboretum can here be explored.

Tilff is the last rural village before reaching the industrial conurbation of Liège (see entry) and is therefore very popular for local excursions by the townsfolk. A very original museum is the Musée de l'Abeille which is concerned with the history and art of raising and keeping bees, illustrated by models, implements and a collection of beehives. Some of the beehives are active so that visitors can see the bees at work.

Vallée de la Semois (Semois Valley) N-P 11–14

Province: Luxembourg, Namur

The Semois rises in the extreme south-east corner of Belgium near Arlon (see entry), it flows first through the plain of Gaume in the Belgian part of Lorraine (Lorraine Belge) and at Tintigny enters the Ardennes. From here onwards it has cut a course deeply into the hills and forms broad curves around forested rocks which again and again offer charming views. Although the distance from its source to its joining the Meuse near the French town of Monthermé is only 80 km (50 mi.) as the crow flies, the total length of the river is over 200 km (124 mi.).

The climate of the Semois valley is relatively mild, as its deep situation protects it from the predominantly westerly winds. Until a short time ago the most important agricultural product was tobacco grown along the lower course of the river, but now this only thrives in the districts further to the south; however, the production of tobacco is becoming increasingly unprofitable.

The valley now lives by tourism and in its beautiful landscape it offers all kinds of attractions: canoe and boat trips, angling, numerous way-marked footpaths, camping sites, hotels and very good restaurants. There are not many cultural sites, the chief being the mighty castle of Bouillon (see entry) and the abbey of Orval (see entry) which is a little way off.

The steep flanks of the valley at times approach the river so closely that the roads are often high above the edge, therefore a trip through the Semois Valley is best done on foot or by boat if one is not to miss the finest parts of the landscape. Many of the larger villages are on the plateau of the Ardennes high above the windings of the river.

For those who are fit cycling through the valley offers fine views.

Jamoigne

A trip along the valley begins in Jamoigne which lies at the junction of the picturesque Vierre Valley and has an old castle (rebuilt in the 19th c.) and a notable church with a beautiful 12th c. font and pictures by Abraham of Orval.

Chiny

From here the Semois winds to the north and flows around Chiny, once the seat of the lords of Chiny, and then becomes wildly romantic. A **trip** in a flat bottomed **boat** is recommended, by means of which it is possible to see picturesque rocks, such as the Rocher du H[a-circum]t, or sail below the Rocher du Paradis (Apr.–Sep. daily 9am–6pm). The trip ends after 7 km (4½ mi.) in Lacuisine from where the return to Chiny can be made on a fine footpath (¾ hour) or by bus.

From a viewpoint about 2.8 km (1¾ mi.) north of Lacuisine (the path has orange-white waymarks on the north of the road to Neufchâteau) there is an excellent view of the stretch which has just been completed by boat.

Florenville

After Chiny the Semois again becomes quieter and there follows Florenville, a tourist centre on the upper course of the river. From the terrace behind the church there is an extensive view of the lovely scenery with its pastures and fields, and this is even more impressive when seen from the church tower. From Florenville a detour of 8 km (5 mi.) to the abbey of Orval (see entry) lying to the south is recommended.

Chassepierre

From Florenville the Semois describes a broad curve and meets the through road again at Chassepierre, one of the prettiest villages on the Semois and a popular holiday resort. Slate-roofed houses surround the Church of Saint-Martin which has interesting choirstalls, probably from Orval. In the surroundings can be seen caves used by hunters in the Stone Age and prehistoric dolmens. About 1 km beyond the village on the right of the road there is a look-out point with a good view of the village to the rear.

The N884 in the direction of Herbeumont leads via Ste-Cécile through the Forest of Conques which belonged to the priory of the same name. This priory, founded in 1694 as a refuge for the monks of Orval, can be seen shortly before reaching Herbeumont on the left of the road; it is now a hotel. Herbeumont village is dominated by the ruins of the counts' castle dating from the 12th c. which was destroyed in 1658 by the French. From the top there is a wonderful **view** of a very narrow reach of the Semois around a rocky ridge which, because of its form, is called the "Tombeau du Chevalier" (knight's tomb). Around Herbeumont there are many footpaths.

Herbeumont

The route continues to Mortehan; from there it is possible to go on to Bouillon via the little tourist resort of Dohan, or to make a detour via Auby to the Saut des Sorcières, a series of waterfalls which fall into pools, and pass the viewpoint of the Mont de Zarton. On the latter stretch the road first passes through Cugnon, where St Remaclus is said to have lived in a grotto in the 7th c. Both detours finish in Noirefontaine, from where Bouillon is reached on the N89. But first visitors should continue from Noirefontaine to Botassart and look down on the bend of the river around the "Tombeau du Géant" (giant's grave).

Direction of Bouillon

After Bouillon the visitor should first take the N810 which is scenically

Poupehan

View of the valley of the Semois

very appealing and which passes the rock called "Hottée du Diable" (devil's basket) to Corbion, where in the 16th c. a certain Monsieur Pistole invented the pistol; and from there take a smaller road towards Poupehan, once an important place of tobacco processing. Shortly before reaching the village a path to the right leads to the viewpoint "Chaire à prêcher" (pulpit), a rock from which monks summoned people to the crusades to Jerusalem and Gottfried of Bouillon heeded their call.

Rochehaut

At a great bend in the river the route reaches Rochehaut situated high up with its Church of Saint-Firmin adorned with frescoes from where there is yet another beautiful **view**, this time of the village of Frahan lying opposite and across to Alle where Joseph Pierret lived; he began tobacco planting in 1855 on the Semois and made Alle his centre.

Vresse

Vresse is almost the end of the trip. Here the Semois receives the Petit-Fays stream which rushes through a narrow valley which can be followed to the north on a minor road. Here can still be seen the bars on which tobacco was dried. Vresse itself has a museum which is primarily concerned with the tobacco world and with smoking.

Parc naturel de Bohan-Membre

Before finally reaching the French frontier the Semois flows through the nature park of Bohan-Membre which is crossed by many footpaths, including one that leads to the viewpoint Jambon de la Semois and to the prehistoric megalithic Table des Fées.

Detour to France

Beyond the frontier the Semois winds its way towards the Meuse. This is the land of the legend of the four Haimon children who set out on the battle charger Bayard from Château Regnault on the banks of the Meuse on their adventures. Near the confluence of the Semois and the Meuse above Monthermé local tradition identifies four crags with the four riders and nearby their battle steed is chiselled in the rock.

Verviers   H 16

Province: Liège
Altitude: 200–240 m (656–787 ft). Population: 53,600
Intercity Station (bicycle rental at station)

Where Limberg, the district of Herve and the foothills of the Ardennes meet extends the industrial town of Verviers, on the slopes of the valley of the Vesdre which flows through it, about half way between Liège and Aachen. Fine civic buildings testify to the prosperity of the town when the woollen industry was flourishing; even today Verviers still has a textile technical school. As well as the textile industry the production of leather goods, agriculture, paper and building materials are of importance. In addition tourism is playing an increasing role, for the town is the gateway to the scenically charming Herve region and to the Ardennes.

History Verviers goes back to a Roman settlement called "Virovirus", but the settlement only acquired importance from 1651 when a charter was given to the town by the prince-bishop of Liège, and the increasing thriving of the woollen industry because of favourable conditions provided by water from the Vesdre and the proximity of sheep rearing areas in the Ardennes and the Eifel. The industrial revolution brought an unexpected impetus and the population rose from 20,000 in 1830 to 53,000 in 1900. Verviers was once the most important place in Europe for wool processing, but the world economic crisis in the 30s put a stop to its prosperity.

Hôtel de Ville

The traffic junction in the heart of Verviers on the left bank of the river is the Place Verte, from which the Crapaurue, the principal street, leads to

The classical Town Hall of Verviers

the Hôtel de Ville in the Place du Marché which is flanked by beautiful Baroque and Rococo houses. This freestanding building in the Classical style dates from the 18th c. and is one of the most elegant of its kind in Belgium. In front of the Town Hall is a perron (raised platform) dating from 1732.

Further to the north in the Rue des Raines there are still a number of fine old burghers' houses dating from the 16th-18th c. which testify to the town's former prosperity. House No. 42, the Maison Cornet, contains the Musée d'Archéologie et du Folklore. Its greatest treasure is the wonderful collection of **lace** from all parts of Belgium; also of great interest are the rooms on the ground and first floors, as well as the Grand Salon in Dutch style and the Salon Louis XIII with three artistic secretaires. Commemorated in the Grand Salon is the violinist Henri Vieuxtemps (1820–81) who was born in Verviers. The second storey is devoted to archaeological finds from the surroundings. (Open Mon.–Thu. and Sat. 9am–noon and 2–5pm, Sun. and public holidays 10am–1pm and 3–6pm.)

Musée d'Archéologie et du Folklore

In a former 17th c. hospice for elderly men in Rue Renier which branches off the Rue des Raines is the interesting Musée des Beaux-Arts et de la Céramique. On the ground floor is exhibited an excellent collection of faience and porcelain from the most important European factories and also china; in other rooms and on the first floor is a considerable collection of pictures including a fine portrait of a child with a lace hood by Cornelis de Vos and works by Pieter Pourbus, Guido Reni and Frans Snyders, as well as more modern paintings by René Magritte and Paul Delvaux; in the courtyard is a lapidarium and in the basement sculptures (open as above).

★ Musée des Beaux-Arts et de la Céramique

Further to the west by the river stands the 18th c. Church of Notre-Dame

Notre-Dame

which was the destination of a pilgrimage in honour of the Black Madonna sculpture of 1692. The tower has a fine carillon of 40 bells.

Musée de la Laine

In the southern part of the town can be found the Musée de la Laine in the building of the textile technical school; it is concerned with the history of wool processing (Rue de Séroule; open Mon.–Sat. 2–5pm).

Limbourg

7 km (4½ mi.) north-east of Verviers is the little town of Limbourg built on a hill. It was situated on the route between Bruges and Cologne and until the Battle of Worringen in 1268 was the chief town of the former Duchy of Limbourg but then it fell to Brabant. Because of its strategic importance it was subsequently fortified but suffered several sieges, especially heavy ones by Louis XIV and in 1703 by the Duke of Marlborough who destroyed the ducal castle which had been built about 1000 in the upper town.

The circular path along the old town walls leads around the upper town and offers fine views. Of interest is the Gothic Église Saint-Georges, of which the predecessor was the 12th c. castle chapel, and this in turn was built above a Romanesque crypt. The church received its present form in the 14th and 15th c.

Dolhain

Not far from Limbourg the Vesdre is spanned by the 20 m (66 ft)-high **viaduct** of Dolhain which was completed in 1843.

Abbaye de Val-Dieu

Nestling picturesquely in the valley of the Berwinne is the Abbaye de Val-Dieu which is reached on a 15 km (9½ mi.) drive via Thimister and Aubel north of Verviers. The abbey was founded around the year 1215 and was very prosperous. Of special interest in the present buildings, which are inhabited by Cistercians, are the refectory, the guesthouse of 1732 and the Renaissance choirstalls in the abbey church.

Barrage de la Gileppe

See Eupen, Surroundings

Veurne · Furnes   E 1

Province: West-Vlaanderen
Altitude: 0–30 m (0–98 ft). Population: 11,300
Inter-regional Station (bicycle rental at station)

The little town of Veurne (French Furnes), not far from the North Sea coast and at the confluence of four canals, is the centre of a legal and administrative district and is worth visiting especially for its lovely marketplace. Its historic monuments dating from the Spanish period were damaged by bombardment during the First and Second World Wars but have been excellently restored. Ham from Veurne is a noted delicacy.

History Veurne grew up around a castle erected by the Counts of Flanders in the 9th c. as protection against the Normans and it became the chief place of the counts' fortified estate of Veurne-Ambacht. It reached its zenith under the regentship of the Archduke Albert and Archduchess Isabella in the 17th c. when most of the stately buildings around the Grote Markt came into being. The French strengthened the fortifications which had been set up in the 14th c. and which, under the Austrians, were razed to the ground in 1783. In the First World War Veurne was the most important town of the small part of Belgium not occupied by German troops and in spite of artillery attack could not be taken. During the Battle of Ypres King Albert I chose the town hall as his headquarters. In the Second World War the town suffered more severe damage than between 1914 and 1918.

The **Penitential procession**, which takes place annually on the last Sunday in July, dates back to the 12th c.; it was first held in 1644 and since 1656 has been celebrated every year. Members of the "Sodaliteit" brotherhood present scenes from the Passion of Christ in a procession, and they are followed by penitents in the garments of Capuchins dragging along heavy crosses. The Way of the Cross processions in Lent and at Easter are connected with Spanish traditions. The Way of the Cross begins at Sint-Walburgakerk and ends at the Sint-Niklaaskerk. During Lent it takes place every Friday at 8pm and during Easter week daily at the same time. On Maundy Thursday it is held at 8 and 9pm.

The impressive centre of the town is the Grote Markt, one of the finest market squares in Belgium. It is lined by several historic buildings in the characteristic west Flanders yellow brick. Interaction of the elements of architectural decoration of Flemish Renaissance and the sober Spanish influence becomes clear and it is for this that Veurne is often called the "Spanish town".

★Grote Markt

The Stadhuis (town hall) in the north-west corner of the square built by Liéviun Lucas between 1596 and 1612 is, with its twin gabled faáade and elegant loggia of bluish stone, is an excellent example of the style of the Flemish Renaissance. Above the roof rises the narrow stepped tower erected in 1599. The rooms of the town hall have largely kept their form and furnishings of the 17th and 18th c. Tours Apr.–Sep. daily 11am, 2, 3 and 4.30pm; Oct.–Mar. daily 11am and 3pm.

Stadhuis

The council chamber on the ground floor is particularly fine and impressive with its leather wall hangings from Mechelen as is the jury room with its linings of blue satin from Utrecht. On the upper floor can be seen the reception hall with leather wall hangings from Córdoba in Andalusia – here King Albert I had his office in 1914 – and the lawcourt

The Grote Markt in Veurne: Stadhuis, Landhuis, Belfry and Sint-Walburga

with a painting by de Vriendt, as well as the marriage room, again with leather hangings from Mechelen and a still life by de Vos.

Landhuis

In the right-hand corner of the square adjoining the town hall is the former Landhuis, built 1613–16 and now the palace of justice (viewing in conjunction with the town hall tour). It is dominated by its mighty Gothic belfry which, however, bears a Baroque spire. The tower, not finished until 1628, was set on fire by bombardment in 1940. Separated only by a narrow road, the Landhuis is adjoined by five very fine stepped gabled houses dating from the beginning of the 17th c.

Sint-Walburgakerk

Along the road mentioned above we come to Sint-Walburgakerk which was begun in 1250 on a magnificent scale but only the 27 m (89 ft)-high sandstone **choir** (14th c.) with its ambulatory and chapels, the lower part of the tower and one arm of the crossing were completed in the Middle Ages. Also from this period date the remains of a pillar which can be seen in the park outside the church. The castle of the counts of Flanders is believed to have stood on this spot.

The transepts and other parts of the church were not added until 1901–04. In the choir which is supported by huge round pillars is some beautiful seating of 1596; also of interest are several paintings (17th and 18th c.), a Baroque pulpit and the reliquary of the cross which Count Robert II of Flanders is said to have brought from Jerusalem in the year 1100.

Noordstraat

In Noordstraat which leads from the market there are several beautiful Renaissance houses, including the house called "Die Nobele Roze" of 1572, one of the oldest hotels in Belgium now occupied by a bank. Opposite a monument commemorates the opening of the IJzer sluices in 1914 by means of which the German advance was stopped.

Spaans Paviljoen

The north-east side of the Grote Markt is taken up by the so-called Spaans Paviljoen. This was built between 1448 and 1452, extended in 1530 and until 1586 served as the town hall. In 1697 it was used to accommodate Spanish officers.

Vleeshuis

The Vleeshuis (meat hall) on the opposite side of the market place dates from 1615 and is a fine example of Late Renaissance architecture.

Hoge Wacht

On the south side of the market place facing the Appelmarkt is the Hoge Wacht, an arcaded building acquired by the town in 1636 for the guard.

Sint-Niklaaskerk

On the Appelmarkt rises the Gothic Sint-Niklaaskerk, the great tower of which dating from the 12-13th c. remained unfinished. It houses a carillon which includes the bell called "Bomtje" of 1379, one of the oldest Flemish bells. It is not known who was responsible for the triptych on the high altar; opinions vary between Jan van Aemstel and Bernard van Orley. In the summer, it is possible to climb the tower.

★Internationaal Bakkerijmuseum

To the south, away from the town centre, an 18th c. farmhouse houses the International Bakery Museum (Albert-I-Laan 2). It is divided into several sections: "Art in the Bakery", "Bread from all the world", an old bakery and a shop in which visitors can buy local delicacies such as "Kletskoppen" (biscuits), "Haantjes" (little chickens made from sandcake pastry, almond bread. (Open Apr.–Sep. daily except Fri. 10am–noon and 2–6pm; Jul. and Aug. also open Fri.; Oct.–Mar. Sun–Thu. 2–5pm.)

Kasteel van Beauvoorde

7 km (4½ mi.) south of Veurne is the Kasteel van Beauvoorde, an attractive Renaissance château surrounded by a moat. It was constructed between 1591 and 1617 on the site of a destroyed castle by the master builder of Archduke Albrecht and Isabella and after a period when it

became dilapidated it was bought by a private citizen Arthur Merghelynck and restored. He is responsible for the present interior furnishing (Renaissance furniture, paintings, objects d'art) which can be seen on a guided tour (guided tours Jun.–Sep. daily except Mon. 2, 3, 4 and 5pm).

In Izenberge, 10 km (6 mi.) to the south, the museum "Bachten de Kupe" should be visited. It is devoted to local culture and divided into three sections: a dwelling house, a museum of popular art and an open-air museum with rural buildings including a smithy and a farmhouse.

Izenberge

The village of Houtem, 10 km (6 mi.) to the south-west was from the beginning of 1915 until the late summer of 1918 the headquarters of the Belgian army.

Houtem

Lo is a pretty little town 15 km (9½ mi.) south-east of Veurne. Its Gothic hall church is richly furnished with artistic features, especially valuable paintings including some by Mittendorf, Boeckhorst and Boucquet. Only a tower remains of the 14th c. fortifications.

Lo

See entry

De Panne

See entry

Koksijde

Virton   Q 15

Province: Luxembourg. Altitude: 230 m (755 ft)
Population: 10,500. Local Rail Station (bicycle rental at station)

The little town of Virton, at the extreme southern tip of Belgium right on the French border, is situated at the confluence of the rivers Vire and Ton. It is the chief place of the peaceful district of Gaume and the **landscape** is reminiscent of Lorraine; it is blessed with a mild climate so that in the extreme south viniculture is possible. Virton is to a large extent dependent on tourism and is an excellent base for excursions in the surroundings.

History Numerous finds testify that the area was settled in Neolithic, Roman and Merovingian times. Virton itself developed from the Roman foundation of Vertunum. From the 16th c. a thriving iron casting industry developed here.

In buildings of a 17th c. monastery is the Musée gaumais which is concerned with the history and culture of the Gaume region (opening times Mar.–Oct. daily except Tue. 9.30am–noon and 2–6pm).
   The various departments exhibit examples of iron casting, including more than 150 fireplace plates, the oldest of which date from the 16th c., firebacks and pothooks; finds from Gallo-Roman times, various items of household furniture and everyday articles typical of Gaume, a collection of Boch stoneware of the 18th c. as well as 16–18th c. woodcarving. Also on view are watercolours by Nestor Outer a friend of Toulouse-Lautrec, oil paintings by Camille Barthélemy, who painted views of Virton, and among other things the painting "Adam and Eve mourn for Abel" by Frère Abraham (18th c.) from the Abbey of Orval (see entry). Three other museums in the vicinity are associated with the Musée gaumais.

★ Musée gaumais

At the Ferme de Huombois, 9 km (5½ mi.) from Virton on the road to Buzenol, it is possible to see kilns and pottery articles dating from the Gallo-Roman era (on enquiry at the Musée gaumais).

Huombois

Buzenol

Near Buzenol, 13 km (8 mi.) north of Virton, there is a 340 m (1116 ft)-high hill called **Montauban** which was already fortified in Roman times. Remains of the fortification walls from this and later periods have been preserved and can be seen in the "Parc archéologique". In the adjoining museum there are fine Gallo-Roman reliefs including a representation of the Celtic reaper mentioned by Plinius the Elder. A number of old smithies and foundries have been preserved in the wooded valley.

Montquintin

4 km (2½ mi.) south-east of Virton lies Montquintin. Here in an 18th c. farm the "Musée de la Vie paysanne" has been set up which, by means of furnishing and implements, brings the old rural existence to life. (Open Jul. and Aug. daily 2–6pm.)

Torgny

Beyond Montquintin we reach Torgny, the most southern parish in Belgium. Around this pretty village vines are grown, the "Clos de la Zolette" which is a Riesling grape.

Latour

Latour, 7 km (4½ mi.) east of Virton, commemorates its past in the Musée Ballet-Latour. The history of the local castle is documented; the battle on the border on August 22nd 1914, as well as events in the First and Second World Wars are described. Several rooms contain everyday and folkloric articles devoted to the culture of the Gaume. (Open Easter–Nov. Sun. 3–6pm; Jul. and Aug. daily 3–6pm.)

Montmédy

Across the French border a detour leads to Montmédy (14 km (8½ mi.)) where can be seen the very well preserved fortification complex of Vauban.

Visé

G 16

Province: Liège. Altitude: 60–85 m (197–279 ft)
Population: 16,800. Intercity Station

Close to the Belgian-Dutch border on the right bank of the Meuse the town of Visé is the most northerly city in Wallonia. It is popular in summer for the water sports centre in the "three countries corner".

History Visé grew up around a wooden bridge over the Meuse and had its flowering between the 9th and the 13th c. In 1330 the town was fortified and subsequently had to defend itself in many sieges, including those against the troops of Charles the Bold in 1468 and Louis XIV in 1663. In the first days of the First World War Visé was set on fire by German troops and almost completely destroyed.

Festivals Visé is rich in folklore. Here is celebrated the "Carnival of the Geese" commemorating the legend of 1334, when the geese of Visé on their search for food made it possible for the besiegers to enter the town: the geese simply chewed up the bolts of the gates.

The three shooting guilds of the town are of great importance: the "Gilde des Anciens Arbalétriers" (Old Cross-bow Shooters Guild), founded in 1310, its successor the "Compagnie Royale des Anciens Arquebusiers" (Royal Company of Arquebusiers) dating from 1579 and the "Compagnie Royale des Francs Arquebusiers" (Royal Company of Free Arquebusiers) which came into being in 1909. Each of these guilds has a festival twice a year.

Collégiale Saints-Martin-et-Hadelin

The collegiate church of Saints-Martin-et-Hadelin was founded by Berta the daughter of Charles the Great in 780. The church was destroyed by German troops and rebuilt from 1925; of the earlier work only the choir (1500) remains. However a visit to the church is well worth while because of its unique art treasures. The **shrine of Saint Hadelinus**, which contains the remains of the priest who preached by the Meuse in the 7th c., is the finest reliquary shrine in the Mosan area. Its gabled ends probably date from the 10th c.; one shows Christ crowning saints Remaclus and Hadelinus, the other an exceptionally rare representation of Christ as the vanquisher of death and the devil. On the sides, which date from 1150, are scenes from the life of Hadelinus and in their execution these are reminiscent of works by Renier de Huy. On the third Sunday in September the shrine is borne in procession through the town.

The present town hall is a reconstruction of the building which dated from the 17th c. in Mosan-Renaissance style. It has a notable onion-shaped tower. On the second floor is the Musée Regional d'Histoire et d'Archéologie (Regional Historical and Archaeological Museum) with a local history collection.

Hôtel de Ville

The three shooting guilds maintain their own museums which are sometimes open on Sunday mornings in summer and which exhibit weapons and documents about the history of their guilds. The museum of the Cross-bow Shooter's Guild is at No. 44 Rue Haute, that of the Old Arquebusiers at No. 11 and the museum of the Free Arquebusiers at No. 3 Rue Dodémont.

Gilden Museum

9 km (5½ mi.) north-west of Visé lies Eben-Emael where the fort was completely destroyed by German troops in May 1940.

Eben-Emael

Walcourt   L 10

Province: Namur
Altitude: 150–238 m (492–781 ft). Population: 15,000
Local Rail Station (bicycle rental at station)

Walcourt is a little place of pilgrimage at the confluence of the Yvres and the Eau d'Heure in the extreme west of the province of Namur. Remains of defence works bear witness to its past as a fortified town.

Processions Every year on Trinity Sunday the "Grand Tour" takes place in Walcourt; this is a procession round the town in honour of the wonder-working statue of Mary. The procession is accompanied by soldiers in Napoleonic uniform together with pipes and drums.

The landscape of Walcourt is dominated by the Basilique Saint-Materne in the Grand-Place. The original church was built about the year 1000 in the Mosan-Romanesque style but in 1220 it burned down. When this happened it is said that the statue of Mary was swept out of the church into a birch tree where it was found by the Count of Rochefort, but he could only recover it after he had vowed to build a new church. This scene is the climax of the annual procession. The new church was built between the 13th and 15th c. in Mosan-Gothic style with five aisles. Only the west of the building and the lower part of the tower date from the time of its predecessor. The north doorway is adorned with a fine sculpture of the Virgin and Child (15th c.); the 63 m (207 ft) high octagonal tower ends in a remarkable spire in a half-domed form dating from the 17th c.

Basilique Saint-Materne

The furnishing of the **interior** is predominantly of 16th c. date; the rood screen (partly Late-Gothic and partly Early Renaissance) of 1533 has sculptures of white Avesnes stone and was a gift of Charles V. The relatively plain choir stalls (1510) are carved with intercession scenes and satirical motifs; the Late-Gothic tabernacle is also of exceptional beauty.

The wonder-working **statue of Notre-Dame du Pélerinage** (Notre-Dame du Walcourt) in the left transept was made in the 11th c. from wood and is covered with silverplate.

Among the treasures of the exceptionally valuable **church treasury** are a reliquary cross of 1300, possibly by Hugo d'Oignies the silversmith born in Walcourt in the 12th c., a 14th c. silver Madonna and several monstrances and reliquary shrines (these can be seen only after enquiry in the basilica).

Musée Communale

The Musée Communale (rue de la Montagne 3) has three sections: the history of the railways, lacework and cultural-religious heritage (open Easter–Oct. Wed.–Sun. 2–6pm).

Thy-le-Château

Thy-le-Château, which lies 8 km (5 mi.) north of Walcourt, had a flourishing iron industry in the 13th c. The fine restored castle (10–13th c.) is well worth a visit.

Barrages de l'Eau d'Heure

About 4 km (2½ mi.) south of Walcourt begins the lake district of the Barrages de l'Eau d'Heure; this was created by building dams to provide energy and as a reservoir for the Sambre and the canal from Charleroi to Brussels; it is the largest connected series of lakes in Belgium. At the same time the area has become popular for leisure activities and water sports including sailing, water-skiing, swimming and diving, and also paragliding. There are more than 100 km (62 mi.) of footpaths for walkers, and short excursions can be made on the lakes in a little steamer.

The longest dam is the 790 m (2592 ft)-long Barrage de la Plate-Taille on the top of which an information centre with a 107 m (351 ft)-high viewing tower has been built. The centre also contains a large aquarium and a relief model of the lake district. Technical details of the complex are provided by means of an audio-visual show (open Easter-Sep. daily 9am-6pm).

Philippeville

13 km (8 mi.) south-east of Walcourt Philippeville is the chief place of the region Entre-Meuse-et-Sambre. The town was constructed in 1555 at the behest of the emperor Charles V in order to counter the building of the French fortification of Mariembourg (see Chimay, Surroundings). The town owes its name to his son Charles V who later became the Spanish king Philip II. However, in spite of its heavy fortifications Philippeville was taken by the French in 1660; Louis XIV had it reinforced by his fortress builder Vauban. In 1860 the ramparts and walls were razed to the ground but even today it is possible to recognise the original layout as a fortification by the concentric roads leading to the Place d'Armes. Of the powerful fortifications only about 10 km (6 mi.) of the subterranean passages and a former powder magazine dating from 1600 remain, the latter has been the Chapelle de Notre-Dame des Remparts since 1922. The passages and chapel can be seen on a guided tour (open Jul. and Aug. daily except Wed. 10am–4pm).

Roly

Roly A well-maintained and almost unaltered fortified estate can be found 11 km (7 mi.) to the south of Philippeville. It was built in 1554 around a large 13th c. keep. The argricultural buildings date from the 16th to the 19th c.

Waterloo   H 9

Province: Brabant. Altitude: 90–130 m (297–427 ft)
Population: 26,900. Local Rail Station

The little town of Waterloo in Brabant, 18 km (11 mi.) south of Brussels, has become world famous through the historic battle of June 18th 1815. This decided not only the fate of France and its emperor Napoleon I but also the future of Europe, when the French army met the united armies of Britain, Hanover, the Netherlands and Prussia. While the British general Wellington spoke of the "Battle of Waterloo", to the Prussian field marshal it was the "Battle of Belle-Alliance" since both generals met after the successful victory at the farm of this name. Every year about June 15th the battles are re-enacted.

The battlefield is situated to the south of Waterloo mainly in the the parish of Braine-l'Alleud and now appears a peaceful scene of pastures and fields of cereals. In summer a tourist train runs from Waterloo station to the Butte de Lion, west of the trunk road to Charleroi.

★ Battlefield

At the foot of Lion Hill lies the visitors' centre, where by means of diagrams and computer screens details of the historic events can be studied. From here there is an entrance to Lion Hill. Open Apr.–Sep. daily 9.30am–6.30pm; Nov.–Dec. daily 10.30am–4pm; Mar. daily 10.30am–5pm; Oct. daily 9.30am–5.30pm.

The Butte du Lion, lion hill, rises above the former battlefield and is visible from afar. It was constructed between 1823 and 1826 on the place where the Prince of Orange was wounded. The hill was built up with 32,000 cu. m (42,000 cu. yd) of earth from the battlefield to a height of 40 m (131 ft) and a circumference of 520 m (1706 ft) on a supporting brick base. On the summit was placed the sculpture of a lion by Arthur-Louis van Geel which weighs 28 tonnes and is more than 4 m (13 ft) long. The lion stands with its right paw on a globe and looks to the south from where the French came. From the platform beneath the monument (over 226 steps to climb) there is a **panoramic view** of the battlefield. Near the visitors' centre stands a circular building which contains a 12 m (39 ft)-high and 110 m (310 ft)-long panorama of the battle. This is a work by the French military painter Louis Dumoulin and dates from 1913/14.

★ Butte du Lion

On the opposite side of the road in a hotel which dates from 1818 is a waxworks museum, where not only the chief figures of the battle but also ordinary soldiers are exhibited in life size (open Apr.–Oct. daily 9.30am–7pm; Nov.–Mar. Sat. and Sun. for groups by appointment tel. (3) 840625).

Musée des Cires

On the extensive area of the former battlefield there are commemorative monuments of the bloody fighting including three around the crossing of the main road with the road to the Lion Hill. These are: a monument erected in 1914 for the fallen of Belgium in the form of a stone column with bronze standards bearing an inscription in French "To those Belgians who fell on June 18th 1815 in the battle for the defence of their standard and the honour of the armies"; a monument surrounded by a railing for the men of Hanover with the inscription "In memory of their brothers in arms who fell on June 18th 1815" and the monument for Lt. Col. Gordon, Wellington's adjutant, who was killed here. Both the last named monuments stand on the level of the former battlefield, the surrounding area was removed for the erection of the Lion Hill. A path to the Lion Hill which passes the monuments corresponds to the course of the sunken road of Ohain. Other interesting monuments can be found further to the south: in Plancenoit is one to the fallen Prussians, a work of Karl Friedrich Schinkel dating from 1819; still further south on the right of the main road the fallen French imperial eagle at the spot where the guard made its last stand which Bellangé emotionally captured in the lithograph (see Baedeker Special, pages 386/87).

Monuments

Further south on the left of the main road is the Ferme du Caillou in which Napoleon set up his headquarters. It is now furnished as a museum with four rooms and exhibit items which the fleeing Emperor

Musée du Caillou

The Old Guard

Following Napoleon's return from Elba and his triumphal entry into Paris the European powers are determined to put an end to his powers once and for all. Their armies are to occupy France in a pincer formation: the English and Prussians through Belgium, the Austrians over the Upper Rhine, the Russians over the Middle Rhine and the Austrian and the Austrian-Sardinian alliance over the Alps. Napoleon sees that his only chance to prevent these armies from joining up is by aiming to defeat one of them quickly. He hopes to surprise the English-Prussian army commanded by Wellington and Blücher south of Brussels.

Marching towards them the first heavy fighting takes place on June 16th 1815: the English are attacked at Quatre-Bras by Marshal Ney's cavalry but not defeated. The Prussians, however, are beaten back at Ligny and withdraw towards Wavre. They are pursued by 33,000 men under Marshal Grouchy who believes the Prussians will fall back at Liege. Two days later Napoleon waits for these 33,000 men in vain.

In the saturated fields of Brabant, on a rainy June 18th 1815 near Waterloo, where Wellington had made quarters, both main armies take up their positions. The French army – 72,000 men and 254 artillery – march up on both sides of Belle Alliance. Facing them on the heights of Mont St Jean are 69,000 British, Dutch, Belgians and Hannoverians, many of whom had already fought against the French in Spain. Towards 11.30am the French go forward and are engaged in heavy fighting at the Ferme de Hougoumont. At 1.30pm the artillery open fire into the middle of the British and four divisions march towards the farmstead of La Haie Sainte, which is doggedly defended along the sunken road of Ohain, and at 4pm 5000 men of Marshal Ney's cavalry attack but are beaten back suf-

The French cavalry attacking at Mont St Jean

fering heavy losses. Only with a further 9000 cavalry and infantry troops does Ney succeed in taking La Haie Sainte. He thinks the British are wavering and without authorisation attacks their centre. In fact the British are struggling and are longing for the support of the Prussians – "I wish it were night or the Prussians would come" – but the French also hardly have any reserves, when the Prussians actually appear at 4.30pm on the right flank of the French and assemble forces. At 7pm Napoleon, seeing the terrible losses suffered by Ney's troops, gambles everything and sends his Old Guard into battle. These veterans, recognisable by their bearskin hats have fought in all the Emperor's great battles, but even they cannot turn things round. They charge, at the same time the Prussians attack with their main army causing panic which soon grips the entire French army. Wellington now mounts the counter attack. The commander of the Imperial Guard, Cambronne, rejects surrender with a brusque

"The Old Guard dies, but it does not surrender" (Lithograph by Bellangé)

"Merde!"; towards 9pm the Imperial Guard form a square with Napoleon in the middle and cover his escape. The veterans of Marengo, Austerlitz, Wagram and all the other battles face death together – "The Old Guard dies, but it does not surrender". Along-side them 33,000 Frenchmen, 15,000 English and 7000 Prussians lie in the now peaceful fields of Brabant.

Unlike almost any other battle in world history Waterloo has become a legend. Here the fate of Napoleon, who had held Europe in his iron grip for years, and that of the French Empire was sealed; it was only here, in front of the gates of Brussels that the European powers finally overcame the French Revolution. Since Waterloo, however, the myth of the battlefield and the heroic commanders has gradually faded from people's thoughts: "The question: 'Why, for what purpose and for whom?' from now on will not fall silent" (Friedrich Sieburg).

In Flanders Fields

IN FLANDERS FIELDS

IEPER
1914-1918

Touring the surroundings of Ypres by car or bike, you will again and again come across the testimonies of the battles in Flanders – the obvious ones such as the shining rows of white crosses of the mostly British military cemeteries, spaced only a few miles apart, and the less obvious ones which you can only detect on closer inspection, for example an idyllic duck pond which was carved into the ground by an exploding grenade. Standing on top of Kemmelberg and looking across the country, it is hard to imagine what it must have looked like over 80 years ago: a landscape pock-marked with craters, literally without a single tree, ploughed over and over again every day by heavy artillery fire.

And every day, hundreds, on some days tens of thousands of soldiers died, on both sides. The dead are buried in 170 cemeteries. The numerous British cemeteries are all situated close to Ypres; the graves for the German casualties were combined in large collective cemeteries in Langemark, Menen Forest, Hooglede and Vladslo-Praetbosch. Many of the British graves are adorned with wreaths of paper poppies, laid there by relatives of the dead. They are a visual quote from the poem written by the British army doctor John McCrae on 8 December 1915 in Boezinge (Essex Farm) to commemorate his comrades-in-arms:

In Flanders fields the poppies blow, between the crosses, row by row ...

"In Flanders Fields" is also the titles of a sign-posted circuit to the most important memorial sites around Ypres. The most important stops are described in brief.

Leaving Ypres on the N 389 in a northerly direction, the circuit turns off at the French memorial site Carrefour des Roses, in the direction of Langemark. In Langemark, thousands of young German volunteers, mostly pupils and students, found their deaths in 1914; a fact still exploited for propaganda purposes by the Third Reich. The large military cemetery holds the graves of nearly 45,000 German soldiers.

The route continues to Poelkapelle, where a memorial in the centre of the village commemorates the French aviator Georges Guynemer who was shot down here in 1917, and then passes the Canadian Forces Memorial which reminds of the 3000 Canadians who lost their lives in the first German gas attack on 22 April 1915. The next stop is at Zonnebeke whose Tyne Cot Cemetery is the largest British military cemetery on the European mainland. It was established by Sir Reginald Blomfield, with almost 12,000 war graves and a memorial for about 35,000 soldiers missing after 16 August 1917. The circuit then returns to Ypres and leaves the town in a southerly direction, on the N 365, to reach Wijtschate and Menen, scene of the infamous mine attack of 7 June 1917 when the British forces exploded 21 giant mines under the German lines. The tremors could be felt as far away as London and Paris; tens of thousands of soldiers were buried within seconds.

From Menen you get to Kemmelberg, the scene of a bitter battle in the spring of 1918 when grenades denuded the entire mountain of trees. On its southern slope is a bone house for over 5000 French soldiers. From the Kemmelberg, the circuit returns to Ypres via Poperinge.

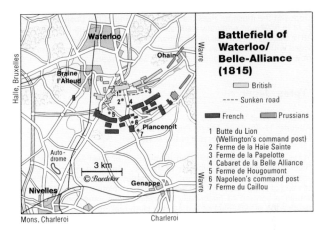

Battlefield of Waterloo/Belle-Alliance (1815)

British

---- Sunken road

French   Prussians

1 Butte du Lion (Wellington's command post)
2 Ferme de la Haie Sainte
3 Ferme de la Papelotte
4 Cabaret de la Belle Alliance
5 Ferme de Hougoumont
6 Napoleon's command post
7 Ferme du Caillou

left behind, including his tent. (Open Apr.–Oct. daily 10am–6.30pm; Nov.–Mar. 1–5pm.)

Musée Wellington In Waterloo itself a visit should be paid to the former headquarters of the Duke of Wellington on the main road to Brussels. Here there is more documentation about the battle and personal possessions of the British commander. (Open Apr.–mid Nov. 9.30am–6.30pm; mid Nov.–Mar. daily 10.30am–5pm.)

Waterloo Town

Waterloo: the Gordon memorial and the Butte du Lion

Opposite the museum rises the domed building of the **Chapelle royale**, built in 1690 and originally dedicated to the Spanish king Charles II. In 1817 the chapel was declared a memorial for the battle and was provided with burial plaques of the Allied soldiers who had died. These can now be seen in the adjoining church of Saint-Joseph.

Ypres · Ieper G 2

Province: West-Vlaanderen
Altitude: 17–45 m (56–148 ft). Population: 35,000
Inter-regional Station (bicycle rental at station)

Ypres (Flemish Ieper) is situated in the plain of West Flanders on the River Ieper (Ieperlee), a tributary of the Iser. The name Ypres is closely associated with some of the most bitter battles of the First World War, at the end of which the town had been almost completely destroyed. It was rebuilt according to historically accurate models, and today it again exudes the atmosphere of a medieval cloth-making town. Tourists are drawn to the city – it serves as a base for bicycle excursions into the surroundings, but also for a large number of tourists who wish to visit the war graves.

History Founded in the 10th c., in the Middle Ages Ypres, together with Ghent and Bruges, was one of the three most important towns in Belgium because of its prosperous cloth-making, reaching the peak of its heyday in the 13th and 14th c. with a population of 40,000. The Cloth Hall, the largest and most beautiful building of its kind in Belgium, symbolises the wealth and power of that period. However, its decline began in 1316 when many of the town's citizens fell victim to a major epidemic. When the town took sides with the King of France against Ghent, which was allied to England during the Hundred Years' War, it was besieged in 1383. It withstood the siege but the massive destruction of the surrounding area and the suburbs forced many of the weavers to leave.

In the 16th c. it was devastated by the Iconoclasts and Duke of Alba's troops, conquered by the Geuzen and the troops of Alexander Farnese and finally, in the 17th c., was taken by the French following many sieges. Under the French Ypres was fortified by Vauban and taken over by the Habsburgs. Not until 1852 were the fortified walls razed and turned into walkways.

Despite all these volatile events Ypres retained most of its ancient buildings, evidence of its former splendour, until the First World War. The inferno broke out in November 1914 in the first Battle of Ypres. Ypres, lying at the junction of important roads, found itself in the middle of the Ypres Salient, the arc of the Allied front, which was bombarded by German and Austrian troops for four years and remained unbroken in the second battle of 1915, in the third of 1917 and during the Kemmel offensive of 1918 even though poison gas was used for the first time in history in April 1915 near Steenstraat to the north. The Allied counter-offensive of 1918 signalled the start of Belgium's liberation from German occupation. During the four years of fighting almost 500,000 soldiers on each side lost their lives; 170 military cemeteries at Ypres and in the surroundings commemorate this mass slaughter. Throughout this time the town stood in the line of fire and was subject to continuous bombardment by artillery so that by 1918 it was reduced to a heap of rubble. It has since been rebuilt according to the original plans, and the damage caused by the air raids in 1940 has been restored. The last building to be rebuilt was the town hall (Nieuwerck).

The Ypres **Cat Festival** which takes place on the second Sunday in May every three years (next 1997) is famous throughout the area. There is a

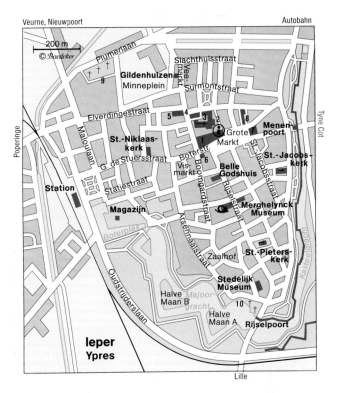

large procession through the town with the giants Goliath, Robrecht the Friesan and Cieper the giant cat. It reaches a climax with stuffed toy cats being thrown down from the belfry.

In the Grote Markt stands the 132 m (433 ft)-long Lakenhalle (cloth hall), rebuilt in 13th c. style. The original building was begun around 1260 and completed in 1304. It was completely destroyed in the First World War, but the new building is one of the finest and largest secular buildings in Europe. The extent of the hall in which the cloth was stored, checked and sold, is indicative of the power wielded by the guilds within the town. Above the entrance door is the statue of the patron saint Onze-Lieve-Vrouw-van-Thuyne; in the niches statues of count Balduin and Mary of Constantinople together with King Albert I and Queen Elisabeth. The large hall on the first floor is open to visitors.

★Lakenhalle

The 70 m (230 ft)-high square **belfry** which projects from the centre of the building is visible from the surrounding countryside. Its carillon of 49 bells is played from June to October at 9pm. From the tower there is a superb view over the plain of Flanders

In Flanders Fields Museum Opened in 1998, on the first floor of the Lakenhalle, this museum commemorates trench warfare in Flanders in the First World War. Its centre are not the large battles and the generals

391

The rebuilt Cloth Hall in the Grote Markt

but the ordinary people – civilians as well as soldiers. The museum makes use of the latest in museum technology, such as computers, video, audio recordings. The room devoted to chemical warfare is particularly impressive (open Apr.–Sep. daily 10am–6pm; Oct–Mar. Tue.–Sun. 10am–5pm).

Nieuwerck On the east wing of the Cloth Hall a new building (Nieuwerck), a town hall, was added in 1619 in the style of the Spanish Renaissance, which has also been reconstructed. It bears the coat of arms of the Spanish King Philip II.

Grote Markt

Opposite the Lakenhalle to the south on the corner of Boomgaardstraat stands the Nieuw Vleeshuis (meat hall), dating back to 1277, where meat was sold on Saturdays until 1947.

At the north end of the Grote Markt on the left is the Kasselrijgebouw (Old Town Hall) with the Seven Deadly Sins represented in the gables; on the east side is the Gerechtshof (County Court), a Renaissance reconstruction, on the site of the 12th c. Onze-Lieve-Vrouwgasthuis.

Sint-Maartens-kathedraal

Behind the Cloth Hall to the north stands Sint-Maartenskathedraal, rebuilt in 1922 (13th c. origin; 15th c. south entrance and tower). Its large-scale proportions are reminiscent of the monumental French cathedrals. The tower is over 100 m (328 ft) high.

Inside are some art treasures which survived the war; a brass font (around 1600) and the picture of Onze-Lieve-Vrouw-van Thuyne, believed to have miraculous powers. Inside the church are buried Bishop Jansenius (founder of Jansenism), Georgius Chamberlain (died 1634; sixth bishop of Ypres) and Count Robrecht of Bethune. The glass paintings are a present from Great Britain to commemorate the war losses.

North of the cathedral, opposite the theatre (Schouwburg) on the corner of Vandenpeerboomplein, the Anglican Church commissioned Sir Reginald Blomfield 1927–28 to build Saint George's Memorial Church to commemorate the soldiers of the British Commonwealth who were killed in battle in Flanders.

Saint-George's Memorial Church

    The entire interior of the church was funded by Great Britain and the Commonwealth, together with the statue of St George and the plaque with the famous poem "In Flanders Field". Nearby the Etonian Memorial School honours the 342 students of Eton College killed in action.

The Stedelijk Onderwijsmuseum (Municipal Museum of Education) in St.-Niklasstraat, west of the Grote Markt, explains daily life in a school.

Stedelijk Onderwijs-museum

At the old fish market with the Fish Gate of 1714, south-west of the Grote Markt the small customs house (Minckhuisje) and two stalls have been reconstructed.

Oude Vismarkt

In Rijselstraat south of the Grote Markt stands the Belle Godshuis, a hospital for the poor founded in 1276 and rebuilt in the 16th and 17th c. It is now a museum about the history of the hospital and has fine paintings, church artefacts and furniture from this period (open Apr.–Oct. 9.30am–noon and 1.30–5.30pm).

Belle Godshuis

Not far south is the Merghelynck Museum, housed in the 1774 building of the Empress Maria Theresa's treasurer, Frans Merghelynck. Part of the splendid Louis XV and Louis XVI interior survived the First World War and was rehoused in the restored house (visits only after prior arrangement tel. 200724).

★Museum Merghelynck

Diagonally opposite the Merghelynck Museum is the Steenhuis, now a post office, the only stone building left standing in Ypres (originally 13th c.).

Steenhuis

At the south end of the Rijselstraat a narrow street leads off to the right to the Stedelijk Museum in a 13th c. poor hospital; it illustrates the town's history (open Tue.–Fri. 2–6pm; Sep. also Sat. and Sun. 2–6pm).

Stedelijk Museum

From the eastern end of the Grote Markt it is only a short way to the Meensepoort through which the British soldiers marched to the front. It was built by the architect Sir Reginald Blomfields in the place of the destroyed medieval town gate. In its arch, the names of 54,896 British soldiers missing in action are inscribed. Since 1928, The Last Post is played here every evening at 8pm, always attended by large crowds.

Meensepoort

From the Meensepoort, you should definitely take a walk on the fortified Vauban ramparts to the Rijselpoort (Lille Gate), a massive fortified gate at the southern limits of the old town, from the Burgundian period. The British general staff had its headquarters in the casemates for a while. Near the gate ruins of the old ramparts can still be seen. Not far from the gate inside the fortifications the "Houten Huis" has been restored, a 16th c. wooden house, one of about 90. The walk will then lead you past the British Ramparts Cemetery to the Majoorsgracht.

Walk on the walls to the Rijselpoort

Surroundings

South of Ypres is the Heuvelland which can only be described as lovely. Its quiet villages are best explored on a bicycle. The only serious ascent being that of the 156 m Kemmelberg with its viewing tower. The Rode Berg and the Zwarte Berg, linked by a cable car, are also favourite excursions. The toy museum bar "Het Labyrint" in the village of Kemmel, and the restaurant on the Dikkebus – which was created in 1320 to supply Ypres with water, are both worth a visit.

Heuvelland

View from the Grote Markt through the Meensestraat to the Meensepoort

Zillebeke

Zillebeke, just outside Ypres to the east, has further reminders of the war: Hill 60, an important artillery observation post and the centre of heavy fighting, The Hooge Crater Museum and the Sanctuary Wood Museum. The Canadian front-line ran along here. The safari park Bellevaerde is also near Zillebeke (see Practical Information, Leisure Parks)

Zeebrugge   C 4

Province: West-Vlaanderen
Altitude: Sea level. Population: 4400
Local Rail Station

Zeebrugge, at the western end of the Belgian coast, belongs to Bruges (see Brugge) and since 1907 has been linked to the latter by the Boudewijnkanaal. It is the only Belgian seaport situated directly on the coast and is therefore of great importance both for freight and for passenger traffic. More recently the town has become increasingly popular as a resort, even if the beach is somewhat small, and Zeebrugge has no historic promenade such as Knokke-Heist (see entry) nor a nature reserve such as De Panne (see entry).

During the First World War Zeebrugge was the most important German U-boat base which was closed in 1918 in a spectacular action on St George's day. This event is commemorated by the St George Memorial at the landward end of the mole. Zeebrugge got into the headlines when on March 6th 1987 the British ferry "Herald of Free Enterprise" on leaving the harbour for Dover overturned about 800 m (2625 ft) from the quayside and 209 people were drowned.

The **port** of Zeebrugge was constructed between 1895 and 1907 and is protected from the sea by a 2.5 km (1½ mi.)-long mole. In the port containers are loaded and unloaded; regular container traffic exists with Great Britain, North America, South Africa, Australia and New Zealand. By means of the Pierre-Vandamme lock, passable by ships up to 125,000 tons, the outer harbour basins are linked with the three inland basins and with the Boudewijnkanaal. For some years an extensive building programme has been in progress which will increase the area of the harbour considerably so that ships up to 250,000 tons can be handled in the port.

Boat trips in the harbour Jul.–Sep. daily 2 and 4pm from the fishing harbour.

Harbours

Ferries to the English ports of Dover, Felixstowe and Hull use the ferry harbour. Zeebrugge is the largest fishing port in Belgium. The departure and arrival of the colourful fishing boats attracts numerous sightseers. The catches of fresh fish and shrimps are auctioned in the fish auction hall with a considerable amount of din.

Today, the harbour also has a tourist attraction. A Soviet submarine of the Foxtrott Class and the fire-boat "Westhinder" built in 1958 can be visited on the Seafront (open Feb.–Apr. and Nov./Dec. daily 1–5pm; May/Jun. and Sep./Oct. 10am–6pm; Jul. and Aug. 10am–9pm).

Seafront

Lissewege, 6 km (3¾ mi.) south of Zeebrugge, is an exceptionally romantic village of West Flanders with its low squat whitewashed brick houses. Worth a visit is the Early Gothic Onze-Lieve-Vrouwkerk (13/17th c.) from the mighty brick tower of which there is a magnificent view. The local museum near the church is also very interesting. Just to the south of the village, an extraordinary example of medieval secular architecture has been pre-served: the great 13th c. barn of the Cistercian abbey of Ter Doest, of which the main gateway and the dovecote (17th c.) also remain.

Lissewege

See entry

Blankenberge

See entry

Knokke-Heist

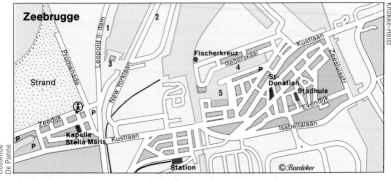

1 Car ferry Zeebrugge–Hull
2 Container Terminal

3 Car ferry Zeebrugge–Dover and Zeebrugge–Felixstowe

4 Fishing Harbour
5 Yacht Harbour

Container terminal in the port of Zeebrugge

Zottegem

See Oudenaarde, Surroundings

Zoutleeuw · Léau   G 13

Province: Brabant
Altitude: 35 m (115 ft.) Population: 7700

The present township of Zoutleeuw (French Léau), between Tienen and Sint-Truiden (see entries) in the extreme east of Brabant, came into being in the 11th c. under the name of Leeuw. It was linked by the little river Kleine Nete with Antwerp and in the 12th c. developed into an important trade centre and one of the principal towns of Brabant. At the same time Leeuw was of great importance for the dukes of Brabant as a frontier fortress, so that in the 12th and 13th c. (and later also in the 17th c.) it was provided with extensive fortifications. Finally Leeuw attracted notable artists as it was a cultural and religious centre with no fewer than eight monastic houses of various orders who left impressive testimony of their skill in St Leonard's Church (Sint-Leonarduskerk). French troops conquered the town in 1678 and destroyed the fortifications.

★★Sint-
Leonarduskerk

St Leonard's Church in Zoutleeuw owes its national importance to the fact that it was one of the very few churches in Belgium which was

Zoutleeuw: the nave of Sint-Leonarduskerk ▶

spared both by the iconoclasts of the religious struggles in the 16th c. and by the French revolutionary troops. For this reason it enables the visitor to realise how richly the churches of the Spanish Netherlands must have been furnished before the mid 16th c.

The building began around 1230 with the west faáade which is flanked by two asymmetrical towers; shortly afterwards the choir and the north transept followed, and in the 14th c. the south transept and the nave. The sacristy was added in the 15th c. to plans by Mattheus de Layens; the building was completed with the side chapels and the belfry above the crossing (today a reconstruction of 1926).

A walk round the **interior** of the church reveals the wealth of paintings, sculptures and other works of art of a religious character; only the more important can be mentioned here:

Marianum A multi-coloured painted wooden sculpture showing "Maria in the Rosary" surrounded by angels hangs from the roof of the nave; it was carved in 1530.

In the **right side-aisle** the first feature of interest is the second chapel dedicated to St Anne. On the left is the St Anne altar of 1565 in the style of the Antwerp school with painted wings dating from the 17th c., and nearby a very fine little triptych with the Crucifixion scene in glass (1535). On the wall opposite there is a triptych of 1525 with a representation of the "Glorification of the Cross" by Spieken.

The adjoining chapel of St Hubertus contains a triptych of the "Sorrow of Our Lady" created by Pieter Aertsen in 1575.

Next comes the sacristy built in Flamboyant style, above the entrance to which is a Romanesque picture of Christ.

In the **right transept** we can first see the extraordinary St Leonard's altar which the Brussels' artist Arnold de Maeler made in 1478. The painted and gilded statue of the saint in the centre of the altar dates from the year 1300.

The original chapel of St Leonard now contains the **church treasury**. It includes brass and copper work, processional crosses (13th and 14th c.), reliquaries, sculptures and liturgical vessels and vestments.

In the niches of the **ambulatory** numerous sculptures have been set up including twelve of saints, dating from the 12th to the 16th c., and a poly-chromatic statue of Mary (15th c.). Also notable is a copper desk in the form of an eagle (Antwerp 1468).

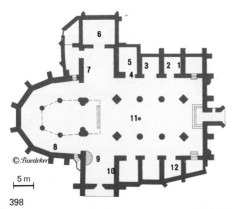

St-Leonarduskerk
Zoutleeuw

1 Triptych: "Glorification of the Cross" (16th c.)
2 Altar of St Anne (1565)
3 Triptych "Our Lady of Sorrows" (1575)
4 Romanesque Christ (11th c.)
5 Sacristy
6 St Leonard's Chapel with Treasury
7 Altar of St Leonard (1478)
8 Easter Candle (1483)
9 Tabernacle (1550–52)
10 Triptych: "Baptism of Christ"
11 Statue of the Virgin (1530)
12 "Seven friends of the Virgin" (1554)

© Baedeker

5 m

A fifteenth-century pietà

The great six-branched **pascal candlestick** which weighs 950 kg (2094 lb) testifies to the fine artistic skill of its creator Reiner of Tienen. This candlestick, almost 6 m (20 ft) tall, was cast in bronze in 1483.

Left transept The left transept houses the finest artistic object of the church, the **tabernacle** created between 1550 and 1552 by Cornelis Floris de Vriendt out of Avesnes stone. The tabernacle is 18 m (59 ft) high and on seven levels more than 200 figures, impressive in their authenticity, represent Old Testament scenes, Paradise, the Last Supper and other scenes of the New Testament, as well as saints, elders of the church and the Virgin Mary. Near the tabernacle are buried its creator, Marten van Wilre, and his wife Maria Pijlepeerts. The triptych opposite showing the baptism of Christ was created by Frans Floris de Vriendt, the brother of Cornelis.

The chapel in the **left side-aisle** is the Erasmus chapel. The triptych "The Seven Joys of Mary" (1554) is attributed to Pieter Aertsen. The wings portray the martyrdom of St Erasmus, St Blasius and St Laurentius.

On the south side of the pretty market place stands the little Renaissance town hall with a stepped gable, a side tower and a balustrade on which the arms of Charles V, Brabant and Leeuw can be seen. The building was erected between 1530 and 1539 to the design of Rombout Keldermans. — Stadhuis

Immediately adjoining the town hall is the former Lakenhalle (cloth hall), a fine building of brick and natural stone of 1314. — Lakenhalle

Of the houses surrounding the market place the Spiegelhuis (1571) is worth mentioning. This house is also constructed of brick and white stone. A curiosity is the gable formed from four ionic pillars. — Spiegelhuis

**Practical
Information
from A–Z**

Practical Information

Air Travel

Belgium is connected to the international network of routes by numerous international airline companies and by its own domestic service Sabena via the Brussels National Airport at Zaventem. There are few charter flights to Belgium.

Belgium's small size means that there is little demand for domestic services.

Airline companies

Sabena

The Belgian national airline company Sabena World Airline offers connections to all important European cities and, mainly through tradition, to Africa.

sabena 〈〉

In Belgium

Sabena Ticketing Center, Hôtel Carrefour de l'Europe,
110 Marché aux Herbes
B-1000 Bruxelles/Brussels, tel. (02) 7238940, fax. 5123974

Appelmansstrat 12–14
B-2018 Antwerpen; tel. (03) 2316825

There are also offices in Bruges, Charleroi, Ghent, Hasselt, Kortrijk, Leuven, Liège, Mons, Namur and Ostend.

In the UK

Gemini House, 2nd floor, West Block, 10–18 Putney Hill
London SW15 6AA; tel. (020) 87801444 (reservations and administration)

In the USA

J. F. K. Airport
New York; tel. (800) 71863210

British Airways

Centre International Rogier, 9th floor, Bruxelles; tel. (02) 2176111

TWA

Boulevard de l'Empereur 5, Bruxelles; tel. (02) 5137916

Air Canada

Boulevard de l'Impératrice 66, Bruxelles; tel. (02) 5136210

Airports

Only Brussels National Airport is of importance for international air travel. The Antwerp Airport has flights from some European cities including London (London City Airport). The smaller airports at Liège and Ostend play little part in this traffic.

◀ *Belgium is a gourmets' paradise*

Brussels National Airport is about 14 km (9 mi.) north-east of the city centre at Zaventem, tel. (02) 7533913; Sabena reservations office, tel. (02) 7232323.

Transfer to and from Brussels: by bus 578-BZ (via Diegem) or 358 and 358b (via Woluwé) to and from Brussels North Station; by the airport express tram to and from Central Station and North Station every 25 minutes (daily 7am–11pm; journey time 30 minutes approximately).

Banks

See Currency

Beaches

The Belgian North Sea coast extends for about 67 km (42 mi.) from the Dutch to the French border. Thirteen seaside resorts are located in this area, a number of which are very popular in the summer such as the largest and most well-known resort of Ostend (long sandy promenade and wide beaches), the elegant Knokke-Heist with five varied beaches or Blankenberge with its 3 km (2 mi.) long and, at low tide, 350 m (1149 ft) wide beach, especially suitable for families with young children. The medium-sized De Panne boasts more than a third of all the dunes along the coast and beautiful national parks (see Nature Reserves, National Parks and Caves). The small, quiet resort of Wenduine has long been well-known as a holiday camp for children.

The fine sandy beaches are gently sloping. Almost all parts of the beaches and dunes are open to the public without charge. The action of the tides has created a permanent beach area.

Composition

In each resort there are fenced-off areas of beach which are supervised throughout the day by members of the rescue service. On the boulevards immediately adjoining beaches members of the Red Cross offer first aid.

Beach facilities

Sun-loungers, windbreaks, etc. can be hired in many resorts. Changing cubicles can also be hired by the week or month.

Red flag = bathing forbidden!
Yellow flag = bathing permitted;
sailing and use of air beds forbidden!
Green flag = no danger

Beach regulations

Nudism on beaches is forbidden in Belgium. Going topless is only tolerated on the beach.

Dogs are generally banned from De Panne beach. This ban is also effective during the holiday period on the beaches at Blankenberge, De Haan, Knokke-Heist, Middelkerke, Ostend and Zeebrugge. Dogs may run freely on Koksijde and Oostduinkerke beaches; at Bredene and Nieuwpoort large dogs must be kept on a lead.

A coastal tram (kusttram) with numerous stops links the two resorts of De Panne (in the west) and Knokke-Heist (in the east) at the extremes of the Belgian North Sea coast.

Coastal tram

Boat Excursions

Excursions on ships or tourist boats on Belgium's lakes and canals, around the harbours of Antwerp and Zeebrugge, or canal tours count among the finest holiday experiences. Such excursions are offered in the following towns and villages described in Belgium from A to Z: harbour and tours on the Scheldt in Antwerp (see entry), canal trips in Bruges (see entry), canal trips from Bruges to Damme (see entry), Ghent (see entry) and Ostend (see entry), trips on the Meuse from Dinant (see entry) to Namur (see entry), excursions on the sloping lock (ship lift) of Ronquières near Ecaussinnes (see entry), towed barge or boat trips at the La Louvière and Strépy-Thieu ship hoists near Binche (see entry), trips on the Meuse departing from Liège (see entry), canal tours departing from Mechelen (see entry), excursions on board fishing boats and canal tours from Nieuwpoort (see entry), canal tours from Veurne (see entry) and harbour tours in Zeebrugge (see entry).

Boat hire

Various firms rent out cabin cruisers for trips on the network of Belgian waterways. Information can be obtained from tourist offices.

Camping and Caravanning

At present there are more than 500 camp sites in Belgium. During the peak holiday period it is advisable to book pitches in advance, especially at sites located along the Belgian coast.

Most Belgian camp sites have been graded into categories and classified by a **star system** which indicates whether the site offers only minimum standards (★), or has simple (★★), comfortable (★★★) or very good (★★★) facilities.

Unofficial camping is forbidden. One-off overnight stops in caravans or camper vans are permitted on picnic sites at motorway service stations.

Separate leaflets for Flanders (northern half of the country) and Wallonia (southern half of the country) **list** camp sites according to the province they are in and are obtainable from tourist information offices (see Information).

Car Rental

The large car rental firms have offices or counters in all of Belgium's larger cities and at Brussels, Antwerp, Liège and Ostend airports. In addition many local car hire firms often charge more modest prices than the well-known firms.

Reservations in Brussels

Avis; tel. (02) 7200944
Europcar; tel. (02) 7210592
Hertz; tel. (02) 7206044
Sixt/Budget; tel. (02) 7208050

Reservations in Great Britain

Avis: (020) 88488733
Budget: (0800) 191191
Europcar: (020) 89505050
Hertz: (020) 86791799

Castles, Monasteries, Béguinages

Most of the castles, monasteries and béguinages listed here are described in the Belgium from A to Z section.

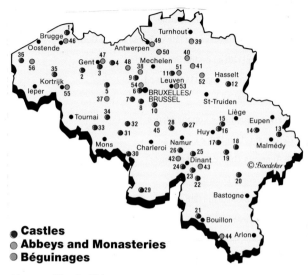

● **Castles**
◐ **Abbeys and Monasteries**
○ **Béguinages**

1 Loppem (Neo-Gothic)

2 Oidonk (13th c.)

3 s'Gravensteen (11th c.), moated castle in Ghent

4 Laarne (12th/17th c.)

5 Leeuwergem (18th c.)

6 Royal palace in Brussels (renovated in 1905)

7 Gaasbeek (13th/16th c.)

8 Beersel (14th c.)

9 Grand Bigard (14th/16th c.)

10 Rixensart (17th c.)

11 Horst (13th c.)

12 Alde Biezen (13th/18th c.)

13 Reinhardstein (medieval; renovated in the 17th c.)

14 Franchimont (12th c.)

15 Aigremont (18th c.) on the Meuse

16 Jehay (16th c.)

17 Modave (17th c.)

Castles, Monasteries, Béguinages

18 Logne (ruins) on the Ourthe

19 Durbuy (16th c.) on the Ourthe

20 La Roche-en-Ardennes (11th c.; ruins) on the Ourthe

21 Bouillon (11th c.) on the Semois

22 Lavaux-Sainte-Anne (14th-18th c.)

23 Vâves (16th c.)

24 Freÿr (16th-18th c.) on the Meuse

25 Spontin (11th/12th c.)

26 Annevoie (16th c.) on the Meuse

27 Franc-Waret (18th c.)

28 Corroy-le-Château (13th c.)

29 Chimay (medieval)

30 Soire-sur-Sambre (13th c.)

31 Le Rœuix (15th/18th c.)

32 Lalaing (11th/15th c.)

33 Belœil (rebuilt in 1900)

34 Attre (18th c.)

35 Rumbeke (16th c.)

36 Beauvoorde (16th/17th c.)

37 Geraardsbergen (12th/18th c.)

38 Grimbergen (12th c.)

39 Postel (12th c.)

40 Tongerlo (19th c.)

41 Averbode (14th c.)

42 Maredsous (19th c.)

43 Chevetogne (19th c.)

44 Orval (11th c.)

45 Villers-la-Ville (12th and 16th/17th c.)

46 Bruges (13th c.)

47 Ghent (13th c.)

48 Dendermonde (13th/16th c.)

49 Antwerp (16th c.)

50 Lier (13th/17th c.)

51 Aarschot (13th c.)

52 Diest (13th/17th c.)

53 Leuven (13th/14th-18th c.)

54 Brussels (16th/17th c.)

55 Kortrijk (13th/17th c.)

56 Diksmuide (12th/17th c.)

Chemists

Belgian chemist's shops (Flemish apotheek; French pharmacie) have either a green cross or the symbol of Aesculapius outside.

The **opening times** of chemists are the same as those of retail shops (see Opening Times). There is an emergency service. Lists of addresses can be found in each chemists.

Currency

The unit of currency is the Belgian Franc (Bfr), which is made up of 100 centimes. There are banknotes for 100, 200, 500, 1000, 5000 and 10,000 Bfr and coins in denominations of ½, 1, 5, 20 and 50 Bfr. Belgian currency is the same in value as the Luxembourgian Franc (Lfr/fLux) and is accepted in the Grand Duchy of Luxembourg.

Since January 1st 1999 the Euro has become the common currecy in eleven European countries. For the time being it is only valid at the stock exchanges and in electronic payments, but from January 1st 2002 it will be the official currency. For Belgium the conversion rate has been fixed at: 1 Euro = 40.34 Bfr.   Euro

Import and export of local or foreign currency is not subject to any limitations.

Banks are usually open Mon.–Fri. 9am–4pm.

Eurocheques can be drawn for amounts up to 7000 Bfr.

Money can be changed in post offices, in banks, at Brussels National Airport or in official exchange offices (bureaux de change) in the large railway stations (higher rates of commission may be charged here).   Changing money

Most international credit cards (American Express, Diners Club, Eurocard, Mastercard and Visa) are accepted by banks, larger hotels, higher-class restaurants and numerous shops. Loss of credit cards should be reported immediately to the police by contacting the credit card security office (tel. 5391502) and to the issuing authority.   Credit cards

Automatic cash-dispensers called "Bancontact" and "Master Cash" with instructions in four languages can be found in all larger towns. These   Cash machines

machines will accept Eurocheque cards and many credit and change cards.

Customs Regulations

In theory there are no limits to the amounts of goods imported from one EU country to another, *provided they have been purchased tax paid in an EU country, are for personal use and are not intended for resale.* However, the customs authorities have issued a list of maximum amounts considered reasonable for persons over 17 years of age of alcoholic drinks, tobacco goods, perfume, etc. These are:

Spirits or strong liqueurs over 22 per cent volume – 10 litres; fortified wines (port, sherry, etc.) – 20 litres; table wine – 90 litres (of which not more than 60 litres may be sparkling wine); beer – 110 litres; cigarettes – 800 or cigarillos 400 or cigars 200 or pipe tobacco 1 kg. Personal use includes gifts, but if a passenger is receiving any payment in return for buying alcohol and tobacco (such as help with travelling expenses) the transaction will be dutiable and the duty must be paid to the Customs authorities.

For those coming direct from a country outside the EU or who have arrived from another EU country without having passed through customs control with all their baggage, the allowances for goods obtained anywhere outside the EU are:

Spirits – 1 litre or fortified wine – 2 litres or table wine – 3 litres plus a further 2 litres of table wine. Perfume – 50 cc; toilet water – 250 cc. 200 cigarettes or 100 cigarillos or 50 cigars or 250 gr. of tobacco.

"Duty-free" goods are still available at major airports, on aircraft and ferries; these are approximately 50 per cent above the limits in paragraph two above and are controlled by the carriers concerned.

Diplomatic Representation

United Kingdom   Embassy: Rue Arlon 85, Brussels; tel (02) 2876211

United States   Embassy: Boulevard du Régent 27, Brussels; tel. (02) 5082111

Canada   Embassy: Avenue de Tervuren 2, Brussels; tel. (02) 7410611

Electricity

Voltage   Belgium is committed to the international voltage regulation IEC 38 (IEC standard voltages) intended to make 230/400 volts a standardised output for 50Hz low-voltage national grid distribution. The country will have converted its electricity supply to 230 volts by the target year of 2003. At present the Belgian electricity system runs on 220 volts AC at a frequency of 50Hz. A voltage transformer is required for American appliances without dual-voltage capability.

An adapter is necessary for British and American-type plugs.

Emergencies

Accident, fire, ambulance; tel. 100

Rijkswacht, police; tel. 101
Breakdown service: tel. (070) 344777

Emergency telephones are stationed at intervals along the motorways.

See Chemists, Medical Assistance and Motoring

Events

The most important events are listed in Belgium from A to Z under the respective heading.

A **calendar** giving the exact dates of individual events is published annually by the tourist information offices listed under Information (see entry). It is available free of charge.

Selected events

January

Antiques Fair	Brussels

February

Carnival with "Gilles" ("Giants") in fancy dress costumes (Mardis Gras and the two days preceeding)	Aalst
Old Woman's Shrovetide Carnival; carnival procession on the Thursday after Ash Wednesday	Eupen
Procession with Haguettes and Happechair (Sunday before Ash Wednesday)	Malmédy

March

Dead Rat's Ball (costume ball in the Kursaal casino)	Ostend
International carnival procession	Hasselt
Carnival procession (Sunday of mid-Lent) including the Blancs Moussis	Stavelot

March/April

Penitential procession to St Peter's Church	Lessines
Golden Egg Festival (egg parade, egg throwing from the church tower and much more)	Kruishoutem
Book Fair	Redu
Flanders' Festival (music and culture) – until the autumn	Flanders

April/May

	Laeken

May

Queen Elizabeth International Music Competition	Brussels
Hanswijk Procession (historic-religious)	Mechelen
Holy Blood Procession (Ascension Day)	Bruges
Cat Throwing Festival (alternate years)	Ypres (Ieper)
St Rolende Hunting Procession (Whit Monday)	Gerpinnes
Notre Dame March (Sunday after Whitsun)	Walcourt
Fiertel Procession (procession with the relics of St Hermes)	Ronse

June

Napoleonic March	Ligny
Golden Carriage Procession and Battle of St George and the Dragon	Mons
Shrimp Festival; procession with folklore groups, decorated coaches, etc.	Oostduinkerke
Day of Four Processions	Tournai
Adriaan Brouwer Festival (beer festival)	Oudenaarde
Penitential procession	Veurne

Duinbergen (Knokke-Heist)	Cartoon Festival (until September)

July

Brussels	Ommegang (procession) – at the end of June-beginning of July
Vielsalm	Bilberry Festival and Witches' Sabbath
Moorsel (Aalst)	Pikkeling (agricultural festival)
Libramont	Libramont Fair (Belgium's largest agricultural fair)
Ostend	Belgium Kite International (model kite festival)
Ghent	Ghent Festival (music and culture second half of the month)
Wallonia	Wallonia Festival (cultural events) – until October

July/August

Brussels	The non-residential parts of the Palace open for visitors

August

Berlare	Flanders Water Festival
Redu	Book Night
Outremeuse (Liège)	Août folklorique en Outremeuse (summer and folk festival)
Knokke-Heist	Blessing of the Sea (parade of ships; historic procession)
Ghent	Patershol Festival in the historic quarter of Het Patershol
Overijse	Grape Festival
Bruges	Historical Golden Tree Procession to commemorate the wedding of Charles the Bold and Margaret of York (every five years, next 1996)
Ath	Ath Public Festival (wedding of Goliath the Giant; procession)
Blankenberge	Flower Parade
Dendermonde	Giants' Procession
Duinbergen (Knokke-Heist)	International Firework Festival (every two days from the middle of the month)

August/September

Saint-Hubert	International Hunting and Nature Days

September

Sint-Niklaas	Balloon Festival
Mechelen	Flower and Vegetable Parade; bell throwing
Tournai	Grand Procession of Notre-Dame des Malades
Poperinge	Hop parade (every three years, next 1996)
Ypres	Music Festival (from classic to pop)
Brussels	Huy, Namur, Liège and Seraing
	Europalia (cultural festival on a European theme; next dates 2001 and 2003)

October

Nivelles	St Gertrude's Tour (procession)
Hasselt	Genever Festival

October/November

Bruges	International Antiques Fair

December

	Christmas fairs in Brussels and towns in the south of the country; in many places (Kempen/Antwerp, Manderfeld and Bullingen) so-called Krippana (exhibitions of Nativity scenes)
Bastogne	Nut Market and Second World War remembrance services

Food and Drink

Belgium has always been the country of the gourmet and people enjoying a festive meal or relishing a picnic often figure in paintings of the Flemish Old Masters. The Belgian of today still seizes on any excuse to enjoy a good meal. The people of Flanders prize their food and drink very highly.

Hotels usually serve a simple breakfast of bread, butter, jam and sometimes cheese. Expensive hotels offer a buffet breakfast. Ample lunches and dinners are optional according to individual requirements. Beer is mainly drunk with these meals, or wine in more modest measures.

Belgian dishes owe their reputation to the combination of French and Dutch influences. Basic dishes alternate with formal haute cuisine. In the Ardennes game and, of course, the famous Ardennes ham is enjoyed, while near the coast fish dominates the menu. A typical Flemish national dish is a large pan of cooked mussels shared by several people, served with pommes frites, which are considered a Flemish invention. Belgium's most commonly-served vegetable is chicory, eaten with boiled ham and cheese sauce.

From the beginning of November until the end of April hotels and restaurants along the Belgian coast and, more recently, a number of inland pubs have staged "Gastronomic Weekends" (cheap weekend flat rates) for gourmets (details available from the Belgian Tourist Office in Brussels, see Information). | Gastronomic weekends

Regional dishes

Flemish carbonnade, lean beef casseroled in beer; smoked ham from the Ardennes; "Heaven and Earth", potato and apple pureé with black pudding or liver sausage; veal kidneys à la liégeoise. | Meat dishes

Hare and rabbit à la flamande, marinated in Gueuze and braised with onions and prunes; pheasant à la brabanáonne; fieldfare à la liégeoise. | Game

Brussels cockerel: particularly tender young birds reared near Brussels; Waterzooi: chunks of chicken stewed with a variety of vegetables and cream; roast goose à la visé: goose first boiled and then roasted. | Poultry

Green eel: boiled eel flavoured with green herbs; herring in cream; cod, pike, trout (particularly in the Ardennes), sole, mussels (especially Jacob mussels), oysters, lobster, crayfish, crab (served with a variety of sauces), Waterzooi with fish. | Fish and shellfish

Hop vegetables (Poperinge); red cabbage à la flamande; asparagus de Maline; chicon (a Brussels endive); Brussels sprouts; Witlof: Brussels chicory with ham and cheese sauce. | Vegetables

Belgian Gouda (St Bernard, Hertog van Brabant); Trappist cheese (Maredsous, Orval, Chimay); Remoudou; Cassette de Beaumont; Pavé de Bastogne (goat's milk cheese); cream cheese curd (fromage blanc) with onions, chives or cress and radishes; Herve à la liégeoise; Remoudou toasted on a slice of bread thinly covered with liégeoise syrup. | Cheese

Spekulatius (small short-crust pastry figures); Diester gingerbread and tartlets; cheesecake; creamed rice; sugar biscuits (e.g. from Namur); almond bread (e.g. from Veurne); Greek bread (a sugar biscuit); Brussels waffles served with sugar, butter, fresh cream and/or fruit; Liége waffles with caramel syrup; apple doughnuts; Kortrijk rusks; Bollen pastries. A well-known speciality from Dinant is Flamiche, a cheesecake. Favourite dainties from Ghent include Gent Mokken, little round cakes made from flour and syrup. Lierse Vlaaikens are typical pastries from Lier. | Pastries and desserts

In Gambrinus' Kingdom

Beer is to the Belgians what wine is to the French. It is an everyday drink in cafés, as a refreshment, but it is also customary to serve one of the many special brands on festive occasions. No other country in the world has such a multitude of different beers as this country between the North Sea and the Ardennes; the taste of some of these takes time to acquire but, nevertheless, they should be sampled. More than 100 breweries now produce over 500 fundamentally distinctive beers. Most Belgian beers are characterised by a top-fermentation process but in many cases fermentation is continued in corked champagne bottles. Many of the beers – such as the white and cherry beers – go back to the days when the use of hops as a flavouring was unknown. St Arnold of Oudenaarde was aware of the importance of beer when in the 11th c. a monastic brewery collapsed and he prayed to his god for an increase in beer. His wish was heard and from then on he was the patron saint of the brewers. Gambrinus, too, the king of beer, is a Belgian. According to legend it was the exceptionally thirsty Duke Jan I of Brabant, Leuven and Antwerp ("Jan Primus") whose name in the 13th c. was parodied to "Gambrinus".

In Belgium most beer is drunk in cafés, but they have nothing in common with cafés in the normal sense of the word. The café is the normal daily meeting place;

here the customers talk, play billiards and, of course, drink beer. Whoever orders a "beer" in a café either gets a normal Pils or he is asked what brand he would like, for every landlord worthy of the name has at least 20 to 30 different beers on offer; good cafés begin with 50 kinds, all of which, of course, are served in a special glass. The beer is accompanied by nibbles, simple sausage or cheese.

Worth a visit for the beer are among others:

Antwerp: Kulminator, Vleminckxveld 32; 't Waagstuk, Stadswag 20; Patersvaetje, Blauwmoezelstraat 1.

Bruges: ★'t Brugs Beetje, Kemelstraat 5 (Belgium – very friendly – "beer university"; an endless beer list with real specialities and nothing mass produced. Served with real knowledge of his subject by Jan de Bruyne and his staff).

Brussels: De Ultime Hallucinatie, 316 Rue Royale (pleasant turn of the century furnishings); ★La Bécasse, Rue Tabora (very unusual specialities: the fruity Lambic and the coriander-flavoured white beer, both served from stoneware jugs into the glass); A la Mort Subite, Rue des Montagnes-aux-Herbes Potagères (wonderful furnishings from the turn of the century; sour Faro).

Ghent: De Hopduval, Rokererlstraat 10; Het Waterhuis an de Bierkant, Groentenmarkt (very friendly; extensive beer list).

Leeuven: Domus, Tiensestraat.

Belgian brewing can be studied in the ***beer museums*** of the country: in Brussels in the Museum of the Brewers' Guild and in the Gueuze Museum; in Leuven in the Brewery Museum; in the exhibition brewery in the Bokrijk open-air museum. A still better introduction to something which is taken for granted is one of the ***beer seminars*** organised by the West Flanders Tourist Office, Westtoerisme (see Information).

The ***bottom-fermented beers*** are generally light and sweet and refreshing beers of the Pilsner kind. The most popular is Stella Artois brewed in the largest brewery of the country in Leuven; then come Cristal Alken, Jupiter and Maes Pils.

"Wild" beers are a unique speciality. They are produced in the Payotte region which is watered by the river Senne south-west of Brussels. It is here that a species of hops grows wild and the local brewers make use of this to produce Lambic. It consists of 30–40 per cent of unmalted wheat and 60–70 per cent of malted barley. The brew, produced according to the classic method is exposed to the air of the Senne valley for one night in open wooden tubs and the hops are added; after this it is drawn off into wooden barrels and left to ferment. Each brewer takes great care to make no alterations in his fermenting cellar so that the combination of micro-organisms in the air and in the barrels are not disturbed. The Lambic is left to mature for between six months to two years in the barrels and then for a further period in bottles. It is generally golden in colour, bitter and with an alcohol content of between 4 and 5 per cent and tastes something like apple juice. One version, sweetened with rock-candy is Faro which like genuine Lambic is generally only obtainable in the little breweries of the Payotte region. However, the Brussels "A la Mort Subite" Brewery always has its own Faro on tap. Generally old and young Lambics are mixed with Gueuze which makes a pleasant sweet and sour refreshing drink in summer.

If cherries are added to Lambic and allowed to ferment with it the result is a Kriek, a very fruity sharp cherry like beer, deep red in colour, the taste of which is sometimes reminiscent of Kir Royal. In the same way raspberry beer (Frambozen) is produced; other more exotic varieties are beers with strawberries, peaches and blackcurrants.

Large Lambic/Gueuze breweries are Belle-Vue in Brussels and St-Louis in Ingelmunster. From the Payotte region the varieties include Eylenbosch, De Neve, De Troch, Timmermans and Vanderlinden. Mort Subite in Brussels brews the best known bitter Lambic and also a Faro and an extremely individual Kriek.

Strictly speaking there is only one **red beer** today, Rodenbach from Flemish Roeselare. It is so sharp that nobody can be blamed for thinking it undrinkable and yet it is a Flemish classic. Its acidity is due to the hops used. Simple Rodenbach is brewed with 4.6 per cent alcohol and Rodenback Grand Cru with 5.2 per cent. If one first gets used to the taste Rodenbach is considered a very good thirst quencher.

There are many **brown beers** in Belgium, but pride of place must go to Liefmans from Oudenaarde, a beer similar to English ale. The simple version has about 4.6 per cent alcohol; Liefmans Goudenband, especially popular at festivals, with bottles wrapped in tissue paper, is sweet and sparkling with 5.5 per cent alcohol. A speciality is Liefmans Kriek, a soft cherry beer based on ale. Other good dark beers include Crombe from Zottengem and Van den Bossche from St-Lievens-Esse.

Belgian **white beers** are draft beers containing up to 45 per cent malted wheat and a low alcohol content of about 3.5 per cent. They are light, fruity and refreshing. The most popular and the best comes from Hoegaarden east of Leuven and its flavourings include coriander. Somewhat stronger is the Grand Cru from the same brewery. Other good white beers are the Dendergemse Wit and the Brugse Wit (Blanche de Bruges).

The monastic breweries can look back on a long tradition. However, today Trappist monks in only five monasteries are still brewing beer, and only these five are allowed to sell their beers as *"Trappist beers"*. The best known Trappist brewery is that of Chimay which brews three beers: Chimay rouge (red Kapsel, 5.5 per cent), Chimnay blanche (white Kapsel, 8 per cent) and Chimay bleue (blue Kapsel, 9 per cent). Similar beers are brewed by the monks of Rochefort. The Flemish monastery of Westvleteren is the smallest of these breweries but produces five different beers, the strongest of which is the heavysweet Abbot with 10.6 per cent alcohol. Also from Flanders comes the Trappist beer of Westmalle with a dark and rather tangy Dubbel (7 per cent) and the light Triple (8 per cent). Finally a quite exceptional beer is the orange coloured Orval from the extreme south-eastern corner of Belgium: very dry, rather acidic and bitter, with its 6 per cent alcohol it is an acquired taste.

As well as these genuine Trappist beers other monastic beers are produced in normal breweries; these include Grimbergen, Leffe and Affigem.

As well as the brands already listed there are many generally **top-fermented beers** which often catch the eye by special bottles, labels and names such as "Lucifer" and "Verboden Vrucht" (forbidden fruit). Traditional is the production of light and dark ales such as De Koninck from Antwerp, the strong Gouden Carolus from Mechelen and the "Saisons" from the Hennegau between Charloi and Mons. A very light and sweet and therefore not to be despised strong beer is Duvel (8 per cent) from the Moortgat Brewery from Breendonk.

Sitting on his barrel of Belgian Beer
Gambrinus says "Cheers"

Babulettes (caramel sweets); pralines; toffees.   Sweets

Drinks

See Baedeker Special pp 412–14   Beers

Wines are usually from the neighbouring countries of France or Luxembourg.   Wine

A speciality of Arlon is the traditional Maitrank – a Moselle wine aperitif flavoured with slices of orange.   Maitrank

Raisin rum and herbal liqueur are two popular drinks as are numerous types of Genever (gin). In the Ardennes a highly prized liqueur from Pumalet de la Roche, a spicey drink made from plums with a dark colour, is known as Ewe di Moûsse.   Spirits and liqueurs

Spa, Bru and Chaudfontaine are the best-known mineral waters.   Mineral water

The Belgian menu

English	French	Dutch/Flemish	General terms
breakfast	petit déjeuner	ontbijt	
lunch	déjeuner	lunch	
dinner	díner, souper	diner	
the bill	addition	rekening	
menu	carte	spijskaart, menu	
wine list	carte des vins	wijnkaart	
soup	potage, soupe	soep	
clear soup	consommé	bouillon	
starter	hors-d'œuvre	voorgerecht	
carp	carpe	karper	Fish (poisson; vis)
cod	cabillaud	kabeljauw	
eel	anguille	aal, paling	
flounder	flet	bot	
herring	hareng	haring	
perch	perche	baars	
pike	brochet	snoek	
salmon	saumon	zalm	
sole	sole	zeetong	
trout	truite	forel	
crab	crevettes	garnalen	Shellfish (crustacés; schelp-en-schaaldieren)
lobster	écrevisse	kreeft	
mussels	moules	mosselen	
oysters	huítres	oesters	
grilled	grillé	gegrilt	Meat (viandes; vleesgerecht)
roast	roti	gebraden, vlees	
beef	bœuf	rund	
ham	jambon	ham	
kidney	rognons	nieren	
lamb	agneau	lam	
liver	foie	lever	
mutton	mouton	schaap	
pork	porc	varken	
pot-roast	bœuf en daube	gestoofd vlees	
sausage	saucisson, saucisse	worst	

Food and Drink

	English	French	Dutch/Flemish
	veal	veau	kalf
	veal cutlet	escalope de veau	kalfsoester
Poultry (volaille; gevogelte)	chicken	poule, poulet	kip
	duck	canard	eend
	goose	oie	gans
Game (gibier; wild)	deer	chevreuil	ree
	rabbit	lapin	konijn
	wild boar	marcasson	wild zwijn
Vegetables (légumes; groente)	beans	haricots	bonen
	Brussels sprouts	chou de Bruxelles	spruitjes
	cabbage	chou	kool
	cauliflower	chou-fleur	bloemkool
	chicory	chicorée	(Brussels)lof
	cucumber	concombre	komkommer
	peas	pois	(dop)erwten
	pickled cabbage	choucroute	zuurkool
	potatoes	pommes de terre	aardappelen
	red cabbage	chou rouge	rodekool
	salad	salade	sla, salade
	spinach	épinard	spinazie
	noodles	nouilles, pâtes	macaroni
	rice	riz	rijst
Desserts (desserts; nagerechten)	cheese	fromage	kaas
	custard tart	flan	pudding
	ice-cream	glace	ijs
	whipped cream	crème chantilly	slagroom
Fruit (fruits; fruit)	apple	pomme	appel
	cherry	cérise	kers
	grapes	raisins	druiven
	orange	orange	sinaasappel
	peach	pêche	perzik
	pear	poire	peer
	plum	prune	pruim
	strawberry	fraise	aardbei
Miscellaneous	bread	pain	brood
	white bread	pain blanc	wit brood
	roll	pistolet, petit pain	broodje
	cake	gâteau	koek
	flan	tarte	taart, gebak
	pastries	pâtisserie	gebak
	butter	beurre	boter
	jam	confiture	jam
	honey	miel	honing
	egg	œuf	ei
	hard	dur	hard gekookt
	soft	à la coque	zacht gekookt
	scrambled egg	œufs brouillés	roerei
	fried egg	œufs sur la plat	spiegelei (gebakken ei)
	salt	sel	zout
	pepper	poivre	peper
	sugar	sucre	suiker
	vinegar	vinaigre	azijn

English	French	Dutch/Flemish	
oil (salad)	huile alimentaire	(spijs)olie	
beer	bière	bier	Drinks (boissons;
coffee	café	koffie	dranken)
milk	lait	melk	
mineral water	eau minérale	mineraalwater	
cream	crème	room	
tea	thé	thee	
water	eau	water	
wine	vin	wijn	
white wine	vin blanc	witte wijn	
red wine	vin rouge	rode wijn	

Getting to Belgium

Those travelling to Belgium from Britain by road can cross by ferry from Hull to Zeebrugge (13 hours 15 minutes) with North Sea Ferries. There are also ferries from Ramsgate to Dunkirk – just over the border in France – (2½ hours) with Sally Line, or Sheerness to Vlissingen – just over the border in Holland – (8 hours by day, 9½ at night) with Eurolink Ferries.

By sea and road

For those without a car there is the fast passenger jetfoil service (1 hour 35 minutes) with Sally Line.

Hoverspeed operate up to seven return sailings between Dover and Ostend daily, with their two catamarans making the crossing in two hours. P&O Stena Line operate a Dover–Calais service in 75 minutes.

An alternative, avoiding the sea crossing, is by car aboard "Le Shuttle" via the Channel Tunnel from Folkestone to Calais (35 minutes/45 minutes at night).

Sally Line, Argyle Centre, York Street, Ramsgate, Kent CT11 9DS; tel. (0990) 595522

North Sea Ferries, King George Dock, Hedon Road, Hull, Humberside HU9 50A; tel. (01482) 377177

Eurolink Ferries, The Ferry Terminal, Sheerness Dock, Sheerness, Kent ME12 1RX; tel. (01795) 581000

Le Shuttle Customer Services Centre, P.O. Box 300, Cheriton Parc, Folkestone, Kent CT19 4QD; tel. (0990) 353535

There is a direct high-speed rail service (EuroStar) between London-Waterloo International and Brussels-Midi/Zuid (3 hours 15 minutes) from where there are frequent connecting services to the rest of Belgium.

By rail

There is also a rail link with ferry and jetfoil services from Ramsgate to Ostende (see above) connecting with Bruges and Brussels.

Brussels has three main railway stations: Bruxelles Nord/Brussel Noord (North Station), Bruxelles Centrale/Brussel Centraal (Central Station) and Bruxelles Midi/Brussel Zuid (South Station).

EuroStar, London-Waterloo International Station; tel. (0345) 881881.

By coach

CitySprint operates a combined coach/hovercraft service from London Victoria Coach Station (via Dover and Ostend) to Antwerp, Bruges and Brussels.

Eurolines has combined coach/ferry services from London Victoria Coach Station (via Ramsgate and Ostend) to Antwerp, Bruges, Brussels, Gent and Liège.

CitySprint, contact: Hoverspeed, International Hoverport, Marine Parade, Dover, Kent CT17 9TG; tel. (01304) 240241

Eurolines, 52 Grosvenor Gardens, Victoria, London SW1W 0AG; tel. (01582) 404511

By air

Brussels Airport at Zaventem is 14 km (9 mi.) from Brussels city centre and has its own rail service in and out of the city (see Air Travel).

There are numerous daily flights into Brussels from Gatwick and Heathrow, as well as frequent flights from Britain's other main airports. North American and Canadian travellers can fly direct to Brussels from New York and Atlanta (daily), as well as from Detroit, Chicago, Montreal, etc. (For Airlines, see Air Travel.)

Help for the Disabled

Help in Belgium

General information from:
Croix-Rouge (Red Cross), Bruxelles/Brussels; tel. (02) 6495010
SOS-Jeunes, Bruxelles/Brussels; tel (02) 5129020
Help Lines (English spoken), Bruxelles/Brussels; tel. (02) 6484014

Social Tourism centres

Inexpensive accommodation for the disabled can usually be found in the Social Tourism centres. These include a number of hotels and holiday homes, run by various organisations for social tourism, which include:

Centrum voor Sociaal Toerisme, Spastraat 8
B-1040 Brussels/Bruxelles; tel. (02) 2303145

Broederlijheid, Charleroisteenweg 145
B-1060 Brussels/Bruxelles; tel (02) 5388300

Help in the UK

A guide entitled "Holidays and Travel Abroad – a guide for disabled people" includes a section on Belgium and is available from:
The Royal Association for Disability and Rehabilitation (RADAR)
25 Mortimer Street, London W1N 8AB

Hotels

Bookings can be made free of charge for hotels throughout Belgium from
Belgium Tourist Reservations, Boulevard Anspach 111;
boite/bus 4 ;
B-1000 Brussels/Bruxelles
tel. (02) 5137484; fax (02) 5139277

The Belgian Tourist Office in Brussels (see Information) publishes an annual list of hotels detailing prices and standards of comfort.

Hotel Categories

The Belgian tourist authorities check hotels by questionnaire regarding their facilities and standards of comfort. They are then classified and approved – indicated on blue plaques with the relevants number of stars. It is important to know that all accommodation without this state approval are illegal.

The following selection is arranged by number of stars although this is not a reliable indication of prices. Even within one category prices may vary considerably. The following is a guide to the average price of a double room with en-suite bath or shower. Breakfast is usually included. R. = number of rooms.

★★★★★Luxury hotel 7000–15,000 Bfr
★★★★First-class hotel 4000–10,000 Bfr
★★★Very good hotel 2500–5000 Bfr

★★ Moderate hotel 1500–3000 Bfr
★/H Simple hotel 1000–2000 Bfr

★★★★ Keizershof   Aalst
Korte Nieuwstraat, 46 r.; tel. (053) 774411, fax. 780097
New building with generous-sized rooms in the centre of Aalst.

★★★★ Rubens Grote Markt   Antwerp
Oude Beurs 29, 36 r.; tel. (03) 2269582, fax. 2251940
Most luxurious accommodation in Antwerp, with a romantic garden and
a tranquil inner courtyard.

★★★★ Antwerp Hilton
Groenplaats, 211r.; tel. (03) 2041212, fax. 2041213
This hotel offer several advantages: excellent central situation on the
popular Groenplats, modern comfort behind the fin-de-siècle façade of
the former Grote Bazaar, terrace with service, great for watching the
world go by on the square.

★★★★ Firean
Karel Oomsstraat 6, 12r.; tel. (03) 2370260, fax. 2381168
A stylish and intimate hotel, established in a town house which man-
aged to preserve its Art Deco interior through the ages.

★★★ Agora
Koningin Astrigplein 43, 27 r.; tel. (03) 2312121, fax. 2321202
Renovated in 1996, this hotel offers a less expensive alternative to the
other hotels.

★★★ Hostellerie de Peiffeschof   Arlon
111, Chemin de Peiffeschof, 6 r.; tel. (063) 224415, fax. 233329
Attarctive small building in rural surroundings, 4 km (2.5 mi.) outside
town; good restaurant with a garden terrace.

★★★★ Helios   Blankenberge
Zeedijk 92, 34 r.; tel. (050) 429020, fax. 428666
Comfortable new designer hotel, directly on the beach.

★★★ Auberge d'Alsace/Hôtel de France   Bouillon
1–3, Rue Faubourg de France, 36 r.; tel. (061) 466588, fax. 468321
Old established hotel at the entrance of town, below the fortress; well
regarded restaurant with terrace.

★★★★ Die Swaene   Bruges (Brugge)
Steenhouwersdijk 1, 24 r.; tel. (050) 342798, fax. 336674
Genuine art on the walls, antiques throughout, even one room with elaborate four-poster bed – this is a hotel for romantic guests who do,
however, need to spend a little more.

★★★★ De Tuilerieën
Dijver 7, 25r.; tel. (050) 343691, fax. 340400
This luxurious hotel is in the heart of Bruges, on the romantic Dijver, in
a patrician house dating back to the 15th c. Rooms have individual
character.

★★★ Maraboe
Hoefijzerlaan 9, 9 r.; tel. (050) 338155, fax. 332928
Cosy hotel on the edge of the old town with an excellent restaurant.

★★★ Ensor
Speelmansrei 10, 12r.; tel. (050) 342589, fax. 342018
Small, inexpensive family hotel in a quiet part of the old town.

Hotels

Brussels

★★★★★Amigo
1–3, Rue de l'Amigo, 186 r.; tel. (02) 5474747, fax. 5135277
This former prison is very popular, especially with politicians and diplomats from the EU-circuit. All the rooms are furnished in Louis XV or colonial style. One of the best hotels in town, only a stone's throw from the Grand'Place.

★★★★★Métropole
31, Pl. de Brouckère, 410r.; tel. (02) 2172300, fax. 2180204
A shrine to the Belle Époque: palm trees, marble, mirrors, stained glass windows, columns, leather and mahogany in the foyer and a tasteful club room. Breathtaking Café. If you can afford it, you should stay here – too good just for sleeping.

★★★★Art Hotel Siru
1, Pl. Rogier, 101 r.; tel. (02) 2033580, fax. 2033303
A must for lovers of art: each floor has its own artistic theme, every room has been individually decorated by a contemporary Belgian artist.

★★★★Argus
6, Rue Capitaine Crespel, 41 r.; tel. (02) 5140770, fax. 5141222
Friendly, modern hotel full of nooks and crannies, conveniently close to Place Louise, Palais de Justice and Marollen.

★★★Arlequin
17–19, Rue de la Fourche, 70 r.; tel. (02) 5141615, fax. 5142202
Friendly, cosy accommodation in the Ilôt Sacré.

★★★Welcome Truite d'Argent
5, Rue du Peuplier, 6 r.; tel. (02) 2199546, fax. 2171887
A very small hotel, beautifully situated on the fish market, with an excellent restaurant; something a bit different.

Chimay

★★★★Host. du Gahy in Momignies (2 km/1.2 mi. to the west)
2, Rue Gahy, 6r.; tel. (060) 511093, fax. 512879
Attractive country guesthouse in quiet situation, with garden restaurant.

Damme

★★★Clio
Gentsesteenweg 86, in the Sijsele part of town, 15 r.; tel. and fax. (050) 353942, fax. 356674
Family hotel in an ideal situation between Damme, Bruges and the coast. Here the landlord cooks.

Dinant

★★Beau Séjour in Houyet (26 km/16 mi. to the south-east)
18, Rue St-Roch; tel. (082) 666635, fax. 667392
Clean country guesthouse, tasty regional cuisine, especially game.

Ghent

★★★Gravensteen
Jan Breydelstraat 35, 17r.; tel. (09) 2251150, fax. 2251850
Based in the former town palais, this hotel offers comfortable accommodation and a view of the Gravensteen castle.

★★★Novotel Ghent Centrum
Goudenleeuwplein 5, 117r.; tel. (09) 2242230, fax. 2243295
Modern, central and comfortable hotel, built on historic foundations: the cellars date back to the 14th c.

★★★H Sint-Jorishof
Botermarkt 2, 26r.; tel. (09) 2242424, fax. 2242640
Comfortable accommodation and upmarket prices despite its low classification – this hostelry in the heart of the old town has been named in 1228 already and is supposed to be the oldest in Europe.

★★★★Parkhotel · Hasselt
Genkersteenweg 350, 29r.; tel. (011) 211652, fax. 221814
Modern, comfortable hotel, 3 km (1.8 mi.) outside town, close to the
open-air museum of Bokrijk.

★★★Scholteshof in Stevoort (5 km/3 mi. to the west)
Kermtstraat 130, 18 r.; tel. (011) 250202, fax. 254328
If you are looking for noble accommodation, this country guesthouse
with its own fruit, vegetable and herb gardens is the place for you. But
most importantly: the restaurant is one of the best in all of Belgium.

★★★St-Yves · Knokke-Heist
Zeedijk 204, in Heist, 8 r.; tel. (050) 511029, fax. 516387
An ideal hotel for holidaymakers – situated on top of the dyke, near the
nature reserve of Zwin, with a homely atmosphere combined with a high
degree of comfort and good cooking by the landlord.

★★★Ter Zaele
Oostkerkestraat 40, in Heist, 18r.; tel. (050) 601237, fax. 611973
Villa-like hotel with garden, swimming pool, sauna and solarium; a little
inland, not directly on the beach.

★★★★Broel · Kortrijk
Broelkaai 8, 61 r.; tel. (056) 218351, fax. 200302
The best hotel in town is situated in the Grachten quarter near the
medieval Broel towers. The interior decoration has been influence by
this setting.

★★★★Begijnhof · Leuven
Tervuursevest 70, 67 r.; tel. (016) 291010, fax. 291022
Stylish accommodation in venerable Leuven. Although the hotel is in a
former béguinage, you won't feel much of the spartan life that the
béguines lived.

★★★★Bedford · Liège
36, Quai St-Léonard, 149 r.; tel. (04) 2288111, fax. 2274575
Large house with all comforts on the banks of the Meuse River, away
from the centre of town.

★★★Simenon
16, Boulevard de l'Est, 11 r.; tel. (04) 3428690, fax. 3442669
A hotel for fans of Commisar Maigret and Georges Simenon: each room
has been individually furnished according to themes and motives from
Simenon's novels.

★★★★Hôtel des Bains, in Robertville (10 km/6 mi. to the east) · · · · · · · Malmédy
2, Rue de Lac de Robertville, 14 r.; tel. (080) 679571, fax. 678143
This rural hotel on the lake of Robertville is an ideal base for excursions
to the nature reserve "Hohes Venn" and the eastern regions.

★★★Parkhotel Blütgenbacher Hof, in Blütgenbach (15 km/9.3 mi. to the
east)
Marktplatz 8, 24 r.; tel. (080) 444212, fax. 444877
Apart from a civilised, quiet stay this large and spacious country hotel
offers an excellent restaurant and an equally superb wine cellar. The
reservoir of Blütgenbach right opposite the front door.

★★★★Alfa Alba · Mechelen
Korenmarkt 22–26, 43 r.; tel. (015) 420303, fax. 423788
The top hotel in town, the Alfa Alba is centrally situated, in historical
surroundings. Non-smoking rooms available.

Hotels

Mons
★★★La Fôret, in Masnuy St-Jean
3, Chaussée de Brunehault, 52r.; tel. (065) 723685, fax. 724144
Very quiet situation in rural tranquillity, garden restaurant.

Namur
★★★Château de Namur
1, Ave. de L'Ermitage, 29 r.; tel. (081) 742630, fax. 742392
You are guaranteed stylish accommodation and excellent cuisine in this large, late 19th c. villa, situated high above the town, in immediate, quiet vicinity of the citadel.

Ostend
★★★★Oostendse Compagnie
Koningstraat 79, 13 r.; tel. (059) 704816, fax. 805316
Truly royal accommodation is on offer in this hotel, surrounded by a park yet centrally situated – it once belonged to the Queen and, accordingly, has been stylishly furnished.

★★★★Thermae-Palace
Koningin Astridlaan 7, 100 r.; tel. (059) 806644, fax. 805274
The recently renovated beach hotel exudes a turn-of-the-century atmosphere.

★★★Du Parc
Marie-Joséplein 3, 43r.; tel. (059) 701680, fax. 800879
Not quite as luxurious, this solid hotel, situated between beach and casino, offers a good-value alternative. It also boasts a beautiful Art deco bar.

Oudenaarde
★★★De Zalm
Hoogstraat 4, 7 r.; tel. (055) 311314, Fax. 318440
Venerable hotel without pretensions, opposite the historical town hall; restaurant with good reputation.

La Roche-en-Ardenne
★★★Claire Fontaine
64, Route de Hotton, 25 r.; tel. (084) 412470, fax. 412111
Very quiet, thanks to its situation slightly outside town, on the banks of the Ourthe River; shady garden for relaxing.

★★★Les Genets
2, Corniche de Deister, 8 r.; tel. (084) 411877, fax. 411893
Another quiet hotel, with good voews and an excellent restaurant.

Rochefort
★★★Trou Maulin
19, Route de Marche, 6 r.; tel. (084) 213240, fax. 221381
Small, inexpensive hotel on the edge of town, with a good restaurant.

★★★★Château d'Hassonvile, in Marche-en-Famenne (13 km/8 mi. to the north-east)
105, Route d'Hassonville, 21 r.; tel. (084) 311025, fax. 316027
Grand accommodation in the 17th c. château, surrounded by a large park with lake.

St-Hubert
★★★ Auberge du Sabotier, in Awenne (9 km/6 mi. to the north-west)
21, Grand Rue, 18 r.; tel. (084) 366523, fax. 366368
Very attractive country guesthouse in a small village. The rooms have rustic furniture; the restaurant is recommended.

Spa
★★★★La Heid des Pairs
132, Ave. Prof. Henri Jean, 11 r.; tel. (087) 774346, fax. 770644
This villa and garden are the right setting for a more luxurious spa holiday.

Stavelot
★★★★Relais du Crouly, in Francorchamps
Ster 306A, 6 r.; tel. (087) 275329, fax. 275539
Country guesthouse in a former farm, dating back to 1780.

★★★★Ambiotel   Tongeren
Veemarkt 2, 22 r.; tel. (012) 262950, fax. 261542
Pleasant town hotel in the centre.

★★★Holiday Inn Garden Court   Tournai
2, Place St-Pierre, tel. (069) 215077, fax. 215078
Good accommodation in the style typical for the hotel chain.

★★★★Le Sanglier des Ardennes, in Durbuy   Vallée de l'Ourthe
14, Rue Comte d'Irse;, 45 r.; tel. (086) 213262, fax. 212465
Quiet, elegant country hotel with excellent cuisine.

★★★Un Balcon en Forêt, in Rochehaut   Vallée de la
120, Rue de Alle, 20 r.; tel. (061) 466530, fax. 466816   Semois
The unusual name describes what is special about this country hotel: its
fantastic situation high above the loop of the Semois River.

★★★Le Relais de la Venerie 3 km (2 mi.) outside, on the N 82)   Virton
Rue au dessus de Rabais, 8 r.; tel. (063) 577084, fax. 571 87
Quiet country guesthouse.

★★★★Grand Hôtel Waterloo   Waterloo
198, Chaussée de Tervuren, 80 r.; tel. (02) 3521815, fax. 3521818
New, sophisticated hotel, behind the façade of a former sugar
factory.

Information

Information outside Belgium

Belgian Tourist Office   In the UK
29 Princes Street, London W1R 7RG;
tel. (0891) 887799, fax. (0171) 629 0454

Belgian Tourist Office   In the USA
Suite 1501, 780 Third Avenue, New York NY 10017;
tel. (212) 7588130, fax. (212) 355 7675

Information within Belgium

Vlaams Commissariaat-Generaal voor Toerisme   Main offices
Office de Promotion du Tourisme Wallonie-Bruxelles
Grasmarkt, Rue Marché-aux-Herbes 61–63
B-1000 Brussel/Bruxelles; tel. (02) 5040390, fax. (02) 5040270

Toerisme Provincie Antwerpen   Antwerpen
Koningin Elisabethlei 16   province
B-2018 Antwerpen; tel. (03) 2406373, fax. (03) 2406383

Fédération Touristique de la Province de Brabant Walloon,   Walloon Brabant
Ch. de Bruxelles 218
B-1410 Waterloo;
tel. (02) 3511200, fax. (02) 3511300

Toeristiche Federatie Vlaams-Brabant, Diestesteenweg 52   Flemish Brabant
B-3010 Kessel-Lo; tel. (016) 267620; fax. (016) 267676

Information

Flanders (Vlaanderen) province	Vlaams Commissariaat-Generaal voor Toerisme, Grasmarkt 61· B-1000 Brussel; tel. (02) 5040390, fax. (02) 5138803
West Flanders (West-Vlaanderen)	Westtoerisme, Provinciale Toeristische Federatie West-Vlaanderen, Kasteel Tillegem, B-8200 St-Michiels – Brugge; tel. (050) 380296, fax. (050) 380292
East Flanders (Oost-Vlaanderen)	Toerisme Oost-Vlaanderen, Woodrow Wilsonplein 3 B-9000 Gent; tel. (09) 2677114/15
Hainaut province	Fédération Tourisique de la Province de Hainaut, Rue des Clercs 31 B-7000 Mons; tel. (065) 360464, fax. (065) 335732
Liège province	Fédération du Tourisme de la Province de Liège, 77 Blvd. de la Sauvinière B-4000 Liège; tel. (04) 2326510
Limburg province	Provinciale Dienst voor Toerisme, Universiteitslaan 1 B-3500 Hasselt; tel. (011) 237450
Luxembourg province	Fédération Touristique de la Province de Luxembourg Belge, Quai de l'Ourthe 9, B-6980 La Roche-en-Ardenne; tel. (084) 411011, fax. (084) 412439
Namur province	Fédération Touristique de la Province de Namur, Parc Industriel-Rue Pieds d'Alouette 18, Boîte 2, B-5100 Naninne; tel. (081) 408010, fax. (081) 408020
Eastern cantons	Verkehrsamt der Ostkantone, Mühlenbachstr. 2 B-4780 St-Vith; tel. (080) 227664, fax. (080) 227539
Local tourist information offices	The tourist information offices within individual towns in Flanders (Vlaanderen) are called Vereniging voor Vreemdelingenverkeer (V.V.V.) or Dienst voor Toerisme and in Wallonia (Wallonië) are called Syndicat d'Initiative or Office du Tourisme.
Aalst	Belfort, Grote Markt 3, B-9300 Aalst; tel. (053) 732270
Aarschot	Demervallei 14, B-3200 Aarschot; tel. (016) 569705
Antwerp	Grote Markt 15, B-2000 Antwerpen; tel. (03) 2320103
Arlon	Pavillon du Tourisme, Place Léopold, B-6700 Arlon; tel. (063) 216360
Ath	Rue du Bouchain, B-7800 Ath; tel. (068) 280141
Bastogne	Place Mac Auliffe 24, B-6600 Bastogne; tel. (062) 212711
Beaumont	1 Rue sous les Cloches, B-6570 Beaumont; tel. (071) 588684
Belœil	Domaine de Belœil, B-7970 Belœil; tel. (069) 689655
Binche	Hôtel de Ville, Grand-Place, B-7130 Binche; tel. (064) 333721
Blankenberge	Leopold III-plein, B-8370 Blankenberge; tel. (050) 412227
Bouillon	Bureau du Château, B-6830 Bouillon; tel. (061) 466257
Bruges	Burg 11, B-8000 Brugge; tel. (050) 448686
Brussels	Hôtel de Ville/Stadhuis, Grand'Place/Grote Markt B-1000 Bruxelles/Brussel; tel. (02) 5138940

Avenue Mascaux 100, B-6001 Charleroi; tel. (071) 866152–57	Charleroi
1 Grand-Place, B-6460 Chimay; tel. (060) 211846	Chimay
Jacob van Maerlantstraat 3, B-8340 Damme; tel. (050) 353319	Damme
Stadhuis, Grote Markt, B-9200 Dendermonde; tel. (052) 213956	Dendermonde
Stadhuis, Grote Markt 1, B-3290 Diest; tel. (013) 312121	Diest
Grote Markt 28, B-8600 Diksmuide; tel. (051) 519146	Diksmuide
Rue Grande 37, B-5500 Dinant; tel. (082) 222870	Dinant
Place du Marché 7, B-4700 Eupen; tel. (080) 227664	Eupen
Stadthuis, Markt 1, B-2440 Geel; tel. (014) 570952	Geel
Caves du Château du Bailly, B-5800 Gembloux; tel. (081) 615171	Gembloux
Stadhuis, Grote Markt 1, B-9500 Geraardsbergen; tel. (054) 414121	Geraardsbergen
Parc Naturel Hautes Fagnes 131 Route de Botrange B-4898 Robertville; tel. (080) 445781	German-Belgian National Park
Crypt of the Belfry Tower, Botermarkt 17A, B-9000 Gent; tel. (09) 2665232	Ghent
Grote Markt, B-1500 Halle; tel. (02) 3564259	Halle
Rue des Sarrazins 1, B-5580 Han-sur-Lesse; tel. (084) 377576	Han-sur-Lesse
Stadhuis, Lombaardstraat 3, B-3500 Hasselt; tel. (011) 239540	Hasselt
22a Rue Champagne, B-5200 Huy-Tihange; tel. (085) 215770	Huy
Zeedijk-Knokke 660, B-8300 Knokke-Heist; tel. (050) 630380	Knokke-Heist
Zeelaan Westendestraat, B-8670 Koksijde; tel. (058) 533055	Koksijde
Schouwburgplein 14A, B-8500 Kortrijk; tel. (056) 239371	Kortrijk
Stadhuis/Grote Markt, B-3000 Leuven; tel. (016) 211539	Leuven
En Féronstrée 92, B-4000 Liège; tel. (041) 219221	Liège
Stadhuis, Grote Markt 57, B-2500 Lier; tel. (03) 4911393	Lier
Markt 1, B-3680 Maaseik; tel. (089) 566372	Maaseik
Place du Châtelet 10, B-4960 Malmédy; tel. (080) 330250	Malmédy
Stadhuis, Grote Markt, B-2800 Mechelen; tel. (015) 297655	Mechelen
Grand Place 20, B-7000 Mons; tel. (065) 335520	Mons
Hôtel de Ville, B-5000 Namur; tel. (081) 246448	Namur
Marktplein 7, B-8620, Nieuwpoort; tel. (058) 234444	Nieuwpoort
Vaux-Hall, Place Albert I., B-1400 Nivelles; tel. (067) 882275	Nivelles

Insurance

Ostend	Monacoplein, B-8400 Oostende; tel. (059) 701199
Oudenaarde	Stadhuis, Markt, B-9700 Oudenaarde; tel. (055) 317251
De Panne	Gemeentehuis, Zeelaan 21, B-8860 De Panne; tel. (058) 421818
Poperinge	Stadhuis, Markt 1, B-8790 Poperinge; tel. (057) 334081
La Roche-en-Ardenne	Rue du Marché 15, B-6980, La Roche-en-Ardenne; tel. (084) 411342
Rochefort	Route de Rochefort 38, B-5580 Han-sur-Lesse; tel. (084) 377716
Saint-Hubert	Rue de la Liberté 18, B-6870 Saint Hubert; tel. (061) 612070
Sint-Niklaas	Grote Markt 45, B-9100 Sint-Niklaas; tel. (03) 777 26 81
Sint-Truiden	Stadhuis, Grote Markt 45, B-3800 Sint-Truiden; tel. (011) 701818
Spa	Place Royale 41, B-4900 Spa; tel. (087) 772510
Stavelot	Rue Neuve 65, B-4970 Stavelot; tel. (080) 862339
Tienen	Stadhuis, Grote Markt 4, B-3300 Tienen; tel. (016) 819785
Tongeren	Stadhuisplein 9, B-3700 Tongeren; tel. (012) 390271
Tournai	Vieux Marché-aux-Poteries 14, B-7500 Tournai; tel. (069) 222045
Turnhout	't Steentje, Grote Markt 44, B-2300 Turnhout; tel. (014) 443355
Verviers	Rue Xhavée 61, B-4800 Verviers; tel. (080) 227664
Veurne	Grote Markt 29, B-8480 Veurne; tel. (058) 330531
Virton	Rue des Grasse Oies 28, B-6830 Bouillon; tel. (063) 578904
Visé	39 Allée des Marguerites, B-4540 Visé
Walcourt	Grand-Place 25, B-6430 Walcourt; tel. (071) 612526
Waterloo	Chausée de Bruxelles 149, B-1410 Waterloo; tel. (02) 3549910
Ypres (Ieper)	Stadhuis, Grote Markt 34, B-8900 Ieper; tel. (057) 200724
Zeebrugge	Zeedijk, B-8380 Zeebrugge; tel. (050) 545042 (open high season, Easter and Whitsun weekends only; other times visit the Bruges office)
Zoutleeuw	Stadhuis, Grote Markt 5, B-3440 Zoutleeuw; tel. (011) 781288

Insurance

Visitors are strongly advised to ensure that they have adequate holiday insurance, including loss or damage to luggage, loss of currency and jewellery.

Health	British citizens, like nationals of other European Union (EU) countries, are entitled to obtain medical care under the Belgian health services regulations on the same basis as Belgians. Before leaving home visitors

should obtain from the post office the leaflet "Health Advice for Travellers" (T5) which contains form E111 which certifies their entitlement to insurance cover. If possible this should be presented to the Local Sickness Funds office (Mutualité/Ziekennfonds) before seeking treatment and 75 per cent of the cost of subsequent treatment by a doctor or dentist (including medicines) will be refunded. for hospital treatment a percentage of hospital costs (excluding the cost of an ambulance) will be paid.

For treatment in Luxembourg charges by doctors and dentists are refundable, though not necessarily for the full amount. Hospital treatment is normally free except for a daily charge that must be paid.

It is nevertheless advisable, even for EU nationals, to take out some form of short-term insurance cover (for example under the AA's Five Star Europe service) providing full cover and possibly avoiding bureaucratic delays. Nationals of non-EU countries should certainly have insurance cover.

Visitors travelling by car should ensure that their insurance is comprehensive and covers use of the vehicle in Belgium.

Vehicles

See also Travel Documents.

Language

Several languages are spoken in Belgium. The Flemings live in the river basin of the Scheldt and the Walloons in the basin of the Meuse. The language frontier between Flanders and Wallonia has hardly changed since the Middle Ages and runs more or less from Visé on the Meuse west across the Waremme, Halle and Ronse to Menin on the French border. North of this line the people speak Flemish, a dialect related to Dutch, south of the line they speak French. Brussels is officially bilingual, although the city centre is becoming a predominantly French-speaking island close to the southern border of the Flemish language area. In the eastern cantons, i.e. in the area around Eupen, Sankt Vith and Arlon, German is mainly spoken.

Language areas

Like Dutch, Flemish is a branch of the Low German language group and in fact only differs from Dutch to the extent that Cockney differs from Geordie in English language terms. Flemish ceased to be used as a written language after the Dutch War of Independence when all Flemish literature was burned by order of the Duke of Alba. It was only under the Dutch administration between 1814 and 1830 that Flemish ceased to be discriminated against. Soon afterwards Dutch was being spoken in the north of Belgium rather than Flemish. After bitter language disputes in the 19th century Dutch also displaced French which had been the official language of the Flemish area. In the forefront of the Flemish movement were several well-known 19th and 20th century writers, among them Felix Timmermans (1886–1947).

Walloon, an ancient French dialect with some elements of Celtic and German, has practically died out. It never became important as a written language, French having tended to fulfil this function since the 12th c.

Walloon

French developed from Vulgar Latin after the Roman Occupation of Celtic Gaul. Although it acquired a number of words of Celtic and later also of Germanic origin, it has kept its Romance character. For centuries it was the most important Romance language spoken by the educated élite and in diplomatic circles. The French polite forms are used when speaking to people, so that "Monsieur", "Madame" and "Mademoiselle" are added to the end of a phrase and *"s'il vous plaît"* (please) is often added when asking for something.

French

Language

	English	French	Dutch/Flemish
Numbers	0	zéro	nul
	1	un, une	een
	2	deux	twee
	3	trois	drie
	4	quatre	vier
	5	cinq	vijf
	6	six	zes
	7	sept	zeven
	8	huit	acht
	9	neuf	negen
	10	dix	tien
	11	onze	elf
	12	douze	twaalf
	13	treize	dertien
	14	quatorze	veertien
	15	quinze	vijftien
	16	seize	zestien
	17	dix-sept	zeventien
	18	dix-huit	achttien
	19	dix-neuf	negentien
	20	vingt	twintig
	21	vingt et un	eenentwintig
	22	vingt-deux	tweeëntwintig
	30	trente	dertig
	31	trente et un	eenendertig
	40	quarante	veertig
	50	cinquante	vijftig
	60	soixante	zestig
	70	septante†	zeventig
	80	quatre-vingt	tachtig
	90	nonante†	negentig
	91	nonante et un†	eenennegentig
	100	cent	honderd
	101	cent un	honderd een
	200	deux cents	tweehonderd
	1000	mille	duizend
	2000	deux milles	tweeduizend

† numbers only used in Belgium; in France they are
70 = soixante-dix; 90 = quatre-vingt-dix; 91 = quatre-vingt-onze

Ordinal numbers	1st	premier (-ière)	eerste
	2nd	deuxième	tweede
	3rd	troisième	derde
Fractions	$-\frac{1}{2}$	un demi	een half
	$-\frac{1}{3}$	un tiers	een derde
	$-\frac{1}{4}$	un quart	een kwart, een vierde
Idioms	Do you speak . . .	Parlez-vous . . .	spreekt u . . .
	I do not understand	Je ne comprends pas	Ik versta niet; ik begrijp u niet
	Yes	oui	Ja
	No	Non	Neen
	Please!	S'il vous plaît!	Alstublieft!
	Thank you!	Merci!	Dank u!
	Thank you very much!	Merci beaucoup!	Dank u wel!
	Excuse me!	Pardon!	Neemt u mij niet kwalijk!
	Sorry!	Excusez!	Pardon!

English	French	Dutch/Flemish	
Good morning!	Bonjour!	Goedemorgen!	
Good day!	Bonjour!	Goededendag! (afternoons)	
Good evening!	Bonsoir!	Goedenavond!	
Good night!	Bonne nuit!	Goedenacht! Wel te rusten!	
Goodbye!	Au revoir!	Tot ziens!	
Mr	Monsieur	Mijnheer	
Mrs	Madame	Mevrouw!	
Miss	Mademoiselle	Juffrouw	
Where is . . . ?	Oó est . . . ?	Waar is . . . ?	
. . . Street	La rue . . .	De . . . straat	
. . . Square	La place . . .	De . . . plaats, het plein	
A travel office	Un bureau de voyage	Een reisbureau	
The church	L'eglise	De kerk	
The museum	Le musée	Het museum	
When?	Quand?	Wanneer?	
When is . . . open?	A quelle heure . . . est ouvert(e)?	Wanneer is . . . open?	
The town hall	L'hôtel de ville	Het stadhuis, het gemeentehuis	
A bank	Une banque	Een bank	
The railway station	La gare	Het station	
A hotel	Un hôtel	Een hotel	
I would like	Je voudrais	Heeft u	
With one bed	A un lit	Met een bed	
With two beds	A deux lits	Met twee bedden	
With bathroom	Avec bain	Met bad	
The key	La clef	De sleutel	
The toilet	La toilette, le cabinet	Het toilet	
A doctor	Un médecin	De arts, de dokter	
Right	A droite	Rechts	
Left	A gauche	Links	
Straight on	Tout droit	Rechtuit	
Above	En haut	Boven	
Below	En bas	Beneden, onder	
Old	Ancien, ancienne, vieux, vieille	Oud	
New	Nouveau, nouvelle	Nieuw	
What does . . . cost?	Combien coûte . . . ?	Hoeveel kost . . . , wat kost . . . ?	
Expensive	Cher, chère	Duur	
Breakfast	Petit déjeuner	Ontbijt	
Lunch	Déjeuner, díner	Middagmaal	
Dinner	Souper	Avondeten	
Eat	Manger	Eten	
Drink	Boire	Drinken	
A lot	Beaucoup	Veel	
A little	Peu	Weinig	
Bill	Addition	Rekening	
Pay	Payer	Betalen	
Immediately	Tout de suite	Dadelijk	
See Food and Drink			The Belgian menu
Departure	Départ	Vertrek	Travelling
Arrival	Arrivée	Aankomst	
Bus station	Gare routière	Autobusstation	
Railway station	Gare	Station	

Language

	English	French	Dutch/Flemish
	Airport	Aéroport	Luchthaven
	Flight	Vol	Vlucht
	Platform	Voie	Spoor
	Stop	Arrêt	Halte
	Connection	Correspondance	Overstappen
	Train	Train	Trein
Traffic signs and warnings	Stop!	Halte! Stop!	Stop!
	Customs	Douane	Tol
	Attention!	Attention!	Pas op! Opgelet!
	Caution!	Prudence!	Waarschuwing!
	Drive slowly!	Au pas! Ralentir!	Langzaam rijden!
	Danger of death!	Danger de mort!	Levensgevaar!
	One-way street	Sens unique	Straat met eenrichtingsverkeer
	No entry!	Route barrée! Passage interdit!	Inrijden verboden, doodlopende straat!
	Roadworks!	Travaux!	Werk in uitvoering!
	Dangerous bend!	Virage dangereux!	Gevaarlijke bocht!
Geographical terms	Stream	Ruisseau	Beek
	Mountain	Mont	Berg
	Bridge	Pont	Brug
	Village	Village	Dorp
	Railway	Chemin de fer	Spoorlijn
	Ferry	Bac	Veer, Pont
	River	Fleuve	Rivier
	Stream	Ruisseau	Beek
	Garden, Park	Jardin, Parc	Tuin, Park
	Summit	Sommet	Top
	Hill	Coline	Heuvel
	Island	Ile	Eiland
	Secondary road	Route	Landweg, Weg
	(Market)Place	Place	(Markt)Platz
	Moor	Tourbière	Veen
	Castle	Château	Slot, Kasteel
	Town	Ville	Stad
	Beach	Plage	Strand
	Road	Rue	Straat
	Bog	Marais	Moeras
	Valley	Vallée	Dal
	Tower	Tour	Toren
	Forest	Forêt	Bos, Woud
	Waterfall	Cascade	Waterval
Months	January	Janvier	Januari
	February	Février	Februari
	March	Mars	Maart
	April	Avril	April
	May	Mai	Mei
	June	Juin	Juni
	July	Juillet	Juli
	August	Août	Augustus
	September	Septembre	September
	October	Octobre	Oktober
	November	Novembre	November
	December	Decembre	December
Days	Monday	Lundi	Maandag

English	French	Dutch/Flemish	
Tuesday	Mardi	Dinsdag	
Wednesday	Mecredi	Woensdag	
Thursday	Jeudi	Donderdag	
Friday	Vendredi	Vrijdag	
Saturday	Samedi	Zaterdag	
Sunday	Dimanche	Zondag	
Holiday	Jour de Fête	Feestdag, vrije dag	
New Year	Nouvel An	Nieuwjaar	Special days
Easter	Pâques	Pasen	
Ascension	Ascension	Hemelsvaartsdag	
Whitsun	Pentecôte	Pinksteren	
Corpus Christi	Fête-Dieux	Sacramentsdag	
Assumption	Assomption	Maria-Hemelvaart	
All Saints' Day	Toussaint	Allerheiligen	
Christmas	Noël	Kerstmis	
New Year's Eve	Le Saint-Sylvestre	Oudejaarsavond	
Post office	Bureau de poste	Postkantoor	At the post office
Main post office	Bureau de poste centrale	Hoofdpostkantoor	
Stamp	Timbre-poste	Postzegel	
Letter	Lettre	Brief	
Postcard	Carte postale	Briefkaart	
Postman	Facteur	Postbode	
Recorded delivery	Recommandé	Aangetekend	
Express	Par exprès	Expres	
Airmail	Par avion	Luchtpost	
Telegram	Télégramme	Telegram	
Telephone	Téléphone	Telefoon	

A small pamphlet entitled "Bienvenue & Merci", which lists the most important idioms in both languages together with their English meaning, is available from the tourist information offices listed under Information (see entry).

Advice

Leisure Parks

Belgium has a large number of leisure/amusement parks offering a broad range of entertainment and opportunities for sports and games. The most attractive are listed here. An admission fee is charged in most parks.

Meli-Park, De Pannelaan 68, with Europe's tallest waterchute.
A family park with numerous attractions such as the waterchute ride Splash, scenes from fairy tales and a nature park.
Opening times: Apr. daily 10.30am–5.30pm (Sun. 10am–6pm); May–early Jul. until 6pm; early Jul.–late Aug. until 7pm; late Aug.–early Sep. until 6pm; early–late Sep. Wed. 10.30am–5.30pm, Sat. 10.30am–6pm, Sun. 10am–6pm.

Adinkerke-De Panne

Antwerpen-Miniatuurstad, Hangar 15a, Scheldekaai
Model of Antwerp on a scale of 1:87 with scale models of ships, which sail along a miniature version of the Scheldt.
Opening times: daily 10am–6pm.

Antwerp

Boudewijnpark, A. De Baeckestraat 12
Contains Europe's largest dolphinarium, an ice-rink and many other family attractions.

Bruges (Brugge)

The Bruparck, with the Atomium in the background

Opening times: late Apr.–Aug. daily 10am–6pm; Sept. Wed., Sat. and Sun. 11am–6pm.

Brussels/Bruxelles	Bruparck, Eeuwfeestlaan, 20 Boulevard du Centenaire (near the Atomium) Mini-Europe: important European buildings on a scale of 1:25; Océade: subtropical waterparadise; Le Village: various refreshment places, play area; Kinépolis (cinema city): the world's largest cinema complex. Opening times: Mini-Europe: daily Apr.–Jun. and Sep. 9.30am–6pm; beginning–mid Jul. until 8pm; mid Jul.–mid Aug. until midnight; mid–end Aug. until 8pm; Oct.–early Jan. 10am–6pm (Sun. and public holidays May–Sep. open 1 hour later). Oceade: Tue.–Thu. (Apr.–Jun. except school holidays) 2–10pm; Fri. 2–11pm; Sat. 10am–11pm; Sun., public holidays and school holidays 10am–10pm.
Coo-Stavelot	Télécoo Bobsleigh run, cable railway, motorcycle track, go-karts, zoo. Opening times: May–Sep. daily and in winter Sat. and Sun. and school holidays 10.30am–6.30pm.
Dadizele	Dadipark, Moorsledestraat 6 Suspension bridge, animation programme Opening times: end Apr.–Jun. daily as well as weekends in Sep. 10am–7pm; Jul./Aug. daily 10am–7.30pm.
Ingelmunster	Aviflora, Bruggestraat 218 Thousands of animals (eg. water fowl) inmidst of green spaces, lakes, waterfalls; exhibition halls with exotic birds, plants and fish; monkey colony. Opening times: May-mid–Sep. daily 10am–6pm.

Bobbejaanland, Steenweg op Olen 45, tel. (014) 557811   Lichtaart
Family park with numerous attractions such as the Mississippi Boat, Wild River; trapeze tower; museum of native Americans.
Opening times: early Apr.–Oct. daily 10am–6pm, (9.30am–7pm in high season).

Rekreatiepark Zoet Water, M. Noëstraat 15   Oud-Heverlee
Play village, open-air theatre, forest pavilion with large aquaria, terrarium, miniature railway, etc.
Opening times: end Mar.–Sep. Mon.–Sat. 10am–7pm, Sun. and public holidays until 8pm; Oct.–Mar. Sat. and Sun. 1–5pm.

Walibi (exit 7 from E411) and Aqualibi (exit 6 from E411)   Wavre
Walibi: water adventure, Kangaroo Land, sea lion and parrot shows, puppet theatre, Lucky Luke City with the 77 m (253 ft) high "Dalton Terror" ride.
Aqualibi: water park with jet stream, breakers, tropical bar.
Opening times: end Mar.–end Sep. daily 10am–6pm for visitors to both establishments, for visitors to Aqualibi only 6–10pm.

Bellewaerde, Meenseweg 497   Zillebeke–Ypres (Ieper)
Safari park, jungle boats, cowboy village, Mexican village.
Opening times: early Apr.–Aug. daily 10am–6pm; Sep.–Mid Oct. Weekends only.

Also of appeal are the SunAquaParks/SunParks which can be found   SunAquaParks/ SunParks
along the Belgian coast. They combine numerous sporting, games and leisure facilities with luxurious holiday homes. Occupants of these homes have free entry to the adjacent SunAquaPark.

SunAquaPark De Haan, Wenduinesteenweg 150
B-8420 De Haan; tel. (050) 429596

SunAquaPark Groendyk, Polderstraat 158
B-8670 Oostduinkerke-Koksijde; tel. (058) 239563

Those interested can find references to popular zoos, safari parks,   Zoological and botanical gardens
aquaria and botanical gardens in the A to Z section.

Markets

In addition to strolling through the picturesque markets which take place once or more a week, a visit to the antiques, flea and flower markets can also prove a delight.

Nearly every Flemish town stages a Kermis: the largest event of this kind   Fairs
in Belgium is Kortrijk's Easter Kermis (from Easter Saturday until the second Sunday after Easter).

One of the most-visited pre-Christmas markets is that which takes place   Christmas markets
on the Place du Grand Sablon in Brussels. Most Christmas markets are to be found in the south of the country.

Selected markets

Antiques market on the Lijnwaardmarkt and art market on the   Antwerp
Dageraadplaats (Easter–Oct. Sat. 9am–5pm)

Flea-market by the Dijver in Bruges

	Flea markets on the Oud Arsenaalplaats, on the Oude Vaartplaats, on the Blauwtorenplein and on the Graanmarkt (Sun. 9am–1pm)
	Junk market on the Vrijdagmarkt (Wed. and Fri. 8am–1pm)
	Bird market on the Oude Vaartplaats (Sat. 9am–4pm, Sun. 8.30am–1pm)
Bruges	Flea market on the Dijver (Apr.–Oct. Sat. 1–5pm, Sun. 10am–5pm)
	Zandfeesten on 't Zand (Flanders' largest antiques and flea market; each for one day at the beginning of Jul., mid Aug. and end Oct. 7am–1pm; see information at the local tourist information office).
Brussels/Bruxelles	Antiques market on the Place du Grand Sablon (Sat. 9am–6pm and Sun. 9am–2pm)
	Flea market on the Place du Jeu de Balle (daily 7am–2pm)
	Crafts market on the Place de l'Agora (Sat. and Sun. 10am–6pm)
	Flower market on the Grand-Place (Tue.–Sun. 8pm–6pm)
	Bird market on the Grand-Place (Sun. 7am–2pm)
Charleroi	Dog market on the Place Charles II and in the Rue Vauban (Sunday mornings)
Ghent	Flower market on the Kouter (daily 7am–1pm)

Animal market (pets, poultry) on the Oude Beestenmarkt (Sun. 7am–1pm)

Flea market around St Jacob (Fri. and Sat. 7am–1pm, Sun. 9am–1pm)

Bird market on the Vrijdagsmarkt (Sun. 7am–1pm)

Art market (Jul. and Aug. Sat. 2–6pm)	Hasselt
"La Batte" flea and grocery market, Quai Batte (Sun. 8am–1pm)	Liège
Flea market on the Boulevard Kleyer (Sat. 9am–noon)	
Flea market on the Tramweglei (every first Sat. in the month 1–6pm)	Lier
Junk market on the Place du Béguinage (Sunday morning)	Mons
Antiques and flea market on the Veemarkt (Sat. 1–6pm)	Sint-Truiden
Flea market in the Galérie Leopold II (Sun. 8am–2pm)	Spa
Antiques and flea market on the Oude Veemarkt (Sun. 5am–2pm)	Tongeren
Antiques and flea market on the Quai des Salines (Sun. 10am–1pm)	Tournai
Grand Flower Market on Good Friday	
Flea market in Warandestraat (Sun. 9am–noon)	Turnhout

Medical Assistance

Belgian medical services are excellent and the country is well supplied with doctors, many of them able to speak English.

British visitors to Belgium will find it helpful before they go to obtain a free booklet from the Post Office, "Health Advice for Travellers" (T5), which gives information about health precautions and how to get medical treatment when abroad.

See also Insurance.

Military Cemeteries

The following list of military cemeteries includes only the most important in Belgium. Further information on Commonwealth sites can be obtained from the Commonwealth War Graves Commission, 2 Marlow Road, Maidenhead, Berks, SL6 7DX; tel. (01628) 34221.

1 Poperinge-Lijssenthoek (WW1)
9,902 Commonwealth, 658 French, 3 American and 223 German soldiers killed in action

2 Ypres-Memorial (WW1)
Menentor (Menin Gate) memorial with the names of 54,359 soldiers missing in action; every evening at 8pm the traffic is stopped and "Last Post" is sounded

3 Tyne-Cot Cemetery and Memorial (WW1)

11,956 soldiers killed in action (including 4 Germans) and a memorial with the names of 34,861 soldiers missing in action

4 Menen (WW1)
47,864 soldiers killed in action
Largest German First World War military cemetery

5 Waregem Flanders Fiels (WW1)
368 soldiers killed in action

6 Poelkapelle (WW1)
7479 British soldiers killed in action (1 in WW2)

7 Langemark (WW1)

8 Houthulster Wald (WW1)

9 Hooglede (WW1)
8247 soldiers killed in action; arcaded hall constructed from material used for the German pavilion in the 1928 World Exhibition

10 Vladslo (WW1)
25,644 soldiers killed in action; sculpture entitled "Mourning Parents" by Käthe Kollwitz

11 Zeebrugge (WW1)
30 Commonwealth and 178 German soldiers killed in action

12 Lommel (WW1, WW2)
541 soldiers killed in action in the First World War and 38,962 soldiers killed in action in the Second World War; also Polish soldiers killed in action in the Second World War

13 Leopoldsburg (WW1, WW2)
769 Commonwealth, 27 Polish and 4 Dutch soldiers killed in action

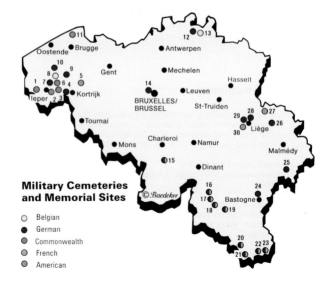

**Military Cemeteries
and Memorial Sites**

© *Baedeker*

○ Belgian
● German
◐ Commonwealth
◑ French
◓ American

French Military Cemetery on the Citadelle of Dinant

14 Bruxelles-Evere (WW1)
1147 German soldiers killed in action are buried in the local cemetery

15 Tarcienne (WW1)
178 German and 446 French soldiers killed in action

16 Maissin-National (WW1)
513 German and 3286 French soldiers killed in action

17 Anloy-Heide (WW1)
1384 German and 594 French soldiers killed in action

18 Bertrix-Heide (WW1)
254 German and 273 French soldiers killed in action

19 Neufchâteau-Malonne (WW1)
340 German and 288 French soldiers killed in action

20 Bellefontaine (WW1)
502 German and 518 French soldiers killed in action

21 Virton-Bellevue (WW1)
1288 German and 2445 French soldiers killed in action

22 Musson-Baranzy (WW1)
511 German and 454 French soldiers killed in action

23 Halanzy (WW1)
44 German and 22 French soldiers killed in action

24 Recogne (WW2)
6785 soldiers killed in action

25 St. Vith (WW1)
173 German soldiers killed in action are buried in the local cemetery

26 Eupen (WW1)
122 German soldiers killed in action are buried in the local cemetery

27 Ardennes Cemetery at Neuville-en-Condroz (WW2)
5310 soldiers killed in action

28 Herstal (WW1)
95 German soldiers killed in action are buried in the local cemetery

29 Liège-Robermont (WW1)
795 German soldiers killed in action are buried in the local cemetery

30 Henri-Chapelle (WW2)
7989 soldiers killed in action, mainly Americans

Motoring

Accidents

Immediate action

However careful a driver is, an accident can always happen. If one does, endeavour to remain calm and polite. Keep a clear head and take the following action.

1. Ensure that the site of the accident is safe, i.e. turn on hazard warning lights, position warning triangle and – if available – warning lights at a sufficient distance.

2. Take care of anyone injured. First-aid advice can be found in a car first-aid kit. If necessary, call an ambulance.

3. Inform the police (tel. 101). They record every accident.

4. Note the names and addresses of other people involved in the accident. Also note the registration number(s) and make(s) of any other car(s) involved and the names and telephone numbers of their insurers. The time and place of the accident are also important as well as the address of the police station alerted.

5. Secure evidence. Note the names and addresses of – if possible, impartial – witnesses; sketch the scene at the site of the accident or, better still, keep a small camera in the glove compartment to take photographs from various angles.

European Accident Report

If possible use the European Accident Report (available from insurance companies) and have it countersigned by the plaintiff for damages. Do not sign any admission of guilt and, above all, do not sign anything written in an unknown language.

Compensation

After an accident the handling of compensation claims should go as smoothly as possible. To achieve this follow this advice.

1. If a claim is made against you, report the damage to your own vehicle insurers. You can also contact the Belgian insurance company named on your Green Card.

2. Make your own claim against the other party and his current insurers. The Green Card is of no help here! Legal costs insurance is useful in helping to pursue such claims.

3. The police accident report is first sent only to the public prosecutor's office. This office will not issue a copy until the conclusion of the investigation.

4. With the exception of minor damage, send an estimate by recorded delivery (with a specialist report if the damage is more severe) to the other party and his insurance company. Request that the insurance company obtains expert advice about the damages within a week. If no reply is forthcoming you are entitled to have the repairs carried out. The other party still has the right to dispute liability but his insurance company cannot refuse a repair bill if you have approved it.

5. If you are summoned to appear in court inform your vehicle insurers immediately. Up to a certain level of damages, claims against the other driver can be made in the criminal court.

6. Is a lawyer required to pursue your compensation claim or to defend you in court? If so your legal costs insurers will issue names of Belgian laywers who speak English and whose fees are then paid by the insurers.

7. In Belgium claims for loss of value are rarely proceeded with. The cost of a rented car is only refunded if it is for commercial use. Out of court costs for a lawyer are also not allowed. In the case of a write-off the appropriate customs authorities must also be notified.

Reporting damage promptly can accelerate any claim.

Breakdown Assistance

Touring Club Royal de Belgique (T.C.B.)
Rue de la Loi 44
B-1040 Bruxelles/Brussels; tel. (02) 2332211

Automobile associations

Royal Automobile Club de Belgique (R.A.C.B.)/Koninklijke Automobiel Club van België (K.A.C.B.)
Rue d'Arlon 53
B-1040 Bruxelles/Brussels; tel. (02) 2870911

Branches of these associations can be found in all larger towns.

Antwerp; tel. (03) 3538888
Ardenne; tel. (062) 212333
Bruges; tel. (050) 811717
Brussels; tel. (02) 2332211
Charleroi; tel. (071) 503838
Hainaut; tel. (064) 663301
Leuven; tel. (016) 461112
Liège; tel. (041) 687991
Limburg; tel. (011) 420545
Namur; tel. (081) 461363
Oostvlaanderen; tel. (091) 626565
Westvlaanderen; tel.(051) 778140

Breakdown help

National Parks, Nature Reserves and Caves

R.A.C.B./K.A.C.B.   Countrywide; tel. (070) 344777

Emergency telephones are stationed along all Belgian motorways.

Failure to observe motoring regulations leads to drivers, even visitors, being fined on the spot by police.

In Belgium vehicles travel on the right and overtake on the left.

Children up to twelve must travel in the back of the car.
    Yellow lines on the kerb mean that parking is forbidden.
    Right of way must be given to police cars, fire engines or ambulances answering an emergency and vehicles on rails.

A **warning triangle** must be kept in the car. In the event of a breakdown on a secondary road it must be placed at least 30 m (99 ft) from the vehicle. On a motorway it must be positioned at least 100 m (328 ft) from the vehicle.

The **maximum blood alcohol level** is 50 grammes per litre.

The use of front **seat belts** is obligatory.

Motorcycle/moped riders must wear **helmets**.

Maximum speed   Within built-up areas 50 k.m.p.h (31 m.p.h); on motorways and dual carriageways for vehicles up to 7.5t (including trailers) 120 k.m.p.h (74 m.p.h), on secondary roads 90 k.m.p.h (55 m.p.h); for vehicles over 7.5t (including trailers) 90 k.m.p.h (55 m.p.h) and 60 k.m.p.h (37 m.p.h) respectively.
    Maximum speed when towing is 25 k.m.p.h (16 m.p.h); this also applies on motorways, where vehicles towing must leave at the first available exit.

Rear fog-lights   Rear fog-lights – if available – have to be used in heavy rain, snow and fog as well as visibility below 100 m (327 ft).

Fuel   Belgium has an extensive network of petrol stations selling 3-star lead-free petrol (92 octane), 4-star lead-free petrol (95 octane) and lead-free super plus petrol (98 octane) as well as Diesel. Leaded petrol is no longer available.

National Parks, Nature Reserves and Caves

National Parks and Nature Reserves

In general plants and animals should not be disturbed in their habitat but should be left in peace. Visitors should not stray from marked paths, bridleways and, if applicable, cross-country ski runs. Rubbish should not be thrown down but must be taken away; dogs must be kept on leads. Picking flowers, camping, radios, night-time walks and fires are banned. The ecologically very sensitive moorland area of Hohen Venn is particularly at risk of fire during summer.

1 Het Zwin (coastal bird reserve)
Location: at Knokke-Heist. Area: 125 ha (309 acres)

2 Kalmthouder Heide

National Parks
Nature Reserves
● **Caves open to the Public**

Location: north of Antwerp. Area: 1700 ha (4201 acres)

3 Molenheide (with zoo)
Location: at Helchteren north of Hasselt. Area: 100 ha (247 acres)

4 Bokrijk (with open-air folk museum and arboretum)
Location: north-east of Hasselt. Area: 514 ha (1270 acres)

5 Maten (bird reserve)
Location: at Genk. Area: 300 ha (741 acres)

6 Mechelse Heide
Location: at Maasmechelen. Area: 400 ha (988 acres)

7 Bois de Soignes (Zonniënwoud)
Location: south-east of Brussels. Area: 4000 ha (9884 acres)

8 Furfooz (nature park)
Location: south-east of Dinant. Area: 819 ha (2024 acres)

9 Lesse et Lomme (national and game park)
Location: at Han-sur-Lesse. Area: 250 ha (618 acres)

10 Hohes Venn-Eifel (nature park)
Location: east of Malmédy. Area: 70,000 ha (172,970 acres)

11 Hohes Venn (nature reserve)
Location: east of Malmédy. Area: 4200 ha (10,378 acres)

The last two areas form parts of the German-Belgian National Park (see
A to Z).

Caves

In southern Belgium slate and limestone form the upper strata of the

Ardennes; in the Condroz, Maas, Ourthe and Lesse in particular and in other rivers fissures have cut into the readily-soluble limestone layer in many places, with the result that water has gradually penetrated through them and formed stalactites. Many of the caves which arose in this way have an underground river flowing through them. The caves are accessible on guided tours.

12 Grotte de Ramioul
Location: Ramet 14 km (9 mi.) south-west of Liège
Pre-historic finds, cave museum

13 Grotte de Comblain-au-Pont
Location: Comblain-au-Pont, 18 km (11 mi.) south of Liège
Sinter formations, find of bones

14 Grotte de Remouchamps
Location: Remouchamps, 13 km (8 mi.) west of Spa
Sinter formations, underground river

15 Grottes des Milles et une Nuits (Caves of the Thousand and one Nights)
Location: Hotton, 23 km (14 mi.) north-east of Rochefort
Sinter formations, dripstones, underground river

16 Grotte de Rochfort
Location: Rochefort
Crystal formations, underground river

17 Grottes de Han
Location: Han-sur-Lesse
Sinter formations, underground river, cave museum in Europe's largest cave complex

18 Grotte "La Merveilleuse" ("The Marvellous")
Location: Dinant
Sinter formations, cave lake

19 Grottes du Pont d'Arcole
Location: Hastière-Lavaux, 23 km (14 mi.) south-west of Dinant
Sinter formations, dripstones, underground river

20 Grotte de Neptune
Location: Couvin, 10 km (6 mi.) east of Chimay
Pre-historic finds, cave museum

21 Grotte de Goyet
Location: Mozet-Goyet, 10 km (6 mi.) east of Namur
Pre-historic finds, sinter formations

Newspapers and periodicals

The principal British and American newspapers are readily available in most parts of Belgium, often on the day of issue.

Among the important Belgian daily newspapers are the Gazet van Antwerpen (catholic-conservative), Het Laatste Nieuws (Brussels, liberal), Het Volk (Brussels and Gent; catholic-conservative), Standaard (Brussels; catholic-conservative), La Wallonie (socialist), La Libre Belgique (Brussels; catholic-monarchist), De Morgen (Brussels, left) and Le Soir (Brussels, independent).

There is a weekly English language magazine, "The Bulletin".

Opening Times

Chemists are open at the same times as retail shops. | Chemists

Banks are usually open Mon.–Fri. 9am–4 or 5pm (some branches closing for an hour or more for lunch); some may open Saturday mornings. | Banks

See below | Post Offices

The law governing trading hours in Belgium is liberal and states that shops need only close for a mere 24 hours a week on the day of their choice. | Shops

In general opening times are between 5am and 8pm; on Fridays late-night shopping is allowed until 9pm. Many shops close between noon and 2pm.

Supermarkets are closed on Sundays. However, by contrast, many small shops (including bakers and greengrocers) open on this day, and close instead on Tuesday or Wednesday.

In most North Sea coastal resorts shops have longer opening hours.

Post

Ordinary letters (up to 20 grams) and postcards cost 17 Bfr within Belgium and 19 Bfr to EU countries (except for Spain and Portugal: 21 Bfr); elsewhere abroad 34 Bfr. Stamps can be bought both in post offices and often in souvenir shops and kiosks.

Belgian post boxes are red and usually marked with a post-horn.

In larger towns post offices are usually open Mon.–Fri. 9am–5pm with smaller offices closing noon–2pm. Some offices are also open on Friday evenings and Saturday mornings. The Brussels X Post Office at the Gare du Midi (South Station), Ave. Fonsny 48A is open continuously.

See entry | Telephone

Public Holidays

If a public holiday falls on a Sunday the following Monday is usually taken as a public holiday.

January 1st: New Year's Day | Fixed public holidays
May 1st: Labour Day
July 11th: Festival of the Flemish Community (only in Flanders)
July 21st: National Day
August 15th: Assumption
September 27th: Festival of the Wallonian Community (only in Wallonia)
November 1st: All Saints Day
November 11th: Armistice Day
December 25th and 26th: Christmas

Easter Monday, Ascension and Pentecost Monday. | Movable holidays

Radio and Television

Belgian radio and television transmit programmes in a variety of languages. Radio-Télévision Belge de la Communauté Française (R.T.B.F.) serves the French-speaking area, Belgische Radio en Televisie (BRT) caters for speakers of Flemish while for German speakers there is the Belgische Rundfunk-und Fernsehzentrum (BRF). There are also very many private stations.

Within Europe Belgium has the largest number of premises linked to the cable network. Almost 95 per cent of all Belgian households have a cable connection and are thus able to receive a wide selection of foreign programmes in addition to Belgian state and private broadcasts.

Railways

In 1835 the first railway line in continental Europe was constructed between Brussels and Mechelen. Since then Belgium has developed the world's densest railway network which makes rail travel highly recommendable.

The operating authority is the Société Nationale des Chemins de Fer Belges (SNCB)/Nationaal Maatschappij van Belgische Spoorwegen (NMBS).

Railway junctions	Since the beginning of the railway age Brussels, with its present four stations, has been the country's most important railway junction. Connections with the French high-speed train TVG to Amsterdam, Paris and Cologne are planned. Together with Brussels, Liège is also of some importance.
Central information In Brussels	Daily 6am–10.30pm: tel. (02) 2192640 (in French) tel. (02) 2192880 (in Dutch)
Trains	Inter-city trains (IC) only stop at large stations, InterRegio trains (IR) also stop at some intermediate stations; both types of train are not subject to supplements. L trains are local trains which stop at almost every station. IC, IR and L trains run throughout the day, usually every hour.
Tickets	There are both first and second class tickets which can be bought up to five days in advance. Buying a ticket on the train is considerably more expensive than buying it at the station. (Day) return tickets cost twice as much as single tickets; the return journey must be made on the same day.
Reductions and special rates	Information about cheap rail travel (including offers for senior citizens, families, groups, the disabled and students) can be obtained from Belgian railway stations.
Children	Children up to the age of six travel free; there is a 50 per cent reduction in price for children aged between six and twelve years.
B-Tourrail	The B-Tourrail ticket permits travel throughout the entire Belgian railway network for five days within one month. This ticket is available for people of all ages.
TTB ticket	The TTB ticket carries the same conditions as the B-Tourrail ticket but can also be used on all buses, trams and underground trains of the narrow gauge railway and the local town/city companies.

To travel through all three Benelux countries the Benelux Tourrail ticket is particularly suitable. This is also valid for five days within one month on all the railway networks of the Benelux countries.

For weekend travel within Belgium (outward journey Fri. noon to Sun. noon; return journey Sat. noon to Mon. noon) there is a 40 per cent reduction in the normal price for the first person and a 60 per cent reduction for those accompanying him/her (2–6 people). The Benelux-Weekend ticket is valid for weekend travel to a particular place within the Benelux countries (outward journey Thu. 4pm to Sun. midnight; return journey Sat. 0.01am to Mon. midnight). The first person gains a reduction of 25 per cent of the normal ticket price, for up to five people accompanying him/her there is a reduction of 50 per cent.

Reduced day tickets to the coast and to the Ardennes are only valid during carnival and Easter holidays, from mid June to mid September, during the week of All Saints' Day and the Christmas holidays. They enjoy the same reductions as weekend tickets (but not only at weekends).

The half-price authorised ticket is valid for a month and entitles the holder to a 50 per cent reduction in the full price of a ticket for one or two people.

The GO-PASS entitles young people (12–25 years) to travel inexpensively on ten journeys within Belgium.

The Belgian railway organises numerous day excursions by train with reductions both on the price of the ticket and on the admission fee to museums, castles, leisure parks, etc.

Cycles can be rented and returned at more than 60 railway stations in Belgium. These are listed in the A to Z section under the relevant town or village. The Belgian railway and the Flemish Central Youth Hostel (see Young Peoples' Accommodation) also offer two to three-day cycling excursions (it is advisable to reserve places a week beforehand). The price includes the return train journey, the rent of the bicycle and overnight accommodation with breakfast in a youth hostel.

Within Belgium there are several opportunities to travel on steam trains and museum trains. The tourist trains which are to be found in many places are not real trains but street cars drawn by tractors.

Museum train "Le Trimbleu". Nostalgic journey on a slow train from Blégny to Mortroux and back.
Information: Freizeitbergwerk "Le Trimbleu"
B-4670 Blégny; tel. (041) 87 44 33

The Venn train travels on Sundays and public holidays in the summer from Eupen/Raeren via Monschau to Bullingen (an extension of the network is planned to Stolberg, Malmédy, Trois-Ponts and Losheim-Jünkerath). Two historic Belgium diesel locomotives pull carriages from the 1930s and two former Mitropa dining cars. In 1993 the German steam locomotive 50366 was added to the collection. The train operates on the first weekend of each month from May to October. The journey is made on both Belgian and German territory.
Information: Vennbahn VOE, Bahnhof Raeren, Bahnhofstrasse
B-4730 Raeren; tel. (087) 85 24 87

Diesel-driven open train from the town centre to the entrance to the grottos (see A to Z, Han-sur-Lesse).

A vintage train in Han-sur-Lesse

Maldegem	Journey on a museum train from the steam centre Maldegem to Eeklo or by narrow-guage railway to Donk. Information: Stoomcentrum, Stationsplein 8 B-9990 Maldegem; tel. (050) 716852
Mariembourg	Steam train "Trois Vallées" Treignes-Mariembourg-Chimay-Momignies Information: 49/51 Chaussée de Givet B-5660 Mariembourg; tel. (081) 221199 and (060) 312440
Rebecq	"Kleiner Glückszug" Journey on a nostalgic steam train through the Vallée des Oiseaux along the Senne. Information: B-1430 Rebecq; tel. (067) 670120
Vilvoorde	Museumstoomtrein der Twee Bruggen Museum steam train between Brussels and Willebroek Information: Museumstoomtrein der Twee Bruggen, Harensesteenweg 494. B-1800 Vilvoorde; tel. (02) 2515476 (2–6pm)

Restaurants

Belgium is a gourmets' paradise. In no other country in Europe – in relation to population – are there so many excellent restaurants rewarded by restaurant guides with stars, chef's hats or cooking spoons as in the small kingdom lying between the Ardennes and the North Sea. The following selection names many such award-winning restaurants

Brussels: the Rue des Bouchers, centre of Belgian cuisine ▶

446

where a simple meal can become an adventure. The countryside inns located in small villages enjoy good to very good reputations. In addition, there are numerous pizzerias, snack bars (frying delicious pommes frites!), sandwich bars and cafés serving light dishes.

A *café* is always an ordinary pub, where beer and lemonade are the most popular drinks, although coffee is also served. Those requiring coffee, tea, cake, etc. should visit a *salon de thé* or a *tearoom*.

Bars are the most popular meeting places. Beer is predominantly drunk here and any landlord worth his salt has at least 20 to 30 varieties at his disposal – all, of course, served in their authentic glasses. Sausages, cheese and sandwiches are available and billiards can be played in many bars.

Selection

Aalst	Hostellerie Mirage, Stationsstraat 21, tel. (053) 774160. Specialities: fish (turbot fillet) and poultry
Antwerp	★'t Fornuis, Reyndersstraat 24; tel. (03) 233 62 70 No. 1 in Antwerp, this restaurant serves outstanding dishes in the rustic ambience of a 17th c. house. Stoofpot, Schuttershofstraat 37, tel. (03) 2 34 39 31. A stronghold of classical Flenish cooking. Hoffys Take Away This eatery in the Kievitsstraat lacks all charme. If, however, you fancy "gefilte" fish or carp fishcakes, this is the place for you – top kosher cuisine in the diamond quarter.
Arlon	Les Forges du Pont d'Oye, in Habay-la-Neuve (14 km/8.7 mi. to the north-west) 6, Rue du Pont d'Oye, tel. (063) 422243. Lamb and veal dishes are the specialities of this excellent restaurant. If the weather permits, you can eat outside.
Beaumont	Hostellerie Le Prieuré Saint Géry, in Solre St-Géry (4 km/2.5 mi. to the south), 9, Rue Lambot, tel. (071) 589700. This quiet country restaurant with terrace is the best place to try some fried pigeons.
Blankenberge	Escapade, J. De Troozlaan 39, tel. (050) 411597. A delight: delicious quality cooking at reasonable prices.
Bruges	De Karmeliet, Langestraat 19; tel. (050) 338259 Chef van Hecke has been awarded three Michelin stars for his cooking – one of only three chefs in Belgium to have gained this distinction. ★Breydel-de Coninck, Breidelstraat 24, tel. (050) 339746. The best place in town to eat the Flemish national dish, mussels and chips ("mosselen"). Eat as much as you can manage. De Stove, Kleine Sint-Amandsstraat 4, tel. (050) 337835. Small, friendly bistro, specially renowned for its fish dishes, for example Ostend fish soup (Hutsepot van vis). Curiosa, Vlamingstraat 22, tel. (050) 342334. Hearty meals to go with the beer, at moderate prices, served in a medieval cellar.

★Au Stekerlaplatte, 4, Rue des Prêtres, tel. 5128681
Belgian cuisine, from hearty to elegant, in a wonderfully relaxed atmosphere. This Marollen district restaurant which has many nooks and crannies is popular with locals.

Bruneau, 73–75 Ave. Broustin; tel. 4276978
The chef, Jean-Pierre Bruneau, who has been awarded three stars for his cooking, is known to be eccentric.

Chez Léon, 18, Rue des Bouchers, tel. 5111415
One of the best places in the mi.-long stretch of restaurants behind the Grand'Place. For more than 100 years, it has guaranteed quality mussels.

★Comme Chez Soi, 23, Pl. Rouppe; tel. 5122921
Chef Pierre Wynants, the doyen of Belgian cooking, promises "home-style" cooking. But whose home cooking can boast a three-star cuisine in an authentic Art Nouveau setting?

★La Femme du Boulanger, 18, Rue Antoine Dansaert, tel. 5024026
Salads, soups and hearty one-pot meals are served up by the baker's wife who, himself, has established a wonderful breakfast bistro in the bakery next door.

★Jacques, 44, Quai aux Briques; tel. 5132762
The best fish dishes in town, in a cosy atmosphere.

De Ogenblik, 1, Galerie des Princes; tel. 5116151
Trendy bistro with ambitious cooking.

't Truffeltje, Bogaerdstraat 20; tel. (052) 224590
The "little truffle" offers a succesful combination of Belgian and French cooking with Far-Eastern influences.

De Nieuwe Haan, Grote Markt 19, tel. (013) 335106
Hearty dishes are tops here, for example rabbit in a beer sauce.

Auberge de Bouvignes, in Bouvignes (2 km/1.2 mi. to the north), 112, Rue Fétis; tel. (082) 611600
Many a Dinant resident who fancies a feast is drawn to this exceptionally pleasant restaurant.

Le Gourmet in the Ambassador Hotel, Haasstr. 81; tel. (087) 740800
Game is the most popular item on the menu.

Jan van den Bon, Koning-Leopold-II-laan 43; tel. (09) 2219085
Best restaurant in town, has been awarded a star. French inspired cooking.

Raadskelder, Botermarkt 11, tel. (09) 2254334
Typically Flemish cooking, for example waterzooi, carbonade and eel in green sauce, in a cellar with Gothic arches.

★Georges, Donkersteeg 23, tel. (09) 2252918
A specialist in seafood since 1924,, and today one of the best fish restaurants in Flanders. Oysters and lobster, served in many different ways, are favourites. Both of these, and other seafood, can also be bought in the adjacent shop.

Het Pakhuis, Schuurkenstraat 4, tel. (09) 2235555
The interior decoration rather than the cooking – decent modern food – are what makes this restaurant a popular meeting place: iron, wood and

basketry dominate, and there is a shiny copper and brass bar, all in a former storage shed.

Hasselt

Gulden Schalmei near Zolder, Sterrenwacht 153, tel. (011) 251750
Excellent Flemish cooking, close to the famous racing track. Always popular with the locals.

★Scholteshof in Stevoort (see Hotels)

Knokke-Heist

Ter Dycken, Kalvekeetdijk 137; tel. (050) 608023
Amongst the numerous restaurants in the resort, this one stands out with its delicious fish dishes and its stylish ambience.

Koksijde

Le Régent, Blieckaan 10; tel. (058) 512110
Another popular fish and seafood restaurant, in a rustic setting.

Kortrijk

Village Gastronomique, Sint-Anna 5, tel. (056) 224756
A very elegant gourmet restaurant.

Français, Grote Markt 2, tel. (056) 222060
An excellent place for the Flemish national dish of mussels.

Leuven

Belle Epoque, Bondgenotenlaan 94; tel. (016) 223389
Best place for the gourmets of Leuven, has been awarded a star.

Domus, Tiensestraat 8, tel. (016) 201449
Visit this establishment for good regional cooking and home-brewed beer.

Liège

As Ouhès, 21, Place Marché; tel. (04) 2233225
On the menu in this restaurant are oysters and Liégois dishes such as kidneys; directly next to the Palais des Princes-Evêques.

La Parmentière, 10, Place Cockerill, tel. (04) 2224359
Belgian classics such as rabbit in beer sauce, but also grilled lobster, are served here in a relaxed atmosphere.

La Ciboulette, in Flémalle (16 km/10 mi. to the south-west), 96, Chemin de Chokier, tel. (04) 2750581
An attractive restaurant in an old building in the Meuse Valley, serving such unusual dishes as Breton langoustines in a crispy coating.

Malmédy

Au Petit Louvain, 47, Chemin-Rue, tel. (080) 330415
Elaborate cooking, for example game dishes, at moderate prices.

Zur Post, in Sankt-Vith (22 km/13.7 mi. to the south), Hauptstr. 39, tel. (080) 228027
A two-star restaurant where the Pankert family serves for example suckling pig with truffles and wild mushrooms.

Mechelen

D'Hoogh, Grote Markt 19; tel. (015) 217553
Mechelen is famous for its green asparagus, and here they know how to prepare it best and at the best prices.

In den Beer, Grote Markt 32–33, tel. (015) 203567
Acceptable prices and excellent eel in green sauce.

Mons

Devos, Rue de la Coupe 7; tel. (065) 351335
Elegant, long established restaurant offering French cuisine.

Namur

La Petite Fugue, 5, Place Chanoine Descamps, tel. (081) 231320

This restaurant offers good prices and unusual dishes such as river eel – hard to find elsewhere.

La Bergerie, in Lives sur Meuse (3 km/2 mi. to the east), 100, Rue Mosanville, tel. (081) 580613
Another two-star restaurant, excelling with dishes such as home-farmed trout and roast lamb, in a beautiful location above the Meuse Valley.

★Villa Maritza, Albert-I-Promenade 76, tel. (059) 508808   Ostend
Ambitious cooking in an elegant town villa dating back to the 19th c.

Old Fisher, Visserskaai 34, tel. (059) 501768
Mussels are on every menu, but shark is a bit more unusual.

Crombé, Markt 30, tel. (055) 311317   Oudenarde
Hearty regional Flemish cooking but also more elegant dishes such as pigeons and quails.

Le Fox, Walckiersstraat 2–4; tel. (058) 412855   De Panne
Try the lobster or coquilles St Jacques.

Hotelrestaurant Palace, Ieperstraat 3e, tel. (057) 333093   Poperinge
Very cosy restaurant serving national dishes.

Auberge des Falizes, Rue de France 90; tel. (084) 211282   Rochefort
Game dishes are the specialities of this restaurant in the Ardennes.

★Auberge du Sabotier, in Awenne (see Hotels)   St-Hubert

Jacques, Luikersteenweg 268, tel. (011) 683965   St-Truiden
It is worth finding this restaurant on the edge of town because of the quality of the Limburg cuisine served here.

Relais du Crouly, in Francorchamps (see Hotels)   Stavelot

★Biessenhuys, Hasseltsestraat 23; tel. (012) 234709   Tongeren
The village alone is worth a visit – the former refuge of the Teutonic Order of Knights – but a visit to this restaurant will make it unforgettable. The cooking is French-inspired Limburg cuisine, and served to the highest standards.

Clos St-Denis, in Vliermaal (5 km/3 mi. to the north-west), Grimmertingenstraat 24; tel. (012) 236096
Family restaurant with two stars, based in a former farm.

Bistro de la Cathédrale, 15 Vieux Marché, tel. (069) 210379   Tournai
Specialities from Tournai and the western Henngau.

Auberge de la Grappe d'Or, in Torgny (6 km/3.7 mi. to the south), 18, Rue Eermitage. tel. (063) 577056   Virton
A surprise in this attractive little village: the art of cooking in a very pleasant atmosphere.

★In den Wulf, in Heuvellan-Dranouter (15 km/9.3 mi. to the south), Wulvestraat 12, tel. (057) 445567   Ypres
A cosy restaurant in a former farm. The chef cooks only local dishes, all from locally sourced products.

Le Chalut, Rederskaai 26, tel. (050) 544115   Zeebrugge
Good fish restaurant.

Road Transport

(Distance Table
see p. 453)

Belgium is a densely populated and important transit country which has been served since the last century by an excellent road network.

All important cities and towns are linked by motorways (A) or through-routes in Europe (E). Motorways usually have three lanes and are illuminated at dusk; there are many petrol stations and services. The numbered main connecting roads (N) are equally as good.

Attractive tourist routes, marked by hexagonal bright green signs with blue lettering, follow to one side of the connecting roads. The routes, which are between 50 km (31 mi.) and 150 km (93 mi.) long and which all have a distinctive name, cross the Belgian countryside. Informative coloured leaflets are obtainable from the offices listed under Information (see entry).

Shopping and Souvenirs

Expensive souvenirs can be found in the high-class shops in the cities and larger towns. Some of Belgium's coastal resorts e.g. Knokke-Heist (Lippenslaan, Dumortierlaan and Kustlaan) also have shops such as jewellers and boutiques selling internationally-known products. The flea markets which take place throughout the country (see Markets) can prove real treasure-houses.

Brussels shopping arcades

The covered shopping arcades in Brussels (e.g. Galeries du Centre, Agora, City 2, Louise, Passage 44, Porte de Namur, Ravenstein, Royales Saint-Hubert and Toison d'Or) do not attract custom only in bad weather. Statuettes of the Brussels Manneken-Pis are among the most popular souvenirs. Articles with the emblem of the European Union are also sought after.

Large shopping centres

Visitors to Brussels should not miss the opportunity of shopping in the Woluwé Shopping Center in Woluwé-Saint-Lambert or the Westland Shopping Center in Anderlecht.

Art and antiques As well as antique shops, the famous art and antiques markets and other markets (see Markets and Events) offer ample opportunities for shopping.

Batist linen from Kortrijk.

Ceramics, brassware from Dinant (especially brassware, so-called dinanderie).

Crystal The world-famous crystal factory of Val-Saint-Lambert is located in Liège-Seraing. Glass-blowing, cutting and decorating can be observed and a valuable souvenir bought.

Diamonds e.g. from Antwerp, an international diamond centre of repute.

Glass From Boom.

Jewellery from Brussels and Kortrijk.

Lace from Bruges (centre of the lace-making industry), Brussels and Mechelen. During the summer months it is possible to see the lacemakers of these towns at work.

Distances in kilometres using Motorways	Antwerpen	Arlon	Bastogne	Brugge	Bruxelles/Brussel	Charleroi	Dinant	Eupen	Gent	Huy	Ieper	Kortrijk	Leuven	Liège	Mechelen	Mons	Namur	Oostende	Tongeren	Tournai	Turnhout
Antwerpen	–	234	195	106	55	115	137	152	60	129	131	101	69	124	28	122	109	123	111	127	47
Arlon	234	–	39	287	188	167	120	142	244	122	300	271	187	131	206	197	127	301	151	242	276
Bastogne	195	39	–	248	149	128	81	102	205	83	261	231	148	92	167	158	88	262	112	203	237
Brugge	106	287	248	–	99	154	190	238	55	182	53	59	129	197	122	136	162	29	189	88	152
Bruxelles/Brussel	55	188	149	99	–	60	91	136	56	83	122	92	28	96	27	69	63	114	88	84	93
Charleroi	115	167	128	154	60	–	55	138	109	64	150	120	68	92	89	46	36	167	95	92	159
Dinant	137	120	81	190	91	55	–	111	147	62	189	159	90	90	109	85	28	205	93	131	175
Eupen	152	142	102	238	136	138	111	–	192	70	266	224	111	37	136	174	99	256	56	216	137
Gent	60	244	205	55	56	109	147	192	–	139	78	48	86	154	80	120	119	70	146	70	106
Huy	129	122	83	182	83	64	62	70	139	–	204	174	69	35	96	100	34	197	38	146	171
Ieper	131	300	261	53	122	150	189	266	78	204	–	29	159	232	145	106	176	56	219	58	177
Kortrijk	101	271	231	59	92	120	159	224	48	174	29	–	129	202	115	76	146	62	189	28	147
Leuven	69	187	148	129	28	68	90	111	86	69	159	129	–	80	24	87	62	144	72	133	111
Liège	124	131	92	197	96	92	90	37	154	35	232	202	80	–	107	128	62	212	25	174	105
Mechelen	28	206	167	122	27	89	109	136	80	96	145	115	24	107	–	90	81	137	90	114	53
Mons	122	197	158	136	69	46	85	174	120	100	106	76	87	128	90	–	72	139	131	48	160
Namur	109	127	88	162	63	36	28	99	119	34	176	146	62	62	81	72	–	177	69	120	147
Oostende	123	301	262	29	114	167	205	256	70	197	56	62	144	212	137	139	177	–	204	91	169
Tongeren	111	151	112	189	88	95	93	56	146	38	219	189	72	25	90	131	69	204	–	192	85
Tournai	127	242	203	88	84	92	131	216	70	146	58	28	133	174	114	48	120	91	192	–	173
Turnhout	47	276	237	152	93	159	175	137	106	171	177	147	111	105	53	160	147	169	85	173	–

Pewter from Huy.

Playing cards from Turnhout (museum).

Puppets from Liège.

Sweets Belgian pralines are famous; the Brussels cake shops Neuhaus and Wittamer ("W"), whose beautiful displays offer very attractively packaged goods, are particularly well-known for their confectionery and gâteaux. Babelutten (caramels) from Veurne and Ypres, Kletskoppen (cakes), Mandelbrot, pancakes and waffles from Veurne are all popular sweets.

Tapestries from Brussels, Ghent, Mechelen, Oudenaarde or Sint-Niklaas.

Wood carvings from Spa.

Smoking

Since September 1st 1987 Belgium has belonged to the group of countries with the strictest anti-smoking legislation.

Chocolates are a Belgian speciality

This bans smoking in all public buildings, hospitals, schools and universities, ministry departments, sports centres, theatres, railway station concourses and underground stations, telephone kiosks, police stations and anywhere where there is a "No Smoking" sign. Failure to observe the smoking ban can result in a heavy fine.

Spas and Relaxation

Chaudfontaine
Complaints: rheumatism, gout in the initial stages, indigestion, neuritis, skin disorders.
Treatments: thermal baths (the only radio-active springs in the country, 36.6°C/97°F), liquid remedies, therapeutic exercises.

Knokke-Heist
Complaints: arthritis, rheumatism, cellulite, oedema.
Treatments: sea-water therapy in the Thalasso Therapy Centre.

Ostend
Complaints: rheumatism, bone and joint problems, rickets, calcium deficiency, neuritis, neuralgia, indigestion, circulation disorders, respiratory problems.
Treatments: fango- and hydro-, helio- and electrotherapies (Thermal Institute), therapeutic exercises and massages, thermal baths and swimming pools with heated sea water (35°C/95°F).

Spa
Complaints: anaemia, gout, arthrosis, rheumatism, cardio-vascular diseases, infections, respiratory problems, neuritis, cellulite.
Treatments: mud-baths, carbonated baths, inhalations, liquid cures, physiotherapy and massages.

Sport

So-called "popular" sports are played throughout Belgium and particularly in Flanders. These sports include Gansrijden (goose riding), Pagschieten (club shooting), Ringsteken (a kind of quoits), Struifvogelspel (a wooden bird must be manœuvred into the goal) and Vinkenzetten (finch's game). Kaatsen, which is also played in public places, consists in shooting an arrow directed vertically upwards at a bar lying horizontally across two poles. The favourite popular sport, however, is cycling and Belgium has some important cyclists, in particular Eddy Merckx.

Billiards should also not be forgotten – different variations of this game are played in many cafés. One of the greats at this game is the several-times world champion Raymond Ceulemans, whose son runs a billiard-café in the Hooverplein in Leuven.

Those interested in one of these sports should contact:
Vlaamse Volkssport Centrale, Tervuursevest 101
B-3001 Leuven (Heverlee); tel. (0 16) 225438 or 237272

Climbing

Alpine climbing sports can be undertaken in Belgium on the cliff faces of the Meuse, Ourthe, Molignée and Samson valleys. Information can be obtained from:
Club Alpin Belge, 19 Rue de l'Aurore
B-1050 Bruxelles/Brussels; tel. (02) 6488611

Cycling

In Belgium a bicycle (French bicyclette, Flemish fiets) is used both for leisure and as a means of transport. The country's network of cycle lanes has been ideally developed, and cycling through the flat landscape of Flanders provides great pleasure for novices at this sport while the more ambitious can have a very good time in the Ardennes.

It is possible to rent a bicycle in many places. Apart from private rental, bicycles can be hired at many Belgian railway stations. These stations are listed under the relevant town heading in the A to Z section. Belgian Railways (see Railways) also offers inexpensive two to three-day cycling holidays with accommodation on offer in youth hostels.

Fishing

Those wishing to fish must be in possession of an angling permit obtainable from any post office and valid for a year. This allows fishing in all state waters. Special permits (issued in post offices) are necessary for fishing in canals. Fishing at sea requires no special permission.

Football

The most popular spectator sport is football. Clubs such as RSC Anderlecht from Brussels, FC Antwerp, KV Mechelen and FC Brugge are among Europe's best.

Tennis

Tennis is a very popular sport with many private and public courts (indoor and outdoor). For further information contact:
Fédération Royale Tennis, Galerie Porte de Louise
B-1050 Bruxelles/Brussels; tel. (02) 5132927

Golf

Information about golf courses is available from:
Fédération Royale Belge de Golf, Chemin de Baudemont 23,
B-1400 Nivelles; tel. (067) 219525

Riding

Riding stables are to be found in most of the resorts along the coast as well as in many other towns or villages. These offer riding lessons and horses for hire. For further information contact:
Fédération Royale Belge des Sports Equestres, Avenue Houba de Strooper
B-1020 Bruxelles/Brussels; tel. (02) 4785056

Telephone

River/canal holidays

A 2000 km (1243 mi.)-long network of rivers and canals crosses Belgium, offering many opportunities for enjoyable holidays on water, e.g. on the Meuse, the Sambre, the Amblève, the Lesse, the Semois or the Ourthe in the Ardennes in private or rented boats. Information leaflets about canoes and kayaks are available from the Belgian tourist information offices (see Information). Motorised cruisers can be rented in many places.

Sailing

Sailing clubs can be found along the coast and inland on the Meuse, the Scheldt and the Leie. Well-equipped yacht harbours with a large number of moorings are located at Blankenberge, Koksijde (St-Idesbald), Nieuwpoort (Euro Yacht Harbour with 2000 moorings), Ostend and Zeebrugge; there are also yacht harbours in Brussels, Antwerp and Maaseik. A unique feature of the Flemish coast is sand sailing in sailcarts (courses are available for beginners). A competition for beach-sailors takes place once a year in November in De Panne.

Walking

Throughout Belgium, and particularly in the Ardennes, there are many beautiful footpaths. A walk along the beach and through the dunes can also be delightful. European Long Distance Footpath 2 leads from the Netherlands through Diest, Liège and Malmédy southwards to Luxembourg. European Long Distance Footpath 3 takes walkers through the Eifel and the Ardennes and includes the Semois valley. Guidebooks and maps can be bought in shops.

Winter sports

Between December and March it usually snows sufficiently for six to eight weeks in the Ardennes to allow winter sports to take place. There are more than a dozen pistes for downhill skiing, around 80 cross-country ski runs and numerous toboggan runs and snow-scooter runs. Cross-country skiing through the beautiful wooded winter landscape can prove especially attractive. The most well-known ski areas are to be found in the Hohe Venn (French Hautes Fagnes; 650 m (2133 ft) above sea level), around Bütgenbach, Eupen and Malmédy as well as at Spa-Francorchamps; further to the south at Vielsalm, on the plateau of the Baraque de Fraiture (Plateau des Tailles), on the Plateau de Bastogne, around Martelange-Anlier, in the Champion/Saint-Hubert district and above Gedinne on the Plateau de la Croix-Scaille. Information and a map entitled "Ski Ardennes" is available from the Belgian Tourist Office (see Information).

Telephone

Pay phones accept 5 and 20 Bfr coins. There are also public telephones which accept phone cards, known as Telecards. These magnetic cards cost 200 or 500 Bfr and can be bought in post offices, at railway station ticket counters, in some of the local tourist information offices and at some newsagents. Callboxes suitable for long-distance telephone calls bear European flags.

Code to Belgium from the UK 00 32
Code to the UK from Belgium 00 44

There are three price bands: zonal, inter-zonal and international. For internal calls between 6.30pm and 8am, at weekends and on public holidays rates are reduced by half. For international calls Monday to Saturday between 8pm and 8am and all day Sunday rates are reduced by a quarter.

Information

Inland; tel. 12 07 (Flemish) or 13 07 (French).
International; tel. 12 04 (Flemish) or 13 04 (French).

Time

In the winter Belgium observes Central European Time (one hour ahead of Greenwich Mean Time) then switches to summer time (two hours ahead of GMT) from the end of March to the end of September.

Tipping

In hotels and restaurants a tip is included in the bill and in taxi fares. A suitable tip should be given for additional services and also to tour guides, maids, porters and cloakroom assistants.

Traffic Regulations

See Motoring

Travel Documents

A passport or identity card is needed to enter Belgium and for a stay of more than three months visitors from outside the EU require a visa.

Driving licence and car registration papers from EU countries are accepted. A Green Card is required for non-EU visitors. All foreign cars must display an approved national identity plate.

Boats over 5.5 m (18 ft) long being brought into Belgium by road, etc. must have a triptych (customs certificate) or Carnet de Passage (customs certificate for several countries).

While Brussels' rich choice of cultural and historical locations makes it suitable for a visit during any season, it is best to visit Belgium between May and September.

When to Go

North Sea bathers most enjoy their sport from June/July to the end of August. Many events (see entry) – in particular the magnificently colourful flower parades organised by the coastal resorts – are worth visiting.

Summer

Most rain falls in the coastal area during autumn and there is often a strong wind. However, even this season can be attractive; for example, for walks or cycle rides in the Ardennes; in addition many beer festivals take place throughout the country at this time of the year.

Autumn

Winters are relatively mild, although during the months from December to March (for between six and eight weeks) good snow conditions in the Ardennes allow the pursuit of a variety of winter sports (see Sport).

Winter

Throughout the country; tel. 17 02 (Flemish) or 17 03 (French).

Weather forecasts

See Facts and Figures, Climate.

Young People's Accommodation

Inexpensive accommodation for all ages, but especially for young people is offered by the numerous youth hostels in Belgium. Foreign youth hostellers must have an International Youth Hostel Federation (IYHF) pass. It is advisable to book places in advance, especially for Easter and the months of July and August.

Information

Flanders:
Vlaamse Jeugdherbergcentrale, Van Stralenstraat 40
B-2060 Antwerpen; tel. (03) 2327218

Wallonia:
Centrale Wallonne des Auberges de la Jeunesse, Rue van Oost 52
B-1030 Bruxelles/Brussels; tel. (02) 2153100

Further youth accommodation is offered by the social holiday centres, whose addresses can be obtained from the tourist information offices listed under Information (see entry). Leaflets listing other inexpensive youth accommodation are also available from these offices.

Index

Index

Index

Picture credits

The Principal Sights of Tourist Interest

★★

Antwerp
Beloeil
Bouillon
Bruges/Brugge
Brussels/Bruxelles/Brussel
Domaine de Mariemont
German-Belgian Nature Park
Ghent/Gent/Gand
Han-sur-Lesse
Het Zwin Nature Reserve near
   Knokke-Heist

Kortrijk
Leuven
Liège
Mechelen
Oudenaarde
Sloping Elevator of Ronquières
Tongeren
Tournai
Vallée de la Meuse
Vallée de l'Ourthe
Zoutleeuw

★

Aalst
Abbaye de Villers-la-Ville
Arlon
Binche
Blankenberge
Château d'Attre
Château de Jehay
Château de Modave
Damme
Dendermonde
De Panne
Dierenpark Planckendael
Diest
Diksmuide
Dinant
Eupen
Fort Breendonk
Halle
Huy
Kalmthoutser Heide Nature
Reserve

Knokke-Heist
Lier
Louvain-la Neuve
Malmédy
Namur
Orval
Ostend/Oostende
Provinciaal Domein Bokrijk
La-Roche-en-Ardenne
Rochefort
Saint-Hubert
Ship-lift near La Louvière
Ship-lift Strépy-Thieu
Spa
Stavelot
Vallée de l'Amblève
Vallée de la Semois
Veurne
Virton
Waterloo
Ypres/Ieper

Note: The above list includes only the more important places of touristic interest in Belgium which are worth seeing either for themselves or for other attractions in the vicinity. In addition there are many other notable sights which are designated by one or two stars within the text of each entry.

Note: A few Belgian towns and two rivers are more familiar to English readers either in a distinct English spelling or in their French form. The following have been used in the text of this book: Bruges, Brussels, Ghent, Ostend, Ypres, and the Rivers Meuse and Scheldt. In all cases in the "A to Z" section both the Flemish and French names appear wherever relevant. The adjective Mosan applies to the River Meuse. The French word Béguinage is preferred as probably more familiar to English readers than the Flemish Begijnhof.

Imprint

198 photographs, 53 maps and plans, 10 drawings, 9 general plans, 1 large map at end of book

German text: Vera Beck, Rainer Eisenschmid, Hans-Dieter Haas, Wolfgang Hassenpflug, Udo Moll, Reinhard Strüber

General direction: Rainer Eisenschmid, Baedeker Ostfildern

Cartography: Franz Huber, Munich; Christoph Gallus, Hohenberg-Niederschopfheim; Mairs Geografischer Verlag, Ostfildern

Editorial work English edition: g-and-w publishing

English translation: Wendy Bell, Julie Bullock, David Cocking, Alec Court, Julie Waller, Sylvia Goulding

Source of illustrations: see Picture Credits

Front cover: James Davis Worldwide
Back cover: AA Photo Library (Alex Kouprianoff)

3rd English edition 2000

© Baedeker Ostfildern
Original German edition 2000

© 2000 The Automobile Association
English language edition worldwide

Published by AA Publishing (a trading name of Automobile Association Developments Limited, whose registered office is Norfolk House, Priestley Road, Basingstoke, Hampshire RG24 9NY. Registered number 1878835).

Distributed in the United States and Canada by:
Fodor's Travel Publications, Inc.
201 East 50th Street
New York, NY 10022

A CIP catalogue record of this book is available from the British Library.

Licensed user:
Mairs Geographischer Verlag GmbH & Co., Ostfildern

Typeset by Fakenham Photosetting Ltd, Fakenham, Norfolk, UK

Printed in Italy by G. Canale & C. S.p.A., Turin

ISBN 07495 2407 3